The Master Musicians Series

HANDEL

SERIES EDITED BY

SIR JACK WESTRUP,
M.A., Hon. D.Mus.(Oxon.), F.R.C.O.

HANDEL THE FASHIONABLE OPERA COMPOSER
From a portrait by Bartholomew Dandridge (d. 1751?)

THE MASTER MUSICIANS SERIES

HANDEL

by

PERCY M. YOUNG

*With eight pages of plates
and music examples in the text*

LONDON
J. M. DENT AND SONS LTD

FARRAR, STRAUS AND GIROUX, INC.
NEW YORK

IN AFFECTIONATE MEMORY OF
GARETH BERNARD BANTING

CONTENTS

ILLUSTRATIONS

'Handel was the Jupiter of music; . . . his hallelujahs open the heavens. He utters the word "Wonderful," as if all their trumpets spoke together. And then, when he comes to earth, to make love amidst nymphs and shepherds (for the beauties of all religions find room in his breast), his strains drop milk and honey, and his love is the youthfulness of the Golden Age.'

LEIGH HUNT (*Table Talk*).

INTRODUCTION

By a happy accident this introduction is written on an auspicious day. Handel appreciated birthday offerings from his disciples, and the author who has lived with his subject for some time is grateful to count himself among their number. The infectious personality of Handel explains the biographical minutiae of this study. He was a 'character,' as were Samuel Johnson and Charles Lamb. An effort has been made, therefore, to relieve his memory of the fictitious estimates (which have accrued despite the devotion of Schoelcher, Chrysander, Streatfeild and Dent, whose labours must be the starting-point of any modern scholar) of pedants and moralists. The intention is to present him as an eighteenth-century citizen. Similarly, his music is treated, so far as is possible, in relation to the audiences for which it was created.

It is hoped that this endeavour to remove a national institution—like all such institutions too frequently taken carelessly for granted—from isolated eminence will promote added enthusiasm for the neglected masterpieces. It is, after all, the music that ultimately matters. Here particular singers and players who have contributed something to this book by accompanying the author on various Handelian excursions must have grateful memorial.

The list of acknowledgments is heavy. If there are omissions they are regretted. The Foreign Office, the Bank of England, the National Library of Ireland, the North Devon Athenaeum, the Fitzwilliam Museum at Cambridge, the Watson Music Library at Manchester and the Birmingham Central Reference Library have been helpful in putting material at my disposal. For the letter, printed for the first time, on page 36 I am indebted to His Grace the Duke of Devonshire and to Mr. Francis Thompson, librarian at Chatsworth. The portrait of Handel by Hogarth is reproduced by permission of the owner, Mr. T. W. Bourne, the Thornhill and Daindridge portraits, and Hogarth's 'A Musical Party,' by permission of the director of the Fitzwilliam Museum.

Dorothy Lady Brabourne, Lady Hatherton, Mrs. Phyllis Brown, Mr. Norman Ault, Mr. G. J. K. Little, Mr. H. Wathall and Canon A. E. Farrow have assisted in supplying detailed information on particular points. Mr. E. H. Dance has co-operated in an attempt to prevent historical inaccuracy and Mr. Edmund Blunden given generously of his vast literary experience. My wife has, as usual, contributed more than can be told.

P. M. Y.

23rd February 1946.

Note to the Third Impression

Since this book was written a great change of climate has occurred in respect of Handel, both in England and Germany. The operas (in England at least, for the German opera-houses have done much pioneer work and put Handel into the standard repertoire) are now performed again, and more authentic styles of presenting the other works are generally preferred; while musicologists have tidied many biographical details—without, however, altering the main outline. I am particularly obliged to Professor O. E. Deutsch and to Herr Konrad Sasse, Director of the Händelhaus, in Halle, for making certain suggestions which I have now been able to incorporate.

P. M. Y.

October 1960.

CHAPTER I

BIRTH AND APPRENTICESHIP

In 1685 Charles II of England died, and with him the prospects of the house of Stuart. In the same year Louis XIV, foreshadowing events to come, revoked the Edict of Nantes and dispersed throughout Europe the skill, intelligence and integrity of unpalatable Huguenotism. In 1685 Handel was born.

An artist may be, and frequently is, oblivious of the vagaries of political machination; but his career, his opportunities and his environment are subject to vicissitudes whose author is the politician. Thus two significant historic events in the year of his birth had some part in the moulding of the future of George Frideric Handel.

The opportunism of Charles II might have staved off the Glorious Revolution, but the stubborn miscalculations of James II, coupled with a respect for the dictatorial technique of the French king, made revolution inevitable. The deposition of James left an ultimate way clear for the Hanoverian succession, the development of modern parliamentarianism, the military achievements of Marlborough, the predominance of Low Church doctrine and such individual qualities *in arte vivendi* as were to excite the later applause of Voltaire and Montesquieu. France, whose habits of depredation stimulated uneasiness throughout Europe in the latter part of the seventeenth century, provoked the enmity not only of princes, but also of peoples by her renewal of religious persecution. England, watchful as ever of the balance of power, viewed with no disfavour the rise of a new, potentially counteractive state: that of Prussia. Under the tutelage of the Hohenzollerns Prussia was beginning to emerge as a unity, and by the time the Great Elector and Frederick I had impressed their personalities on various scattered German domains which had languished in semi-feudal torpor since the Peace of Westphalia she was a great power, with the third army in Europe, an imposing list of achievement in the arts and the sciences, and the competent continental check to future French ambitions in the east. But all this was purchased at a cost. The lives and liberties of her subjects passed from the inert or inefficient control of local princes to that of a centralized and efficient bureaucracy.

It was for the very reason that England provided a tolerable life for a man of independent proclivities that Handel made this country for the greater part of his life his home. It is, however, wrong to consider him an Englishman. It is equally wrong to consider him a German. He was neither, but rather a European, and as such a glory to his own age and an example to others.

The independence to be discerned in Handel's character was (*pace* scientific scepticism) a hereditary endowment. The Händels in general pursued life with a superb faith in their own destinies. And since they were successful they aroused envious respect. Valentin, the first who comes into our field, was born at Breslau in 1583. Thence, having learned his trade as a coppersmith, he migrated to the more prosperous town of Halle, of which he was enrolled as citizen early in 1609. As a tradesman—that is the signification of the family name—Valentin Händel contracted an advantageous marriage with Anna Beichling, daughter of a master coppersmith. Thereafter he prospered, his money went into property, and he nurtured a large family in the fear of God—the upbringing was Lutheran—in bourgeois respectability and in a sound belief in the efficacy of balanced budgets. In 1622 his fifth son, Georg, was born.

As the coppersmith business eventually passed to his elder brothers Georg was constrained to attempt new fields of endeavour. Influenced, no doubt, by the prevailing needs of the times and by the contemporary carnage of the Thirty Years War, he chose surgery (with its ancillary craft of barber). Left fatherless at the age of fourteen Georg Händel developed that degree of self-dependence which necessity so often mothers. He was first apprenticed to Andrew Beger, whose wife was daughter of the English musician William Brade. Next he assisted Christoph Oettinger. After his death, in 1643, Händel acquired both his practice and his widow, who thus became Frau Händel. Of this *mariage de convenance* six children were born, of whom two survived the perilous passage of infancy. With that ambition induced by paternity Händel progressed in dignity to appointment as surgeon to the suburb of Giebichenstein and as surgeon-in-ordinary and *valet de chambre* to the Duke Augustus of Saxony. Three years later an episode occurred to show that municipal and individual rights had their eighteenth-century prot-agonists. Händel purchased a house-cum-wineshop (a commend-able departure in medical practice), the *Zum gelben Hirsch* in the Schlamm, but the civic authority refused to renew the wine-selling licence. Händel referred the matter to the elector, who referred it back to Halle. But the indomitable Händel refused to be reduced by his fellow townsmen and shuttlecocked his grievances back to the elector, who thereupon, exhausted by the strain of attempting de-cisions of such magnitude, settled the matter in the plaintiff's favour. The town council was promised military occupation and monetary penalties should the matter be raised again. Nor was this the only occasion on which Händel asserted his rights. In 1680, on the death of the duke and consequent political changes, attempts were made, unsuccessfully, to deprive him of his court appointments. Whether, as a matter of fact, this would have entailed much loss of emolument is doubtful. Princes and dukes were conspicuous for the splendour of their surroundings rather than for their capacity for adequately recompensing their *aides*. However, Händel intended to conserve his personal dignity and in so doing ensured his unborn son's first entry into romantic anecdote.

By the Peace of Westphalia Halle had been assigned from Saxony to Prussia, but this arrangement became operative only on the death of Augustus. The local effects of this change were that the court was transferred to Weissenfels, where the new duke, Johann Adolf, set up the customary pathetic illusion of a *petit Versailles,* and that Halle resumed its more stolid characteristics, changing, incidentally, the Ritter-Akademie—an establishment exclusively devoted to the propagation and preservation of aristocratic privilege—into a univer-sity. Halle-an-der-Saale was a pleasant town, anciently a member of the Hanseatic League, with a sturdy tradition documented in its principal buildings. These included a medieval Rathaus; the re-mains of the castle of Moritzburg, established in 1478 by the Arch-bishop of Magdeburg and largely destroyed by fire during the Thirty Years War; the Moritzkirche; the Liebfrauenkirche (church of

Our Lady), conspicuous by its curious twin-spired and bridged façade; and the ancient but altered Dom, Calvinist since 1689. The natural situation of Halle, which was a centre of salt manufacture, gave trading advantages, a certain cultural independence and a dignity which its most distinguished alumnus recollected gracefully in later years.[1] But part of the price paid by the seventeenth and eighteenth centuries for such cultural blessings as excite the envy of later generations was plague, famine and sudden death. Georg Händel himself was given up for dead in 1681. His recovery possessed, so far as his kinsfolk were concerned, elements of the miraculous. His eldest son, Gottfried, perished in a general and alarming epidemic in the following year. His wife died in 1683.

Giebichenstein, where Händel worked, had as its Lutheran pastor Georg Taust, of Bohemian descent. He had two daughters. One, Dorothea, became Händel's second wife a few months after the passing of the first. The other, Anna, followed to the Schlamm when the onset of pregnancy demanded sisterly sympathy and domestic reinforcement. In 1684 a son was born to Dorothea. He died almost immediately.

On 23rd February 1685 a second child was born who did survive. He was christened on the following day at the Liebfrauenkirche. The names given to him were Georg Friedrich. Confusion with the old-style calendar (in which the year began on 25th March) impelled earlier authorities, including the engravers of the memorial inscription in Westminster Abbey, to place the date of Handel's birth in 1684.[2] A further digression may here be relevant. The family name was susceptible of various orthography: thus we meet Händel, Hendel, Händeler, Hendler, Hendtler, and the charming feminine form of Händelin (to Christiana Susanna Händelin Handel ultimately bequeathed £300). The commonest English usage was, and is, Handel. Hereafter the composer shall be called, as he styled himself in England, George Frideric Handel.

Those who, in the period under review, survived the hazards of infancy were, beyond doubt, hardy. Handel, who inherited a good

[1] *Vide* reference to the coat of arms of the Foundling Hospital on page 83.

[2] The Gregorian or new-style calendar was introduced in England in 1752. It was welcomed with the reserve accorded to all innovations.

deal from his father, received therefrom the benefit of a tough constitution. Old Händel mercifully survived his illness of 1681: at the same period of his own life his son recovered from a severe and paralytic disorder. They were, literally, a breed of diehards. In later years Handel's physique became one source of anecdote. More important than this is the fact that his bodily powers had particular reference to his creative activities, his capacity for hard work and his resilience in the face of misfortune being directly consequential. The bowed legs of maturity may suggest a vitamin deficiency in childhood, otherwise the parents may be exonerated from any suspicion of early neglect.

The incidents of youth are germane to the later development of the biographic subject. Accordingly the Händel household needs to be set in proper perspective. Episodes imperfectly recollected from John Christopher Smith by the gullible Mainwaring have furnished material for romantic screeds of significance only to the unmusical.

A not unnatural affection for an estimable mother and a later aversion from the bonds of holy matrimony have been construed into psychological jargon as 'mother-fixation,' while a fatherly inclination to suggest a career other than that of music has had the elder Händel arraigned for tyranny. Such facts as are available suggest that Georg Händel had excellent good sense, pride in his son's potentialities, and a willingness to provide for educational opportunity. His surviving portrait adds to these qualities a grave, patrician dignity. If the percussion instruments of the nursery really were incinerated and the clavichord acquired only against interdict the natural desire of an elderly surgeon for a quiet home may be held responsible. The lusty presence of George Frideric's younger sisters provided distraction enough.

Somewhere about his seventh or eighth year George Frideric accompanied his father to the court of Weissenfels. There, with a precocity not uncommon to the children of elderly parents, he proposed to the duke his intention of becoming a musician.[1] The duke sensibly advised that self-expression should find its natural outlet

[1] One connection with music was through Cyriacus Berger (related by marriage), musician at Zeitz.

under competent guidance. Handel was put, therefore, under that of Zachau, organist of the Liebfrauenkirche. At the same time his general education proceeded classically and conservatively at the Lutheran Gymnasium, a grammar school. An incident of these years which appropriately stuck in the mind was the operation which his father performed in 1692 on Andreas Rudloff, the 'Halle Sword-swallower.' The incident may be quoted as demonstrating either the incredible surgical gifts with which Händel was endowed or the mythical propensities of many Handeliana.

Halle had enjoyed that sort of musical reputation which would now promote complacency in a similarly placed English provincial town. Before the reign of Zachau it had possessed two notable organists in Wolff Heintz, a friend of Luther's, and Samuel Scheidt, the son of a salt-works manager and a father of German music.[1] In the palmy days before pietism stepped on such displays Halle had gone some way in the inauguration of the *Singspiel* as opposed to the infiltrating Italian opera. Zachau himself combined competence with sobriety, was painstaking and friendly, and had a good collection of Italian and German music.[2] Young Handel learned the organ, the harpsichord, the violin, the hautboy, composition and common sense. The contemporary attitude to music was utilitarian. Much was required for ceremonies of church and state and, library facilities being non-existent, had to be composed *ad hoc*. The embryonic organist was early initiated into the mysteries of ecclesiastical tradition, and Handel, as a matter of course, wrote a weekly cantata as exercise. But sacred music was hardly his first love. 'I used to write like the devil in those days, but chiefly for the hautbois, which was my favourite instrument,'[3] he is reported to have said. A set of sonatas, written at the age of ten, were discovered by Lord Polwarth later in Handel's life in Germany, but have since disappeared again. Another loss to the biographer is the exercise book which was compiled under Zachau's direction. This contained copied extracts from such models as Froberger, Krieger, Kerl, Ebner and Strungk. As a historic figure Strungk is worth momentary consideration. He was a conspicuous composer, a

[1] For his knowledge of English music see p. 223.   [2] Mainwaring, p. 14.
[3] Burney, *Commem.*, p. 3 n.

member of the German resistance party fighting at Hamburg the cause of native opera, who left a large catalogue of works which quickly passed into the limbo of forgotten achievement. Some of his titles have a familiar ring, *Nero* (1693) and *Agrippina* (1699) in particular. Handel no doubt spent the impressionable years of his youth reflecting on the splendour of their associations. His own copies of Strungk were probably made from *Ein hundert auserlesene Arien zweyer Hamburgischen Operen, Semiramis und Esther. Mit beigefügten Ritornellen* (1689).

Three or four years of Zachau's able tuition, absorbed together with the nearby schooling of the Gymnasium, qualified Handel for inclusion among the ranks of the prodigies. In this capacity he visited Berlin in 1696.[1] There Frederick,[2] later to become by imperial grace King of Prussia, held court. While he continued his father's work of Prussian organization and diplomatic opportunism—he had previously supported the claims of William III to the English throne and was later to aid the allied cause in the War of Spanish Succession—his second wife, Sophia Charlotte, occupied herself with the department of *Kultur*. Lest, however, it should be thought that the elector himself was a Philistine, it should be recorded that he was responsible for the foundation of the University of Halle and of the Academy of Science in Berlin, that he appreciated French culture despite political antagonism and that he was ready to extend a welcome to Berlin to victims of political and religious discrimination. Across this scene Handel flitted meteorically. He impressed the court, the electress, herself a practising musician, and the elector. The latter made an offer not unusual for a period in which crowned heads felt easier with a maximum *entourage* of sycophantic retainers. He suggested a further course in musical education, inevitably in

[1] It was not on this visit that Handel met Ariosti and Buononcini, as neither was in Berlin in 1696. Ariosti arrived in 1697 and Buononcini in 1702. Mainwaring was probably right in recording a meeting between Handel and these musicians, but, as usual, he gets his dates wrong. Mainwaring may be credited with the invention of the bed-time story about the youthful Handel sitting on Ariosti's knee.

[2] As Elector of Brandenburg this ruler was Frederick III, as King of Prussia, Frederick I.

Italy. Old Händel, however, was not enthusiastic. Still supporting the conventional thesis that the precarious possibilities of music offered improbable avenues of worldly success, he emphasized the advantages of a legal career. It may be urged that, as a matter of fact, jurisprudence formed a better training for musicians than music: among German musicians Schütz, Walther, Mattheson, Kuhnau, Telemann, Emanuel Bach, as well as Handel, were 'spoiled' lawyers. Georg Händel died on 11th February 1697. The melancholy event was commemorated by his son in a poetic effusion duly published.

Georg Händel was something of Horace's *justus et tenax vir,* and the value of independence, a quality which dictated his reaction to the electoral offer, he impressed on his son. The University of Halle, under the progressive leadership of Thomasius, further stimulated intellectual adventure, and the pietistic teaching of Francke, head of the theological faculty, laid stress on the necessity for freedom in spiritual experience. Handel entered the university in 1702 and, while his academic attainments may have been slight, he could hardly have remained impervious to the new liberalism of thought which characterized the foundation. Music was simultaneously pursued with added zeal. In the same year as entering the university Handel became organist of the Dom, in succession to the intemperate Leporin.

The composition of ecclesiastical music being an organist's necessary duty, Handel produced the proper sequence of cantatas for the Dom. The sole authentic survivor is a *Laudate pueri.* These Halle activities created a reputation that was not merely local. So that Georg Philipp Telemann, a young man of varied abilities, called on Handel round about the year 1700. Telemann was four years older than Handel, a native of Magdeburg, a nominal student of law and an undergraduate of the University of Leipzig.

A capacity for loyal friendship was a characteristic of Handel, and that with Telemann was lifelong. Forty years on they were still in amicable correspondence with each other. These early days were days of serious intent and, whereas the latest letters were devoted to horticulture, between 1701 and 1703 they engaged their pens technically on the 'working-out of melodious compositions.'[1] At that

[1] Mattheson, *Grundlage einer Ehren-Pforte.*

8

time melody was the *fons et origo* of all music. Personal intercourse also took place, and if this was not at Halle then it was at Weissenfels, for which court Telemann wrote a number of operas. The reciprocity of musical thought in the eighteenth century is indicated by the extent of Telemann's studies. Being as fluent in literature as in music —and Handel commented that he 'could write a motet for eight voices more quickly than one could write a letter'—Telemann left valuable evidence in this respect. His recorded models were Kuhnau's fugues, the French overtures of Lully and Campra, 'the true and barbaric beauty' of such Polish music as he came across while sojourning in Upper Silesia and the ubiquitous productions of Italy.

But experience of foreign schools could only come to the home-staying student fortuitously. The proper way to learn was to travel, and this, influenced by Telemann's example and irked by the monotony of the Calvinistic round at the *Dom*, Handel proposed to do. He finished his year's probation as organist in the spring of 1703, leaving his place to Johann Kolhart, disconnected himself from the university, took leave of his family and started on the first stage of his Odyssey.

CHAPTER II

'IL CARO SASSONE'

THE magnetic town of northern Germany was Hamburg, handsomely prosperous and culturally progressive. There would be met travellers from overseas and ample opportunities for intellectual exercise. By 1703 the onslaught of Italy was biting into the inner defences of German opera, despite the vigorous protective measures undertaken in Scholt's opera house. But this fact was an inducement to the young. Artistic theories worried Handel little. His career, law being now finally rejected, was to be that of a musician, which then implied craftsman. Music was required and therefore must be written, and if a particular style was in vogue then it must be obeyed; although later on Handel sometimes indulged in anti-popular stylistic dictation. The Italian manner was favoured because it exalted melody. Therefore throughout the century we find great stress being laid on 'air.' In view of the later genius of the age it cannot on the whole be complained that public taste miscalculated in its postulations. Handel arrived at Hamburg with a provincial reputation and with provincial deficiencies. From a metropolitan point of view his achievement was thus summarized: 'He was strong in the organ, stronger than Kuhnau in fugue and counterpoint, especially *extempore,* but he knew very little about melody until he came to the Hamburg operas.'[1]

Thus the first stage in Handel's emancipation from German influence opened. Over the period with which this chapter is concerned presides the benign influence of one of the most remarkable of eighteenth-century worthies: the abbate Steffani. Born in 1654 in obscurity, carried off to the Bavarian court as a promising choir-boy, tutored by Johann Caspar Kerl and Carissimi, Steffani acquired a high musical reputation by his twentieth year. But in addition to music he studied theology, mathematics and philosophy with equal

[1] Mattheson, *Grundlage einer Ehren-Pforte.*

10

success. He became a priest in 1680, after which he left Munich for Hanover, where an appointment as *Capellmeister* awaited him. There he wrote operas for Giusti's new and elegant theatre, and in so doing increased the artistic reputation of Hanover. His operas were also performed at Brunswick and Hamburg. For the latter town, significantly, they were translated into German.

But this was only one side of Steffani's life. In 1698 he became the elector's ambassador at Brussels, and thenceforth his duties as plenipotentiary overshadowed his artistic activity. But not so much as to prevent the continuance of his enthusiasm therein. If there was one figure in Europe whose acquaintance and encouragement were worth a young man's acquisition it was Steffani. Handel was fortunate.

Precisely when he first met the abbate is doubtful. His own statement, as recorded by Hawkins,[1] reads:

When I first arrived in Hanover as a young man, under twenty, I was acquainted with the merits of Steffani, and he had heard of me. I understood something of music, and could play pretty well on the organ; he received me with great kindness, and took an early opportunity to introduce me to the princess Sophia and the elector's son, giving them to understand that I was what he was pleased to call a virtuoso in music; he obliged me with instructions for my conduct and behaviour during my residence at Hanover; and being called from the city to attend to matters of a public concern, he left me in possession of that favour and patronage which himself had enjoyed for a number of years.

The latter part of this statement applies to 1709, in which year Handel attached himself to the Hanoverians. But the first part refers to an earlier period: prior, in fact, to 1705. Remembering that Handel had left Germany at least thirty years before Hawkins obtained this statement, it is reasonable to assume that what were two separate events had unified in mental coalescence. By emending Hawkins's punctuation [2] the antithesis becomes quite clear. Brenet suggests that Handel called at Hanover *en route* for Hamburg in 1703 and that then he made the acquaintance of Steffani. Such a meeting, resulting in mutual respect, would have been profitable.

[1] Hawkins, v. 267.

[2] e.g. '. . . a virtuoso in music. He obliged me . . .'

Steffani's good opinion would help to explain the trail of glory which Handel blazed at Hamburg and, to a greater degree, in Italy. And the later offer of the Hanoverian *Kapellmeister* post is more comprehensible if understood as the result of a more or less prolonged interest on the part of Steffani.

Arrived at Hamburg during the summer of 1703 Handel quickly made the acquaintance of Johann Mattheson, an aspiring singer, composer, author and man of the world. In the latter capacity he was serviceable to Handel: as an author to posterity. He left sufficient information in his encyclopaedic *Grundlage einer Ehren-Pforte* for a full-size portrait of the young Handel (an individual too seldom considered) to be re-created.

In this we discern a youth as much characterized by industry as by brilliance. Handel wrote arias, which were apparently interminable, and cantatas, visited organs, did the round of choirs, operas and concerts, became domesticated 'at a certain house, in which music was practised with the utmost devotion,' absorbed the correct dramatic style from Mattheson, to whom—after sociable meals at the expense of Mattheson's father—in return he gave contrapuntal assistance. 'I learned from him as he learned from me. *Docendo enim discimus.*' [1] In his capacity as second violin (perhaps after this example it will no more be regarded as undignified to sit at a second violin desk) in the theatre orchestra he 'behaved as if he couldn't count five, being naturally inclined to a dry humour.' His manner was engagingly modest, it being only with difficulty that he was induced to substitute for an absent harpsichordist. But life was punctuated by such pleasant trivialities as river excursions. And Mattheson, writing in 1740, looked back wistfully and whimsically on the occasion which brought them together at the Maria Magdalen church, where the organ-blower was a pastry-cook's son. 'I know well enough,' he says of Handel, 'that he will laugh heartily when he reads this, though as a rule he laughs but little.' And then there was the August expedition to Lübeck, in the pigeon-fancier's company. At Lübeck the bait was the prospect of succeeding the great Buxtehude. And this was made additionally attractive by the municipality who, alive as always to the possibility of rate reduction,

[1] Mattheson, op. cit.

12

offered not only an organ stool but also a marriage bed to the successful applicant. The intended pensioner was Buxtehude's daughter,
whose lack in allurement and wealth in years recommended a quick
return to Hamburg. What was refused by Handel and Mattheson, and
three years later by Sebastian Bach, came eventually to one of Keiser's
juniors—Johann Christian Schieferdecker.

The later months of 1703 passed less excitingly but more profitably.
Handel became music tutor to the family of the English resident—
John Wich.[1] This dignitary was an amiable soul, whose wine a
few months previously had filled Addison with satisfaction and whose
swollen legs with concern.[2] In addition to his tutorial activities
Handel was composing a Passion, for next Holy Week, at the behest
of Postel, an old librettist now turned Pietist. More time for composition was afforded by Mattheson's absence in Holland. Handel,
however, missed his companionship and wrote accordingly on 18th
March 1704. He finishes his letter: 'I therefore beg you to notify
me of your departure so that I may have the opportunity of fulfilling
my duty, and come and meet you with Mlle Sbulens.'[3] The lady
has this solitary entry in history. Whether she came, as has been
suggested, from Halle is a matter for speculation, as is the possibility
of her having exercised particular claims on the affections of Handel.
It may be suspected that some good reason prompted a joint welcome
home for the nomadic Mattheson. However that may be, he deferred
his return until after the production of the Passion. This work,
relatively inconspicuous as it was, disturbed the *amour-propre* of
Keiser, an older man prone to dissipation and jealousy, and
spurred him to the composition of a similar work: *Der blutige und
sterbende Jesus*. Mattheson thought little of Handel's Passion and
indulged in its critical anatomy in his *Critica Musica* of 1725.

The Handel-Mattheson friendship went through rather rough

[1] John Wich continued in office until 1713, in which year he was succeeded by Cyril (afterwards Sir Cyril) Wich.

[2] Letter from Addison to Wich, May 1703.

[3] A Mr. Sbuelen is twice mentioned in letters from Handel to Michaelsen
(10th August 1731 and 28th August 1736). On the second occasion we
learn that wedding presents to Handel's niece were sent to Sbuelen at
Hamburg.

waters in 1714. First Mattheson usurped his friend's place in the Wich household and then brawled with him in the theatre. The circumstances leading to this much publicized incident are peculiar, and one suspects more than meets the eye. On 20th October Mattheson produced his *Cleopatra,* in which he sang the part of Antonius. His custom was, having (dramatically speaking) expired, to descend to the orchestra and to supplant Handel at the harpsichord. The opera ran smoothly, with this curious arrangement not apparently disapproved, until 5th December. On that night Handel suddenly refused to resign his place at the harpsichord, and the irate composer took the opportunity, when outside the theatre, of slapping his colleague on the face. Anticipating Hawkins's bloodthirsty charge[1] at a later date Mattheson archly commented that 'a dry slap on the face was no assassination, but rather a friendly hint, to put him on his guard.' He further described Handel as 'tall, strong, broad-shouldered and muscular; consequently well able to defend himself.' The sequel was a Sheridanesque duel in which tradition assigns Handel's deliverance to a fortunately placed button or score[2] which broke Mattheson's sword. The spectators must have repined at so anticlimactic a dénouement. A happy ending was effected by a dinner of reconciliation on 30th December engineered by a pacifically minded town councillor who also held shares in the theatre. Brawls, bloodshed and hot emotion were part of the eighteenth-century mode of life, and Handel was not immune from their incidence.

Tranquillity again prevailing, Handel and Mattheson turned to the business of wage-earning. This centred round Handel's first opera *Almira,* to a libretto by Feustking in mixed German and Italian. Mattheson was the *primo uomo.* After *Almira,* which ran from 8th January 1705 to 25th February, came *Die durch Blut und Mord erlangte Liebe, oder* (less sensationally) *Nero.* This had a run of three nights, and then came off. But Handel had achieved two things. First the opportunity of demonstrating to himself and to Hamburg in general that he was possessed of an exceptional dramatic flair; secondly and consequently the sour enmity of Keiser. Keiser was much annoyed and began work on new settings of both

[1] Hawkins, v. 265.   [2] Mainwaring, p. 35.

He leaves Germany

Nero and *Almira*. Neither was a success but, reading between the lines, Handel came to the conclusion that life would be more tolerable in another place. His mind turned to the prospects of an Italian journey. Steffani would have urged this; Ariosti and Buononcini,[1] whose acquaintance Handel had made in the days of his apprenticeship, would similarly have advised; and a new friend, Prince Giovanni Gastone de' Medici, still more importunately.

Gastone de' Medici was Micawber-like in impecuniosity, in good nature and in constant optimism. He had few grounds for optimism, which, doubtless, is why he was optimistic. His father was the despotic Cosimo III, who handed Tuscany to the bondage of clerical taskmasters; his wife, tied to him by statecraft and not by love, the stout, unrefined Anna Maria of Saxe-Lauenburg; his official home an isolated castle in the hinterland of Bohemia. Not surprisingly Gastone dedicated one half of himself to Venus and the other, less dangerously, to opera-going and flute-playing. It was these latter occupations which brought him into contact with Handel.

Thus encouraged to look south Handel took practical steps to implement his desires. He set to work on a third opera, an opera of such proportions that for practical purposes it needed dichotomy and became therefore *Florindo* and *Daphne*. Leaving behind him these scores and, according to Mainwaring, a good many other miscellaneous compositions, he packed his bag, counted his savings— 200 ducats—and shook the dust of Hamburg off his feet. His travelling companion was an acquaintance named von Binitz who, if Mattheson's testimony is correct, subscribed the travelling expenses.

Italy in the eighteenth century was, like Greece at a more remote period of history, in process of conquering her conquerors. Fragmented, Venice a nominally independent state of consequence to Europe in general as a pleasure resort, Lombardy and Naples subject to Spanish viceroys, Florence and Tuscany under Austrian attention, Savoy on uneasy terms with France, and the Papal States perpetuating reaction and obscurantism, she left practical affairs to the northern nations, setting herself the task of cultural diffusion. Which, in the realm of music, she did so inexorably that opposition was impossible.

[1] It is probably correct to assume that Handel met Ariosti and Buononcini during his residence at Hamburg.

The schools of music were the courts, both lay and ecclesiastical, and the patrons-in-chief were such as Handel encountered.

His career in Italy was so unnaturally successful (for a Saxon to outshine the Italians on their own ground was surely unthinkable) that one is tempted to see behind it influence, then as now a surer guide to popular acclamation than ability. The influence, it might reasonably be surmised, was that of Steffani. First Handel went to Florence, where Gastone's brother Ferdinand, a patron of Alessandro Scarlatti, controlled the aesthetics ignored by his father. This was towards the end of 1706. A short sojourn at the Pratolino left time for some emendations to *Almira* and for the composition of some cantatas. But early in the new year he was in Rome, where he completed a *Dixit Dominus*.[1] In July a new opera, probably begun when Handel first arrived at Florence, *Rodrigo,* was produced at the Florentine court. The reward from Ferdinand, who had come to the recent conclusion that Scarlatti had deteriorated in amusement value, was a hundred sequins and a service of porcelain. Judging by the social assets which stood him in such good stead at this period an amorous interlude, detailed with customary factual inconsistency by Mainwaring, would not be out of place. Mainwaring's heroine —Vittoria Tesi—is ruled out by reason of immaturity: she was born in 1700. Although it may be that Mainwaring's lady was right, but his date wrong. Handel probably met her again in 1719. Vittoria Tarquini, the prima donna of *Rodrigo* (an alternative candidate to Tesi), was well ensconced in the good graces of the Prince Ferdinand, and therefore unlikely to have spent her energy in chasing an impecunious composer, however flashing his immediate reputation, all over Italy. Thus in uncertainty dies a promising anecdote.

Venice was the next port of call. There Handel made the pleasant acquaintance of Domenico Scarlatti, who later reappeared in Handel's London life in 1720. An attractive trait was this capacity for remembering old friends with affection, and often with gratitude. Instances occur so frequently that the underlining of their incidence may be forgiven in that thus the conventionally drawn Handel is softened in outline. Handel also met Scarlatti's tutor Gasparini, Lotti and possibly (we may like to think) the young Canaletto.

[1] See 'Handel among the Carmelites,' J. S. Hall, *Dublin Review,* 1959.

There was also in Venice the Earl of Manchester.[1] The earl was an incompetent diplomat—he had previously failed in missions to Paris and Venice—but well-mannered: therefore, after normal convention in these matters, he was given full opportunity to continue in the wrecking of his own professional reputation and his country's interests. At this time he was negotiating the adherence of the Venetians to the Grand Alliance. They for their part were entertaining him with diversionary operations. Thus he came into contact with Handel and commenced an interest in his music which was maintained in later years. The advantage of the Grand Tour, whether for rich or poor, was a healthy diminution in chauvinistic intention. The intelligent were not over-conscious of nationality. The Earl of Manchester loved the Venetians, while deploring their policy of *attentisme,* and approved their opera in which the rising star was the German Handel. English lack of artistic perception, a deficiency more rare than is commonly believed, did not disgrace Her Majesty's representative. His lead was followed by another English resident. Joseph Smith, whose address Handel made use of on a later visit to Italy,[2] was beginning to lay the foundations of his bibliophilic reputation in 1707. And a final stimulus came to English affairs in Venice during Handel's visit, through the presence of Ernest of Hanover, brother to the future George I, who was basking in the glory attached to his house by the Act of Settlement (1701) and in the official satisfaction of diplomacy at its loyalty to the allied cause.

From Venice, having established useful contacts, Handel went with Domenico Scarlatti to Rome. Temporarily papal authority was frowning on opera and inferior princes of the church were compelled to divert their interest to a more godly form of recreation. Cardinal Pietro Ottoboni was the principal connoisseur of the arts and, being also a friend of Ferdinand of Tuscany, he welcomed Handel on his arrival. With the entrée to the cardinal's musical evenings Handel added to his growing list of acquaintances Corelli, in charge of the Ottoboni music, Pasquini and (if he had not previously met him) Alessandro Scarlatti. Handel was not only a musical but a social success. He proceeded from Ottoboni's to

[1] Created duke 1719.
[2] *Vide* letter from Handel to Michaelsen, 11th March 1729.

the favour of the Prince Ruspoli, prince by papal dispensation, and in the luxury of his palace stayed for the most of March and April 1708.[1]

In the Palazzo Bonelli Handel wrote *La resurrezione,* which was performed in succession to Scarlatti's *Della Santissima Annunziata. La resurrezione* was received with satisfaction: the only discord was struck by the Holy Father, who dispatched a pained note to Ruspoli complaining of the employment in the oratorio of a female singer.[2] The next work was contrived with less care. It was a setting of Cardinal Pamfili's *Il trionfo del tempo e del disinganno,* fifty years later to be remodelled into *The Triumph of Time and Truth.* Although *Il trionfo* was a relative failure Handel felt sufficiently sure of his standing in Italy to remonstrate with Corelli for his inability to cope with the overture. 'My dear Saxon,' complained Corelli, 'this music is in the French style, of which I have no knowledge.' Nor was there any reason why he should have had in view of Italy's prerogative of supplying music to the rest of Europe. *Il trionfo,* per-formed for Ottoboni's Arcadians, was given under the shadow of political discontent and the imminence of yet another of the many sieges of Rome. Therefore Handel went south to compose *Aci, Galatea e Polifemo* for the marriage of the Duca d'Alvito, which was solemnized on 19th July at Naples. While in Naples Handel dallied with another lady, of whom no more is known than that her name was Donna Laura.[3] He also met the Viceroy of Naples, Cardinal Grimani, a friend of Lady Mary Wortley Montagu's, a connection of the family which built the San Giovanni Crisotomo theatre at Venice and a good librettist. Grimani prepared the libretto for Handel's next opera, *Agrippina.* This overshadowed all the other events of the Carnival season which opened at Venice on 26th December 1709, running for twenty-seven nights. Two of the singers later came to London. They were Margherita Durastanti,

[1] The Ruspoli archives are precise regarding hospitality to Handel, even detailing charges for the hire of his bed.

[2] See letter quoted in 'New Sources for Handel—*La Resurrezione,*' Rudolf Ewerbert, in *Music and Letters,* April 1960, p. 128.

[3] ' . . . whether a Portugueze or a Spanish Princess I will not be cer-tain.'—Mainwaring, p. 66.

whose appearance in *Agrippina* at the age of fourteen or fifteen was less remarkable then than it would be now, and Giuseppe Boschi, the possessor of a Gostling-like voice of immense profundity.

Agrippina was Handel's greatest achievement to date, and he let it be his valediction to Italy. After the hysteria of 'Viva il caro Sassone!' which punctuated every pause in each performance he determined to try his fortunes elsewhere. Invitations from Hanover were pressing, Prince Ernest had seen the success of *Agrippina,* and Steffani was pleased with the progress of his protégé. He had learned something of the favourable impression Handel had made when in Rome a year earlier. Steffani was too involved by now in affairs of church and state to continue his *Kapellmeister* office. Therefore he vacated it, applied himself to episcopal duties—he had been consecrated Bishop of Spriga, *in partibus infidelium,* and appointed the pope's representative in Northern Germany—and deposited Handel at Hanover.

The three years in Italy were to Handel as a post-graduate course. He had previously learned the fundamentals of musicianship in good schools, those of Halle and Hamburg, but Italy provided the opportunity of absorbing, at first hand, the principles which were to dominate the eighteenth century. Stylistic considerations will be dealt with at a later juncture, but a sufficient guarantee of the value of this experience is denoted by the manuscripts collected of works by Alessandro Scarlatti, some of which eventually found their way into the library of Charles Jennens. In Italy Handel was reminded of the welcome which would greet him in England, when he cared to make the journey. He left the country having gained in knowledge, in friendship and in reputation. The laity impulsively referred to him as 'L'Orfeo del nostro secolo,' which Germany subsequently thought of as 'a rare honour, for no German is spoken of thus by an Italian or a Frenchman, these gentry being accustomed to scoffing at us'; the clergy with commendable zeal looked on him not only as a great musician, but as a worthy subject for proselytism. Handel reacted to this compliment by resolving 'to die a member of that communion, whether true or false, in which he was born and bred.' At the same time he produced a large number of effectively apposite works, some of which, motets, are preserved in the Santini collection at Münster (Westphalia).

CHAPTER III

ENGLISH PATRONAGE

LIKE other employers of labour the eighteenth-century disciples of Maecenas had their faults. But Johnson's letter to the Earl of Chesterfield and Mozart's humiliation at the hands of the Archbishop of Salzburg have been allowed to overshadow the positive benefits accorded to numerous artists more fortunate in their selection of patron. The good and bad of the system will be evident from the progress of this book; with Handel's appointment to Hanover we enter upon a period in his life singular for its pleasant association with the great. It was in the middle of June 1710 that he took up his duties in place of Steffani. His emoluments amounted to 1,000 thaler per annum. Within a month or so he was, however, again peripatetic. First a dutiful call at Halle and then a visit to the electoral court at Düsseldorf. Here he already had contacts: the Electress Anna Maria was sister to Ferdinand and Gastone de' Medici; Steffani was a regular correspondent of the elector; and Corelli was *persona grata* there. For a short time the splendour of Düsseldorf, apparent in its opera and its picture galleries, beguiled Handel, but during the autumn he made his way to London. As a cultural demonstration this visit would have met with Hanoverian approval and Handel's success in London been regarded as of slightly more than artistic value. Handel did one important thing. He impressed many people of influence with what to them was a singular fact: that a foreigner, possessed of certain attributes, could override that insular prejudice which insisted that aliens were of necessity comic and/or offensive.

Heidegger, manager of the Opera, was both.[1] A Swiss by birth,

[1] Heidegger's appearance can be wondered at in Hogarth's 'Cuzzoni, Farinelli and Heidegger' (1734) or in Pope's succinct

'And lo! her bird (a monster of a fowl,
Something betwixt a Heideggre and owl).'

Dunciad, i. 289–90.

HANDEL THE PERFORMER
From a portrait by Sir James Thornhill (1676–1734)

he essayed various professions speculatively and graduated to opera by way of a privacy in Queen Anne's Life Guards. This he judiciously relinquished to invest his wits in the new potentialities of Italian opera. Thus he met Handel in 1710 with a view to establishing a fortune out of the latter's high reputation and the whims of the aristocracy. They, indignant at any suggestion that England (particularly after Blenheim and Ramillies) could be bettered in any department of life, but none the less slaves to continental fashion, were sympathetic to the newer form of operatic entertainment. The nearest contemporary parallel to the influence of Italian opera is that of the American domination of the film industry. If in some measure the reader understands the further implications of this parallel the difficulties of Handel's career will be better appreciated.

Had he lived, Purcell might have prevented the overwhelming success of foreign opera. But in the interregnum between his death in 1695 and Handel's arrival in 1710 developments had taken place which eased the way for Heidegger, Handel and the consequent combined operations of continental singers and composers. That Purcell went so soon was a permanent regret to the discriminating, and Henry Carey, a keen enough Handelian, was to voice the feelings of many who loved opera but had a shrewd idea that England, given a chance, could do it as well as anybody:

> Ev'n heaven-born Purcell now is held in scorn;
> Purcell, who did a brighter age adorn.[1]

It was not only, however, the dearth of composers which was responsible for a changed outlook. It was first such singers as Francesca de l'Épine and Francesco Tosi who demonstrated the histrionic possibilities of the Italian language. Superimposed was snobbery, which assumed that what was presented unintelligibly in a foreign tongue must be a symbol of high cultivation. Italian influence was insidious. *Arsinoe,* produced at Drury Lane in 1705, had English words and Italian music. A year later came Buononcini's *Camilla,* in translation. In 1707 the same work was done macaronically; l'Épine and Valentini sang in Italian, Mrs. Tofts, Mrs. Lindsey, Mrs. Turner, Leveridge and Ramondon in English.

---

[1] 'The Poet's Resentment,' from *Poems on Several Occasions,* 1729.

Addison's *Rosamund* did nothing to set the clock back. Addison had himself principally to blame. The text of *Rosamund* is a flaccid effort. In Italian the ridiculous would have passed unnoticed, but in English verse Addison descends below banality with such lines as

> Here will I stand
> With hat in hand
> Obsequiously to greet him.

Nor was Thomas Clayton a composer who could get over the textual difficulties. The only interest of *Rosamund* is in its anticipation of romantic historiography and the revived balladry of Percy. Addison put his defeat down to stupidity on the part of others and upheld his dignity by poking through the chinks in the Italian armour. He had a prejudice, but his remarks on *Rinaldo* are very funny and not point-less. In 1709 Nicolini, 'the first truly great singer who had ever sung in our theatre,'[1] arrived and took London by storm.[2] Early in 1710 the first three operas to be done entirely in Italian were given: *Almahide, L'Idaspe fedele,* in which Nicolini strangled a lion with great gallantry,[3] and *Etearco.* The conductor was Pepusch.

This new form of entertainment won the approval of society as a whole, but the intellectuals were against it from the start. Addison for obvious reasons, Tickell because he was a henchman of Addison. Elijah Fenton gave vent to England's latent Puritanism by recalling nostalgically in 1711 that

> There was an age, (its memory will last!)
> Before Italian Airs debauch'd our taste;[4]

Hogarth came later, and Pope with him, to protest that opera had damaged the true tradition of native drama. English singers ranged themselves, if not against Italian opera as such, at any rate against imported singers. Mrs. Tofts had expressed their point of view with

---

[1] Burney, *History,* iv. 208.

[2] For Nicolini's acting ability, *vide* Steele, *Tatler,* No. 115.

[3] Letter from Lady Mary Wortley Montagu to Mrs. Hewet, 1711.

[4] Elijah Fenton, 'An Epistle to Mr. Southerne, from Kent, January 28, 1710–11.'

some emphasis by employing a domestic to throw oranges at l'Épine during a Drury Lane performance as long ago as 1704.

> Effeminate in dress, in manners grown,
> We now despise whatever is our own.[1]

So Carey put forward the moral issue which was energetically thrashed during the years to come with particular regard to the exotic and repulsive race of *castrati*. All this being taken into consideration, Handel's success in opera is remarkable. But in these circumstances may be discerned the seeds of destruction.

Heidegger acted as Handel's cicerone in 1710. Among the quality to whom Handel was introduced was Sir John Stanley, a minor court official, to be precise a commissioner of customs, whose moderate Jacobitism ensured his subsequent rustication. With him lived his ward—Mary Granville. At this time she was a volatile child of ten, and her first impressions of Handel were later memorialized:

> I was struck with his playing, but struck as a child, not a judge, for the moment he was gone, I seated myself at the instrument, and played the best lesson I had then learnt: my uncle archly asked me whether I thought I should ever play as well as Mr. Handel. 'If I didn't think I should,' cried I, 'I would burn my instrument.'[2]

So began a lifelong friendship.

Handel's first opera in England was *Rinaldo*,[3] commissioned by Aaron Hill for the company which he had a year or two earlier transferred from Drury Lane to Vanbrugh's new theatre in the Haymarket. The libretto was adapted by Giacomo Rossi from Tasso; Handel, with a characteristic burst of energy, wrote his music, much too fast for the unfortunate librettist, in a fortnight. The singers included Boschi, his wife, Vanini and Nicolini. The work was first produced on 24th February 1711. The *éclat* was terrific. For this the singers should claim as much responsibility as the composer: fashionable audiences at all times have a habit of paying devotion not to the quality of music so much as to its extraneous embellishments. It was Nicolini who carried the house away. Addison's

---

[1] *Vide* Carey, 'The Poet's Resentment.'
[2] Mrs. Delany, *Life and Correspondence*, pp. 5 and 6.
[3] *Vide* Addison, *Spectator*, Nos. 5, 29 and 31.

trunk-maker 'upon Nicolini's first appearance was said to have demolished three benches in the fury of his applause.'[1] The absence of Nicolini two years later led to the failure of *Il pastor fido*. But in 1711 Handel could not foresee the possibility of failure.

At that time Thomas Britton's musical evenings in Clerkenwell were one of the wonders of London, demonstrating how common interest could unite in amiability individuals of widely contrasted social status. Courtesy and intelligence intermingled at Britton's to form a pattern of democratic behaviour. Britton himself was a seller of small-coal: outside of business hours a bibliophile, rubbing shoulders at Bateman's bookshop by St. Paul's and at the stalls in Little Britain with earls and dukes. He was also an amateur in chemistry, a Rosicrucian and a musician. 'There goes the famous small-coal man,' they used to cry after him, 'who is a lover of learn-ing, a performer in music, and a companion for gentlemen.' Among his visitors in 1711 was Handel, who must have been surprised at the unconventional music-room over the coal-store, at the numerous quality who used to clamber shin-dangerously up the narrow stair, at the standard of amateur performance and at the sensitive under-standing of contemporary music.

At Britton's Handel met, though he could hardly have missed meeting him before, Pepusch; Abiel Whichello and Philip Hart, organists and harpsichord players; Obadiah Shuttleworth,

> Envy of foreigners, thy country's pride,
> Whose soul is harmony, nor ought beside,
> Oh! could Corelli hear thy charming lays,
> He'd hug thee in his arms, and give thee praise;
> For thou such justice to his works has done,
> He need not blush to call thee son.[2]

Also John Banister, the younger, the leader of the opera orchestra, and the little prodigy Dubourg. Outside the ranks of professional musicians were Woolaston, a portrait painter; John Hughes,[3] poet

[1] Addison, *Spectator,* No. 235.

[2] Henry Carey, *To Mr. Obadiah Shuttleworth. Made and Spoken Extempore, on hearing him perform a Solo of Corelli with great Propriety.*

[3] Johnson's essay on Hughes (*Lives of the Poets*) contains the immortal phrase concerning 'an exotick and irrational entertainment.'

and dramatist; and Henry Needler, recently appointed accountant for the candle duty at the excise office, who drank and fiddled by turns at the 'Crown' in the Strand and rattled off Corelli to his boon companions at the Academy of Vocal Music. Add the bibulous Ned Ward, the eccentric Duchess of Queensberry and Justice Robe, and the gallery is reasonably complete. Such experience as this taught Handel that below the surface of English society ran an undercurrent of sympathy and understanding, and that between posing nobility and crapulent rabble came a middle class of friendly philosophers with whom he could find much in common. This section of the community was strengthened by the progress of national tradition and without parallel in any other part of Europe. With such protagonists of independence Handel felt himself at home.

The passing of the season reminded Handel of his Hanoverian commitments. Therefore he returned, but by way of hospitable Düsseldorf, and with a sufficiently long stay there to concern both himself and the elector over his reception at Hanover. However, he eased his conscience by writing for the Princess Caroline acceptable duets and for the court chamber music. During the year he was in correspondence with his English friends. This correspondence, couched in the lingua franca of the time, demonstrates Handel's faculty for pertinent expression without too precise attention to orthographical detail. 'Faites bien mes compliments à Mr. Hughes,' he wrote to Andrew Roner in July.

Je prendrai la liberté de lui écrire avec la prémiere occasion. S'il me veut cependant honorer de ses ordres, et d'y ajouter une de ses charmantes poésies en Anglois, il me fera la plus sensible grace. J'ai fait, depuis que je suis parti de vous, quelques progrés dans cette langue.

So another visit to England was in the wind. But before this was undertaken Halle called. Handel's sister Dorothea, married to a rising lawyer,[1] produced a daughter whose christening provided an opportunity for compassionate leave. Another year at Hanover followed, and then came the complete translation.

---

[1] Dr. Michael Michaelsen, later a member of the Prussian Imperial Service and the War Council. Handel was always on the most cordial terms with him.

In the autumn of 1712 Handel was back in London. On 26th November *Il pastor fido* disappointed him by its failure. Nicolini was away in Italy, and the new *castrato* Pellegrini, on his first visit, was too little known to attract a sufficiency of hero-worship. There was another reason why this opera failed. On 15th November the Duke of Hamilton had been murdered after a duel with Lord Mohun. This was more sensational than a new opera, and the after-gossip precluded other activities. *Teseo,* produced on 10th January, restored Handel's prestige. This was dedicated by its librettist, Haym,[1] to the Earl of Burlington. An astute move, as Burlington was on the point of setting up as the general director of all the fine arts. His inherited wealth, his palace in Piccadilly, his acquaintance with Italy and his personal charm fitted him for this self-appointment. 'He possessed every quality of a genius and artist except envy,' said Horace Walpole. It was to Burlington that Handel owed the establishment of his reputation during the declining years of Queen Anne. Handel was a close friend of Henry Needler, a familiar drinking-companion, and a frequent caller at Needler's house in Clement's Lane. Needler was a useful friend. He was, as a gentleman, so qualified by his clerkship in excise, and a musician, on terms of friendship with many of the nobility, a frequent performer at the town houses of the Duke of Rutland, Lords Burlington,[2] Essex and Percival. He had probably brought Handel into touch with Burlington. The concerts at which Needler played are worthy of mention as factors of importance in musical education. Uffenbach[3] describes one enthusiastically: 'The famous Pepusch often gets up such a concert at the request of some noble lords. The orchestra was not very strong, consisting of not more than 16 persons [an average-size band in those days], but it was incomparable.' L'Épine sang, but not so well as at the opera because 'she sang whatever was put before her and did not take much trouble.' The instrumental music, however, was very beautiful and the whole concert lasted for two hours. 'I could have listened the whole night with the greatest pleasure.'

[1] Who based his text on one prepared for Lully by Quinault in 1675.
[2] Handel frequently had the direction of these concerts. Hawkins, v. 410.
[3] *London in 1710, from the travels of Zacharias von Uffenbach,* pp. 66–7.

Handel became a great citizen of London. In these early years of his residence therein we can visualize him as spending his off-duty hours at Britton's, until 1714, when Britton died, at the concerts at the 'Swan' and at the 'Crown,' at Lœillet's séances in Hart Street and with the choirmen from Saint Paul's at the nearby 'Queen's Arms.' He was a frequent visitor to the cathedral, completely finished only in 1710, and pushing past the ballad-singers and vendors of nuts, apples and ginger-bread who shouted their wares at the west doors, would go in to hear the organ and the music of Purcell. In Italy Handel showed himself a master of Italian style; in England he paid like tribute to his hosts by taking as model the most brilliant (and how they lamented him at Britton's!) of recent composers. Purcell's *Te Deum* and *Jubilate* of 1694 encouraged the *Te Deum* and *Jubilate* which Handel wrote to celebrate the overdue Peace Treaty of Utrecht.[1] This, however, followed another work of particular significance, the *Birthday Ode* for the queen. This was done on 6th February (a very wet day), and the *Te Deum* at St. Paul's on 7th July. By this time Handel had progressed considerably in his English studies. We may presume friends at court to have engineered these occasional works, for it was unusual for alien musicians to write ceremonial music, and without proper influence being brought to bear we can hardly imagine an obstinate woman like Queen Anne, and no particular lover of the prospective Hanoverian succession, prejudicing herself in Handel's favour, and so far forgetting herself as to settle on him a pension of £200. Thus obviously in the good graces of the English, Handel had no particular desire to return to his somewhat less exhilarating duties at Hanover. He did not return.

He was intoxicated by social success and by the free-and-easy life of London. Prospects in the opera were generally good, the nobility was obliging, other people were generous in hospitality—Andrews of Barn Elms had given him house-room for a year—money was flowing in. In 1716 he started his investments by putting £500 into the South Sea Company. And he was living well. He appreciated the gouty results of the Methuen Treaty of 1703, which brought port into the country almost duty free, and respected the

[1] Noted in a provincial paper, the *Worcester Post Man,* 27th February.

enthusiasm of the English for the pleasures of the table. The times had altered less in some respects than might be imagined since the classic remark of Erasmus: 'Britanni, praeter alia, formam, musicam, et lautas mensas proprie sibi vindicent.'

The death of Queen Anne on 1st August 1714 involved Handel less than other notabilities. Bolingbroke, for instance, having been engaged in dictatorial aspirations and king-making negotiations, was caught most uncomfortably, and so were all the high Tories. The new king had more to do than to contemplate the caprices of an errant *Capellmeister,* a minor official whose activities could have been of little consequence set against the panorama of politics. Hitherto Handel's desertion of Hanover has been rated too dramatically and the picture has been heightened by the legend of the *Water Music.* It is true that this was performed for the gratification of George I, that fifty players did add to the delights of a seductive evening spent with the Duchess of Bolton, Countess Godolphin, Madame Kiel-mansegge and Madame Ware, and that Kielmansegge arranged at considerable cost to himself the order of the evening. But that was long after George's accession: it was on 17th July 1717.[1]

The king's accession produced neither ode nor anthem. Handel was busy concocting with Heidegger another opera for the Hay-market. In the meantime *Rinaldo* was revived as a contribution to the coronation festivities. The king came to *Rinaldo,* with one or other of his mistresses, and to *Amadigi,*[2] the new opera, on a number of occasions during 1715.

Handel had written no opera for three years, from *Teseo* to *Amadigi,* except for the miniature *Silla,* which, if performed at all, was done in privacy, possibly at Burlington House. This sabbatical period may be accounted for by the anarchic state of affairs, which reigned at the Haymarket after the Irishman MacSwiney, an able producer but, like so many of his countrymen, possessed of no financial acumen, had left his management of the theatre in haste and bankruptcy in the middle of the run of *Teseo.* Poor MacSwiney was more sinned against than sinning. He had left the army in 1705 in the optimistic belief that Rich would live up to his promise to provide ' 100 Guineas

---

[1] Newman Flower, p. 104 et seq.   [2] Produced 25th May.

per annum Salary, a place at Court, and the Devil and all.'[1] Only
the last clause matured, and MacSwiney took his grievances and the
contents of the box-office to Italy. After this episode Handel kept
off the Haymarket, but occupied his time in consolidating his social
bridge-heads.

Amadigi, so Heidegger tells us in his dedication, was composed by
Handel at Burlington House. From 1715 to 1718 Handel lived
there a good deal. He had rooms at the back of the house where, so
nearly rural was Piccadilly, he enjoyed a pleasant prospect of open
country. A fellow pensioner was the lively architect Kent, who
came under the earl's wing in 1716. More distinguished beneficiaries were Pope and Gay. Another intimate was Dr. Arbuthnot,
'a man of great comprehension, skilful in his profession, versed in the
sciences, acquainted with antient literature, and able to animate his
mass of knowledge by a bright and active imagination.'[2] Arbuthnot was one of Handel's greatest friends.

Gay's *Trivia* (1716) has often been quoted for

> There *Hendel* strikes the strings, the melting strain
> Transports the soul, and thrills through ev'ry vein;

but the whole poem should be read for the complete picture it affords
of Handel's London. Splendour, squalor, misery, disease, vice and
a little virtue all in proportion quietly blended. The *eheu fugaces*
romanticists would do well to feel Gay's stabbing couplets on the
seamy side. Heroic couplets is a misnomer. And those who overestimate the comfort of Burlington House might be reminded of Lord
Hervey's opinion that it was

> Possessed of one great hall of state,
> Without a room to sleep or eat.

But then Hervey was no lover of Burlington. Pope found Handel's
fame and popularity perplexing. With a distaste for music, a heartier
distaste for foreign musicians and a complete contempt for opera, he
so far lacked confidence in his judgment as to apply to Arbuthnot on
the score of Handel's reputation. Was all the rapture displayed by
his audiences genuine or was it not?[3] 'Conceive the highest you can

---

[1] Grove, v. [2] Johnson.
[3] Warton's *Pope's Works*, v. 235 n.

of his abilities,' said Arbuthnot, 'and they are far beyond anything you can conceive.' However, Pope interested himself in preparing libretti for Handel, and protested when in due course he learned that the composer was being traduced by those who were both fashionable and ignorant.[1] But Arbuthnot's good opinion was worth more than Pope's. Formerly physician-in-ordinary to Queen Anne, a political pamphleteer, an occasional poet and a shining light in the company of wit or wealth, he was capable of placing opportunities in the way of the young and ambitious.[2] Years later he proved the endurance of his loyalty by whipping Handel's detractors in *Harmony in an Uproar*.

Amadigi brought back to London Nicolini. With him in the cast was Anastasia Robinson. She was driven to a profession by indigence and, having chosen singing, acquired her technique from Croft and Sandoni. At the time of the production of *Amadigi* she was little more than seventeen and at the outset of a career brief, glorious and not unprofitable. Gay rallied round with a somewhat commonplace compliment:

> When *Anastasia's* voice commands the strain,
> The melting warble thrills through ev'ry vein;
> Thought stands suspense, and silence pleas'd attends,
> While in her notes the heav'nly Choir descends.[3]

Success on the stage and a modest behaviour recommended Anastasia to the gallant and erratic Earl of Peterborough, Swift's hang-dog whom he loved dearly. Peterborough married Anastasia in 1722, but disallowed her the title of countess until 1735, when he assembled his friends, informed them of the lady's merits and announced his thirteen-year-old marriage. So ended with universal satisfaction the mystery of the virtuous lady who had apparently permitted herself the licence of noble concubinage.

By 1715 Handel was regarded as a great composer, but also as a

[1] W. Coxe, *Anecdotes of Handel*, 1799, p. 40.

[2] 'The doctor has great power with the queen.'—Swift, op. cit., Letter XXXI.

[3] 'To the Right Honourable William Pulteney Esq.' (*Epistles on Several Occasions, 1720*).

great performer. As the best available harpsichord player he re-
entered the immediate entourage of the king. Geminiani, an old
client of George I, brought himself to the notice of Kielmansegge
and, having insinuated himself into that gentleman's graces and been
invited to play at St. James's, insisted that he would play to no other
accompaniment than Handel's. As a result of his renewed association with royalty Handel was granted a further £200 a year (titles
and emoluments fell thick on German subjects in the king's English
service), and this sum was added to, in like measure, by the Princess
Caroline, who put the musical education of her daughters in his
hands.

On 9th July 1716 George retired to his electorate as a respite
from the responsibilities of constitutional monarchy imposed on him
by an English parliament. Handel went with him. Here was an
opportunity for him to air his English accent, a vile one according to
his biographers but apparently effective enough for general purposes
at Halle. For a visit to Halle formed part of this itinerary. Mother
and aunt must have found it difficult to apportion their pride as
between a relatively prodigal but clearly distinguished son and a
wholly prosperous and respectable son-in-law. Old Zachau was
dead, but Handel, with characteristic generosity, went out of his way
to relieve the widow's straitened circumstances.

Correspondence was going on at this time between Mattheson and
Handel,[1] and Hamburg was looking forward to a performance of
the newly written setting of Brockes's Passion. Mattheson avers
that this was written in London 'and was sent by the post in a score
written very minutely.' Later writers cast doubts on this statement
and preferred to have the Passion written in Germany during this tour.
In default of positive evidence it is uncharitable to question Mattheson's veracity on this point. In any case Handel was clearly
travelling a good deal during this vacation.

He was, among other places, at Ansbach, on some mission contrived by the Princess Caroline. Here he met an old associate in
Johann Christoph Schmidt. Schmidt was impecunious, and Handel
recommended London as a city in which broken fortunes might be

---

[1] Mattheson, *Ehren-Pforte*.

mended. Schmidt accordingly went to London, shortly afterwards sending for his family to join him. Thus Handel combined self, interest (he needed a secretary) and charity.

Handel's Passion was performed at Hamburg after he left Germany. Its later history is not without interest. Bach came across it and, with the help of Anna Magdalena, made a copy for use at Leipzig.[1]

In January 1717 King George, refreshed by beer and oysters, solaced by Mesdames Schulenburg and Kielmansegge, and rested from the unconscionable English, who disapproved paraded para, mours who were fat and foreign, returned to London. Back went Handel.

---

[1] Schweitzer, *J. S. Bach*. i. 94. Twenty-three pages were copied by Bach and thirty-seven by Anna Magdalena. Telemann also thought highly of this work, for once withholding his own music in its honour in a performance given at the Collegium Musicum at Hamburg in 1722. (Rolland, op. cit., p. 116.)

CHAPTER IV

'AN ACT FOR NATURALISATING . . . ?'

THE principal profiteer out of the War of Spanish Succession was James Brydges, who had paid the accounts, as Paymaster-General to the Forces, of Marlborough's overseas armies and kept a good deal of the change. In 1711 the disappearance of £35,000,000 caused a parliamentary stir, and Brydges, though defended with warmth by Mr. Secretary,[1] was named as partly responsible. Nevertheless, the fuss died down, and like many military heroes whose duties keep them at a safe distance from the firing-line, Brydges won the customary rewards of successful peculation. In 1714 he became Viscount Wilton and Earl of Carnarvon, and five years later Marquis of Carnarvon and Duke of Chandos. In the middle of this prosperity (retribution later overtook him in ill-judged speculation in the South Sea Bubble and lost him £300,000) he built a palace at Canons, by Edgware, and as a necessary adjunct a chapel.

The Chapel is a singularity not only in its building and the beauty of its workmanship, but in this also, that the Duke maintains there a full Choir and has the Worship performed there with the best musick, after the manner of the Chapel Royal, . . . Nor is this chapel only furnished with such excellent musick, but the Duke has a set of them to entertain him every day at dinner.[2]

The duke's first director of music was Pepusch. The maxim

He wins this Patron, who can tickle best,[3]

however, worked to his disadvantage, and Handel soon after his return from Germany superseded him. His royal associations—he still continued in his capacity as music-master to the king's grandchildren—and his virtuosity in performance and composition fitted Handel better for the baroque atmosphere of Canons than did learning Pepusch. From Handel's point of view this appointment was a welcome

[1] Swift, op. cit., Letter XXI.   [2] Defoe, *Tour in England*, 1725.
[3] Pope, *Dunciad*, ii. 196.

33

addition to his emoluments, there being a lull in operatic interest in town. He celebrated the grand duke worthily in the Chandos anthems as well as in the *Te Deum*. In the early days at Canons he collected a number of harpsichord pieces, those which perplexed royal fingers, and other pieces with which he had been accustomed to impress his select audiences; these he published in 1720 with Cluer under the title of *Suites de Pièces pour le Clavecin*. 'I have,' wrote Handel in an introductory note which reflects the amoral habits of piratical publishers, been obliged to publish some of the following lessons, because surrepticious and incorrect copies of them had got abroad. I have added several new ones to make the work more useful, which if it meets with a favourable reception, I will still proceed to publish more, reckoning it my duty, with my small talent [tongue well in cheek here!], to serve a nation from which I have received so generous a protection.

Two significant works of larger stature were produced under the ducal aegis; *Acis and Galatea* and *Haman and Mordecai*, or *Esther*. The libretto of the first was done by Gay, though assisted by Hughes and Pope,[1] and was prompted by Handel's previous affection for this Sicilian fable. *Esther*, reputed to have been performed in August 1720 and to have brought from the duke a gift of £1,000, was prepared by Pope (in 1732 it was added to by Humphreys) from Racine. These two works, privately rehearsed, indicated new direction: towards landscape and towards oratorio. But in 1720 their significance was not apparent to their author. He was by now newly involved in an illfated operatic adventure.

The Hanoverian dynasty securely fixed, Jacobitism gone underground or to SaintGermain since the miscarriage of 1715, the Tories suffering political exclusion and no greater excitement than could be provided by the Mohocks to hand, aristocracy turned its head towards culture. Therefore was launched the Royal Academy of Music. This, in 1719-20, appeared a no less profitable speculation than anything else. In fact, more than in the case of most newly formed companies of that time, there was a definite chance of the thing working. There were composers, librettists and managers available and there was a probable market. A capital of £50,000 was raised

---

[1] Passages from Pope's *Autumn* (ll. 43-6) and *Iliad* (xiii. ll. 17-33) appear almost unaltered in *Acis and Galatea*.

in £100 shares, and the king was induced to contribute £1,000 to the scheme.

Under the governorship of the Duke of Newcastle, and with Lord Bingley as his second-in-command, twenty directors were elected. These included the Dukes of Portland and Queensberry, the Earls of Burlington (who apparently didn't mind Handel's desertion to Canons), Stair and Waldegrave, Lords Chetwynd and Stanhope, a collection of military gentlemen, including the celebrated roadmaker General Wade and Scarlatti's pupil Colonel Blathwayt, Sir John Vanbrugh and William Pulteney. Burlington, whose voice was raised authoritatively on artistic matters, had the bright idea of inviting Buononcini to come from Rome; somebody else suggested Attilio Ariosti. By 1720 they were banded with Handel in brief amiability. The next development was the engagement of singers. To effect this Handel was dispatched abroad.

A new lease of life to opera was a congenial prospect to Handel. He undertook his responsibilities in connection therewith with high seriousness. He complains in letters to Mattheson, whose request for a biographical entry for the *Ehren-Pforte* he disappointingly refused and whose questions on Greek modes receive a pragmatic answer,[1] and to his brother-in-law, of pressure of work.

Do not [he writes to Michaelsen,[2]] judge of my desire to see you by the delay connected with my departure; for, to my great regret, I find myself detained here by indispensible business, on which it is not too much to say that my whole fortune depends, and which lasts much longer than I expected.

Handel's sister Dorothea had lately died of consumption, so that personal grief overshadowed the excitement of the inception of the Royal Academy. However, shortly after writing Handel was *en route* for the Continent.

[1] Letter from Handel to Mattheson, 24th February 1719: 'As to the Greek Modes, Sir, I find that you have said all that can be said upon the subject. It is no doubt necessary that those who wish to practise and execute Music composed in those Modes should study them: but, since we have escaped from the narrow bounds of antient Music, I cannot see in what way the Greek Modes can be useful in connection with the Music of modern times. This, Sir, is my opinion: . . .'

[2] 20th February 1719.

Business took him to Düsseldorf and Dresden, and painful pleasure to Halle. Here he stayed for too short a period to allow of a meeting with Bach who, hearing of his presence there, undertook a fruitless walk from Anhalt-Cöthen. At Düsseldorf Handel impressed Baldassari, at Dresden Durastanti. In the middle of his Dresden negotiations Handel wrote to the Earl of Burlington. Because the letter has not previously been published it is given in full:

My Lord

C'est toujours autant par une vive reconnoissance, que par devoir, que je me donne l'honneur de Vous dire le zele et l'attachement que j'ay pour Vôtre personne. Je Vous dois de plus un conte exact de ce que j'ay entrepris, et de la reussite du sujet de mon long voyage.

Je suis icy à attendre que les engagements de Sinesino, Berselli, et Guizzardi, soyent finis, et que ces Messieurs d'ailleurs bien disposés, s'engagent avec moy pour la Grande Bretagne. tout sera decidé en quelques jours; j'ay des bonnes esperances, et dès que j'auray conclû quelque chose de réel, je Vous l'ecrirai My Lord comme a mon bienfaiteur, à mon Protecteur. Conservez moy, My Lord, Vos graces, elles me seront pretieuses, et ce sera toujours avec ardeur et fidelité que je suivray Vôtre service, et Vos nobles volontés. C'est avec une soumission egalement sincere et profonde que je serai à jamais

à Dresde	My Lord
ce 26/15 de Juillet	Vôtre
1719	tres humble tres obeissant, et tres devoue
	Serviteur
	GEORGE FRIDERIC HANDEL [1]

The negotiations with Senesino and Berselli went satisfactorily, but not with Guizzardi, who never came to England. However, Salvai and Boschi made up for that deficiency. In addition to contriving these arrangements Handel was playing the harpsichord at the Dresden court. For this the elector, with generosity under the circumstances, made him a present of 100 ducats. As for German noblemen, Handel found them inferior to the English variety, and the Count von Fleming, annoyed at shallow excuses for inability to be social, wrote to Melusine von Schulenburg [2] in London, that

[1] Devonshire MSS., 1st Series, 150, 0.

[2] She was a daughter of the Duchess of Kendal, formerly Madame von Schulenburg, a pupil of Handel's, and in 1733 married the Earl of Chesterfield.

Handel was a little mad. That was on 6th October, so Handel had been a long time at Dresden. His newly engaged singers relieved themselves quickly of electoral responsibility by displaying such bouts of temperament that the elector was glad to terminate their contract.

Back in London Handel began *Radamisto*, his first contribution to the reportory of the Royal Academy. His librettist was Haym and the story from Tacitus. Handel's optimism for the new scheme led him to take the house in Lower Brook Street, No. 57,[1] which was his home for the rest of his life.

The opera season opened on 2nd April 1720 with Porta's *Numitor*, which gave way after half a dozen performances to *Radamisto*. This attracted a tremendous first-night audience: the royal family was there, and so great was the crush that free fights ensued in the admission queues with damage to persons and property: women fainted, and of those who didn't many had their dresses torn off their backs. In view of impending developments and disappointment it should be mentioned that this opera season came, with more than a fair share of publicity, after a fallow period in the entertainment world. *Radamisto* is notable among Handelian operas, but fine craftsmanship was beside the point to the majority of those whose lives were governed by a sequence of events whose primary purpose was to relieve boredom. Handel took himself seriously: only a few other people of discernment did. When Dr. William Stukeley told Sir Isaac Newton that he had attended a rehearsal of *Radamisto*, Newton expressed a distaste for the subject.[2] As for Handel's playing Newton was reported to have found 'nothing worthy to remark but the elasticity of his fingers.'[3] But that Newton got so far as to comment on Handel is symptomatic of the pressure of the Handel cult. Nothing, however, is more delusive than to be the temporary hero of fashion.

Radamisto came and went and was followed by Domenico Scarlatti's *Narciso*, conducted by that unhappy genius Thomas Roseingrave. The chief singers during the season were Baldassari,

[1] As renumbered, No. 25 Brook Street.
[2] William Stukeley, *Family Memoirs*, i. 59.
[3] Hawkins, *Life of Johnson*, iii. 176 n.

Durastanti, Anastasia Robinson, Mrs. Turner Robinson—wife of the organist of Westminster Abbey—and the athletic Gordon.

In March the singers from Dresden arrived. Of these the most eagerly awaited was Senesino, who came to fill the void left by Nicolini. The cult of the *castrato* helped to ruin opera in England, where men were preferred as men. From Handel's point of view, however, considerations of masculinity were secondary to those of vocal ability and the box-office. The great *castrati* could sing magnificently, and their Mediterranean manners engaged the attention of the ladies. This encouraged such vainglorious idiosyncrasies as Handel found unbearable. *Radamisto* in the meantime was published with Meares and Christopher Smith (formerly Schmidt) and *Esther* was got ready for Canons.

The next opera to be performed at the Haymarket was Buononcini's *Astarto*, one of the Earl of Burlington's favourite works. The combination of Buononcini and Senesino was irresistible. In the patchwork operas of Queen Anne's day Buononcini's arias had been highly popular. He was a good composer, an elegant melodist, a competent judge of the requirements of public opinion and an astute courtier. His style, says Hawkins, 'was tender, elegant, and pathetic. Handel's had all these qualities, and numberless others, and his invention was inexhaustible.' [1] Unfortunately Handel had a superfluity of excellence, so that vociferous and ignorant critics were always able to find something to displease them in the differences which separated Handel from Buononcini. That his orchestration was heavy and his counterpoint severe was therefore relatively true. All this tended towards the division of the musical into two factions. *Radamisto* was again revived after *Astarto*, but Buononcini's opera, which had run for ten nights before and ten after Christmas, put him in the ascendant. The season closed with him well pleased, and he disappeared to Twickenham in an aura of self-satisfaction to idle the summer away with Senesino and Mrs. Robinson. He cultivated the quality and supped occasionally with Lady Mary Wortley Montagu.[2]

[1] Hawkins, v. 276.

[2] Letter from Lady Mary Wortley Montagu to the Countess of Mar, 6th September 1721.

The Buononcini faction was largely Whig, his chief support coming from the disgruntled Marlboroughs with the Duke of New-castle furnishing a good second string. Handel's associates were of the discredited Tory school and, while his political ideas were necessarily not particularly bound, the fact that he had been among the Arbuthnot, Swift (although there is no direct evidence of a meet-ing between Handel and Swift it is inconceivable that they were not acquainted),[1] Pope, Gay and Parnell circle would not have gone unnoticed. Moreover, he was a king's man, and that was not con-ducive to popularity; nor was a character unpliable to condescension. The letter to Burlington may appear Heep-like, but in private conversation Handel spoke to all and sundry as man to man.

In the spring of 1721 *Muzio Scevola,* of which the acts were com-posed in turn by Filippo Mattei, Buononcini and Handel, afforded an opportunity to view the protagonists in close juxtaposition. Handel's *Floridante,* later in the season, was a failure, and Buononcini was able to establish a commanding lead by the popularity of his *Crispo* and *Griselda.*

At this juncture Handel fell back on the expedient of introducing a new singer. This was Francesca Cuzzoni, an ugly little Venetian virago with a dominating personality, a flair for self-advertisement, a pathetic husband (Sandoni her accompanist, whom she married on landing in England) and 'a nest of nightingales in her belly.' This pregnant remark was bawled from the gallery by a groom privileged to hear Handel's *Ottone,* which at the beginning of 1723 introduced Cuzzoni to an enraptured public. *Ottone* undermined Buonon-cini's operatic future, which had already suffered from his arrogant demands on the directorate of the Royal Academy. He retreated to enjoy a handsome pension from the Duchess of Marlborough. Cuzzoni drove from the stage Anastasia Robinson, whose voice had been reduced by illness and her interest in the theatre by the importunities of the Earl of Peterborough. Handel thus survived his first depression and celebrated it by a fit of choler at the expense of his new prima donna.

Having refused to sing the first air in *Ottone* in rehearsal, Cuzzoni

[1] Swift was a particular friend of Mrs. Pendarves's uncle, Sir John Stanley, to whom frequent reference is made in the *Journal to Stella.*

Handel

suffered: 'Madame, je sais que vous êtes une véritable diablesse, mais je vous ferai savoir, moi, que je suis Béelzebub, le chef des diables.' This was followed up by an intention to throw her through a conveniently open window. But at that point she capitulated.

After *Ottone* came *Flavio,* in which Gordon's threat to jump on the harpsichord provoked Handel to comment that that would be more attractive an entertainment than his singing. And after *Flavio* came *Giulio Cesare.* Cuzzoni and Senesino were carrying all before them; but the latter suffered some diminution in fame by his abjection at the disturbance caused by a falling piece of scenery in *Giulio Cesare* and by his recent horse-whipping at the hands of Peterborough. On 25th May 1724 Ambrose Philips let Cuzzoni know that her tenure of popularity was not eternal:

> Little *Siren* of the stage
> Charmer of an idle age,
> Empty warbler, breathing lyre,
> Wanton gale of fond desire,
> Bane of every heavenly art,
> Sweet enfeebler of the breast,
> O, too pleasing is thy strain,
> Hence to southern climes again;
> Tuneful mischief, vocal spell,
> To this island bid farewell;
> Leave us as we ought to be,
> Leave the *Britons* rough and free.[1]

A year earlier Philips had put a straw in the wind by his publication of *A Collection of Old Ballads,* including *Robin Hood* and *The Children in the Wood.* There were others. Hogarth,[2] at the outset of his career, was, in 'Masquerades and Operas,' displaying a righteous indignation at the sympathies of high society. His butts were Burlington, whom he regarded as an effete play-boy, and Heidegger, who was promoting *ridotti* and masquerades of lewd distinction. Easeful life and the Walpolian policy of a peaceful England were reducing morality to shreds. Heidegger was doing his best to complete the

[1] 'To Signora Cuzzoni May 25, 1724,' *Pastorals, Epistles, Odes,* 1765.
[2] Hogarth joined the Academy of Vocal Music in 1729.

40

process. 'The rules that are observed by this new society,' says Addison acidly, 'are wonderfully contrived for the advancement of cuckoldom.'[1] Handel looked on at the attacks on the opera and considered *Esther* an insurance against the religious revival which Heidegger would undoubtedly stimulate. Already the Bishop of London was inveighing against him and Fielding was coming in to the attack.

Tamerlano, Rodelinda and *Scipione* kept the Academy precariously afloat until 1726. *Rodelinda* was sensational for no other reason than that in it Cuzzoni scored a sartorial triumph by appearing in a brown and silver dress which set the pace for ladies' fashions for a long time. Handel found refuge from such irrelevancies in a nostalgic letter,[2] the first for some time as he ruefully admits, to his brother-in-law. Michaelsen was acting *in loco filii,* but Handel was anxious to revisit Halle. In England, however, he saw trouble ahead if he did not take adequate measures to safeguard the future: therefore he filed a petition to the House of Lords which ran as follows:

To the Right Honourable The Lords Spiritual and Temporal in Parliament assembled. The Humble Petition of George Frideric Handel sheweth That your Petitioner was born at Halle, in Saxony, out of His Majesty's Allegiance, but hath constantly professed the Protestant Religion, and hath given Testimony of his Loyalty and Fidelity to His Majesty and the Good of this Kingdom.

Therefore the Petitioner humbly prays That he may be added to the Bill now pending entitled 'An Act for Naturalising Louis Sechehaye.' And the petitioner will ever pray, etc.

GEORGE FRIDERIC HANDEL.

On 20th February 1726 the king signed the Bill. Having made his *civis britannicus sum* gesture, Handel was now eligible for employment as 'Composer of Musick for the Chapel Royal,' from which aliens were debarred, and 'Composer to the Court.'

The affairs of the Academy languishing, the directors committed themselves to the further extravagance of engaging a new singer, at £2,000 a year, in the person of Faustina Bordoni. Considering the eminence in military circles of so many of the directors, it can only be regarded as providential that their inane tactical behaviour was

[1] *Spectator*, No. 8.   [2] 11th/22nd June 1725.

confined to the realm of artistic operations. 'The umbrage given to Cuzzoni by her [Faustina's] coming hither, proves that as Turkish monarchs can bear no brother near the throne, an aspiring sister is as obnoxious to a theatrical Queen.'[1] The degree of enmity engendered between these two was worse 'than even the theological and political parties of high church and low, or Whig and Tory, which then raged in this country.'[2] The main supporters of Cuzzoni were the Countess of Pembroke, Sir Wilfred Lawson, Sir William Gage and Mr. Simon Smith; of Faustina, more impressively, Sir Robert Walpole, the Countess of Burlington, Lady Delawar and Lady Cowper.

They were jointly featured by Handel in *Alessandro,* which ran from 5th May until the end of the season on 7th June. Not unnaturally there were good houses. Handel's preoccupation on this score was to effect such division of virtuosity that neither of his ladies felt affronted. The only casualty was Senesino, who, forgotten in this welter of new adulation, advertised his chagrin in the conventional way by falling ill and retiring to Italy for a rest cure.

During the season Quantz was in London. He observed the battle of the singers, but was on the whole more interested in the orchestra which, led by Castrucci and directed by Handel, impressed him. Handel played the harpsichord and the organ; other players were

Geminiani, a great master on the violin; Dubourg, his scholar, an Englishman, who was a pleasing performer on that instrument; the two Castrucci's, who were brothers, and tolerable solo players; Weidemann, a German, and Festing, an Englishman, on the German flute, with Mauro d'Alaia, who came to England with Faustina; he was an excellent performer on the violin, and an excellent leader; his manner of playing was clear and distinct, but he never ventured at great difficulties.[3]

Quantz had an idea of staying in London and received encouragement from Handel, but—and we may hope that Handel appreciated this—'as he was still a servant of the King of Poland, he did not chuse to perform in public, thinking it a duty to his prince to offer him the first fruits of his travels.'[4]

[1] Burney, *History,* iv. 306.   [3] Burney, *Travels,* ii. 191 et seq.
[2] Ibid, iv. 309.   [4] Ibid.

Senesino returned from Italy in time for Ariosti's *Lucio Vero* on 7th January 1727. In succession to it came Handel's *Admeto*, which kept the flames of Cuzzoni-Faustina animosity well ablaze until Buononcini's *Astyanax* provided the grand conflagration. Polly Peachum and Lucy Lockit behaved as ladies in comparison with the rival singers, who delighted a vast audience with a hair-tearing display which not only stimulated Gay but also Arbuthnot, who celebrated it in *The Devil to pay at St. James's,* and Cibber, who produced honorifically *The Rival Queens.*

On 11th June George I died in his electorate, of apoplexy, at Osnabrück. On the 15th, the news having tardily reached England, George II was proclaimed. For his coronation in October Handel wrote what must be the paragon of all ceremonial music, not less than four anthems. This was a busy period. Music for the court balls was also requisitioned, and *Admeto* was put on at the Hay-market on 3rd October. On 11th November a *pièce d'occasion* was presented in the shape of *Riccardo primo, re d'Inghilterra.*

I was yesterday at the rehearsal of Mr. Handel's new opera called Richard I —'tis delightful. There I saw Captain Elliot. I was in Lady Sutherland's box . . . and he came and sate behind me. . . . Masquerades are not to be forbid, but there is to be another entertainment *barefaced*, which are balls. . . . There is to be a handsome collation, and they will have Heidegger's rooms to perform in. Some prudes already have attacked the reputation of those ladies that will accept of the tickets, but as all the sub-scribers are men, I don't see what scandal can ensue, only spiteful people make harm of everything.[1]

Not even Mrs. Pendarves (*née* Mary Granville and later to be Mrs. Delany) could resist the counter-attractions. Small wonder, then, that *Richard I* played for only eleven nights. And round the corner was another surprise.

[1] Mrs. Pendarves to Anne Granville, 11th November 1727.

CHAPTER V

ENGLISH OR ITALIAN?

There's Madam Faustina, Catso
And eek Madam Cuzzoni;
Likewise Signor Senesino
Are *tutti Abbandonni*:
Ha, Ha, Ha, Ha, Do, Re, Mi, Fa,
Are now but farce and folly;
We're ravish'd all with Toll, Loll, Loll,
And pretty, pretty Polly.[1]

THUS cheerfully Harry Carey epitomized the state of affairs at the beginning of 1728. *The Beggar's Opera* had its *première* on 29th January. To his title-page Gay added, over-modestly, from Martial: 'Nos haec novimus esse nihil.' The influence of this work, under-taken at the suggestion of Swift, was tremendous. Italian opera, the philandering Walpole, corrupt politicians and lascivious courtiers all came under the lash, and English drama was enriched. In the rumbustiousness of the text Ben Jonson was recalled, in the sharp-edged satire Dryden, in the songs the open-air artlessness of the natural pastoralist. Of all poetry English is, according to Voltaire, the most moral: *The Beggar's Opera* is the prime example. The music was not of less consequence than the libretto. Herein lies Gay's genius. Only a musician could have contrived it. Pepusch scored the work, but the tunes were those to which Gay had been brought up. Handel must often have heard the same tunes, which ravished the general ear when Gay fluted privately at Burlington House. Moreover, Gay knew the ways of opera. Prison scenes were common-place. Handel provided them in *Tamerlano, Radamisto, Floridante* and, most movingly, *Rodelinda,* while in *Floridante* an excellent fare-well scene between Elmira and Floridante suggested that between Polly and Macheath.

[1] 'Polly Peachum,' Carey, op. cit.

44

But of malice towards Handel Gay must be acquitted, nor was Handel the sort of person to have suggested it. At Burlington House they had got on excellently well together and later Handel had subscribed for a copy of *Poems on Several Occasions*.[1] Further, they were linked by a mutual friendship for Aaron Hill, a fellow Devonian with Gay. That *The Beggar's Opera* ran for sixty-three nights was a surprise to everybody: in advance Rich, who produced it at Lincoln's Inn Fields, had been very dubious, so had Bolingbroke when acquainted with the project, so had Gay's patron the Duke of Queensberry, and so had Jimmy Quin, who refused Macheath. However, in the curious fashion of literary-dramatic affairs it defied the previous dismalling and exceeded its author's most sanguine expectations.

Handel's *Siroe,* produced in February, containing nothing more extraordinary than Signora Mignotti trousered, lasted nineteen performances, and its successor *Tolomeo* only seven. And that was the end of £50,000, the Royal Academy and apparently of Faustina, Cuzzoni, Senesino and Handel. Faustina, fortified by the energy of London life, went off to Venice. There she disappeared into respectability and matrimony. She married Hasse in 1730. Senesino also went to Venice, where for a time he sang with Faustina. At another Venetian theatre at the same time could have been found Cuzzoni, Boschi, Nicolini and Farinelli.

Carey solemnized the departure of Senesino in *A Sorrowful Lamentation for the Loss of a Man and No Man*.[2] Handel settled down with customary determination to revive the faded glories by proposing partnership with Heidegger and by taking the King's Theatre for a five-year period. The first step was to replace the vanished singers, and this necessitated another Italian visit. In Italy he signed on— the whole business seems to foreshadow latter-day commercial sport technique—Bernacchi, a *castrato*; Fabri, a tenor (tenor singers had not yet arrived at idolization); Signora Fabri; Merighi and Bertolli, *contralti*; and Strada, to whom the English with their usual flair for graceless observation promptly attached the loveless sobriquet of 'The Pig.'

[1] Phoebe Fenwick Gaye, *John Gay,* p. 201.
[2] Carey, op. cit.

In Italy Handel renewed acquaintance with Joseph Smith[1] and exhibited a nice tact in declining an invitation from Colonna[2] at Rome on account of the Pretender's holding court in the city. From Italy to Germany. At Hamburg Gottfried Riemschneider was persuaded to come to England to take the place of Boschi. At Halle Handel saw his mother for the last time, blind and paralysed. Again he received overtures from Bach, who wished Handel to visit him at Leipzig; but there was no opportunity for a *rencontre*. To be truthful, it looks as though Handel was lacking in enthusiasm. He was a busy man, he probably reasoned, and provincial cantors had a habit of tedious severity in conversation unpalatable to the travelled and worldly-wise.

Handel went before and the singers followed after, arriving in London in time for *Lotario,* which was to open the 1729–30 season on 16th November. 'Being thus embarqued on his own bottom,'[3] as Mainwaring picturesquely puts it, Handel proceeded to forget the misdemeanours of the former Academy directorate in the enthusiasm of his new scheme. Not that affairs were, at the outset, particularly propitious. *Lotario* and *Partenope* were indifferently received despite the splendid songs written for Fabri. The moderate capacity for stimulation possessed by the singers is instructively indicated by Mrs. Pendarves:

Bernacchi has a vast compass, his voice mellow and clear, but not so sweet as Senesino, his manner better; his person not so good, for he is as big as a Spanish friar. Fabri has a tenor voice, sweet, clear, and firm, but not strong enough, I doubt, for the stage: he sings like a gentleman, with-out making faces, and his manner is particularly agreeable; he is the greatest master of musick that ever sung upon the stage. The third is the bass, a very good distinct voice, without any harshness. La Strada is the first woman; her voice is without exception fine, her manner near perfection, but her person is *very bad*, and she makes *frightful mouths*. La Merighi is the next to her; her voice is not so extraordinarily good or bad, she is tall

---

[1] Letter from Handel to Michaelsen, 11th March 1729. 'You have only to address your letters to Mr. Joseph Smith, Banker, at Venice (as I have already explained), and he will forward them to me, in whatever part of Italy I may be staying.'

[2] Mainwaring, p. 113.   [3] Ibid.

and has a very graceful person, with a tolerable face: she seems to be a woman about forty, she sings easily and agreeably. The last is Bertoli, she has neither voice, ear, nor manner to recommend her; but she is a perfect beauty, quite a Cleopatra, that sort of complexion with regular features, fine teeth, and when she sings has a smile about her mouth which is extreme pretty, and I believe has practised to sing before a glass, for she has never any distortion of her face.[1]

Bernacchi was dismissed and Senesino re-engaged, through the intermediary offices of His Majesty's Envoy Extraordinary at Florence, Francis Colman,[2] at a fee of 1,400 guineas for the season. The amount is large in view of the fact that Handel had no directors behind him: but his financial transactions were conducted on a large scale,[3] and what he earned by music was increased by judicious investment. The re-engagement of Senesino worked, despite the rumblings of abuse which came from those who subscribed to Carey's

> Curse on this damn'd Italian pathic mode,
> To Sodom and to Hell the ready road,[4]

and trundled off to take pugilistic advice from Figg, to enjoy manly sports at Hockley-in-the-Hole, and to demonstrate Macheath-like the benefits to be conferred on a virile nation by the pursuit of strumpets. Senesino brought large audiences to the Haymarket during the 1730-1 season who were regaled with revivals of *Scipione,* the evergreen *Rinaldo,* whose name *The Beggar's Opera* had done much to make familiar, *Rodelinda* and the new *Poro.* The second act of this opera was composed in a week, and if any reason is required to explain the speed of Handel's execution none other is necessary than his busyness. When he wasn't discussing his finances with his City friends, or struggling with the vagaries of singers (in general

[1] Mrs. Pendarves to Anne Granville, 1728.

[2] Letters from Handel to Colman, 19th/30th June 1730 and 7th/16th October 1730.

[3] A summary of Handel's financial transactions is given in Appendix E.

[4] 'A Satire on the Luxury and Effeminacy of the Age,' Carey, op. cit. Carey, like Addison, writes his prejudices with magnificent anger. The reason therefor is contained in a couplet of universal application:

> But such is the good-nature of the town,
> 'Tis now the mode to cry the English down.

'he resolved to subdue these Italian humours, not by lenitives, but sharp corrosives'[1]), or teaching, or performing at private concerts, he was engaged in the normal pleasures of a normal person.

From here and there fragments may be pieced together to form a composite picture of the man. He had no great library,[2] one small book-case mentioned in the inventory of his effects after his death appears to have sufficed; but his views on literature were put to shrewd use in his later dealings with oratorio librettists. Pictures were a source of considerable pleasure, and two Rembrandts eventu-ally found their way into the hands of Bernard Granville (who had given them to Handel in the first place), while Jennens received his Denners. Among the fleshly pleasures eating and drinking were conspicuous. Many anecdotes abounded concerning his intemper-ance in these respects, and Goupy perpetuated it by a malicious cartoon. It may be that Goupy had a private score to settle, for he had had dealings with Handel years before 1730, when his cartoon appeared, when he was employed as a scene-painter for the Royal Academy.[3] Mainwaring parsonically proclaims that 'he paid more attention to it [food] than is becoming in any man.'[4] Which, if true, suggests that the capacity of the eighteenth-century stomach was less than the general evidence leads us to suppose.[5] In most respects Handel was a typical Georgian, and such exaggeration as finds its way into fable is that which inevitably follows the name of a con-spicuous member of society. And by this period of his life Handel was conspicuous. The roughness of his manners was limited to

[1] Mainwaring, p. 108.

[2] Hawkins, v. 410. 'His attainments in literature cannot be supposed to have been very great . . . but . . . Of the English also he had such a degree of knowledge, as to be susceptible of the beauties of our best poets. . . .'

[3] Goupy must have been forgiven (what a capacity for this virtue Handel must have possessed!), as Hawkins (v. 412) mentions him as one of Handel's intimates.

[4] Mainwaring, p. 140.

[5] Ned Ward and his friends (*London Spy,* Chapter III) could manage two calves' heads and a couple of geese as a *first course,* and then, without notifiable discomfort, follow it up with a 'stately Cheshire cheese, of a groaning size.'

professional points of exasperation; otherwise his relationship with friends and acquaintances is marked by amiability. So he frequented country houses (Handel's rural painting, such as shown in *L'Allegro*, was based on ample experience of the English countryside): he used to stay at Salisbury with the Harris family, [1] at Ashford, in Kent, with Sir Wyndham Knatchbull,[2] with Jennens in Leicestershire[3] and as far afield as Calwich,[4] in Staffordshire, with Bernard Granville or at Teddesley Hall in the same county with Fisher Littleton.[5] His favourite house, however, was that of Mrs. Pendarves. Mrs. Pendarves, whose first marriage was turbulently miserable and whose second was quietly uneventful, had a wealth of sympathy, wit, literary and artistic sensibility and musical knowledge. She could also achieve the conquests of flippant flirtation. All these things attracted Handel and, while we have no reason to doubt that the friendship was of other than the platonic order, he would call frequently to play over new works, to interrupt Mrs. Pendarves in her correspondence or to *desipere in loco*. The parties which Mrs. Pendarves gave had that blend of entertaining refreshment and refreshing entertainment to which we may glance nostalgically:

I must tell you of a little entertainment I had last week; I never wished more heartily for you and my mother than on that occasion. I had Lady

---

[1] Streatfeild, pp. 185–6 n.

[2] At the end of August 1734 Handel had to decline a week-end at Merstham-le-Hatch, near Ashford; but the friendship was a durable one in that we find Handel sending his respectful compliments to Sir William (Wyndham?) Knatchbull via Jennens in 1741. Lady Knatchbull was a daughter of James Harris, of Salisbury, and was married in 1730.

[3] Newman Flower, *passim*.

[4] *History of Ashbourne*, 1839, and Lady Mary Fortescue, *History of Calwich Abbey*.

[5] The father of the late Lord Hatherton, of Teddesley Hall, who lived to the age of ninety, used to relate that Handel was accustomed to play with Fisher Littleton's amateur band at concerts at Teddesley. An interesting and detailed account of a visit by Handel to Lord Gainsborough's country seat at Exton, Rutland, is given in a letter from James Noel (23rd January 1745) quoted in 'Unpublished Letters concerning Handel,' Betty Matthews, *Music and Letters*, July 1959, pp. 264–5.

Rich and her daughter; Lady Cath. Hanmer and her husband, Mr. and Mrs. Percival, Sir John Stanley and my brother, Mrs. Donellan, Strada and Mr. Coot. Lord Shaftesbury begged of Mr. Percival to bring him, and being a *profess'd friend* of Mr. Handel (who was here also) was admitted: I never was *so well* entertained at *an opera* ! Mr. Handel was in the best humour in the world, and played lessons and accompanied Strada and all the ladies that sung from seven o' the clock till eleven. I gave them tea and coffee, and about half an hour after nine had a salver brought in of chocolate, mulled white wine and biscuits. Everybody was easy and seemed pleased, Bunny [Bernard Granville] staid with me after the company was gone, eat a cold chick with me, and we chatted till one o' the clock.[1]

The curious conclusion has frequently been drawn that Handel's sole mistress was Art (always with a capital A). Handel was a bachelor, but that condition did not preclude the eighteenth-century gentleman from becoming acquainted with the delectable possibilities of female companionship. Pope, Gay, Congreve, Prior, Atterbury and Savage were all bachelors: it was not unfashionable to avoid the rigours of matrimony. Regarding Handel an anonymous commentator, said to have been George III, observed that he 'scorned the advice of any but the Woman he loved, but his Amours were rather of short duration, always within the pale of his own profession . . . .' [2] Rolli, in a scurrilous outburst, made rude insinuations concerning Handel and Strada.[3] It may be remarked, as a matter of fact, that the only creditor who pressed hardly on Handel in a period of financial instability was Strada's husband.

But this is to anticipate. Returning to the opera, we find the 1731-2 season less successful than its predecessor despite the début of yet another remarkable bass in the person of Antonio Montagnana, who graced the first performances of *Ezio* and *Sosarme*.

In 1732 a fortuitous set of circumstances diverted Handel from a

[1] Letter from Mrs. Pendarves to Anne Granville, 1734.

[2] *Vide* Newman Flower, p. 188 n. Is Mrs. Pendarves indicated?

[3] Letter to *The Craftsman*, 7th April 1733. '. . . *Strada del Pò*, who is much in his favour. . . .' In *Anecdotes of Handel* (p. 28) two anonymous ladies are mentioned who would have married Handel had he been willing to eschew his undignified profession of musician. They were of rank and fortune.

too rueful contemplation of his operatic disappointments. On 23rd February, Bernard Gates, Master of the Chapel Royal, a member of the Academy of Vocal Music and a zealous Handelian, performed *Esther* at his house in Westminster as a birthday offering. Gates had been one of the original singers in the Canons performance. In 1732 he used the services of his choir-boys. The debt owed by English drama and music to generations of singing-boys is incalculable. A further private performance was given in the rooms of the Academy of Ancient Music at the 'Crown and Anchor.' Emboldened by appreciation Handel took a further step. The *Daily Journal* advertised at the beginning of April as follows:

Never performed in public, at the great room in Villar's Street, York-buildings, by the best vocal and instrumental Musick, Esther an Oratorio, or sacred drama, will be performed, on Thursday, April 20th., as it was composed for the most noble James Duke of Chandos, by George Frederick Handel. Each ticket five shillings.

The evening before this event a further advertisement appeared to the effect that

By his Majesty's command, at the King's Theatre in the Haymarket, on Tuesday the 2nd. day of May, will be performed the sacred story of Esther; an oratorio in English, formerly composed by Mr. Handel, and now revised by him with several additions, and to be performed by a great number of voices and instruments. N.B. There will be no acting on the stage, but the house will be fitted up in a decent manner, for the audience. The Musick to be disposed after the manner of the coronation service. Tickets to be delivered at the usual prices.

That the oratorio was performed in static undress was due to the Bishop of London, who, fearful lest true religion should founder on the rocks of histrionic excess, forbade a production after the operatic manner. It is unjust to cavil at the bishop's veto. He, not unaware of the reputation of the Haymarket, must have been much exercised in mind at the projected liaison between the Word of God and the music of the theatre. The wonder is that the performance ever took place. However, it did and was approved by king and court.

On 17th May a pirated version of *Acis and Galatea* was done at the Little Theatre in Lincoln's Inn Fields, under the management of Rich, at the instigation of the eccentric Arne—father of Thomas and

Susanna and, according to Addison, an arm-chair politician [1] who made his own arm-chairs—who saw money in the new-style Handel and an opportunity of starting his daughter on her career. Handel retaliated against this exploitation of his labour and promptly put on at his own theatre a refurbished *Acis*

by a great number of the best voices and instruments. There will be *no action* on the stage [did Handel mistake his hero and heroine for *St. Acis* and *St. Galatea*?], but the scene will represent, in a picturesque manner, a rural prospect, with rocks, groves, fountains, and grottos, among which will be dispersed a chorus of nymphs and shepherds, the habits and every other decoration suited to the subject.

The singers were Strada, Senesino, Montagnana, a choir-boy for the part of Damon, Mrs. Davis, Miss Robinson (? Anastasia's sister). An enlarged cast was necessary, for Handel, forced to expand his original score by Arne's thunder-stealing, had incorporated part of his Italian *Aci, Galatea e Polifemo*. Thus the audiences who pat-ronized the King's Theatre enjoyed macaronically the best of both works. Susanna Arne's appearance had given a fillip to the growing school of English protagonists, and Handel might have done well at this juncture to jettison Italian libretti altogether. Aaron Hill thought so, and later in the year proposed

that you would be resolute enough to deliver us from an Italian bondage, and demonstrate that English is soft enough for opera, when composed by poets who know how to distinguish the sweetness of our tongue from the strength of it, when the last is less necessary.[2]

Hill had in mind, no doubt, the skill of the lately deceased Gay, whose opera *Achilles* was still awaiting performance and whose heroic theme was ill suited to the pleasant jingle of ballad tunes suggested by the author. But English opera had taken a side turning in 1728 and Handel was reluctant to bring it back to the main road. Italian opera had its vicissitudes, but at best it was extremely remunerative, and at worst no more disastrous than unsuccessful English opera. Besides which oratorio was the new delight. Its record in 1732 was propitious: on 2nd August Handel paid £2,300 into his account at the Bank of England.

[1] Addison, *Tatler,* Nos. 155 and 160.
[2] Letter from Aaron Hill, 5th December 1732.

'Deborah'

Orlando was completed on 20th November and produced on 27th January 1733; it was followed by a revival of *Floridante*. In Lent *Deborah,* the text being by Samuel Humphreys, who had had a hand in the 1732 version of *Esther,* came next in the oratorio succession. The royal family was in attendance, which at this juncture was unfortunate. Handel, as has previously been noticed, was often the victim of circumstances over which he could have had no direct control. That Walpole was proposing the introduction of an Excise Bill, and that the Prince of Wales, in the best tradition of his family, was in opposition to his father and therefore to his father's prime minister, were factors for which Handel could hardly be held responsible. But Handel's loyalty to the Crown, combined with the increased price of admission to the oratorios, necessary, so Handel and Heidegger protested, to meet the increased expenses in production, were sufficient to call forth Rolli's letter in the *Craftsman* of 7th April, concluding:

> Quoth W——e to H——l, shall We Two agree,
> And *excise* the whole Nation?
>> H. *Si, Caro, Si.*
> Of what use are *Sheep* if the Shepherd can't shear them
> At the *Hay-market* I, you at *Westminster.*
>> W. Hear him!
> Call'd to order, their *Seconds* appear in their place;
> One fam'd for his *Morals,* and one for his *Face.*
> In half they succeeded, in half they were crost:
> The EXCISE was obtained, but poor DEBORAH lost.

This crude attack, supervening on a house of no more than 260 persons, and a growing deterioration in health worried Handel.

In June the nobility under the direction of Frederick, Prince of Wales, and Marlborough[1] set up a rival opera to Handel's, substituting Porpora for their former champion Buononcini, now thoroughly in disgrace for palming off a madrigal of Lotti's as his own. Singers were seduced from Handel's service, first Senesino, then Cuzzoni and then Montagnana: only Strada remained faithful. In this wretched year two gestures relieved the gloom. The first

[1] Charles Spencer, succeeded to the title on the death, in 1753, of his maternal aunt Henrietta, who had been duchess in her own right since the death of her father, the first duke, in 1722.

was a vigorous polemic by Arbuthnot in defence of Handel and entitled *Harmony in an Uproar*; the second an invitation from the University of Oxford which, in honouring Handel, was paying lip-service to the house of Hanover and thereby giving the lie to its alleged Jacobitism. If Handel was offered a degree he refused it, possibly because tact forbade receiving the honour from a politically suspect institution or possibly because so many people of whom he disapproved, including Maurice Greene, were doctors. Handel preferred the less honorific Mr. to being associated with Greene.[1]

On the whole Oxford greeted Handel with warmth, and what he made out of a series of concerts there amply compensated for the lean period in the earlier part of the year. On 5th July *Esther* was given, on the 7th it was repeated, on the 8th the *Utrecht Te Deum* at St. Mary's, on the 10th 'a spick and span new oratorio, called *Athaliah*,' on the 11th *Athaliah* again, and on the 12th, to conclude the festival, *Deborah*. Earless dons, purse-empty undergraduates and recalcitrant Jacobites might carp at the attention paid to 'Handell and (his lousy crew) a great number of foreign fiddlers,'[2] but the *Gentleman's Magazine* reported that *Athaliah* was greeted 'with vast applause, before an audience [this must have been the sum of the two audiences] of 3,700 persons.'

But after this interlude the ugly business of fighting the operatic opposition had to be faced. The nobility put in Porpora to bat first. *Ariadne* filled Lincoln's Inn Fields from 29th December. Handel responded with a similarly titled opera (*Arianna*) of his own on 26th January. In this he featured a new *castrato*—Carestini, who had been engaged during a continental tour undertaken after Oxford with this end in view. Lady Bristol described Carestini as 'an extream good singer. The rest are all scrubbs, except old Durastanti, that sings as well as ever she did.' Nor was Lady Bristol far wrong.

---

[1] *Vide Harmony in an Uproar*: 'Why Dr. Pushpin [Pepusch] and Dr. Blue [Greene] laugh at you, and scorn to keep you company; and they have vowed to me, that it is scarcely possible to imagine how much better they composed after the commencement gown was thrown over their shoulders than before; it was as if a musical —— had laid hands upon them, and inspired them with the enthusiasm of harmony.'

[2] Hearne, *Reliquiae Hearnianae*.

Handel faced the nobility with an inferior team, and he had played into their hands by preferring Carestini to the much more famous Farinelli.

Meanwhile opera in English was improving in popularity if not always in quality. In the tradition of ballad opera came Charles Johnson's *Village Opera* and Bickerstaff's *Love in a Village*. In direct competition with Handel Carey produced, in 1732, *Amelia* and *Teraminta,* the first to music by Lampe and the second by John Christopher Smith. *Amelia* gave Susanna Arne her first opportunity, and not only encouraged her father in Handelian depredation, but also put ideas into her brilliant brother's head. He proceeded to take the threadbare script of Addison's *Rosamund* and to give it another trial. With no more famous singers than old Leveridge, a relic of the Purcellian era, one of Rich's pantomimers, a reliable drinker and a massive *basso* who lived ripely on to the age of eighty-eight; Mrs. Barbier, more celebrated as the heroine of an elopement escapade than as a singer; Mr. Corfe; Miss Chambers; Mrs. Jones; Miss Arne; and a younger brother, Master Arne, *Rosamund* achieved ten performances and a benefit night for the composer. Carey with his genius for lampoon was at the same time handling grandiose exoticism in general extremely roughly in *Chrononhotonthologos* which, with its nomenclature (Aldiborontiphoscophornio, Rigdum-Funnidos, the Queen of Queerum-mania), its rude allusions to

A sudden diarrhoea's rapid force

which stimulated disastrously the peristaltic motion of the queen, and with its 'Rough Music of Salt-boxes and Rolling-pins, Grid-irons and Tongs, Sow-gelders Horns, Marrow-bones and Cleavers' (an orchestration later adopted by Burney) sent gusts of ribald laughter round London at the expense of more serious entertainment.

Nor was oratorio left as a Handelian monopoly. Defesch, a Fleming and leader of the band at Marylebone, composed a work in this *genre* to a text by Huggins. The work is known to posterity through Hogarth's castigation in caricature. Maurice Greene, to whom, as has been noted, Handel was particularly allergic, tried his hand at part of *The Song of Deborah*. And Porpora was in the same occupation as a relief from opera.

Yesterday [wrote Mrs. Pendarves] in the afternoon Phil and I went to the oratorio at Lincoln's Inn, composed by Porpora, an Italian, famous for church music, who is now in England: it is a fine solemn piece of music, but I confess I think the subject too solemn for a theatre. To have words of piety made use of *only* to introduce good music, is *reversing* what it ought to be, and most of the people that hear the oratorio make no reflection on the meaning of the words, though God is addressed in the most solemn manner; some of the choruses and recitatives are extremely fine and touching, but they say it is not equal to Mr. Handel's oratorio of *Esther* or *Deborah*.[1]

Mrs. Pendarves was a fair critic and Handel would not have had it otherwise.

In the spring of 1734 Handel fulfilled an occasional engagement by compiling out of *Athaliah* a *Parnasso in festa* and by writing an anthem to celebrate the marriage of the Princess Royal with the Prince of Orange. At the end of the season Handel's agreement with Heidegger was terminated, and before he had had time to readjust his affairs the nobility rushed into the Haymarket. There was in their party sound business direction. They took the best theatre and then produced a sensational addition to their company—Farinelli. With Farinelli, Montagnana, Cuzzoni and Senesino the directorate could confront Handel with the ace, king, queen and knave of hearts.

[1] Letter to Anne Granville, 28th March 1734.

CHAPTER VI

THE TRANSITION

On his [Farinelli's] arrival here, at the first private rehearsal at Cuzzoni's apartments, Lord Cowper, then principal manager of the opera under Porpora, observing that the band did not follow him, but were all gaping with wonder, as if thunder-struck, desired them to be attentive; when they all confessed, that they were unable to keep pace with him: having not only been disabled by astonishment, but overpowered by his talents. This band was small, consisting only of Carbonelli, Mich. Christ. Festing, Valentine Snow, afterwards sergeant-trumpeter, and Mr. Vezan, a dancing-master, who was likewise a steady and excellent player on the violin, and constantly employed whenever Carbonelli or Festing was the leader: it was from this worthy that I had this anecdote.[1]

The prince of *castrati* stayed in London for three years, sufficiently long to be in at the kill of Italian opera, to see Handel reduced to financial disorder and society to a state of emotional exhaustion. The incredible furore his presence created is without parallel in the long history of stage idolatry. He happened to be the best singer of his kind in Europe, but this was not entirely relevant. His acclamation came because he was the Farinelli. Towards the end of his sojourn he had the mortification of playing to near-empty houses, but his fortune was made and he could retire to Spain to endorse the truth of Mattheson's remark that 'he who in the present time wants to make a profit out of music betakes himself to England.' Handsome fees were dispensed by private purses when the presence of Farinelli was indicative of social standing. Among his patrons were the Spanish ambassador, the Portuguese chaplain for whom Farinelli sang 'on the occasion of the Princess of Brazil's being brought to bed of a daughter,' the Duke of Leeds and the Prince of Wales.

His Royal Highness the Prince of Wales was pleased to make a present of a fine wrought snuff-box, richly set with diamonds and rubies, in which was inclosed a pair of brilliant diamond knee-buckles, as also a purse of one hundred guineas, to the famous Signor Farinelli, who had constantly attended all his Royal Highness's concerts since he came from Italy. [2]

---

[1] Burney, *History*, iv. 380.   [2] Ibid., iv. 384.

'One God, one Farinelli!' shouted Lady Bingley with accurate impiety at the opera, thus achieving immortality in Hogarth's denunciation of the whole disgusting orgy of *castrato* worship in the fourth scene of 'Marriage à la Mode.' In 'The Rake's Progress' (Scene ii) the gifts enumerated above are listed, with T. Rakewell both pertinently and impertinently named as donor, as the eleemosynary outcome of *Artaserse,* Farinelli's first opera at the Haymarket. This scene of Hogarth's illuminates distressingly the degeneracy of fashionable artistic proclivities. There are Figg, the instructor in quarterstaff, Dubois the fencing-master, Essex the professor of dancing, hatters, tailors and other miscellaneous clients, a horn-player blowing indiscriminate noises and Handel (the wig is of the ripe variety favoured by him, although the figure is less massive than we have been accustomed to imagine). The latter rehearses with blissful unconcern the score of *The Rape of the Sabines* at the harpsichord. The repulsiveness of Farinelli exercised a particular fascination on Hogarth, who lashed the idol again in his 'Farinelli, Cuzzoni and Senesino' of 1734.

Handel, excluded from the King's Theatre, took the smaller house, under Rich's management, in Lincoln's Inn Fields. It is suggested by Streatfeild that this theatre was temporarily taken [1] for the benefit of the Princess of Orange, who was anxious to hear some music before leaving for Holland. He stayed at Lincoln's Inn Fields until 18th December with *Arianna* and *Il pastor fido,* the latter being re-arranged to include dances for the Parisian ballerina, if the term is not too euphemistic, Sallé, who had been used for her talents of dubious propriety in earlier pantomime. After 18th December Handel moved to Covent Garden.

For the new year his singers were Carestini, Beard, Waltz, Stoppelaer, Strada, Negri and Cecilia Young. John Beard was a former chorister of the Chapel Royal under Gates. He was a singer of charm and intelligence, but of limited technique. Cecilia Young was one of three sisters, all of whom sang themselves into marriage: Cecilia with Arne, Isabella with Lampe and Esther, less notably, with one Jones. Waltz, the other singer who calls for comment, was reputed to have served Handel as cook,[2] and had certainly sung in the

[1] Streatfeild, p. 134.
[2] See 'Gustavus Waltz: was he Handel's cook?' in *Concerning Handel,* W. C. Smith, 1948.

E. H. Gooch

'THE RAKE'S PROGRESS' (SCENE II)

Oxford celebrations in place of the miscreant Montagnana. Previously Waltz had put himself in temporary disgrace by taking part
in Arne's *Acis and Galatea* production.

Against *Artaserse* and *Polifemo* at the Haymarket Handel set
Ariodante at Covent Garden. The king generously, and with a
deprecatory sigh at those of the nobility who made such sacrifice
necessary by attempting 'the ruin of one poor fellow,' contributed
£1,000 towards the running expenses. For Lent, Handel, 'as his
capital singers were inferior in number and renown to those of his
rival . . . very wisely discontinued the performance of operas for a
considerable time, and rested his fame and fortune on his choral
strength in the composition of oratorios.'[1] Burney felt strongly here:
after all as a young man he had had the honour of playing for
Handel, and as a schoolboy he had experienced the greater thrill of
witnessing the great man so ordinarily engaged as in drinking a cup
of coffee and smoking a pipe. He continued his communiqué with
gallant satisfaction at Porpora's discomfiture after sending a *David*
into the oratorio sector of the battle. 'In this attack he seems to have
sunk under his antagonist's superior force and fire. For this oratorio
was executed but three times. . . .' *Esther* was given six times, *Athaliah*
five and *Deborah* three. Between the acts of *Esther* Handel 'performs a
part in two concertos, that are the finest things I ever heard in my life.'

In introducing organ concertos Handel was wise. Many would
come to hear him play who found less to interest them in the singing
of indifferent singers. Handel was a great organ-lover with modern
tendencies and was apparently instrumental in inducing the Germans
to adopt the English-invented swell-box. As far back as 1722 his
playing stimulated the Rev. Daniel Prat, M.A., to Browningesque
enthusiasm:

> Yet as thy volant touch pursues
> Through all proportions low and high
> The wondrous fugue, it peace renews
> Serene as the unsullied sky.[2]

The concertos indicate that the touch was still volant [3] in 1734.

[1] Burney, *History*, iv. 383.

[2] 'Ode to Mr. Handel, on his Playing on the Organ, 1722' in Nichols's
Select Collection of Poems, 1781, vii. 150–6.

[3] *Vide* Hawkins, v. 413.

On 16th April *Alcina,* with a preliminary puff in the *London Daily Post* stating that 'the new opera will exceed any composition of Mr. Handel's hitherto performed,' completed the season. In the other house, during the performance of *Polifemo,* unnecessary notoriety was gained by a show of anarchy on the part of the footmen who terrified the ladies 'by crowding into the lobby with lighted flambeaux, and refusing to retire when ordered by the gentlemen.' The assistance of the guards was called for and 'the Marquis of Tweedale's servant received a wound of which he died a few days after.' [1] An episode such as this often enlivened the theatre of the heroic age. With Handel's triumph in *Alcina,* a lightweight among his operas designed more than was usual with Handel to suit popular taste, and including more dances for the disreputable Sallé, was mingled the by now familiar touch of disillusionment. Carestini, affronted by his director's corrosive treatment (the old story of the singer refusing to sing an aria and being subjected to a salutary course of browbeating repeats itself), affirmed his intention of leaving the cast. Handel thereupon took £300 from the bank and left town for the summer. Some time during the recess he had another of Mattheson's periodic requests for autobiographical matter. To this Handel returned his customary polite refusal: 'It would be impossible for me to recall the events of my past life, since continued application to the service of this Court and Nobility prevents me from giving my attention to any other matters.' [2] Which wasn't quite true, as a letter written to Jennens at the same time shows:

I received your very agreeable letter with the inclosed oratorio. I am just going to Tunbridge; yet what I could read of it in haste, gave me a great deal of satisfaction. I shall have more leisure time there to read it with all the attention it deserves. There is no certainty of any scheme for next season, but it is probable that something or other may be done, of which I shall take the liberty to give you notice, being extremely obliged to you for the generous concern you show upon this account. . . . [3]

In 1736, after diplomatic disappointment over the miscarried 'double marriage project,' designed to detach Prussia from Austria, the Prince of Wales was married to the Princess of SaxeGotha on 27th April. Handel carried out his proper duties and added a

[1] Burney, *History,* iv. 384.   [2] 29th July 1735.   [3] 28th July 1735.

wedding anthem to his list of royal offerings. *Sing unto God* was about the only token of piety in a sordid affair. The prince, indifferent to considerations other than those of unpleasant consequence to his father and to women who were honest, seized the opportunity to make the occasion a parliamentary issue in which his financial position gave the Opposition a stick with which to beat the Government. The debate was notable for the appearance on the floor of the House of Cornet Pitt, who was, for his championship of the prince, deprived of his rank. Occasional music was in these conditions a minor issue. Nevertheless Porpora put on *The Feast of Hymen* to keep the scores even, anticipating that Handel would cap his wedding anthem with a piece of secular *réjouissance*.

At the beginning of this year Handel, embarrassed by the late secession of Carestini, had turned Purcellian in a setting of one of Dryden's odes for St. Cecilia. *Alexander's Feast*, in a version prepared by Newburgh Hamilton, was highly successful, probably for no other reason than that it was in English. In May *Atalanta* brought back the opera under princely protection, as it was by way of being the expected *Festgesang*. The description of this work in the *Daily Post* recalls the glories of the Jonsonian masque. There

was a new set of scenes painted in honour of the union, which took up the full length of the stage; the fore part of the scene represented an avenue to the temple of Hymen, adorned with statues of heathen deities. Next was a triumphal arch, on the summit of which were the arms of their Royal Highnesses. Under the arch was the figure of Fame on a cloud [under it would have been more fitting], sounding the praises of the happy pair. The names Fredericus and Augusta appeared above, in transparent characters. The opera concluded with a grand chorus, during which several beautiful illuminations were displayed.

The prince and princess from now on were staunch Handelians, to the temporary annoyance of the king, who felt, as a matter of principle, obliged to withdraw his support.

In the summer and autumn Handel took comfort from the obviously declining fortunes of the opera of the nobility. Senesino had already gone and Farinelli was on the point of departure. Handel himself had lately engaged new singers—Gioacchino Conti (alias Gizziello), a soprano who had appeared in *Atalanta* and possessed, according to Burney, delicacy and tenderness; and Domenico Annibali, a con٬ tralto from Dresden. The scores of the operas for the coming season were prepared and as completed were taken round for Mrs. Pen٬ darves's approval.[1]

By November the scene was set for the final show٬down between the rival schools: Handel in good heart, although his health was a source of anxiety; the nobility banking on their new arrivals— Merighi, Chimenti and Francesina. The new singers on both sides were paraded before the queen and the princesses at Kensington and impartially approved. Strada, back from a vacation in Holland, acclimatized herself by singing at the Swan Tavern.

Handel got off this season to a flying start with revivals of *Atalanta* (with 'several fine devices in fireworks' in honour of the Princess of Wales's birthday) and *Poro,* whose production was somewhat delayed by Strada's sore throat, under royal patronage. In the new year came *Arminio* (12th January), *Giustino* (16th February) and *Berenice* (18th May). But little success attended these works, and Handel's health was no longer proof against rapid deterioration. He survived the oratorio performances during Lent—the days were Wednesdays, Fridays and the first four days of Holy Week—but on 30th April the *London Daily Post* referred to Mr. Handel's indisposition with rheumatism and his hopes of being sufficiently recovered to accom٬ pany *Giustino* on 4th May. During his illness his cast staged an untraceable *Dido. Berenice,* which had been composed between 18th December and 18th January, was the season's last opera. Handel closed his theatre on 1st June.

At the Haymarket affairs were in no better state. Operas failed with monotonous regularity, operas with intermezzi (*Il Giocatore,* introduced between the acts of Hasse's *Siroe,* was the first ever seen on the stage in England) failed, Hasse, Porpora, Pescetti failed, and Farinelli, perturbed by houses worth no more than £35, developed a cold, thus preventing further performances of the concluding *Sabrina,* and cleared out of the country having completely knocked the bottom out of the aspirations of the nobility.

[1] Streatfeild, p. 140.

Giustino had featured a sea monster. Harry Carey grinned broadly, picked up his ready pen, scribbled a farce, dragged in the agreeable Lampe and threw into London the pleasant ribaldries of *The Dragon of Wantley*. To visualize Handel enjoying this burlesque[1] is to recognize the greatness of his heart and the instinct for chivalry which prompted him to approve Carey's opportunism. The Dragon was killed by a kick on the backside. This (sixty-three performances during the season) was also the death-blow of Italian opera. Carey refreshed his audiences by action and words which were intelligible, by a Yorkshire accent and by slapstick comedy. His final chorus mocked at the noise of Italian vowels, and winked wickedly at the new Lenten occupation of oratorio. Thus was morale restored:

> Sing, sing, and rorio
> An Oratorio
> To gallant Morio,
>   Of More-Hall.
> To Margereenia
> Of Roth'ram Greenia,
>   Beauty's bright Queenia
>   Bellow and bawl.

Upon which supervened a concluding salvo of loud huzzas.

Handel's illness has previously been referred to as rheumatism. In the summer it culminated in a paralytic disorder which affected his right side and, more disastrously, the balance of his mind. For cure he was recommended to the waters of Aix-la-Chapelle. Having been soused with (sulphurous) holy water by attendant nuns, he returned to England much restored, miraculously so they said, in health early in November. It is worth remarking that those who refer to Handel as bankrupt at this period do him an injustice. He had lost pretty heavily by operatic misadventure, but in 1737 his banking account was in credit, nor did his name appear in the published lists of bankrupts.[2]

He returned to London in time to celebrate the obsequies of Queen

---

[1] *Wentworth Papers,* p. 539.

[2] 'Bankruptcy is the status of a debtor who has been declared by judicial process to be unable to pay his debts.'—*Ency. Brit.,* iii. 56.

Caroline in *The Ways of Zion do mourn.* 'This fine anthem of Mr. Handel's', says the *Daily Post* in reference to the melancholy events of 17th December,

> was performed about nine; the vocal parts were performed by the several choirs of the Chapel Royal, Westminster Abbey, St. Paul, and Windsor, and the boys of the Chapel Royal and Westminster Abbey; and several musical gentlemen of distinction attended in surplices, and sung in the burial service. There were near 80 *vocal* performers and 100 *instrumental,* from His Majesty's band and from the Opera, etc.

The queen's death sent the town into mourning, and Handel's *Faramondo,* which had been begun early in November, was set aside until the new year. Neither this nor the patchwork *Alessandro Severo* nor *Serse (Xerxes)* materially improved Handel's fortunes; but a benefit concert, given in March, did. More than this (and more than the fact that its receipts enabled Strada to be paid and her husband quieted), the concert, consisting of oratorio excerpts and organ concertos, renewed Handel's confidence in his friends. A further demonstration in his favour occurred when, a little later in the year, Tyers, the prosperous proprietor of Vauxhall Gardens, spent £300 on the erection of that Roubiliac statue [1] which now greets the customers of Messrs. Novello. Tyers's gesture was prompted by the use he had made of Handel's music in enhancing the pleasures of his playground. According to the Russian Nkarinstev Handel was a 'people's composer.' If so, no better evidence can be afforded than by the amount of his music presented to the citizens and citizenesses who nightly flocked to Vauxhall for a variety of diversions, some innocent, others not. There, said a gentleman of Oxford,

> . . . plac'd marmoric in the vocal grove
> He guides the measures listening throngs approve.

In view of the major events of biography which are chronicled in headlines it may tend to be assumed that in between opera and oratorio production Handel was lacking in occupation. The present period is a case in point. Nothing of great significance appears, but all the time Handel is engaged fully: preparing material for

[1] See 'Handel and Roubiliac,' M. Whinney, *Musical Times,* February 1961, pp. 82-3.

publication (Handel was the most frequently published of all eighteenth-century composers), interviewing Heidegger as to the prospects of renewed partnership, exercising his charitable instincts, as in the foundation, in 1738, of the Society of Musicians, or essaying collaboration with Jennens.

To refer to the century under review as the Age of Reason, or as the Classical Era, is to obscure its principal attributes. It was the age of high romance, of glorious irrationality, of the novel. Above all, it was the age of the individual. The life of London (population in 1750 was 676,250[1]) was still sufficiently compact for people to be known, and the precision of classical education, which impinged even on the relatively illiterate, combined with a native genius for idiosyncratic observation enlarged names into characters. And conversation, not then a lost art, took leisurely opportunity at coffee-house, tavern or pleasure garden to embellish familiar characters with picturesque anecdote. When the royal linen, that perennial source of indignant amusement, had been disposed of, conversation turned to this and that. Handel stories were frequent. Sometimes his appetite set the inventive going. One day Handel ordered dinner for three and, on being asked whether he would wait for the company, replied pontifically: 'Bring up the dinner *prestissimo*. I am the company.' Stories like this were improved by being put into the pidgin-English which Handel was reputed to have spoken. (So far as can be judged from quoted examples of Handel's speech it would seem that he changed his consonants as in the Halle dialect of boy-hood German.) In 1738 the clubbable were diverted to hear that Handel and Jennens were on agreeable terms.

Charles Jennens, of Gopsall in Leicestershire, was a notable conversation piece. Rich and a bachelor, he could afford to live in undisturbed and luxurious eccentricity. In town Jennens graced Great Ormond Street and impressed the impressionable by the ostentation of his wealth on the one hand (he used to drive the distance of a penny bus ride with four footmen in attendance, one deputed on descent to clear the footpath of garbage) and his patronage of the polite arts on the other. He understood, although Steevens and

[1] M. Dorothy George, *London Life in the XVIIIth Century*, p. 329.

Johnson held a different opinion, literature, music and painting. And in time they called him 'Solyman the Magnificent.'

Jennens met Handel and projected ideas for oratorios. He sent a libretto, which may well have been that of *Saul,* to Handel in 1735. (*Saul* was in other people's minds as a possible subject, and one act of a dramatic work thereon, by Aaron Hill, appeared in the *Gentleman's Magazine* for February 1736.) A good deal of the autumn of 1738 was spent in fruitful collaboration, the outcome being *Saul* and *Israel in Egypt.* The important partner, according to Jennens, was Jennens. While we may sympathize with Handel for having to work with an opinionated poetaster we should not overlook the fact that in matters of art he was not slow in expressing himself with rough dogmatism. And the aftermath of his illness was often disturbing in social reper- cussions. However, Jennens had the grace to keep his opinions private and to circulate them only in family correspondence. A letter to the Earl of Guernsey, written by Jennens on 19th September 1738, hints at domestic disorder:

Mr. Handel's head is more full of maggots than ever. I found yesterday in his room a very queer instrument which he calls carillon (Anglice, a bell) and says some call it a Tubalcain, I suppose because it is both in the make and tone like a set of Hammers striking upon anvils. 'Tis played upon with keys like a Harpischord and with this Cyclopean instrument he designs to make poor Saul mad. His second maggot is an organ of £500 price which (because he is overstocked with money) he has bespoke of one Moss of Barnet. This organ, he says, is so constructed that as he sits at it he has a better command of his performers than he used to have, and he is highly delighted to think with what exactness his Oratorio will be per- formed by the help of this organ; so that for the future instead of beating time at his oratorios, he is to sit at the organ all the time with his back to the Audience. His third maggot is a Hallelujah which he has trump'd up at the end of his oratorio since I went into the Country, because he thought the conclusion of the oratorio not Grand enough; tho' if that were the case 'twas his own fault, for the words would have bore as Grand Musick as he could have set 'em to: but this Hallelujah, Grand as it is, comes in very nonsensically, having no manner of relation to what goes before. And this is the more extraordinary, because he refused to set a Hallelujah at the end of the first Chorus in the Oratorio, where I had placed one and where it was to be introduced with the utmost propriety, upon a pretence that it would make the entertainment too long. I could tell you more of his maggots: but it grows late and I must defer the rest till I write next, by which time, I doubt not, more new ones will breed in his Brain.

The maggots came from mental derangement on the one hand and flooding inspiration on the other. So that any host was likely to have had his patience stretched. The Tubalcain (the name was surely a joke at Jennens's expense) is indicative of Handel's Straussian outlook on orchestral colour and is a warning to extreme purism. Through mention of the organ a glimpse can be obtained of the anarchic conditions which obtained in choral singing, and which justified Carey's 'roratorios.' Moreover Mr. Moss's new organ explains the prominence given to the instrument in the score of *Saul*, where there are two more or less complete organ concertos.[1] Both *Saul*, finished on 27th September, and *Israel in Egypt*, finished on 1st November, are impressive in their intensity. Handel fought the nightmare of mental disturbance with deep concentration.

The completion of these works was therefore the triumph which their author desired. That neither succeeded worried him little. Some of his critics complained of the noise, a perennial annoyance to the witless who regarded any instruments which overpowered conversation as supernumerary. The kettledrums borrowed from the Tower would have effectively put an end to gossip. Then some of the singers were castigated. But the truth was that the psychological insight of *Saul* and the *Lear*-like vasture of *Israel in Egypt* were out of time and out of place. Nor did the latter succeed when Handel interspersed it with operatic arias for Beard and prefaced it with the *Funeral Anthem*. Beard, incidentally, had stimulated drawing-room tittle-tattle by marrying, above his station, Lady Harriet Herbert in the previous year. Lady Mary Wortley Montagu was much distressed. The failure of his two oratorios drove Handel to his side line of pasticcio: *Jupiter in Argos*, based on the libretto of Lotti's opera of that name, which Handel had seen twenty years before at Dresden, was advertised for performance on 1st May. It was never performed. The year 1739 was a bad one altogether. No one was in the mood

[1] See *Saul*, H.H.A. edition (Bärenreiter, 1962).

for music. As Jenkins was bringing his ear out of pickle, and opinion was hardening against foreigners in general and Spaniards in particular, opera and oratorio became insignificant against the necessity for moving the stubbornly pacific Walpole to declare war.

In October the king moved to St. James's from Kensington and on the night of the 27th went to the Play-house with the duke and the princesses, 'where the Tune of Britons Strike Home, etc. being played for a Dance the House seconded it with a loud and long Huzza.'[1] That was the feeling of the times. In Lincoln's Inn Fields on 22nd November 'it being St. Cecilia's day [Handel] first performed *Dryden's Second Ode*,[2] with two concertos for several instruments, preceded by *Alexander's Feast*, and a concerto on the organ, at opera prices.' A month later *Acis and Galatea* was again revived and two more *Concerti grossi* (all twelve were written this year) appeared.

In the winter the roasting of oxen on the frozen Thames was a familiar sight, but the elements responsible for so elevating and so olfactory a spectacle put the draught-riddled seats of Lincoln's Inn Fields out of bounds. Handel was a notable curser: his vocabulary was fully exercised at this time. Nevertheless he picked up Jennens's 'improvements' to Milton and turned out the enchanting music of *L'Allegro*. And still dallying with his old love he prepared two more operas. *Imeneo (Hymen)* had two performances in November. *Deidamia*, the last of his operas, three in January and February 1741.

An advertisement during March 1741 in the *London Daily Post* read:

For the benefit and increase of a fund established for the support of decayed musicians and their families, at the King's Theatre, on Saturday next (14) will be performed, with the original scenes and habits, *Parnasso in festa*, composed by Mr. Handel for Her Royal Highness the Princess of Orange's wedding.

So Handel eased his discontent by helping to alleviate the misfortunes of others.

On 8th April *L'Allegro* and the *Ode for St. Cecilia's Day* furnished the programme for a farewell concert.

[1] *Gentleman's Magazine*, October 1739.
[2] i.e. The *Ode* (Dryden's *Song*) *for St. Cecilia's Day*; cf. pp. 61 and 71.

CHAPTER VII

'SACRED GRAND ORATORIO'

DUBLIN in 1741 had not yet reached its peak in architectural achieve/
ment: Gandon's crowning glories were still to come. But among
European capitals Dublin held high place, despite the Liberties, for
elegance in town/planning and for beauty in situation. Trinity
College focused attention in the city centre; medieval Dublin spoke
proudly through the curiously Irish crenellations of her parish churches;
Christ Church sat in grave ruination on its own eminence overlooking
the changing colours of the Liffey; not far away St. Patrick's nursed a
sick dean and entertained the lords of state. The bay of Dublin, flanked
by its headlands, welcomed the English visitor and the quiet serenity of
the Wicklow mountains hinted at not/too/distant rural enchantment.
Society in Dublin was feverishly gay. For many years appointment
to the Irish service had been a pleasant insult to those who had failed,
or proved disagreeable in other ways, in English government or
diplomacy. The rusticated, therefore, concentrated on the pleasantest
way of killing time. Posterity should be grateful that this took the
form of building houses, making libraries, beautifying a city, engaging
in that brilliance of conversation which was the foundation of the
great Anglo/Irish literary tradition, patronizing the fine arts in general
with taste and understanding and in reading nostalgically the news
from England.

The great name in English music was that of Handel. Handel's
fortunes were declining. What better opportunity could there be,
then, argued Castle circles, for Dublin to restore his fame by fêting
him in Ireland? Dr. Delany, who, when he wasn't in London
dancing attendance on Mrs. Pendarves, was in Dublin, knew all
about Handel. He approved him as a friend of Mrs. Pendarves and
reflected that a course in oratorio would help to spread godliness
among a society not conspicuous for its cult. The lord lieutenant,
William Cavendish, fourth Duke of Devonshire, was impressed by
what he heard and issued an invitation which Handel gratefully
accepted.

Between 22nd August and 14th September Handel, again with the collaboration of Jennens, had written a new oratorio: *Messiah*. By 11th October he had done the most of *Samson,* the text ably extracted from Milton by Newburgh Hamilton. After this furious burst of energy Handel went north. For some days he waited at Chester for the contrary winds to subside before hazarding the notorious waters of St. George's Channel. Young Burney saw Handel at the 'Golden Falcon' in Bridge Street and got all the details of the *Messiah* rehearsal, at which mediocrity and self-satisfaction were pricked by Handelian sarcasm, from Baker, the cathedral organist and Burney's music-master. And so to Ireland.

Among old friends there were Dubourg, leader of the viceroy's band, and Mrs. Cibber (*née* Susanna Arne), whose exquisite Polly Peachum excused those moral lapses which had driven her to Ireland out of the range of the anger of Theophilus and the scandals of litigation. Other performers went with Handel. A new concert hall had lately been built not far from Christ Church: Neal's Music Hall in Fishamble Street. The architect was a German immigrant—Richard Cassels—who had already designed Leinster House, the Rotunda, the dining hall of Trinity and a series of mansions for the wealthy. He was, as the examples quoted still show, a good architect, and in his concert hall he triumphed, where most architects fail, in producing good acoustics. This pleased Handel. Indeed, everything pleased Handel (except when they miscalled him doctor), and he wrote with old-time enthusiasm to Jennens on 29th December:

The Nobility did me the honour to make among themselves a Subscription for 6 Nights, which did fill a Room of 600 Persons, so that I needed not to sell one single ticket at the Door, and without Vanity the Performance was received with a general Approbation. Sig^{ra.} Avolio, which I brought with me from London, pleases extraordinary. I have found another Tenor Voice which gives great Satisfaction, the Basses and Counter Tenors are very good, and the rest of the Chorus Singers (by my Direction) do exceedingly well. As for the Instruments they are really excellent, Mr. Dubourgh being at the Head of them, and the Musick sounds delightfully in this charming room, which puts me in good Spirits (and my Health being so good) that I exert myself on my Organ with more than usual success.

I open'd with the *Allegro, Penseroso, and Moderato,* and I assure you that the words of the *Moderato* are vastly admired. The Audience being composed (besides the Flower of Ladies of Distinction and other People of the greatest Quality) of so many Bishops, Deans, heads of the Colledge, the most eminent People in the Law, as the Chancellor, Auditor General, etc. etc., all of which are very much taken with the Poetry, so that I am desired to perform it again the next time. I cannot sufficiently express the kind treatment I receive here, but the Politeness of this generous Nation cannot be unknown to you, so I let you judge of the satisfaction I enjoy, passing my time with honour, profit, and pleasure.

These six subscription concerts were followed by six more. And Dublin, which had previously welcomed [1] such of Handel's music as had come its way, rallied round a god's-plenty of *Alexander's Feast*, the *St. Cecilia Ode, Esther,* a revision of *Imeneo,* renamed *Hymen,* and unspecified orchestral works. In one of these latter occurred Dubourg's celebrated cadenza which, having returned from labyrinthine modulation to the safe haven of the tonic, provoked Handel's 'You are welcome home, Mr. Dubourg.' That was the sort of comment which went (and still goes) down well in Dublin. Handel's rooms in Abbey Street, near a later centre of laudable artistic achievement, were a hive of activity in February and March. *Messiah* was coming. On 8th March a crowded rehearsal greeted it with acclamation. The first performance was given, and to increase the accommodation ladies were requested to attend hoopless,[2] on 13th April.

On Tuesday last Mr. Handel's Sacred Grand Oratorio, *The Messiah* [*sic*] was performed in the New Musick Hall in Fishamble Street; the best judges allowed it to be the most finished piece of Musick. Words are wanting to express the exquisite Delight it afforded to the admiring crowded Audience. The Sublime, the Grand, and the Tender, adapted to the most elevated, majestick and moving Words, conspired to transport and charm the ravished Heart and Ear. It is but Justice to Mr. Handel that the World should know he generously gave the Money arising from this

---

[1] *Vide Pue's Occurrences*, 1st April 1736, and *Dublin News-Letter*, 12th–16th January 1741.

[2] The wording of the 'hoopless' advertisement in *Faulkner's Journal* (6th–10th April 1742) suggests that *Messiah* was a commissioned work: 'Many Ladies and Gentlemen who are well-wishers to this Noble and Grand Charity *for which this Oratorio was composed* . . .' (my italics—P. M. Y.).

Grand Performance, to be equally shared by the Society for relieving Prisoners, the Charitable Infirmary, and Mercer's Hospital, for which they will ever gratefully remember his Name; and that the Gentlemen of the Two Choirs [Christ Church and St. Patrick's], Mr. Duburg, Mrs. Avolio, and Mrs. Cibber, who all performed their Parts to Admiration acted also on the same disinterested Principle, satisfied with the deserved Applause of the Publick, and the conscious Pleasure of promoting such useful and extensive Charity. There were above 700 People in the Room, and the Sum collected amounted to about £400, out of which £127 goes to each of the three great and pious Charities.

What the self-conscious correspondent of *Faulkner's Journal* fails to note is the Christian charity which Dr. Delany was impelled to display at Mrs. Cibber's 'He was despised.' His comment was: 'Woman, for this thy sins be forgiven thee.'

Messiah was performed again on 3rd June, and other summer activities were *Saul* (25th May), Avolio's benefit on 16th July and Mrs. Arne's benefit on 21st July. In between whiles Handel told funny stories to Dr. Quin and Mrs. Vernon and exercised their understanding in Italian, French, German and English, all of which languages he used indiscriminately. What else he did we should know had his letters from Ireland to Bernard Granville not been lost. He went away with the full intention, unfulfilled, of returning to Ireland the next year.

Back in London early in September Handel was at something of a loose end. A report that he was to take over the opera again was without foundation in fact. He had left opera for good and had arrived at the stage when he could laugh at its absurdities.[1] The ageing Handel—he was by now fifty-seven—looked at life more gravely. Added piety came resultant on recovery from illness, and a new evangelical spirit infused his outlook on his work. 'My Lord,' he said to Lord Kinnoul after the London production of *Messiah*, 'I should be sorry if I only entertained them; I wished to make them better.'

Samson was quickly finished on returning home and with *Messiah*

[1] Letter to Jennens, 29th December 1741: 'The first Opera [*Alessandro in Persia*] I heard myself before I left London, and it made me very merry all along my journey. . . .'

formed the mainstay of the 1743 season. *Samson* went down well, *Messiah* badly. *Samson* was sufficiently pagan to avoid damaging the susceptibilities of piety, induced by William Law and John Wesley, whereas *Messiah* had a blasphemous look in the title which was accordingly disallowed on the play-bills. None the less, *Messiah* impressed the eclectic and at its first performance—it had three this season as against eight of *Samson*—George II set the fashion (which might quite well now be discontinued) of standing during the 'Hallelujah' chorus.

In 1743 the king was a man of war and distinguished himself by being the last reigning monarch in England to appear at the head of his troops in the field. In the war, which had been greeted so ecstatically four years before, things were going badly, but at Dettingen, de Noaille's pincers movement going wrong, a surprising and unwarranted victory was snatched from defeat. Hence the *Dettingen Te Deum,* which enraptured all who heard it and which was pronounced by Mrs. Pendarves 'heavenly.' During the year Handel had another bout of illness. 'Handel has had a palsy and can't compose,' noted Horace Walpole.

At this period Mrs. Delany (on 9th June 1743 the *Gentleman's Magazine* advised the world of the marriage of the Rev. Dr. Delany 'to the Relict of Alex. Pendarvis Esq.') was very busy. Marrying a clergyman, seconding his efforts to gain preferment, cutting down unbecoming flirtation and writing for and about Handel took the best part of her time. In May 1744 she was pleased for her husband's sake that he was elected to the vacant deanery of Downpatrick, but her pleasure was permanently tempered with anxiety for Handel. She records a row, of short duration, between Handel and the Prince of Wales—it was at Carlton House, where rehearsals frequently used to take place—and praises *Semele.* 'But it being a profane story D.D. [Dr. Delany] does not think it proper for him to go.' *Semele,* a reversion to the masque form of *Acis and Galatea,* suffered, like all Handel's music, opposition—from 'the fine ladies, petit [*sic*] maitres, and *ignoramus's.* All the opera people are enraged at Handel, but Lady Cobham, Lady Westmoreland, and Lady Chesterfield never fail it.' [1]

---

[1] Letter to Mrs. Dewes (*née* Anne Granville), 21st February 1744.

On 10th March Mrs. Delany wrote to her sister a letter which has greater interest:

The oratorios fill very well, notwithstanding the spite of the opera party; nine of the twelve are over. Joseph is to be performed (I hope) once more, then Saul, and the Messiah finishes; as they have taken very well, I fancy Handel will have a second subscription; and how do you think *I have lately been employed*? Why, I have made a drama for an oratorio, out of Milton's *Paradise Lost,* to give Mr. Handel to compose to; it has cost me a great deal of thought and contrivance; D.D. approves of my performance, and that gives me some reason to think it is not bad, though all I have had to do has been collecting and making the connection between the fine parts. I begin with Satan's threatenings to seduce the woman, her being seduced follows, and it ends with the man's yielding to the temptation; I would not have a word or a thought of Milton's altered [a rare act of eighteenthcentury selfdenial]: and I hope to prevail with Handel to set it *without* having *any of the lines put into verse,* for that will take from its dignity.'[1]

Handel, however, avoided the task set for him. The story was hardly in his line: not sufficiently strong in that clash of heroic personality which was his especial province. What happened to Mrs. Delany's text is not known. Professor Dent suggested the possibility that it furnished the original of Haydn's *Creation*, and that Lidley was the nearest that German scholarship could approximate to Delany.

From Covent Garden Handel returned to the Haymarket in November 1744. The theatre had again become available through the inability of Lord Middlesex, whose efforts at opera management had amused Handel previously, to succeed where better than he had failed. Subscription concerts, *Hercules* and *Belshazzar* were ill received, to Handel's 'great loss, and the nation's disgrace,' and once again he was taken ill.

Lady Shaftesbury went to *Alexander's Feast,*

but it was such a melancholy pleasure as drew tears of sorrow to see the great though unhappy Handel, dejected wan and dark, sitting by, not playing on the harpsichord, and to think how his light had been spent by being overplied in music's cause. I was sorry, too, to find the audience so insipid and tasteless (I may add unkind) not to give the poor man the benefit of applause; but affectation and conceit cannot discern or attend to merit.[2]

---

[1] Letter to Mrs. Dewes, 10th March 1744.   [2] *Malmesbury Papers,* i. 2.

Society wanted amusement and novelty. Handel to the generality was too familiar, too severe and too incomprehensible. In his youth he had provided gay fantasy; in his old age, so it seemed, his line was moral philosophy. Lord —— saw in the oratorio an opportunity to attack the outworks of Amelia's virtue.[1] The bucks at the masquerade gave their opinion of oratorio when they discovered Dr. Harrison's philippic against adultery:

'Tom,' says one of them, 'let us set the ditty to music; let us subscribe to have it set by Handel; it will make an excellent oratorio.'
'D——n me, Jack,' says another, 'we 'll have it set to a psalm-tune, and we 'll sing it next Sunday at St. James's Church, and I 'll bear a bob, d——n me.'[2]

In the summer of 1745 Charles Edward Stuart landed at Moidart. For six months he kept England in agitated suspense. He 'liberated' Scotland, passed through Carlisle and Manchester, and reached as far south as Derby. At Ashbourne he was proclaimed king in the market-place. For Handel this was an uncomfortable thought. He knew Ashbourne, for Calwich Abbey near by, in what is now known as the George Eliot country, was the seat of Bernard Granville. Handel was a frequent visitor. The local tradition that *Messiah* was written at Calwich is improbable in view of the fact that Granville's new house was not yet ready in 1741. However, it may be reasonably assumed that Handel's fullest inspiration did not always come in London. Between Prince Charlie and London, as he had by-passed Wade's forces, lay only the indomitable volunteers. In them only insobriety would have reposed confidence. They had changed little since the early days of the century when they were affectionately designated 'The Cuckolds-all-in-a-row' and thus pleasantly delineated by the effervescent Ned Ward:

I could not forbear laughing to see so many greasy cooks, tun-bellied lick-spiggots, and fat wheezing butchers, sweating in their buff doublets, under the command of some pig-faced brewer, whose belly was hooped in with a golden sash, which the clod-skulled hero became as well as one of his dray-horses would an embroidered saddle.[3]

---

[1] Henry Fielding, *Amelia,* iv, Chapter IX.
[2] Ibid., x, Chapter II.   [3] Ned Ward, *London Spy*.

But the train-bands, despite Handel's exhortation in a 'Song made for the Gentlemen Volunteers of the City of London,' were not called on. Charles Edward misjudged his strategy, retreated from Derby to have his forces finally routed by the bloody Duke of Cumberland at Culloden, on 16th April 1746. In 1745 Handel had been unable to complete his series of subscription concerts. The disappointment of his patrons he mitigated by giving them the *Occasional Oratorio*. This successfully celebrated the duke, who

> allur'd by glory's charms
> Flew with a lover's haste to arms [1]

and gave disappointed ticket-holders their money's worth. Thus honourably did Handel always keep to the spirit of his commitments.

The year 1745 is significant in Handel's life. It divides the old unhappiness and disappointment from an autumnal season of mellowed brilliance and general esteem. The *Occasional Oratorio* preluded a period of *ad hoc* composition. Its successor was *Judas Maccabaeus*. The librettist was Thomas Morell, D.D. Like other librettists Morell had no high standing in letters. Writing to Walpole of some odes, Mason remarked: 'They are so lopped and mangled, that they are worse now than the productions of Handel's poet, Dr. Morell.' [2] But, as Garrick said, he was a scholar,[3] and what was more he could see Handel's point of view.

Fortunately his observations on the inception of an oratorio are extant. They make illuminating reading:

. . . As to myself, great lover as I am of music, I should never have thought of such an undertaking (in which, for the reasons above, little or no credit is to be gained) had not Mr. Handel applied to me when at Kew in 1746, and added to his request the honour of a recommendation from Prince Frederick. Upon this I thought I could do as well as some who had gone before me, and within two or three days carried him the first act of *Judas Maccabaeus*, which he approved of. 'Well,' says he, 'and how are you to go on?' 'Why, we are to suppose an engagement, and that the Israelites have conquered, and so begin with a chorus as "Fallen is the foe," or something like it.' 'No, I will have this,' and began working it, as it is, upon the harpsichord. 'Well, go on.' 'I will bring you more

---

[1] *Gentleman's Magazine*, May 1746.   [2] Walpole, *Letters*, **v**. 420.
[3] Hill, *Boswell*, **v**. 350.

to-morrow.' 'No, something now.' 'So fall thy foes, O Lord——'. 'That will do,' and immediately carried on the composition as we have it in that most admirable chorus. That incomparable air, 'Wise men, flattering, may deceive us' (which was his last chorus) was designed for *Belshazzar*, but that not being performed, he happily flung it into *Judas Maccabaeus*. N.B.—The plan of *Judas Maccabaeus* was designed as a compliment to the Duke of Cumberland, upon his returning victorious from Scotland. I had introduced several incidents more apropos, but it was thought they would make it too long, and they were therefore omitted. The Duke, however, made me a handsome present by the hands of Mr. Poyntz. The success of the oratorio was very great, and I have often wished that at first I had asked in jest for the benefit of the 30th night instead of a 3rd. I am sure he would have given it to me; on which night there was above £400 in the house. He left me a legacy, however, of £200.[1]

Judas was produced on 1st April 1747 at Covent Garden. Rosenberg, with his 'This *Judas Maccabaeus* (composed on the occasion of the great battle won by the English over the Scots) was simply a song of praise on victory,'[2] would have been disturbed at the enthusiasm with which Handel was on this occasion greeted by the Jews. There were in England at that time probably 5,000 Jews: their chief synagogue had been established in Duke's Place, Aldgate, in 1722.[3] Persecution had brought them or their forbears to England, and Handel's flamboyant glorification of the Maccabees filled them with pride and gratitude. It would appear that George Amyand, Handel's friend and executor, had Jewish blood,[4] so that an interest

[1] Historical MSS. Commission, Report XV, Appendix, Pt. 2.

[2] Alfred Rosenberg, *Georg Friedrich Händel* (Berlin, 1937). 'Dieser Judas Maccabaeus — komponiert aus dem Anlass der gewonnenen grossen Schlacht der Engländer gegen die Schotten—war ein einziger Lobgesang des Sieges.'

[3] M. Dorothy George, op. cit., p. 126.

[4] George Amyand, after Handel's death M.P. for Barnstaple and created baronet in 1764, was the second son of Claudius Amyand and his wife Mary Rabache, and grandson of Isaac Amyand and Anne Hottot, refugees from Mornac, Saintonge. He was a 'Hamburg merchant' and married in April 1746 the daughter of the 'late John Abraham Korten.' Handel met Amyand at court, where Claudius was principal surgeon to George II from 1729-40.—*Gentleman's Magazine* and Daphne Drake, *Members of Parliament for Barnstaple.*

in Jewry was of personal origin. Morell, therefore, was instructed to choose another Jewish subject. The result was *Alexander Balus*.

Burney saw a good deal of Handel domestically at this time. He had lately come to London and was preparing his own literary career by noting the characteristics of the great whom it was his privilege to meet.

Handel's general look was somewhat heavy and sour; but when he did smile, it was his sire the sun, bursting out of a black cloud. There was a sudden flash of intelligence, wit, and good humour, beaming in his countenance, which I hardly ever saw in any other.[1]

Thus we can picture Handel. At Carlton House in rehearsal, severe and concentrated; tempestuous at the prince's late arrival; swearing at undertones of maid-of-honour conversation ('Hush! hush! Handel's in a passion,' urged the Princess of Wales); wig vibrating in moments of satisfaction, discarded as a sign of dissatisfaction. In the afternoons walking in the park, talking to himself. 'The devil! the father was deceived; the mother was deceived —but I was not deceived; he is a damned scoundrel—and good for nothing,' he was once heard to mutter after a charity boy entrusted to his care had betrayed his testimonials and absconded. In the evenings, and particularly on Sundays, occupied in amiable conversation at Mrs. Cibber's or Frasi's. If he was a little in love with Mrs. Cibber his taste was commendable. She was a lovely woman, honest—hence she cast off the odious Theophilus, intelligent, full enough of conviction to defy convention in more ways than one. She was a Catholic. She was also a great actress with an unrivalled career as Juliet to her credit and a singer of attractive accomplishment.

No person of sensibility, who has had the good fortune to hear Mrs. Cibber sing in the oratorio of *The Messiah*, will find it very difficult to give credit to accounts of the most wonderful effects of music produced from so powerful a union. And yet it was not to any extraordinary powers of voice (whereof she has but a moderate share), nor to a greater degree of skill in music (wherein many of the Italians must be allowed to exceed her) that she owed her excellence, but to expression only, her acknowledged superiority in which could proceed from nothing but skill in her profession. [2]

---

[1] Burney, *Commem.*, p. 53.
[2] Sheridan, *British Education*, p. 369.

Varied Activities

With Mrs. Cibber should be mentioned Jimmy Quin, a staunch friend of Handel's since the day on which he walked out of *The Beggar's Opera* to devote his Hibernian affection to the destruction of the anti-Handelians. He too was a great actor: a notable Othello, Falstaff and Lear. Handel went to the theatre sometimes, and in addition to his two particular friends would have seen David Garrick.

Occasionally Handel still went for recreation to the opera, more often to St. Martin's-in-the-Fields to hear Kelway play the organ. Kelway was a great player, possessed of 'a masterly wildness' and a highly individual style, 'bold, rapid, and fanciful.'[1] He was also a devotee of Domenico Scarlatti. But Handel went to church not only for the purpose of listening to the organ. His piety was not inconsiderable. It was reported that he prayed twice a day. He certainly exhibited his faith beneficially through works. He was rarely absent from the charity concerts for the benefit of decayed musicians and their families and was a great supporter, as the next chapter will show, of Captain Coram's new foundation.

Handel still worked in terrific bursts, spasmodically. A libretto was ready. He put everything on one side and wrote his music in a fortnight or three weeks. He was no believer in cold iron. *Alexander Balus* took from 1st June to 4th July 1747; *Joshua* from the end of July to 19th August; *Solomon* from 5th May to 13th June 1748; *Susanna* from 11th July to 24th August. The precision with which Handel's works can thus be dated is due to his methodical habits of annotation. *Susanna* bears the following inscriptions:

> Ouverture Sussana Oratorio angefangen 11 July ·) 17. . . . .
> Fine della parte prima geendiget July 21 ♃ 1748
> Fine della parte 2ᵈᵃ | völlig Agost 21 —
> Fine dell Atto 3ᶻᵒ | S.D.G.   G. F. Handel Agost 9 ♂ 1748
> aetatis 63 völlig geendiget | Agost 24 ☿ 1748 [2]

The five languages here employed give some hint of Handel's linguistic capacity which, in conversation (plus a wealth of broad oaths), must have been impressive.

[1] Burney, *History*, iv. 665.
[2] The astrological signs for the days of the week were consistently used by Handel after 1737.

In October 1748 the Peace of Aix-la-Chapelle was signed. So ended another war. No doubt on the conclusion of this egregious campaign Handel reflected on Jonathan's air:

> From cities storm'd, and battles won,
> What glory can accrue;
> By this the hero best is known,
> He can himself subdue.

But dutifully he turned his attention to a royal command for fitting music.

CHAPTER VIII

TELLUS SUPERATA

Country Tradesman
    When will Profusion leave a Bankrupt realm?
    When Folly cease? and Prudence guide the helm?

Court Politician
    O! When will dull mechanics cease to prate,
    With blind presumption, on affairs of state!
    To break a glorious peace lest *France* should dare,
    'Tis right to shew, We've powder still to spare.[1]

To celebrate the return of peace with a royal salute of 101 brass ordnance (viz. 71 six-pounders, 20 twelve-pounders and 10 twenty-pounders), with a near-lethal display of fireworks, and with music arranged for warlike instruments obviously was not everybody's idea of propriety. But it was that of George II and his masters of cere-monies. Handel, who wrote music with godlike detachment for any occasion attractive to puny mortality, flung all the wind and per-cussion he could lay hands on into the April celebrations of 1749. Twenty-four hautboys, twelve bassoons, nine trumpets, nine horns, three pairs of kettledrums, a serpent (although this is crossed out) and a double bass are all listed in the score of the *Fireworks Music*.

The wonder is that this virtuous age, which has brought to bear all the resources of musicology on Tchaikovsky's *1812 Overture*, has been able to resist a proper-scale, near-original performance of the *Fireworks Music* in Hyde Park (the Albert Hall if wet). Judging by what happened on 21st April 1749 the result would be highly diverting. On that day a rehearsal at Vauxhall drew 12,000 people, stopped the traffic over London Bridge for three hours, and led to disorderly queues in which heads were duly broken. This rehearsal was one sensation in a bout of glorious licentiousness. Another was the masquerade at Ranelagh. There George II, disguised in an old English habit, viewed with lewd satisfaction the classical

---

[1] *Gentleman's Magazine*, January 1749.

nudity (emphasized by a modest covering of flimsy gauze) of Elizabeth Chudleigh arrayed as 'Iphigenia for the sacrifice but so naked, the high priest might easily inspect the entrails of the victim. The MaidsofHonour (not of maids the strictest) were so offended they would not speak to her.' The Princess of Wales threw a shawl over the lady and a veil over the proceedings.[1]

On 27th April Peace came into her own with impressive salvos from the aforementioned guns (a bombardier lost his life in preparing them[2]), with Handel's music, with fireworks which would not at first function and which, when they did, set ablaze the great temple erected *ad hoc* by the Chevalier Servandoni, and with lesser orgies of Georgian amusement.

A few days later Handel turned his thoughts to the Foundling Hospital. He attended a committee on 5th May and offered for performance in aid of the foundation the *Fireworks Music*; the anthem on the peace; selected pieces from *Solomon* relating to the dedication of the temple; and several pieces composed for the occasion. With this began (publicly speaking) an association which still happily persists: the genius of Handel still honours the hospital and the hospital with charming fidelity still remembers its greatest governor. The foundation was due to two widely contrasted facets of eighteenthcentury life: on the one hand gin,[3] which reduced women to depravity and their unwanted offspring to the dubious hospitality of the pavement; on the other to the crescent power of middleclass initiative. Captain Coram urged that something must be done (the wheels of government eventually turned, but not before amateur organization had achieved a monument of empirical piety), and something was done. This independence of action was after Handel's own heart. He did not place much trust in governments, as his anger at the hospital's intention to have its interest in *Messiah* safeguarded by Act of Parliament shows. 'Mine musick shall not go

[1] Mrs. Elizabeth Montagu.

[2] *Gentleman's Magazine,* April 1749.

[3] Because of the prevalence of gindrinking children were 'starved and naked at home' and 'either become a burthen to their parishes or . . . are forced to beg whilst they are children, and as they grow up learn to pilfer and steal.'—*Order Book,* Middlesex Sessions, January 1735–6.

HANDEL IN MIDDLE AGE
From a portrait by Giuseppe Grisoni

to the Parliament.' But added to an appreciation of Coram's gesture was lonely bachelordom and growing age, both of which helped to turn the full magnificence of a broad sympathy to the fatherless and destitute. In 1750 he presented an organ to the hospital and opened it himself with *Messiah*. Thereafter he presided annually at a Foundling Hospital *Messiah* and was instrumental thereby in enriching the hospital to the extent of nearly £7,000.[1] A fair copy and parts of the oratorio were bequeathed to the foundation in his will. The suggestion frequently made that Handel was segregated from intellectual activities outside of music is not borne out by his connection with the Foundling Hospital. On 9th May 1750 he was elected a governor. In this capacity he was called into consultation, not only on musical matters, but 'also in affairs connected with the interior ornamentation of the Chapel.'[2] And an interest in heraldry, attached to a nostalgia which naturalization and long residence never entirely removed, is romantically signified in the coat of arms granted to the hospital in 1749. This contains a 'Crescent Argent between two Mullets of six points Or': a part also of the arms of the town of Halle.[3]

In 1749 Handel mourned the death of his old friend Sir Wyndham Knatchbull, who died on 23rd July. But being given to sublimating his private griefs in assistance for the living he busied himself with the composition of *Theodora*, in the consideration of music for Smollett's *Alceste* (which was never performed but which was rehashed in *The Choice of Hercules*) and in advising Jennens on the subject of organ specification. The clergy, who are frequently anxious for information on this head, are recommended to Handel's good sense and austerity. He wrote to Jennens on 30th September:

Yesterday I received Your letter to which I hereunder specify my Opinion of an Organ which I think will answer the Ends you propose, being everything that is necessary for a good and grand Organ, without reed Stops, which I have omitted, because they are continually wanting to be tuned, which in the Country is very inconvenient, and should it remain useless on that account, it would still be very expensive althou' that may not be

---

[1] Burney, *Commem.*, p. 43.

[2] Nichols and Wray, *The History of the Foundling Hospital*, p. 204.

[3] Ibid., p. 250.

your consideration [herein out-peers German frugality]. I very well approve of Mr. Bridge who without any objection is a very good Organ builder, and I shall willingly (when he has finished it) give you my Opinion of it. I have referr'd you to the Flute Stop in Mr. Freeman's Organ being excellent in this kind, but as I do not referr you in that Organ.

The System of the Organ I advise is. Vizt.

The Compass to be up to D and down to Gamut,
    full Octave, Church Work,
One Row of Keys, whole Stops and none in halves.

STOPS

An Open Diapason	—	of Metal throughout to be in Front
A Stopt Diapason	—	the Treble Metal and the Bass Wood
A Principal	—	of Metal throughout
A Twelfth	—	of Metal throughout
A Fifteenth	—	of Metal throughout
A Great Tierce	—	of Metal throughout
A Flute Stop	—	such a one is in Freeman's [1] Organ.

Theodora came off with indifferent success in March 1750. Handel was annoyed. Among his oratorios the work was his favourite. But he chose the wrong year for its production. It was the year of the great earthquake, and superstition having been so little eradicated by the rationalism of the age people began to set their affairs in order against the apparent imminence of the last trumpet. Handel was angry or amusing. It depended on his gout. 'Oh, your servant, mine Herren!' he said to two gentlemen who applied for 'orders of admission' to the May performance of *Messiah*, 'you are damnable dainty! You would not go to *Theodora*—there was room enough to dance there, when that was perform.' To another who remarked on the exiguity of audience: 'Never mind; the music will sound the better.'

In this year's *Messiah* Cuzzoni, old and voiceless, was charitably given an engagement. But she was a shadow from another world. She sang for Handel and for the newly arrived Giardini at the Little Theatre in the Haymarket and 'returned to the continent, more miserable than she came,' to die in a short time in the pauper's ward of a

[1] William Freeman, to whom the libretto of *Alexander Balus* is inscribed, donor of the Oxford Music Room organ, 1748.

Bolognese hospital.[1] Other ancient history was revived by the defalcations of Dr. Croza, the latest in the tribe of opera managers. On 15th May Handel would have smiled sardonically at a newspaper advertisement, signed by Henry Gibbs, a tea-merchant of Covent Garden, offering £30 for the production of the person of the said Croza.[2]

During the summer Handel left England for a holiday in Germany. A coach accident between The Hague and Haarlem nearly achieved a second remarkable coincidence of history. Bach, born within a month of Handel, died in that year. But on 21st August the *General Advertiser* announced that Handel was out of danger.

At the beginning of 1751 *Jephtha* was written. As he wrote Handel had some idea that this might be his last major work. On 13th February he had to stop work because of his failing sight. Ten days later he felt better and resumed his score with a determination that this should be a fitting close to a career which he knew to be not without distinction. *Jephtha* is (in one opinion at all events) the most magnificent of all the oratorios. On 18th April and 16th May there were *Messiah* performances at the Foundling Hospital, and afterwards an unavailing effort to recapture elusive health by a visit to Cheltenham. By the end of the year sight was so far gone as to admit of none but drastic treatment. Handel resigned himself to the hands of Samuel Sharp.

Sharp, lest all medicine and surgery of the eighteenth century should be regarded as a compound of old wives' tale and elemental butchery, was an influential figure in medical history. He was the first great surgeon of Guy's, to which he was elected in 1733, a lecturer to naval surgeons and the author of learned works which proved him to be an innovator in surgical technique. As a traveller, a *littérateur* and the husband of a wealthy wife he anticipated later consultative practice.[3] But he was unable to cure Handel. The best he could do after operating unsuccessfully was to suggest that Handel should go into partnership with John Stanley. 'If the blind lead

[1] Burney, *History,* iv. 460.

[2] Ibid.

[3] Wilks and Bettany, *Biographical History of Guy's Hospital,* p. 120, et seq., and *Gentleman's Magazine.*

the blind, shall they not both fall into the ditch?' was the observation of Handel's grim humour.

By 1753, despite the further attentions of William Bramfield and the Chevalier Taylor, blindness was complete. Indeed reports got about that Handel was preparing for death by composing his own funeral anthem to be sung in the chapel of the Foundling Hospital. This rumour distressed the governors of the hospital so that they issued a statement saying:

the said Paragraph has given this Committee great concern they being highly sensible that all well-wishers to this Charity must be desirous for the continuance of his life, who has been and is so great and generous a benefactor thereto.

> Total eclipse! No sun, no moon!
> All dark amid the blaze of noon.

When Beard sang those words a great wave of sympathy swept over his audience and many were seen in tears. But Handel was courageous as ever. If Gay had ever told him stories of the old sea-dogs of Devon Handel would have recognized in them men after his own heart. He carried on, calling in Christopher Smith to manage his affairs, to act as amanuensis and to control the rough edge of his tongue,[1] playing at the oratorio, corresponding with his friends and composing.

Habit rather than inspiration kept the latter faculty in operation, and nothing of greater moment than a duet and chorus for *Judas Maccabaeus* ('Zion now her head shall raise') and a revision of the *Trionfo del Tempo* (*The Triumph of Time and Truth*) appeared.

In 1754 we are reintroduced to Telemann.[2] He had been reported as dead, so that, on confirmation of the falseness of this report, Handel wrote to him with relief and promising to send some flowers which Telemann had requested. So a friendship of fifty years draws to its close, fragrantly and in the garden.

The last years of Handel's life were uneventful. He rested in the satisfaction that his music was the most durable of all that was written in England during his lifetime. He heard with pleasure of the

---

[1] Particularly when Handel had a sudden quarrel with old Smith, which led to the (temporary) withdrawal of Smith's name from his will.

[2] Letter from Handel, 20th September.

popularity of his oratorios in the west country where the Three Choirs Festival was emerging to occupy its particular niche in the history of English music. In 1757 *Messiah* was first performed at this festival. With the faithful Beard new singers appeared, and among them a high preponderance of English: there were Mence and Wass, Baildon and Denham, Miss Turner and Frasi; among the players Adcock, Millar, Vincent, Malchair, Richards and Storace.[1] Mention of the last-named, father of Ann and Stephen, indicates the passing of the years. A new era was opening, that of Haydn and Mozart. In the world too events were inexorably pressing forward. The Great Commoner was in power at the close of Handel's life, the Seven Years War was in progress, imperial conquests were at hand, and Josiah Wedgwood was prefacing the Industrial Revolution with rural spoliation and exquisite craft. Of all these things Handel was only dimly aware. His life was in his music and among his friends.[2]

On 30th March and 6th April 1759 *Messiah* was, as usual, performed for the Foundling Hospital. Handel was present on the first occasion, and this was his last appearance in public. He was taken home unwell. On 11th April he added a third codicil to his will. On 14th April, being the Saturday before Easter Day, he died.

According to your request to me when you left London [wrote James Smyth to Bernard Granville], that I would let you know when our good friend departed this life—on Saturday last, at eight o'clock in the morn, died the great and good Mr. Handel. He was sensible to the last moment; made a codicil to his will on Tuesday; ordered to be buried privately in Westminster Abbey, and a monument not to exceed £600 for him. I had the pleasure to reconcile him to his old friends[3]: he saw them and forgave them, and let all their legacies stand! In the codicil he left many legacies to his friends; and among the rest he left me £600, and has left to you the two pictures you formerly gave him. He took leave of all his friends on

---

[1] Lysons, *Origin and Progress of the Meeting of the Three Choirs* (1895 edition), p. 36. Portions of *Messiah* had been performed in Salisbury Cathedral in 1752.

[2] To those already mentioned should be added 'one Hunter, a scarlet-dyer at Old Ford' and Gael Morris, 'a broker of the first eminence.'—Hawkins, v. 410–11.

[3] Including old Smith, presumably.

Friday morning, and desired to see nobody but the doctor, and apothecary, and myself. At seven o'clock in the evening he took leave of me, and told me we 'should meet again.' As soon as I was gone, he told his servant not to let me come to him any more, for that he had now done with the world. He died as he lived, a good Christian, with true sense of his duty to GOD and man, and in perfect charity with all the world. If there is anything that I can be of farther service to you, please let me know. I was to have set out for Bath to-morrow, but must attend the funeral, and shall then go next week.

London made amends for earlier lapses in its behaviour by sending 3,000 of its citizens to the obsequies. These took place with due solemnity in Westminster Abbey on the evening of 20th April. The music, including Dr. Croft's *Funeral Anthem,* was sung by the Gentlemen of His Majesty's Chapels Royal, the choirs of St. Paul's and the Abbey. The sermon was preached by Dr. Zachary Pearce, Dean of the Abbey and Bishop of Rochester. The grave was placed in the Poets' Corner and now has as near neighbour that of Charles Dickens. The proximity of their ashes may, perhaps, be symbolic of the similar massive influence which each has exercised on the hearts and minds of generations they never knew. The fitting epitaph for Handel (Roubiliac added none to his monument) was written over a thousand years before his time by another musician—Boethius:

Tellus superata
Sidera donat.

CHAPTER IX

STYLE

THERE exists a popular fallacy that all music of the first half of the eighteenth century not written by Bach was written by Handel. Thus a song cast in this mould:

being obviously non-Bachian, would provoke the averagely well-read to father it on Handel. In fact, the responsible composer was James Oswald,[1] a relatively obscure figure in musical history whose misfortune it is, alongside Greene, Arne, Boyce, Carey and any other English musician of the period, to be counted out as insignificant because an imitator of Handel. *The Moderate Wish*[2] is chosen, more or less at random, to illustrate particular qualities characteristic of the eighteenth century. Balance, proportion, mellifluence, lyrical aptness and harmonic insouciance are combined so as to satisfy the hedonistic ear. And, peeping through, comes the amiable modesty of urban pastoralization. Now to dismiss so charming a by-product as merely *Ersatz* Handel is to misunderstand the basis of eighteenth-century

[1] A Scotsman, an assiduous editor, a music-seller and publisher in St. Martin's Lane. Founder of the Society of the Temple of Apollo and a putative composer of 'God save the King.' The above quotation comes from *Ten Favourite Songs sung by Miss Formantel at Ranelagh* (1747).

[2] Oswald's title. The poem is, of course, Pope's juvenile *Ode on Solitude*.

style and to allow the romantic picture of the great Cham of music to obscure that clarity of intellectual vision which the age consciously invites.

That a family likeness is apparent between the works of Handel and any contemporary of his is due not to the fact that Handel was the prime source of formal inspiration, but that homogeneity of thought prevailed with regard to the purpose of music in the community and the style in which it should generally be cast. That music should convey more or less specific ideas was the keystone of musical philosophy and that lucidity of expression should prevail was regarded as a necessary symbol of good breeding. In emphasizing the necessity for clear communication the eighteenth century was doing service to art if disservice to itself. It rendered music generally intelligible, but invited the later charge of uninspired uniformity. At this point Dryden's apophthegm that 'a great thought comes dressed in words so commonly received, that it is understood by the meanest apprehensions, as the best meat is the most easily digested' may be introduced to indicate the deeper significance of the classical outlook. Style may remain constant, but the underlying ethos can still preserve independence and individuality. Thus it is that in Handel we meet the paradox of an individualist without obvious individuality.

A common mode of speech is the ideal towards which art perpetually aspires, and at certain stages in history the ideal has not been far from realization. Dante's master, Brunetto Latini, writing in the days when the romance-poem carried itself to universal comprehension through the medium of French, commented that 'la parleuse en est plus délitable et plus commune à toutes gens.' A similar community of expression led the medieval pilgrim to find in the ubiquity of Gothic architecture a genius making every foreign city a home from home. After the Renaissance a particular set of circumstances developed a mode of musical address more than at any other period in the history of music *plus commune à toutes gens*. Under those conditions which obtain when a style is generally accepted and approved a major artist tends to be accepted as representative of his age. Chaucer, Leonardo, Goethe are cases in point. Each is more than himself, confluential. All the tributaries of the eighteenth century flow into Handel and so he stands apotheosized.

A robust and generative period concerns itself more with the summarization of anterior effort than with the novelty of experiment. Therefore most of what appears characteristically eighteenth-century is in fact discoverable in the seventeenth. The simple mechanics of both centuries involved melody, counterpoint, the harmonic basis of triadic repose interspersed with regulated discord and utilitarian rhythm controlled by dance and poetry. In the later period emphasis was laid on certain points so that retrospectively we recognize inevitable mannerisms. It may, however, be considered that superior observation on the presence of such mannerisms is the result of mental restlessness rather than of objective criticism. The perfect cadence and the easeful modulation, to take two obvious and easily recognized habits, were to the style of Handel as the pointed arch to Gothic architecture, essential to large-scale and monumental planning.

The tripartite aria, regularized by Alessandro Scarlatti, the forms of recitative peculiar to seventeenth-century dramatic music, the conventions of suite, sonata, fugue, overture, ground-bass were all ready for Handel's employment, but on whatever form he used he impressed a sense of fluency only comparable to that of Mozart. Fluency, however, is not *per se* a complete virtue: Handel achieved fluency, but he did more. Matthew Arnold added to Chaucer's other qualities a 'large, free, simple, clear yet kindly view of human life—so unlike the total want, in the romance-poets, of all intelligent command of it.' The observation fits Handel and should be borne in mind throughout any attempt to estimate his significance.

The language of Handel was that of his contemporaries, but often they were lacking in the capacity for deep penetration. In so familiar an example as the 'Dead March' from *Saul* Handel's profundity of sympathy extends itself through nothing more complex than a four-bar sequence of tonic and dominant harmony. Placing this movement by the side of a not dissimilar passage from the overture to Clayton's ill-fated *Rosamund* music, we shall see that what Clayton achieved is negative:

This is merely not unpleasant and has no particular dramatic sense.

Handel was pre-eminently a dramatic writer, and in the simplest passages he demonstrates the two essentials of dramatic intention: timing and placing. Among the moving passages in Handel one of the most intense occurs in *Hercules* where Iole laments her dead father in the strangely Schubertian 'Peaceful Rest.' With grave memory Iole reflects:

The extension of thought engendered by the orchestral repetition of the operative phrase is miraculous. Nothing could be simpler nor more obvious, yet placed in its setting of poignant pulsation the spacious crotchet movement is entirely fitting. Inspired simplicity of this order recalls the emotional finality of Lear's 'I am a very foolish fond old man.' Within this aria Handel reserves one more telling blow until the end:

This aptitude for realizing unerringly the point of climax was partly the gift of the gods and partly—industry is rarely neglected by the great—the result of extensive experience, wide reading and absorbent memory. It has already been stated that the eighteenth century was a recapitulatory epoch, and the scholar will not be slow to point out that Handel was so typical in this respect that he reiterated often the spirit and sometimes the substance of other men's music. And yet the unassailable fact remains that what he wrote was so dramatically synthesized that it never leaves the impression of being the music of any one but Handel. At this point we may tread lightly round the plagiaristic slough which has led so many 'sapient trouble-tombs' from the contemplation of music to the anatomy of morals and merely comment that the two common and alternative theses, (1) that it was a great blemish to copy out Muffat, Erba, Kerl, Stradella, Urio or Habermann, (2) that since Handel turned mediocrity into perfection it was satisfactory behaviour (although not too prominently so), ignore the major issues of musical philosophy.[1]

In the eighteenth as in the thirteenth and the sixteenth century there was, despite such contrary appearances as are indicated by

[1] This matter is treated more fully in Appendix F, pp. 233–4.

political rivalries, a reciprocity which viewed artistic achievement with massive impartiality. The achievement was the thing, and whether Pope employed agents to translate his Homer or Handel represented an incorporated society mattered as little to their audiences as did the fact that Shakespeare looked over Marlowe's shoulder and quarried in Holinshed to his. Epochal literature came because it outcropped from the seams of lively conversation. Music of comparable quality also grew from the fecundity of commonplace phraseology. The desiccation of both music and literature by the academies leads sometimes to the suppression of this vital point, but without its absorption the rapidity of Handel's creation and the normality of his clichés become of inflated significance. The speed in execution was inevitable when mastery of language was so complete, and the continual appearance of particular idioms equally inevitable when each was universally regarded as a useful vehicle of competent expression. Triteness develops not when clichés are used, but when they are used in the wrong place. There is a resemblance in method and achievement between Handel and Virgil. Virgil was dependent on what earlier poets had said: words, stories, technical devices came from everywhere; complete lines from Homer and Ennius.

> The impulse to say the verse or tell the story over and over again [came], partly because there was a mysterious, self-sufficient delight in the poetry, and partly because it fitted Virgil's own feelings, expressed them, clarified them, and made them acceptable and friendly to himself. . . . Everything went into the dream world . . . the 'hooked atoms' parted and recombined.[1]

So in Handel's case the 'esemplastic' imagination worked in fertility to produce new combinations of integrative miracle.

The places of Handel's residence explain his technical antecedents in the main. The influence of Italy, however, is proportionately more significant than his brief sojourn there would suggest, the reason being that from the beginning of the seventeenth century all music was tending towards the Italianate. Italy was the first home of madrigal, opera, oratorio and the major instrumental forms of sonata, concerto and suite: these and their virtuosic exponents were nurtured under the shadow of Renaissance humanism and at the expense of princely

[1] *The Times Literary Supplement,* 1st April 1944.

patrons whose interest came not entirely from ostentation. Under enlightened patronage circumstances were helpful and music was subjected to a degree of refinement unknown since the monastic organization of polyphony. The tendency of the age was away from the austerity of the ancient *a cappella* style (which was as out-moded then as Stainer is now) towards virtuosic display, an obvious adjunct of specialization, and towards that expressiveness perceived through the medium of musico-dramatic performance. Reacting against the inherent moralization of old counterpoint, Galuppi, Vivaldi, Corelli and the Scarlattis evolved a new melodic sensibility in long, sensuous melismatic lines, pointed with wit, grace, fire or whatever dramatic quality was considered proper, and supported by slender pillars of conventional chording. The revolution was noteworthy in the same way as that which produced walls of painted glass in late Perpendicular. The insistence on melodic integrity which culminated in the Scarlatti-Handel aria was an unconscious reversion to the self-sufficiency of Gregorian chant, to the popular approach of troubadour art and to the simpler urge of folksong. Once again the nature of the melody in Handel depends on environ-ment, and on further examination the range suggested will not seem extravagant. The outlook of the age was summed up by Telemann thus: 'Singen is das Fundament zur Music in allen Dingen.'[1]

Although aristocratic in setting, seventeenth- and eighteenth-century music aimed at popular understanding in that its basic concern was with that interplay of tonal nuance such as can hardly leave un-affected even the confessedly unmusical. Handel learned more than formality from Italy: he learned the theory that what is to be quickly influential must be effective in immediate application. Thus his melodies are ever warmed with the rich voluptuousness of the south and are readily apprehensible. The danger in Italian teaching lay in the facility it promoted, and on occasion Handel fell victim to that 'Deluge of unbounded *Extravaganzi*, which the unskillful call Invention, and which are merely calculated to shew an Execution, without either Propriety or Grace.'[2] Hence the fluent emptiness of

[1] 'Singing is the foundation of music in all things.'—Romain Rolland, op. cit., p. 73.

[2] Avison, *An Essay on Musical Expression*, 1753.

the following in *Hercules,* where for a moment the customary irradiation of personality is lacking:

That Handel so seldom pursued fluency for its own sake was due to influences other than that of Italy. He had early been nourished on the strong meat of Teutonic severity. Rugged Lutheranism turned the attention of art to the power of personal experience and to the continual wrestling of contrary mental forces: thus *Sturm und Drang* imbue religious music from Schütz to Bach. Handel betrays his German origin when he leads us into agony with Iole:

or when he sacrifices dramatic logic to massive counterpoint as in the stupendous 'Wretched lovers' of *Acis and Galatea*. Elsewhere, chorale influence [1] serves to make direct reference to Germany, and dramatic recitatives recall the forgotten talent of Keiser.

Between the extremes of German intensity and Italian virtuosity English style characteristically steers a middle course. And it is the influence of England which acts catalytically for Handel. The particular may be taken first. Purcell was not forgotten when Handel first arrived in London. His music could be still heard in the cathedrals, at Britton's, where also scores were available for reference, [2] and elsewhere domestically. From Purcell Handel learned the possibilities of rhythmic extension along the lines of resilient syncopation. The lesson was well learned for it was Handel who wrote:

in *Theodora*, and casual listening will reveal that Handel uses this turn of rhythm with continual enthusiasm. [3]

[1] Passion music and Funeral Anthem. Whether the second subject of the 'Hallelujah' chorus in *Messiah* is derived from 'Wachet auf' must be decided by the reader. Some authorities are fervent in support of this thesis, but direct quotation from a German chorale would seem to have been a pointless procedure.

[2] Britton's well-stocked library included the music for *Dioclesian, Ode for St. Cecelia's Day, Te Deum and Jubilate,* two volumes of *Harmonia Sacra,* airs from the operas, catches and miscellaneous music, all by Purcell.

[3] This, of French origin, also serves to remind us that Handel was aware of French music of the age of Lully, for it was much cultivated in Germany in his youth.

In 1745 Gluck visited England and Handel, but was discouraged by the latter in a moment of disillusionment from extending his visit. He did, however, discover that England had some contribution to make to the development of musical thought.

> He then studied the English taste; remarked particularly what the audience seemed most to feel; and finding that plainness and simplicity had the greatest effect upon them he has endeavoured to write for the voice, more in the natural tones of the human affections and passions, than to flatter the lovers of deep science or difficult execution; and it may be remarked, that most of his arias in *Orfeo* are as plain and simple as English ballads; and the additions made to it when first performed in England, by Messrs. Bach [J. C.] and Guglielmi, were of so different a texture, though excellent in another way, that they destroyed the *unity* of style and characteristic simplicity, for which, when performed at Vienna, this production was so much admired.' [1]

It was simplicity and directness of approach which Handel too detected and admired in the English response: hence the primeval strokes of triadic majesty in the Jews' chorus 'Recall, O King' in *Belshazzar,* in 'Make them to be numbered with Thy saints' in the *Dettingen Te Deum,* in 'Moses and the Children of Israel' in *Israel in Egypt* and in the superlative 'But their name liveth evermore' in the *Funeral Anthem* for Queen Caroline.[2] This last chorus, with its cross-rhythms (throughout Handel conductors may be urged to treat bar-lines without exaggerated respect) consciously renews the glories

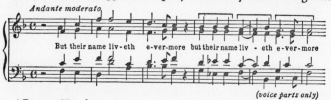

Andante moderato

But their name liv-eth e-ver-more but their name liv - eth e-ver-more

(*voice parts only*)

[1] Burney, *Travels,* 1. 268–9.

[2] 'In this, and the preceding movement, HANDEL has made a happy use of a modulation which was very frequent in the sixteenth century: the giving a common chord to the flat seventh of a major key, just before a close.' This chorus is, in fact, a transcription of the motet *Ecce quomodo moritur justus,* by Jacob Handl, a work which was sung at Passiontide at the Thomaskirche in Leipzig when Handel lived in neighbouring Halle.— Burney, *Commem.,* p. 37 n.

of Renaissance polyphony. Here it may be interjected that with rare exceptions, one of which is the clumsy handling of

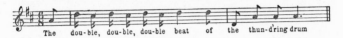

The dou-ble, dou-ble, dou-ble beat of the thun-d'ring drum

in the *Ode for St. Cecilia,* Handel's treatment of the English language is, from an accentual point of view, so meticulous as to suggest that he not only understood it as well as most Englishmen but that he loved it. Could otherwise

which with its succeeding chorus recalls the first scene of *The Fairy Queen,* have been penned? This leads to the observation that the English outlook on music is largely literary, with the result that songs from Dowland to Warlock have a studied lyricism based on the dictation of melodic and rhythmic contour by the shape and situation of individual words. Handel's extension of the Purcellian technique in this respect softens the Italian-inspired roulades and divisions so beloved by contemporary singers, so indifferently mastered by those of later generations, and gives point to virtuosic embellishment. Frequently Handel allowed the delicacy of verbal rhythm to catch his imagination and proceeded to eliminate bar-line tyranny. One instance, from *Jephtha,* will serve representatively in this respect:

Laud her, all ye— vir-gin train,— In glad songs of— choicest strain:

Handel

Charles Lamb and Handel are odd bedfellows, but in one respect they are well matched—in a philosophic realization that the surface of life runs at every turn over the main springs of human emotion. Eclecticism belonged to Italy, large-eyed wonder to Germany; to England an eccentricity that saw silk purses in every sow's ear. 'I have sat through an Italian Opera,' says the unrepentant and unmusical Elia,

till, for sheer pain, and inexplicable anguish, I have rushed out into the noisiest places of the crowded streets, to solace myself with sounds which I was not obliged to follow, and get rid of the distracting torment of endless, fruitless, barren attention! I take refuge in the unpretending assemblage of honest common-life sounds; and the purgatory of the Enraged Musician becomes my paradise.[1]

Handel took inspiration from, rather than refuge in, honest common-life sounds. Therefore he rushes to meet Hercules with the noise of bucolic bagpipery:

David, in *Saul,* with the cheering glitter of Flemish carillon; the infant Jesus with the recollected naïveté of the *pifa*. A Roman holiday in *Theodora* is celebrated with a ripe tavern song—hiccups in the rhythm and top Cs indicate that English tenors should hesitate to essay 'Venus laughing from the skies' when sober—whose fitting place is in those collections of catches and glees, catholicly embracing almost every composer from Morley to Harrington, which when pleasure was taken gladly used to keep the tap-room alive with harmonious gurgitation. That Handel recognized degrees in intoxication may be gathered from a comparison of this plebeian revelry with the dignified Commemoration Dinner merriment of Belshazzar's court: his nobles invoke their tutelar gods with well-trained octave passages and the king sings the praise of wine in the sort of

[1] *A Chapter on Ears.*

rum-tum-tum measure one might have expected from an eighteenth-century don. It may be suspected that the picture was truer of London than of Babylon.

Handel himself confessed that street cries fascinated and inspired him:[1] the direct evidence is in *Serse*, and the flower-seller's song, honoured frequently enough by reference but never by quotation, may be found below on page 138. The quality of rusticity achieved in *L'Allegro* and *Susanna* suggests that Handel was susceptible to the influence of folksong.[2] The sunny charm of

(Susanna)

When first I saw my love-ly maid, be-neath the cit-ron's shade

and the Helston Furry excitement of

(L'Allegro)

Come, Come, thou god-dess fair and free, fair and free, In

Heav'n y-clep'd Eu phro-sy-ne

summarize this aspect of Handelian universality. The merry bells of *Saul* have already been heard: in later contrast come the thunderous peals of ominous profundity which darken the canvas in 'Envy, eldest born of Hell' and threaten the wicked with a horrific *Dies irae* prospect. *L'Allegro* places all sorts of bells in happy neighbourhood: there are the pleasant Sunday morning chimes of 'Or let the merry bells,' the rich urban ring of 'Populous cities,' the distant enchant-ment of the faintly heard curfew and the domestic jangle of the bell-man's instrument of office. Clearly one might say *nullum tetigit quod non ornavit*.

The synoptic outlook of Handel, which is his most distinctive

---

[1] Lady Luxborough to Shenstone: 'The great Handel has told me that the hints of his very best songs have several of them been owing to the sounds in his ears of cries in the streets' (*Luxborough Correspondence*, 1775, p. 58).

[2] An Irish folksong, 'The poor Irish Boy,' appears in Handel's Fitz-william MSS.

quality, recalls Waller's epitaph on Ben Jonson: 'Mirror of poets! mirror of our age!' Therein we may leave the comprehensiveness of Handel temporarily suspended.

In a period so prolific as the eighteenth century supply and demand were particularly interdependent. The consideration of what Handel, or anybody else for that matter, wrote cannot be fully undertaken without some conception of the obligations laid upon them by society. When art functions actively in a community which regards some degree of artistic endeavour as normal rather than abnormal it is not unhealthy that those who pay the piper should take some responsibility for calling the tune. Frequently Handel outdistanced his patrons in imaginative exploration, but from time to time he called himself back to the standards required. What these standards were is defined by Burney at the outset of his *History*. His definitions may help us to discover to what extent Handel was representative of his age and to what extent he outgrew its limitations.

MUSIC is an innocent luxury, unnecessary, indeed, to our existence, but a great improvement and gratification of the sense of hearing. It consists, at present, of MELODY, TIME, CONSONANCE, and DISSONANCE.

By MELODY is implied a series of sounds more fixed, and generally more lengthened, than those of common speech; arranged with grace, and, with respect to TIME, of proportional lengths, such as the mind can easily measure, and the voice express. These sounds are regulated by a scale, consisting of tones and semitones; but admit a variety of arrangement as unbounded as imagination.

CONSONANCE is derived from a coincidence of two or more sounds, which being heard together, by their agreement and union, afford to ears capable of judging and feeling, a delight of a most grateful kind. The combination and succession of CONCORDS or SOUNDS in Consonance, constitute HARMONY; as the selection and texture of Single Sounds produce MELODY.

DISSONANCE is the want of that agreeable union between two or more sounds, which constitutes Consonance: in musical composition it is occasioned by the suspension or anticipation of some sound before, or after, it becomes a Concord. It is the DOLCE PICCANTE of Music, and operates on the ear as a poignant sauce on the palate: it is a zest, without which the auditory sense would be as much cloyed as the appetite, if it had nothing to feed on but sweets.

Of MUSICAL TONES the most grateful to the ear are such as are produced by the vocal organ. And, next to singing, the most pleasing kinds are those which approach the nearest to vocal; such as can be sustained, swelled, and diminished, at pleasure. Of these, the first in rank are such as the most excellent performers produce from the Violin, Flute, and Hautbois. If it were to be asked what instrument is capable of affording the GREATEST EFFECTS? I should answer, the Organ; which can not only imitate a number of other instruments, but is so comprehensive as to possess the power of a numerous orchestra. It is, however, very remote from perfection, as it wants expression, and a more perfect intonation.

With respect to EXCELLENCE OF STYLE AND COMPOSITION, it may perhaps be said that to practised ears the most pleasing Music is such as has the merit of novelty, added to refinement, and ingenious contrivance; and to the ignorant, such as is most familiar and common.

There, in a fair-sized nutshell, is a monument to the rational hedonism which Handel sought to serve.

It may be complained that morality, such as should surely fit a composer of oratorio, is ignored. Avison does something to fill this gap when he speaks of 'the peculiar Quality of Music to raise the *sociable* and *happy Passions,* and to *subdue* the *contrary ones.*' But a musician's first duty was to please: after that he could take a risk and, like Dr. Johnson and the B.B.C., try his hand at instruction through pleasure. The glory of Handel is that he worked through all these stages until he arrived by intelligible steps at the *ne plus ultra* of musical expression. This was because he worked in a style which had, so far as music ever can have, utilitarian significance. A utilitarian style, approved and generally understood by an intelligent and not insensitive community, is indivisible. Therefore opera and oratorio use the same language. A comparison may not be inapt with the architectural style of the Tudors wherein both God and man were served in the same homely, well-bred idiom.

CHAPTER X

THE ORCHESTRA

AT the beginning of the eighteenth century there was, as we understand it, no orchestra: there were instrumentalists who on occasion
played together. Their function, both individually and collectively,
was a subordinate one; to assist prandial conversation, to enliven the
pageantry of city streets, to serve the gaiety of the dance, to enwrap
the amorous excursions of royalty, to furnish pompous atmosphere
for military display, to support ecclesiastical ceremony, to add zest to
holiday and to sauce the conceit of operatic heroes and heroines. For
each of these purposes music was necessary, and what in the way of
players happened to be available was united in relative concord.
This relativity varied from place to place, but a general deduction is
that those were congenial days for players to whom faulty tonality
came naturally. Cacophonous memories are contained in Avison's
remark about 'the irremediable Disagreement of their [wind instru-
ments] rising in their Pitch, while the others are probably falling.'[1]
That strings had their limitations too is indicated by Corelli's protest
against Handel's impatience. This episode immediately suggests that
Handel had orchestral vision beyond what was then considered
normal. But whatever his aspirations, he was constrained always
to make the best use of the material to hand.

It is always the privilege of one generation to regard previous
generations as barbaric. It happened in the eighteenth century, it
happens to-day, and in no respect more markedly than when eyes
accustomed to the systematized scoring of the contemporary orchestra
review a Handel score. To see such a score in proper perspective
it is necessary to see it from an eighteenth-century angle.

The first factor for realization is that then music possessed a unique
sense of homogeneity. Sophistication had not so far progressed as to
remove music from the focal position it should occupy in life in
general. There was still apparent an Elizabethan or Jacobean

[1] Avison, op. cit.

influence which contained music, despite the forward-looking aspirations of the virtuosic, within almost universal limits of comprehension. Airs from opera and oratorio with movements from concertos kept in agreeable spirits the patrons of Vauxhall, Ranelagh or Marylebone: the same works, together with divers suites, sonatas and lessons, found their way into the editions of Walsh, Arnold or Cluer, or else less expensively through supplements to the *Lady's* or the *Gentleman's Magazine*, to the hands of the Sophia Westerns of the countryside. Amateur music-making flourished so extensively that it was possible for teachers of instrumental music to make fortunes from their teaching, the flautist John Festing, for instance, leaving the sum of £8,000 as a monument to his industry.[1] It was also not regarded as improper by professional players that the quality should associate with them on equal terms. In country houses music was indulged in with such frequency that, were we to fall victim to jingoism, we should protest that English music in a practical way had a spirited reply to make to the Continent. James Harris at Salisbury and Fisher Littleton at Teddesley each had bands in which it is recorded that Handel used to play. Court Dewes, who married Mrs. Delany's sister and lived at Wellesbourne in Warwickshire, had a concert daily at which the vicar, presumably as a necessary part of his pastoral function, played the bass viol. Hogarth's 'Music Party' mixes tea-drinking, conversation, the cat's milk and music in the proportions which might have been expected at Mrs. Delany's. A later picture by Zoffany shows the Sharp family making water music. In the eighteenth century it was difficult to escape the sound of music, and so much energy being apparent in its culture compels the opinion that it was then more likely to be understood than when, as in the succeeding century, musicians were regarded as 'ingenious puppets, sir, who live in a box and look out on the world only when it is gaping for amusement.'

The variety of instruments used by Handel in combination related to the improvisatory character of performances of the time. Whether in private house or theatre, there were always differences in the number and quality of instruments available; but this factor of uncertainty partly led to the mastery achieved by Handel over the

---

[1] Every English town had its concert society at this period.

orchestral forces at his disposal. The variety met with in his scores may be gathered from a survey of selected works. In the autograph copy of *Messiah* strings, trumpets and drums are employed (a harpsichord should be taken as constant in every score, whether expressly indicated or not); in 1759 the Foundling Hospital noted with uncommon precision the number of players involved in a *Messiah* performance—and a new scoring is apparent: twelve violins, three 'tenners,' three cellos, two double basses, four hautboys, four bassoons, two horns, two trumpets, kettledrums and organ. In *Esther* provision was made for flutes, hautboys, bassoons, theorbo, harp and organ. In *Orlando* are used *violette marine, per gli Signori Castrucci*. *Alexander's Feast* has three bassoon parts, *Alexander Balus* a mandoline, the *Fireworks* music a double bassoon, *Semele* a side-drum and *Saul* three trombones. Clearly the period was one of experiment: thus archaic and startlingly modern effects stand side by side. Handel, as will be seen shortly, was a founder of orchestral music, and if we ignore his manipulation of different *ensembles* in performance we lose a great part of his music. With him each player or singer has a potentiality not to be disregarded in the working-out of his plot, and where his genius for transmuting the conventional into the extraordinary appears most prominently is in his orchestration.

The prestige of an instrumentalist was lower than that of a successful singer; consequently the names of the majority of Handel's orchestral performers are lost in anonymity. Nevertheless some remain. Of violinists the most celebrated were William Corbett, Bannister, Carbonelli, Castrucci, Veracini, Pasquali, Michael Festing, John Clegg, Richard Charke, Defesch and Richard Collet. Caporale, Pasqualino, Filippo ('Pippo') Mattei—one of the *Muzio Scevola* collaborators—Abaco and the long-nosed and long-lived Cervetto [1] established the cello. Caporale was a notably expressive player, Cervetto and Pasqualino technically finished but tonally raw. The great flautists were Lœillet, Jack Festing and Weidemann. Among oboists we hear of Kytsch, San Martini, Galliard and Richard Vincent, among bassoonists Karba, Lampe, Hebden and Miller, while the surpassing trumpeter was Valentine Snow,

[1] Of whom there is an excellent portrait by Zoffany.

sergeant trumpeter in the king's service. Most of these players per-formed on more than one instrument, so that, in the case of a special instrument being required for an exceptional effect, changes were made in performance in similar manner to that familiarized by the contemporary dance-band musician. Some of them were also com-posers. There could have been few complaints concerning lack of employment. The king's band, the theatres, the pleasure gardens, Hickford's Music Rooms, the taverns and private clients gave as much work as most had time for.

Music which may be supposed to have been 'popular' is recorded in this programme of Carbonelli's benefit concert in 1722[1] (the division into acts signifies the omnipotence of operatic design):

Act I. A new concerto for two trumpets, composed and performed by *Grano* and others; a new concerto by *Albinoni*, just brought over; song by *Mrs. Barbier*; concerto composed by Signor *Carbonelli*.

Act II. A concerto with two hautbois and two flutes, composed by *Dieupart*; a concerto on the base-violin by *Pippo*; song, *Mrs. Barbier*; by desire, the eighth concerto of *Arcangelo Corelli*.

Act III. Concerto by *Carbonelli*; solo on the arch-lute by Signor *Vebar*; song, *Mrs. Barbier*; a new concerto on the little flute, composed by *Wood-cock,* and performed by *Baston*; solo, Signor *Carbonelli*; and for *finale,* a concerto on two trumpets by *Grano,* etc.

It is not specified how long this concert lasted, but it is evident that the virtuosic and the bizarre were principal attractions. In 1729 the hearts of those who revelled in these qualities must have been gladdened by the appearance of one Joachim Frederic Creta, who at several concerts 'blew the first and second treble on two French-horns, in the same manner as is usually done by two persons.' It is to be regretted that this singular art died with its creator.

Handel dealt tactfully, from an artistic point of view, with singers, leaving them their exhibitionism but sublimating it to higher ends. In the same way he made use of the mechanical inventiveness of his instrumentalists while keeping in check their aptitude for music-hall display. And so their acrobatic feats fitted naturally into a more idealistic setting. Conspicuous examples are the trumpet parts, of which those to 'And the trumpet shall sound' and 'Let the bright

---

[1] Programme from the *Daily Courant,* quoted by Burney, *History,* iv. 648.

Seraphim' will be immediately familiar. Then there are the magnificent canonic entry at the beginning of the *Dettingen Te Deum* and the brief flourish which follows 'Thou shalt come to be our Judge':

This latter is indicative of so many aspects of Handel that it merits closer attention. Obviously the trumpeters enjoyed it and so did the audience. On the other hand there is more to it than this simple equation of enjoyment. The passage is dramatically impressive. It halts the flow of *Te Deum* at the sombre and leaves the judicial vision of the hereafter poised in mid thought while by the association of ideas the crimson dignity of the assize court is evoked.

It will be remembered that Handel was a collector of pictures, that he had an eye as well as an ear. The conclusion drawn from his music at many points is that

whether life or nature be his subject . . . he has seen with his own eyes: he gives the image which he receives, not weakened or distorted by the intervention of any other mind: the ignorant feel his representations to be just, and the learned see that they are compleat.[1]

In music as in literature the classical theory of *mimesis* had particular validity in the eighteenth century. 'Every man's performance,' says Johnson, 'must be compared with the state of the age in which he lived, and with his own particular opportunities.' Therefore the response of Handel to the theory that music in general and orchestral music in particular held up the mirror to nature must now be considered.

There is, from our point of view, a naïveté in

[1] Johnson, *Preface to Shakespeare.*

in the bucolic

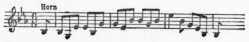

in the harp *obbligato* in 'Praise the Lord with cheerful noise' from *Esther*, in the murmurous insect life of *Israel in Egypt*, in the lute and flute dialogue of St. Cecilia's 'Soft complaining flute' and in countless similar descriptive passages. But such behaviour was part of the eighteenth-century stylistic convention. Avison, in summarizing contemporary thought, writes:

> Thus Music, either by imitating these various Sounds (of Nature) in due Subordination to the Laws of *Air* and *Harmony*, or by any other Method of Association, bringing the Objects of our Passions before us (especially where those Objects are determined, and made as it were visibly, and intimately present to the Imagination by the Help of Words) does naturally raise a Variety of Passions in the human Breast, similar to the Sounds which are expressed. . . .[1]

By the side of this may be placed Mattheson's statement from *Der Musikalische Patriot*: 'All that produces an effect upon men is theatrical. . . . The whole world is a gigantic theatre.' The working out of this general theory brings us to the inevitable fact that 'there are various instruments suited to the different Kinds of musical Compositions.' Trumpets, horns, kettledrums are meet for 'the rough handling proper for Battles, Sieges, and whatever is great or terrible,' while love, tenderness and beauty are the province of the lute or harp. Of descriptive sounds Avison [2] comments first that

> their Tendency is rather to fix the Hearer's Attention on the Similitude between the Sounds and the Things which they describe, and thereby to excite a reflex Act of the Understanding, than to affect the Heart and raise the Passions of the Soul.

Yet such sounds are legitimate so long as the 'expression' is contained in the vocal line and the bird and allied noises are placed at a discreet distance in the accompanying parts. This was at Handel's expense. Handel could never refrain from giving his singers some share in the picturesque.

[1] Avison, op. cit.   [2] op. cit.

It is difficult to see how the orchestra would have developed but for programmatic considerations, and Handel's large palette was in large measure, like those of Berlioz and Wagner, the result of the search for verisimilitudinous colour. Thus the little flute breaks into bird-song in *Riccardo I*; clarinets make tentative pastoral entry in *Tamerlano* (thirty years before, or thereabouts, Denner had produced the clarinet, although it was not until about 1770 that it became finally accepted as a member of the woodwind fraternity); the double bassoon, first made by Stanesby in 1739 and probably at Handel's suggestion, is introduced in *L'Allegro*; four horns exotically enhance the scoring of *Giulio Cesare*; three trumpets imperially add their ardour to the coronation music and to the *Dettingen Te Deum* (one marked 'Principal' indicates, according to Heinrich Christoph Koch,[1] a particular 'crashing (or martial) Style of performance, for which only the middle tones of this instrument are used'; three trombones are uniquely employed in *Saul,* a work which holds incredible fascination in its opulent instrumentation and the ready answer to those who ignorantly rail at the indifference of Handel's orchestral technique. Realism led Handel, who had a notable habit of following every idea to its logical conclusion, to anticipate Tchaikovsky in producing gun-fire as a musical climax. 'Handel,' wrote Mrs. Elizabeth Carter, 'has literally introduced firearms . . . and they have a good effect.' The reference was to *Judas Maccabaeus,* and the innovation was so startling as to provoke Sheridan at a later date to explain off-stage gun-shots thus: 'See, I borrowed this from Handel.'[2] It was not every one who approved these experiments: it was in fact a customary complaint that Handel made too much noise with his orchestra. Pope glances sidelong at the vogue for noisy theatrical effects in that passage in the *Dunciad* which begins:

> 'Tis yours to shake the soul
> With Thunder rumbling from the mustard bowl,
> With horns and trumpets now to madness swell,
> Now sink in sorrows with a tolling bell.

[1] Heinrich Christoph Koch, *Musikalisches Lexicon,* 1802. While on the subject of trumpets, it may be noted that in the *Rinaldo* march Handel uses four.

[2] Sheridan, *Jupiter.*

This may or may not have some connection with Handel's zest for massive and unprecedented orchestral climaxes, but it does indicate how effects in drama and in music were of inspiring variety. The tendency towards extravagance was not confined to Handel, nor to England. 'One no longer hears the voice; the orchestra is deafening,' complained the conservatives in Germany.[1]

Before dismissing such criticism as unreasonable, it may be noted objectively that in general string tone was inadequate to cope with large additions of brass and woodwind: as a rule, about a dozen strings with harpsichord were expected to hold their own. Moreover, obscuration of the melodic line was regarded as an unpardonable offence against the canons of good taste, and without considerable augmentation of the string department such obscuration was at times inevitable.

The fact remains, however, that Handel was indicating progress in the employment of new combinations of colour. After directing attention to the mimetic a second factor supervenes. Avison laid down in brief that certain instruments were apt for certain forms of direct imitation; he also hinted at the attachment of other instruments to more indefinite and more philosophic ideas. Not that this represented anything new. In the Shakespearian theatre flutes made funereal impact on the mind; from the earliest times hautboys or their ancestors had stood for pastoral atmosphere; God, in the mystery plays, had been haloed by string tone. These ancient associations held point in the eighteenth century, as indeed they obviously do to-day; but Handel, with the keenest dramatic insight of his age, subtilized these general impressions. In so doing he urged romanticism from the wings.

'He was the first,' said Volbach, 'to assert the expressive personality of the violoncello.' Thus rich melancholy steals into *L'Allegro*, clad sombrely in cello and bassoon tone:

<hr>

[1] Romain Rolland, op. cit., p. 76.

and sadness and virginity at a later point in the same work find sympathetic delineation in the voluptuous folds of a solo passage which any cellist would relish as an exercise in soulful dissertation. The viola was accepted in the eighteenth-century orchestra only on sufferance and it was the custom to insist on 'placing one of the worst hands to the Tenor,' much to Avison's annoyance. If Handel failed to raise this instrument to its true dignity, he did indicate the importance he attached to its particular timbre by withholding violins at the beginning of the second act of *Alexander's Feast* and by painting the ghostly with a dark combination of two violas, three bassoons, cello, basses and organ. In *Giulio Cesare* Caesar's 'Dall' ondoso periglio' is introduced with this dialogue in the strings:

Therein the viola receives more attention than was then common.

The gently suggestive use of woodwind colour is ubiquitous, and in such music as 'As steals the morn' in *L'Allegro,* where the oboe sings its own aubade, or 'Ferma l'ali' from *La Resurrezione,* where two flutes and muted violins undulate over a pedal, or in Oriane's 'Dolce vita' from *Amadigi,* where the picture of distressed beauty is thus delicately flavoured:

or in the colloquy between voice and oboe in Melissa's 'Ah! spietato!' from the same opera:

the delicacy of aquarelle invites an intimacy between performer and listener which is not apparent unless the fact that in Handel's day the orchestra had not left the domestic atmosphere of chamber music is realized.

At the opposite pole comes Handel's sense of tonal climax: instrument piled on instrument to achieve the golden enchantment of Parnassus in *Giulio Cesare*. Two orchestras are used with strings, oboes, harp, gamba, theorbo and bassoons. The music runs:

and then the second orchestra enters with answering phrase. The dramatic perfection of this movement lies less in the actual music than in the seductive colouring. Another point to be noted is that Handel was sensible that the numerical strength of the instruments employed was not necessarily in relation to the dynamic power intended. Mozart struck at the truth, even though by his supererogation he endeavoured to undermine it, when he observed 'Handel understands effect better than any of us—when he chooses, he strikes like a thunderbolt.' The last part of this has been remembered, the first part too often inconveniently forgotten. The mastery of effect was all-embracing.

As for the thunderbolts, we look for them chorally. But the massive trumpet climaxes which crown the full choral fury are overlooked, largely because they can never be heard. When they can they possess an Elgarian inevitability, as when they surprise the imagination in the Gloria of *Messiah* or when they anoint the regality of 'Thou hast set a crown of pure gold upon his head' in the first *Coronation Anthem,* or when, undarkened either by horns or trombones, they help the acclamation of 'God save the King.' With regard to his brass Handel had clear-cut ideas: trumpets were noble, horns—four of them at any rate—exotic, trombones priestly. The secret of their effectiveness lay in their rarity of appearance. When they did appear they were felt.

CHAPTER XI

CHAMBER MUSIC

THE essence of chamber music is domesticity. Handel wrote at a time when most music still retained something of its *camera* origins and for that reason, and because Handel was of amiable disposition in congenial company, his suites, sonatas and concertos are pleasantly evocative of fireside warmth. This is a great though often neglected quality, for when music loses its fraternal power to 'fetch out in smiles the mutual soul,' as Leigh Hunt wrote of it to Thomas Alsager, the graciousness of courteous hospitality is denuded of one of its chief agents. The proper setting for Handel's music, other than that obviously designed for public performance, was between Mrs. Delany's conversation and her mulled white wine: the two extremes of extemporaneous sagacity, wit and philosophy and discriminating hedonism. Music in the eighteenth century was disposed to stimulate pleasure, but an unwritten law decreed that pleasure should have such blend of intellectual and sensual appeal as became a set of comfort-able eclectics. With the eclectics Handel was at home, and his music is monumental to his clubbableness; it is not esoteric like so much of Bach, nor shot with the febrile brilliance of Domenico Scarlatti, nor overrun with the tintinnabulations of the vulgar who, like the Rev. William Felton, had no more than 'a neat finger for common divisions and the rapid multiplication of notes,' but plainly pleasing.

It is symptomatic that the most eligible party piece for the not too precociously musical schoolgirl is the set of variations from the E major (No. 5) Suite (Set I, 1720), commonly miscalled *The Har-monious Blacksmith*. The long story of why this title and the attendant fable are mythical will do no good by repetition (a generation bred on Hollywood will be loth to believe that pretty inaptness in nomen-clature is no great aid to musical appreciation), so let it simply be stated that there is no recorded instance of Handel's having had dealings with blacksmiths, harmonious or otherwise, at Edgware or anywhere else. The music of these variations has that artless, narrative pleasantry equally attractive to the child and to the naïve adult who enjoys the simplicity of innocent pleasures. Handel was not above taking children seriously, nor did he underestimate their capacity for understanding. His educational interests showed their effectiveness in the loyalties of the Princesses Anne and Amelia and of Frederick, Prince of Wales, while a nice piece of prescience prompted this anecdote of the future George III in Southey's *Commonplace Book*:

Handel asked the King, then a young child, and listening very earnestly while he played, if he liked the music, and the Prince warmly expressed his pleasure. 'A good boy, a good boy,' he cried, 'you shall protect my fame when I am dead.'

It was for those *in statu pupillari* that many of the harpsichord pieces were written: some clearly betray their *étude* origin and need no long critical examination. But elsewhere Handel speaks for himself more particularly. In the Prelude to the first Suite, in A major, the characteristic flourish of extemporization is represented in little more than a shorthand abstract. In the succeeding Allemande that gentle quality which, for want of a term of nearer precision, had best be defined as pastoral, demonstrates how much more musical thought meant to Handel than the implications of a set form. The suave counterpoint of the opening:

and the sinuosity of the last cadence:

have a cool French quality of rationalized whimsicality. The Courante has similar poise and recollects in its closing bars the particular note-disposition of the Allemande cadence. If inspiration fails, it is in the gigues of the harpsichord suites, which with their slickly tailored efficiency please once. An exception is the rum-bustiously percussive finale to the Suite in G minor (No. 6, Set II, 1733). This, unbuttoned and Beethovenian, is of more than nor-mally generous proportion and elbows its rough way thus impulsively:

If this defeats the capacity of the harpsichord the same may be said of the Ouverture, also in G minor, to Suite VII (Set I). This intense prelude is too tragic for its context and suggests a sketch for some epic tale of high passion. Fuguing was a constant delight to Handel, but not as an exercise in academic rectitude. The purpose of a Handelian fugue was to demonstrate the personality of his subject. If students would learn how not to satisfy examiners they should model their counterpoint on that of Handel; if, however, they would realize the incentive to musical thought given by epigram they should study the suggestiveness of such themes as:

or the darkly anachronistic romanticism of the second movement of the Suite in F minor (No. 8, Set I). The third fugue in the set of six published in 1735, which also furnishes most of the Sinfonia to the Passion of 1716, gives further publicity to the St. Anne motif and, underlining the common sources of eighteenth-century musical diction, emphasizes the dangers of recognizing personal influence by fortuitous thematic coincidence.

Those who have looked at the suites will realize that often as between movement and movement there is some philosophic con-nection which imposes a sense of unity on what would otherwise be a collection of heterogeneous fragments. This is not simply a matter of key consistency, but an offshoot of Handel's fertile dramatic ability to present problems and situations with comprehension. An interest in the dramatic capacity of melody led inevitably to experiment with *Leitmotive*. The possibilities of this artificial aid to consistency were foreseen tentatively long before Handel's day, in fact the folksong-dependent mass-writers of the sixteenth century were first in this field; but Handel had a habit of anticipating Berlioz and Wagner in so many other respects that this practice, not fundamentally of the eighteenth century, cannot pass without notice. In Handel's case, however, it may often be attributed to accident rather than design. Thematic identity at the outset of successive movements, such as occurs in Suite 4 (Set I):

suggests the improviser calculating the future plan of development while automatically delivering what remains fresh in the mind. Sometimes, on the other hand, thematic reiteration comes as the result of deliberation: the most effective instance being in the 'Se mai turbo' duet in *Poro*, 'in which the lovers, Porus and Cleosilda, are ironically repeating the former promises which they had made to each other of fidelity and confidence.'[1]

In contrast to this subtlety lies the conservatism which generally pervades Handel's use of variations. Here too often the volant finger has little to proclaim except its own dexterity. Here and there, however, a masculine perversity recalls the acidulous flavour of the Elizabethan virginalists. The Chaconne in F is thus antiquely reminiscent, while elsewhere, and particularly in the organ concertos, monotony is relieved by Chippendale delicacy. Variations were to Handel a recreation. High seriousness he reserved for opera and oratorio, though accidents sometimes happened and let into the drawing-room an occasional glimpse of tragedy; and the ground basses which symbolize intensity of feeling in *Poro*, *Orlando*, *Hercules* and *Saul* demonstrate Handel's outlook on the relative functions of

[1] Burney, *History*, iv. 351.

opera and oratorio on the one hand and domestic music on the other.

This sense of fitness for purpose is one of the keys to Handel's omnipotence. It was not that opera and oratorio had a higher sanction than chamber music, but that when they were performed there was more likelihood of listening being more attentive than in the case of that homely music which entered the one ear not engaged in the absorption of whispered scandal. From all accounts Quin was a mighty Lear, but conversely he was a delicious raconteur. Handel had the same zest for rich expression, and the necessary complement to profundity may be discovered in the violin sonatas, written for Dubourg or possibly for Dubourg's pupil, the Prince of Wales, in the oboe sonatas, characteristically available for German flute or violin, and in the various works for trio. Of these it may be said that they implicitly express approval of Telemann's 'Wer auf Instrumenten spielt muss des Singens kundig seyn.' [1] Otherwise they impress by high technical competence and by mellifluence which jointly predominate over imaginative adventure.

In the smaller chamber works there are many instances of recol-lection or anticipation of ideas familiarized in other settings. The 1735 collection of fugues presents those which fit horrifically into *Israel in Egypt* ('He smote all the first-born in Egypt' and 'They loathed to drink of the river'); the *Allegro* of the violin Sonata in D major appears symphonically in *Jephtha*; 'Why so full of grief' from the sixth Chandos anthem is reflected in the first of the 1733 trio sonatas and the fourth of the 1738 set remodels the overture to *Athaliah*.

If the organ concertos are considered among the chamber works organists may feel encouraged to regard them without pomposity, and to refrain from enveloping their clarity in orgiastic outbursts from the swell reeds. The largest organs of the eighteenth century, in England at any rate, where choral singing was well able to dispense with massive accompanimental support, were slight of build, clear-voiced, bright-eyed with mutation work, effective in contrast with the string ensemble and accordingly acceptable in theatre or house as well as in church. Pedal boards were rare in England; that they were not altogether unknown is shown by Handel's note that pedals should be

[1] Whoever plays an instrument must be conversant with singing.

used in Concerto I of the second (1740) set. In general, the style of writing for the organ was that proper for the harpsichord. In relation to modern interpretation this suggests a reduction of tone-colour to near conformity with eighteenth-century standards. This makes evident the integrity of the melodic line, the delicacy of contrast and ornamentation, the gentle persuasiveness of the orchestral scoring (how eloquently flutes and oboes can maintain silence!) and the intimate dialogue. And sufficient is left unsaid—this is important in all Handelian interpretation and particularly in *ff* which should never be pushed to the vulgar extremity of *fff* with the solo tuba— for the listener to be able to follow the direction of the thought in his own imagination. It may be that the best way of presenting the organ concertos to a modern audience is via pianoforte or harpsichord and chamber orchestra. That is so long as the alternative combines the violence of the out-voluntary with the clamour of 'full' orchestra.

'Our Composers,' said Avison,[1] 'have run all their concertos into little else than tedious Divisions.' The unsympathetic may hold this generalization to Handel and suspect that it applies. But once again it is necessary to view the matter from an eighteenth-century angle: then purpose will begin to appear. Concertos were an exhibition of skill (presumably they still are) into which the orchestra entered as a foil to pyrotechnic display. This display often stood out in a strong light because the concertos were, as Avison remarks, generally under-rehearsed. Concertos in which the solo instrument was the organ and in which the soloist was Handel were different in one important respect. They were conceived as ancillary to a larger scheme, as intermissions in oratorio. Therefore while the concerto relieved the tension of the oratorio plot its technical flights were projected against a particular background. Thus the divisions never ran out of control.

The organ concertos were works of maturity. Op. 4 was published in 1738; Op. 7 in 1740.[2] They accordingly carry the flexibility conspicuous in all Handel's later music. Normally they possess four movements, but the length and character of each move-

---

[1] op. cit.   [2] A third set appeared posthumously.

A MUSIC PARTY

By Hogarth

ment varies from work to work. A significant step in the direction of poetry is indicated by the frequent tendency to emphasize the slow movements at the expense of the more or less formal allegros. It is evident that these works were approved. Hawkins leaves this tribute:

> When he gave a Concerto, his method in general was, to introduce it with a Voluntary movement on the Diapasons, which stole on the ear in a slow and solemn progression; the harmony close wrought, and as full as could possibly be expressed; the passages constructed with stupendous art; the whole, at the same time, being perfectly intelligible, and having the appearance of great simplicity. This kind of prelude was succeeded by the Concerto itself, which he executed with a degree of spirit and firmness that no one even pretended to equal. Such, in general, was the manner of his performance; but who shall describe its effects on his enraptured auditory? Silence, the truest applause, succeeded, the instant that he addressed himself to the instrument; and that was so profound, that it checked respiration, and seemed to controul the functions of nature [whatever that may mean!], while the magic of his touch kept the attention of his hearers awake only to those enchanting sounds to which it gave utterance.[1]

It remains to detail the enchantment. As for a 'slow and solemn progression,' there is none of greater beauty than the opening *Larghetto* of the Concerto in F major (No. 5, Set I): here is the consummation of simplicity. Of almost equal simplicity, but of more profound feeling, is this enhanced repetition of the opening bars of the *Largo, e piano* from the B flat major Concerto (No. 1, Set II), a movement which follows the sober optimism of the first *Andante* in the remoteness of D minor:

[1] Hawkins, v. 413.

The preceding movement, in two sections, is a free fantasia on this commonly used bell motiv:

which serves as an impressive ground. Another interesting ground-bass treatment occurs in the G minor Concerto (No. 5, Set II), where the Olympian tread of the octave-spacing continues from beginning to end of the *Andante larghetto, e staccato,* the only relief lying in the counterpoint in the organ. That the orchestra was more than a sleeping partner becomes apparent when in the twelve-bar *Adagio* of the G minor Concerto (No. 3, Set I) a *concertino* carries more or less extravagant modulations in contrast both to the organ and the *ripieno,* when in the D minor Concerto (No. 4, Set II) veiled melancholy is enshrined thus:

or when in the last little Concerto of the first set the organ is alternative to the harp, the violins are muted, the lower strings are *pizzicato* and flutes are added to a Botticellian atmosphere of fair-weather ingenuousness. For the sake of completion it should be added that precisely what we most desire, Handel's extemporized cadenzas, are lost for ever. A concerto without its embellishments and with subsequent editorial accretions is as near the original as is a medieval church stripped of its wall paintings and made to look dismally religious by pitch pine and garish glass.

The surprising variety of orchestration suggested in the organ concertos is evident throughout Handel's larger-scale chamber works. The reason was the different conditions which prevailed when the works were written. The six *Concerti Grossi* (Op. 3), written at Hanover, at Canons or for the marriage of the princess royal in 1733, employed flutes, oboes, bassoons and strings disposed in the normally contrasting arrangement of *concertino* and *ripieno*. The open-air music, that for the *Water Music* and the *Royal Fireworks,* naturally lays more insistence on the wind. More or less experimental combinations exist in various sketches. An organ concerto with choral termination, intended for the 1737 revival of *The Triumph of Time and Truth*; a concerto for two *concertini,* each consisting of two horns, two oboes and a bassoon, and supported with the customary string ensemble; concertos for trumpets and horns and for horns and side-drums. But the crowning works in concerto form are the great set written in 1739 and published as Op. 6.

In these works it is tempting to see the peak of Handel's creative genius. Elsewhere the flame of inspiration may leap momentarily higher, but nowhere else has consistency of imaginative thought so triumphal a progress. It is generally evident that Handel was on good terms with his orchestral players (it is encouraging to find no anecdotes to suggest the contrary). Understanding their point of view— after all, Handel started life as a fiddler at Hamburg—he was able to maintain that subtle balance between all departments which pleases the players and likewise the audience. With no more than strings and *continuo* a wealth of light and shade is achieved by the subtle interplay of *concertino* and *ripieno*. Elgar follows the pattern with magnificent fidelity to Handelian ideals in the *Introduction and Allegro* and underlines the lesson of the concertos that economy in material leads to amplification of musical thought. This economy imposes one sort of unity on the *Concerti grossi*: key relationship (in allowing the principal key to dominate all the movements Handel was following Corelli); and another, larger unity: that of action or idea. This is apparent in performance where any one of the concertos impresses as a complete essay and not, as in the case of so many suites, as a series of heterogeneous items thrown into accidental contiguity. It is not quite satisfactory to contain, as Romain Rolland does, the music within objective limits by the erection of somewhat arbitrary concrete imagery. More philosophically it may be suggested that each concerto concerns itself with one facet of the pattern of life, and that what variety is apparent rises from cognate impressions associated with the central idea.

This centrality of outlook, the capacity for representing largely and truthfully one aspect of the universal, is the supreme mark of greatness, and if Handel and Beethoven are to be in any way associated, as by Beethoven's admission they should,[1] it is by referring the concertos to Beethovenian standards of expression. Frequently in his overtures Handel leads us to suppose that the introductory slow movement is more than a conventional curtain-raiser: here are two quotations which contain in little space the conviction that the prelude was of parallel importance with its companion movements:

The tremendous rhythmic vigour here contained is urged insistently throughout the respective movements, the first declining into the mystery of this coda:

<hr />

[1] *Vide* p. 177.

the second sweeping into spacious scale progressions cousinly to those in the first movement of Beethoven's seventh Symphony.

Writing fugues was not Handel's forte; writing fugally was. The contrapuntist who won early respect from Mattheson spreads himself throughout the *Concerti grossi*, although not in the construction of school fugues. In the last movement of the second Concerto the subject walks briskly through its exposition until halted by the ingenuousness of:

which the *concertino* projects against a plain chordal background in the accompanying parts. The two ideas eye each other like a couple of unintroduced mongrels and finally join together in boisterous merry-making which happens to involve double invertible counterpoint. The principal subject—Handel favoured fugues with two subjects—of the *Andante* of the third Concerto has Bachian tautness and resolves its dolours into a passionate climax of great power:

The whole of this Concerto is cast in severity, the prevailing darkness of the colouring being emphasized by the delicate detail of the *Polonaise*, the bright robe of which sets off the grief of the *mater dolorosa*. The *Allegro* shows the forward-looking Handel engaged in rough violation of all the accepted clauses relating to key change:

This ellipsis is characteristic, as in the eighth Concerto the *Andante* shows:

while the *Grave* proceeds with similar brusqueness from one scene to another:

This last passage contains the clue to the process. In choral music of the older schools such abruptness had grown naturally out of the juxtaposition of unrelated triads. Handel borrowed the idea, used it frequently and with majestic effect in his choral music, and translated it orchestrally. His harmonic sense led him to pursue courses which are effective by their unexpectedness. In the fifth Concerto the pedal-points of the second movement and the nine consecutive bars of tonic seventh, dangerously near the end, in the third movement speak with picturesque accent on romanticism. Students of elementary harmony may like to take up a set of consecutive fifths from the third bar of the *Minuet* in the ninth Concerto and inquire of their tutors wherein lies the crime.

Ingenuity in harmony and counterpoint should not blind us to the fact that Handel's chief blessing was a capacity for containing his text in a single line of melody. Apprenticeship to the theatre had taught that intensity of thought had more significance when memorably placed within the scope of the melodically minded listener. But melody gets pushed out to the limits. Wide intervals indicate mystery in the first movement of the ninth Concerto and wild spirits in the fifth movement of the fifth Concerto. In contradistinction, however, Handel can turn a one-note subject, as in the second section of the seventh Concerto, into a matter for jesting. This comic fugue terminates with cellos and basses wagging their bows over the diminution of minim to crotchet and crotchet to quaver.

The attention to landscape detail so familiar in the oratorios and the operas pervades the concertos, so that in the *Andante larghetto* of the eleventh Concerto this is placed after an opening of vigorous octave strides:

and a little later another corner is turned to reveal the insistent chatter of

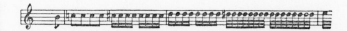

The truth is that tunes cropped up as if by accident, and where Handel had only meant a servant-boy episode he set a Sam Weller on an irresistible career.

CHAPTER XII

CHARACTERIZATION

FROM his biography it is clear that Handel was a realist. From his music a similar deduction, though with a certain difference in emphasis, may be drawn. In general his music had close associa/ tion with the façade of life, being in seven cases out of ten concerned with more or less obvious description. From a Platonic point of view what we receive may be twice removed from reality, but despite that we conceive a fresh and vital reality of a new musical order. The purpose of music has defied the efforts of philosophy and theology to discover it. The most we may with certainty conclude is that it deals with the antithesis of ideas. In abstract music (this arbitrary term is here used on account of its relative convenience in definition), such as Bach's *Art of Fugue* or Mozart's G minor Symphony, the motivating ideas are of purely musical significance. It will be re/ membered that Berlioz to show his distaste for Handel dragged in a reference to a 'tub of pork and beer': a phrase which intends rudeness but points complimentarily to the *nihil humani alienum puto* thesis which is the substance of this chapter. The Russian writer referred to earlier claims Handel as a people's composer. The non/ideological side of this thought will be endorsed by the least musical, who will explain that the only music which for them has significance is Handel's. The incredible influence Handel holds, ruefully we must confess by means of the one or two fragments which duly pass from school hall to parish hall and from parish hall to town hall, is indicative of a particular capacity for understanding human nature. This came from an observation not of what people wanted, but of what people were, and are. Whether Handel succeeded in passing through the stages enumerated in the *Symposium* to arrive at ultimate goodness and beauty is a matter of opinion; what is certain is his shrewd observation of the world around him. Not only was he gifted in observation, but also in narrative expression, which being easeful and friendly breeds familiarity.

There were few crimes of greater magnitude in the eighteenth century than that of unsociability; therefore the easiest way to mis-understand Handel is to regard him as a detached creature addicted to supernal communion. Romantic anecdotes, in single setting assuming alarming significance, about the tears which accompanied the parturition of the Messianic Hallelujah disguise the fact that Handel was rarely at ease with God and sought general inspiration from what was epigrammatically considered the proper study of mankind.

It has already been indicated that music in the eighteenth century had greater relevance to everyday life than has been the case since. Thus in the most typical of eighteenth-century composers we should unravel part of the intelligence of the music by consideration of this point in its most graphic expression.

Handel left no diary and only a handful of polite letters, but a solitary inscription in one of his sketch-books to be found in the Fitzwilliam Museum has some compensatory value. The psycho-logist may care to enlarge on its significance: here it is sufficient to draw attention to the secret of well-oiled counterpoint, to the mental contiguity of work and play, and to the bachelorly preoccupation with details of hospitality (unless we accept Brown's libellous sugges-tion of addiction to secret drinking) which speak through this terse memorandum:

12 Gallons Port
12 Bottles French   Duke Street
                       Meels.

Handel engaged in decanting the port, in handing it round, in genial conversation, preludes the optimistic philosophy which imbues his music with infectious confidence, good nature and tolerance. And such convivial intimacy gave precisely those opportunities for observation which, from a wordly point of view, elude the more pietistic. And then supervenes the direction of Handel's education in opera and his own natural enthusiasm for that form of expression.

An opera is a story about people and their emotions intensified through the use of music. What people happen to be called on the stage is immaterial: what they are in fact are projections of the personality and emotional excitement of the audience which attends the opera. The heroic puffs up the manly breast; the villainous attracts anger or else that sneaking affection for daring wickedness which we all entertain; beauty provokes wonderment; distress draws tears; and so we might proceed through the gamut of conventional opera types. In more senses than one audience and actor were closer together in the eighteenth century than to-day, and Handelian audiences were fully competent to rival the players in histrionic endeavour. Thus, although the horseplay would have tried the patience of the earnest, there was a directness in approach to the project of opera which by-passed academic philosophies and took all that we may lecture about as read. The main requisites were colour, novelty, hot emotion and virtuosity: the requisites in fact of any popular art whose existence is dependent on satisfaction in the box office. Handel's triumph and failure were due to his practice of achieving more than was expected from him, but because he did this he rose above his environment and left for posterity an enlargement of the better attributes of contemporary outlook. This he did by avoiding writing with deliberation for posterity and by keeping his finger on the public pulse.

FitzGerald refers to Handel as 'a good old pagan at heart' and, in tacit agreement with Leigh Hunt, who makes kindly observation on his Theocritan aptitude for dropping milk and honey, puts a pen accurately on the side of truth when writing:

I think Handel never gets out of his wig, that is, out of his age: his Hallelujah Chorus is a chorus, not of angels, but of well-fed earthly choristers, ranged tier above tier in a Gothic cathedral, with princes for audience, and their military trumpets flourishing over the full volume of the organ. Handel's gods are like Homer's, and his sublime never reached beyond the region of the clouds.[1]

Bach invaded the *Himmelreich*; Handel found *Lebensraum* on earth. The fact is clear if Handel's music is regarded as a whole. Operas, oratorios and other works of cognate character form an immense

---

[1] This FitzGerald wrote after seeing Macready's stage revival of *Acis and Galatea* in 1847.

portrait gallery and an inexhaustible fund of carefully catalogued human emotion. For reasons which will in due course be made apparent oratorio provided a better framework for extended psycho-logical study, but opera was the first experimental laboratory. Unless the nature of Handel's operatic style is in some way understood the oratorios are lacking in point.

The people whom Handel was initially constrained to represent were of a conventional type. Kings and princes of a most excellent goodness, in the portrayal of whom a careful eye was cocked court-wards, for the seventeenth-century habit of incidental flattery had not entirely passed out; bad kings and princes, who were possibly Jacobites in disguise; beauty in distress; sorcerers and sorceresses whose presence was often necessary for the smooth operation of the improbabilities which had to culminate in happy endings; occasional retainers, prophets, priests and warriors. It was the greatness of Handel to turn these vehicles of varied aria—*cantabile, di portamento, di mezzo carattere, parlante, di bravura* or *d'imitazione*—and recitative into people.

If Handel's characters sometimes stand stiff-jointed and stylized, it is because such behaviour was expected and because had this connection with normality been ignored the operas would have suffered immediate relegation to the realm of impracticability. As it was, differences of opinion with singers and audience led to the ill acceptance of much of the finest music. But when Handel's people pose they do so with magnificent full-blooded theatricality. The angel of *La Resurrezione* ends with Grinling Gibbons florescence the aria 'Disserratevi, oh porte d'Averno!' thus:

2 Trumpets & Strings

Rinaldo strikes the heroic in what George Eliot would have called the 'mechanical dramatic' manner:

Com - bat - ti da for - te, com - bat - ti da for - te, che fer-mo il mío sen

and Galatea trails self-pity behind her like a representation of Rossettian charm.

The end-stopped theatrical presentation of personality was inevitable so long as Handel referred to the conventions by which recitative, although Keiser had educated him in the dramatic possibilities latent herein, and aria fulfilled the functions of plain narration on the one hand and onomatopoeic virtuosity on the other, while the incongruity of *da capo* provided a further handicap. But despite these obstacles Handel rarely leaves his characters solely mechanical. Into his arias he pours corpuscular energy, an achievement rare in the fluent Buononcini or in any other contemporary composer. For the most part it is possible to dislike Handel's feather-brained heroines—as helpless in the grip of circumstance as any of Hardy's—but, for all their supine resignation, they are attractive in lineament, and in their decorative subordination they reflect something of the eighteenth-century attitude towards women. Representative heroines of this order are the pallid Magdalena of *La Resurrezione,* the child-like Asteria of *Tamerlano,* the vapid Queen of *Solomon* and the obedient Merab of *Saul.* In depicting these women Handel seizes on the obvious, achieves skilful and apt portraiture, but hardly touches subtlety. On a first hearing this static quality may seem to define all Handelian characters: royalty has its vocabulary of apposite dignity: the hieratic, as in Valens in *Theodora* or that impressive song of the Levite in *Solomon,* 'Praise ye the Lord,' its Anglo-Catholic poise of cultured superiority; while braggarts storm in the same strain of cheerful anger from Argante to Harapha. To continue this catalogue is merely to indicate that, as all Handel's characters are in some measure self-projective, a family likeness is not to be unexpected.

The excuse of narrative, whether in drama, in literature or in dramatically conditioned music, is that emotional behaviour is naturally settled by the tendencies of plot. In the period under review the plot as such was subsidiary to the circumstances evolved by its often ductile meanderings. Sterne, Richardson, Fielding, Smollett and clearly Hogarth concerned themselves with the kaleidoscope of life, and in selecting incidents from their *milieu* endeavoured to portray faithfully what they saw, what was, rather than what they thought ought to be. This latter was left to the imagination of the beholder. Handel's music was complementary to the art of the above-mentioned, and his strength must lie in his capacity to express his sensibility to human passion. The moral purpose which he began to experience towards the end of his life was the natural outcome of extensive observation, a development of sympathy with what he described, and that attractive brotherliness which Leigh Hunt ascribed to Abou Ben Adhem.

What happened to Polissena in *Radamisto* is neither here nor there, but her anguish of soul, the result of her husband's attachment to Zenobia, is thus portrayed:

There is a universality about this which immediately makes the turgid plot development irrelevant and provokes sympathy with the victim of misfortune whoever she may be. Burney remarks some-where that no one could use octave and unison passages with such effect as Handel. The rests, the melodic intervals, the ambiguous tonality of Polissena's opening are all symptomatic of the complex simplicity which Handel used in moments of strained emotion. In *Floridante* Orante similarly speaks agonizingly through the terseness of

This form of direct repetition links the Handelian style of musical development with that of twentieth-century practice: the fundamental

idea is represented in one short and pregnant theme which then impresses the listener not by evolution in the academic way, but by stark alliteration. Of this habit no more expressive example can be found than in the accompaniment to the 'Monster Atheist' of *Saul*. Accompaniment is the wrong term: the more intense Handel's thought the more coalescently vocal and instrumental parts unite in balanced symmetry. It was this insistence on the necessity for orchestral partnership which led Handel into trouble with his contemporaries, but the truth is that his vision looked forward to a new form of expression. Tolomeo's 'Stille amare,' for instance, is not so much a song as a tone-poem the opening of which

leaves in the unsubstantial terms of pure music what Tolomeo endeavours, in inchoate mixture of recitative and aria and with death on his lips, to put into coherence. On the side of tragedy Dejanira's 'Where shall I fly,' in *Hercules*, Samson's 'Total Eclipse' and Orlando's mad scene are the most penetrating and awe-inspiring examples of Handel's capacity for uncovering the raw nerve-centres of mental agony. Sheer despair, haunting and spectral fear, mad desires translate the personality from humanity to bestiality or to primeval chaos. Dejanira expels her evil spirits. Orlando passes the region of reclamation except for the intervention of magic. Once again bare octaves suffice to carry the voice; once again the music is peremptorily occupied in reiteration; and for the first time in history the time-signature 5-8 appears. The catastrophic passage, so frequent in reference and so rare in appearance, stands thus:

Was it prevision of personal misfortune or simply the observation of kindled imagination which prompted this anachronistic *scena*? The craft is superb. Mental affliction crosses recitative and aria, ebbs to exhaustion through the healing influence of the 'Vaghe pupille' gavotte and finally reposes Orlando in troubled sleep over the time-honoured motif of chromatically descending ground-bass. The return to sanity is achieved through the mediation of Zoroaster. Necromancy plays its superficial part, but the emotional picture is larger than the obvious limits of opera allow. Handel comes near, at this juncture, to the fundamental and unanswerable problems of life and death. Both in matter and manner there is an occasional tinting of Elgar. While Orlando is tossed into unhappy uncertainty the beneficent powers are arranging his release from suffering, the high priest officiates pontifically with solemn appeal to the unknown gods:

and supernatural agents bring restorative to the shadowy beauty of this soothing interlude:

The music for this scene is, perhaps, the most profound essay in characterization in the whole of Handel. But one point remains abundantly clear: Handel judged not his fellow men, but extended to them the full warmth of his sympathy. It is this sympathy, coupled with an abiding affection, which embraces all the moods in which we find the figures of opera and oratorio. Old age in mellowed serenity in the 'Nel riposo' of *Deidamia* or in the Manoah music of *Samson*; spirited chaperonage in the two Irenes of *Tamerlano* and *Theodora*; leafy amorousness in Dorinda's music at the beginning of the second act of *Orlando*; the bucolic jollity of *Hercules*; the apt representation of Ben Jonson's bluster in *L'Allegro*; even the *sic semper tyrannis* of Haman in *Esther* or of Tiridate in *Radamisto*; and the below-stairs comedy of *Serse* and *Almira*. The grateful antidote to the common-place thesis that Handel principally enjoyed pious occupation in the production of endless Hallelujahs for the faithful is Elviro's Mozartian (albeit the cries of London exude in springtime vivacity) flower-selling song from *Serse*:

The student of Handel will be readily able to add to this list of varied character studies and in so doing he will realize Handel's kinship with the diarist. But Handel was not only a diarist, he was a dramatist, and drama depends on the relationship evolved between one character and another. Because he was not satisfied in leaving his people in splendid isolation Handel proceeded to bring them into a psychological relationship typical of Mozart and to divest the opera of its more obvious function of providing a concert in fancy dress.   Love-making, for the benefit of those who read autobiography in every bar, did not rouse Handel to considerable enthusiasm.   But when jealous suspicion and possible infidelity appear the music warms up to the pitch of painful realism evident in the duets between Porus and Cleosida or Samson and Delilah.   In *Rinaldo* and *Teseo* there are masterly contrasts between the two women in each opera, who respectively duel with each other over the possession of the men. In *Hercules* Iole and Dejanira are similarly brought together, but with greater subtlety, and their unsought rivalry is projected against a more significant background wherein the mutability of human nature and the vicious turns of inexorable fate are tragically intermingled.   And at the climactic moment the shadow overhanging the scene takes recognizable shape as the chorus, that element which Handel required to fulfil his dramatic intentions with complete fidelity, after the foreboding of an octave introduction utters:

One more example of Handel's psychological insight must suffice. It is in that scene in *Solomon* where the two women appear: impudent harlotry and rich motherhood can rarely have had such representation.

This counterpoint of ideas is turned into triple counterpoint by the presence of Solomon, whose judicial behaviour at this point is perfect.   To present three or more strands of thought simultaneously is the most involved problem in musical drama.   Handel achieved the trio in *Acis and Galatea*, the quartets in *Radamisto, Semele* and *Jephtha,* all of which would appear superb at any period, but incredible in an age when such extravagantly truthful demonstrations of human frailty and perplexity were regarded as improper interpolations in an evening's enjoyment.

The libretti with which Handel had to deal were frequently of infuriating puerility, but they served as incentive to the composer to recreate from his imagination the types of personality there collected.

Characters and situations were so arranged in Handel's capacious and orderly mind that they were ready for any contingency: hence the speed of execution receives additional sanction. The operas were often episodic—the plots were to blame for this; the oratorios hardly ever. In general the texts on which he worked for oratorio composition possessed a singleness of direction never evident in the complex organization of the eighteenth-century opera; moreover, and this will receive amplification in a later chapter, the introduction of the chorus enabled additional matter relevant to the argument and impossible of mention by the principal characters to be adduced. The main difference between opera and oratorio lies in the capacity of the latter form to show not only isolated moments of inspired characterization but continuity in emotional development. Samson remains Samson through all vicissitudes and is musically recognizable at any given moment. Nicotris, like Storge in *Jephtha*, adjusts herself to whatever situation may arise, but stands perpetually fixed in an incredible pattern of grief, righteousness and forbearing motherhood. And in those late works *Theodora* and *Jephtha* Handel takes youth in hand with consummate understanding, leading Theodora and Iphis from the feckless innocence of newly awakened love through anxiety, bred of principle on the one hand and devotion on the other, to certainty in the value of values and to the uncommon climaxes of death in the one case and conventual immuration in the other. Their name should be Cordelia.

CHAPTER XIII

'TONMALEREI'

IF there is one aspect of Handel which reveals him more than any other as sharing the traditional philosophy of the English it is his outlook on nature. The revival of romanticism belonged to his period, as the preoccupation of music with details of illustration— itself an inevitable outcome of the development of instrumental technique—the realistic essays in scenic adventure and the transition of poetic thought all indicate. 'What this increased interest in nature signified,' writes Professor Ifor Evans,

is difficult to record. Part of it was a delight in 'prospects,' in scenes which a painter might use. Now that roads were improving, gentlemen and ladies could look out from their carriages on the views, and many of them they found good. Some even constructed 'views' on their own estates and parklands. The delight was often not for the pretty and regular design, but for the more wild and rugged aspects of nature. It was as if the human mind were in revolt against the increasing rationalism of the century.[1]

In isolating Handel's approach to nature emphasis is once again laid on his genius for expressing the motions of eighteenth-century thought and equally on his genius for transcending the common-place and rising superior to his contemporaries by integrating fragmentary facets of imaginative exploration into unity. It is not uncommon to note that Handel conscribed a company of frogs, lice and locusts and that he brought down hailstones and fire from heaven for the discomfiture of Pharaoh's hosts, that he emulated Marvell's 'green thought in a green shade' in *Semele*, that he com-manded thunder and lightning in *Riccardo I* and *Joshua*, that he shared with the Almighty the governance of the sea in the Chandos anthem 'The Lord is my Light' and in *Israel in Egypt*, and that in a hundred other instances he demonstrated powers of observation such as rarely find so adequate an expression. But it is less frequent to observe that Handel not only contemplated nature picturesquely, but also with a conviction that the mind of man and the operations of nature were of a piece in the universal design. Handel was by no means

[1] B. Ifor Evans, *A Short History of English Literature* (Pelican Books), p. 39.

lacking in religious faith, but his faith of an elementary and practical order left ample room for the expansion of a free will into those realms of speculation uncongenial to the theologically dogmatic.

From a technical point of view Handel invented nothing: he merely did what other people did, but generally better. Many eighteenth-century composers were exploring the possibilities of realism. Vivaldi had written seasonable music, in concerto form, to illustrate spring, summer, autumn and winter. Kuhnau had put sections of the Old Testament into sonatas. Werner had produced the detailed preciosity of an *Instrumental-Kalender* and Telemann had invested opera and oratorio with large portions of elementary scene-painting. Such experiments served a double purpose: on the one hand the freedom of music was safeguarded against the encroachments of pedantry, and on the other the theatre was saved from operatic atrophy. In any form of drama continual adjustment of the scales is necessary for the preservation of true balance or rather, since drama has never fixed itself in absolute equipoise, for a semblance of true balance. Elizabethan drama accommodated itself to the inn-yard by expressing the scenic setting in the text. Eighteenth-century opera overcame the disadvantage of a tale told in an alien tongue by rendering narrative superfluous by elegance in back-cloths, by extravagance in properties, by conventional plot-arrangement (one opera being very much the same as any other in the number of persons employed and in the order and function of the various types of aria enumerated on page 131) and by the transference of antithesized ideas from the medium of words to that of music. In this latter respect the particular of verbal expression was losing itself in the universal of musical exegesis. In the meantime, however, music was going half-way to meet the situation by embracing particularity. By nineteenth-century standards, which set opera religiously enthroned in the ultimate theories of Wagner, the eighteenth century was lacking in sense. Opera as an entertainment, opera as a diversified concert, opera without action (singers as a rule quitted the stage after each appearance) was all wrong, but only by the arbitrary standards of later generations. Viewed objectively the opera of Handel's day should be regarded as a necessary stage in the development of aesthetic perception. It was the training-ground of singers and orchestral musicians. It may be that, looking backwards,

Debussy, Mussorgsky, Wagner, Meyerbeer, Berlioz, Mozart and Gluck were chief agents in the evolution of opera; but what they in turn achieved was at least hinted at by Handel.

Handel's delineation of character was exact and meticulous. He threw on his canvas universal types of men and women such as we find elsewhere defined in the works of Memling. It happened that Memling's types were dressed as Flemish citizens, Handel's as heroes or heroines of classical or Hebraic tradition. Behind both sets was placed the background of nature. Memling's countryside shone in jewelled beauty and contrast; Handel's implied, Hardy-like, an influence over the characters it supported. Solomon, in the oratorio of that name, is a study not so much of a ruler skilled in jurisprudence as of a naturalist turning pantheist. *Acis and Galatea* is an essay less in personal than in landscape charm, and the metamorphosis of Acis into a river appears a proper sort of poetic justice. In the opening scene of *Orlando* Zoroaster stands majestically on his mountain-side, and whether the music directs attention to the one or on the other it is impossible to decide. Burney was sensitive to something strange and new when he referred to the scene as having 'a wild grandeur in it of a very uncommon kind.' [1]

In the second act of *Orlando* the summer lightness of Dorinda's 'Quando spieghi':

- men - ti a - mo - ro - so ro - si - gno - lo,

and the whole murmurous nature of the forest music exert an influence on the musical progress of the opera by throwing Orlando's later madness into the most poignant relief. Wherever we look the presence of nature as a separate, subtle and enveloping personality is evident. The *Nachtmusik* of *Floridante* and *Amadigi* combines Schumann and Weber in a sensuous blend of mingled starlight and feminine charm; the garden path, up which most of us are led and beyond whose end we seldom explore, presents the tree prospect of 'Ombra mai fù'; moonshine reflects in the nocturnal intermezzo of *Ariodante*; *Susanna* is a gossip piece interlaced with the sounds and sights of village life; sunrise and sunset inspire the loveliest of the arias in *Theodora* and *Samson*; *L'Allegro* has the vivacity of a seventeenth-century *genre* painting, but also the more fragile poetry of Constable.

The intention of theoreticians was that music should, as Avison suggests, depict nature; but the operations of emotional behaviour were also considered to be susceptible of direct expression. Mattheson wrote that

One can represent all the passions of the heart by simple harmonies and their concatenation, without words, so that the hearer grasps and understands the development, the meaning and the ideas of the musical utterance as though it were in actual spoken utterance.[1]

To this philosophy was linked the whole of Handel's achievement, and viewed in this light his music dissolves into a profounder heart-search than modern conditions of performance allow. The majestic, leonine Handel is but part of an immeasurably greater whole. The subtlety of theatrical chiaroscuro and the subtlety of life in general drew from him a new orchestral technique. This has been discovered already in incidental music which reveals something more than mere appositeness and suggests that the composer saw, in part

[1] Mattheson, *Die neueste Untersuchung des Singspiels,* 1744.

at any rate, the substance which casts the shadow on the wall of the cave. This intensity of contemplation shows up again in the overtures which preface opera and oratorio. Starting from the original curtain-raising function of such music they proceeded to vary in outline (the outline bequeathed from Lully through Steffani) as the needs of the whole work decreed and even to summarize the emotional direction of the plot. The overture to *Messiah*, greyly contrasting its E minor with the E major of the first aria, holds Advent in its sober dignity and refrains from anticipating festivity by omitting the customary third movement in minuet form; that to *Saul* foretells the opening *epinicion* by turning into an organ concerto; that to *Deborah* presents Baalites and Israelites in immediate antipathy by quoting their particular thematic material from the later stages of the oratorio; that to *Esther* preludes obviously the tyranny, despair and triumph which furnish the life of the plot. The overture to the *Occasional Oratorio* is so familiar that its military zest needs no emphasis. In the overture to *Serse* the comedy is drawn out in the humour of the fugue subject:

and in the playfulness of its succeeding dialogue:

Alcina was a combination of opera and ballet and preludes its *élan* in an overture of fitting vivacity. The lines of the minuet:

epigrammatize the sparkling quality of this work and recall Mrs. Delany's exclamation that 'whilst Mr. Handel was playing his part I could not help thinking him a necromancer in the midst of his own enchantments.'

From orchestral we may turn to choral *Tonmalerei*. And here it would appear necessary to discuss the general principles which influenced Handel in his choral technique. This is always impeccable, and because the approach to the orchestra is at apparent variance with that of later schools and the balance of choir and orchestra has in large-scale performances altered to the disadvantage of the latter an undue emphasis is laid on the magnificence of those exceptional choral movements which appeared to justify their performance in the Crystal Palace. Handel himself was accustomed to small and relatively capable companies of singers for his choral movements which initially, except for works written for ecclesiastical use exclusively, were incidental. In opera and oratorio the eighteenth century followed in the wake of the seventeenth and aptly produced a chorus for the representation of crowd effects. Soldiers, sailors and attendants formed the basis of secular and observant congregations of faithful Christians of sacred choralism. Handel enjoyed crowds, appreciated the effectiveness of combined voices as an addition to orchestral colour, lived among people whose pleasure often led to the conviviality of collective singing, and accordingly expanded choral music into greater significance than hitherto. But the intention was not to exclude the orchestra at any time: it was to treat the one with the other on equal terms just as in later times the woodwind or the brass *ensemble* came to a reciprocal understanding with the strings. The Handelian view of the function of chorus is illustrated more simply in the operas than in the oratorios, where other considerations supervene.

In *Il pastor fido* may be noted the minuet pleasantry of the final chorus (choruses as finales were *de rigueur* in the system) 'Quel ch' il cielo' which, if not remarkable, is at all events fitted with the airy Arcadianism apt for pastoral drama. The Athenians have a cheerful welcome song for Theseus in the second act of *Teseo*. Burney observes of 'Ogn' un acclami' that it is not like the oratorio choruses, for an evident reason:

In these the subject being generally solemn, and in the church style, should partake of choral complication; whereas an opera chorus, being in action, and committed to memory, must necessarily be short, easy and dramatic.[1]

The importance of the choral writing, whether in opera or oratorio, lies not so much in complexity or in lack of complexity as in its dramatic situation. The short bursts of choral observation in *Messiah*, in *Israel in Egypt,* in the *Funeral Anthem* are simple in process but momentous in setting. In general this is true of Handel's music as a whole, and we cannot but deplore the practice of cutting amiable patterns for public offering while ignoring the texture to which the patterns belong. There is a chorus in *Alcina* which runs thus:

This has lately been put into the trimness of high-school uniform. It belongs to the naughty ravishment of Alcina's palace, Alcina being another of Handel's seductive heroines who combined the functions of princess and sorceress for the bewitchment of Ruggiero. There is no doubt that if some headmistresses were aware of Handel's mind-picture as he wrote 'Questo il cielo,' with what effectiveness can only properly be deduced from the score, the purified school song would be banned forthwith. This is not a complaint against the practice of encouraging the young to sing Handel so much as an objection lodged against the refusal, on the part of those who should know better, to take Handel seriously when he intended seriousness of artistic purpose. Of all the opera choruses that which is most telling is the 'Viva, viva il nostro Alcide,' with which *Giulio Cesare* opens. Here we have the tremendous exhilaration which infects the festive crowds of *Deborah, Solomon* and *Saul* and sets in immediate view the hot heroism of romanticized royalty. The oratorio choruses, possessed of a larger significance than those of the operas, will be

[1] Burney, *History*, iv. 241.

treated in greater detail, but it must be urged that they too had their origins in dramatic propriety.

Chromatic harmony is another weapon in the dramatic armoury, and reference must be made to Handel's dependence thereon in particular moments. The chromatic ground-bass usage, as in *Orlando, Poro* and in the magnificent petitionary pessimism of the Israelites' 'How long O Lord' in *Susanna,* follow familiar models: Purcell, in fact, is immediately recalled. Where, however, there is no ground-bass to impose a regulated course, Handel breaks the bonds of conformity and allows the urge of inspiration to dive into uncharted waters. In *Israel in Egypt* there is the 'He sent a thick darkness' chorus, of whose modulations Tovey has to say that

they are as expressive as the modulations in Bach's Chromatic Fantasia, inasmuch as they traverse most of harmonic space. On the other hand, they differ profoundly from the Chromatic Fantasia, and from Handel's own Passion recitatives in *The Messiah,* because they are not enharmonic—that is to say, each step is known as far as it goes, but there is no general aim and the end of the groping is incalculably remote.[1]

Herein we may emphasize 'each step is known as far as it goes'— a dictum applicable to the whole range of Handel's technical accomplishment and indicative of the perplexity in which we so frequently find ourselves, discovering how much we know of Handel and, at the same time, how little. As in the chorus of darkness Handel intrudes deep mystery into 'How are the mighty fallen' and 'Their bodies are buried in peace' in the *Funeral Anthem.* In twenty bars or so an immense profundity is stirred, by means which are perfectly obvious save in one respect. That is in the ellipticism of modulation already mentioned in connection with the *Concerti grossi* which takes us from key to key with this degree of suddenness:

The feeling is seventeenth-century [2] and on this form of behaviour

---

[1] Tovey, *Essays in Musical Analysis,* v. 97.   [2] See p. 98.

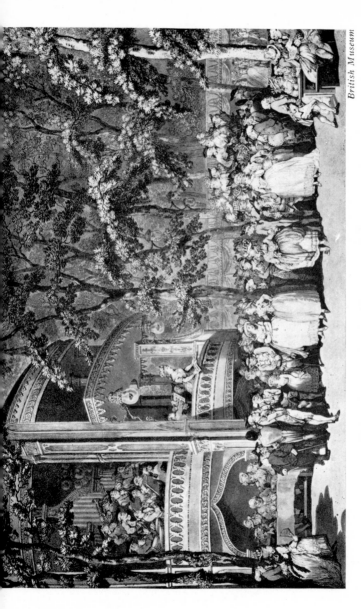

VAUXHALL, WHERE HANDEL WAS A POPULAR COMPOSER

After Thomas Rowlandson (1756–1827)

the eighteenth-century modernists no doubt looked deprecatingly. It savoured of archaism. When, however, school logic conflicted with emotional tension Handel preferred to follow the latter. In respect of this we may look at the second part of 'Tyrants now no more shall dread,' a chorus from *Hercules* which produces

> Horrid forms of monstrous birth
> Again shall vex the groaning earth;
> Fear of punishment is o'er,
> The World's avenger is no more.

These words, provoked by the death of Hercules under signally un-fortunate circumstances, were sufficient to set Handel on a course symbolic of the bewilderment of the leaderless:

which terminates thus:

It is passages such as this to which we may like to think Cowper points.[1] It is in passages like this that Handel shows his complete

---

[1] Cowper, *The Task,* book vi:

> Remember Handel? Who, that was not born
> Deaf as the dead to harmony, forgets,
> Or can, the more than Homer of his age?

mastery of technique and his intellectual capacity for psychological interpretation.

We have all had our Handelian training in church, and the perfect church-going mood is one of pure abstract reverence. A mood of active intelligence would be scandalous. Thus we get broken in to the custom of singing Handel as if he meant nothing; and as it happens that he meant a great deal, and was tremendously in earnest about it, we know rather less about him in England than they do in the Andaman Islands, since the Andamans are only unconscious of him, whereas we are misconscious.[1]

The misconsciousness arises from a misconception that Handel was more interested in God than in man. The reverse is the truth. If this is by now established we may turn to the oratorios with clearer vision.

[1] Shaw, *Music in London 1890–4,* i. 110.

CHAPTER XIV

THE ORATORIOS

So involved are the motions of human thought that what is entertainment to some is instruction to others and what passes as amusement to one generation serves the next with didactic purpose. In music the difficulty of appreciation lies in the fact that the component elements are of both orders simultaneously, so that the last quartets of Beethoven or the operas of Mozart are at once fit for philosophic scrutiny on the one hand and plain enjoyment on the other. Handel's purpose was primarily to amuse, to embellish life with leisurely occupation—how leisurely it was is clear from the inability of subsequent admirers to survive uncut masterpieces—but he also had in mind the enigmatic capacity of art for ethical interpretation and direction. He spoke out on this point to Lord Kinnoul. This being the case, sympathy may be extended both to those who treat *Messiah* sacramentally and to those who, ignoring doctrinal implications, surrender themselves to an orgy of aural titillation. That the pious and the hedonistic sit side by side at such performances of Handel's 'sacred' music as are familiar is not, as they so often consider it, a tribute to them, but to Handel's vast instinct for universal companionship. This sense of fraternity would be better understood if the whole of Handel's output were known; even, if we accept the point of view that the operas are unperformable (which they are not), were the whole of the oratorios known.

If choral societies were filled with initiative and with versatile singers and took it upon themselves to produce works of such diversity as the Passion of 1716, *Saul, Theodora, Susanna* and *Jephtha*—*Israel in Egypt* is only here excluded because it is relatively familiar—it would be seen that Handel, so far from being among the Lord's anointed, which is where idolatry places him, is very mortal in his approach to immortality. At home with the elemental passions of men and women, he fails to get nearer to God than do most of us who have no

F   151

special claim to spiritual superiority. Bach imposes humility, seeming so frequently to see into eternity; Pergolesi inspires ardour because he is burnt up with the heat of his Mariolatrous devotion; Palestrina implies, almost Jesuitically, the logic of God; Byrd details philosophy. Handel does none of these things. He stands before the unknown in bewildered sorrow at suffering, in joy at virtue triumphant, in anger, of a particular paternal and sympathetic order, at moral turpitude, in simple wonder at whatever is incomprehensible. He shouts 'Hallelujah' from pure *joie de vivre,* sings praises with the robust vigour of a prosperous churchwarden and prays with the variable intensity of those who look to supernaturalism under stress of despair. The Handelians may complain that this undervalues Handel. On the contrary, it indicates his special claim to supremacy. He understands human nature in its strength and in its weakness with more acuteness than any other of the great composers. This is why there can be no division between opera and oratorio in his case. The concern of both is with human affairs.

The pedigree of oratorio takes us back inconveniently far to trace in detail. In any case the normal encyclopaedists can present it with ramified exactitude. Here it may be recapitulated that towards the end of the sixteenth century opera, sanctified solely by verbal indication, was impressed into the service of the Counter-Reformation with due caution by Filippo Neri, a priest whose behaviour matched his birth in nobility and led to his canonization. Neri's intention was to make intelligible to the illiterate youth of Rome the mysteries of theology by their presentation in terms of drama and music. His innovation, which in view of medieval religious drama was not really an innovation, stimulated Italian composers of the seventeenth century to issue many works of this kind. Thus from Cavalieri to Scarlatti a steady flow of picturesque essays in dramatic-musical form appeared to grace varied episodes of ecclesiastical association, from the *mater dolorosa* to the life-story of St. Philip himself. Among the vast array of oratorios and cantatas then composed those of Giacomo Carissimi were particularly significant, blending recitative, aria and chorus into narrative interest suitable for ecclesiastical performance. Hawkins expresses an opinion which immediately directs attention to the Handelian contact: 'Carissimi excelled in imitating

H. H. Tansley

HANDEL
From a portrait by Hogarth

the inflexions of the human voice, and in uniting the charms of music with the powers of oratory.'[1] As the score of *Jephte* is easily accessible the Handelian student is urged to take the opportunity of making contact with this precursor of later oratorio. Handel knew his Carissimi sufficiently well to adapt 'Plorate filiae Israel' for the chorus 'Hear Jacob's God' in *Samson*.

The style of Carissimi was, however, outmoded when Handel lived in Italy. Its severity hardly commended itself to the worldlings who, opera having been prevented in the theatre by edict of Pope Innocent XII, dictated that oratorio should select such episodes from holy writ as would stimulate eroticism in the operatic tradition. Hence such pleasing' subjects as Susanna and Bathsheba and the secularity of Handel's first contribution to oratorio in Italy.

It is to be regretted that *La Resurrezione* is no more than a library curiosity. Completely operatic, with a lovable Lucifer (Handel could never find the heart thoroughly to dislike villainy and shared the modern belief that sinners in general are victims of causality), a sweet-voiced little Magdalene, an agreeable—if somewhat Tennysonian—St. John, an angel of pleasant virtuosity, and with delicious water-coloured orchestration, this *oratorio sacro* imbues religious exercise with an easefulness which may be reprehensible to the austere, but which suggests a degree of comfort in heaven not to be despised by the world-weary. Renaissance painters believed less in heaven on earth than in earth, that well-fed and well-housed earth represented by the cardinals' standards of living, in heaven. The only improvements possible were in sanitation.

Germany countered Italy with religious music of different significance. The social history of Reformation and Thirty Years War, together with the natural consequences of a northern climate, induced deeper reflection on the problems of suffering and of pain. Therefore there arose the tradition of setting the story of the Passion with its concentration of congregational interest in, and not merely on, the subject by the employment of chorales. Before Bach the representative names were Schütz and Keiser, but Handel wrote two Passions, of which one, that of 1716, deserves consideration. It is interesting

[1] Hawkins, iv. 92.

in that it demonstrates how de-germanized Handel had become by long residence abroad, yet, in contrast, how strongly he endeavoured to construct his music so as to be acceptable in the place of its presentation. The framework is German, but not the content. Chorales appear in severe unemotion. A daughter of Zion shows herself, but with little concern for the tragedy she witnesses. St. Peter is present in unseemly high spirits; Judas in obvious contrition which rings with little conviction in empty roulades:

Flames, chas-tize _____ me

and Christ. Here we may pause and consider in greater detail Handel's reaction to the central figure of the Crucifixion. The part of Christ redeems this Passion from the charge of complacency, which otherwise, and with propriety, might be directed at it. But Christ is the Man of Sorrows, with manhood as Handel's exclusive wonder. We view Him pictured with dignity, virility and affection as a companion of men sacrificed as a man on the altar of uncertain and extraneous circumstantial operation. The consecration of bread and wine is portrayed with massive simplicity:

and with a tenderness redolent of Handel's quick intensity of emotion before the shrine of friendship. 'Lo! I will smite the shepherd' is angry with the vigorous integrity which sweeps through 'Why do the nations' in the face of wilful disobedience and with the same breadth of arpeggio-fired inspiration. The Agony in the Garden produces the awe-laden sympathy of:

This is scrupulous portraiture, but lacking in the larger hope which sees not so much immolation of manhood as the triumph of the god-head. Thus Handel shows how his vision suffers general limitation in incomprehension of deep theology, but also he displays it limitless in human understanding.

It was fortunate for the subsequent history of oratorio that during his years of Burlington-Chandos patronage opportunities occurred for conversations with Pope, Gay and the surrounding constellation of wits and worthies. Human affairs are so frequently set in motion by accidents of companionship that it is safe to assume that had Handel not been on amiable terms with practitioners of arts other than his own *Esther* would not have appeared. Had this not happened, the possibilities of an English variant of *oratorio sacro* would have remained latent.

It may be imagined that Racine's *Esther*[1] came into conversation by chance, that Pope considered it an attractive proposition for translation, that Handel was sufficiently interested in what he had overheard to borrow a copy of the work, and that after reading it he suggested its further possibilities as a libretto. Here it may be interposed that he would have acknowledged in Racine a reflection of many of the ideas which were also his own. Racine was a drama-tist whose strength lay in humanizing the conventional figures of classical mythology. Therefore he emphasized matter at the expense of form and acquired a solidity of expression in the same way as did ultimately Handel. It is further worthy of mention that not only Racine's *Esther*, but also his *Athalie* prompted music by Handel.

---

[1] An English version of *Esther* was done in 1715 by Thomas Brereton, a graduate of Brasenose College, Oxford, and a 'gentleman of Cheshire.'

Esther (Handel's *Esther*) is an uneven work. Its principal defect is that it lacks the cohesion which marks the later oratorios. The solo music is tentative, except where Handel in Haman's cataclysmic opening looks prophetically forward through the years:

Let Jew-ish blood . dye ev-'ry hand, Let Jew-ish blood dye ev-'ry hand, Nor

age, nor sex I spare

and much is in fact transferred from the Passion. The choruses similarly vary in quality so that the first with its ingenuous contra-puntal interjections and its anthem derivation carries not very much of personal conviction. The mannered use of the ♩ ♩ idiom in 'Shall we of servitude complain' is also symptomatic of conscious adaptation to English usage. Passing by 'Ye sons of Israel, mourn,' which has a histrionic plaintiveness akin to that of the coeval funereal chorus in *Acis and Galatea,* and the handsome jingle of 'Hallelujah' (an Italian 'Hallelujah'[1] whose coruscations are a relief from the lumbering of later choruses to this text) as possessing potentialities of extreme effectiveness in performance, we must draw up in astonishment at the final, cantata-like 'The Lord our enemy has slain,' which, with its *canto fermo* to crown the concluding 'for ever blessed,' is magnificent.

The years passed, and Handel forgot the existence of *Esther.* In 1732 it was without his foreknowledge revived. In that same year Aaron Hill inscribed his plea for opera in the vernacular. Handel witnessed the success of the revival, took note of his friend's admonition and called Humphreys into consultation. It may be that further incentive to oratorio came from the publication four years earlier of John Ernest Galliard's *Morning Hymn of Adam and Eve,* a slender cantata, but a hint that Milton was a possible source of libretto inspiration. However, Milton does not just yet come into the Handel field. In 1733 it was Humphreys's version of the story of Deborah which called his attention. With the best will in the world it is difficult to arouse very much enthusiasm for this work, and the point of view of those who complained at the increased prices must

[1] Borrowed from the brilliantly attractive motet *Silete venti.*

be considered reasonable. In *Deborah*, however, Handel did discover the effectiveness of contrast between two choirs representing different philosophies: his Israelites unfortunately are possessed of an inapt docility which dulls their music and which enlists support for the Baalites who, if obtuse, are spirited in utterance. Dramatically, despite its apparent unification by the introduction of *Leitmotive*, *Deborah* is a poor sequel to *Orlando* which appeared at about the same time. It is seldom that Handel really touches banality, but when the priests of Baal can do no better than this:

the palm for heathen exaltation must temporarily rest with Mendelssohn.

In *Athaliah* Handel reverts more happily to his operatic vein, and while Baalites and Israelites again present a background of conflict, with more subtlety defined in extravagances of languor and charm, the personalities of Athaliah, a character tied up with Storge and Dejanira in a primitive state of subjection to irrational projections from the fearful dream-world, Josabeth, Joash and Joad (a knowledgeable sort of person) play in the forefront parts of attractive individuality. Up to this point there is, if one may ever say it of Handel, an immaturity in the disposition of oratorio: in each there is a specialized interest but no real fusion of the disparate elements such as is met with, after a space of two years, in *Saul*.

Saul is one of Handel's most extensive studies of human nature in primitive form. It holds the stylized libretto in contempt and deals in the same terms of epical eloquence with a story of heroic proportions as does the writer of the book of Samuel. Jennens was neither better nor worse than most of the poetasters who constructed libretti to order, but the fiery clash of ancient arms defeated his decorous transcription. However—and here a case may be made out for texts which in this way are incomplete—there was scope for Handel to revivify the dry bones. Handel went back to the Authorized Version and made an oratorio the music of which carried the same dignity, poetry and ripeness as the seventeenth-century words. Interest starts with the people of the plot, people delineated with the exactness of photogravure. But while we study the gnawing deceit of Saul, the pert independence of Merab (who puts ideas into her father's head by refusing to marry one 'of poor, plebeian parents born'), the pretty romanticism of Michal, the somewhat evirated mutual affection of Jonathan and David, the witch of Endor and the prophetic apparition of Samuel, the chorus saves itself for more or less abstract commentary. It is true that the chorus is also participant in the drama, with what effect is manifest in the opening chorus, but its detachment from the immediate scene is adroitly controlled so that the strictures laid on Saul by his subjects and in his presence have no incongruity. In this respect actionless oratorio has the advantage over opera, and *Saul* produces the choruses which are neither fit for opera, being too prodigious, nor for church, because too unkempt, but entirely proper to their intended setting: the theatre during Lent. 'Envy, eldest born of Hell' and 'O fatal consequence of rage' are terrible in their particular and in their universal application. The decadence of Saul as described in the latter is presented in terms which bear superficial resemblance to a not dissimilar mood survey in the *Schicksalslied* of Brahms. Thus the chorus follow the demented turmoil of the mind of Saul:

The affection possessed by Handel for Saul raises that monarch to the full heroic stature necessary for tragedy—'a man who is not eminently good and just, yet whose misfortune is brought about not by vice or depravity, but by some error or frailty.'[1] Saul is kept free from exaggeration, and when he displays anger it is anger redolent of quick temper and free from unspoken malignity of thought. 'A serpent in my bosom warmed' is illustrative of this point and also of the further point that Handel treated formal considerations with scant courtesy when it suited his dramatic purpose. This aria terminates abruptly in G minor, without a *da capo,* as Saul hurls his javelin at a too agile David. The anger becomes uncontrollable, and as jealousy mingles with despair there comes the sudden impulse to invoke the powers of darkness. Thus Saul, whose recitatives are dramatically the most cumulative in tension in the whole range of oratorio, turns the corner to final moral dissolution:

If heav'n de-nies you aid,   seek it from hell!

The soldierly death of Saul calls from David, hitherto an exemplar of sickly virtue, his best song, 'In sweetest harmony they lived,' and treachery passes out of the picture as the maids of Israel are reminded that it was to Saul's indulgent care they owed the scarlet and gold they wore. The oratorio should end with the chorus 'O fatal day,' but the necessity for a cheerful finale imposed on Handel the task of setting 'Go on,' at least twenty times repeated, which the Israelites shouted at David together with sundry exhortations and guarantees of divine favour as he girded on his sword for the next campaign.

The companion work to *Saul* was *Israel in Egypt.* Here is simply the story of a people in their progress from adversity to victory, epically related in what is to all intents and purposes a choral symphony. Whether Handel borrowed other men's ideas or not is not

[1] Aristotle, *Poetics,* xiii.

so important as the thankfulness to God, nowhere else so patent, which infuses the music, leads to the overwhelming impact of the ageless paean which prefaces the final chorus, and symbolizes the recovery of Handel himself from illness, the triumphant passage of the Children of Israel and, more than this, that of all peoples who have come through the darkness of oppression and subjugation. This is music of which it might truly be said that 'the touch of life has turned to truth.' The first chorus, in which the tremendous effect of the withheld bass part when it sets the earth rumbling with its cry to God should be noted as born of genius, is the representation of Europe as I remember it in 1941.[1]

Why in 1741 Handel forsook his natural field of dramatic and heroic narrative for the solemn libretto of *Messiah* is difficult to decide. That it was entirely due to evangelistic zeal is improbable. The possibility is that the cause was more personal. At a period when disillusionment preyed on his mind his thoughts took flight to happier times, and the memory of his dead sister came back to him. And with her memory came that of her favourite text—'I know that my Redeemer liveth.' Therefrom possibly sprung the conception of a commemorative work—a *Trauerode,* which however should see death swallowed up in victory. Handel could see death in no other way.

The first triumph in *Messiah* is the text. Here one wonders at the felicity of extraction—in one detail the mixture of Job and Corinthians in the text above mentioned is so happy that it passes even the learned unnoticed—and whether Jennens really possessed the devotion

---

[1] A letter eulogizing *Israel in Egypt* appeared in the *London Daily Post,* dated 18th April 1739. The following extract indicates the writer's approval of my thesis. I apologize to my Catholic friends for the particular example of evil. They will, I am sure, judge the writer charitably and allow his comments validity in essence while making allowances for the prejudices of the period:

'Did such a Taste prevail universally in a People, that People might expect on a like Occasion, if such Occasion should ever happen to them, the same Deliverance as those praises celebrate; and Protestant, free, virtuous, united, Christian England need little fear, at any time hereafter, the whole Force of slavish, bigotted, united, unchristian Popery, risen up against her should such a conjuncture ever hereafter happen.'

to Holy Writ to produce so masterly an abstract of Christian thought. It has reasonably been suggested [1] that the text owed to Nonjuror practice (Jennens being a Nonjuror), but one reflects also that Handel once observed over the selection of words for the coronation music: 'I have read my Bible very well and shall choose for myself.' Accordingly it may be presumed that Handel had a good deal to do with the textual compilation of *Messiah*. This is supported by the fact that the central figure of the work appears only in the background. Partly this may have been due to subservience to public feeling, but partly to Handel's lack of ease in the neighbourhood of divinity. Thus the music bears an impersonality, an eighteenth-century and Protestant quality as Handel throws aside, except for the 'He trusted in God' chorus, the intense passion and fire of *Saul* and *Israel in Egypt*. A Wren-like monument is the result: a temple of marble on which Mozart was later to hang stucco ornaments.

Messiah is a careful and awe-inspired work. The scoring is indicative of this in its ferial nature. More thrilling choruses may be found in *Israel in Egypt* or in *Belshazzar,* finer arias in *Samson* or *Theodora,* recitative of greater musical significance in *Saul* or *Jephtha,* but nowhere else is there a firmer homogeneity. This is due to Handel's evocation of ceremonial dignity. And this in turn explains the English affection for *Messiah*: it represents what, since the Reformation, they have generally felt obliged to feel about God in public. Because it is representative of a nation's thought *Messiah* is a notable work, but also, inevitably, it is not Handel at his greatest. Jennens expressed an opinion that Handel might have done better with the subject. Jennens was wrong. Handel could have done no more with *Messiah,* but with a different text and with a less abstract theme he could have written music which, considered on its own merits and without the subtle influence of familiar words of acknowledged genius and specific religious association, was more intrinsically poetic.

The confirmation lies in the next oratorio—*Samson,* where music once again runs into the familiar channels of heroic narrative. Here we have an anthology of Milton, ingeniously doctored by Newburgh

[1] 'The Text of *Messiah*,' Geoffrey Cuming, in *Music and Letters,* July 1950, p. 226 et seq.

Hamilton,[1] running into the full tide of Handel's inspiration. The constant comparison of Handel with Homer has fullest significance in attachment to this oratorio, in which the clash of personalities is developed amid the tumult of many voices, both human and divine. There is also evident that particular capacity of Handel for living with the ancients and at the same time for placing both them and us, the listeners, in the same timeless pattern. Thus the priests of Dagon and those of Jehovah, well matched in strenuous earnestness, champion all the characters who immortalize the eternal struggle between the powers of darkness and of light. The choral writing which enshrines this meta‚physical duality is sublime in picturesqueness and inflexibility. The voices move with the sinuous grace of strings, a quality not so con‚sistently achieved by Handel until he wrote *Samson,* and yet in so doing lose nothing of the mountainous grandeur apparent twenty years before. The urgency of 'Awake the trumpet's lofty sound,' the expression of plea and counter‚plea in 'Fix'd in His everlasting seat'—with this exalted exploitation of rests to suggest astonished contemplation:

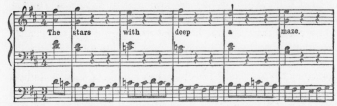

the extension of *da capo* formality to 'With thunder arm'd,' with

[1] Newburgh Hamilton was related to (the relationship may be guessed at) and lived with the Duke of Hamilton. Before his association with Handel his fame had precariously rested on *The Doating Lovers, or The Libertine Tamed* and *The Petticoat Plotter* (Thomas Winchop, *Scanderbeg*). It looks as though Handel selected his text for those works which had Hamilton's collaboration. In the first codicil to his will it is stated: 'I give to Mr. Newburgh Hamilton, of Old Bond Street, who has assisted me in adjusting words for some of my compositions, one hundred pounds.' Which was a hundred pounds less than Morell received. *Samson* borrows from *Samson Agonistes,* the odes 'On the Nativity,' 'On the Passion,' 'On Time,' 'At a solemn Musick,' the 'Epitaph on the Marchioness of Winchester' and the translations from the Psalms.

insight into the minds of those who reinforce the humility of prayer with more vigorous methods of advising the Almighty, the contrapuntal genius which contains a nation's grief in the twelve bars of 'Weep, Israel, weep' and the finality of the concluding hymn of praise are tokens of the complete mastery of choral technique.

In *Samson,* however, the emancipation of the chorus is not at the expense of the solo singers. Far from it. Each has his or her personality tightly packed into recitatives and arias in which untidy ends of virtuosity no longer trail about deprived of dramatic point. Samson with his tragic strength, Manoah with the virility of his paternal affection, Harapha, who stamps through the score with superb ὕβρις, and Dalila, whose truculent amorousness is implied as much as stated, are among the most heroic of all the persons of opera or oratorio.

The athletic quality of *Samson* leaves *Joseph and his Brethren* immobile and generally unattractive, but the old barbaric spirit returns in full glory in *Belshazzar,* an oratorio in which the contrast between vicious pleasure and Godinspired virtue, appropriately armed with effective weapons of offence, is demonstrated in the plain manner of an old morality play with keen emphasis on the inevitable wages of sin. Despite the coloured pageant of riotous living centred in the carousal music, *Belshazzar* holds a greater sense of personal obeisance before the divine will than do many of the other oratorios. The keynote is sounded initially by Nicotris, a tragic queen of immense power and courage on whom Handel lavished music of unsurpassable quality, in an extensive *recitativo accompagnato,* whose subject is the decline and fall of empires. The 'sprung rhythm' of Jennens's verse at this point momentarily attaches him to poets of greater fame. Handel's treatment of the closing bars of this recitative may be quoted as demonstrating the richer implications of his tonepainting faculty:

runs the same shad-ow-y round of fan-cied

A further instance of this developed symbolism occurs in the scene during which Daniel interprets the writing on the wall:

The perfect dramatic setting of the chord of the diminished seventh.

The *Occasional Oratorio* served its ardent purpose by collecting contributions from earlier works: the overture survived the occasion and may still be enjoyed by those who like sublimated bellicosity. *Judas Maccabaeus* has little to commend it (Handel disliked a story devoid of love interest) and *Joshua* is fairly dull. 'See the conquering hero,' text by Morell out of Dryden,[1] provoked a dialogue which may be taken to heart by those who neglect the greater works of Handel. Sir John Hawkins was asked by Handel how he liked this chorus. 'Not so well as some things I have heard of yours.' Then said Handel: 'Nor I neither, but, young man, you will live to see it a greater favourite with the people than my other fine things.'

Alexander Balus, the third of the conscious tributes to Jewry, was less popular than either *Judas Maccabaeus* or *Joshua*. This may be

---

[1] Cf. *Alexander's Feast* :

> The jolly god in triumph comes !
> Sound the trumpets, beat the drums !

ascribed to the inability of the oratorio public, which by 1748 was setting up limited piety and prudery as standards of criticism, to reconcile themselves to a love story, albeit with biblical sanction, arrayed in the persuasive delicacy of Longus. Lest, however, it should be thought that Handel was indulging in unhealthy fancies, it should be duly noted that *Alexander Balus* is a bright celebration of conjugal fidelity and, while an influx of brigandage affords some excellent and dramatic relief, the central theme of matrimonial propriety is responsible for Cleopatra's sweet songs and for the cheerful connubiality of the epithalamium chorus 'Hymen fair, Urania's son.' *Susanna* is a companion monument to chastity. The artlessness of this charming work is epitomized in:

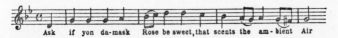

Ask if yon da-mask Rose be sweet, that scents the am-bient Air

a ballad strain which might have come from Somerset. The decline of the elders into senile maudlinity is consummately portrayed and the etching of 'Away, away, ye tempt me both in vain,' a trio for Susanna and the two elders, is perfect. Behind the plot stands the awful severity of 'How long, O Lord,' a magnificently contrived prayer expanded over a ground bass, the mystical union of the brute passions of man of and nature in 'The torrent that sweeps in its course,' and the rustic backchat of village gossips. The theme of the work is summarized hopefully in the final operatic and four-square chorus which emphasizes that

> A virtuous wife shall soften fortune's frown,
> She's far more precious than a golden crown.

Public morality, if affected at all by works of art, is less likely to be disturbed by *Susanna*, whose title has kept it immured for the private delectation of scholars, than by *Solomon*, in which the dalliance of Solomon with the Queen of Sheba contrasts violently with his relationship with his own vapid queen. *Solomon* has a considerable number of double choruses of great splendour, but their omnipresence is inclined to add an overplay of sententiousness to a work of uneven quality.

Regarding *Theodora* there remains evidence of Handel's private opinion. Handel possessed a rare perspicuity in self-criticism, and his judgment should be respected. He, so Morell wrote,

valued it more than any performance of the kind, and when I once asked him, whether he did not look upon the Grand Chorus in *The Messiah* as his masterpiece? 'No,' says he, 'I think the chorus at the end of the second part in *Theodora* far beyond it, "He saw the lovely Youth."'

Theodora has the maturity and the same mellowed courtesy that Shakespeare displays in *The Winter's Tale*. A Christian story, a rare choice for Handel, *Theodora* looses the gloom from eighteenth- and nineteenth-century religion by seizing on the attractiveness of the first Christians—an attractiveness which embraced courage. In the springtime of the faith the devout had not forgotten the pleasances of paganism. The geniality of 'Come, mighty Father' is worship of a more affectionate order than that to which the more ecclesiastical choruses in other oratorios admit us and springs in refinement from the rites of Venus and Flora, which also find eloquent expression in this work. There is in *Theodora* a contemplative quality and an intimacy revealing old Handel detached personally from the conflict of life, but in complete sympathy with the victims of catastrophe.

Finally there comes *Jephtha*: the *summa summarum*. The greatness of *Jephtha* reposes in Handel's philosophic absorption in the vast problem propounded by the plot—the obedience of man to the legislation of eternity. The abstract philosophy is carried by the chorus whose utterances, nine of them, lie rooted in the earthly actions of Jephtha, but offshoot towards the universal. The climactic, quadripartite 'How dark, O Lord, are Thy decrees,' placed (let it be noted) after Jephtha's desperate 'Deeper and deeper still,' contains the human acknowledgment of divine supremacy, achieved only after mystified and even angry protestation against the uncertainty of the pilgrimage. Handel, with blindness imminent (indeed, it was the above-mentioned chorus which suffered interruption on this account), had reason to follow his argument closely, for he knew himself to be in the inexorable grasp of destiny. The averting of a tragic denouement is accomplished in *Jephtha* by the intermission of an *angelus ex machina,* but the low-level drama of Jephtha, Iphis, Storge and Hamor is of small consequence beside that traced by the finger of God. Against the severity of the Almighty, however, Handel places a tranquillity in heaven which draws peace over the final stages of life. The opening of the 'Cherub and seraphim,' with its arpeggio-wrought effulgence, first cousin to the opening of *Zadok the Priest*, paints a picture which finds reflection in the lambent beauty of 'Waft her, angels,' the serene token of Jephtha's ultimate acceptance of the beneficence of divine governance, and in the music with which Iphis prepares to leave the world.

It is easy and natural to have talent at twenty; to have talent still at forty, that is the best; to keep it until old age, when it has been enriched by the experience of a lifetime, that is to be something more than a man of talent. Genius is always rare, and always admirable; but most admirable when it has matured into something that is uniquely personal.[1]

What Handel wrote at twenty and at forty may be easily discovered. What he wrote after the age of sixty reveals the unique genius of the man, and no work more than *Jephtha*, which secretes immortality in an awareness of spiritual adventure, in the hopefulness of perennial youth, and in the expression of the experience of a full life.

[1] R. C. Trevelyan, *Windfalls*.

CHAPTER XV

A MISCELLANY

BEYOND the pale of oratorio lies a sequence of works, neither opera nor oratorio, though related to both, which may only be ignored at the risk of falling victim to the Chadband-Handel myth. We move round the periphery which bounds the familiar terrain to discover a variety of entertainment reminiscent more of the spontaneity of the seventeenth than of the sophistication of the eighteenth century. The boundary between one age and another or between one form of art and another—Quiller-Couch's analogy with the limits which administratively settle where one county ends and the next begins may aptly be remembered—only assumes *raison d'être* when a certain distance from the arbitrary dividing line is covered on one side or the other. In respect of Handel rigid categorization, except where the cataloguer orders his lists, is impossible. Difficulties were early encountered. *Acis and Galatea* was variously described as a serenata (*Daily Journal*, 5th June 1732), which term also belonged to the earlier *Aci, Galatea e Polifemo*, as a pastoral (*Daily Journal*, 13th March 1731), as a pastoral opera (*Daily Post*, 2nd May 1732) and as a 'Mask' in Walsh's edition of 1730. Twenty-six years later the last term reappeared. The *Norwich Mercury* of Saturday, 28th February 1756 recorded:

Cambridge, Feb. 26. On Thursday night the Mask of Acis and Galatea was performed at Trinity Coll: Hall before a very numerous audience and was conducted by Dr. Randall, Professor of Music in this University.

From masque, the thoroughbred seventeenth-century stock, came the ideals of English opera. English opera, that is, as it was to develop under Purcell and receive its most extensive, elegant, odd and moving expression in *The Fairy Queen*. Masque entailed poetry— how exquisite may be judged from reference to the occasional offerings of Ben Jonson, Campion, William Browne of Tavistock and others of their courtly order. And it was poetry incapable of affiliation with the necessary music for the glamorous atmosphere of the public theatre. Masque also entailed dancing, the culmination of whose music was in *The Fairy Queen,* and the painting of scenery. The back-cloths of Inigo Jones are the finest things of this sort in the history of the English stage. The place for masque was at court on the occasion of a royal wedding, a coronation, the visit of a foreign potentate or a royal coming-of-age. Some pearls were produced, but as they were cast before swine they were disallowed by the Cromwell regime. To be fair to the Puritans it should be admitted that Inigo Jones's landscapes concealed many scenes of lechery. The idea of the masque, however, never died, so that Purcell depended on it, as later did Rich in his pantomimes (with music by Galliard) and Arne in *Alfred,* which properly fitted a garden party given by the Prince of Wales. Handel caught the spirit and when first presented with a piece of really lyrical poetry inscribed the music of *Acis and Galatea.*

Appropriateness, according to Dionysius of Halicarnassus, is the chief source of beauty. This thought may be applied justly to whatever Handel wrote, but in the particular instance of *Acis and Galatea* it will be seen that his appreciation of Gay's poetry—an echo of the whimsy of Jonson's *Oberon*[1] and a Jonsonian transmutation of classical into English country scenes—a feeling of affection for a legend which may at one time have impinged on a classical education, plus the knowledge that his finished work would adorn a *fête champêtre,* produced a masterpiece of Arcadianism, refined yet mixed with a natural zest which kept the music free from preciosity. The whole thing, excepting that voluminous 'Wretched lovers' chorus, catches at the heart like a memorable verse by Chaucer. *Acis and Galatea* is no oratorio, nor should it be performed like an oratorio. Put it on a sunny lawn on a summer's day.

Holst wrote of *Acis and Galatea* and that even sunnier companion work *L'Allegro:* 'Why didn't the old chap write more of that sort of thing?' He did. He wrote notably *Semele.* Congreve designed *Semele* as an opera libretto in 1710. The year is perhaps worth noting and it may be speculated whether Handel, possibly knowing Congreve through his other literary associates, was on the point of treating this promising theme when the Academy project came to monopolize his attentions. However that may be, *Semele* remained untouched

[1] Which masque was used by Arne in 1771 as the basis of *The Fairy Prince.*

until 1744. Then it served as an antidote to piety. It was, said Mainwaring, 'after the manner of an oratorio an English opera, but called an oratorio'—a pretty jugglery with nomenclature. But whatever *Semele* may be called it is, as the argument indicates in the word-book, a characteristic Renaissance flirtation with paganism.

After Jupiter's amour with Europa, the daughter of Agenor, king of Phoenicia, he again incenses Juno by a new affair in the same family, viz., with Semele, niece of Europa, and daughter to Cadmus, king of Thebes. Semele is on the point of marriage with Athamas, a prince of Boeotia; which marriage is about to be solemnized in the temple of Juno, goddess of marriages, when Jupiter, by ill omens, interrupts the ceremony, and afterwards transports Semele to a private abode prepared for her. Juno, after many contrivances, at length assumes the shape and voice of Ino, sister to Semele; by the help of which disguise, and artful insinuations, she prevails with Semele to make a request to Jupiter, which, being granted, must end in her ruin.

The surprise is that this was allowed in English, and in Lent.

Semele has its moments of tension, as in the lengthy recitative of Cadmus, 'Ah wretched Prince,' which culminates in the terse description of the seizure of Semele by Jupiter, with versatility appearing here as an eagle, and in the aerial ascent of raped and raper to the 'Waft her, angels' formula; in Juno's magnificent 'Awake Saturnia'; in the concluding scene which grows out of Semele's request and Jupiter's oath. But the same diversionary air overhangs the music as in *Acis and Galatea*. The story, indicates Handel, is a fable of no consequence, so what he allows to remain freshest in the memory is a distillation of nature's charms. 'Where'er you walk' in fact is the perfect summary.

A year later Handel once again retreated into classical antiquity. *Hercules,* done from Sophocles (*The Women of Trachis*) by the Rev. T. Broughton,[1] in contrast to *Semele,* is a work accurately described by its first advertisement as 'a new musical drama.' Like *Saul, Hercules* is a study in jealousy. It is also, like *Saul,* a commentary on human impotence. Dejanira's murder of her husband (one may agree with her in her judgment of Hercules's motives in bringing back captive the beautiful Iole from Oechalia) illustrates this impotence in simple

[1] A well-known scholar and translator of *Don Quixote*.

form. Hercules is done to death painfully, and after cremation, a process warmly described in 'Oh Jove! What land is this?' lands safely among the senior deities with easy access to nectar and ambrosia. Dejanira, however, wins more sympathy than Saul. She is richer in portraiture, more heroic and defeated by a problem which might beset any woman passing the prime of her beauty and encountering an apparent rival of Iole's calibre. The whole of Dejanira is contained in the honest-to-goodness scolding of 'Resign thy club' (a title which should not be misinterpreted): an upright woman with a rasping tongue and a malignant impetuosity. Iole is a fitting foil to the older woman; graceful in movement, dignified in rebuttal of the false charges laid against her, sympathetic to Dejanira when she should have forfeited all claims to sympathy and courageous in grief. Iole is the ripest of Handel's young women, and marriage with Hyllus, son of Hercules, is (we may hope) a deserved reward for virtuous living under conditions of difficulty. Hercules himself is a bluff soldier with equal zest, if we read the music aright, for battle, murder and sudden death (provided that he is the dispenser) and bucolic sports. He also has a simplicity of character which places him immediately within the environs of sympathy.

The chorus appropriately holds a Greek position in abstract commentary. The quality of the individual choruses is uniformly high and, as in *Samson*, there is a pervasive flexibility. Thus a passage in doubled sixths illuminates the festivities which, at the end of Act I greet the returning Hercules:

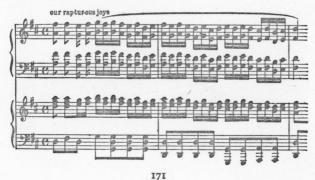

And thus with subtle insinuation comment is made on the affection of Hyllus for Iole:

The uniqueness of *Hercules,* however, rests not so much on high technical competence as on the sensitive response of the music to changes of mood in the drama. Dejanira holds tragedy in mind in her first aria. Anxiety for her lord and master is the immediate source of melancholy, but deeper lies the intensity of the unknown grief. Notice the chromatic suspense—and Handel used such effects only rarely:

De - plore, in thick-est gloom ____ of grief,

Parallel with this is the acridity of Iole's lament for her father:

the sword in-flicts the dead - ly wound

with which dissonant discomfiture Handel points the despair which
resolves itself in the anaesthetic resignation of 'Peaceful rest.' One
more illustration must suffice to indicate the dramatic integrity of
Hercules. During Act II Dejanira recalls that she has possession of a
robe, dipped in the blood of Nessus which

> boasts a wondrous virtue, to revive
> The expiring flame of love: so Nessus told me,
> When dying to my hand he trusted it—
> I will prevail with Hercules to wear it,
> And prove its magic force—

So Dejanira in good faith endeavours to overcome her fears of infidelity (that her fears were groundless heightens the dramatic tension)
and the chorus respond with delicious satisfaction at so happy a
denouement:

Love and Hy-men, hand in hand, Come, re - store the nup-tial band!

This completes the second act. From such a climax of contentment
Act III immediately plunges us into disaster. The robe was poisoned.

173

Act III is a drama within a drama. Hercules dies in agony: Dejanira maddens as Handel lashes her with the snakes of Alecto, with the vision of 'Megaera fell, and black Tisiphone' in an aria which carries the unearthly impress of terror Blake understood. But from the trough of despair all are led by Jupiter, who sends his messenger to terminate the drama. An inevitable conclusion, but more appropriate to this excursion into antiquity than to the oratorios. That is if art and philosophy must be bounded by theology.

Another classical adaptation, the *Alcestis* (*Alcides* in the edition of Arnold), was arranged for Handel by Smollett. This English opera was metamorphosed into *The Choice of Hercules,* as for some reason or other Rich's projected performance never came off. With the minor works of attractive parts must be placed the incidental music to Ben Jonson's *The Alchymist* which, although reduced from *Rodrigo* in some part, has an antique simplicity in its airs and dances:

recalling the flavour of Lupo or Coperario, intimates of Jonson's and his particular composers, and pioneers whose honour has been neglected. Then there is the *Terpsichore* music which Arnold, with an eye unconsciously directed at the progenitors of so much music of the class, again designated 'A Masque.'

There are a hundred or so Italian cantatas and duets, whose composition at various times provided exercise in conventionality and ephemeral pleasure for the eclectic. The cantatas, after the manner of operatic scenes, and the duets, after the model of Steffani, were easy carriers of mellifluence. Their influence was ubiquitous.

The Independence of his Music

The genius of Handel was so pervasive that no work of his may entirely be ignored and we must be reluctant to draw the line at any point short of the complete pilgrimage. Yet here it must be done. This chapter was designed to segregate fine secularity and to free Handel from the eternal curse attached by the sentimental to a 'sacred' musician. The final conclusion is that in Handel there is neither Jew nor Gentile, neither bond nor free: there is a corpus of integrated membership, which, transcending critical definition, can only be comprehended by those who believe in the final independence of music and are willing to lay aside the dark glass of prejudice and pedantry to see the music—and the man—face to face.

CHAPTER XVI

L'ENVOI

'THERE, Sir, is the portrait of the inspired master of our art; when I open my eyes in the morning, I look upon him with reverential awe, and acknowledge him as such, and the highest praise is due to your country for having distinguished and cherished his gigantic genius.' [1]

So Gluck, in his bedroom, delivered his private thoughts to Michael Kelly as they stood before a rich-framed painting of Handel. A man may be judged from the quality of his friends, and Handel's represent a catholic assortment. The tributes of those who followed the same vocation may be considered, not because they are of necessity the most valuable, but because they display a degree of unanimity unusual in artists. The man commanded universal respect and indeed affection, but so too did his art. So much so that Handel was regarded by his greatest successors as the *fons et origo* of music and the tutelary genius of musicians. Intellectual genuflection was first made by Gluck. The gesture was impressive in that his reception by Handel in London—in 1747—was brusque and hardly encouraging.

'You have taken too much trouble over your opera,' said the old man, having eyed the score of *La caduta dei giganti*. 'Here in England that is mere waste of time. What the English like is something they can beat time to [Charles II was, according to Evelyn, the founder of the pulsatory school of appreciation], something that hits them straight on the drum of the ear.' [2] Which is, after all, a legitimate and homely interpretation of a fundamental of musical expression. If there was one lesson taught by Handel to posterity, and to Gluck according to Burney, it was that periphrasis is anathema.

[1] Kelly, *Reminiscences*, i. 255. One assumes that Gluck meant England and not Ireland, although it would be attractive to think that Gluck regarded an Irishman as an Irishman and not as an Englishman, and that he intended some tribute to the politeness of the generous nation which welcomed Handel in 1742.

[2] Schmid, *C. W. von Gluck*, p. 29.

An early and notable victim of Handel's straight-hitting faculty was Haydn. After hearing 'The nations tremble' from *Joshua* he told Shield that 'He had long been acquainted with the music, but never knew half its powers before he heard it, and he was perfectly certain that only one inspired author ever did, or ever could, pen so sublime a composition.' On another occasion Shield compli-mented Haydn on the quality of his recitatives in *Il ritorno di Tobia.* 'Ah!' exclaimed Haydn with that engaging habit of his of self-denigration, '"Deeper and deeper," in *Jephtha,* is far beyond that.' The obvious influence of Handel on Haydn produced *The Creation,* the text for which had been lying about since before Handel's death. Haydn undertook this work after having experienced a Lenten season of Handel in 1794.

Mozart's counterpoint frequently reflected that of the master whose music he recollected having to read at sight under the critical eye of George III. An imitative fugue (the fugues of Handel were frequent companions to his studies) and the re-orchestrations of *Acis and Galatea, Messiah, Alexander's Feast* and the *Ode for St. Cecilia's Day* betokened affection. It was these versions which started the canard about Handel's impotence in orchestration. The responsibility was van Swieten's, who in enthusiasm ordered the new scoring. Handel might have cursed van Swieten for his effrontery, but he would have complimented Mozart on his acceptance of a welcome commission. Handel, unlike many who profess to be Handelians, deplored indigence among artists and considered that it was the duty of a composer to undertake the particular tasks set by his patrons.[1]

Of his peers Beethoven was perhaps the most generous in his appraisal of Handel. 'He was the greatest composer that ever lived. I would uncover my head, and kneel before his tomb.' And again, when forty volumes of Arnold's edition came to him on his deathbed: 'There is the truth.'

Handel was never so much alive as when he was dead. For this

---

[1] Samuel Wesley was the first to suggest keeping to Handel's orchestration in preference to Mozart's. See *Lectures* (B.M. Add. MS. 35015, f. 63), where he says that no other accompaniments are needed beyond 'what their immortal author deemed proper and necessary'.

there were two principal reasons. The first was George III; a dis-criminating music-lover and consistently generous in his promotion of Handel's posthumous fame. He supported the commemoration performances of 1784—that mammoth progenitor [1] of all musical festivals and choral constipation—encouraged Arnold's edition and was graciously pleased to accept from Christopher Smith those manuscripts which now glorify the royal collection. But with George III there was more to it than mere monarchic patronage. He could pen a critical memorandum to Burney's account of the commemoration:

Dr. Burney seems to forget the great merit of the choral fugue 'He trusted in God,' by asserting that the words would admit of no stroke of passion. Now the real truth is, that the words contain a manifest pre-sumption and impertinence, which Handel has, in the most masterly manner, taken advantage of. And [this observation throws interesting light on Handel's methods of extemporization] he was so conscious of the moral merit of that movement, that, whenever he was desired to sit down to the harpsichord. if not instantly inclined to play, he used to take this subject; which ever got his inspiration at work, and made him produce wonderful capriccios.

It may be suspected that the court grew a little weary of the subject of Handel. When the king left off Mrs. Delany, a royal pensioner, would lapse into fond reminiscence.

On a memorable day in 1789 Fanny Burney ran into the king in the gardens at Kew. Fanny was terrified. The king was not well and under restraint. On this morning, however, an interval of tired sanity prevailed. The king called to Fanny, kissed her cheek, and 'What a conversation followed! When he saw me fearless, he grew more and more alive, and made me walk by his side. . . .' The conversa-tion eventually turned to Dr. Burney and the *History*.

This brought him to his favourite theme, Handel; and he told me in-numerable anecdotes of him, and particularly that celebrated tale of Handel's saying of himself, when a boy: 'While that boy lives, my music will never want a protector.' And this, he said, I might relate to my father.

Then he ran over most of his oratorios, attempting to sing the subjects

---

[1] Upwards of five hundred musicians participated.

of several airs and choruses, but so dreadfully hoarse that the sound was terrible.

The second principal to Handel's immortality was the revivification of religious fervour. The Catholic church in its wisdom affords ample opportunity for emotional exultation, both in its liturgy and its furniture. The Protestant creeds, having renounced these riches, were obliged in the course of time to find compensation in other ways. Hence the inauguration of romantic hymnody in the eighteenth century. Handel had written a chorus which had brought even a king to his feet. If it were necessary to summarize the religious character of the English people during the late eighteenth and early nineteenth centuries one word would suffice—Hallelujah. Hallelujah, which split the establishment, opened the eyes of the blind, brought sinners to tearful repentance, lit the ceremonial fires on Mow Cop, inspired the erection of a thousand conventicles and sent Handel rampaging the country like one of his Old Testament heroes. When a rich sequence of Hallelujahs was discovered to belong to a work entitled *Messiah* the terminology caught at the imagination of those whose spiritual pabulum was the Old Testament. It was part of Handel's misfortune, and part too of his glory, that his music should readily have become an integral part of the Englishman's religion. Anecdote was useful in supporting the position. There were memories of the aged and beloved Handel presiding in his latter days over performances for the benefit of the foundlings, of the constant worshipper at St. George's, Hanover Square, of the visionary who was reported to have seen the opened heavens in the white heat of inspiration, of the sublime deathbed and of the last wish that he might die on Good Friday 'in hopes of meeting his good God, his sweet Lord and Saviour on the Day of His Resurrection.' The Great (and Good) Mr. Handel was born in 1759. In that year *Messiah* began its provincial course with a celebrated performance at Church Langton, Leicestershire.[1]

In the *Chester Courant* for 9th June 1772 appeared a notice which will serve to show what stimulus Handel gave to the provinces both in religious and in musical development. Many who remembered

[1] See Hanbury's *Charitable Foundations at Church Langton* (1767), pp. 80–7.

Handel's encounter with the saucy Johnson (precisely entered by one treasurer of the cathedral as Ap John) thirty years before would have been provoked to reminiscence by the following:

> On Tuesday, the 16th instant will be performed in the Broad Isle of the Cathedral, of this City, the Oratorio of
>
> ### 'MESSIAH'
>
> On Wednesday Evening, the 17th, will be performed in the Exchange,
> A Miscellaneous Concert of Select Pieces of Music, Vocal and Instrumental, the particulars of which will be expressed in the bills of the day.
> The principal vocal parts by Miss Linley, Miss M. Linley, Messrs. Norris, Price, Matthews, etc.
> The Instrumental by several of the most eminent performers from different parts of the Kingdom.
> On Thursday the 18th, will be performed, the Oratorio of
>
> ### 'SAMSON'
>
> And on Friday, the 19th, will be performed the Oratorio of 'JUDAS MACCHABAEUS.' No person to be admitted without tickets, which may be had at Messrs. Smith and Green's offices, opposite the White Lion, and all the Book Sellers' shops; where likewise may be had Books of the Several Oratorios.
> N.B. The South Door and the Cloister Door of the Cathedral will be opened each morning at Ten o'clock, and the performance will begin exactly at Eleven.[1]

And that, more or less, has been going on ever since. Occasionally the higher powers showed their approval by contributing to the orchestration. Once Jupiter capped Handel's thunderbolt. It was during a performance in 1791 at York of *Israel in Egypt* that a storm burst. Michael Kelly related how

> never before or since did I behold such a tremendous night,—such bursts of Heaven's artillery, and such sheets of fire, combined with the sacred words and the majestic music of the mighty master, were altogether appalling and magnificent.[2]

---

[1] The history of Handel at Chester is admirably told in Dr. J. C. Bridge's 'The Organists of Chester Cathedral': *Journal of the Architectural, Archaeological and Historic Society* (Chester), vol. xix, and in R. V. H. Burne's *Chester Cathedral*, London 1958, p. 200 et seq.   [2] Kelly, op. cit., ii. 8.

HANDEL
Pottery bust ascribed to Enoch Wood (1759–1840)

Religion and Handel were not confined to cathedral churches. There were the new foundations of the Methodists to which a hitherto musically disfranchized class were gradually drawn. Singing brought vision into the new squalor of industrial England and dignity to the singers. Handelian choruses levered latent talent into opera tion and became the priceless property (via the tonic sol fa class) of the factory workers of Lancashire and Yorkshire, the potters of Staffordshire and the miners of Wales. Handel, who had among his early friends an unashamed coalman from Clerkenwell, would have been pleased. Here we may tread out of music into sociology to contemplate our grandparents escaping from the muck of Manchester to the vision of the glory of the Lord as revealed to them by Handel. Here the cynic stands dumb. We have heard what Gluck, Mozart, Haydn and Beethoven said about Handel. What they did in the Potteries may be remembered as a greater tribute. In 1892 the Hanley Glee and Madrigal Society received an invitation to sing Gaul's *Israel in the Wilderness* at the Crystal Palace. The invitation was declined because the choir preferred to stay at home to practise *Israel in Egypt*.

Almost without noticing it we have traversed a hundred years in a couple of paragraphs. A hundred years during which the settle ment of oratorio left as well as its positive aspect a negative legacy. Under the impact of that newly cultivated vice of respectability—a quality which in the eighteenth century was literally laughed out of court—the Victorians lost the vivacity of Handel (nor has it yet been regained) and let choral singing deteriorate to the standards of com munity singing: they habituated themselves, as Bernard Shaw puts it, to 'lumbering along with Hallelujah as if it were a superior sort of family coach.'[1] Worse than that, they welcomed the fitful enlighten ment of the twilight corybantic Christianity by the lucubrations of repressed academists. Israel went with Gaul to the Wilderness and stayed there for a long time. The enemies of sacred music are not the religious but the religiose.

Rejecting an excellent book a friend commented the other day: 'There's too much imagination about this. I like facts.' Which is a

---

[1] Shaw, op. cit., i. 110.

fair and concise exposition of the artistic creed mistakenly believed by the English to be the one they follow. The truth is that our imagination proceeds from a pragmatic terminus. But as we look at the world around us we allow a fertilization of fancy. Thus poetry exudes from common things. Unconsciously we take the validity of poetry for granted and therefore tend to deny its existence. Because he too starts from earthly phenomena and from commonplace actions and invests them with the imagery of poetic aspiration Handel finds house-room with us. This is the secret of his genius.

Matthew Arnold preached that poetry should be a criticism of life. It is not clear that he knew precisely what he meant himself. We may, however, approximate to his idealism if we contemplate the uniqueness of Handel. He was, above almost all other composers, lively because he was full of life. His music, moreover, is a part of life. The least literate among music-lovers will appreciate this. Epping Forest on a summer's day recalls a song from *Semele,* or perhaps from *Serse*; the Thames at Richmond the *Water Music*; civic or military festivity the march from *Rinaldo*; athletic victory a chorus from *Joshua*; surpliced choir-boys an air from *Theodora*; the burial of the dead a march from *Saul*. No other music serves in quite the same intimate and yet universal way. No other music, so far as we are concerned, is so oblivious of time. Handel, like Shakespeare and Dante, wrote for his audience:

their glory is that they have outlasted the conditions they observed. Yet it was by observing them that they gained the world's ear. Let us, who are less than they, beware of seeming to belong to our own time.[1]

Handel was a Londoner, the musician laureate of the *beau monde*. But into the stifling air of the city he brought the fragrance of the country. Not all his time was spent in Brook Street. This is too often forgotten. The eye of fancy follows the coach routes. Handel views the garden of Kent, stands on the spaciousness of Salisbury Plain, looks at the royal antiquities of Chester and dreams by the Dove. Did they tell him about Izaak Walton? At Calwich, in the freshest country in England, they put a monument to Handel—an eighteenth-century pavilion. They call it still—Bernard Granville's house is

[1] Quiller-Couch, *On the Art of Writing*, p. 44.

gone, but the pavilion remains in quiet testimony to the fragrance of a near-forgotten friendship—with divided dedication the Temple of Handel and of fishing.

Handel was a Londoner, but he loved England. He became an Englishman, but he loved Europe. The story of this book is of a lover of humanity, of one who understood his fellow men and wrote their character with affection and optimism in the imperishable terms of great music. Manly music which springs from the contemplation of man. Is that not the source of the philosophy of the Augustans?

They wrote of him after his death:

Such was Handel, in whose character whatever there was wrong there was nothing mean; though he was proud his pride was uniform; he was not by turns a tyrant and a slave: a censor in one place and a sycophant in another; he maintained his liberty in a state in which others would have been vain of dependence: he was liberal even when he was poor, and remembered his former friends when he was rich. . . .[1]

---

[1] *Gentleman's Magazine*, May 1760.

APPENDICES

APPENDIX A

CALENDAR

(Figures in brackets denote the age reached by the person mentioned during the year in question.)

Year	Age	Life	Contemporary Musicians
1685		Georg Friederich Händel born Feb. 23, at Halle, son of Georg Händel (63), district surgeon and barber.	Bach born, March 21; Scarlatti (D.) born, Oct. 26. Abaco aged 10; Albinoni 11; Ariosti *c.* 25; Blow 37; Böhm 24; Buononcini 13; Buxtehude 48; Caldara *c.* 15; Campra 25; Charpentier *c.* 50; Clarke *c.* 25; Corelli 33; Couperin 17; Croft 7; Desmarets 23; Destouches *c.* 13; Durante 1; Eccles *c.* 22; Fux 25; Geminiani 5; Keiser 11; Kerl 57; Kuhnau 25; Lalande 28; Legrenzi *c.* 60; Lotti 18; Lully 53; Muffat (sen.) *c.* 40; Pachelbel 32; Pasquini 48; Pepusch 18; Purcell 26; Rameau 2; Reinken 62; Scarlatti (A.) 26; Steffani 31; Telemann 4; Vivaldi *c.* 15.
1686	1		Marcello born, July 31/ Aug. 1; Porpora born, Aug. 19.
1687	2		Graupner born, Feb.; Lully (55) dies, March 22; Senaillé born, Nov. 23.
1688	3		Fasch (J. F.) born, April 15; Foggia (84) dies, Jan. 8.
1689	4		
1690	5		Carey born (approx.); Legrenzi (*c.* 65) dies, July 26;

Appendix A—Calendar

Year	Age	Life	Contemporary Musicians
			Muffat (jun.) born, April; Vinci born.
1691	6		d'Anglebert (63) dies.
1692	7	Learns to play the clavichord. His father (70) has no intention of encouraging a musical career.	Tartini born, April 8; Vitali (G. B.) (*c.* 48) dies, Oct. 12.
1693	8	Visit to court at Weissenfels, where he plays the organ so well that the duke advises his father (71) to let him have competent tuition. To this no objections are raised.	Kerl (65) dies, Feb. 13; Locatelli born; Sammartini (G.) born (approx.).
1694	9	Begins to study under Zachau (31). He progresses on the clavier and organ, and takes up the violin and oboe. His general education proceeds at the Gymnasium.	Daquin born, July 4; Leo born, Aug. 5.
1695	10	Makes great progress and begins to compose. 6 Sonatas for two oboes and bass.	Greene born; Purcell (36) dies, Nov. 21.
1696	11	Visit to Berlin, where he plays at court. An offer of assistance in respect of advanced musical tuition is refused by his father (74), who wishes him to take up legal studies. The boy returns to Halle.	
1697	12	Death of H.'s father (75), Feb. 11. He continues musical studies and writes a number of church cantatas and organ pieces.	Leclair born, May 10; Quantz born, Jan. 30.
1698	13	Composes much in his spare time.	Francœur born, Sept. 28.
1699	14		Hasse born, March 25.
1700	15		Strungk (60) dies, Sept. 23.
1701	16	First contact with Telemann.	Graun born, May 7; Sammartini (G. B.) born.

Year	Age	Life	Contemporary Musicians
1702		Enters Halle University as a law student, Feb. 10. Leporin, who makes a habit of defaulting, is dismissed from the cathedral and H. is appointed organist, March 13. Large number of church cantatas composed.	
1703	18	Ends his University studies and resigns his organist's post, spring. Meets Steffani at Hanover (?). He goes to Hamburg, where Mattheson (22) assists him to become known as organist and clavier player, and he becomes second violin at the Opera under the management of Keiser (29). Visit to Lübeck, Aug., to see if the succession to Buxtehude (66) can be secured; but as this means marrying Buxtehude's daughter, Anna Margreta (28), both H. and Mattheson refrain from applying for the succession. Return to Hamburg.	Lampe born.
1704	19	Passion according to St. John performed, Lent. Opera, *Almira*, begun. Quarrel with Mattheson (23) over the playing of the continuo in the latter's opera, *Cleopatra*, Dec. 5, and reconciliation, Dec. 30.	Biber (60) dies; Charpentier (c. 69) dies, March; Muffat (sen.) (c. 59) dies, Feb. 23.
1705	20	*Almira* produced at Hamburg, Jan. 8. It is very successful, and is repeated some twenty times. Second opera, *Nero*, produced, Feb. 25.	

Year	Age	Life	Contemporary Musicians
		The Hamburg Opera begins to deteriorate under Keiser (31). H. dissociates himself from it and takes pupils.	
1706	21	Many songs, harpsichord pieces and cantatas composed, also (approx.) the operas *Florindo* and *Daphne* (originally one work, but divided because of its length). Departure for Florence. Secular cantatas composed there. He is introduced to Prince Ferdinando de' Medici at Pratolini, near Florence, and (?) meets Alessandro Scarlatti (47) there, Sept.	Galuppi born, Oct. 18; Martini born, April 24.
1707	22	Leaves Florence for Rome, Jan. (approx.). Psalms, *Dixit Dominus, Laudate pueri* and others composed there. Return to Florence, July, where his first Italian opera, *Rodrigo,* is produced with great success. Visit to Venice, autumn.	Buxtehude (70) dies, May 9; Clarke (c. 47) dies, Dec. 1.
1708	23	Meeting with Lotti (41), Steffani (54), Gasparini (40) and Earl of Manchester in Venice and friendship with Domenico Scarlatti (23). Return to Rome, early spring, where he is received by the Arcadians. There he meets Corelli (55), Marcello (22) and Pasquini (71). He is also received by Prince Ruspoli and Cardinal Pietro Ottoboni (40). Oratorio, *La Resurrezione,* and cantata, *Il Trionfo del tempo e*	Blow (60) dies, Oct. 1.

187

Year	Age	Life	Contemporary Musicians
		del disinganno, composed in Rome, also secular cantatas to words by Cardinal Bene detto Pamfili (55), including *Apollo e Dafne* and *Fillide ed Aminta.* Departure for Naples, end of June. French can zonets in the style of Lully composed there. Meets Don na Laura. Pastoral play, *Aci, Galatea e Polifemo,* composed.	
1709	24	Meeting with Cardinal Vin cenzo Grimani, who com missions an opera for Venice from H. Third visit to Rome, spring. H. hears Calabrian shepherds sing and play their Christmas songs, end of year. Second visit to Venice for the carnival. Opera, *Agrip pina,* produced there, Dec. 26.	Benda (F.) born, Nov. 25; Colasse (60) dies, July 17; Duni born, Feb. 9; Richter (F. X.) born, Dec.
1710	25	There he is encouraged by Eng lish and Hanoverian visitors, including Prince Ernest of Hanover and Baron Kiel mansegge, to go to London. He makes the journey by way of Hanover, where he goes with Steffani (56), who re sumes his duties at the elec toral court there. He is appointed musical director by the Elector Georg Ludwig (50) and the visit to England is postponed until the autumn, when (?) he visits his mother at Halle and leaves for Lon don. He is presented to Queen Anne (45), and Aaron	Arne born, March 12; Avi son born (approx.); Bach (W. F.) born, Nov. 22; Boyce born, Feb. 7; Pasquini (73) dies, Nov. 22; Pergolesi born, Jan. 3.

Year	Age	Life	Contemporary Musicians
		Hill (25), manager of the King's Theatre, suggests an opera, *Rinaldo,* to him, which he composes, to an Italian libretto by Rossi, in a fortnight, using many earlier pieces.	
1711	26	Production of *Rinaldo,* Feb. 24. It is given fifteen times before the opera season closes on June 2. H. appears at Thomas Britton's (*c.* 67) musical club, meets Babell (*c.* 21), who arranges harpsichord lessons on airs from *Rinaldo,* and influential amateurs. Return to Hanover, early summer, after another visit to Düsseldorf. Visit to Halle, June. Steffani (57) shows him much kindness and influences him musically. Chamber duets composed for Princess Caroline of Ansbach. Oboe Concertos and 12 cantatas.	Holzbauer born.
1712	27	Asks leave of Georg Ludwig (52) for a second visit to England. It is granted on condition that he return within a reasonable time. Arrival in London, late autumn. Production of the opera, *Il pastor fido,* at the King's Theatre, Nov. 22. Opera, *Teseo,* finished, Dec. 19.	Zachau (49) dies, Aug. 14.
1713	28	Production of *Teseo* at the King's Theatre, Jan. 10. The manager, Owen MacSwiney, fails and decamps, leaving H. and the singers unpaid; but	Corelli (60) dies, Jan. 10; Dauvergne born, Oct. 4; Krebs born, Feb. 10; Terradellas born, Feb.

they continue to give the opera
at their own risk. *Te Deum* for
the Peace of Utrecht finished,
Jan. 14. Uncertain whether
a work by a foreigner will be
sung at the peace celebrations, H. writes a birthday
ode for Queen Anne (48),
which is sung, with one by
Eccles (*c.* 50), Feb. 6. The
queen is so delighted with it
that she commands H. to have
the *Te Deum* and a *Jubilate*
ready for the celebrations.
These take place at St. Paul's
Cathedral, July 7. Anne is
too ill to attend, but hears the
works privately later, granting
H. a yearly salary of £200.
The *Te Deum* is modelled on
one by Purcell. The Earl of
Burlington (18) invites H. to
live at his house in Piccadilly
and introduces him to society.
Meeting with Pope (25), Gay
(28) and Arbuthnot (46).

1714 29   Opera, *Silla,* (?) composed   Bach (C. P. E.) born, March
and performed at Burlington   8; Gluck born, July 2;
House. Accession of the Elec-   Homilius born, Feb. 2; Jom-
tor Georg Ludwig of Hanover   melli born, Sept. 10.
(54) to the English throne as
George I.

1715 30   Opera, *Amadigi,* produced at   Alcock born, April 11;
the King's Theatre, May 25.   Nares born, April; Wagen-
Geminiani (35) introduces H.   seil born, Jan. 15.
(who for obvious reasons had
kept out of the king's way) to
court by insisting on being
accompanied at the harpsichord by him.

Appendix A—Calendar

Year	Age	Life	Contemporary Musicians
1716	31	Departure for Hanover in the suite of George I (56), July. Visit to Dresden in search of singers for London. Composition of a Passion Oratorio by Brockes (36). Visits to Hamburg, Ansbach and Halle. Return to London, end of year. *Concerto grosso*, F major (Op. 3, No. 4), composed for the benefit of the opera orchestra.	
1717	32	After revivals of *Rinaldo* and *Amadigi*, the opera season closes without any prospect of renewal, end of June. Music by H. played to the court on the Thames (*Water Music*), July 17.	Nichelmann born, Aug. 13; Purcell (Daniel) (*c.* 57) dies, Nov.; Stamitz (J. W.) born, June 19.
1718	23	The Earl of Carnarvon (45) invites H. to take up his residence at Canons, near Edgware, in succession to Pepusch (51). He is to conduct the band, play the organ and compose the *Chandos Anthems*.	Vitali (T. A.) (*c.* 53) dies (approx.).
1719	34	A Royal Academy of Music formed for the production of opera, Feb. The Earl of Carnarvon (47) created Duke of Chandos, April. H. goes to Germany in search of singers. He finds one at Düsseldorf. Letter to Burlington. Summer spent at Hanover. Visit to Dresden, July–Sept. There he secures several Italian singers for the London season of 1721, meets Lotti (52) again and plays before the Elector	

Year	Age	Life	Contemporary Musicians
		Frederick Augustus I (49) of Saxony. Visit to Halle, autumn, where his sister, Dorothea Sophia Michaelsen, has died in 1718. Return to London. Composition of the pastoral cantata *Acis and Galatea,* the poem by Gay (34).	
1720	35	Italian opera season under the auspices of the Royal Academy of Music opens at the King's Theatre under H.'s direction, April 2. Opera, *Radamisto,* produced there, April 27. The masque, *Haman and Mordecai* (*Esther,* H.'s first English oratorio), performed at Canons, Aug. 29. First book of Suites for harpsichord published, Nov. 14. Opening of the second Royal Academy season with *Astarto* by Buononcini (48), who comes to London, Nov. 19. Most of the *Concerti grossi* (Op. 3) composed at Canons.	Agricola (J. F.) born, Jan. 4.
1721	36	Production of the opera, *Muzio Scevola,* at the King's Theatre, April 15. The third act is by H., the second by Buononcini (49) and the first either by Ariosti (*c.* 61) or by the cellist Filippo Mattei. The public begins to be divided in its adherence to H. or Buononcini. The latter gains the upper hand after the opening of the third Royal Academy season, Nov. 1, the public, un-	Kirnberger born, April.

Year	Age	Life	Contemporary Musicians
		settled by the bursting of the South Sea Bubble, favouring lighter entertainments. Production of the opera, *Floridante*, Dec. 9.	
1722	37	H.'s popularity diminishes. Opening of the fourth Royal Academy season, Nov. 7. The opera, *Ottone*, on a libretto by Nicola Haym, is postponed until the arrival of Francesca Cuzzoni (*c.* 22), which has been delayed. She arrives end of Dec., but proves extremely obstinate, refusing to sing the aria 'Falsa immagine' until H. seizes her and threatens to throw her out of the window.	Benda (G.) born, June 30; Kuhnau (62) dies, June 25; Nardini born; Reinken (99) dies, Nov. 24.
1723	38	*Ottone* produced at the King's Theatre, Jan. 12. It does much to reinstate H. in the public favour. But *Flavio*, produced May 14, has no great success. Fifth Italian season opens, Nov. 27.	Gassmann born, May 4.
1724	39	Ariosti's (*c.* 64) opera, *Vespasiano*, produced Jan. 14, proves such a failure as to threaten the existence of the Italian Opera. H., to save the situation, hastily finishes *Giulio Cesare*, which is produced Feb. 20. He plays the organ at St. Paul's Cathedral before the Princesses Anne and Caroline, his pupils, Aug. 24. Sixth Royal Academy season opens, Oct. 31.	Theile (78) dies, June.

Handel

Year	Age	Life	Contemporary Musicians

Buononcini (52) has been dismissed. Production of the opera *Tamerlano*, Oct. 31.

1725 40 Opera, *Rodelinda*, produced at the King's Theatre, Feb. 13. It has an immense success. Seventh Italian season opens, Nov. 30. Ariosti's (c. 65) engagement is not renewed. John Christopher Smith (Schmidt) (13), son of H.'s treasurer, becomes his pupil.

Krieger (J. P.) (76) dies, Feb. 6; Scarlatti (A.) (66) dies, Oct. 24.

1726 41 H. becomes a naturalized Englishman, styles himself George Frideric Handel and is created, next to Croft (48), Composer of Musick to the Chapel Royal. Opera, *Scipione*, finished March 2 and produced March 12. Production of the opera, *Alessandro*, in which Faustina Bordoni (33), who has been newly engaged, appears as well as Francesca Cuzzoni (c. 26), May 5. A dangerous rivalry between the two singers develops.

Lalande (69) dies, June 18; Philidor born, Sept. 7.

1727 42 Eighth season of Italian opera opens at the King's Theatre, Jan. 7. Opera, *Admeto*, produced, Jan. 31. There is much disturbance, the public having split into two parties supporting either Bordoni (34) or Cuzzoni (c. 27). Opera, *Riccardo I*, finished, May 16. The two prima donnas engage in a hand-to-hand fight, to the delight of the audience, on the

Croft (49) dies, Aug. 14; Traetta born, March 30.

Year	Age	*Life*	*Contemporary Musicians*

stage during a performance of Buononcini's *Astianatte*, which brings the season abruptly to a close, June 6. Coronation of George II (44), at which H.'s Coronation Anthems are sung, Oct. 11. Ninth opera season opens, Sept. 30. H. is now sole musical director, but the Royal Academy of Music is so disorganized by intrigues among the singers, and the public so discouraged by the violent demonstrations for and against the artists, that it is impossible to secure enough subscriptions. *Riccardo I* is produced, Nov. 11.

1728 43 Opera, *Siroe,* produced at the King's Theatre, Feb. 17, and *Tolomeo,* April 30. The King's Theatre closes, June 1, and the Royal Academy of Music in its original form is wound up. The public is tired of Italian opera and transfers its affection to Gay's (43) satire on it, *The Beggar's Opera,* which, with music arranged by Pepusch (61), has had an enormously successful run since its production on Jan. 29. A New Royal Academy of Music is formed for the production of Italian opera, summer, with Heidegger as manager and H. as musical director.

Hiller (J. A.) born, Dec. 25; Lœillet (*c.* 53) dies; Marais (72) dies, Aug.; Piccinni born, Jan. 16; Steffani (74) dies, Feb. 12.

1729 44 H. goes to Italy to hear new

Monsigny born, Oct. 17;

Year	*Age*	*Life*	*Contemporary Musicians*
		operas and engage singers, Jan. He visits Florence, Milan, Venice, Rome and other cities and hears works by Porpora (42), Vinci (38), Hasse (29) and Pergolesi (18). He also becomes acquainted with the librettos of Metastasio (30). At the conclusion of his Italian tour, H. goes to Halle, where he finds his mother blind and infirm, June. Bach (44), who is ill at Leipzig, sends his son Wilhelm Friedemann (19) to Halle to invite H. to go and see him, but H. is unable to do so. Return to London, end of June. The new Italian season opens at the King's Theatre with the production of the opera, *Lotario*, Dec. 2. It has no great success and the new prima donna, Anna Strada del Pò, does not please.	Sarti born, Dec. 1.
1730	45	Opera, *Partenope*, produced at the King's Theatre, Feb. 24. Second New Royal Academy season opens with a revival of *Scipione*, Nov. 3, in which Senesino (*c.* 50) reappears.	Aylward born; Jackson born, May 29; Senaillé (43) dies, Oct 15.
1731	46	Opera, *Poro*, set to Metastasio's (33) *Alessandro nell' Indie*, produced, Feb. 2. Stage performance without choruses of *Acis and Galatea* at John Rich's (*c.* 49) theatre in Lincoln's Inn Fields, March 26. Third New	Cannabich born.

Year	Age	Life	Contemporary Musicians
		Royal Academy season opens, Nov. 13.	
1732	47	Operas, *Ezio* and *Sosarme,* produced at the King's Theatre, Jan. 15 and Feb. 15. Performance of the oratorio, *Esther,* at the house and under the direction of Bernard Gates (*c.* 47), on H.'s birthday, Feb. 23. It is repeated at the 'Crown and Anchor' under the auspices of the Academy of Ancient Music and, May 2, at the King's Theatre under H.'s own direction. Incidental music to Ben Jonson's *The Alchymist,* produced by John Rich (*c.* 50) at Covent Garden, March 7. It is mainly an adaptation of the dance tunes from *Rodrigo* of 1707. Stage performance of *Acis and Galatea* with choruses, May 17. Arne (22) conducts and his sister, Susanna Maria (18), sings the part of Galatea. H. himself gives another performance at the King's Theatre with a mixed cast of English and Italian artists, June 10. Some numbers of the earlier Italian version of 1708 are used. Fourth New Royal Academy season opens, Nov. 4. Opera, *Orlando,* finished, Nov. 20. A series of Sonatas for violin, flute or oboe and harpsichord (Op. 1) begun.	Haydn born, March 31/ April 1; Linley born.
1733	48	*Orlando* produced at the	Couperin (65) dies, Sept. 12.

King's Theatre, Jan. 27. Oratorio, *Deborah,* produced there, March 17. H. dismisses Senesino (*c.* 53), who succeeds, with the help of his noble admirers, in opening a rival Italian opera in Lincoln's Inn Fields. Several singers forsake H., and the Prince of Wales's side of the court adheres to Senesino. Porpora (47) is engaged as musical director. Visit to Oxford, where he gives several performances and finishes the oratorio, *Athaliah,* which is produced there, July 10. He declines the title of Mus.D. offered him by the university. Visit to Italy to engage singers, including Carestini (*c.* 28). Opera, *Arianna,* finished, Oct. 5. H. opens his season of Italian opera before his opponents are ready, Oct. 30. 6 Sonatas for two violins, flutes or oboes with harpsichord (Op. 2) published by Roger (Amsterdam) and reprinted by Walsh, who also brings out a pirated edition of a second series of Suites for harpsichord, consisting of 'lessons' for Princess Anne.

1734 49 Opera, *Arianna,* produced at the King's Theatre, Jan. 26. H.'s undertaking, being patronized by the unpopular court in opposition to the adherents of the Prince of

Ayrton born; Carter born; Cooke (B.) born; Gossec born, Jan. 17; Sacchini born, July 23.

Year	Age	Life	Contemporary Musicians

Wales, is deserted by many members of society, in spite of the momentary success of Carestini (*c.* 29). First performance of a new version of *Il pastor fido* (*see* 1712), May 18. H. quits the King's Theatre, the lease of which is at once disposed of to the rival company by Heidegger. H. makes an arrangement with Rich (*c.* 52) to produce Italian opera alternately with English Drama at Covent Garden at popular prices, summer. The season opens in Lincoln's Inn Fields, Covent Garden not being ready, Oct. 5. Covent Garden opens with *Il pastor fido,* preceded by a ballet, *Terpsichore,* composed by H. at the request of Rich, who wishes Mlle Sallé to dance on this occasion, Nov. 9. 6 *Concerti grossi* (Op. 3) published, Dec. 7.

1735 50 Opera, *Ariodante,* produced at Covent Garden, Jan. 8, and *Alcina,* April 16. During Lent H. gives a series of fourteen concerts, at which he performs various oratorios and for which he composes two organ Concertos. Farinelli (30) being now attached to the rival company, H.'s losses become alarming and the season closes on July 2. After a cure at Tunbridge Wells, he retires from public life,

Bach (J. C.) born, Sept. 5; Eccles (*c.* 72) dies, Jan. 12; Krieger (J.) (83) dies, July 18.

Year	Age	Life	Contemporary Musicians

autumn, and composes a version of Dryden's *Alexander's
Feast* by Newburgh Hamilton.
6 Fugues for harpsichord published by Walsh.

1736 51 *Alexander's Feast* finished,
Jan. 17, and first performed
at Covent Garden, Feb. 19.
Wedding Anthem performed
at the marriage of the Prince
of Wales, April 27. Opera
season opens at Covent Garden, May 5. Production of
the opera, *Atalanta,* in honour
of the royal wedding, May 12.
Farinelli's (31) success at the
rival house is rapidly waning,
and Fielding's (29) satirical
play, *Pasquin,* deals a serious
blow to Italian opera. Operas,
Arminio and *Giustino,* finished,
Oct. 14 and 20. Another
season opens at Covent Garden, Nov. 6, and the rival
company opens, Nov. 23,
under the direction of Hasse
(37), who has taken the place
of Porpora (50).

Contemporary Musicians (1736): Anfossi born (approx.); Cal-
dara (*c.* 66) dies, Dec. 28;
Fasch (C. F. C.) born, Nov.
18; Pergolesi (26) dies, March
17.

1737 52 Production of the operas,
Arminio, Jan. 12, and *Giustino,* Feb. 16. During Lent
H. gives performances of
Esther, Alexander's Feast and
a new version of *Il Trionfo
del tempo* of 1708, also several
new concertos for organ
and other instruments.
Worn out by financial cares
and excess of work, he has a

Contemporary Musicians (1737): Mysliveček born, March 9.
Carey (*c.* 47) and Lampe (34)
produce *The Dragon of Wantley,* a parody of *Giustino,*
Oct. 26.

Year	Age	Life	Contemporary Musicians

stroke which paralyses his right arm, April 13. Production of the opera, *Berenice*, May 18. H. undergoes a cure at Aix-la-Chapelle, late summer. He returns to London in better health, Nov. Heidegger, collecting the remains of the two failing Italian opera companies, opens a season at the King's Theatre on his own account, Oct. 29. He invites H. to write two new operas and a pasticcio. Funeral Anthem for Queen Caroline sung in Westminster Abbey, Dec. 17.

1738 53 Production of the opera, *Faramondo*, at the King's Theatre under Heidegger's management, Jan. 7, of the pasticcio, *Alessandro Severo*, Feb. 25, and of the opera, *Serse*, April 15 (?). Concert at Vauxhall, where Roubiliac's (42) statue of H. in unveiled, May 2. First meeting of the Royal Society for the Support of Decayed Musicians founded by Greene (43) and Festing, of which H. becomes a member, April 19. Arne (28), Boyce (28), Carey (c. 48) and Pepusch (71) are present. Oratorios, *Saul* and *Israel in Egypt*, finished, Sept. 27 and Nov. 1. 6 organ Concertos (Op. 4) published by Walsh, Oct. 4. 7 Sonatas for two violins, flutes or oboes

Battishill born, May; Murschhauser (75) dies, Jan. 6.

Year	Age	Life	Contemporary Musicians
		and harpischord (Op. 5) composed.	
1739	54	Oratorio, *Saul*, produced at the King's Theatre, Jan. 16, and *Israel in Egypt*, April 4 and 11. Italian opera being now almost completely obliterated, H., who is now at the theatre in Lincoln's Inn Fields, adds oratorios, serenades and odes to his repertory. Composition of Dryden's *Ode for St. Cecilia's Day* finished, Sept. 24. 12 *Concerti grossi* for strings (Op. 6) composed, Sept. 29–Oct. 30. First performance of the *Ode for St. Cecilia's Day* at Lincoln's Inn, Nov. 22. H., like Hogarth (42), takes an active interest in the Foundling Hospital just founded by Captain Coram (71).	Dittersdorf born, Nov. 2; Keiser (65) dies, Sept. 12; Marcello (53) dies, July 24; Rust born, July 6; Wanhal born, May 12.
1740	55	First performance of *L'Allegro, il Penseroso ed il Moderato* for solo voices, chorus and orchestra, at the theatre in Lincoln's Inn Fields, Feb. 27. Opera, *Imeneo*, finished Oct. 10 and produced Nov. 22, without a suitable Italian company and without success. His last opera, *Deidamia*, finished, Nov. 20. 12 *Concerti grossi* (Op. 6) and 6 organ Concertos (Op. 7) published by Walsh.	Arnold born, Aug. 10; Böhm (79) dies (approx.); Lotti (73) dies, Jan. 5; Webbe born.
1741	56	Production of the opera, *Deidamia*, Jan. 10. It is given	Arne (Michael) born; Desmarets (79) dies, Sept. 7;

Year	Age	*Life*	*Contemporary Musicians*

only three times, Italian opera being now definitely out of fashion. H., utterly discouraged and financially ruined, decides to retire from his public activities and gives a farewell concert, April 8. Oratorio, *Messiah,* begun Aug. 22 and finished Sept. 12. Oratorio, *Samson,* finished, except two numbers, Oct. 29. *Messiah* rehearsed at Chester. H. arrives in Dublin, where he has been invited by the Duke of Devonshire, who is Lord Lieutenant of Ireland, Nov. 18. Series of subscription concerts opened in Dublin, Dec. 23. 6 orchestral Concertos by H., Tartini (49) and Veracini (*c.* 56) published by Walsh.

Contemporary Musicians: Fux (81) dies, Feb. 13; Grétry born, Feb. 8; Naumann born, April 17; Paisiello born, May 9.

1742 57 *Hymen,* an English concert version of *Imeneo* (*see* 1740), produced March 24. Production of *Messiah* in Dublin, April 13, and repeated, June 3. Return to London, Aug. 13. Oratorio, *Samson,* completed, Oct. 12.

Abaco (67) dies, July 12.

1743 58 Production of *Samson,* at Covent Garden, Feb. 18. First London performance of *Messiah,* at Covent Garden, March 23. Secular oratorio, *Semele,* finished, July 4. Oratorio, *Joseph and his Brethren,* finished, Sept. *Te Deum* and Anthem for the victory of

Boccherini born, Feb. 19; Carey (*c.* 53) dies, Oct. 4; Vivaldi (*c.* 73) dies.

Year	Age	*Life*	*Contemporary Musicians*
		Dettingen performed in the Chapel Royal, Nov. 27.	
1744	59	Production of *Semele* at Covent Garden, Feb. 10, and of *Joseph and his Brethren,* March 2. Secular oratorio, *Hercules,* finished, Aug. 17. Oratorio, *Belshazzar,* finished, autumn (approx.). H. again takes the lease of the King's Theatre, autumn.	Campra (84) dies, June 29; Leo (50) dies, Oct. 31.
1745	60	Production of *Hercules* at Haymarket, Jan. 5. Production of *Belshazzar* at one of H.'s subscription concerts at the King's Theatre, March 27. H. is again ill. He is again obliged to give up the performances at the King's Theatre, which his opponents have done their best to damage, April. Meeting with Gluck (31) on his visit to England, autumn. Loyalty of H. during the '1745.'	Albinoni (71) dies (approx.); Dibdin born, March 4.
1746	61	Production of the *Occasional Oratorio,* specially written for the Covent Garden season, which again proves unprofitable, Feb. 14. H. appears with Gluck (32) at a concert and plays a Concerto of his own, March 25. Oratorio, *Judas Maccabaeus,* finished, Aug. 11.	Hook born, June 3; Stamitz (C.) born, May 7.
1747	62	In Lent H. again takes Covent Garden Theatre for a series of subscription concerts. The season is more successful and *Judas Maccabaeus,* produced	

Year	Age	Life	Contemporary Musicians
		April 1, is repeated five times. Oratorios, *Alexander Balus* and *Joshua,* finished, July 4 and Aug. 19.	
1748	63	*Joshua* and *Alexander Balus* produced at Covent Garden, which Handel has again taken for a series of Lenten Concerts, March 9 and 23. Oratorios, *Solomon* and *Su-sanna,* finished, June 13 and Aug. 24.	Shield born, March 5
1749	64	*Susanna* and *Solomon* produced during Lent at Covent Garden, Feb. 10 and March 17. Music written for the fireworks to be held in Green Park in celebration of the Peace of Aix-la-Chapelle, April 27. H. offers the governors of the Foundling Hospital the proceeds of a concert. The concert held in the chapel of the hospital, May 27, and an Anthem composed for the occasion performed. Oratorio, *Theodora,* finished, July 31.	Cimarosa born, Dec. 17; Destouches (*c.* 77) dies (approx.); Vogler born, Jan. 15.
1750	65	H. finishes music to *Alcestis,* a dramatic piece by Smollett (29), to be staged by Rich (*c.* 68) at Covent Garden, Jan. 8. It is withdrawn, and he uses nearly all the music for the interlude, *The Choice of Hercules,* which is finished, July 5. *Theodora* produced at Covent Garden without success, March 16. H. for the first time plays the	Bach (65) dies, July 28; Buononcini (78) dies (approx.); Salieri born, Aug. 19; Sammartini (G.) (*c.* 57) dies (approx.); Veracini (*c.* 65) dies.

Year	Age	Life	Contemporary Musicians
		organ presented by him to the Foundling Hospital, and conducts *Messiah* there, May 1. Elected a governor of the Foundling Hospital, May 9. He pays his last visit to Germany, summer. Coach accident in Holland.	
1751	66	*The Choice of Hercules* produced at Covent Garden, March 1. H. visits Cheltenham to take the waters, the symptoms of his illness of 1737, recurrent ever since, making themselves strongly felt, spring to June 13. His eyesight begins to fail. Oratorio, *Jephtha,* finished, Aug. 30. On seeking medical advice, H. finds that blindness is imminent, winter.	Lampe (48) dies, July 25; Terradellas (38) dies, May 20.
1752	67	Production of *Jephtha* at Covent Garden, Feb. 26. His Lenten seasons there now enjoy universal recognition. Unsuccessful operation to his eyes, May 3.	Clementi born, (?) Jan.; Pepusch (82) dies, July 20; Reichardt born, Nov. 25; Zingarelli born, April 4.
1753	68	Is now almost totally blind. John Christopher Smith (41), acts as his amanuensis.	Dalayrac born, June 13; Viotti born, May 23.
1754	69	Unable to write new works, he is able, with the help of Smith (42), to revise and add to old ones. He also appears at concerts occasionally, playing harpsichord and organ from memory or extemporizing.	Kozeluch born.
1755	70		Durante (71) dies, Aug. 13; Winter born.

Appendix A—Calendar

Year	Age	Life	Contemporary Musicians
1756	71		Mozart born, Jan. 27; Umlauf born.
1757	72	Production of *The Triumph of Time and Truth*, a new version of *Il Trionfo del tempo* of 1708 and 1737, produced at Covent Garden, March 4, with additional numbers dictated to J. C. Smith (45).	Pleyel born, June 1; Scarlatti (D.) (72) dies; Stamitz (J.) (40) dies, March 30.
1758	73	His health deteriorates. Towards the end of the year his appetite leaves him and he has premonitions of his approaching end. But he still appears at some concerts.	Dagincourt (74) dies; Zelter born, Dec. 11.
1759	74	In spite of his failing health, H. attends a performance of *Messiah* on March 30. He is seized with faintness afterwards and has to take to his bed. Handel dies in London, April 14. Handel Festival at Church Langton, Leicestershire, Sept. 26, 27.	Graun (58) dies, Aug. 8. Agricola (J. F.) aged 39; Alcock 44; Anfossi *c.* 23; Arne (T. A.) 49; Arne (M.) 18; Arnold 19; Avison *c.* 49; Aylward 29; Ayrton 25; Bach (W. F.) 49; Bach (C. P. E.) 45; Bach (J. C.) 24; Battishill 21; Benda (F.) 50; Benda (G.) 37; Boccherini 16; Boyce 49; Cannabich 28; Carter 25; Cimarosa 10; Clementi 7; Cook (B.) 25; Dalayrac 6; Daquin 65; Dauvergne 46; Dibdin 14; Dittersdorf 20; Duni 50; Fasch (J. F.) 71; Fasch (C. F. C.) 23; Francœur 61; Galuppi 53; Gassmann 36; Gazzaniga 16; Geminiani 79; Gluck 45; Gossec 25; Graun 58; Graupner 72; Grétry 18; Hasse 60; Haydn 27; Hiller (J. A.) 31; Holzbauer 48;

Year	*Age*	*Life*	*Contemporary Musicians*

Hook 13; Jackson 29; Jommelli 45; Kirnberger 38; Kozeluch 5; Krebs 46; Leclair 62; Linley 27; Locatelli 66; Martini 53; Monsigny 30; Mozart 3; Muffat (jun.) 69; Mysliveček 22; Nardini 37; Nares 44; Naumann 18; Nichelmann 42; Paisiello 18; Philidor 33; Piccinni 31; Pleyel 2; Porpora 73; Quantz 62; Rameau 76; Reichardt 7; Richter (F. X.) 50; Rust 20; Sacchini 25; Salieri 9; Sammartini (G. B.) *c.* 58; Sarti 30; Shield 11; Stamitz (C.) 13; Tartini 67; Telemann 78; Traetta 32; Umlauf 3; Viotti 6; Vogler 10; Wagenseil 44; Wanhal 20; Webbe 19; Winter 4; Zelter 1; Zingarelli 7.

APPENDIX B

Operas

Admeto (1727) (73).

Agrippina (1709), Vincenzo Grimani [2] (57).

Alcina (1735) (86).

Alessandro (1726), Antonio Rolli (72).

Almira, Königin von Castilien (1704), Friedrich Feustking (55).

Amadigi (1715), Heidegger (62).

Arianna (1734), Francis Colman (83).

Arminio (1737) (89).

Ariodante (1735), Antonio Salvi (85).

Atalanta (1736) (87).

Berenice (1737) (90).

Deidamia (1741), Rolli (94).

Ezio (1732), Metastasio (80).

Faramondo (1738), Apostolo Zeno (91).

Flavio (1723), Nicola Haym (67).

Floridante (1721), Rolli (65).

Giulio Cesare (1724), Haym (68).

Giustino (1737), Count Beregani (88).

Imeneo (1740) (93).

Lotario (1729), Matteo Noris (77).

Muzio Scevola (1721), Rolli (third act only by Handel) (64).

Orlando (1733), Braccioli (82).

Ottone (1723), Haym (66).

Partenope (1730), Silvio Stampiglia (78).

Pastor fido, Il (first version, 1712), Giacomo Rossi (59).

Pastor fido, Il (second version, 1734) (84).

Poro (1731), Metastasio's *Alessandro nell' Indie* (79).

Radamisto (1720), Haym (63).

Riccardo primo, re d'Inghilterra (1727), Rolli (74).

Rinaldo (two versions, 1711 and 1731), Rossi (58).

Rodelinda (1725), Haym (70).

---

[1] The numbers of the appropriate volumes in Chrysander's Händel-gesellschaft edition are given in brackets.

[2] Names given after the dates are those of the librettists.

Rodrigo (1707) (56).
Scipione (1726), Rolli (71).
Serse (1738) (92).
Silla (1714) (61).
Siroe (1728), Haym, after Metastasio (75).
Sosarme (1732), Noris (81).
Tamerlano (1724), Haym (69).
Teseo (1713), Haym (60).
Tolomeo, re d'Egitto (1728), Haym (76).

Lost Hamburg Operas:
   Daphne (*c.* 1706), Hinsch.
   Florindo (*c.* 1706), Hinsch.
   Nero (1705), Feustking.

Advertised in 1739, but probably never performed:
   Jupiter in Argos (MS. in the Fitzwilliam Museum, Cambridge).

Unperformed and unpublished:
   Alfonso primo.
   Flavio Olibrio.
   Honorius.
   Tito.
   Unnamed Opera (MS. in the Fitzwilliam Museum).

Recitatives to 11 Pasticcios compiled by Handel from works by various
   composers (1730–47).

BALLET

Terpsichore (1734) (84).

INCIDENTAL MUSIC

Alceste (1750), Tobias Smollett (46).
Alchymist, The (1732), Ben Jonson.

SERENATAS, MASQUES, PASTORALS, ODES AND INTERLUDES

Aci, Galatea e Polifemo (two versions, 1708 and 1732) (95).
Acis and Galatea (1719), John Gay (3).
Alexander's Feast (1736), Dryden (12).

Allegro, il Penseroso ed il Moderato, L' (1740), Charles Jennens, after Milton (6)
Choice of Hercules, The (1751) (18).
Haman and Mordecai (first version of *Esther*) (1720), ? Pope, after Racine (40).
Hercules (1745), Rev. T. Broughton (4).
Hymen. English concert version of the opera *Imeneo* (1742).
Ode for the Birthday of Queen Anne (1713) (46).
Ode for St. Cecilia's Day (1739), Dryden (23).
Parnasso in festa, Il (1734) (54).
Praise of Harmony (c. 1739), Newburgh Hamilton.
Semele (1744), after Congreve (7).

ORATORIOS

Alexander Balus (1748), Rev. Thomas Morell (33).
Athaliah (1733), Samuel Humphreys (5).
Belshazzar (1745), Charles Jennens (19).
Deborah (1733), Humphreys (29).
Esther (second version of *Haman and Mordecai*, 1732), Humphreys (41).
Israel in Egypt (1739), words from the Bible (16).
Jephtha (1752), Morell (44).
Joseph and his Brethren (1744), Rev. James Miller (42).
Joshua (1748), Morell (17).
Judas Maccabaeus (1747), Morell (22).
Messiah (1742), words from the Bible (45).
Occasional Oratorio (1746), ? Morell (43).
Resurrezione, La (1708) (39).
Samson (1743), Newburgh Hamilton, after Milton (10).
Saul (1739), Jennens (13).
Solomon (1749), ? Morell (26).
Susanna (1749) (1).
Theodora (1750), Morell (8).
Trionfo del tempo e del disinganno, Il (1708 and 1737), Benedetto Pamfili (24).
Triumph of Time and Truth, The (1757) (20).

PASSION MUSIC

Der für die Sünden der Welt gemarterte und sterbende Jesus (1716), Barthold
  Heinrich Brockes (15).
Johannespassion (1704), Gospel of St. John and arias by Wilhelm Postel (9).

CHURCH MUSIC

Ach Herr, mich armen Sünder, Church Cantata (*c.* 1696).
Chandos Anthems (1716–18) (34–5):
1. *O be joyful in the Lord.*
2. *In the Lord I put my trust.*
3. *Have mercy upon me.*
4. *O sing unto the Lord a new song.*
5. *I will magnify Thee.*
6. *As pants the hart.*
7. *My song shall be alway.*
8. *O come, let us sing.*
9. *O praise the Lord with one consent.*
10. *The Lord is my light.*
11. *Let God arise.*
12. *O praise the Lord, ye angels of His.*

Coronation Anthems (1727) (14):
1. *Zadok the Priest.*
2. *The King shall rejoice.*
3. *My heart is inditing.*
4. *Let Thy hand be strengthened.*

Dettingen Anthem (1743) (36).
Dettingen *Te Deum* (1743) (25).
Dixit Dominus (1707) (38).
Foundling Hospital Anthem (1749) (36).
Funeral Anthem for Queen Caroline (1737) (11).
Haec est Regina virginum (*c.* 1707–8).
Hymns. Rev. C. Wesley (MS. in the Fitzwilliam Museum):
 O Love divine, how sweet thou art.
 Rejoice, the Lord is King.
 Sinners, obey the Gospel Word
Lobe den Herrn meine Seele (1719).
Laudate pueri, F major (1702) (38).
Laudate pueri, D major (1707) (38).
Nisi Dominus (1702–7) (38).
O praise the Lord, anthem (36).
Salve Regina, G minor (38).
Seuiat tellus inter vigores (?).
Silete venti, motet (? 1715–20) (38).
Te Deum, A major (*c.* 1727) (37).
Te Deum, B flat major (1716–18) (37).
Te Deum, D major (*c.* 1714) (37).
Utrecht *Te Deum* and *Jubilate* (1713) (31).
Wedding Anthem for Princess Anne (1734) (36).
Wedding Anthem for the Prince of Wales (1736) (36).

Appendix B—Catalogue of Works

Vocal Chamber Music

6 *Alleluias* for voice and harpsichord (*c.* 1735–45) (38).

72 Italian Cantatas for one or two voices and instruments (50–3).

7 Italian Cantatas (MSS. in the Fitzwilliam Museum).

20 Italian Duets with continuo (1707–8, 1741–5) (32):

    1. *Caro autor di mia doglia.*

    2. *Giù nei Tartarei regni.*

    3. *Sono liete, fortunate.*

    4. *Troppo cruda, troppo fiera.*

    5. *Che vai pensando.*

    6. *Amor gioie mi porge.*

    7. *Va, speme infida.*

    8. *A mirarvi io sono intento.*

    9. *Quando in calma.*

    10. *Tacete, ohimè, tacete.*

    11. *Conservate, raddoppiate.*

    12. *Tanti strali al sen.*

    13. *Langue, geme, sospira.*

    14. *Se tu non lasci amore.*

    15. *Quel fior che all' alba ride.*

    16. *No, di voi non vo' fidarmi.*

    17. *No, di voi non vo' fidarmi.*

    18. *Beato in ver.*

    19. *Fronda leggiera.*

    20. *Ahi, nelle sorti umane.*

2 Italian Trios with continuo (32):

    1. *Se tu non lasci amore.*

    2. *Quel fior che all' alba ride.*

Instrumental Chamber Music

Hornpipe for the Concert at Vauxhall (1740) (48).

8 *Sinfonie diverse* (48).

15 Solos for a German flute, oboe or violin and continuo, Op. 1 (*c.* 1724) (27).

Sonata for 2 violins, bass and organ, G minor (48).

Sonata for *viola da gamba* and cembalo, C major (*c.* 1705) (48).

3 Sonatas for flute and cembalo (*c.* 1710) (48).

9 Sonatas for 2 violins, oboes or flutes and continuo, Op. 2 (1733) (27).

7 Sonatas for 2 violins or German flutes and continuo, Op. 5 (1738) (27)

6 Sonatas or Trios for two oboes and continuo (1696) (27).

Handel

6 *Concerti grossi,* for flutes, oboes, bassoons and strings, Op. 3 (1729) (21):

 1. B flat major-G minor. 2. B flat major. 3. G major. 4. F major.
 5. D minor. 6. D major-minor.

12 *Concerti grossi,* for strings, Op. 6 (1739) (30):

  1. G major. 2. F major. 3. E minor. 4. A minor. 5. D major.
  6. G minor. 7. B flat major. 8. C minor. 9. F major. 10. D
  minor. 11. A major. 12. B minor.

Concerto, C major, for 2 oboes, bassoon, 4 horns, strings and continuo
 (47).[1]

Concerto, D major, for 2 oboes, bassoon, 4 horns, 2 trumpets, drums,
 strings and continuo (47).[1]

Concerto, F major, for 2 oboes, bassoon, 2 horns, strings and continuo (47).

Concerto grosso, C major, for 2 oboes and strings (21).

Concertos:

 1. B flat major, for oboe and strings (21).

 2A. B flat major, for oboe and strings (21).

 2B. F major, for 2 horns and strings (21).

 3. G minor, for oboe and strings (21).

 4. (Sonata) B flat major, for solo violin, oboes and strings (21).

Double Concerto (*a due cori*), E flat major (? 1740–50) (47).

Double Concerto, F major (? 1740–50) (47).

Fireworks Music (1749) (47).

Overture for the pasticcio, *Alessandro Severo* (1738) (48).

Overture for the pasticcio, *Oreste* (1734) (48).

Overture in B flat major (48).

Water Music (c. 1717) (47).

6 Concertos, Op. 4 (1738) (28):

 1. G minor. 2. B flat major. 3. G minor. 4. F major. 5. F major.
 6. B flat major.

6 Concertos, Op. 7 (1740) (28):

 1. B flat major. 2. A major. 3. B flat major. 4. D minor. 5. G
 minor. 6. B flat major.

5 Concertos (48):

 F major. 2. A major. 3. D minor. 4. D minor. 5. F major.

---

[1] These two works are identical, and both are used in the *Fireworks Music.*

Appendix B—Catalogue of Works

Capriccio, F major (2).
Capriccio, G minor (2).
Chaconne, F major (2).
Courante e due Minuetti, F major (2).
Fantasia, C major (2).
6 Fugues (*c.* 1720) (2).
Lesson, A minor (2).
Preludio ed Allegro, G minor (2).
6 Short Fugues (48).
Sonata, C major (2).
Sonata, C major (2).
Sonatina, B flat major (2).
Suite, D minor (2).
Suite, G minor (2).
Suites (or Lessons) (1720) (2):

    1. A major. 2. F major. 3. D minor. 4. E minor. 5. E major.
      6. F sharp minor. 7. G minor. 8. F minor.

Suites (or Lessons) (1733) (2):

    1. B flat major.[2] 2. G major. 3. D minor. 4. D minor. 5. E minor.
      6. G minor. 7. B flat major. 8. G major. 9. G major (*Chaconne*).

Various Suites (48).

There was a tradition that, during his 1737 visit to Aix-la-Chapelle, Handel wrote a *Jubelkantate* for the city of Elbing in East Prussia, and that the music was subsequently lost. The facts are that for the fifth centenary of the foundation of the city a libretto was compiled by one Seiler, head-master of the Gymnasium, and that music was arranged for it by Johann Jeremias du Grain. The work was entitled *Hermann von Balcke.* The recitatives were supplied by du Grain and the arias, some of which were also by du Grain, were in part adapted from Handel's *Partenope, Riccardo I, Ottone, Admeto, Scipione* and *Alessandro.* Handel himself was unaware of this pasticcio, at any rate before its performance. The MS. was discovered at Elbing by Irmgard Leux (*vide Archiv für Musikwissenschaft,* vol. vii, pp. 441–51). *Hermann von Balcke* was broadcast from Königsberg in 1933.[3]

---

[1] Containing the so-called *Harmonious Blacksmith* variations.

[2] Containing the air (with variations) on which Brahms wrote variations of his own for piano.

[3] I am indebted to Professor O. E. Deutsch for permitting me to use this information.

APPENDIX C

PERSONALIA

Abaco, Giuseppe dall' (1709–1805), Italian cellist, born in Brussels, son of the violinist Evaristo dall' Abaco. He worked at Bonn, London, Vienna and elsewhere, and composed cello sonatas.

Albinoni, Tommaso (1674–1745), Venetian violinist and composer.

Ariosti, Attilio (born c. 1660), Italian operatic composer, who produced his first opera, *Dafne,* at Venice in 1686.

Arne, Cecilia. See Young.

Arne, Susanna Maria. See Cibber.

Avison, Charles (c. 1710–70), organist at Newcastle-on-Tyne. Pupil of Geminiani and author of *An Essay on Musical Expression,* in which Handel is sometimes adversely criticized.

Avolio (or *Avoglio*), *Signora,* Italian soprano singer of whose career nothing is known apart from its coincidence with that of Handel.

Baldassari, Benedetto, Italian tenor singer, in London 1720–2.

Banister, John (died 1735), English violinist and teacher of his instrument, composer for the theatre, son of John Banister (1630–79).

Beard, John (c. 1717–91), English tenor singer, chorister at the Chapel Royal under Gates (q.v.) in his boyhood, appeared first as a mature singer in works by Handel in 1736.

Bernacchi, Antonio (1685–1756), Italian male soprano singer and teacher, first heard in London in 1716.

Berselli, Matteo, Italian tenor singer, who came to London with Senesino (q.v.) in 1720.

Bertolli, Francesca, Italian contralto singer, first heard in London in 1729.

Bordoni, Faustina (1693–1783), Italian mezzo-soprano singer, made her first appearance in Venice in 1716 and came to London ten years later. Married Hasse (q.v.) in 1730.

Boschi, Giuseppe, Italian bass singer, member of St. Mark's, Venice; (?) sang Polyphemus in Handel's *Aci* in Naples, 1709. First appeared in London in 1711.

Boyce, William (1710–79), English composer and organist, boy chorister at St. Paul's Cathedral in London and later pupil of Greene (q.v.), whom he succeeded in 1755 as Master of the King's Band. Organist of the Chapel Royal from 1758. Published a collection of English *Cathedral Music*, 1760–78.

Brade, William (1560–1630), English string player and composer who worked in Germany. In 1618 he was in Halle and his daughter Magdalene married a surgeon to whom Handel's father was apprenticed.

Brockes, Barthold Heinrich (1608–1747), poet and important official in Hamburg.

Buononcini (or *Bononcini*), *Giovanni Battista* (born 1672), Italian opera composer, son of Giovanni Maria Buononcini (*c.* 1640–78), whose pupil he was and whom he succeeded as chapel-master of the church of San Giovanni in Monte at Modena, his birthplace. Attached to the court of Vienna in 1692 and of Berlin in 1696; produced his first operas in Rome in 1694. Vienna and Italy, 1706–20; London, 1720–32.

Burney, Charles (1726–1814), composer and historian. His Handel comments are valuable in that he had played the violin in Handel's orchestra.

Buxtehude, Dietrich (1637–1707), Swedish composer and organist, settled in Denmark and from 1668 organist of St. Mary's Church at Lübeck.

Campra, André (1660–1744), French composer of Italian descent. He became musical director at Notre-Dame in Paris, but was also famous as an opera composer.

Caporale, Andrea (died *c.* 1756), Italian violoncello player who came to London in 1734 and joined Handel's opera orchestra in 1740.

Carestini, Giovanni (*c.* 1705–*c.* 1759), Italian male soprano singer, afterwards a contralto. Came out in Rome in 1721 and made his first London appearance in 1733.

Carey, Henry (*c.* 1690–1743), English poet, composer and dramatist, pupil of Roseingrave (q.v.) and Geminiani (q.v.).

Carissimi, Giacomo (? 1604–74), Italian composer who cultivated the forms of oratorio and cantata in their early stages.

Castrucci, Pietro (1679–1752) and *Prospero* (died 1760), Italian violinists, who came to London in 1715, Pietro becoming leader of Handel's opera orchestra and Prospero a member of it.

Cervetto, Giacomo (1682–1783), Italian violinist and composer, who settled in London in 1728. He wrote violin and chamber music.

Cibber, Susanna Maria (*née Arne*) (1714–66), English contralto singer and actress, sister of Thomas Augustine Arne. She first appeared on the London stage in 1732 and married Theophilus Cibber in 1734.

Clari, Giovanni Carlo Maria (1677–1754), Italian composer. He was chapel-master in turn at Pistoia, Bologna and Pisa.

Clayton, Thomas (c. 1670–c. 1730), English composer and adapter, who set Addison's opera, *Rosamond*, in 1707, and for whom Pope wrote his *Ode for St. Cecilia's Day* in 1713.

Clegg, John (1714–c. 1750), English violinist of outstanding gifts, who became insane in 1744.

Coperario, Giovanni (*John Cooper*) (c. 1570–1627), English lutenist, violist and composer who worked under an assumed Italian name after his studies in Italy, whence he returned to England c. 1604.

Croft, William (1678–1727), English organist and composer, pupil of John Blow at the Chapel Royal, organist at St. Anne's, Soho, from 1700 and organist with Jeremiah Clarke at the Chapel Royal from 1704; Master of the Children there from 1715.

Cuzzoni, Francesca (c. 1700–70), Italian soprano singer, first appeared in Venice in 1719 and in London in 1722.

Defesch, William (died c. 1758), Flemish organist, violinist and composer, who settled in London in 1731, having been organist at Antwerp cathedral.

Dieupart, Charles (died c. 1740), French violinist, harpsichord player and composer settled in London.

Dubourg, Matthew (1703–67), English violinist, pupil of Geminiani (q.v.), for many years in Dublin and towards the end of his life in London, his birthplace.

Durastanti, Margherita (born c. 1695), Italian soprano singer, who came to London in 1720 and again in 1733. The text of a cantata sung by her at a benefit concert was by Alexander Pope.

Ebner, Wolfgang (c. 1610–65), German organist and composer who worked in Vienna, both at St. Stephen's Cathedral and in the court chapel.

Épine, Francesca Margherita de l' (died 1746), Italian or French singer, who first came to England in 1692, remaining there until her death and marrying Pepusch (q.v.) in 1718.

Erba, Dionigi, Italian composer, chapel-master at the church of San Francesco, Milan, in 1692.

Fabri, Annibale Pio (1697–1760), Italian tenor singer also known under the name of 'Balino,' who first came to England in 1729. He was also a composer.

Appendix C—Personalia

Farinelli (Carlo Broschi) (1705–82), Italian male soprano singer, made his first appearance in Rome in 1722, when he had already acquired some fame in southern Italy, and went to Vienna in 1724. His first appearance in London was in 1734.

Ferrabosco, Alfonso (c. 1575–1628), English composer of Italian descent, educated at Queen Elizabeth's expense. He became a musician at the court of James I.

Festing, Michael Christian (died 1752), English violinist and composer for his instrument in London, pupil of Geminiani (q.v.). Made his first appearance about 1724 and became a member of the king's private band in 1735. Musical director of Ranelagh Gardens from 1742.

Frasi, Giulia, Italian singer, who first appeared in London in 1743.

Froberger, Johann Jacob (c. 1617–67), German organist and composer. He was a pupil of his father at Halle, court organist in Vienna in 1637–57, visited Italy and England, and died in France.

Galliard, John Ernest (c. 1687–1749), German composer, settled in England c. 1706. Oboist, composer of pantomimes, anthems and cantatas.

Galuppi, Baldassare (1706–85), Venetian composer, who produced his first opera at Vicenza in 1722. He was in London in 1741–3, became vice chapel-master at St. Mark's in Venice in 1748 and chapel-master in 1762.

Gasparini, Francesco (1668–1727), Italian composer, pupil of Corelli and Pasquini (q.v.), chorus master at the Ospedale di Pietà in Venice, and appointed chapel-master of St. John Lateran in Rome in 1725.

Gates, Bernard (1685–1773), English theorist, singer and composer, Gentleman of the Chapel Royal from 1708 and Master of the Children some time before 1732.

Gaul, Alfred (1837–1913), English organist and composer, pupil of Zachariah Buck at Norwich Cathedral and later organist at various churches in Birmingham.

Geminiani, Francesco (1667–1762), Italian violinist and composer, pupil of Corelli in Rome, came to England in 1714 and lived in London, Dublin, Paris and again in Ireland until his death.

Giardini, Felice de (1716–96), Italian violinist and composer. He studied at Milan Cathedral and wih Somis at Turin, played in various Italian opera orchestras, visited Germany and settled in London, where he succeeded Festing as leader of the Opera orchestra in 1752.

Gizziello (Gioacchino Conti) (1714–61), Italian male soprano singer, who first appeared in Rome in 1729 and made his first London appearance in 1736.

Graun, Karl Heinrich (1704–59), German singer and composer. Studied at Dresden, went into the service of the court at Brunswick and later worked at that of Frederick II of Prussia, first at Rheinsberg and after the king's accession at Potsdam and Berlin.

Greene, Maurice (1695–1755), English organist and composer in London, chorister at St. Paul's Cathedral as a boy, where he became organist in 1718. In 1727 he succeeded Croft (q.v.) as organist and composer to the Chapel Royal.

Grimaldi. See Nicolini.

Habermann, Franz Johann (1706–83), Bohemian composer, who published six masses in 1747.

Harington, Henry (1727–1816), English physician and an amateur musician. He was a doctor at Bath and composed vocal music, including probably the familiar setting of Ben Jonson's 'Drink to me only.'

Hasse, Johann Adolph (1699–1783), German composer of Italian operas, born near Hamburg, where he came out as tenor at Keiser's (q.v.) Opera. Afterwards sang at Brunswick, where he produced his first opera in 1721. Then went to Italy to study dramatic music under Porpora (q.v.) and Alessandro Scarlatti. Appointed musical director and manager of the royal opera at Dresden in 1731. Married Faustina Bordoni (q.v.) in 1730.

Heintz, Wolff (*fl. c.* 1540), organist at Halle.

Keiser, Reinhard (1674–1739), German composer, studied under Schelle at St. Thomas's School in Leipzig. Went to the court of Brunswick in 1692 and to Hamburg two years later, where he made the Opera the most distinguished in Germany for a time and composed 116 works for it. He also wrote church music, including oratorios and a Passion according to St. Mark.

Kelway, Joseph (died prob. 1782), organist of St. Martin's-in-the-Fields, harpsichordist to Queen Charlotte. Devoted to the music of Scarlatti.

Kerl (or *Kerll*), *Johann Caspar* (1627–93), German organist and composer, born in Saxony, but settled early in Vienna as a pupil of Valentini. Then studied in Rome under Carissimi (q.v.) and probably the organ under Frescobaldi.[1] In the service of the Elector of Bavaria in Munich, 1656–74. Went to Vienna as private teacher and was appointed court organist there in 1677.

Krieger, Johann Philipp (1649–1725), German organist and composer. Studied at Venice and became chamber musician to the Duke of Saxe-Weissenfels.

Kuhnau, Johann (1660–1722), German organist, clavier player, composer and

---

[1] But Kerl was only sixteen when Frescobaldi died.

writer on music, cantor at Zittau, went to Leipzig in 1682, became organist at St. Thomas's Church in 1684 and cantor in 1701, in which post he preceded Bach.

Lampe, John Frederick (Johann Friedrich) (1703–51), German bassoon player and composer at Brunswick; came to England about 1725 and settled in London, but went to Dublin in 1748 and to Edinburgh in 1750.

Leveridge, Richard (c. 1670–1758), English bass singer in London, who made his first appearance before Purcell's death in 1695 and sang until a few years before that of Handel, his last recorded appearance being in 1751. He was also a composer of songs and theatre music.

Linley, Elizabeth Ann (1754–92), English soprano singer, daughter of Thomas Linley of Bath, where she sang as a child. She made her first important appearance at the Worcester Festival in 1770 and married Sheridan in 1773.

Linley, Mary (1759–87), English singer, sister of the preceding. She sang in oratorio and at festivals until her marriage to Richard Tickell.

Locke, Matthew (c. 1630–77), English composer. He was a choir-boy under Edward Gibbons at Exeter Cathedral and settled in London *c.* 1650, becoming an important stage and chamber composer.

Lœillet, Jean Baptiste (1680–1730), Flemish flautist, oboist and composer. He settled in London in 1705 and joined the orchestra at the King's Theatre. Later he went to Munich as chamber musician to the Elector of Bavaria, but returned to London some time after 1725.

Lotti, Antonio (c. 1667–1740), Venetian composer, singer in the Doge's chapel as a boy, produced his first opera at the age of sixteen. Became second organist at St. Mark's, Venice, in 1692 and first in 1704. He was at Dresden in 1717–19.

Lupo, Thomas (16th–17th century), English lutenist, singer and composer, member of a large family of musicians of Italian origin.

Mainwaring, Rev. John (1724–1807), rector of Church Stretton, Salop, and Professor of Divinity at Cambridge. Author of many theological works and (for no very obvious reason) Handel's first biographer. He was thirty-six and not, as is frequently stated, twenty-five, when he wrote his biography.

Mattei, Filippo, Italian violoncellist and composer at the Opera in London.

Mattheson, Johann (1681–1764), German writer on music, organist and composer, first sang female parts at the Hamburg Opera, then composed two operas (1699 and 1704), became cantor at Hamburg Cathedral in 1715, wrote several books on music, the most important being *Das neu eröffnete Orchester* (1713), *Der vollkommene Capellmeister* (1739) and *Grundlage einer Ehrenpforte* (1740).

Merighi, Antonia, Italian contralto singer, who first appeared in London in 1729.

Montagnana, Antonio, Italian bass singer, who first appeared in London in 1731.

Muffat, Gottlieb (1690–1770), German composer, pupil of Fux in Vienna, where he became court organist and music master to the imperial children.

Nicolini (Nicola Grimaldi) (born *c.* 1673), Italian male soprano singer, later a contralto, made his first appearance, in Rome, about 1694. First came to England in 1708.

Pasquali, Francesco (16th–17th century), Italian composer who studied and worked in Rome.

Pasquini, Bernardo (1637–1710), Italian composer, who as a young man became organist of Santa Maria Maggiore in Rome.

Pepusch, John Christopher (Johann Christoph) (1667–1752), German composer and theorist born in Berlin, appointed to the Prussian court at the age of fourteen, emigrated first to Holland and came to England about 1700, where he settled in London for the rest of his life. Married Margherita de l'Épine (q.v.) in 1718.

Pescetti, Giovanni Battista (*c.* 1704–*c.* 1766), Italian composer, pupil of Lotti at Venice. He lived in London from *c.* 1737 to shortly after 1750 and then worked at St. Mark's in Venice.

Porpora, Niccola Antonio (1686–1767), Italian composer, theorist and singing teacher, came to London as Handel's rival in 1729.

Porta, Giovanni (*c.* 1690–1755), Italian composer. Having been in the service of Cardinal Ottoboni in Rome, he lived in London in 1720–36 and then went to Munich.

Quantz, Johann Joachim (1697–1773), German flautist and composer. He studied at Dresden and Vienna, worked at the Saxon-Polish court at Dresden and Warsaw, travelled in France and England, taught the flute to Frederick II of Prussia, to whose court at Potsdam and Berlin he was attached from 1741.

Ramondon, Lewis (died *c.* 1720), English or French bass singer and composer, who sang in London until *c.* 1711 and then made a success as a song composer.

Randall, John (1715–99), English organist and composer, pupil of Gates (q.v.) at the Chapel Royal, organist of King's College, Cambridge, from 1743 and professor there in succession to Greene (q.v.) from 1755. Possibly encouraged Mainwaring (q.v.) to write a biography of Handel.

Appendix C—Personalia

Robinson, Anastasia (c. 1698–1755), English singer, made her first stage appearance in 1714 and retired ten years later, having married the Earl of Peterborough in 1722.

Roseingrave, Thomas (1690–1766), English or Irish composer and organist, son of Daniel Roseingrave (c. 1650–1727). Organist of St. George's, Hanover Square, London, 1725–38.

Scheidt, Samuel (1587–1654), organist and composer at Halle, and one of the important figures in German music. His acquaintance with English music is shown in variations on a theme of John Dowland. In Halle he was for a time a colleague of William Brade.

Schütz, Heinrich (1585–1672), German composer. Studied at Cassel and Marburg University, also with G. Gabrieli at Venice. He returned to the court of Hesse-Cassel, but in 1614 was appointed musical director to the Elector of Saxony at Dresden.

Senesino (Francesco Bernardi) (c. 1680–c. 1750), Italian male soprano singer, attached to the court opera at Dresden in 1719 and there invited by Handel to London, where he first appeared in 1720.

Shield, William (1748–1829), English violinist and composer. Pupil of his father and of Avison at Newcastle-on-Tyne. He went to London in 1772 to join the Opera orchestra as second violin and the following year became principal viola. He composed stage pieces and in 1817 became Master of the King's Music.

Smith, John Christopher (1712–95), English organist and composer of German descent, son of Johann Christoph Schmidt of Ansbach, who came to England as Handel's treasurer and copyist.

Snow, Valentine (died 1770), English trumpeter, appointed Trumpeter to the King in 1753 in succession to John Shore (died 1752).

Stanley, Charles John (1713–86), English organist, blind from the age of two, pupil of Greene (q.v.), later organist of several London churches.

Steffani, Agostino (1654–1728), Italian composer and diplomat, who spent much of his time in diplomatic missions at German courts, but was a remarkable composer as well as a scholar and priest.

Strada del Pò, Anna, Italian soprano singer, who first appeared in London in 1729.

Stradella, Alessandro (c. 1645–82), Italian composer of noble birth who appears to have held no regular musical appointments, and what is known of his career seems to be based more on legend than on fact.

Strungk, Nikolaus Adam (1640–1700), German violinist, organist and composer, who opened an opera-house at Leipzig in 1693.

Swieten, Gottfried van, Baron (1734–1803), Austrian diplomat, physician and musical amateur in Vienna.

Telemann, Georg Philipp (1681–1767), German composer, studied at the University of Leipzig 1700–4, was appointed organist to the New Church there and founded a Collegium musicum. After holding various posts at Sorau, Eisenach and Frankfort, he was appointed cantor of the Johanneum and musical director to the five principal churches at Hamburg, posts which he held until his death.

Tesi-Tramontini, Vittoria (1700–75), Italian mezzo-soprano singer, who made her first stage appearance at a very early age. In 1719 she was at Dresden, where Handel met her, but did not engage her.

Turini, Francesco (c. 1595–1656), Italian composer. He studied in Prague, Venice and Rome, became chamber musician to the Emperor Rudolph II in Prague and later cathedral organist at Brescia.

Urio, Francesco Antonio, Italian composer at Milan, whose first published work, a set of motets, appeared in 1690.

Valentini (*Valentino Urbani*), Italian male contralto singer, afterwards a counter-tenor, who first came to London in 1707.

Veracini, Francesco Maria (1690–c. 1750), Italian violinist and composer. Studied with his uncle, Antonio Veracini, and with Tartini, lived in London in 1714–17, then worked at the Saxon court at Dresden, went to Prague in 1723 and returned to London c. 1735.

Vivaldi, Antonio (c. 1675–1741), Italian violinist and composer. Studied under his father and under Legrenzi at Venice, where he held various posts all his life, except for visits to Mantua and Vienna.

Waltz, Gustavus, German bass singer, who was (?) for a time Handel's cook.

Weideman, Charles (*Carl Friedrich Weidemann*), German flute player, settled in London about 1726.

Werner, Gregor Joseph (1695–1766), Austrian composer. He was appointed director to the Esterházy family in 1728, being Haydn's predecessor at Eisenstadt.

Whichello, Abiel (died c. 1745), English organist and composer. He was organist at a London church, taught the harpsichord and appeared at Thomas Britton's concerts.

Young, Cecilia (1711–89), English singer, married Arne (1710–78) in 1736.

Zachau, Friedrich Wilhelm (1663–1712), German composer, theorist, and organist at Halle, first teacher of Handel.

APPENDIX D

BIBLIOGRAPHY

Arbuthnot, John, 'Harmony in an Uproar.' (London, 1732.)

Avison, Charles, 'An Essay on Musical Expression.' (London, 1752.)

Bairstow, E. C., 'Handel's Oratorio "The Messiah."' (Oxford and London, 1928.)

Bayne-Powell, Rosamond, 'Eighteenth Century London Life.' (London, 1937.)

Bingley, W., 'Musical Biography.' (London, 1714.)

Bishop, John, 'Brief Memoirs of George Frederick Händel.' (London, 1856.)

Bredenförder, Elisabeth, 'Die Texte der Händel-Oratorien: eine religionsgeschichtliche und literar-soziologische Studie.' (Leipzig, 1934.)

Brenet, Michel, 'Haendel.' (Paris, 1912.)

Burke, Thomas, 'The Streets of London.' (London, 1940.)

Burney, Charles, 'A General History of Music.' (London, 1776–89.)

—— 'An Account of the Musical Performances in Westminster Abbey and the Pantheon in Commemoration of Handel.' (London, 1785.)

Carey, Henry, 'Poems.' Edited by F. T. Wood. (London, 1930.)

Carse, Adam, 'The Orchestra in the XVIIIth Century.' (Cambridge, 1940.)

Chrysander, F., 'G. F. Händel.' 3 vols. (unfinished). (Leipzig, 1858–67.)

Cibber, Mrs. Susannah Maria, 'The Life of' (London, 1887.)

Clark, Richard, 'Reminiscences of Handel, the Duke of Chandos, etc.' (London, 1836.)

Coxe, J. C., 'Anecdotes of G. F. Händel and J. C. Smith.' (London, 1799.)

Delany, Mary, 'Autobiography and Correspondence of Mary Granville, Mrs. Delany.' Edited by Lady Llanover. (London, 1861–2.)

Dent, Edward J., 'Handel' ('Great Lives' Series). (London, 1934.)

Flower, Newman, 'George Frideric Handel: his Personality and his Times.' (London, 1922; new ed. 1948.)

Förstemann, Karl Eduard, 'G. F. Haendels Stammbaum, nach Originalquellen und authentischen Nachrichten.' (Leipzig, 1844.)

Franz, Robert, 'Ueber Bearbeitungen älterer Tonwerke, namentlich Bachscher und Händelscher Vokalmusik.' (Leipzig, 1781.)

—— 'Der Messias, unter Zugrundelegung der Mozartschen Partitur.' (Leipzig, 1884.)

Handel

Handel, G. F. Letters and Writings. Edited by Erich H. Müller. (London, 1935.)

—— 'Messiah.' Edited from the Original Sources by J. M. Coopersmith. (New York, 1947.)

Händel-Jahrbuch. Herausgegeben von Rudolf Steglich. (Leipzig, 1929, etc.)

Hawkins, John, 'A General History of the Science and Practice of Music.' (London, 1776 and 1853.)

Heinrich, E., 'G. F. Händel, ein deutscher Tonmeister.' (1884.)

Hoyle, John, 'Dictionarium Musica.' (London, 1770.)

Ireland, John, 'Hogarth Illustrated.' (London, 1806.)

Irving, W. H., 'John Gay's London.' (Harvard, 1928.)

Leichtentritt, Hugo, 'Händel.' (Stuttgart, 1924.)

Loewenberg, A., 'Annals of Opera: 1597–1940.' (Cambridge, 1943.)

Lysons, Rev. D. (and others), 'Annals of the Three Choirs.' (Gloucester, 1895.)

Mainwaring, J., 'Memoirs of the Life of the late G. F. Handel.' (London, 1760.)

Mattheson, Johann, 'Grundlage einer Ehrenpforte.' (Hamburg, 1740; Berlin, 1910.)

—— 'G. F. Händels Lebensbeschreibung.' (Hamburg, 1761.)

Milnes, Keith, 'Memoir relating to the Portrait of Handel by Francis Kyte.' (London, 1829.)

Müller-Blattau, J., 'Georg Friedrich Händel.' (Potsdam, 1933.)

Nichols and Wray, 'The History of the Foundling Hospital.' (Oxford, 1935.)

Nkarintsev, 'Pictures from the Life of Handel.' (Moscow, 1937.)

Prout, Ebenezer, 'The Orchestra of Handel.' (Proceedings of the Musical Association, Leeds, 1885–6.)

Reichardt, J. F., Georg Friedrich Händels Jugend.' (Berlin, 1785.)

Robinson, J. R., 'The Princely Chandos.' (London, 1893.)

Robinson, Percy, 'Handel and his Orbit.' (London, 1908.)

Rockstro, W. S., 'Life of Handel.' (London, 1883.)

Rolland, Romain, 'Haendel.' (Paris, 1910.)

—— 'Handel.' Translated by A. Eaglefield Hull. (New York, 1923.)

Rosenberg, Alfred, 'Georg Friedrich Händel.' (Berlin, 1938.)

Sasse, Konrad, 'Händel Biographie.' (Leipzig, 1963.)

Appendix D—Bibliography

Schoelcher, Victor, 'The Life of Handel.' (London, 1857.)

Schultz, W. E., 'Gay's Beggar's Opera.' (New Haven, 1923.)

Squire, W. Barclay, 'Catalogue of the King's Music Library: Vol. I, Handel's MSS.' (London, British Museum, 1927.)

Stevens, D. H., 'Some Immediate Effects of the Beggar's Opera.' (Chicago, 1923.)

Streatfeild, R. A., 'Handel.' (London, 1909.)

—— 'The Case of the Handel Festival.' (London, 1897.)

Taut, Kurt, 'Verzeichnis des Schrifttums über Georg Fr. Händel. (Leipzig, 1934.)

Taylor, Sedley, 'The Indebtedness of Handel to Works by Other Composers.' (Cambridge, 1906.)

Tobin, John, 'Handel at Work.' (London, 1964.)

Townsend, Horatio, 'An Account of Handel's Visit to Dublin.' (1852.)

Uffenbach, Zacharias von, 'London in 1710 from the Travels of.' Translated by W. H. Quennell and Margaret Mare. (London, 1934.)

Ward, Ned, 'The London Spy.' Edited by A. L. Hayward. (London, 1927.)

Weissebeck, J. M., 'Der grosse Musikus Händel im Universalruhme.' (Nuremberg, 1809.)

Weissenborn, B., 'Das Händelhaus in Halle.' (Berlin, 1938.)

Winchop, Thomas, 'Scanderbeg—with a List of all the Dramatic Authors, etc.' (London, 1947.)

APPENDIX E

HANDEL'S FINANCES

RECORDS relating to the banking account of 'George Frideric Handel [the signature in the Firm Book], in Brooke Street Hanover Square' are still extant in the Record Office of the Bank of England (fo. 97/2674). With the exception of a period from 28th March 1739 to 14th February 1743 a fairly complete statement is available from 2nd August 1732 until 21st March 1758. As details of payments are sparse ('By Cash' on the one side and 'To Cash Him' on the other have little helpful significance), an extract is only given to cover the alleged bankruptcies. It will be clear that Handel was not at any rate insolvent either in 1737 or 1745–6.

1734					1732		
June 26 To Cash Him				£1300	Aug. 2 By Cash		£2300
1735							
June 30	,,	,,	,,	300			
Sep. 15	,,	,,	,,	100			
Dec. 8	,,	,,	,,	50			
1736							
Aug. 20	,,	,,	,,	150			
Sep. 28	,,	,,	,,	200			
1737							
Sep. 1	,,	,,	,,	150			
1739							
Mar. 28 yᵉ balance				50			
				£2300			£2300

1743				1743			
Feb. 21	To Cash		650	Feb. 14	By Cash		650
	Chambers [1]			Mar. 6	„	„	250
1744				1744			
Apr. 5	„ do.		226.5.6	Nov. 3	„	„	500
17	„ Him		23.14.6	9	„	„	100
Jan. 19	„ do.		200	Dec. 11	„	„	50
May 4 [2]	„ Robinson [3]		210	Jan. 5	„	„	50
May 11	„ Francesina [4]		400	Feb. 1	„	„	150
13	„ Jordan [5]		140				
				1745			
				May 9	„	„	100
			£1850				£1850

1747			1746			
Apr. 29	To Cash Him	1000	Feb. 28	By Cash		400
			Mar. 7	„	„	100
			21	„	„	100
			1747			
			Apr. 9	„	„	250
			24	„	„	150
		1000				1000

These are the only payments specified in the whole of the banking account.

---

[1] Possibly Robert Chambers of Hackney (d. 1761), with whom Handel had dealings in 1752.

[2] Obviously 1745.

[3] Fees to Miss Robinson, daughter of John Robinson, organist of Westminster Abbey, and of Mrs. Turner Robinson. Miss Robinson (Hawkins, v. 182) sang in *Hercules* and other oratorios.

[4] Alias Mlle Duparc who, having left the opera, 'attached herself to Handel, was first woman in his oratorios for many years.' (Burney, *History*, iv. 667.)

[5] ? Abraham Jordan, the organ-builder.

In addition to this series of statements concerning his account at the Bank there are other documents indicative of Handel's shrewd financial sense.[1] Between 4th June 1728 and 22nd June 1732 he bought and sold South Sea Annuities [2] (1751) to the value of £4,622 (fo. 71/124). Between 6th May 1748 and 9th November 1749 his turnover in 4% Annuities (1748) (fo. 877) was £7,750 and between 10th April 1744 and 6th May 1748 3% Annuities (1743) (fo. D.1468) involved him to the extent of £3,000. By 2nd January 1753 he held £12,000 in 4% Annuities (1746) (fo. 874). Handel had commenced an interest in these on 22nd February 1749 with an investment of £7,700, which would appear to have come from the sale of the 1748 Annuities. On 2nd January 1753 the £12,000 were transferred to Reduced 3% Annuities. By 1759 these savings grew to £17,500. (fo. D.2646 M.2583).

In the Register Office Book A–K 1348 we read:

MEMORANDUM that GEORGE FRIDERIC HANDELL of Brooke Street Hanover Square, Esq. in the Probate late of the Parish of St. George Hanover Square In the County of Middx. Esq. died possessed of SEVENTEEN THOUSAND FIVE HUNDRED POUNDS Reduced Annuities at £3 per cent & by his last Will and Testament dated 1st June 1750 appointed JOHANNA FRIDERICA FLOERCKEN Sole Executrix with four Codicils respectively dated the 6th. Aug. 1756, 22nd. March 1757, 4th. Aug. 1757 & 11th. April 1759 wherein he appoints GEORGE AMYAND Esq. Co Executor making no mention of the said Anns. they are at the disposal of the said George Amyand Esq. he only having proved the Will.

Power reserved to make the like grant to Johann Friderica Floercken Wife of   Floercken the Neice of the said decd. & Executrix named in the said Will when she shall apply for the same.

Probate dated at Doctrs. Comm. 26 April 1759
Regd. 30th. April 1759

The final story of the dispersal of Handel's fortune in Reduced 3% Annuities is told in the following statement (D.2646 M.2583). It will be seen that the legatees mentioned hereunder did better than the terms of the will specify.

---

[1] Or that of his advisers.

[2] All these loans were managed by the Bank of England.

1759 £

2 May. To Christopher Smith [1] of Dean St. Soho, Gent. 2470

John Duburk of Hanover Sq., Gent. [2] 600

16 May. Peter Gallier, senior. Christian Reich of Westminster. Gents. Thomas Wood, Gent. of St. Giles in the Fields } 1254

25 May. To William Delacreuse of Castle Street, Esq. 400

Henry Monk of Dublin, Esq. 100

8 June. William Prevost, jnr. of Shad., Thames, Gent. 500

27 June. Edward Shewell of Lombard St. Goldsmith 500

28 June. James Smyth [3] of New Bond St. Perfumer 700

11 Oct. Johanna Friderica Floerken Wife of Johan Ernst Floerken. Director of the University of Halle in Saxony 9000

31 Oct. To James Sinclair [4] of Shadwell. Mariner 500

Lewis Morel of Fleet St. Goldsmith 876

Edward Shewell of Lombard St. Goldsmith 600

_____

17500

£

2 Jan. 1753. By Anns. 1746 Con' 12000

19 July 1754. Benjamin Jones of Bow, Gent. 1500

14 May 1755. Philip Hale of Basing Lane. Sugar Refiner 500

23 June 1756. Stephen Gardes of Rathbone Place, Gent. 1000

19 May 1758. John Jones of St. Anns, Soho, Gent. 2500

_____

17500

[1] Was left £2,000 in the will.   [2] Was left £500 in the will.
[3] Was left £500 in the will.
[4] Died in 1789 *aetat.* 85, was a senior master in the Navy.

Other legacies included:

£1,000 to the Royal Society of Musicians.

£500 to James Hunter. [1]

£600 for his monument in Westminster Abbey.

£300 each to the five orphan children of his cousin Georg Taust, Pastor of Giebichenstein.

£300 each to his cousins Christiana Susanna Handelin, and Rachel Sophia; Thomas Harris [2] of Lincoln's Inn Fields; the widow of his cousin Magister Christian Roth.

£200 each to Dr. Morell; George Amyand; Reiche, Secretary of Affairs of Hanover.

£100 each to John Hetherington, of the Middle Temple; Matthew Dubourg, the violinist; Newburgh Hamilton; Mrs. Palmer, widow, of Chelsea; Thomas Bramwell, his servant.

Fifty guineas each to Benjamin Martyn, of New Bond Street; John Cowland, apothecary; John Belcher, surgeon; Mrs. Mayne, widow, of Kensington; Mrs. Downalan,[3] of Charles Street, Hanover Square.

The will and codicils are in Schoelcher and Rockstro in full.

---

[1] The scarlet-dyer of Old Ford.

[2] Of the Salisbury family and a master in Chancery.

[3] Or Donellan: an Irishwoman and an intimate of Mrs. Delany.

APPENDIX F

THE PROBLEM OF PLAGIARISM

THERE are two considerable books which set with admirable clarity two different points of view concerning Handel's loans from other composers. One is *The Indebtedness of Handel to Works by other Composers* by Sedley Taylor (Cambridge, 1906); the other—in counterblast—*Handel and his Orbit* by Percy Robinson (London, 1908). The passages in Handel (detailed in Sedley Taylor) which appear to refer to music by Muffat (1690–1770), Habermann (1706–83), Clari (1669–1740) and Graun (1711–1759) are of no great significance except in so far as they show Handel's awareness of more or less contemporary publications. To employ other people's thematic material was a usual practice, as Bach often enough indicates. Where Handel's 'borrowings' were obvious his contemporaries noted the fact without censure.

'And here it may be noted that the chorus in Mr. Handel's oratorio of *Samson* "Hear, Jacob's God" is taken from that in [Carissimi's] *Jephtha*, "Plorate filiae Israel."' (Hawkins, iii. 92.)

'Handel is supposed to have availed himself of Clari's subjects, and sometimes more, in the choruses of Theodora.' (Burney, *History*, iii. 36.)

'In this work [by Turini] there is a canon, upon the subject of which Handel has composed one of his finest instrumental fugues; but, *according to his usual practice* [my italics—P. M. Y.], whenever he adopted another man's thought, he has enlivened and embellished this theme, like a man of true genius, with a counter subject, and shewed that he saw farther into its latent fertility than the original inventor.' (Burney, *History*, iii. 521.)

So far so good. But when we come to *Israel in Egypt* we discover that most of the work owes to a Magnificat attributed to one Erba and to a Serenata by Stradella. This means that, if we accept the Sedley Taylor ruling, *Israel in Egypt* should be announced as by Stradella and Erba (edited and arranged by Handel). With regard to the *Dettingen Te Deum* the attribution should be 'Urio, arr. Handel.' Mr. Robinson, however, suggests, by brilliant reasoning, that Erba, Stradella and Urio were not the composers of the works ascribed to them, but Handel himself. Readers of detective fiction would enjoy following the deductions by which Mr. Robinson proves that one work was written at the house of Benedetto Erba, an Arcadian, that one was simply mis-attributed to the shadowy Stradella and that one was written at Urio on Lake Como: that all, in fact, were really by Handel.

To revert to the more orthodox doctrine of borrowing, we find Professor Edward J. Dent suggesting that, as Handel used other people's music more intensively after 1737, he needed thematic stimulus of this order on account of the paralysis which had affected the state of his mind. This led specu-lation up an unpleasant avenue. That form of paralysis which has the direst effect on the mind is syphilitic paralysis. This would have blunted Handel's moral sense and accounted for large-scale depredation of other men's thoughts to an unprecedented degree. Moreover, Handel went to recuperate at Aix-la-Chapelle, which was the European centre for the treatment (such as it was in those days) of venereal disease. Fortu-nately for Handel's reputation, he did not decline into general paralysis of the insane, which would certainly have been the case had he con-tracted the French pox. He suffered on two occasions a severe cerebral thrombosis, and recovered in quick time because of efficient vascularity. Such recovery would have left his mentality unimpaired. His 'maggots' and his moroseness should therefore not be exaggerated. Since it is the fashion of the day to associate genius with either homosexuality or venereal disease, it had better be stated that there is no particle of evidence to suggest that Handel was tainted by either. Examination of what evidence there is in respect of Handel's physical and mental health has led Dr. Eliot Slater, of the National Hospital for Nervous Diseases, to the conclusion that Handel was a cyclothymic personality—with a fair, but not abnormal, range of mood changes.[1]

[1] 'Contributions to a Pathography of the Musicians: 2. Organic and Psychotic Disorders,' Eliot Slater and Alfred Meyer, in *Confinia Psychiatrica*, vol. iii, No. 3, pp. 129–145.

INDEX

237

Index

Index

DATE DUE			

GERMANY'S DRIVE TO THE WEST

(*Drang nach Westen*)

A STUDY OF GERMANY'S WESTERN WAR AIMS
DURING THE FIRST WORLD WAR

GERMANY'S DRIVE
TO THE WEST

(*Drang nach Westen*)

A STUDY OF GERMANY'S WESTERN WAR AIMS
DURING THE FIRST WORLD WAR

HANS W. GATZKE

BALTIMORE

THE JOHNS HOPKINS PRESS

TO

FRITZ T. EPSTEIN

ACKNOWLEDGMENTS

THE IDEA for this book was suggested by Professor William L. Langer of Harvard University. I am deeply indebted to the guidance I received in his seminar and to his always helpful criticism and encouragement. Professors Sidney B. Fay and Heinrich Brüning of Harvard University, Ralph H. Lutz of Stanford University, Kurt Riezler of the New School for Social Research, and the late Professor Veit Valentin made valuable suggestions on various aspects of the work while it was in progress. Professor Harry Rudin of Yale University, during a busy year as visiting professor at Harvard, gave generously both of his time and ever-friendly advice. Professors Edward W. Fox of Cornell University and Frederic C. Lane of The Johns Hopkins University read and criticized the completed manuscript. I wish to thank all of the above for being so kind and helpful. A special debt of gratitude belongs to my friend Dr. Fritz Epstein. His innumerable suggestions and constructive criticism proved as invaluable to me as they have to so many other specialists in the German field. Without his loyal help, this study could never have been written. Harvard University, where a first version of this work was submitted as a doctoral dissertation, through its generous grant of a Sheldon Traveling Fellowship, enabled me to carry on research at the leading American libraries, notably the Hoover Library at Stanford University. To the latter I am indebted for most of the material on which this study is based. I have never found a more congenial and hospitable place. Thanks are due, finally, to Miss Lilly Lavarello, for much-needed and ably-performed editorial assistance.

H. W. G.

Baltimore, Maryland
September, 1949

CONTENTS

INTRODUCTION

THE QUESTION of war aims was the most important problem of German foreign and domestic policy during the First World War. All other issues, in comparison, were of secondary significance but in some way related to this central issue. Yet to this day no comprehensive study, which attempts to present and co-ordinate the many different facets of this particular problem, has been made. The present study intends to fill this gap.[1]

The problem of war aims, of course, is primarily one of foreign policy. As such it presents a significant chapter in the history of German territorial expansion, and had far-reaching effects on German and Allied attempts at a negotiated peace settlement. But like all foreign affairs, the war aims problem ultimately has its roots in the nation's domestic affairs, whose issues, tensions and discords we find reflected in the bitter controversy over war aims between the German Right and Left. There was a direct relationship, notably, between Germany's war aims and her most important domestic problem, her need for governmental reform. Bethmann Hollweg, reflecting upon his experiences as Chancellor during the World War, wrote in 1921: " Partisanship for large war aims and opposition against the so-called *Neuorientierung* usually went hand in hand. At least such a relationship developed during the course of the war." [2]

The history of Germany's war aims, therefore, covers a wide territory, much more than could be competently handled in a single volume. This, plus the fact that there are no monographs on several important subsidiary aspects of the war aims problem, necessitated a certain topical limitation.[3] But instead of treating the entire range of war aims from the vantage point of a single

---

[1] One of the most rewarding sources for the study of German war aims is the minutes of the Fourth Sub-Committee of the Parliamentary Investigating Commission, published as: Germany, Nationalversammlung,. *Das Werk des Untersuchungsausschusses,* 4. Reihe, " Die Ursachen des Deutschen Zusammenbruchs im Jahre 1918 " (12 vols., Berlin, 1925-29). Henceforth cited as *U. A.,* 4. Reihe. Of special significance is vol. XII (1) in this series: Volkmann, " Die Annexionsfragen des Weltkrieges " (Berlin, 1929). The equally important vol. XII (2) by Martin Hobohm, dealing with German Annexationist Propaganda, has never been published.

[2] Th. von Bethmann Hollweg, *Betrachtungen zum Weltkriege* (2 vols., Berlin, 1921), II, 31.

[3] There is no study, for instance, of the " Independent Committee for a German

1

group or party, it was considered more meaningful to examine only the western aspects of the question, and at the same time to make this examination as thorough and exhaustive as possible. Such a division of German aims into Eastern, Western, and Central European, has been quite common in the past; and though it holds the dangers of most over-simplifications, it still is a logical method of dealing with a very complicated subject.[4]

There already exists a study of Germany's plans for some kind of *Mitteleuropa* under her leadership.[5] As far as eastern aims are concerned, they did not really become prominent until the war was well under way, after Germany had made considerable eastward advances. From then on, the annexation of vast areas along Germany's eastern frontier became part of most expansionist programs. Yet compared to the west, much less internal disagreement was aroused and consequently much less propagandist effort was expended over these eastern aims. What controversy did arise in connection with this question was not so much over the principle of annexation as over the future organization of the eastern lands. It is this latter problem that makes Germany's eastern war aims a profitable field for further research.

Germany's wartime plans for expansion to the west (on the continent and overseas) had important repercussions both at home and abroad. Internally, the controversy over western war aims soon destroyed the unity of all classes and parties, which the outbreak of war had created. Externally, the projected annexation of western areas found strong opponents not only among those nations immediately affected, but beyond in England and the United States. These nations considered Germany's westward expansion a direct threat to their own political and economic independence. A negotiated peace between Germany and any of her western enemies was impossible, therefore, so long as her annexationists continued to adhere to their western dreams. It is because of these effects at home and abroad that Germany's western war aims have been considered more important than those involving any other region.[6]

Peace," one of the important annexationist pressure groups. Also such studies as exist of the "Pan-German League" for the war period and of the "German Fatherland Party" are highly biased.

[4] See E. R. Bevan, *German War Aims* (New York, 1918), pp. 4-13.

[5] H. C. Meyer, "Mitteleuropa Concept and Reality" (New Haven, 1942), Typescript at the Yale University Library.

[6] Dr. Bredt, "Der Deutsche Reichstag im Weltkrieg," *U.A.*, 4. Reihe, VIII, 295;

Something should be said about the term *Drang nach Westen*. It was not an expression current among World War annexationists.[7] Nor does it have the same validity which its eastern counterpart, the *Drang nach Osten*, has gained. Yet it is not an entirely arbitrary term. Germany's western, like her eastern ambitions, have their antecedents, which may be traced from the late eighteenth and early nineteenth centuries through the formative years of the German Empire into the World War and beyond. Originally this *Drang nach Westen* was exclusively cultural, nebulous in its aims and of special intensity in periods of political and intellectual unrest. During the Wars of Liberation, for instance, as during the 1840's, men like Ernst Moritz Arndt, Ludwig Jahn, Joseph Goerres, Friedrich List, Helmuth von Moltke, David Hansemann, Gustav von Höfken, and many others, looked for some sort of federation between the states of Germany and the people of " Germanic " stock in Switzerland, the Netherlands, and Denmark.[8] There were some strategic and economic reasons given for such a " re-union," but the main arguments were cultural, ethnographic, and historical. As the nineteenth century progressed, these arguments found additional support from the pseudo-scientific racial theories of Count Gobineau and Houston Stewart Chamberlain, and they continued to play a prominent part in annexationist propaganda.[9]

At the same time, the growing industrialization of Germany, the resulting quest for markets and raw materials, and the simultaneous increase of population gave added impetus to this desire for westward expansion. Bismarck's annexation of Alsace-Lorraine in 1871 for the first time contained all the elements of the *Drang nach Westen*. Historical, cultural, and strategic considerations predominated; but the economic advantages of the Lorraine iron deposits

E. Direnberger, *Oberste Heeresleitung und Reichsleitung 1914-18* (Berlin, 1936), p. 29; Max von Baden, *Erinnerungen und Dokumente* (Stuttgart, 1927), pp. 665 ff.

[7] The term may be found in the annexationist *Deutsche Tageszeitung*, Aug. 25, 1916, 2d ed.

[8] No comprehensive study has yet been made of this phase of German expansionism. The following touch on the problem: R. Haufe, *Der deutsche Nationalstaat in den Flugschriften von 1848-49* (Leipzig, 1915); O. Wagner, *Mitteleuropäische Gedanken und Bestrebungen in den vierziger Jahren 1840-1848* (Marburg, 1935); W. L. Langer, " When German Dreams Come True," *Yale Review*, XXVII (1938), 678 ff.

[9] During the World War German annexationists frequently referred back to the early nineteenth-century exponents of the *Drang nach Westen*. For examples see: W. Müller-Eberhart, *Jahn's Vermächtnis für unsere Zeit* (Berlin, 1918); also by the same author: *Ernst Moritz Arndt und der Friede* (Berlin, 1918).

were not overlooked.[10] This is not the place to go into the justification or advisability of any such plans for German westward expansion. But if viewed not merely as an extension of the Prusso-German sphere of power, but as an attempt at re-uniting and integrating political areas which historically, ethnically, geographically (especially in regard to natural lines of communication), and economically seem predestined for some kind of union, then the *Drang nach Westen* loses some of its sinister implications.

The first decades of the new German Empire saw all roads to further continental expansion closed, and the energies of a rising industrial and commercial class found its outlet largely in overseas expansion, in imperialism and *Weltpolitik*. But such expansion, no matter how much it might increase the economic strength of Germany, did nothing to increase her European basis of power. To create not merely a more prosperous but also a " Greater Germany " was the aim of the " Pan-German League " and its affiliated organizations, which developed at the turn of the century. It was these organizations that kept alive the hope for an eventual satisfaction of German land-hunger on the European continent. Because of their negligible membership and the " unrealistic " character of their aims, the Pan-Germans and their friends have not always been taken as seriously as they deserve.[11] Yet when war broke out in 1914 and the rich lands on Germany's frontiers were overrun by her victorious armies, these " unrealistic " aims suddenly seemed most realistic and possible of fulfillment. A century-old dream seemed to have come true.

While the *Drang nach Osten* was the phenomenon of an agricultural age in which land was the chief source of wealth and political power, the *Drang nach Westen* is a phenomenon of our own industrial age, in which land, though still an important commodity as such, has been surpassed in importance by mineral wealth and industrial potential.[12] Much of German pre-war history

[10] W. Bowden, M. Karpovich, A. Usher, *An Economic History of Europe since 1750* (New York, 1937), pp. 495-97.

[11] The term " Pan-German," often used to describe German annexationists in general, is used throughout this study in its strict meaning, referring to the Pan-German League. Examples of annexationist propaganda before the war may be found in: Great Britain, Foreign Office, *German Opinion on National Policy prior to July 1914*, Part I (London, 1920); M. Hobohm and P. Rohrbach, *Die Alldeutschen* (Berlin, 1919). The best available study of the Pan-German League, M. Wertheimer, *The Pan-German League 1890-1914* (New York, 1924) tends to underestimate the significance of the organization.

[12] For a suggestive, though biased, discussion of these general aspects of the *Drang nach Westen* see: W. Kundt, *Deutsche Westwanderung* (München, 1929).

can be viewed as a struggle between these two divergent movements, with the latter constantly encroaching on the former and finally becoming a formidable rival for leadership in the German Empire. The East-Elbian *Junker*, economic and political backbone of Hohenzollern Prussia and (through an antiquated political system) of Germany, at last had found his match in the western German industrialist. The latter derived his power not from birth and privilege but from education and wealth, *Bildung und Besitz*, with emphasis on the latter.

Despite their divergent interests, however, the aristocracy of blood and the aristocracy of coal and iron (ranged respectively behind the Conservative and National Liberal Parties) had much in common. In the domestic field they shared their determined opposition against the political and economic demands of the German masses. In the foreign field they shared (although for different reasons) a common hatred of Great Britain.[13] Germany's industrial and commercial interests saw England as their most dangerous competitor; while Germany's agricultural interests looked upon England as the birthplace and embodiment of that liberal and democratic tradition which threatened the maintenance of their privileges. This common opposition against Great Britain, better than anything else, explains the support which the *Drang nach Westen* of German industry, especially during the World War, found among German Conservative circles. The adherence of a party, whose main interests were in Eastern Europe, to a policy of westward expansion, shows better than anything else the deep significance of the *Drang nach Westen*. It was against England that agricultural and industrial magnates " let the dog of Pan-Germanism off its leash." Lissauer's " Hymn of Hate " against Great Britain became the battle hymn of the western annexationists.

Yet at the same time many Conservatives realized that an exclusively westward expansion would neither increase their material basis of power, nor check permanently the advance of " western " ideas in Germany. In the end it would benefit solely their commercial and industrial " allies," who hated England for economic reasons but had a hidden admiration for her political system. To maintain the existing balance between Germany's ruling classes, between industrial (and " liberal ") and agricultural (and

---

[13] P. R. Anderson, *The Background of Anti-English Feeling in Germany 1890-1902* (Washington, D. C., 1939), p. 72; E. Kehr, *Schlachtflottenbau und Parteipolitik 1894-1901* (Berlin, 1930), p. 331; E. Kehr, " Englandhass und Weltpolitik," *Zeitschrift für Politik*, XVII (1928), 515-16.

reactionary) interests, the Conservatives looked for material gains adjacent to their eastern holdings.[14] That such gains could be made only at the expense of Russia, for whom they felt a deep and implicit affinity, gave the matter a certain irony. Nor was such eastward expansion necessarily a pure blessing, as some agrarians well realized, since it would decrease the value of land and the price of agricultural produce.[15]

If we remember these facts, we understand why the terms " Easterners " and " Westerners," often applied to denote the factions in Germany favoring expansion in one or the other direction, have only partial validity. For the agricultural " Easterners " and the industrial-commercial-maritime " Westerners " each had great admiration for the governmental systems of those powers—Russia and England respectively—against whom they hoped to realize their material ambitions.

The alliance between the two groups before and during the war was but a *mariage de convenance*; it was a mutual bargain, but as such it was far from equitable. The hatred of the Conservatives for Great Britain, based not merely on ideological grounds, but on an equally important element of patriotism (Anglo-German naval rivalry, after all, was not merely a matter of commercial competition but equally one of national prestige), was not counterbalanced by any comparable feeling on the part of the National Liberals against Russia. The counterpart to the Conservatives' ideological Anglophobia, ironically enough, was the Russophobia of the Social Democrats! The " Westerners " thus received from their " Eastern " allies a great deal more than they were giving in return. Their support of the Conservative *Drang nach Osten* was much less ardent than the Conservatives' support of the industrialist *Drang nach Westen*. This, plus the fact that the liberal political philosophy of the " Westerners " appealed to a much larger section of the German people than did the reactionary attitude of the " Easterners," we must keep in mind if we want to understand the dominant position which western expansionism held throughout the war.

[14] It is not always possible, of course, to draw a sharp line between German agrarian and industrial interests. In certain regions, notably in Silesia, agrarians owned stock in industrial enterprises while industrialists owned large estates. See Anderson, p. 68.

[15] K. Jentsch in *Kunstwart* (1917), p. 141, as quoted in G. von Below, *Kriegs- und Friedensfragen* (Dresden, 1917), pp. 36-37.

CHAPTER I

THE EVOLUTION OF WESTERN WAR AIMS
(AUGUST 1914–MAY 1915)

THE GERMAN offensive against the West, based on the "Schlieffen Plan," rolled off with expected precision as soon as war was declared on August 1, 1914. Violating the neutrality of Belgium, six German infantry brigades reached Liège by August 5, and two days later took this strongest obstacle to Germany's projected encircling move. On August 18 the five armies of invasion had taken up positions and began their gigantic turning move around the pivot of Diedenhofen. Their advance in the north was marked by a succession of victorious battles, while at the same time the left wing of Germany's western army, under Crown Prince Rupprecht of Bavaria, repulsed the French in the Battle of Lorraine.[1] "Thirty-five days since mobilization," the Kaiser could boast, "and Rheims has been occupied, the French government has moved to Bordeaux, and the advance-guards of our cavalry stand fifty kilometers from Paris."[2] Yet the very same day, Germany's Commander-in-Chief, Generaloberst von Moltke, observed: "We have had successes, to be sure, but we have not won. Victory means the destruction of the enemy's power of resistance. When millions of soldiers meet, the victor should take prisoners. Where are our prisoners?"[3] This ineffectual heir to a proud military tradition had failed to carry out his great predecessor's last will. The Schlieffen Plan had failed.

After September 4, the French launched their counter-offensive, the "Battle of the Marne," climaxed by the famous "miracle," the sudden withdrawal of German forces on September 9. There followed the somewhat misnamed "race to the sea," and by the middle of October, when the Germans reached the Atlantic, warfare in the west had changed from a war of movement to a war of position.

[1] For a brief discussion of military events in 1914 see E. O. Volkmann, *Der grosse Krieg 1914-1918* (Berlin, 1938), pp. 35 ff.
[2] K. Helfferich, *Der Weltkrieg* (Berlin, 1919), p. 143.
[3] *Ibid.*

7

The Kaiser's army had failed to deliver a knock-out blow to the Allied forces, and for the next few months, in view of the added Russian pressure in the east, Germany was in a by no means enviable military position.

Yet the majority of Germans were quite unaware that things had not gone according to schedule. They believed what they saw, namely, that their armies had carried the war deep into enemy territory and had conquered vast areas—almost all of Belgium and the most valuable regions of eastern France. No wonder, then, that many Germans looked longingly towards the west. The table had been set for the annexationist feast.

The Government and Western War Aims

The declared aim of the German government at the outbreak of war was a negative one—the defense of the Fatherland. Most Germans felt that their country had become involved in a war against her will, a feeling to which the Emperor's speech on August 4 gave voice: " Not lust of conquest drives us on," he said. " We are inspired by the unalterable will to protect, for ourselves and all coming generations, the place which God has assigned to us." [4] His Chancellor, von Bethmann Hollweg, fully agreed. It had always been Germany's aim, he held, to fight only " in defense of a just cause." " The day has now come," he said, " when we must draw our sword, against our wish, and in spite of our sincere endeavors." [5] Yet at the same time, much to the dismay of German patriots, Bethmann admitted that Germany's invasion of Belgium was " a breach of international law." " The wrong—I speak frankly —the wrong we thereby commit, we will try to make good as soon as our military aims have been attained." [6] And as if to live up to his promise, Germany, on August 7, offered Belgium a peace which would not interfere with a continued war against France. But Belgium preferred to stay on the side of the Allies.[7] Germany's hopes of concluding a similar peace with a defeated France were dashed at the Marne.[8]

[4] R. H. Lutz, ed., *Fall of the German Empire* (2 vols., Stanford, 1932), I, 8.
[5] *Ibid.*, p. 10.
[6] *Ibid.*, p. 13.
[7] E. Caukin-Brunauer, " The Peace Proposals of Germany and Austria-Hungary " (Stanford, 1927), pp. 2-3. Typescript at Stanford University Library.
[8] A. von Tirpitz, *Politische Dokumente* (2 vols., Hamburg, 1926), II, 62.

The initial successes of Germany's armies in the west soon changed the official attitude of moderation. A first hint came as early as August 26, when Bethmann asked his Secretary of the Interior for a report on the French iron deposits in the Briey-Longwy region and on the extent of Germany's pre-war share in their exploitation.[9] Two weeks later, the Chancellor apparently had decided to annex these districts, together with certain strategic regions along the Franco-German border and the fortress of Belfort.[10] As far as Belgium was concerned, Bethmann's aims during these early days of the war are not quite so clear, though there is evidence that he was ready to consider the annexation of parts of northern Belgium, leaving the southern section as a buffer state between Germany and France.[11]

When it became clear in early September, however, that Germany's western offensive had failed to reach its objective, Bethmann Hollweg temporarily abandoned whatever annexationist aims he had. The disaster on the Marne had spoiled all chances for a quick military decision, and the only hope now was for a separate peace with one of Germany's adversaries, to lighten the burden of a war on two fronts. Although the Chancellor's pre-war foreign policy of rapprochement with Great Britain had proved a fiasco, Bethmann's first peace efforts in 1914 and early 1915 were directed towards England.[12] In this he had the support of most Germans, who at this time still considered Russia and not England Germany's chief enemy.[13]

The best way to achieve such a separate understanding with Great Britain, probably, was to engage first in a show of military and naval force, and then to offer an acceptable compromise, especially on the crucial question of Belgium.[14] Instead, Bethmann Hollweg not only opposed all strong measures and demonstrations against England, but he slowly maneuvered himself into a most

---

[9] *U. A.*, 4. Reihe, XII (1), 35.

[10] *Ibid.*, p. 36.

[11] Tirpitz, *Dokumente*, II, 65.

[12] Brunauer, " Peace Proposals," pp. 1 ff.; R. Stadelmann, " Friedensversuche im ersten Jahre des Weltkrieges," *Historische Zeitschrift*, CLVI (1937), 485 ff.; R. G. Swing, " First World War Peace Offer," *Esquire*, April 1939, pp. 56 ff.

[13] E. Dahlin, *French and German Public Opinion on Declared War Aims 1914-1918* (Stanford, 1933), pp. 14-17.

[14] H. Stegemann, *Erinnerungen aus meinem Leben und aus meiner Zeit* (Stuttgart, 1930), pp. 305-06.

ambiguous position on the future of Belgium.[15] A first step in this direction was the publication of documents from the Belgian archives, intended to prove that Belgium had forfeited her pre-war neutrality when she entered into military discussions with Great Britain. Published in October and November of 1914, these documents seemed to revise Bethmann's earlier admission of guilt towards Belgium.[16] At the same time, in justifying Germany's invasion of Belgium, they supplied the annexationist element with potent arguments against restoring the latter's independence. Even the more moderate groups felt indignant over the " perfidy " of Belgium and demanded that measures be taken to keep her from ever again becoming an ally of France and England.[17]

While the German people thus slowly developed an appetite for annexations, Bethmann Hollweg preferred to remain vague. On the one hand he called the Grand Duke of Oldenburg's program for the annexation of Belgium " a great mistake," and continued to be evasive on the future of eastern France; yet on the other he still insisted in a Reichstag speech of December 2 on a " stronger Germany," so powerful and secure that " no one would dare again to disturb " her peace.[18] As for other leading statesmen, their war aims during this early period were almost exclusively moderate. This was especially true of Foreign Secretary von Jagow and his chief assistant, Zimmermann, as well as of the Kaiser and his military staff.[19] Moltke, in a letter to the Emperor, recommended that Germany not expect much territory in Europe but instead extend her holdings in Central Africa.[20] Moltke's successor, General

[15] A. von Tirpitz, *Erinnerungen* (Leipzig, 1919), pp. 258 ff.

[16] *Norddeutsche Allgemeine Zeitung*, Oct. 13 and Nov. 25, 1914.

[17] *U.A.*, 4. Reihe, IV, 251-52; B. Schwertfeger, *Der geistige Kampf um die Verletzung der belgischen Neutralität* (Berlin, 1925), *passim*.

[18] *U.A.*, 4. Reihe, XII (1), 36; C. Haussmann, *Schlaglichter* (Frankfurt a. M., 1924), p. 14; A. Rechberg, *Reichsniedergang* (München, 1919), p. 28; F. Thimme, ed., *Bethmann Hollwegs Kriegsreden* (Stuttgart, 1919), pp. 14, 23.

[19] Graf J. H. Bernstorff, *Deutschland und Amerika* (Berlin, 1920), pp. 118-19; Haussmann, p. 17; H. Kanner, " The Papers of Dr. Heinrich Kanner " (3 vols. of typescript at Hoover Library, Stanford, Cal.), II, 65, 92; Bethmann Hollweg, II, 18; Ch. Seymour, *The Intimate Papers of Colonel House* (4 vols., N. Y., 1926), I, 371, 391; Tirpitz, *Dokumente*, II, 176; M. Hoffmann, *Die Aufzeichnungen des Generalmajors Max Hoffmann* (2 vols., Berlin, 1930), I, 64, 69; Rupprecht von Bayern, *Mein Kriegstagebuch* (2 vols., München, 1929), I, 332; L. Ganghofer, *Reise zur Deutschen Front* (Berlin, 1915), pp. 48-49.

[20] G. von Moltke, *Erinnerungen, Briefe, Dokumente 1877-1916* (Stuttgart, 1922), p. 412.

von Falkenhayn, repeatedly expressed concern over the people's optimism and stressed the vast difficulties still ahead.[21] Similar views were held on the eastern front by Hindenburg and Hoffmann.[22] Only Admiral von Tirpitz, eagerly awaiting an opportunity to use his navy against Great Britain, came forth with a series of annexationist demands: Antwerp, the Flanders coast, and a substantial colonial empire (as additional *raison d'être* for a powerful German fleet).[23]

Such colonial war aims, though strictly speaking in a separate category, are often included in continental annexationist programs. But while almost all western annexationists advocated some degree of colonial expansion, many people in favor of such expansion did by no means favor annexations in Western Europe as well. To many Germans the western conquests were a kind of pawn (*Faustpfand*), to be exchanged at a future peace conference against the former German colonies (most of which had fallen into allied hands soon after the outbreak of war) plus some additional colonial holdings. The most noted representative of this group was the Colonial Secretary, Wilhelm Solf. He was opposed to German annexations on the continent, but throughout the war he stressed the need for a larger colonial empire in Africa, advocating a general re-distribution of all colonial holdings on that continent.[24] These colonial aims found wide support among annexationists of all classes, especially from members of the *Deutsche Kolonialgesellschaft*.[25]

The declared war aims of Germany's statesmen during the first months of war, as these examples show, were on the whole moderate. But this does not exclude the existence of more detailed and far-reaching plans for the future of Western Europe. In October of 1914 the Prussian Minister of the Interior, von Loebell, wrote a lengthy memorandum on the future peace settlement; and in December a similar document was prepared by Germany's Secretary

---

[21] K. Westarp, *Konservative Politik im letzten Jahrzehnt des Kaiserreiches* (2 vols., Berlin, 1935), II, 93.

[22] Hoffmann, *Aufzeichnungen*, I, 69, 180.

[23] Tirpitz, *Dokumente*, II, 58-59, 65, 144-5, 179; Tirpitz, *Erinnerungen*, pp. 422, 440; see also *Dokumente*, II, 142 for similar views of Admiral von Pohl, the navy's representative with the Supreme Command.

[24] *U..A.*, 4. Reihe, XII (1), 36; S. Grumbach, *Das annexionistische Deutschland* (Lausanne, 1917), pp. 9-10.

[25] Dahlin, p. 69; Hoffmann, *Aufzeichnungen*, I, 64; Westarp, II, 46; *Vorwärts*, May 28, 1915.

of the Interior, Clemens von Delbrück, and Under-Secretary Zimmermann.[26] Both memoranda are important steps in the evolution of western war aims.

Von Loebell looked upon France and England rather than Russia as Germany's natural enemies, and demanded that these two be weakened as much as possible. To become a truly great world power, Germany, according to Loebell, had to strengthen her continental position against England and at the same time gain unconditional freedom of the seas, defensible colonies, and the necessary naval stations to maintain overseas communications. As far as Western Europe was concerned, France had to be beaten and rendered harmless once and for all. Strategic frontier rectifications, surrender of her coal and iron districts, and a high indemnity would bring about such permanent weakening. As to Belgium, her fate depended largely on the outcome of Germany's conflict with England. Only by the defeat of England could Germany hope to keep Belgium. But this possibility von Loebell doubted, because he realized that England would fight to the very last against a German annexation of the Lowlands. The final contest would thus be postponed, though it was inevitable. " Great Britain now has pitted her vital interests against ours. She is the enemy with whom sooner or later we shall have to force a showdown; because she will never tolerate at her side a strong Germany, actively engaged in world affairs." [27]

The idea that the World War was only the preliminary step in the final overthrow of Great Britain, the " First Punic War " as the Kaiser called it, was quite current among German annexationists. Its proponents suggested that Germany should first of all strengthen and consolidate her position on the continent, thus preparing herself for the final bout with England. Such continental strength had to be won at the expense not only of France but of Russia as well; and to achieve this it might even be necessary—as Bethmann Hollweg had tried—to come to a temporary understanding with England, so as to be able to concentrate all forces against the east. But at the same time there were other annexationists who felt that Germany could defeat England and thus take her place as a world power in this first world war. To these exponents of the

[26] U. A., 4. Reihe, XII (1), 36, 187 ff., 193 ff.
[27] U. A., 4. Reihe, XII (1), 188.

Drang nach Westen England was the immediate enemy, the *Haupt-feind*, and they advocated a separate peace with Russia to make possible a concentration of forces against the West. Throughout the war, the question of who could best be annihilated first and who best appeased temporarily, England or Russia, played an important part in Germany's debate on war aims.[28]

Of still greater interest than von Loebell's memorandum were the proposals of Delbrück and Zimmermann for " the treatment of Belgium in case of a decisive German victory." Written at the request of the Chancellor, the general idea of the memorandum was to find a way short of open annexation by which Belgium could be put completely under German domination. As a result this document (which should be viewed as an impartial report rather than a manifestation of the two Secretaries' war aims) stands as the most specific elaboration of the expression " military and economic guarantees," through which Germany hoped to maintain her influence over Belgium.

The main purpose of German " military guarantees," according to Delbrück and Zimmermann, should be to make sure that Belgium would never again serve as a· base of operations against Germany. To prevent this, the following measures were suggested:

(1) All fortresses, the whole Belgian coast and its defenses, must remain under German control. The same applied to all means of transportation and communication.

(2) In addition, Belgium must give up her army. The money she thus saved could be used to maintain Germany's army of occupation.

(3) German military domination of Belgium also required certain limitations of Belgian sovereignty. German troops must be subject to their own jurisdiction. There must be no independent foreign policy for Belgium, and in internal matters Germany must have a veto over all laws and administrative acts conflicting with her military interests. Under certain conditions the Kaiser must have power to decree martial law for all or part of Belgium.

So much for Germany's military control. What little freedom Belgium retained would be taken away through " economic penetration." This would involve the following measures:

[28] For a discussion of this problem see S. Eggert, " Die deutschen Eroberungspläne im ersten Weltkrieg," *Neue Welt*, II (1947), 45-47

(1) Belgium must join the German customs union as a non-voting member.

(2) The Belgian system of rail- and waterways must be closely integrated with that of Germany.

(3) Germany's monetary system must be extended to Belgium.

(4) To impose identical burdens on German and Belgian industries (preventing unfavorable competition which might result from a customs union) Germany must introduce her system of taxation and social legislation into Belgium.

Here, in brief outline, we have the 1914 version of Germany's "New Order" for Belgium. It is the clearest and most ruthless official definition of "veiled annexation" available for the period of the World War. In comparison, as a memorandum from the Ministry of Public Works pointed out, "complete annexation appears as a milder form of securing influence." [29] At the time it was drafted, of course, this memorandum was a mere theoretical discussion of a possible solution in case of complete German victory. But before long, references to this type of solution began to appear in Bethmann Hollweg's statements on war aims. In the spring of 1915, for instance, the Socialist Deputy Scheidemann, alarmed by the widespread annexationist propaganda, asked the Chancellor about his plans for the future of Belgium. Bethmann in reply clearly dissociated himself from the wild schemes of the Pan-German annexationists and assured Scheidemann that he had no intention of annexing Belgium.

I imagine that we might obtain closer economic relations with Belgium and, perhaps, also agreements of a military kind; and if I should succeed in obtaining a slight adjustment of the frontier in the Vosges which now runs below the crest of the range, that in itself would be of great importance, just as the dismantling of Belfort would be, if we could obtain it. We have had to make terrible sacrifices on those parts of the frontier.[30]

Note the reference to closer economic and military agreements. As Bethmann's stand against outright annexation of Belgium became known in annexationist circles, Count Westarp (leading Conser-

---

[29] *U. A.*, 4. Reihe, XII (1), 22, note 1.

[30] Ph. Scheidemann, *Memoiren eines Sozialdemokraten* (2 vols., Dresden, 1928), I, 350-51. Bethmann, at the time, seemed genuinely disturbed over the growing annexationist sentiment: R. von Valentini, *Kaiser und Kabinettschef* (Oldenburg, 1931), pp. 226-27.

vative in the Reichstag) wrote him a worried note, asking for further clarification. The Chancellor's reply, according to Westarp, left nothing to be desired. It did object to the annexation of large areas in northern France; but the statements on Belgium went further than those made to Scheidemann:

If a lasting peace is to be won, Belgium must be rendered harmless. We must gain military, political [!] and economic guarantees that England or France will not be able to use Belgium against us in future political controversies. Such guarantees require at least [!] the military and economic dependence of that country upon Germany.[31]

To make completely sure of the Chancellor's position, a delegation of deputies from the annexationist parties of the Right and Center visited Bethmann on May 13, 1915, to request a definite statement on the government's war aims. The similarity between the Chancellor's views expressed on this occasion and the Delbrück-Zimmermann Memorandum is unmistakable. " Belgium," he said, " must be rendered harmless, she must become Germany's vassal state." Here is Count Westarp's summary of the statement:

Occupation of the whole country and complete economic domination. His statement did not make it quite clear whether he was thinking of political independence, i. e. some kind of federal relationship, or of annexation, the latter in any case without conferring any political rights. Economically, the Chancellor is considering a customs union, German influence over [railway?] rates—the acquisition of railways he considers difficult, since 80,000 German employees would have to be moved to Belgium—complete economic domination over the port of Antwerp, introduction of German civil law, legal procedure (doubtful) and social legislation, to ensure to German industry the ability of competing with that of Belgium. . . . Imposition of German Imperial laws, administration through one or several military governors.[32]

In regard to France, Bethmann did not go quite so far as the annexationist deputies should have liked to see, though his statement to the effect that " France had to be weakened as much as possible, regardless of any later sentiment in the matter " recalls the tone of the Loebell Memorandum. The Chancellor also intended

---

[31] Westarp, II, 46-50; see also Under-Secretary Wahnschaffe's reassuring letter to the Pan-German Franz von Bodelschwingh, who had expressed similar concern over Bethmann's weak aims in regard to Belgium: F. von Bodelschwingh, *Innere Hemmungen kraftvoller Aussenpolitik* (Hannover, 1919), p. 44.

[32] Westarp, II, 37, 51-52.

to take the ore region of Briey and Longwy, the fortress of Belfort, and to require some small rectifications of the Vosges frontier. Count Westarp's general impression of Bethmann's aims was that they were essentially the same as his own. Yet the Count, as we shall see, was one of the most radical German annexationists.

Up to this point, all of Bethmann's statements on the future of Western Europe had been made in private. The first public pronouncement on the subject did not come until May 28, five days after Italy had declared war on Austria-Hungary. " We must persevere," he said in an address to the Reichstag, " until we have created and won for ourselves all possible real guarantees and securities that none of our enemies . . . will again dare to engage us in armed conflict." [33] This statement certainly was ambiguous enough; yet both the Reichstag and the German press applauded it as an acknowledgment of Germany's need for annexations. " The demonstrative applause which this statement found among all bourgeois parties," the Socialist *Leipziger Volkszeitung* wrote on May 29, " made it plain to everybody that the Chancellor has now come out in favor of some sort of annexationist policy and has thus revoked his declaration of August 4, 1914." [34]

The significant change that Bethmann Hollweg's attitude on the future of Western Europe underwent, at least outwardly, during the first ten months of war, was the direct result of external and internal factors. Externally, this period proved the futility of Germany's first attempts at a negotiated peace. The history of the various peace moves is too intricate to be discussed here. [35] It is sufficient to say that the first efforts, between September 1914 and April 1915, primarily directed at England, were unsuccessful. [36] " If there were possibilities of peace during the first months of 1915," Bethmann wrote in 1921, " which I personally doubt, then surely at the most for a peace based on the *status quo ante*, with reparations for Belgium, that is, for just the opposite of the programs

[33] Thimme, p. 35.

[34] For similar press comments from Right to Left see: *Deutsche Tageszeitung*, May 29, 1915; *Post*, May 29, 1915; *Kreuzzeitung*, May 30, 1915; *Vorwärts*, June 1, 1915.

[35] For a discussion of the subject see K. Forster, *The Failures of Peace* (Washington, D. C., 1941).

[36] R. Stadelmann, " Friedensversuche im ersten Jahre des Weltkrieges," *Historische Zeitschrift*, CLVI (1937), 498-516.

proclaimed at that time." [37] To give up a country whose past neutrality was doubted and whose future neutrality was doubtful, would have aroused "the most bitter feeling among the German people." Yet this very thing, plus a possible indemnity to Belgium was the *conditio sine qua non* for England's willingness to discuss peace.[38]

When by spring and early summer of 1915 negotiations in the west had proved unsuccessful, similar moves were made towards Russia. These moves, significantly enough, coincided with Bethmann's change of attitude towards Belgium. But despite continuous German military successes in the east, these moves were likewise condemned to failure.[39] The more important reasons for Bethmann's change, however, are to be found in the German domestic scene. Here the Chancellor was subjected to the pressure of a public opinion which became increasingly annexationist during this early period. To a study of this pressure, both spontaneous and artificially stimulated, we must turn for a real understanding of Bethmann's change of position.

The Reichstag and Western War Aims

Because of the strict censorship imposed on the discussion of war aims soon after the outbreak of war, it is difficult to determine the extent of annexationist sentiment among the German people. Contemporary observers agree, however, that most Germans soon abandoned their passive attitude of the first days of war and demanded the annexation of enemy territory, especially in Western Europe. These popular aims, however, were nebulous at first and had to undergo a formative period of several months before they crystallized into a series of definite demands. To understand these German hopes for annexations, we must remember the apparent military successes of the first months of war, the publication of Belgian documents already mentioned, and the sanguinary character of warfare in Belgium which cost the lives of many German soldiers. To give up "the soil which had been won with so much German blood," many Germans felt, would be ungrateful to the soldiers who gave their lives to secure it.[40]

---

[37] Bethmann Hollweg, II, 26-27.
[38] *Ibid.*, p. 27; Brunauer, "Peace Proposals," pp. 13 ff.
[39] Forster, pp. 21 ff.; Stadelmann, *Historische Zeitschrift,* CLVI, 516 ff.
[40] Bethmann Hollweg, II, 27.

The influence of this annexationist opinion on the conduct of the German government is difficult to measure. In Germany people had even less direct influence in governmental affairs than elsewhere, and even the voice of their elected representatives in the Reichstag played only a small part in the formation of policy, at least until the pressure of events forced the government to make some concessions in the course of the war. But despite its lack of direct power, the Reichstag debates remained the most significant single expression of public opinion in the country.

The Kaiser's words on August 4, 1914: "I no longer know parties, I only know Germans," and the Socialist vote for the war budget, these two events symbolized the closing of a long-standing gulf between Germany's classes and masses.[41] But this *Burgfriede* was a truce rather than a peace; it did nothing to remove some of the most blatant political injustices, and its days were numbered from the start. The first event to disturb this precarious domestic peace, significantly enough, was the controversy over war aims.

The majority of Social Democrats, true to their ideals of universal peace and international conciliation, soon adopted a more or less consistent stand against annexations and in favor of a " peace of understanding " or a " Scheidemann Peace " as it was called after its leading proponent. They had made clear this stand as early as August 4 in a declaration which said: " We demand that, as soon as the aim of protection shall have been attained and the enemies be inclined toward peace, the war be ended by a peace which shall render possible friendship with our neighbors." [42] But we must not assume that this Socialist opinion was predominant among the German people or even its lower classes this early in the war.[43] Even a number of Socialists soon began to modify their views, though the party itself reiterated its earlier stand on several later occasions.[44] Beginning in late September, several members began to express approval of annexationist aims and by March 22, 1915, the Socialist *Frankfurter Volksstimme* held that " the renunciation of all demands of annexation is in itself not a serviceable program.

[41] Lutz, *German Empire*, I, 9.
[42] *Ibid.*, p. 16.
[43] *U. A.*, 4. Reihe, XII (1), 34; V, 97; Scheidemann, *Memoiren*, I, 260.
[44] Germany, Reichstag, *Verhandlungen des Reichstages*, XIII. Legislaturperiode, II. Sitzung, Stenographischer Bericht (henceforth cited as *Reichstag*), vol. 306, p. 21; Scheidemann, *Memoiren*, I, 370.

Social Democracy must put forward positive demands, and these demands can and must include modification in maps. All must not remain as it was." [45] There was Paul Lensch, for instance, Socialist Reichstag deputy and editor of the hyperradical *Leipziger Volkszeitung*, who in 1914 had voted against war credits; then suddenly his position changed—he wrote a book *Weltkrieg und Sozialdemokratie* in which he defended the government's war policy, and later in the war he joined his fellow socialists Haenisch and Winnig (who had undergone a similar change of heart) in the editorship of a Socialist periodical with annexationist leanings, *Die Glocke*, financed by the enigmatic "Parvus" Helphand. The end of Lensch's leftist affiliations came in 1925, when he was made editor of the nationalist *Deutsche Allgemeine Zeitung*.[46] The Socialist trade unions were equally reluctant to declare themselves against any and all annexations, considering the close community of interests between the working class and heavy industry, both of whom stood to gain from annexations in the west.[47]

Besides these right-wing, annexationist Socialists (sometimes called "Imperial Socialists") there developed, in the course of the war, two left-wing factions within the Socialist Party. The smaller and more radical one, under Karl Liebknecht and Rosa Luxemburg, not only was violently opposed to annexations, but hoped to stir up the lower classes against the annexationists of the Right, using the resulting discontent and disorder for the overthrow of the Hohenzollern regime. These "Spartacists," as they were later called, never became very influential and their activities were seriously curtailed by government interference in the spring of 1915.[48] The other, less radical group, rallied around Haase, Bernstein, and Breitscheid. They were just as strongly opposed to annexations as the Liebknecht group, but advocated protests and strikes rather than outright violence.[49] We shall see how this second group finally seceded and formed its own Independent Socialist Party.

[45] H. Ströbel, *Die deutsche Revolution* (Berlin, 1922), p. 16; Grumbach, pp. vi-vii, 111.

[46] A. Winnig, *Der weite Weg* (Hamburg, 1938), pp. 339 ff.; Scheidemann, *Memoiren*, I, 254. On Helphand see K. Haenisch, *Parvus* (Berlin, 1925).

[47] Grumbach, p. 118; A. Mendelssohn Bartholdy, *The War and German Society—The Testament of a Liberal* (New Haven, 1937), p. 221.

[48] Forster, p. 24; Grumbach, p. 432.

[49] *U. A.*, 4. Reihe, XII (1), 59.

The attitude of the bourgeois parties of the Reichstag was neither as moderate nor as consistent as that of the Socialists. Most of them refrained from definite statements on war aims this early in the war; though the declarations of their leaders and newspapers made it perfectly plain where they stood. The majority of the Progressive Party took a middle course between extreme annexationism and renunciation of all territorial expansion. Some members like Heckscher, Wiemer, Müller-Meiningen, and Pachnicke were definitely for large annexations, while others like Dove, von Payer, Gothein, and Haussmann were opposed to all but colonial aggrandizement and small frontier rectifications.[50] The Center Party during this period was, on the whole, annexationist, although there was a moderate faction as early as 1915.[51] Its chief organ, the *Kölnische Volkszeitung*, and its most influential member, Mathias Erzberger, because of their close ties with the industrialist Thyssen, were extremely annexationist. The case of Erzberger is an example of the clever methods employed by German industrial interests to further their territorial ambitions. Through native intelligence and extreme diligence, Erzberger had created for himself a position of great but hidden influence.[52] Alfred Hugenberg called him " the most powerful man in Berlin. With his recommendation one gets everywhere, without it one gets nowhere." [53] It is not surprising, then, that old August Thyssen, leading Ruhr industrialist and member of the Center Party, chose Erzberger to present his annexationist plans to the German government. Officially the Erzberger-Thyssen affiliation did not begin until June 1915, when the Centrist deputy, for a salary of 40,000 marks, joined Thyssen's board

[50] H. Ostfeld, *Die Haltung der Reichstagsfraktion der Fortschrittlichen Volkspartei zu den Annexions-und Friedensfragen in den Jahren 1914-1918* (Kallmünz, 1934), Diss. Würzburg, pp. 10-11; *Vorwärts*, Oct. 23, 1914; Grumbach, pp. 104-05.

[51] F. Wacker, *Die Haltung der Deutschen Zentrumspartei zur Frage der Kriegsziele im Weltkrieg 1914-1918* (Lohr, 1937), Diss. Würzburg, pp. 5-6; Haussmann, p. 31.

[52] Besides being a leading member of his party, Erzberger ran a semi-official, government-supported propaganda agency in Berlin; he went on secret missions to Rome and Vienna, tried to buy a French newspaper during the war, and was instrumental in Bethmann Hollweg's dismissal in 1917. See M. Erzberger, *Erlebnisse im Weltkrieg* (Stuttgart, 1920), pp. 1 ff., 41 ff., 110 ff.; *U. A.*, 4. Reihe, VII (2), 108-09.

[53] H. Class, *Wider den Strom* (Leipzig, 1932), p. 329. There are a number of character sketches of Erzberger, mostly unfavorable: " A " [Adolf Stein], *Gerichtstage über Erzberger* (Berlin, 1920); Wacker, pp. 28-29; for a more favorable view see M. Harden, *Köpfe* (4 vols., Berlin, 1924), IV, 431 ff.

of directors.[54] But already on September 2, 1914, Erzberger had drafted a memorandum for the government which set forth the following minimum aims for a German peace: Military domination over Belgium, the French coast to Boulogne, and the Channel Islands; German annexation of the region of Briey-Longwy and the fortress of Belfort; large annexations in the East; an extensive German colonial empire in Central Africa; and finally a high indemnity to repay Germany's war costs.[55] There is no proof for Erzberger's later claims that he withdrew this memorandum soon after he had written it; though his subsequent public utterances on war aims were somewhat less radical.[56]

The further we move to the Right, the more annexationist Germany's parties become. The National Liberals, party of big business and heavy industry, refrained from any very specific statement on war aims and merely declared " that the tremendous results of our incomparable army and our death-defying fleet must be fully utilized politically." [57] Their leaders, however, were somewhat more specific. Professor Hermann Paasche, Vice-President of the Reichstag and connected with numerous industrial concerns, refused " to give up the enemy territory conquered with so much German blood." [58] The head of the party, the lawyer Ernst Bassermann, who had been very pessimistic at the outbreak of war but had changed his mind after Germany's military successes, made several almost identical statements.[59] Of special interest is an address by Gustav Stresemann, which stressed the favorite Pan-German idea that England was the *Hauptfeind*. Stresemann demanded expansion to the east and west, especially the annexation of the Channel coast, including Calais! Like Paasche, Bassermann and Stresemann were closely tied up with industrial interests.[60]

---

[54] *Erzberger gegen Helfferich* (Berlin, n. d.), pp. 13-14, 18-20, 22-23; S. Löwenstein, *Der Prozess Erzberger-Helfferich* (Ulm, 1921), *passim*.

[55] Tirpitz, *Dokumente*, II, 69 ff.

[56] Erzberger, p. 228; Westarp, II, 53; *Allgemeine Rundschau*, XI (1914), 709; *Der Rote Tag*, March 28, 1915, as cited in *U. A.*, 4. Reihe, XII (1), 67.

[57] D. Schäfer, *Der Krieg 1914-16, 1916-18* (Leipzig, 1916-20), II, 5; Grumbach, p. 38; P. Fuhrmann, *Das deutsche Volk und die gegenwärtige Kriegslage* (n. pl, n. d.).

[58] *Chronik des Deutschen Krieges*, IV, 422-23.

[59] *U. A.*, 4. Reihe, VII (2), 215; *Vorwärts*, Dec. 5, 1914; *Hamburger Fremdenblatt*, April 9, 1915.

[60] G. Stresemann, *Deutsches Ringen und Deutsches Hoffen* (Berlin, 1914); *Vorwärts*, Feb. 17, 1915. For annexationist views in the Nat. Lib. press see *Freiburger Tageblatt*, March 4, 1915; *Leipziger Neueste Nachrichten*, May 17, 1915.

On the extreme Right, both Conservative Parties, the smaller and less important Free Conservative Party as well as the main German Conservative Party, were openly annexationist. The former worked in close collaboration with the Pan-German League, and its leader, Baron von Zedlitz-Neukirch, expressed hope for indemnities and other compensations, such as the iron deposits of French Lorraine.[61] The German Conservatives, on the other hand, remained vague in their public statements on war aims, and although keeping in touch with the Pan-German League, they refused to endorse its far-reaching program. The two leading Conservatives, von Heydebrand und der Lasa and Count Westarp, opposed premature declarations of German war aims and refused to consider areas as possible annexations before they had been conquered.[62] Heydebrand merely asked for " securities worthy of our sacrifices," and Westarp demanded " free access to the sea." [63] In a memorandum to Bethmann Hollweg, the latter became somewhat more specific. " Belgium," he held, " must be permanently and securely kept in our hands . . ." as a protection against England and France. " This can only be achieved through far-reaching political and economic attachment (*Angliederung*) ." Westarp's letter ended in the veiled threat: " A government which, without urgent necessity . . . relinquishes Belgium, will lose the support of the largest and best sections of the German people and thus endanger the monarchy and the future of our country." [64]   Other Conservatives—notably von Grumme-Douglas, Prince Salm-Horstmar, Roesicke, and von Gebsattel—went even further in their demands; while the Conservative members of the Prussian Upper House, men like Counts Schulenburg, Groeben, and Seidlitz, were more moderate.[65]

To sum up briefly the attitudes of the various political parties towards war aims, we may say that there was a definite divergence between the non-annexationist stand of most of the Social Democrats and the more or less annexationist programs of the remaining parties. This divergence of opinion first came into the open after

[61] Class, *Strom,* pp. 358-60; Grumbach, pp. 50-53.

[62] Westarp, II, 43, 45-46; O. Hoetzsch, *Der Krieg und die grosse Politik* (2 vols., Leipzig, 1917-18), I, 86-87.

[63] Westarp, II, 41; Grumbach, p. 46; *Vorwärts,* April 7, 1915; for similar views by other leading Conservatives see *Vorwärts,* Jan. 3, 1915, Jan. 30, 1915.

[64] Westarp, II, 46; see also his Reichstag speech on May 29, 1915 in *Reichstag,* vol. 306, p. 172.

[65] Westarp, II, 309-11.

the Chancellor's Reichstag address of December 2, 1914.[66] On the one hand the Socialists, through their spokesman Haase, declared that the facts which had become known since the publication of Belgian documents, in the opinion of the Social Democrats, " did not justify any change of attitude in regard to Belgium and Luxemburg from that taken by the Chancellor on August 4." [67] The bourgeois parties, on the other hand, in a declaration read by the leader of the Center Party, Peter Spahn, made veiled allusions to an indemnity for the sacrifices of war: " In this most difficult of all wars, wantonly forced upon us, we shall hold out until we have won a peace which corresponds to the immense sacrifices made by the German people. It must give us lasting protection against all enemies." [68]

The controversy thus begun between Socialist and bourgeois parties was continued in similarly vague statements by Haase and Spahn in the Reichstag session of March 10, 1915.[69] The following day, in a closed meeting of the Budget Committee, the issue emerged somewhat more clearly. While the Socialists opposed annexations of any kind, and the Progressives declared the whole discussion premature, the remaining parties all came out in favor of more or less far-reaching war aims. The National Liberal Bassermann demanded radical corrections of Germany's western frontier, but left the annexation of Belgium open. Gröber, for the Center Party, wanted " veiled annexation " of Belgium through military and economic penetration. Westarp was for outright annexation.[70]

The Chancellor's speech of May 28, in which he demanded for the first time " real guarantees and securities " for Germany's future was followed the next day by declarations much like those of December 2 and March 10.[71] By now the annexationist parties— National Liberals, Conservatives, and the Center Party (occasionally joined by the Progressives) had formed a definite parliamentary bloc, a *Kriegszielmehrheit* (as Westarp calls it) in favor of expansionist war aims. This bloc, deciding on a course of action in each case, worked together until the end of 1916 and was able to wield

[66] Thimme, *Bethmann Hollweg*, pp. 13 ff.
[67] *Reichstag*, vol. 306, p. 21; *U.A.*, 4. Reihe, VIII, 54.
[68] *Ibid.*, p. 55.
[69] *Ibid.*, p. 56; *Reichstag*, vol. 306, pp. 47-48.
[70] Haussmann, p. 31; Westarp, II, 54.
[71] *Reichstag*, vol. 306, pp. 172 ff.; Grumbach, p. 69; Westarp, II, 56.

considerable influence.[72] We have already seen it in operation on May 13, when Bassermann, Spahn, Baron von Gamp (Free Conservative) and Count Westarp brought its views before the Chancellor with the, apparently successful, intention of converting him to annexationism. Here, then, in the *Kriegszielmehrheit* of the German Reichstag, we have one of the pressure-groups which help account for Bethmann's change of position during the first year of the war.[73]

The Pan-German League

A much more important factor than the Parliamentary *Kriegszielmehrheit* in the evolution and propagation of western war aims was a number of small but influential groups outside the Reichstag. Collectively these groups have been referred to as the *Kriegszielbewegung* to express the close collaboration among different annexationist groups and individuals in the hope of influencing the policy of the German government. There was often considerable overlapping between this *Kriegszielbewegung* and the *Kriegszielmehrheit*, since the members of both had identical social and economic backgrounds. Among the various forces that went into the making of the *Kriegszielbewegung*, two stand out most prominently—the Pan-German League and the great industrialists of Western Germany.

The League was founded in 1890 by a group which included the future director of Krupp's, Alfred Hugenberg. It had been led, since 1908, by Heinrich Class, who is best characterized by his deep admiration for Treitschke, from whom he inherited the anti-semitism which he made part of the Pan-German program.[74] When asked by von Heydebrand, why he did not join the Conservative Party, Class replied: " Because the Conservative Party is too democratic for my taste." [75] The membership of the Pan-German League

[72] *Ibid.*, II, 52-54.

[73] In both Houses of the Prussian Diet the majority was equally in favor of strong war aims. See *U.A.*, 4. Reihe, V, 61; *Vorwärts*, March 25, 1915; Grumbach, p. 43; Graf von Schwerin-Löwitz, *Kriegsreden-und Aufsätze* (Berlin, 1916), pp. 8, 10, 39 ff.

[74] Class, *Strom*, pp. 15-16, 87; see also p. 131 for Class' relations with Professor Schemann, propagator of Gobineau's racial theories.

[75] Class, *Strom*, p. 267; see also Class' anonymous, highly anti-democratic books: " Einhart," *Deutsche Geschichte* (Leipzig, 1909), and " Daniel Frymann," *Wenn ich der Kaiser wär'* (Leipzig, 1912).

usually fluctuated between 15-25,000, but during the war it increased considerably until by 1917 it numbered some 34,000. It was not so much its size, however, but the social and economic position of its members which gave the League its importance. They were drawn almost exclusively from the upper bourgeoisie and nobility, with a majority of teachers, professors, industrialists, business and professional men. Various attempts to gain a following among the lower classes had proved unsuccessful.[76] The importance of the League was further increased through a number of subsidiary and allied organizations, numbering 84 in 1914. Often these organizations were founded by Pan-Germans themselves, and though nominally independent, they worked in close co-operation with the League. Among these organizations were the Army League, the Navy League, the Association against Social Democracy, and the Association for Germans abroad (*V. D. A.*). The leaders of most of these groups held prominent positions in the Pan-German League, and their members increased its direct and indirect following to over 100,000.[77]

The League had no daily paper, but among its members were the editors of some of the most important German dailies—Reismann-Grone of the industrialist *Rheinisch-Westphälische Zeitung,* Rippler of the *Tägliche Rundschau,* Pohl of the industrialist *Post,* and Liman of the *Leipziger Neueste Nachrichten.* During the war a group headed by Class bought the *Deutsche Zeitung* and made it into an organ of annexationist propaganda. There were also a number of Pan-German journals—the official *Alldeutsche Blätter, Das grössere Deutschland* under Bacmeister, the *Deutsche Zeitschrift,* and several anti-semitic magazines—*Die Nornen, Heimdall, Der Hammer,* and *Deutschlands Erneuerung.*[78]

Politically, the League's main support came from the National Liberals (notably Gustav Stresemann), and only secondarily from the Conservatives. In 1916 fifteen of its members sat in the Reichstag, among them eight National Liberals and three Conservatives. Its strength in the western, more highly industralized regions of

---

[76] L. Werner, *Der Alldeutsche Verband* (Berlin, 1935), pp. 43, 62, 64, 287; Wertheimer, p. 214; W. Wenck, *Alldeutsche Taktik* (Jena, 1917), p. 29.

[77] Wertheimer, p. 237; Class, *Strom,* pp. 221, 273; *U. A.,* 4. Reihe, XII (1), 49; " Junius Alter " [Franz Sontag], *Nationalisten* (Leipzig, 1930), pp. 16-17; *Handbuch des Alldeutschen Verbandes* (Mainz, 1914), pp. 56 ff.

[78] Wenck, p. 24; Werner, pp. 77-78.

Germany, was greater than in the agricultural east. The majority
of its members were Protestants.[79]

This brief survey of the Pan-German League shows that it was
not a popular movement but a pressure group, the " shock troop
of German nationalism," the " national conscience of the German
people." [80] One of its most active members, the publicist Franz
Sontag, close friend of Class' and editor of the *Alldeutsche Blätter*,
refers to the League as the " germ-cell " of post-war German nationalism. " Whoever holds a prominent position in our national or
völkisch movement today [i. e. 1930] belonged, with few exceptions,
at one time to the Pan-German League, or at least maintained close
relations with the League and its leaders." [81]

While the majority of Germans had no very clearly defined war
aims at the outbreak of war, the Pan-Germans could draw upon a
vast array of pre-war plans and writings; they constituted a kind
of " general staff for war aims propaganda," which carried its aims
into the war and was received enthusiastically by the parties of the
Right.[82] Immediately upon the outbreak of war, while the government was still talking of a " war of defense," a special edition of the
Alldeutsche Blätter on August 3, 1914, already called the war " a
struggle for our greater future " which " cannot end through a weak
compromise." [83] Right afterwards, Class and his chief assistant in
the administration of the League, Baron von Vietinghoff-Scheel,
began to work on an outline of Pan-German war aims. By August
28, barely four weeks after the outbreak of war, they were ready to
call a meeting of the League's Executive Committee, to discuss
these aims.[84] In his opening address Class launched an impassioned
attack upon those individuals and groups most hated by the Pan-
Germans. Besides Bethmann Hollweg, these included " the bankers,
the socialists, the intellectuals, and the Jews." Class particularly
bemoaned the possibility of Prussian electoral reform in the direction of greater democracy, as propagated by these people. Such
reform, Class held, would mean the loss of the war on the home

[79] *Handbuch des Alldeutschen Verbandes* (Mainz, 1916), p. 39; Class, *Strom*,
pp. 240, 355-56; Werner, p. 66.

[80] " Junius Alter," *Nationalisten*, p. 15; Class, *Strom*, p. 306.

[81] " Junius Alter," *Nationalisten*, p. 13; F. W. Heinz, *Die Nation greift an* (Berlin,
1933), pp. 178-79.

[82] *U. A.*, 4. Reihe, VII (1), 378.

[83] *Alldeutsche Blätter*, Sondernummer, Aug. 3, 1914.

[84] Class, *Strom*, p. 319.

front. The only means of counteracting and silencing the proponents of these reforms was a far-reaching movement in favor of annexations, diverting people's attention from domestic to foreign affairs.[85] Here we have a first example of the close relationship between the problems of war aims and domestic reforms. To most German annexationists, a "Greater Germany" seemed necessary not only for military and economic reasons, but because it helped to justify and maintain the existing political order. "The monarchist," according to Count Westarp, "was afraid that the radicalization which had to be expected after the war, would assume dangerous proportions, if the returning soldier found nothing but an increased tax bill as a reward for his deeds. He might easily think that the government of the Empire did not know sufficiently well how to make use of our military successes."[86] The result of such widespread disappointment might be revolution and the overthrow of the Hohenzollern regime. We shall encounter this same theme throughout this study.

The main body of Class' speech was devoted to his program of war aims. Except for large agricultural areas in the east, most of these aims were directed towards the west. France must hand over her remaining mineral deposits and must agree to an extension of Germany's frontier to the mouth of the Somme. Belgium, in its entirety, was to be brought under German domination, with differing treatment for the Walloons and the "Germanic" Flemings. England must relinquish her domination of the seas, and in addition must make colonial concessions to Germany.[87] These aims, of course, are not really so different from the ones we have already encountered. Remarkable about them is only the early date at which they appeared and the cruel procedure which Class proposed for the Germanization of the conquered areas. Not only did he want to close Germany's frontiers against further immigration of Jews, but he demanded all new lands free from their inhabitants. The vanquished nations would have to care for their unfortunate compatriots thus driven out by Germany's "rightful need for expansion."[88] The leaders of the Pan-German League, after thorough discussion, expressed complete agreement with Class'

---

[85] *Ibid.*, p. 321.
[86] Westarp, II, 41; *U. A.*, 4. Reihe, VII (2), 350.
[87] Class, *Strom*, p. 322.
[88] *Ibid.*, pp. 363-64.

speech and he was given full powers to take any action necessary
for the propagation of his aims and for gaining annexationist allies
in other quarters.[89]

Many Pan-Germans changed their minds, however, when Germany's western offensive did not proceed according to original
expectations. As a result, a second meeting was called in October,
this time of a larger and more representative group of members.
Again the demands of Class, now in printed form, found unanimous
and enthusiastic approval.[90] When favorable news from the Russian
front in December seemed to make the collapse of that country
merely a matter of time, Class decided to put his views before a
still wider audience. On December 22, 1914, copies of his memorandum were sent to 1,950 influential public figures, among them the
Supreme Command and the Chancellor. Though officially suppressed, the Class memorandum became one of the most effective
and influential weapons of annexationist propaganda during the
war, with profound influence on other similar programs.[91] " My
memorandum," Class tells us, " started the discussion of war aims
. . . and gained for myself a great number of new personal
contacts." [92]

The League officially adopted an abbreviated version of the Class
memorandum as its own official program, and in turn this document was sent to Bethmann, this time with a letter by the League's
Vice President, General von Gebsattel. The General reiterated the
idea that a weak peace would bring revolution to Germany, because
the soldiers would expect rewards for their heroic deeds. If instead
they merely found a larger tax bill, they would revolt and perhaps
abolish the monarchy.[93] Here again is the idea of war aims as a
lightning-rod to avert domestic discontent and as an indirect means
of perpetuating the disproportionate political influence of the prop-
ertied classes which made up the bulk of the League's membership.
The League's memorandum itself differed little from the speech of
Class on August 28, 1914. Again the emphasis was on western aims.
" To secure our future," it read, " at least one of our flanks must be

[89] *Ibid.*, pp. 322-23.

[90] *Ibid.*, p. 343; H. Class, *Denkschrift betreffend die national-, wirtschafts-und
sozialpolitischen Ziele des deutschen Volkes im gegenwärtigen Kriege* (n. pl., 1914).

[91] Class, *Strom*, pp. 344-46; *U. A.*, 4. Reihe, XII (1), 49-50.

[92] Class, *Strom*, p. 394.

[93] *Ibid.*, pp. 404 ff.; *Alldeutsche Blätter*, Dec. 9, 1916, no. 50.

permanently liberated. Since there will always be a large Russian people and hundreds of millions of Mongols in the east, the lasting liberation of our flank cannot be sought there but only in the west." [94]

Of the various subsidiary organizations of the Pan-German League, it was primarily the Army League which raised its voice in favor of annexations during the first months of the war. As early as August 29, 1914, its founder, the Pan-German General Keim, asked for a " peace worthy of the immense sacrifices "; the same line was subsequently taken by its official magazine, *Die Wehr* (circulation 108,000).[95] On December 5, 1914, the Army League held its first national convention at which it demanded " a peace which will permanently secure Germany's leading position in the world." [96] In February, it passed a more specific resolution which asked " not only for financial indemnities but also for an increase of German territory and influence inside and outside of Europe." [97] A memorandum in March was still more specific: " Germany's permanent possession of Belgium," it said," is an absolute necessity for military, *völkisch*, and economic reasons." [98] A simultaneously issued circular expressed the same idea. " Belgium," it said, " is ours. Our self-preservation demands that she remain in German hands." [99] A meeting of the Army League in May dealt almost exclusively with problems of Belgium and France. The Pan-German Kurd von Strantz, President of the League in the absence of General Keim (who was military governor of the Belgian province of Limburg), used linguistic arguments to urge German westward expansion as far as " Boonen " (his " Germanic " version of Boulogne).[100] Finally Keim himself, in a newspaper article, added his demands for " a large prize of victory." [101]

---

[94] *Ibid.*, p. 478.
[95] *Tägliche Rundschau*, August 29, 1914; Grumbach, pp. 151, 170; A. Keim, *Erlebtes und Erstrebtes* (Hannover, 1925), pp. 174-76.
[96] *Vorwärts*, Dec. 9, 1914.
[97] *Ibid.*, Feb. 23, 1915; Grumbach, pp. 152, 170.
[98] *U. A.*, 4. Reihe, VII (2), 334.
[99] Auskunftsstelle Vereinigter Verbände, *Gedanken und Wünsche deutscher Vereine und Verbände zur Gestaltung des Friedens* (Berlin, 1915), p. 19.
[100] *Vorwärts*, May 23, 1915; Grumbach, pp. 152-53.
[101] *Ibid.*, p. 24.

The Western Industrialists and their War Aims

The second important element of the *Kriegszielbewegung*, Germany's western industrialists, is not so clearly defined a group as the Pan-Germans. A number of outstanding individuals, they were united not through membership in a political or expansionist pressure group, but through common and very tangible ambitions in Western Europe. They were not concerned with finding *Lebensraum* for Germany's growing population, or maintaining, through annexations, the power of Germany's ruling class. Their foremost aim was to secure for themselves and their industries the considerable supplies of iron ore, which the Franco-Prussian War had left in the hands of France. When Bismarck came to make peace in 1871, he was at first unaware of the fact that Alsace-Lorraine contained the most valuable iron deposits on the European continent. Only when Wilhelm Hauchecorne, Director of the Prussian Academy of Mines, called his attention to this fact, was the new frontier drawn to include the richest of the iron beds.[102] The remaining deposits, partly undiscovered, and consisting of a highly phosphorus ore called "minette," were of little use until after the invention of the Thomas converter in 1879. At that date, France again became the possessor of important metallurgical resources, concentrated chiefly in the regions of Briey, Longwy, and Nancy. Of Europe's reserves of iron ore, France, before the World War, held 33 per cent as compared to Germany's 22 per cent.[103]

If France was superior to Germany in her resources of iron ore, Germany was superior in the extent and quality of her coal deposits. The Ruhr valley, one of the world's largest coal regions, only gained in importance because of its close proximity to the iron mines of Lorraine. This happy marriage of coal and iron, facilitated by extremely favorable communications, made Germany one of the chief iron producing nations of the world. Between 1860 and 1910, she climbed from fourth place to second, while during the same

[102] D. C. McKay, " The Pre-War Development of Briey Iron Ores," *Essays in the History of Modern Europe* (N.Y., 1936), pp. 170 ff.

[103] M. Ungeheuer, " Die industriellen Interessen Deutschlands in Frankreich vor Ausbruch des Krieges," *Technik und Wirstschaft*, IX (1916), 160; A. H. Brooks and M. F. Lacroix, " The Iron and Associated Industries of Lorraine, the Sarre District, Luxembourg, and Belgium," *U. S. Geological Survey* (Washington, 1920), Bulletin 703, p. 16.

period France fell from second to fourth.[104] But since Germany's supply of iron ore was limited, ˉer iron industry came to depend increasingly on foreign sources. In 1871 all the iron produced in Germany had been smelted from German ore. By 1890 this was true for only three-quarters of Germany's iron production; and by 1913 about half the needed ore had to be imported.[105]

Germany's chief sources of supply were Spain, Sweden, and France. The greater distance of the first two increased the cost of transportation, but the high quality of their ore made up for this disadvantage. During the last years before the war, however, Spain's reserves of the highest grades of iron ore began to approach exhaustion. At the same time Sweden imposed restrictions on her export of that commodity.[106] Increasingly, therefore, Germany became dependent on her third chief foreign source. Between 1900 and 1913, Germany's imports of iron ore from France increased from *ca.* 20,000 to 3,811,000 metric tons. To keep this source, on which their industries depended, from drying up, and to gain additional supplies elsewhere, were two of the most important problems facing the industrialists of western Germany.[107] The Moroccan crises of the pre-war decade in some respects were but a series of unsuccessful attempts to solve this question. The simultaneous agitation of the Pan-German League and of heavy industry (notably the firm of Mannesmann) for the acquisition of Morocco, foreshadow the later collaboration between these two groups in the *Kriegszielbewegung*.[108]

More successful, however, than these Moroccan ventures, were the pre-war attempts of Germany's industrial magnates to gain indirect control over the French iron mines in Lorraine and Normandy. As a background to Germany's western war aims, this slow economic infiltration is of immense importance. Between 1900, when the firm of August Thyssen acquired the concession of Batilly

---

[104] Ungeheuer, *Technik und Wirtschaft,* IX, 98.

[105] F. Friedensburg, *Kohle und Eisen im Weltkriege und in den Friedensschluessen* (München, 1934), p. 39.

[106] Brooks-Lacroix, *U. S. Geological Survey,* p. 16; " Die schwedische Eisenerzfrage," *Stahl und Eisen,* vol. 27 (1907), pp. 533-34.

[107] Ungeheuer, *Technik und Wirtschaft,* IX, 166; Friedensburg, p. 40; P. Krusch, *Die Versorgung Deutschlands mit metallischen Rohstoffen* (Leipzig, 1913), p. 125.

[108] C. H. Mannesmann, *Die Unternehmungen der Brüder Mannesmann in Marokko* (Würzburg, 1931), Diss. Würzburg, *passim.*; Friedensburg, pp. 46-48; Class, *Strom,* pp. 104-07, 202-15, 217-18, 222 ff.

in the Briey region, and the outbreak of war in 1914, about 18 such concessions had passed either completely or partly into German hands. Most of these mines were situated in the Briey district, richest and most productive of the minette deposits. Although specific data are difficult to obtain, it has been estimated that *ca.* 15 per cent of France's iron reserves in this region were under German influence by 1914.[109]

In this exploitation of French resources, the pioneering efforts of Thyssen were followed up by most of the prominent industrial concerns of western Germany. The brothers Röchling controlled half the mines of Valleroy and in addition held the concession of Pulventeux. The *Deutsch-Luxemburgische Bergwerks A. G.* of Stinnes owned one-fourth of the *Société de Moutiers* and part of the *Société des Forges de Brévilly.* Four-fifths of the *Société des Mines de Murville* were controlled by Peter Klöckner's *Aumetz-Friede*, and three-fourths of the *Société des Mines de Jarny* and parts of the concession of Sancy were in the hands of a group made up of Haspe, Hoesch, and Phönix. The *Dillinger Hüttenwerke* of Stumm owned one-third of the *Société des Mines de Conflans.* And finally— Kirdorf's *Gelsenkirchener Bergwerks A. G.* controlled *ca.* 2,000 hectars in French Lorraine, surpassed only by Thyssen's holdings of 2,200 hectars in the same region.[110]

Among the deposits in Normandy, German influence was still more prevalent. The first concessions in that region had been granted as far back as 1875, but technical difficulties had prevented their exploitation. When the mines were finally made productive around the turn of the century, it seems to have been due largely to German initiative, since French industry did not dare risk the large investments necessary to make the mines profitable.[111] Again Thyssen led the way. In 1907 he acquired the concessions of Dielette, Soumont, and Perrieres. Phönix, Haspe, Hoesch, Deutsch-Luxemburg, and the *Gutehoffnungshütte* followed his example in 1907-11. The firm of Krupp bought Larchamp in 1909, and a combine of Krupp, Thyssen, and Stinnes, using the Dutch financier de Poorter as a front, jointly acquired control over Jurcques, Oude-

---

[109] L. Bruneau, *L'Allemagne en France* (Paris, 1915), pp. 11 ff., 87; Brooks-Lacroix, *U. S. Geological Survey*, pp. 44 ff.; McKay, pp. 177-81.

[110] *Vorwärts*, Feb. 23, 1915; Bruneau, *passim.*; C. Streit, *Where Iron is there is the Fatherland* (New York, 1920), p. 10.

[111] Bruneau, pp. 79 ff.; Ungeheuer, *Technik und Wirschaft*, IX, 161 ff.

fontaine, Bourberouge, and Mortain in 1911.[112] Of twenty concessions granted prior to the war, only two were exclusively in
French hands. Roughly three-fourths of Normandy's iron fields
were under German influence, Thyssen alone holding one-sixth of
the total area.[113] The latter's contracts with Swedish iron mines
were to expire in 1917, a fact which explains his special eagerness
to find substitute sources of supply elsewhere.[114]

August Thyssen, in many ways, was a typical example of the
great West-German industrialist. Of simple tastes and insignificant appearance, he combined great ability and resourcefulness with
a passion for work.[115] Living in outward splendour at his castle of
Landsberg, where, among his famous Rodin collection, he received
his friends the Ludendorffs, his real home was among his workers,
who deeply respected " the old gentleman," even though in labor
matters his heart was " as hard as his steel." [116] His life's sole
purpose and ambition was the success of his firm, and nothing was
allowed to interfere with it. As long as his own interests and those
of Germany were identical, August Thyssen was a patriot. But
when they disagreed, he (and for that matter his favorite son
Fritz) did not hesitate to join the enemies of their country.[117]

The French, naturally, were alarmed at this growing German en-
croachment upon their mineral resources, and a flood of articles and
books during the first decade of the century warned against the
dangers of such infiltration.[118] To counteract this agitation and to
evade the enforcement of a law prohibiting direct foreign ownership
of French mines, the Germans were forced to camouflage their
French holdings, employing French citizens as intermediaries, or
making use of the close relations between French and German
banking houses.[119] Again Thyssen showed the greatest ingenuity

[112] *Ibid.*, pp. 225 ff.; *Vorwärts*, Feb. 18, 1915.

[113] Friedensburg, p. 44.

[114] Ungeheuer, *Technik und Wirtschaft*, IX, 223.

[115] On Thyssen see R. Gaston, *Krupp et Thyssen* (Paris, 1925).

[116] P. Arnst, *August Thyssen und sein Werk* (Leipzig, 1925), pp. 69 ff.

[117] F. Engerand, *Le Fer sur une frontière* (Paris, 1919), pp. 221 ff. cites an
article from the Danish *Aftenpost*, Sept. 8, 1918, in which August Thyssen denounces
the Hohenzollern regime. After being partly responsible for the rise of Hitler, his
son Fritz again left the sinking ship: F. Thyssen, *I Paid Hitler* (New York, 1941).

[118] Bruneau, pp. x, 10, 129 ff.; *L'Echo de Paris*, Oct. 19, 1907.

[119] Ungeheuer, *Technik und Wirtschaft*, IX, 220; Friedensburg, p. 45; on Germany's influence over French banking see: J. E. Favre, *Le Capital français au*

and enterprise. His *Société des Mines de Bouligny*, for instance, was run by the Belgian *Société Métallurgique de Sambre et Moselle*, in which August Thyssen himself was vice president, and in which his son Fritz and several of his German directors held leading positions.[120] Thyssen even went so far in 1909 as to consider French citizenship for one of his sons, so as to evade all future legal restrictions.[121] Thyssen's rival, Hugo Stinnes, was equally skillful at this game of economic penetration. "Give me three or four years of peace," he boasted to Class in 1911, "and I shall silently secure Germany's European predominance." To shield himself against losses in a future war, he carefully selected trusted Frenchmen as directors for his foreign enterprises.[122]

Compared to France, Germany's penetration of Belgian pre-war economy was much less spectacular. Economic relations between the two countries were most active; but such relations—consisting in the investment of capital, the sending of commercial representatives, and the founding of industrial branches on foreign soil—are common phenomena of our industrial age. Their existence is not necessarily proof of some sinister plot on the part of one nation for the exploitation and eventual extermination of another, as has sometimes been asserted.[123]

There were no German interests, comparable to those in the Briey and Normandy regions, in pre-war Belgium; no interests, that is, on whose maintenance the continued prosperity of one of Germany's most important branches of industrial production depended, as did (or at least it thought it did) the iron industry of western Germany upon the iron deposits of eastern France. There were sufficient industrial and commercial advantages to be gained from an annexa-

---

service de l'étranger (Paris, 1917), esp. pp. 145-48; K. Strasser, *Die deutschen Banken im Ausland* (München, 1925), *passim.*

[120] Ungeheuer, *Technik und Wirtschaft*, IX, 230. A still greater masterpiece was Thyssen's camouflage of his steel works in Caën: Bruneau, pp. 123 ff.

[121] Streit, p. 9.

[122] Class, *Strom*, pp. 217-18, 329.

[123] On Germany's economic interests in Belgium see R. de Weerdt, *Supermania* (London, 1915); R. de Weerdt, *The Spider's Web* (London, 1915); J. Claes, *The German Mole, A study of the art of peaceful penetration* (London, 1915). For more realistic appraisals see Handelskammer Frankfurt a. M., *Belgiens Wirtschaftsleben und Handelsbeziehungen zu Deutschland* (Frankfurt a. M., 1915); H. Davignon, *Belgien und Deutschland* (Lausanne, 1916); H. Davignon, "German methods of penetration in Belgium before and during the war," *Quarterly Review*, vol. 225 (1916), pp. 130-47.

tion or " assimilation " of Belgium, however, to make it a welcome addition to the war aims of German industry. In many respects, Germany was the economic hinterland of Belgium, and the actual economic interdependence of the two countries was considerable. It is difficult to determine the exact extent of Germany's share in Belgium's industry prior to the World War. Existing estimates differ widely. In the iron and steel industry, " the capital stock held in 1914 by German interests is estimated at 60 million francs, representing 17 per cent of the total value." [124] The main German shareholders in Belgian heavy industry, apparently, were Thyssen, Stinnes, and Klöckner.[125] Another branch of Belgian industry, in which Germany had a large share, was armament works, e. g., the *Fabrique nationale d'armes de guerre* and the *Ancien établissement Peiper*, both at Herstal. Chemical, shipping, and metal industries likewise showed prominent German influence.[126]

Besides these industrial ties, German banking houses had a strong foothold in Belgium, either directly through branch offices (so the *Deutsche Bank, Dresdener Bank,* and *Diskontogesellschaft*), or indirectly through control of Belgian establishments. The *Banque d'Outremer,* the *Banque Belge de Chemin de Fer,* the *Crédit Anversois,* and especially the *Banque Internationale de Bruxelles,* were partly in German hands.[127] The most numerous and important links between Germany and Belgium, however, were commercial. Germany held first place among the receivers of Belgian goods, and her own exports to Belgium, 5 per cent of her total exports, were surpassed only by those of France.[128] German influence was particularly stong in the port of Antwerp, which was almost as much a German as it was a Belgian port, particularly vital as an outlet for Germany's western industries.[129]

Economic relations between the two countries were not entirely

---

[124] Brooks-Lacroix, *U. S. Geological Survey,* p. 84.

[125] *Ibid.,* p. 110; O. Kessler, *Das deutsche Belgien* (Berlin, 1915), p. 30.

[126] Handelskammer Frankfurt, pp. 17-18, 39; Brooks-Lacroix, *U. S. Geological Survey,* p. 110; Kessler, p. 30; Davignon, *Quarterly Review,* vol. 225, pp. 137 ff.

[127] Strasser, p. 64; Favre, pp. 42-43; Handelskammer Frankfurt, p. 18.

[128] E. Oppermann, *Belgien einst und jetzt* (Leipzig, 1915), pp. 12-13; Handelskammer Frankfurt, pp. 11-12, 69.

[129] H. Schumacher, *Antwerpen, seine Weltstellung und Bedeutung fuer das deutsche Wirtschaftsleben* (München, 1916); K. Wiedenfeld, *Antwerpen im Weltverkehr und Welthandel* (München, 1915); R. de Rautlin, *Les Allemands au port d'Anvers en 1912* (Paris, 1913).

without their negative aspects, however. There was considerable competition, for instance, between certain branches of Belgian and German industry, and in case of articles produced by mass-production, Belgium with her lower wages definitely held the upper hand. Furthermore, Belgium's economy depended as much on England and France as it did upon Germany, and a German-dominated Belgium might easily prove a heavy liability, since these important commercial ties would be broken. It is not surprising, therefore, that some German industrialists were not quite so enthusiastic about the annexation of Belgium as they were about the Briey-Longwy region in eastern France.[130]

This latter region, because of the rapid German advance in August 1914, had suddenly been delivered into German hands. There is no evidence to suggest that this immediate German occupation was due to any preconceived plan. Nor was the importance of this acquisition so great for Germany at this time as it has been made out to be. Before the war, Germany had imported *ca.* 10 per cent of her iron ore from French Lorraine; and although after a victorious war she would undoubtedly have drawn much more heavily on these resources, due to war conditions she actually took less from the mines of Briey than she normally did in time of peace.[131] Even so, it was most annoying to many Frenchmen that Germany seemed able to enjoy freely the fruits of her conquest. They asked particularly, why their armies did not destroy their own mines and thus make German exploitation impossible. When no satisfactory explanation came forth, it was rumoured that a plot had been hatched between French and German industrialists in which the Germans on their side bound themselves not to shell the French coal mines opposite their lines in northern France.[132] Continuous demands of the French public finally resulted in a parliamentary investigation, which failed to substantiate these suspicions; but the story has persisted into the present.[133]

[130] Handelskammer Frankfurt, *passim.*

[131] Friedensburg, pp. 119, 182.

[132] Friedensburg, pp. 90 ff.; Streit, pp. 7, 27, 36 ff.; K. Graf Hertling, *Ein Jahr in der Reichskanzlei* (Freiburg, 1919), pp. 94-95.

[133] *Le Rôle et la situation de la métallurgie en France,* Question de Briey, Annales de la Chambre des Députés, Documents Parlementaires 1919, Annexe No. 6026, pp. 225 ff.; see also *New York Times,* Nov. 18, 1942: Obituary for M. Eugène Schneider. For an interesting account of a similar failure to destroy the French

In the light of their pre-war interest in these regions, it should cause little surprise to find Germany's industrialists demanding the annexation of Briey and Longwy as well as some sort of control over Belgium, as soon as these regions were in German hands. As early as August 28, 1914, the firm of Thyssen (already supported by Erzberger) approached the government with an appropriate petition, and a few days later August Thyssen repeated his demands in person.[134] The brothers Röchling, in a memorandum addressed to Bethmann Hollweg, likewise demanded their share of the Briey district.[135] Hugo Stinnes made clear his stand when he called on the President of the Pan-German League in early September, in order to express his complete agreement with the latter's memorandum on war aims and to promise his support of these aims. " This promise," Class tells us, " he kept faithfully." In some respects Stinnes even went beyond the Pan-German aims. To strengthen Germany's strategic position against England, and to gain the iron deposits of Normandy, he proposed the annexation of the whole northern coast of France.[136] Emil Kirdorf, founder of the *Rheinisch-Westphälisches Kohlensyndikat* and head of the *Gelsenkirchener Bergwerksgesellschaft* likewise subscribed to the aims of the Pan-German League, of which he was a leading member.[137] Krupp von Bohlen agreed with Class' aims, until German reverses on the Marne temporarily changed his attitude.[138]

This individual agitation in favor of western annexations was supplemented by public statements and petitions of various economic and industrial organizations. Since they had to comply with censorship regulations, their tone was usually quite vague. In this category belongs the speech, in December of 1914, of Dr. Schweighoffer, Secretary of the *Zentralverband Deutscher Industrieller*, as well as a number of addresses delivered by industrial leaders before the *Industrieklub* of Düsseldorf.[139] In February of

mines during the Second World War see E. Taylor, *The Strategy of Terror* (New York, 1942), Pocket Book Edition, pp. 161-62.

[134] " A " [Adolf Stein], *Erzberger*, p. 19; *U.A.*, 4. Reihe, XII (1), 36.

[135] *Ibid.*

[136] Class, *Strom*, pp. 327-29.

[137] W. Bacmeister, *Emil Kirdorf, Der Mann, Sein Werk* (Essen, 1936), p. 138; Class, *Strom*, pp. 354-55.

[138] *Ibid.*, pp. 326-27, 329-30, 352-54.

[139] *Norddeutsche Allgemeine Zeitung*, Dec. 10, 1914; W. Hirsch, *Wirtschafts- und Verkehrsfragen im Kriege* (Essen, 1915), speech delivered Jan. 20, 1915; M. Schinkel,

1915, the *Verein Deutscher Eisen- und Stahlindustrieller,* leading
organization of heavy industry, demanded the usual peace " worthy
of the immense sacrifices," a " greater Germany," and more specifically, an increase of Germany's colonies.[140] The various Chambers
of Commerce (*Handelskammern*) of Western Germany, under the
direction of Hugenberg, likewise expressed their approval of Pan-
German war aims and at a joint meeting in April 1915, demanded
the extension of Germany's territory to increase her military, maritime, and economic strength.[141] Finally, on April 1, 1915, the four
most important organizations of business employees joined the
ranks of their employers and demanded a rectification of Germany's
frontiers and territorial expansion both in Europe and overseas.[142]

The most specific and effective of these industrialist statements
in favor of annexations, however, was the so-called " Petition of the
Six Economic Organizations," first issued on March 10, 1915, and
repeated, in a slightly altered version, on May 20, 1915. It was one
of the landmarks of German annexationist propaganda and the
result of the *Kriegszielbewegung,* i. e., the close collaboration between the Pan-German League and German industry.

The Kriegszielbewegung

The close community of interests and personnel between the Pan-
German League and German heavy industry necessarily suggested
concerted action. An alliance between the financial resources of
the latter and the effective propaganda machine of the former
naturally presented obvious advantages to both. The first to think
of such an alliance was Heinrich Class, who brought it to the attention of Alfred Hugenberg, representative of heavy industry, as
early as August 1914. Hugenberg, Class tells us, shared his views:
" So we went to work immediately; the German *Kriegszielbewegung,*

Unsere Geldwirtschaft (Essen, 1915), speech of March 6, 1915 by the head of the
Discontogesellschaft and the Norddeutsche Bank; W. Beumer, *Eine Bismarckrede
zum 1. April 1915* (Essen, 1915). Beumer, like Hirsch, was member of the Prussian
Lower House.

[140] *Vorwärts,* Feb. 19, 1915.

[141] Class, *Strom,* p. 352; *Vorwärts,* April 22, 1915. As promoter of commercial and
industrial interests, the German *Handelskammer* is of vastly greater importance
than the American Chamber of Commerce. The two, actually, have very little in
common.

[142] Auskunftsstelle Vereinigter Verbände, *Gedanken und Wünsche,* 1915 edition,
pp. 8-9.

which played an important role in the course of the great conflict, had begun." A plan of campaign was drawn up in subsequent discussions between Class and Hugenberg.[143]

Hugenberg, whom we have already encountered, had himself been one of the founders of the Pan-German League. In 1909 he had become Chief Director of Krupp's, a position which made him particularly suitable as a link between the two leading annexationist factions. His talent for organization, moreover, made him a valuable asset not only to the Krupps, but to German heavy industry in general. In some ways he might be considered its most influential and most typical figure. Reserved, immobile, stubborn, and ruthless, he quickly gained the confidence of all the great in Germany's iron, steel, and coal industry. " Hugenberg is not a man, he is a wall," secretive and strong like " the vault of a great bank." [144]

Shortly after he began his work with Krupp, Hugenberg was made joint chairman of the Chambers of Commerce of Essen, Mühlheim, and Oberhausen. In 1912 he became President of the *Bergbaulicher Verein*, which represented the interests of all large Ruhr concerns. Hugenberg, in co-operation with Emil Kirdorf, used this position to build up a most important organization, the so-called *Wirtschaftsvereinigung*. Its purpose was to concentrate in one hand the various financial contributions which the Ruhr industrialists were constantly called upon to make to charitable and political organizations. A committee under the direction of Hugenberg decided in each case whether a cause warranted the financial backing of heavy industry. Many political and other groups, by accepting such backing, put themselves under the control of the Hugenberg committee. Hugenberg had thus become the holder of the Ruhr industry's purse strings, a position which he held until long after the war.[145]

As the opening move of the *Kriegszielbewegung* Class instigated

[143] Class, *Strom*, pp. 319, 330, 352-53.

[144] D. Jung, *Der Alldeutsche Verband* (Würzburg, 1936), Diss. Bonn, p. 2; O. Kriegk, *Hugenberg* (Leipzig, 1932), pp. 27-28; L. Bernhard, *Der Hugenberg Konzern* (Berlin, 1928), pp. 54-55; " Junius Alter," *Nationalisten*, pp. 144 ff.

[145] Bernhard, pp. 56 ff.; " Morus " [R. Lewinsohn], *Das Geld in der Politik* (Berlin, 1930), p. 172. Hugenberg also set up a number of news and propaganda agencies—the *Auslands G. m. b. H., Vera, Ala,* and *Telegraphen Union*. In 1916 he was instrumental in buying the Scherl publishing house as another propaganda agency for his nationalist-industrialist sponsors.

a meeting, in late September of 1914, of various industrial, commercial, and agricultural organizations, to express the unanimous
confidence of Germany's economy in the successful completion of
the war. The list of speakers was impressive (Dr. Kaempf, Progressive and President of the Reichstag, Count von Schwerin-
Löwitz, President of the Prussian Lower House, Roetger, head of
the *Bund der Industriellen*, and Wolfgang Kapp, famous annexationist) and the general tenor of the speeches delivered was annexationist, though in rather veiled terms. In a telegram addressed to
the Emperor, the participants expressed hope for a peace " which
will correspond to the enormous sacrifices of this war and make its
repetition impossible." [146]

In October 1914, the *Zentralverband Deutscher Industrieller*, the
Bund der Landwirte, and the Conservative Party met, on invitation
from Hugenberg, to discuss the problem of food supply. In November the Pan-German League joined in, and the discussion shifted
from grain to war aims. As its first action this newly-constituted
group asked Class and Hugenberg to prepare a program of war
aims based on the Class memorandum of September 1914. This
program was presented at a meeting of these organizations on
December 15, 1914. The mention of Stinnes indicates that probably
other industrialists besides Hugenberg were present. On this occasion the Conservatives, led by Westarp, opposed some of the more
far-reaching among the Class-Hugenberg proposals, and when they
found no sympathy among the other delegates present, they withdrew at a later meeting their active participation in the *Kriegszielbewegung*. This did not mean that the Conservative Party was
opposed to annexations, but merely that its leaders objected to
some of the exaggerated aims of the Pan-Germans and their friends,
considering them unrealistic and utopian. Several Conservatives
moreover, such as Roesicke and von Wangenheim, did not share
their party's views and continued to take part in future meetings.[147]

In the meantime, as we have seen already, Class had sent out
the 1,950 copies of his own memorandum. Among the many enthusiastic replies was a letter from Hugenberg, expressing the agree-

---

[146] Class, *Strom*, p. 342; Deutscher Handelstag, *Versammlung aus Anlass des
Krieges* (Berlin, 1914), pp. 4-23; E. Jäckh and K. Hoenn, eds., *Schulthess' Europäischer Geschichtskalender* (henceforth cited as *Schulthess*), vol. 55 (1), p. 398h.
[147] Westarp, II, 42-46, 382; Class, *Strom*, pp. 360-61.

ment of himself and of "the other industrial gentlemen."[148] In late January 1915, the annexationists got together again, to continue their discussion of the memorandum which Class and Hugenberg had worked out during the preceding months.[149] Their plan was to use this memorandum as a declaration of the leading industrial and agricultural organizations, and, if possible, of the parties of the *Kriegszielmehrheit* as well. The January meeting was attended by some thirty persons, Hugenberg presiding. Of leading industrialists, Kirdorf, Stinnes, Beukenberg, Reusch, and von Borsig were present. The *Bund der Industriellen*, in which Stresemann played a leading role, was represented by its chairman Friedrichs, and the *Bund der Landwirte* by Baron von Wangenheim and Roesicke. Besides Class, the Pan-Germans had sent General von Gebsattel, Admiral von Grumme-Douglas, and Johannes Neumann, a Lübeck senator.

Class delivered the main address, based on his own memorandum. It was received in deep silence and without comment, until Hugo Stinnes rose to speak. Here is Class' description:

Stinnes was no speaker. His sentences kept flowing evenly, without a raising or lowering of his voice. . . . But there could be no doubt—in spite of his cold and businesslike manner, he was quite aware of the importance of our age. One can imagine, therefore, the impression it made when he put the whole weight of his personality behind my proposals . . . promising to use his influence with the *Zentralverband Deutscher Industrieller* to urge their acceptance by that group.[150]

Hugo Stinnes, whose speech made such an impression, was the youngest at the meeting. Barely 44 years old, he already was one of the wealthiest and most influential of European industrialists. In addition to his chief enterprise, the *Deutsch-Luxemburgische Bergwerks—und Hütten A. G.*, covering large regions in the Ruhr and in Alsace-Lorraine, he controlled—together with Thyssen—the *Rheinisch-Westphälische Elektrizitätswerks A. G.*, which supplied most of western Germany with electricity. During and after the war he expanded his holding to include not only additional mines and iron-works, but also shipping companies, power plants, paper works, hotels, and newspapers, building up one of the world's

---

[148] A. Hugenberg, *Streiflichter aus Vergangenheit und Gegenwart* (Berlin, 1927), pp. 203-05.

[149] For this and the following see Class, *Strom*, pp. 354 ff.

[150] *Ibid.*, pp. 354-55.

largest vertical trusts.[151] Albert Ballin once said: " As some children cannot let alone a piece of cake, or some men a beautiful woman, so Stinnes cannot let business alone; he wants to make everything his own, even if it should happen to belong to somebody else." [152]

Like most of his colleagues among Germany's captains of industry, Stinnes preferred the actuality of power to its outward manifestations. He never abandoned the simplicity of dress and manner which made him like one of his workers, " a walking piece of coal." His business transactions were usually carried on in an atmosphere of secrecy, which only helped to magnify their importance in the eyes of outsiders. Already during his lifetime, and still more so after his early death in 1924, the figure of Stinnes, unlike that of any of his colleagues, became almost legendary. His pale face, his black, pointed beard, and his manner of speaking coolly and dispassionately in a " weary whisper," earned him names like " Assyrian King," " Flying Dutchman," or " Christ of Coal." [153] His influence on the political affairs of Germany is difficult to determine, since most of his political, like his economic activities, were carefully hidden from public scrutiny. That his influence was considerable can be gathered from numerous references in contemporary accounts. Especially during the second half of the war, when much of the Government's actual power was centered in the Supreme Command, Stinnes paid frequent visits to headquarters and seems to have been consulted on many questions. His friendship with General Ludendorff was particularly close.[154]

To return to the annexationist meeting in Berlin—once Stinnes had endorsed the views of Heinrich Class, they found immediate and full support of those present. Baron von Wangenheim, welcoming the possibility of large-scale German settlements, notably in the east, pledged the support of the Agrarian League. Friedrichs

---

[151] G. Raphaël, *Hugo Stinnes, Der Mensch, Sein Werk, Sein Wirken* (Berlin, 1925), *passim.*; P. Ufermann and C. Hueglin, *Stinnes und seine Konzerne* (Berlin, 1924), pp. 27 ff., 57; C. Geyer, *Drei Verderber Deutschlands* (Berlin, 1924), pp. 27, 34, 52-53; M. Lair, " Hugo Stinnes," *Revue des Sciences Politiques,* vol. 49 (1926), pp. 167 ff.; H. Brinckmeyer, *Hugo Stinnes* (München, 1921), *passim.*

[152] Harden, *Köpfe,* IV, 425.

[153] Harden, IV, 412-13; R. Oertmann, *Hugo Stinnes, ein Künstler und ein Vorbild* (Berlin, 1925), *passim.*

[154] Raphaël, *Stinnes,* p. 93; M. Ludendorff, *Als ich Ludendorffs Frau war* (München, 1929), p. 21; J. Fischart, " Hugo Stinnes: An Industrial Ludendorff," *Living Age,* vol. 308 (1921), pp. 148-51.

added his approval in the name of German industry. After general agreement had thus been registered, a detailed discussion of each point of the Hugenberg-Class memorandum followed, in which everybody took part. At the close of the meeting, its oldest participant, Emil Kirdorf, urged the dissemination of the war aims agreed on at the meeting among the whole German people, regardless of governmental opposition.

Kirdorf was another outstanding member of the aristocracy of coal and iron, in a class with Thyssen and Stinnes. Founder of the *Gelsenkirchener Bergwerks A. G.* (the largest Ruhr enterprise, employing 65,000 workers) he was the only great industrialist who openly and consistently supported the annexationists.[155] A small and unpretentious man, much like his chief rival, August Thyssen, this " Bismarck of German coal mining " concealed, behind a genial front, an iron will and ruthless determination, which appeared in his many conflicts with Thyssen and in his stubborn fight against labor unions.[156]

Class and Hugenberg, with the help of the latter's associate, Hirsch, now incorporated the results of the January meeting into a second draft of their memorandum. In a later session, this version was adopted and signed by the representatives of the various economic organizations which had participated in the preliminary discussions—the *Zentralverband Deutscher Industrieller*, the *Bund der Industriellen*, the *Bund der Landwirte*, the *Deutscher Bauernbund*, and the *Reichsdeutscher Mittelstandsverband*. On March 10, 1915, this declaration of the five economic organizations was presented to the German Chancellor.[157] Simultaneously, the same organizations, with added support from the commercial *Hansa Bund*, petitioned the Reichstag to permit the public discussion of peace aims, expressing the hope " that our German Fatherland shall emerge from its fight for existence—which has been forced upon it—greater and stronger, with secured frontiers in the west and the east and with the European and colonial extensions of

---

[155] Class, *Strom*, pp. 247-48.

[156] Ufermann-Hueglin, p. 18; R. Martin, *Deutsche Machthaber* (Berlin, 1910), pp. 429 ff.; *Vorwärts*, April 18, 1915. See also the favorable biography by W. Bacmeister, *Emil Kirdorf, Der Mann, Sein Werk* (Essen, 1936).

[157] *Alldeutsche Blätter*, Dec. 23, 1916, no. 52; *Vorwärts*, March 12, 1915.

territory necessary for the maintenance of our sea power as well as for military and economic reasons." [158]

It should be noted that for tactical reasons the chief annexationist wire-pullers, the Pan-Germans and industrialists, do not appear in either petition, except indirectly. To remedy this omission, Hugenberg, Stinnes, and Kirdorf, together with several historians and geographers and with the Westphalian branches of the National Liberal and Center Parties, issued an additional memorandum in favor of annexations in March of 1915.[159] As a further consolidation of the annexationist front, the collaborator of Class and Hugenberg, Dr. Hirsch, also tried to establish an alliance between the signatories of the Hugenberg-Class memorandum and the bourgeois and annexationist parties of the Reichstag. At a meeting on May 1, however, both the Conservatives and the Center expressed their preference for independent action. The result of this decision, the conversation between Bethmann and the representatives of the annexationist parties on May 13, 1915, we have already discussed.[160]

But even if this attempt to link the *Kriegszielbewegung* and the *Kriegszielmehrheit* failed, the annexationist parties, especially the National Liberals and the Free Conservatives, were very much in favor of the aims proclaimed by the Pan-Germans and the Economic Organizations.[161] Even the Conservatives, in spite of their earlier secession, still maintained " close contact and agreement " with the *Kriegszielbewegung*. Roesicke and Admiral von Grumme-Douglas, besides holding leading positions in the Agrarian and Pan-German Leagues respectively, also played prominent roles in the Conservative Party.[162] Further co-operation between the various annexationist groups was maintained through the *Auskunftsstelle Vereinigter Verbände*, founded by Dr. Poensgen, which counted among its members Professor Dietrich Schäfer, Bassermann, Stresemann, and Mathias Erzberger. Its purpose was the collection and co-ordination of the various annexationist programs and pronouncements and their propagation through meetings and publications.[163]

[158] Lutz, *German Empire*, I, 311; Auskunftsstelle Vereinigter Verbände, *Gedanken und Wünsche*, 1915 edition, p. 7.
[159] *U. A.*, 4. Reihe, XII (1), 50.
[160] Westarp, II. 50. See above, pp. 15-16.
[161] Class, *Strom*, pp. 355, 358.
[162] Westarp, II, 44, 162, 164; *U.A.*, 4. Reihe, VII (1), 124. For collaboration between Pan-German and Agrarian Leagues see Class, *Strom*, pp. 270-71.
[163] D. Schäfer, *Aus meinem Leben* (Berlin, 1926), p. 174. Poensgen was chairman of the Oberbilk Steel Works, affiliated with the firm of Thyssen.

On May 20, 1915, the petition of March 10, in almost its original form, was again addressed to the Chancellor and the Ministries of the various federal states. Besides the original five organizations, a sixth, the *Christliche Deutsche Bauernvereine* added its signature, thus making it the well-known "Petition of the Six Economic Organizations." Although not quite so radical as the memorandum of Heinrich Class, it clearly shows the influence of its Pan-German and industrial godfathers.[164] To satisfy commercial circles it demanded "a colonial empire adequate to satisfy Germany's manifold economic interests." [165] Agrarian needs were to be met "by annexation of at least parts of the Baltic Provinces and of those territories which lie to the south of them. . . . The great addition to our manufacturing resources which we anticipate in the west, must be counterbalanced by an equivalent annexation of agricultural territory in the east."

It was in regard to the west that the petition was most emphatic and specific. The future which it painted for Belgium was much like the proposal Bethmann Hollweg had made to the representatives of the bourgeois parties on May 13, 1915. From France the Six Associations demanded the coastal districts, including the hinterland, as far as the mouth of the Somme, to improve Germany's strategic position against England. In addition they asked for the district of Briey, the coal country of the *Départements du Nord* and *Pas-de-Calais*, and the fortresses of Verdun, Longwy, and Belfort. Class' suggestion for "land free from inhabitants" was not included in the petition, a fact for which the Conservatives claim credit.[166]

The total area that the Six Organizations demanded from Western Europe amounted to some 50,000 square miles, with a population of *ca.* 11 million. The arguments used to justify these annexations ranged from the rather vague—"the prize of victory must correspond to our sacrifice"—to most specific military and economic considerations:

The iron-ore and coal districts mentioned above are demanded by our military necessities and not by any means in the interests only of our manufacturing development. . . . As a raw material for the production of pig

---

[164] Auskunftsstelle Vereinigter Verbände, *Gedanken und Wünsche,* 1915 edition, pp. 117 ff.; *U. A.,* 4. Reihe, XII (1), 50.

[165] For this and the following see Lutz, *German Empire,* I, 314 ff.

[166] Westarp, II, 43.

iron and steel . . ., minette is being employed more and more. . . . If the output of minette were interrupted, the war would be as good as lost.[167]

This, however, might easily happen, since the mining and industrial region of Lorraine was directly in the shadow of French guns:

Does anyone believe that the French, in the next war, would neglect to place long-range guns in Longwy and Verdun and would allow us to continue the extraction of ore and the production of pig-iron? . . . Hence the security of the German Empire in a future war imperatively demands the possession of the whole minette-bearing district of Luxemburg and Lorraine, together with the fortifications of Longwy and Verdun, without which this district cannot be held.[168]

Most of these arguments were demolished almost immediately.[169] It was maintained, for instance, that strategically the possession of the French coast would not in the least ensure Germany's domination of the English Channel, especially in the age of the airplane of which people were just becoming aware; and economically, Belgium and northern France, far from having an excess of coal, had to import that commodity to meet the needs of their considerable industries, and thus were an economic liability. Still, we must realize that there were considerable advantages to be gained for German industry from these western annexations, such as the domination, and, if necessary, elimination, of Belgian and French industrial competition; or the assurance to Germany's iron masters of a continued supply of ore from eastern France. We have already treated the significance of this last question during the pre-war period and have traced the attempts of Germany's industrialists to solve it by economic penetration of French Lorraine and Normandy. The growing French demand for the elimination in the future of this German influence threatened German industry with the loss of these valuable sources of supply, even if the war ended on a *status quo ante* basis.[170] For Germany's heavy industry, therefore, it was a question of all or nothing. Either Germany would gain complete

[167] Lutz, *German Empire*, I, 317-18.

[168] *Ibid.*

[169] P. H. von Schwabach, *Aus meinen Akten* (Berlin, 1927), pp. 274-8; Friedensburg, p. 50; Grumbach, pp. 375 ff.

[170] E. Thaller, " Esquisse de réforme de la législation des étrangers, particulièrement dans les rapports franco-allemands, individus et sociétés," *Révue Politique et Parlementaire*, XCII (1917), 297-336; XCIII (1917), 5-37; Ungeheuer, *Technik und Wirtschaft*, IX, 101; L. Férasson, *La Question du fer* (Paris, 1918), p. 131.

control of France's iron supply, or else she would lose even the small foothold she had gained before the war. It is this fact which explains the deep interest of German industry in the war aims problem.

Annexationist Propaganda

The question as to how far the views of the annexationists expressed the opinion of the majority of Germans, is difficult to answer. For reasons of censorship, most annexationist programs could not be put before the general public. The publication of the Six Economic Organizations, for instance, was prohibited by the government, though it became known in other ways.[171] Yet despite censorship restrictions, the amount of articles, pamphlets, and speeches during the first months of the war, dealing with German westward expansion, was considerable. Whether this propaganda was the result of a widespread popular demand, or whether it was intended to help create and increase such a demand, is again difficult to determine. The average citizen has little real opportunity of voicing his approval or disapproval of the propaganda to which he is subjected. Many observers testify, however, to the artificial character of German annexationist propaganda; and its origin among the annexationist pressure groups certainly lends credence to this view.[172] Whether artificial or spontaneous, however, the result of these writings was to popularize the idea of territorial expansion and direct the nebulous hopes of the German people into specific channels.

The most important means of influencing opinion, of course, was the press. We have already seen how the *Tägliche Rundschau, Leipziger Neueste Nachrichten, Rheinisch-Westphälische Zeitung,* and *Post* were indirectly under Pan-German influence.[173] It should not surprise us, therefore, to find more or less veiled hints in favor of annexationist aims in these papers, even while the public debate of such aims was still prohibited by the German government.[174]

---

[171] Westarp, II, 165-66; Class, *Strom,* p. 395.

[172] Kanner, II, 42-44 and *passim.*; S. B. Clough, *A History of the Flemish Movement in Belgium* (N. Y., 1930), pp. 182-83; Grumbach, p. 376.

[173] See Jung, p. 25, for a list of Pan-German papers.

[174] For references to such articles see *Vorwärts,* Oct. 16, 17, 29, 1914; Feb. 16, 23, March 16, 25, 29, April 18, May 6, 8, 1915; *Tägliche Rundschau,* May 1, 1915; *Leipziger Neueste Nachrichten,* March 24, 1915.

At times these articles lost all their vagueness and became openly and bluntly annexationist. The *Post* on October 25, 1914 wrote: " The German Reich . . . may and must annex Belgium and must under no circumstances show any leniency when it comes to the imposition of an indemnity. The German people expect the Germanization of Belgium as a matter of course and a physical necessity. . . ." [175] Other prominent papers with annexationist leanings, the *Tag*, the *Kölnische Volkszeitung*, and the *Kreuzzeitung* wrote in a similar vein. The latter, under the editorship of the Conservative Party's secretary, Schroeter, was a direct outlet for Count Westarp's views on war aims.[176] Even the semi-official *Norddeutsche Allgemeine Zeitung* and the *Berliner Lokalanzeiger* dropped occasional hints that a " greater Germany " should result from the war.[177]

One of the outstanding annexationist papers was the *Deutsche Tageszeitung*. Its editor was Ernst Georg Oertel, a leading Conservative and member of the *Bund der Landwirte*, which mainly supported his paper. The outstanding contributor was " E. R.," i. e., Count Ernst von Reventlow. A former columnist on foreign affairs for the liberal *Berliner Tageblatt* and Maximilian Harden's *Zukunft*, Reventlow had used his position for frequent attacks upon the naval policy of Admiral von Tirpitz. Suddenly, in 1908, for reasons never satisfactorily explained, he changed his attitude and became an ardent supporter of the Admiral. He severed relations with his former employers and took over the foreign desk of the *Tägliche Rundschau* and later of the *Deutsche Tageszeitung*. He also served his time with the Pan-German League, as head of its Berlin branch and editor of the *Alldeutsche Blätter*; and though he left the League in 1910, he maintained contact and resumed collaboration during the World War.[178]

Reventlow's relations with the *Reichsmarineamt* of Admiral von Tirpitz were close, although both he and the Admiral denied the rumor that Reventlow was the paid propagandist of Tirpitz and

---

[175] On the industrial affiliations of the *Post* see H. Wehberg, *Die internationale Beschränkung der Rüstungen* (Berlin, 1919), p. 344.

[176] *Tag*, Feb. 13, 1915; March 22, 1915; *Kölnische Volkzeitung*, Sept. 17, 1914; May 29, 1915; O. Hoetzsch, *Der Krieg und die grosse Politik* (Leipzig, 1917), vol. I contains H.'s weekly editorials in the *Kreuzzeitung* during this early period. For a list of Westarp's articles see Westarp, II, 32, note 1.

[177] *Norddeutsche Allgemeine Zeitung*, April 24, 30, 1915; *Vorwärts*, Oct. 17, 1914.

[178] L. Persius, *Graf Ernst zu Reventlow* (Berlin, 1918), *passim*.

his naval policy.[179] The similarity of their aims was, to say the least, suggestive of some sort of collusion. Both Tirpitz and Reventlow considered Great Britain Germany's most dangerous enemy, and both demanded the coast of Belgium and northern France as base for a powerful German fleet. Such a fleet would be the only means of securing their version of the " freedom of the seas," substituting Germany's naval predominance for that of Great Britain.[180] The elusive concept " freedom of the seas " reappeared continually in the writings of most western annexationists, because it gave an excellent excuse for the annexation of extensive coastal areas and eventually of the hinterland as well.[181] Such annexation would prevent another English blockade, the pinch of which was increasingly felt by the Central Powers. We shall run across the demand for "freedom of the seas" in many variations throughout this study. Its constant reiteration by " E. R." 's quick and biting pen won a large following both for western annexations and for the *Deutsche Tageszeitung*.[182]

Periodical literature in Germany, especially if known for its annexationist leanings, was more seriously affected by governmental censorship regulations than the press. The *Alldeutsche Blätter*, as we have seen already, wanted a " greater future " for Germany.[183] *Das grössere Deutschland* published articles on German eastward expansion by Paul Rohrbach, on a large colonial empire in Central Africa by Paul Arndt, and on annexations in France and Belgium by Count Reventlow.[184] Rohrbach, as the war progressed, became increasingly opposed to the Pan-Germans and their *Drang nach Westen*. But at this early stage he was by no means averse to complete German domination of Belgium.[185] *Des neue Deutschland*, a Free-Conservative weekly edited by Adolf Grabowsky, was still more outspoken than either of these two journals.[186] *Die Grenzboten* had advocated co-operation between Germany and her west-

[179] Tirpitz, *Dokumente*, II, 628 ff.

[180] *Deutsche Tageszeitung*, Sept. 7, Oct. 27, 1914; March 20, 28, April 14, 1915.

[181] For a discussion of the question and for various writers on the subject see Ch. Meurer, *Das Programm der Meeresfreiheit* (Tübingen, 1918), esp. 101 ff.; A. Gray, *The Upright Sheaf* (London, 1915), pp. 45 ff.

[182] Westarp, II, 180-81.

[183] *Alldeutsche Blätter*, Aug. 3, 1914.

[184] *Das grössere Deutschland*, Sept. 19, 1914; April 3, May 8, 1915.

[185] Kanner II, 118.

[186] *Das neue Deutschland*, Sept. 30, Oct. 28, Dec. 22, 1914; Feb. 27, 1915.

ern neighbors ever since the early nineteenth century, and it continued this policy during the war. Specifically it suggested the extension of Germany's political and economic sphere by incorporating parts of Belgium and Holland into the German Reich.[187] *Handel und Industrie* published a series of articles by Kurd von Strantz, president of the Army League, in which he demanded the annexation of Belgium as a counterweight against Great Britain.[188] Even the Catholic *Hochland* wished for the annexation of Belfort, and (in an article by Professor Martin Spahn, son of the prominent Centrist) for the economic and military domination of Belgium and the annexation of sections of eastern France.[189]

This list of annexationist articles could be considerably enlarged. Even the sophisticated *Zukunft* of Maximilian Harden temporarily was affected by the annexationist mania. As early as August 22, 1914, Harden defended Germany's " right to extend her territory." In September he reminded Belgium that she owed her culture, her colonies, and her independence to Germany, and that she had forfeited her privileges because of her cruel warfare against the invading Germans. A month later, Harden joined the most radical of the annexationists: " We shall remain in the Belgian Netherlands," he wrote, " to which we shall add a thin coastal strip up to and beyond Calais . . . From Calais to Antwerp, Flanders, Limburg, Brabant, and beyond the line of the Meuse: Prussian. . . ." [190]

More effective than this periodical literature, however, were the innumerable books and pamphlets which dealt with a post-war settlement. It is impossible to determine their exact number, but a conservative estimate would put such writings during the first year at close to a hundred.[191] Not all were of equal significance, of course, nor did they all reach an equally wide audience. Some were sent out by mail to a limited number of important persons, a practice started by Heinrich Class, to evade the watchful eye of the censor. Professor Fabarius, for instance, Pan-German and director

[187] *Die Grenzboten,* Oct. 17, Nov. 11, Dec. 23, 1914.

[188] *Handel und Industrie,* Sept. 12, Oct. 10, 1914; March 6, 1915.

[189] F. Otto, " Belfort," *Hochland,* Oct. 1914; M. Spahn, " An den Pforten des Weltkrieges," *ibid.*

[190] *Die Zukunft,* Aug. 22, 1914, p. 251; Aug. 29, 1914, p. 291; Sept. 19, 1914, p. 379; Oct. 17, 1914, p. 96; May 1, 1915.

[191] For a bibliography of annexationist writings during this period see F. Passelecq, *La question flamande et l'Allemagne* (Paris, 1917), pp. 318-29.

of the *Deutsche Kolonialschule*, expressed his war aims (Belgium, Northern France, French and Belgian colonies) in a typescript which was privately distributed.[192] Another example was the Pan-German Franz von Bodelschwingh, whose memorandum to Bethmann, asking for the annexation of Belgium, was privately printed and widely circulated by mail.[193] But the majority of annexationist propaganda was carried on quite openly, reaching a considerable audience.

It is unnecessary for our purposes to discuss each publication in detail, since the aims advanced are little different from the ones we have already encountered. The National Liberal imperialist Arthur Dix, for instance, advocated that Belgium " in one form or another " should " come under German influence." As for France, " the German and French mines in both parts of Lorraine already to a large extent encroach upon each other. To join them together in German possession appears an appropriate step to make France economically dependent." Colonies in Central Africa and naval stations all over the globe were to complete Germany's gains.[194] Pamphlets by Gustav Stresemann, Professor Max Apt, and Professor Conrad Borchling made similar suggestions, though not always in such outspoken manner.[195] The role of university professors in German annexationist propaganda, as we shall see, was considerable. Already shortly after the outbreak of war, a number of them had pledged their support to the government's war policy.[196] Now they went one step further and joined the annexationists in their demands for German expansion. Julius Wolf, economist and founder of the *Mitteleuropäischer Wirtschaftsverein*, in addition to territorial demands, wanted a substantial indemnity.[197] Colonial expansion, often in connection with annexations

[192] E. A. Fabarius, " Deutsche Friedenshoffnungen (n. pl., 1915), Vertrauliche Handschrift, Typescript, esp. pp. 32, 40, 52 ff.

[193] F. von Bodelschwingh, *Innere Hemmungen kraftvoller Aussenpolitik* (Hannover, 1919), pp. 37 ff.; Schäfer, *Leben*, p. 168.

[194] A. Dix, *Der Weltwirtschaftskrieg* (Leipzig, 1914), pp. 32 ff.

[195] G. Stresemann, *Deutsches Ringen und Deutsches Hoffen* (Berlin, 1914); M. Apt, *Der Krieg und die Weltmachtstellung des Deutschen Reiches* (Leipzig, 1914), esp. pp. 30-31; C. Borchling, *Das belgische Problem* (Hamburg, 1914), pp. 4 ff., 28.

[196] Schäfer, *Leben*, pp. 166-67.

[197] J. Wolf, *Die französische Kriegsentschädigung* (n. pl., 1914); J. Wolf, *Die Kriegsrechnung* (Berlin, 1914); on the problem of an indemnity see also Freiherr von Zedlitz und Neukirch, *Reichs-und Staatsfinanzen im Kriege* (Leipzig, 1914), pp. 25-26.

on the continent, was the subject of books or pamphlets by Professors Mirbt (Theology), von Liszt (Law), Backhaus (Agriculture) and even the well-known editor of the *Preussische Jahrbücher*, Hans Delbrück.[198] The idea of some of these writers, that Germany's continental conquests should be exchanged against a more extensive colonial empire, found little favor with the majority of the Pan-German and industrial annexationists.[199]

In dealing with the future of Western Europe, some of these writers advanced solutions which had a novel ring. We have already run across references to the division of Belgium's population into the Germanic Flemings and the Romanic Walloons. The German government, as we shall see, was much aware of this dualism and the advantages it offered. To the annexationists, the historic and ethnographic arguments in favor of a division of Belgium into its component parts, and a rapprochement of the Flemish section with its Germanic " mother country " supplied welcome material for propaganda. " We have not indeed begun the war [one of them writes] to support the Germanic Flemings in their struggle against French tendencies; but after we have been forced to war, and after making such an astonishing acquaintance with the Belgian people, it is our duty to make good old omissions, and to pay closest attention to the national claims of the Belgian people." [200] The Flemish state, some writers held, should become part of a Teutonic federation under German leadership.[201] Other Germanic nations—Holland, Switzerland, Denmark, and parts of Austria— might also be included in such a federation.[202] Another plan called for the separation of Belgium into her Flemish and Walloon components and their inclusion into an economic *Mitteleuropa* under German domination.[203] The Pan-German Rudolf Theuden went

[198] C. Mirbt, *Der Kampf um unsere Kolonien* (Braunschweig, 1914), p. 20; F. von Liszt, *Ein mitteleuropäischer Staatenverband* (Leipzig, 1914), p. 7; A. Backhaus, *Der Krieg eine Notwendkeit für Deutschlands Weltstellung* (Berlin, 1914), p. 39; H. Delbrück, *Bismarck's Erbe* (Berlin, 1915), p. 202.

[199] G. W. Schiele, *Überseepolitik oder Kontinentalpolitik* (München, 1917), pp. 13 ff.

[200] Borchling, p. 5.

[201] A. Ruhemann, " Die Zukunft Belgiens: Vlamen und Wallonen," in K. L. van der Bleek, ed., *Die Vernichtung der englischen Weltmacht* (Berlin, 1915), pp. 142-43; see also Borchling, p. 28.

[202] E. Deckert, *Panlatinismus, Panslawismus, und Panteutonismus in ihrer Bedeutung für die politische Weltlage* (Wien, 1914), p. 29.

[203] H. L. Losch, *Der mitteleuropäische Wirtschaftsblock und das Schicksal Belgiens* (Leipzig, 1914), pp. 34-37.

still further. " If Belgium should participate in the war [he wrote in August 1914], she must be struck off the map." [204] The Walloons should be handed over to France and the Flemings to Germany or to Holland, if the latter would consent to become a German federal state.

This and other similar proposals to solve the Belgian problem caused considerable concern to the Dutch.[205] Under-Secretary Zimmermann tried to allay these fears in an interview with the Dutch Socialist Troelstra in October 1914.[206] But when the output of propaganda continued, the Secretary found it necessary to address a reproachful letter to the Pan-German League. " The largest share of the suspicion [he wrote], which meets our efforts to create some understanding abroad for Germany's aims, results from the boundless character of Pan-German writings and speeches. I say this on the basis of my observations over many years." [207]

To the list of annexationist writings (which could be much enlarged) [208] we should add the many speeches and public statements to which Zimmermann referred in the letter just quoted. Many of these we have already discussed. Next to the politicians, Pan-Germans, and industrialists, it was the university professors who were most vociferous. Already in August 1914, Ernst Haeckel, by now over eighty years old, asked for the division of Belgium, the annexation of northern France, and even the occupation of London.[209] Johannes Haller, noted historian, opposed a peace which would leave Germany territorially unchanged. Other speeches by Professors Schwalbe, Ruge, von Gruber and Ostwald made similar demands, the latter advocating a United States of Europe under the presidency of the German Emperor.[210]

In conclusion, there are one or two general observations that should be made on this annexationist propaganda during the first

---

[204] R. Theuden, *Was muss uns der Krieg bringen?* (Berlin, 1914), p. 10; see also Ph. Muench-Born, *Was uns der Weltkrieg bringen muss* (Leipzig, 1914), p. 37.

[205] *Frankfurter Zeitung*, May 23 and 28, 1915; Schwabach, p. 285.

[206] Gray, p. 65.

[207] Jung, pp. 30-31.

[208] For further writings see Grumbach, pp. 265 ff.; Great Britain, Foreign Office, *German Opinion on National Policy since July 1914* (London, 1920), *passim.*

[209] H. von Gerlach, *Von Rechts nach Links* (Zürich, 1937), p. 235; E. Haeckel, *Englands Blutschuld am Weltkriege* (Eisenach, 1914), *passim.*

[210] J. Haller, *Warum und wofür wir kämpfen* (Tübingen, 1914); Grumbach, pp. 170-71; 290; Class, *Strom*, p. 376; Gerlach, p. 235.

few months of the war. Both the large number and the early date
of these publications indicate that, while to the average German
the war was at first one of defense, to a small minority it was almost
immediately converted into a struggle for territorial gains. Another
fact worth pointing out is that so many of the annexationist plans
showed such striking similarities, which has been attributed to the
influence of Heinrich Class' basic memorandum.[211]   There was
general agreement, for instance, on the desirability of colonial gains,
especially in Central Africa. There was widespread demand for
sections of eastern France. The only region over which there was
considerable disagreement was Belgium. But even here most annexationists agreed that Germany should maintain some hold,
direct or indirect, over Belgium's political and economic life.

The " Moderates "

One of the most interesting insights into the extent of annexationist opinion in Germany can be gained from a study of those organizations and individuals who were generally attacked because of
their moderate attitude on the question of war aims. Because surprisingly enough, to be a moderate or a *Flaumacher* (as the Pan-
Germans called it), did not necessarily mean the rejection of any
and all annexations.

We have already discussed the most prominent and consistent
group among the anti-annexationists, the Social Democrats, particularly their more radical members. As early as August 1914, Karl
Liebknecht had organized meetings to oppose the growing clamor
for territorial expansion.[212] In November, Klara Zetkin, Secretary
of the Women's International, published a manifesto against all
annexations, while Eduard Bernstein turned specifically against the
annexation of Belgium, which was demanded, he said, by " large
sections of the people, including the ranks of the workers." [213] The
Socialist press took a similar stand, especially in its leading organ,
the *Vorwärts*.[214]

Compared to the Social Democrats, the various non-political
organizations opposed to annexations were too small to be of much

[211] *U. A.*, 4. Reihe, XII (1), 50.
[212] Dahlin, p. 29.
[213] Grumbach, pp. 448, 448.
[214] *Vorwärts*, Oct. 1, 3, 4, 1914; Jan. 30, Feb. 5, 1915.

practical significance. The first of them, the *Bund Neues Vaterland*, was founded in October 1914 under the leadership of Baron von Tepper-Laski and Otto Lehmann-Russbüldt.[215] Its importance has been much overrated.[216] It did oppose the ultra-annexationist programs current in Germany and produced a detailed memorandum against the " Petition of the Six Economic Organizations." [217] But even the *Bund Neues Vaterland*, so violently persecuted by its Pan-German adversaries, did not completely forego all hope for German aggrandizement after the war:

We can and must gain real guarantees [!] to secure our position. If peace should be concluded under present military conditions, we must use the territories occupied by our troops as pledges or objects of compensation. The most obvious thought in this connection would be of colonial acquisitions, improvements of our frontiers for military protection, and indemnities; perhaps also naval and coaling stations.[218]

Germany's leading Pacifist organization, the small *Deutsche Friedensgesellschaft*, was equally opposed to large-scale annexations on the European continent and advocated a peace " which does not contain the seeds of new wars." [219] Many of the society's writings and its journal *Der Völkerfriede* were subsequently prohibited for the duration of the war.[220] Yet again this very moderate organization was not entirely averse to German expansion overseas. Its president, Professor Quidde, suggested the principles of the " open door " and " freedom of the seas " as alternate war aims, and in return for the evacuation by Germany of the occupied areas in Western Europe, he hoped to gain a German colonial empire in Central Africa, consisting of the Belgian Congo and additional territories, plus naval stations and strategic improvements of Germany's western border.[221]

---

[215] Forster, p. 27; K. Wortmann, *Geschichte der Deutschen Vaterlands-Partei 1917-18* (Halle, 1926), p. 12; O. Lehmann-Russbüldt, *Der Kampf der Deutschen Liga für Menschenrechte vormals Bund Neues Vaterland für den Weltfrieden 1914-1927* (Berlin, 1927), *passim*.

[216] For a humorous description of one of the *Bund*'s meetings see Kanner, II, 189.

[217] Grumbach, pp. 375-409.

[218] *Ibid.*, pp. 407-08.

[219] G. Fuchs, *Der deutsche Pazifismus im Weltkrieg* (Stuttgart, 1928), pp. 61-62.

[220] *Reichstag*, vol. 307, p. 1289.

[221] L. Quidde, *Reale Garantien für einen dauernden Frieden* (n. pl., 1915), pp. 20 ff.; Fuchs, p. 61.

In the same category as the two previous organizations belongs the *Freie Vaterländische Vereinigung*, founded in February 1915, which arranged for discussions among its members and representatives of various parties, to arrive at a moderate program of war aims.[222] Its president, Professor Kahl, made it perfectly clear that he was not averse to " territorial expansion to gain military, political, and economic security." [223]

What we have just discovered for the so-called " anti-annexationist " organizations—namely that they were by no means opposed to all, but merely to large-scale continental annexations— also holds true for certain prominent individuals who, in the course of the war, became the leading opponents of Pan-German expansionism. In his speech before the leaders of the Pan-German League on August 28, 1914, Heinrich Class had mentioned, besides the Socialists, the intellectuals, Jews, and German high-finance as chief opponents of Pan-German war aims.[224] Admiral von Tirpitz subsequently defined this group somewhat differently as " the *Hapag*, the banks, all former ambassadors and diplomats, and the Wilhelmstrasse." [225] We must not think in this connection, however, of a well-organized opposition group with a clearly defined program. Socially and politically, these moderates differed little from their annexationist adversaries. Both groups recruited their main following from the upper levels of society and the parties of the Right. The main difference was in their attitude towards Germany's domestic and foreign policy. In opposition to the ultra-annexationists and their reactionary domestic policy, the moderates advocated a conciliatory, more liberal policy, both at home and abroad. Their cultural, financial, or commercial ties with Great Britain made most of them, if not actual Anglophiles, at least admirers of the British Empire and its institutions. They hoped for some kind of agreement with their Anglo-Saxon cousins, giving Germany a due share in the colonial wealth and the commercial activities of the world. In return she would refrain from annexing Belgium and thus upsetting the balance of power on the continent. Such an agreement, they held, would best serve Germany's wide commercial and industrial

[222] *Die Tat*, IX (1917), 187.
[223] *U. A.*, 4. Reihe, XXI (1), 52-53; W. Kahl, *Die Freie Vaterländische Vereinigung* (Berlin, 1915), *passim*.
[224] Class, *Strom*, p. 321.
[225] Tirpitz, *Erinnerungen*, p. 469.

interests. Even so, during the early days of the war, many of these moderates hoped to maintain some sort of control even over Belgium. Count Wedel, formerly *Statthalter* of Alsace-Lorraine and in 1916 to be president of the moderate *Nationalausschuss für einen Deutschen Frieden* wrote in January of 1915: " I agree that Belgium (which in addition must be induced to cede some of its territory) must be secured in some fashion. But I think this can be achieved through economic *Anschluss* and a military convention." [226] The former Colonial Secretary Dernburg, later known for his moderate views on war aims, stated in April 1915, that " Germany cannot renounce Belgium," since that country " had been conquered with great sacrifices of blood and money and offers Germany's western trade the only free access to the sea." [227] Count Monts, formerly ambassador to Italy, whose moderation and Anglophilism aroused the ire of the German Empress and her confidant, Admiral Tirpitz,[228] had his eye on both the French and Belgian Congo. In a letter to Theodor Wolff, editor of the liberal *Berliner Tageblatt*, he added the French railways in Anatolia, a war indemnity, and the iron fields of Briey; also Liège and Luxemburg as necessary protection for Germany's western industrial area.[229] Theodor Wolff himself had hinted at annexations as early as August 10, 1914.[230] And even the *Frankfurter Zeitung*, leading organ of liberal and moderate elements in Germany, wrote as a comment on Bethmann's speech of May 28, 1915: " The question is not annexations or no annexations. The question is, how can Germany best secure the fulfillment of her world tasks? If the annexation of foreign districts is necessary in order to secure our military position or to get closer to our aim, we favor it." [231]

One of the outstanding opponents of German continental expansion was the Berlin historian Hans Delbrück. " May God prevent Germany," he wrote in October 1914, " from following the

---

[226] F. Lienhard, ed., " Statthalterbriefe aus Elsass-Lothringen," *Der Türmer,* XXVI (1924), p. 536.

[227] *Chronik des Deutschen Krieges* (München, 1915), IV, 437-38.

[228] Tirpitz, *Erinnerungen,* p. 474. The influence of the Empress, though difficult to determine, was an important element in German policy; see also T. Wolff, *Der Marsch durch zwei Jahrzehnte* (Amsterdam, 1936), p. 249; O. Braun, *Von Weimar zu Hitler* (New York, 1940), pp. 45-47.

[229] Wolff, *Der Marsch,* p. 92.

[230] *Berliner Tageblatt,* Aug. 10, 1914.

[231] *Frankfurter Zeitung,* May 31, 1915 (2d ed.); also March 12, 1915.

course of Napoleon's policy after the victory which we expect! Wars without end would be the result. However heavily we might chain other nations, we cannot keep them in fetters forever. Europe is agreed on this one point, never to submit to the hegemony of one single state." The aim of the war, he declared, should be " that on land the balance of power must be maintained as it is, and that on the sea a similar balance must be attained." [232] These moderate views which, as the *Vorwärts* pointed out, " demanded exactly what Emperor William formally proclaimed at the beginning of the war," caused violent outbursts in annexationist circles. The *Tägliche Rundschau* called the article a " crime against the German cause." The *Post* more explicitly accused Delbrück of criminal subserviency to Germany's enemies. Reventlow in the *Deutsche Tageszeitung* wrote in a similar vein.[233] At this point the censor intervened, the author was reprimanded and his article confiscated. Delbrück appealed to the censorship board headed by a close friend of the annexationist Conservatives, General von Kessel, contending that Bethmann Hollweg held the same views on war aims as he, Delbrück, did. " So much the worse for the Chancellor," the General replied, " but that does not change my views in the least." [234]

The moderation among Germany's intellectuals and former diplomats, as this brief survey has shown, was by no means so great as the attacks of the Pan-Germans may lead us to believe. The same can be said for her financial and commercial interests. Although the war seriously curtailed the international activities of Germany's leading banks, the boom of domestic industries helped to make up for any losses abroad. Their attitude during the early days of the war, therefore, was definitely optimistic.[235] The leadership of German high finance, according to Class, was in the hands of director

[232] H. Delbrück, " Der zukünftige Friede," *Preussische Jahrbücher,* vol. 158 (1914), p. 191.

[233] For a summary of press comments on Delbrück's article see *Vorwärts,* Oct. 3-4, 1914.

[234] Germany, Nationalversammlung, Untersuchungsausschuss über die Weltkriegsverantwortlichkeit, *Stenographische Berichte über die öffentlichen Verhandlungen des 15. Untersuchungsausschusses* (2 vols., Berlin, 1920) (henceforth cited as *U. A.,* 15. Ausschuss), I, 182; Kanner, II, 47; Westarp, II, 181. A colleague of Delbrück's, Friedrich Meinecke, hoped for colonial expansion but advocated the complete independence of Belgium. F. Meinecke, *Strassburg, Freiburg, Berlin 1901-1919 Erinnerungen* (Stuttgart, 1949), p. 198.

[235] Kanner, II, 19.

von Gwinner of the *Deutsche Bank*.[236] Gwinner, who became considerably more moderate as the war progressed, was sufficiently impressed by Germany's early victories to hope for a large indemnity and France's colonies as possible German gains.[237] His colleague, Paul von Schwabach of the *Diskonto-Gesellschaft* was still a better example of the moderately annexationist German financier. He opposed the exaggerated aims of the ultra-annexationists, especially the Six Economic Organizations.[238] Instead he wrote a detailed memorandum of his own, in which he revealed himself as by no means averse to certain moderate war aims. The annexation of the French mining region of Briey, he felt, was desirable and presented few geographical obstacles. As to Belgium, he was against outright annexation and instead suggested German economic domination and military control. The few specific suggestions which he made in this connection, such as German supervision over Belgian tariffs, railroads and canals, the dismantling of her fortresses, and the reduction of the Belgian army to a bare minimum, were but a weaker version of the aims current among radical annexationists.[239]

Walter Rathenau, head of Germany's leading electrical trust, the *A. E. G.*, and member of more than a hundred German and foreign business concerns, was the chief industrial exponent of a moderate peace. This was due partly to the nature of the " light " industries he represented. While the " heavy " industry of coal and iron stood much to gain from a prospective German expansion to the west, the lighter industries, such as chemicals, railways or electrical interests, had few economic stakes in that region. Rathenau's personality, a curious blend of shrewd businessman, artist and philosopher, likewise helps to explain his moderation. Though at the same time, the drastic efficiency he showed in the creation and administration of the *Kriegsrohstoffabteilung* (whose purpose was the co-ordination of the various sources of German raw-materials, and which led to the confiscation of large amounts of enemy property) made a moderate peace settlement considerably more difficult.[240] " Rathenau," a con-

---

[236] Class, *Strom*, 321.

[237] Tirpitz, *Dokumente*, II, 67.

[238] Schwabach, pp. 281-82.

[239] *Ibid.*, pp. 274 ff.

[240] On Rathenau see Harry Graf Kessler, *Walter Rathenau, his Life and Work* (New York, 1930), esp. pp. 117 ff.; H. Brinckmeyer, *Die Rathenaus* (München, 1922), pp. 11 ff.

temporary observed, " when it came to politics, was an industrialist
first and last." [241] Rathenau deplored the exaggerated expectations
of the annexationists. Instead he wanted the German government
to issue a reassuring declaration concerning the future of Belgium,
realizing that to England this question was of foremost concern. A
Central European economic union with both France and Belgium
participating, might be a more organic and lasting achievement
than the annexation of Belgium; especially if one believed, with
Rathenau, " that the economic union between these neighbors
would eventually include a political union." [242] " To destroy and
annex Belgium," he said to Conrad Haussmann in December 1914,
" would be the greatest mistake Germany ever made." [243]

Of the various economic groups affected by the outbreak of war,
none suffered more severely than Germany's commercial and
shipping interests. Cut off from the rest of the world through
Britain's naval blockade, their policy, naturally, was directed
towards a speedy termination of the war. Their spokesman was
Albert Ballin, Director of the *Hapag* and close friend of the
Emperor. In the enthusiasm of the first weeks of war, Ballin had
hoped for large financial indemnities and colonial concessions.[244]
Yet a few weeks later, when Germany's knock-out blow against
France had failed, his enthusiasm declined noticeably. " I was in
Berlin during the week," he wrote to Admiral von Tirpitz on
October 1, " and I was alarmed when I became acquainted with
the wild schemes which are entertained not only by the people of
Berlin, but by distinguished men from the Rhineland and Westphalia." [245] Ballin, more than most people, realized how much
Germany's success depended on a quick military decision. " My
opinion is that the result of this world war, if it lasts twelve
months, will be exactly the same as if it lasts six months. If we
do not succeed in acquiring the guarantees for our compensation
demands within a few months, the further progress of events will
not appreciably improve our chances in this direction." As to war
aims, Germany " must find compensation by annexing valuable
territories beyond the seas; but for the peaceful enjoyment of such

[241] Mendelssohn Bartholdy, p. 224.
[242] W. Rathenau, *Briefe* (2 vols., Dresden, 1926), I, 164-65, 170.
[243] Haussmann, p. 20.
[244] Tirpitz, *Dokumente*, II, 68.
[245] B. Huldermann, *Albert Ballin* (Berlin, 1922), p. 240.

overseas gain, we shall be dependent on the good-will of Great Britain." To assure this good-will, we must aim at "a new grouping of powers around an alliance between Germany, Great Britain, and France. This alliance will become possible as soon as we shall have vanquished France and Belgium, and as soon as you [i. e., Admiral von Tirpitz] have made up your mind to bring about an understanding with Great Britain concerning the naval program." [246]

Here we have a clear expression of the moderates' creed: the colonization and commercial exploitation of the world not in opposition to, but in friendly competition with Great Britain. That such a policy, which had the sympathy and support of the government, was possible, Anglo-German relations on the eve of war had proved.[247] Yet the voices of moderation and conciliation were drowned by the clamor of Anglophobe annexationists, patriotic Pan-Germans, naval enthusiasts, and greedy industrialists for the complete and final defeat of the British Empire.

At the beginning of January 1915, Ballin wrote an article for the *Frankfurter Zeitung* which caused considerable discussion.[248] Its title, "The Wet Triangle," together with such terms as "real guarantees and securities" or "freedom of the seas," soon became one of the clichés of annexationist propaganda. The term referred to that section of the North Sea between the island of Heligoland and the mouths of the Elbe and Ems. Hemmed in between the narrow confines of this triangle, the German fleet, according to Ballin, lacked effective bases from which to operate successfully against the blockading British navy. "We must, therefore, find a naval base beyond the limits of the North Sea," he wrote, "which will secure us in the future the same opportunities in this part of the world as England now possesses and ruthlessly exploits."

Although this latter statement, as Ballin's friend and biographer Huldermann points out, probably referred to a naval base on the Atlantic, in Northern Africa perhaps, it was sufficiently vague to be applicable to the coast of Belgium. This was promptly done by the supporters of Belgian annexation.[249] Nor was Ballin himself

---

[246] *Ibid.*, pp. 237-40; Tirpitz, *Dokumente*, I, 131, 134.
[247] E. F. Willis, *Prince Lichnowsky, Ambassador of Peace* (Berkeley, 1942), chs. IV and V.
[248] A. Ballin, "Das nasse Dreieck," *Frankfurter Zeitung*, Jan. 4, 1915.
[249] Huldermann, pp. 234-35; Hoetzsch, I, 51.

as disinterested in the acquisition of a German foothold in Belgium as Huldermann would have us believe. Since he was against outright annexation, he suggested that Germany acquire a lease over the port of Zeebrugge as well as a voice in the administration of Antwerp.[250] On February 8, 1915, Ballin, in a memorandum to the government, suggested far-reaching economic co-operation between Germany and Belgium.[251]

In concluding this brief survey of moderate opinion in Germany we may say that any real opposition to territorial aggrandizement was rare, even among people known as anti-annexationist. Return to the *status quo ante bellum* seemed desirable only to the Social Democrats; and even here, as we have seen, opinion was divided. Some concessions, perhaps in the colonial field, some territorial or financial indemnity, appeared justifiable even to the most moderate German. Because he believed, just as strongly as most of his annexationist compatriots, that the Fatherland had suffered a premeditated encirclement and attack from a conspiracy of jealous enemies. It was a question of degree and not of principle that separated the ultra-annexationists from their moderate opponents.

The Government and the Annexationists

It has been necessary to treat the formative period of Germany's war aims in some detail, because it helps us to understand the changing attitude of the German government, as represented by Bethmann Hollweg, towards western expansionism. We have seen how, when war broke out, both government and people had no aim beyond that of defending the Fatherland. The initial victories and sacrifices of Germany's army, however, soon created an almost universal, though still vague hope for some kind of tangible reward. Except for the majority of Social Democrats, almost all Germans expected an increase in colonial holdings and, perhaps, a few minor improvements along the frontiers.

Yet despite this growing sentiment in favor of some degree of expansion, the government maintained its initial attitude of vagueness, hinting at the necessity for " real guarantees and securities," but failing to define that term, at least publicly. It was possible,

[250] Tirpitz, *Erinnerungen*, p. 443; Wolff, *Marsch*, p. 266; P. F. Stubmann, *Ballin, Leben und Werk eines deutschen Reeders* (Berlin, 1926), p. 258.
[251] *U. A.*, 4. Reihe, XII (1), 37.

therefore, for the moderate section of the German people, especially the Socialists, to claim official support and to set the government against those of their countrymen who hoped for considerable and tangible gains on the European continent as well as overseas.[252] At the same time, however, we find the German Chancellor committing himself in private to a program of western expansion which, to be sure, only called for the annexation of parts of eastern France, but which also outlined a plan for the political, economic, and military domination of Belgium which, in some ways, was more extreme than outright annexation.

To explain the rise of annexationist hopes among the German people and political parties entirely as a natural phenomenon, however, in which the expansionist appetite developed as the table was set with increasingly inviting territories along the western border, would be much too superficial. Still less would it be correct to attribute the changes in Bethmann Hollweg's attitude to such a cause. For he, more than the rest of the German people, was deeply aware of the artificiality of Germany's initial military successes. To understand the rise of annexationism in its more extreme forms, we had to turn to those groups within Germany in which this annexationism was not entirely spontaneous: the Pan-Germans and the representatives of heavy industry. The pre-war writings of the former and the pre-war economic policy of the latter point towards Western Europe as the most desirable field for expansion. This, plus the fact that the war was barely a month old before both groups had voiced their specific demands, belies the assertion that with them, as well, the rise of annexationist aims was a spontaneous affair.

However the advantages to be gained from this more extreme annexationism were by no means equally obvious to the whole German people. To convince those parts of the population who were either opposed to it, who held moderate views, or who were undecided (perhaps the largest number, and often referred to as *Laubfrosch Annexionisten*, tree-frog annexationists, " who jumped up when the war news was good, and jumped down when it was bad "), a propaganda barrage was let loose which soon made it appear as though the whole German people in equal spontaneity demanded the annexation of large sections of Western (and Eas-

[252] *Ibid.*, p. 66.

tern) Europe. How far this propaganda succeeded and what share it had in converting already existing vague demands into a definite program is hard to say. At the very least, the expansionists made the government and many people believe that the majority of Germans demanded the annexation of Belgium and parts of north-eastern France.

It was towards the German government that most of the annexationist propaganda was directed, since the government, and not the people, was responsible for the conduct of war and the conclusion of peace. It was for the government's benefit primarily that innumerable memoranda and petitions were drawn up and presented and that cleverly concealed pressure-group tactics were employed. Germany's annexationists suspected, with good reason, that their Chancellor did not fully share their territorial ambitions. Bethmann definitely belonged in the camp of the moderates. Germany's successful pre-war policy, especially in her economic and commercial gains, was ample proof to the Chancellor that she did not need any considerable expansion to gain her place in the sun. Imperialism, *Weltpolitik,* while leading to international conflict, might just as easily lead to a type of international co-operation, of which international finance and the international working-class movement were already existing examples. One of Bethmann's closest associates had laid down some of these ideas in a most interesting book, which had great influence on the Chancellor.[253]

Here was one of the chief causes for the annexationist attack upon Bethmann. To the influence of some of his colleagues, notably Tirpitz, and the pressure of " public opinion," we must add the uninterrupted bombardment with propaganda from annexationist quarters, if we want to understand Bethmann's change of attitude between August 1914 and May 1915. Most of these plans for westward expansion, though primarily concerned with France and Belgium, really aimed at the defeat of the one nation most deeply hated by the protagonists of the *Drang nach Westen*—Great Britain. Napoleon's dictum: " Antwerp is a pistol, directed at the heart of England," became a much-used cliché to express this ultimate aim of westward expansion.[254] Anyone opposing this

---

[253] " J. J. Ruedorffer " [Kurt Riezler], *Grundzüge der Weltpolitik in der Gegenwart* (Berlin, 1913); see also Bethmann Hollweg, II, 16; Schäfer, *Leben,* pp. 168-69; Stubmann, p. 265; Kanner, II, 120.

[254] *U. A.,* 4. Reihe, XII (1), 50.

Anglophobia, of course, laid himself open to the merciless attacks of the annexationists. The government's failure both to take strong military or naval measures against England, and to declare itself openly in favor of far-reaching western annexations, to serve as bases against the British Isles, fostered malicious rumors among its opponents. Perhaps the fact that the Kaiser was related to the British royal family, or his investments in the Bank of England, or the indebtedness of Bethmann Hollweg to "international Jewish finance" (to meet the debts of his son) might help to explain the mildness of Germany's policy towards England? [255] In this connection we should also mention the mysterious and abortive attempts in the fall of 1914 to overthrow the Chancellor "because he refused to keep Belgium." They were led by Dr. Witting, director of the *National Bank,* formerly mayor of Posen, and brother of Maximilian Harden (their real name being Wittkowski), in collaboration with various annexationist newspapers and members of the Army League.[256] It is interesting to note that the change in Bethmann's attitude towards the future of Belgium between March and May 1915, coincided with a period of intensified annexationist propaganda and attacks, and in one instance at least (Bethmann's answer to Westarp's letter of April 17, 1915) had a direct connection with such an attack.[257]

If, despite Bethmann's concessions to the annexationist spirit of the period, the ultra-annexationists still persisted in their attacks upon his person and his policy, we find a partial explanation in the fact that the Chancellor's sympathies and traditional policy were friendly towards Great Britain. Yet there was a still deeper cause for this annexationist antagonism against Bethmann. We have already pointed out the relationship between expansionist aims and domestic reforms. While the annexationsts denied the necessity for such reforms and hoped to divert any demands for more representative government by the promise of territorial expansion, the Chancellor believed that, no matter how the war ended, governmental reforms had to be one of its lasting results. "Even

---

[255] Westarp, II, 36. For other attacks on Bethmann see Class, *Strom,* p. 391, and Bodelschwingh, pp. 37 ff.

[256] Haussmann, p. 17; Scheidemann, *Memoiren,* I, 396-97; Stubmann, p. 255.

[257] See above, p. 15. Professor Schäfer admits the possible connection between the numerous annexationist petitions in May and Bethmann's speech on May 28: Schäfer, "Kriegszielbewegung," *Der Krieg,* II, 5. Bethmann himself stated that he felt helpless before the propaganda campaign of the Pan-Germans: Valentini, pp. 226-27; Wolff, *Marsch,* p. 93.

the most perfect victory," he wrote after the war, "had to secure the influence of the lower classes in the state, their co-operation and joint responsibility." [258] To him the Kaiser's words of August 4, 1915: "I no longer know parties, I only know Germans," represented a most binding obligation. At this he hinted in his Reichstag speech of December 2, 1914: "When the war is over," he said, "parties will reappear. For without parties, without controversy, there is no political life, even for the freest and most united people. But we want to fight—and I for one promise to do so—we want to fight for one aim: that in this controversy there will be only Germans." [259]

To the Pan-Germans and the parties of the Right, this threat of impending governmental reforms, through which they would lose most of their disproportionate political influence, could only be averted by getting rid of Bethmann Hollweg. It is here that we have to look for the real cause of opposition against the Chancellor. "My God," Class exclaimed, when he read the Kaiser's August proclamation, "we have lost the war on the domestic front!" [260] It was the mission of the Pan-German League, he and his friends decided, to "lead the fight against Bethmann Hollweg." In this he was joined by industrialists, Conservatives, and many National Liberals. [261] Hugenberg, his brother-in-arms, even went so far as to attempt an alliance between the Six Economic Organizations of the famous petition and the bourgeois parties (such as Hirsch had contemplated in the field of war aims), to counteract Bethmann's democratizing domestic policy. The plan, according to Westarp "too beautiful to be true," came to nothing. [262] It was more popular and ultimately just as effective, to launch patriotic attacks against the Chancellor's weak foreign policy, instead of reactionary and unpopular attacks against his liberal and far-sighted domestic policy.

Bethmann Hollweg, instead of taking the determined leadership in a policy which expressed his ideals of moderation abroad and reform at home, followed a course of vagueness, which satisfied

[258] Bethmann Hollweg, II, 33 ff. On the whole problem of domestic reform see U. A., 4. Reihe, VII (1), 229 ff. and VIII, 156 ff.

[259] Reichstag, vol. 306, pp. 17 ff.

[260] Class, Strom, pp. 306-07.

[261] Ibid., pp. 328, 355-56; Westarp, II, 24-25; T. Wolff, Vollendete Tatsachen (Berlin, 1918), p. 24.

[262] Westarp, II, 51.

everyone and no one. The term " real guarantees and securities " which he used in his speech on May 28, 1915, to describe Germany's war aims is a case in point. Yet he was guilty at times of more than mere vagueness. In the question of Belgium, for instance, he showed an amazing ingenuity in adapting his statements to the taste of his audience, without basically changing them. In early March 1915, he received the Socialists Haase and Scheidemann. " The war aims, which the Pan-Germans demand, are nonsense! " he proclaimed. " I don't think of realizing them. To annex Belgium! A country with an entirely foreign population." [263] Yet a few weeks later, the Chancellor presented the annexationist Count Westarp with a program of war aims, " against which [according to the Count] no objection could be raised." [264] Again in May, Bethmann told his aims to an annexationist delegation, which was entirely satisfied with his statement. To the Socialists, a few days later, he presented a milder version of the same views, which " breathed sincere and deep longing for peace." [265]

Behind the Chancellor's vacillation stood his desire to maintain the artificial unity of the *Burgfriede*, and thus the strength of the German nation in time of war.

For the sake of German unity [Bethmann wrote after the war] no policy could be conducted during the war but a policy of the ' diagonal.' Especially in times of excitement and restlessness, in which extremes fight each other, thus increasing their antagonism, such a policy is an ungrateful task. It is attacked from both sides, must seek its followers according to circumstances, and lacks the glamor as well as the momentary force which are characteristic of a more reckless policy. . . . Decisive measures, open controversy in domestic questions, were possible and perhaps necessary when peace was secured and the external struggle was ended. During the war, I considered it my patriotic duty, to walk the narrow path of cool-headedness among passions, tensions, and delusions.[266]

Bethmann's middle-of-the-road policy turned out badly, as we shall see. Yet that it was the result of his sincere endeavor for the well-being of his country cannot be denied. His honesty, experience, knowledge, thoroughness, and patriotism were recognized even by some of his most bitter political opponents.[267]

---

[263] Scheidemann, *Memoiren*, I, 34.
[264] See above, pp. 15-16.
[265] Scheidemann, *Memoiren*, I, 349.
[266] Bethmann Hollweg, II, 34-36.
[267] Westarp, II, 361; W. Ziegler, *Volk ohne Führung* (Hamburg, 1938), p. 43.

Chapter II

A PERIOD OF CONFLICT —
CHANCELLOR VS. ANNEXATIONISTS
(JUNE 1915–AUGUST 1916)

SINCE WE ARE dealing with a subject which does not show any clear subdivisions, organization may easily seem arbitrary. There are no natural highlights in the history of German war aims during the first part of the war as there are during the second with the Peace Note of December 1916, or the Peace Resolution of July 1917. The end of May 1915, was simply chosen as a convenient break since at this time we find the first clear and public statement on the part of the German government (i. e., Bethmann Hollweg) in favor of an expansionist peace. There was no change in developments after this date. The main trends continued: growing support of large war aims in the public statements of the government, paralleled, strangely enough, by an increasing cleavage between the German Chancellor and the more violent annexationists. The explanation for this paradox is that, as Bethmann's statements on war aims grew stronger, his private views on the subject yielded to his increasing pessimism and became more and more moderate. His fatal vacillation, keynote of the early period, thus lasted into the second year of the war.

Certain new elements, however, were injected into the controversy over war aims during this period. The hardships resulting from heavy fighting on several fronts, and the growing scarcity of vital necessities of life due to the blockade, aroused in the majority of Germans a longing for the speedy termination of war. Whether this was to be achieved through a peace of understanding on the basis of the *status quo ante* (involving the renunciation of all territorial gains), or through a peace of victory, dealing a deadly blow to Germany's most dangerous adversary, Great Britain (by means of the newly developed submarine weapon) were questions which helped to intensify the already existing strife inside Germany and to widen the split which the controversy over war aims had reopened among the German people. Another factor, first promi-

68

nent in this period, was the development of a German administration in the conquered regions of the west. Beginning shortly after the outbreak of war, Germany's policy, especially in Belgium, began to show certain marked trends which, better than mere governmental declarations, indicated her true aims in those regions. And finally, it is in this period that the first traces appeared of that rivalry between the civil authority vested in the Chancellor, and the military authority which, though theoretically vested in the Emperor, came increasingly under the influence of the Chief of the General Staff. This dualism did not become acute until after the change in the army's Supreme Command at the end of August 1916, when General von Falkenhayn was replaced by Field Marshal von Hindenburg and his close associate, General Ludendorff. Yet the first indications of a difference of opinion between the civil and military departments of the government about the future of Western Europe already appear in the second year of the war. With the change of command in August 1916, the division of opinion, which ran through the whole German people, definitely invaded the government of the German Reich.

Dualism of Bethmann Hollweg's Policy

The vacillation which the German Chancellor had shown in his statements on war aims during the first year continued during the second. There was moderation, such as his promise to Hungary's Foreign Minister Count Tisza, that Germany would not endanger the chances for an early peace through exaggerated territorial demands; [1] or again his statement to Conrad Haussmann that he " wanted only as much Belgian territory as was absolutely necessary for political and strategic reasons." [2] Yet in his public statements the Chancellor reiterated and even enlarged, the vague promises of his early speeches. On August 1, 1915, first anniversary of the outbreak of war, an Imperial proclamation, approved by Bethmann, promised the German people " a peace which offers the necessary military, political, and economic securities for our future, and which fulfills the conditions for the unhindered development of our creative forces at home and on the free seas." [3] The " real

[1] *U. A.*, 4. Reihe, XII (1), 42.
[2] Haussmann, p. 42.
[3] *Norddeutsche Allgemeine Zeitung*, Aug. 1, 1915 (2d ed.).

guarantees and securities " of May 28, are here more closely defined as " military, political, and economic," and the concept " freedom of the seas " has been added. Before this proclamation appeared, the annexationists were quite worried, because it was rumored that it would again state that the war was not one of conquest and that Germany did not intend to expand her continental frontiers.[4] But only the first part of the rumor turned out to be true, and then the reference was in the past tense: " It was not lust for conquest that brought us into the war," the proclamation read. To such a statement the annexationists had no objection.

Shortly afterwards, on August 14-16, the Social Democrats framed their own declaration in which they demanded " the restitution of Belgium." [5] One of Bethmann's aides, Under-Secretary Wahnschaffe, managed to suppress this section of the manifesto, even though he knew that the Chancellor was in absolute agreement with it. What he was afraid of was that " the military authorities might raise objections." [6] Here we have a first indication that the government's war aims policy was opposed not only by the annexationists but by its own military men as well.

In the meantime, Bethmann Hollweg's vacillation continued. On August 19 he told the Reichstag: " Germany must so cement and strengthen her position, that the other powers will lose their taste for a renewal of their encirclement policy. We must gain the freedom of the seas for our own protection and that of all peoples." [7] These words found the undivided approval of the annexationist press.[8] Yet when he was discussing the future of Belgium privately with Crown Prince Rupprecht of Bavaria, the Chancellor reverted to his moderate views.[9]

A further example of the Chancellor's straddling on war aims came on the occasion of a Socialist interpellation in the Reichstag on December 9, 1915, which asked the government to enter into peace negotiations as soon as possible.[10] Bethmann made two speeches, one before and one in answer to the interpellation. The

[4] Westarp, II, 308; Tirpitz, *Erinnerungen,* p. 481.
[5] *U. A.,* 4. Reihe, XII (1), 61.
[6] *U. A.,* 4. Reihe, XII (1), 62.
[7] *Reichstag,* vol. 306, p. 219.
[8] For a summary of these press comments see Thimme, *Bethmann Hollweg,* pp. 60-61.
[9] Rupprecht, I, 395.
[10] *U. A.,* 4. Reihe, XII (1), 68; Westarp, II, 59.

first speech ended on the usual vague note: " We continue with determination the struggle which our enemies have wished upon us, so as to attain what Germany's future demands from us." [11] Later, after the Socialist Scheidemann's speech, the Chancellor became more specific:

One thing our enemies must realize: the longer and more ardently they wage this war against us, the more the guarantees, necessary for ourselves, will increase. Neither in the East nor in the West shall our present enemies have at their disposal gates of invasion, through which to threaten us anew and more seriously than in the past. . . . We must defend ourselves politically and militarily and must secure the possibility of our economic development. . . . This war can only end with a peace which, as far as is humanly possible, will give us securities against our adversaries.[12]

The jingo press acclaimed the speech and gave it the usual annexationist slant.[13] Yet in the very same speech, Bethmann also said: " We do not carry on this struggle, which has been forced upon us, to subject foreign peoples, but to protect our life and our liberty! For the German government, this war has remained what it was from the beginning and what it has remained in all our proclamations: the defensive war of the German people." [14] It was this latter statement which caused Scheidemann to say: " With this speech the Chancellor once again had moved away from the German annexationists, whose hatred, consequently, pursued him to an ever growing extent." [15]

The favorable reactions of both annexationists and anti-annexationists to Bethmann's speech are an excellent illustration of the dual interpretation to which the Chancellor's views on war aims lent themselves. However, in this case, the reactions were not entirely accidental or unforeseen. The speech of Bethmann had been conceived from the start as a compromise.[16] A week before it was delivered, the Chancellor granted an interview to delegates from the annexationist parties, to agree on the procedure to be followed during the session of December 9. On this occasion, Bethmann gave an outline of his contemplated speech, to which

[11] *Reichstag,* vol. 306, p. 433.
[12] *Reichstag,* vol. 306, pp. 436-37.
[13] Thimme, *Bethmann Hollweg,* p. 89; Great Britain, General Staff, *Daily Review of the Foreign Press,* Dec. 22, 1915, pp. 10-11
[14] *Reichstag,* vol. 306, p. 437.
[15] Scheidemann, *Memoiren,* I, 380.
[16] For this and the following see Haussmann, p. 52.

Bassermann and Westarp objected because it did not sufficiently stress Germany's territorial ambitions. The Chancellor, in turn, opposed the more radical demands of the annexationists, not on general principle, but because too heavy demands might spoil the chances for a negotiated peace. Finally a compromise, suggested by the Progessive leader von Payer, was accepted by all present. To make sure that this compromise would also meet the approval of the anti-annexationist Socialists, Bethmann discussed his speech of December 9 with Scheidemann as well. The latter, in return, gave Bethmann the contents of his interpellation and the Chancellor expressed his approval.[17] On December 9 both men delivered their pre-arranged speeches.[18]

Despite this continuous ambiguity in Bethmann Hollweg's statements on war aims, however, there can be little doubt that the Chancellor's views were closer to those of the Socialists than to those of the annexationists. In a memorandum to the Prussian Minister of the Interior, dated December 9, 1915, Bethmann warmly defended the Socialists against von Loebell's accusation, that it was they who had started the controversy over war aims and that the *Kriegszielbewegung* of the Right was merely a counter-move against this Socialist agitation. Bethmann Hollweg, on the contrary, held that the moderate position of the Socialists gave the parties of the Right a welcome excuse to reopen their traditional fight against the Left, temporarily interrupted by the *Burgfriede*.[19]

Nevertheless the Chancellor's vacillating policy continued. Shortly after his Reichstag speech he suggested to the Foreign Affairs Committee of the German *Bundesrat* " the creation of a customs union and a mutually protective alliance between Germany and Belgium." [20] Towards the end of January 1916, in a conversation with Colonel House (who was then on his second European mission), " the Chancellor intimated that Germany would be willing to evacuate both France and Belgium, if an indemnity were paid." [21] In March, speaking to the representatives of the press, Bethmann advised moderation in the discussion of

[17] *U. A.*, 4. Reihe, XII (1), 62-63.
[18] Scheidemann, *Memoiren*, I, 380.
[19] Westarp, II, 282-83.
[20] Rupprecht, I, 30.
[21] Seymour, II, 142.

war aims. " He did not consider it wise to bluff with far-reaching annexationist demands and then become more and more modest." [22] Still the Chancellor failed to take his own advice; because in his address on April 5, 1916, he made his most specific reference to the future of Western Europe in general and of Belgium in particular:

Can anyone believe that we shall give up areas which we have occupied in the west, on which the blood of our people has been spilled, without gaining complete security for our future? We shall secure real guarantees for ourselves, so that Belgium will not become an Anglo-French vassal state, and be made a military and economic outpost against Germany. Here, too, will be no *status quo ante*. Here, too, fate will not retrace its steps. Germany cannot again abandon to *Verwelschung* [Latinization] the tribe of the Flemings, which has been kept down so long.[23]

Again the annexationist press hailed the Chancellor's stand, in which some papers saw an endorsement of the famous demands of the Six Economic Organizations.[24] The reference to the Flemings gains added significance in the light of simultaneous governmental policy in Belgium, which we shall discuss at greater length below.

In view of the constant discrepancy between Bethmann Hollweg's public and private views, it should not surprise us to find him making one of his most pessimistic statements only a little more than a week after he had given the above speech. On April 13, 1916, he wrote on the margin of a petition demanding the free discussion of war aims:

We should not think of something very wonderful in connection with this famous discussion of war aims. Our situation at the end of the war will not be such that we can choose freely among a series of entirely different possibilities. We shall rather try to make of the situation whatever we can. As far as there will be a choice, it will be limited by the fact that Belgium, colonies, and a large indemnity cannot all be had. The value of colonies and an indemnity will have to be balanced against the value of Belgian guarantees.[25]

Such were the German Chancellor's public and private declarations on war aims up to the spring of 1916. As the year progressed, they became more and more pessimistic, a fact easily explained

[22] *U.A.*, 15. Ausschuss, II, 166.
[23] *Reichstag*, vol. 307, pp. 851-52.
[24] Thimme, *Bethmann Hollweg*, p. 103; *U.A.*, 4, Reihe, XII (1), 66.
[25] Westarp, II, 191.

by military reverses—the failure of the German army to win a decisive victory at Verdun, and the entry of Rumania into the war in August. But how are we to explain his previous vacillating policy in the second half of 1915 and early 1916?

Here also military factors played an important part. After Germany's advance in the west had been halted in late 1914, and the Russian threat in the east had been overcome, the war had become one of position, in which existing military strength was pretty evenly distributed between the Central and Allied Powers. As far as intrinsic military power and potential were concerned, however, the Allies definitely held the upper hand. It was merely a question of time before their superiority of matériel and manpower would crush the resistance of Germany and her allies, whose only salvation lay in a concentrated use of all forces on land and sea. Consequently on February 4, the German Admiralty stepped up its U-boat activity in the waters adjacent to the British Isles, thus embarking on a course which had the gravest consequences. Simultaneously, the Army Supreme Command decided to direct its main land offensive against the eastern front. Between May and September 1915, the concerted efforts of German and Austro-Hungarian armies pushed the Russian forces out of Poland and Galicia and advanced the front far into the plains of Eastern Europe. They failed, however, to achieve the decisive annihilation of the Russian army, partly due to differences of opinion between the Chief of the General Staff, von Falkenhayn, and the commanders of the eastern front, Hindenburg and Ludendorff. At the same time, a concentrated Anglo-French offensive in the west near Arras and on the Champagne sector made exclusive operations on the eastern front impossible. Italy's entrance into the war and the Allied expedition against the Dardanelles, further limited the freedom of action of the Central Powers.

Yet the military results of 1915, though not decisive, were sufficiently impressive outwardly to keep alive the optimism of a large section of the German people. It is this very fact which further helps to explain the Chancellor's dual attitude towards war aims. The military situation was never bad enough to make possible a public renunciation of all annexationist aims (such as the Socialists demanded). At the same time, extremely annexationist statements were equally unwarranted. None of the military successes had dealt a decisive blow to one of Germany's adversaries, and it became increasingly clear that perhaps the only way to break a link of the chain which the Allies had forged around Central Europe was through a negotiated peace with one of the encircling powers. Such a peace, however, would have necessitated the abandonment of at least some of Germany's war aims and would have called for a certain moderation in the government's public statements. Instead, these statements became ever more extreme.

Before we analyze further the policy of Bethmann Hollweg a few words about the attempts at a negotiated peace. We have already seen how negotiations with Russia were started in early 1915. These efforts, favored by certain groups within the army and navy, and pursued through the remainder of 1915 and into 1916, had no success.[26] The vast areas Germany held after the summer offensive in Eastern Europe, plus the hardships which East Prussia had suffered at the hands of the Russians in the early days of the war, made an extension of Germany's frontier in the east equally, if not more desirable than expansion to the west. To curtail the power of Russian despotism was looked upon with favor by the Social Democrats, to whom Russia was the chief enemy. It was in the east, finally, that German agrarian interests hoped to reap tangible rewards for their support of industrial aims in Western Europe.

As to the chances for a separate peace with the western powers, the numerous attempts at a settlement with Russia naturally limited Germany's efforts in that direction. France's aim to recover the lost provinces, moreover, made peace with her difficult, if not impossible, since the majority of Germans, including most Socialists, were against the return of Alsace-Lorraine.[27] " Whoever raises the knife to cut pieces from the body of the German people," the Socialist Landsberg had said in the Reichstag, " no matter where he applies it, will meet the German people, united in defense, and ready to knock the knife from his hand." [28]

The popular hatred of England and the simultaneous interest

[26] Forster, pp. 24 ff., 42 ff.; Brunauer, *Peace Proposals,* pp. 41 ff.; W. K. von Korostowetz, *Lenin im Hause der Väter* (Berlin, 1928), pp. 185-90; Bethmann Hollweg, II, 42; Tirpitz, *Erinnerungen,* p. 262; E. Hölzle, " Die Ostfrage im Weltkrieg," *Vergangenheit und Gegenwart,* XXVIII (1938), 208 ff.

[27] Dahlin, pp. 21, 64.

[28] *Reichstag,* vol. 306, p. 445.

in Belgium made a settlement with the second great western power equally difficult. The British blockade and the German submarine retaliation all added fuel to the flames. The time was not ripe as yet for an agreement with England.[29] In February 1916, the Allies guaranteed the restitution of Belgium, and in May made a similar declaration on the integrity of the Belgian Congo.[30] The *Drang nach Westen*, like the *Drang nach Osten* was incompatible with a separate peace. Yet even so, innumerable minor efforts, direct and through neutral channels, were made to bring about the end of war. They did not assume serious proportions until late in 1916, when Germany's attempt to exhaust her western opponents through the Verdun offensive had proved equally costly to both sides.[31] When in the second half of 1916 the initiative suddenly shifted from the Central Powers to the Allies, when the Russian offensive in the Bukovina, the Italian attacks on the Isonzo front, and the Anglo-French offensive on the Somme were followed up by Rumania's declaration of war in August, a quest for peace began in Germany which culminated in the official peace offer of the German government on December 12, 1916.

If the military situation was sufficiently favorable until early 1916 to justify the hope for German territorial gains, it was by no means favorable enough to justify the hopes for the far-reaching expansion which the Chancellor's official statements aroused. Why, then—we must qualify our earlier question—did Bethmann Hollweg not present the moderate aims which he uttered privately, to the German people? One explanation we have already found in his sincere desire to maintain domestic peace and internal unity through a middle-of-the-road policy. To this we must add as influential factors pressures of two kinds: On the one hand pressure from governmental agencies and individuals, public opinion and annexationists, and on the other hand, pressure of circumstances growing out of Germany's policy in the occupied areas of Western Europe.

---

[29] Brunauer, *Peace Proposals*, pp. 14-15; Dahlin, p. 38; Max von Baden, *Erinnerungen und Dokumente* (Stuttgart, 1927), pp. 21, note 1, 24, 36 ff.

[30] *Schulthess*, vol. 57 (2), pp. 333, 336.

[31] One of the reasons given for this offensive was that the fortress of Verdun threatened Germany's occupation of the French iron regions; see M. Schwarte, ed., *Der Grosse Krieg 1914-18* (10 vols., Leipzig, 1921-33), II, 481; Friedensburg, pp. 117-18.

The War Aims of Other Public Figures

As far as pressure from other governmental agencies is concerned, it may seem strange that in our discussion of Germany's war aims policy thus far we have concentrated on the Reich's Chancellor and have almost completely ignored the Kaiser. The reason is that William II, weighed down by many responsibilities, withdrew almost entirely as the war progressed, accepting the policy of his Chancellor and his Chief of Staff instead of suggesting his own. As a result, Bethmann Hollweg gained a political position such as no other Chancellor had ever held under William II. In the field of war aims, the Emperor, except for occasional oratorical outbursts, followed closely in the footsteps of his Chancellor, at least during the first years of the war. Since the Battle of the Marne, so Bethmann Hollweg tells us,

the Kaiser always agreed with me, that if we only held our own, we had already won the war. Once in a while, when his generals announced great victories, his impetuous temperament carried him away into making different statements. . . . But never did the unequalled military feats of his army seriously give him the faintest idea of satisfying with German blood a desire for world domination, which was alien to him.[32]

The heir to the German throne, Crown Prince Wilhelm, under the influence of Conservative expansionists, at first tended to be less moderate than his father. His political adviser, Baron von Maltzahn, helped temporarily to make him the rallying point of Conservative opposition against the moderate policy of the government.[33] Yet as early as December 1915, young William showed signs of moderation in a memorandum which advised the conclusion of a separate peace, preferably with Great Britain.[34]

While the Kaiser was in accord with his Chancellor's moderation, the heads of some of the other federal states were more radical. We have already mentioned the demand to annex Belgium, which the Grand Duke of Oldenburg tried to bring before the Kaiser via the King of Bavaria.[35] In March 1915, he added to this demand a large section of northern France.[36] Duke Johann Albrecht of

---

[32] Bethmann Hollweg, II, 18. See also Kanner, III, 210; E. Stern-Rubarth, *Graf Brockdorff-Rantzau* (Berlin, 1929), p. 57; *U.A.*, 4. Reihe, XII (1), 74.

[33] Westarp, II, 187.

[34] Kronprinz Wilhelm, *Erinnerungen* (Berlin, 1922), p. 156.

[35] *U.A.*, 4. Reihe, XII (1), 36.

[36] *Ibid.*, p. 373.

Mecklenburg, as president of the *Deutsche Kolonialgesellschaft*, hoped for a powerful African Empire as well as a series of naval and commercial stations.[37] By far the most numerous annexationist pronouncements were made by King Ludwig III of Bavaria. As early as August 1914, he had visited Imperial Headquarters trying to urge upon William II the annexation of Belgium and northern France and their incorporation into Prussia. Bavaria, in that case, should be given compensations in the south, perhaps Alsace-Lorraine. Bethmann at the time managed to prevent the King from bringing the matter before the Kaiser.[38] In October and December 1914, Ludwig began dropping vague hints to the effect that after a German victory all would not be as before the war.[39] His most important statement came on June 7, 1915, at a dinner given by the *Bayrischer Kanalverein* in Fürth. " Russia's declaration of war," he said, " was followed by that of France; and when in addition the English fell upon us, I said: I am happy about it, I am happy, because now we can settle accounts with our enemies, because now—and that particularly concerns the *Kanalverein*— we gain a direct outlet from the Rhine into the Sea." [40] This reference to the mouth of the Rhine did little to soothe the already existing fears of the Dutch about their future in case Germany should annex Belgium. To cover up this blunder, it was said that old Ludwig did not realize the mouth of the Rhine was in the hands of the Dutch.[41] But still, the fact that the King of Bavaria " who surely must be most reliably informed on our military situation," made such optimistic statements, left little doubt in the minds of less well-informed people " that we shall be able, at the conclusion of peace, to put our hand on Belgium." [42] Ludwig III continued throughout 1915 and 1916 to adhere to his earlier aims.[43] The hope for western annexations and for a corresponding Bavarian hold over Alsace also increased the always prominent particularism

---

[37] Grumbach, p. 6.

[38] Tirpitz, *Erinnerungen*, p. 448.

[39] W. Zils, *König Ludwig III. im Weltkrieg* (München, 1917), pp. 21-22, 30-31.

[40] *Schulthess*, vol. 56 (1), pp. 215-16; V. Naumann, *Profile* (München, 1925), pp. 116-17.

[41] *U. A.*, 4. Reihe, VII (2), 335.

[42] *Münchner Neueste Nachrichten*, June 8, 1915.

[43] Zils, pp. 67, 98; Grumbach, p. 6; B. Graf von Hutten Czapski, *Sechzig Jahre Politik und Gesellschaft*, (2 vols., Berlin, 1936), II, 317.

of Bavaria during the war.[44] In contrast to his father, the Bavarian Crown Prince Rupprecht soon gave up his initial hopes for an annexationist peace. From the beginning of 1915 he maintained that Germany should not only give up and completely restore Belgium, but that she should renounce all conquests and seek a peace of understanding.[45] Rupprecht ultimately became one of the leading forces of moderation in German war aims policy.

Except for such influence as they had on the formation of public opinion, the views of these various rulers had no bearing on the policy of the Empire. What influence there was of the federal states was exerted through the Committee on Foreign Relations of the *Bundesrat,* which likewise did not amount to much. The committee held some thirteen meetings during the war, of which the first did not take place until November 3, 1915. The procedure at each meeting was for the Chancellor or his Foreign Secretary to report on the foreign affairs of the Empire, after which questions might be asked. Opposition to or criticism of the government's policy was never expressed.[46]

Another element of influence upon Bethmann Hollweg's policy came from his various colleagues in the government, military and civilian. The Foreign Office followed closely the policy laid down by the Chancellor. The few private statements we find during this early period from Secretary of State von Jagow and Under-Secretary Zimmermann show the moderation we have already found in the Chancellor's unofficial utterances. What official statements were made during the first part of the war were mainly the work of Bethmann Hollweg. In August 1915, and again in May 1916, von Jagow complained to Conrad Haussmann about the exaggeration shown in annexationist claims.[47] On June 7, 1916, however, he wrote to the German ambassador in Washington, Count Bernstorff, expressing his skepticism of Wilson's attempts at mediation, adding that " if the progress of the war were to continue favorable for us, a peace founded on the absolute *status quo ante* would be unacceptable." [48] Zimmermann's views in various conversations with

[44] Haussmann, pp. 62-63; Ziegler, p. 181.

[45] Rupprecht, I, 394; Naumann, *Profile,* p. 150; V. Naumann, *Dokumente und Argumente* (Berlin, 1928), p. 254.

[46] *U. A.,* 4. Reihe, VIII, 49.

[47] Haussmann, pp. 44, 61-62; Erzberger, p. 228.

[48] *Official German Documents relating to the World War* (2 vols., New York, 1923), II, 978.

the Austrian journalist Kanner were similar.[49] Colonial Secretary Solf continued his agitation for the return and extension of Germany's colonial possessions.[50] There was a general increase of colonial propaganda around the middle of 1916.[51] In May, Solf hoped that Germany might " fill the gaps in her existing colonial empire." [52] A month later he added a new idea for which he was much maligned by various annexationists. To the latter German colonial expansion was only possible in conjunction with a strong anti-British naval policy. On the other hand, Solf, in an article published in the *Weserzeitung*, held that the control of the seas was not necessary to Germany's colonial policy. " It is not Germany alone which possesses overseas colonies. Other nations do so too, and are not troubled about England's dominion over the seas. . . . We ought to be able to make some day as strong a coalition against England as she has now made against us." [53] The press of the Right objected to such a solution.[54] " Colonial and overseas policy," Otto Hoetzsch wrote in the *Kreuzzeitung,* " are impossible without a fleet and a coast and unthinkable without the opposition against England." [55]

The only real opposition within the government to the Chancellor's moderation did not come from civilian, but from naval and military circles.[56] For the navy, the annexation of the Belgian coast was of vital significance, since it considerably extended Germany's coastline and in Antwerp presented her with one of the world's outstanding ports. Admiral Tirpitz continued his agitation for the Flanders coast up to the time of his resignation over the submarine controversy in March of 1916.[57] This controversy, though not directly related to the problem of war aims, helped to intensify the existing split between annexationists and moderates. The unlimited use of the submarine weapon was increasingly considered the only means of achieving a victorious

[49] Kanner, II, 212, 257-58, 283.
[50] Grumbach, p. 9; *Schulthess,* vol. 57 (1), pp. 123, 202.
[51] Great Britain, *Daily Review,* May 27, 1916, pp. 11 ff.; W. H. Solf, *Die Lehren des Weltkrieges für unsere Kolonialpolitik* (Berlin, 1916).
[52] *Frankfurter Zeitung,* May 30, 1916.
[53] Bevan, *War Aims,* p. 29; Great Britain, *Daily Review,* July 6, 1916, pp. 9 ff.
[54] *Ibid.,* July 12, 1916, p. 8.
[55] Hoetzsch, II, 346.
[56] Bethmann Hollweg, II, 43.
[57] Tirpitz, *Erinnerungen,* p. 500; Tirpitz, *Dokumente,* II, 263-64, 400.

end of the war, without which, so the annexationists felt, the whole German system would collapse. It was over the question of submarine warfare that the civil and military heads of the German government ran into one of their first serious disagreements.[58] Up to 1916, Moltke, and after him Falkenhayn, had been too much preoccupied with military matters to interfere with problems beyond the sphere of their own department. They had made no official statement of their war aims, though in private conversation in February 1916, Falkenhayn stated: " If we give up Belgium, we are lost." [59] In a subsequent letter to Bethmann Hollweg, he became still more specific:

As far as the future of Belgium is concerned, there can be no doubt that the country must remain at our disposal as an area for the initial assembly of our troops, for the protection of the most important German industrial region, and as a hinterland for our position on the Flanders coast, which is indispensable for our maritime importance. From this demand automatically arises the necessity of unconditional military domination of Belgium by Germany. . . . Without this . . . Germany would lose the war in the West.[60]

These strategic arguments for keeping a firm hold over Belgium after the war had considerable military justification and it was understandable that the Chief of the General Staff should be eager to improve the unfavorable strategic position of his country.[61] Nor were these aims of Falkenhayn in any way different from those stated by Bethmann Hollweg.

The policy of non-interference by the military in the governmental affairs of Germany came to an end after August 1916, when Hindenburg and Ludendorff took over the Supreme Command. In the light of subsequent developments, it is interesting to examine the relations between Bethmann and these two men, especially Ludendorff, during the early part of the war. Since their military skill (and that of General Hoffmann) had first halted and then pushed back the Russian forces during 1914-15, Hindenburg had become the most popular figure in Germany, and both he and his associate had become important political factors. " There was hardly a day," a contemporary relates, " when minis-

---

[58] *U. A.*, 4. Reihe, VIII, 64 ff.
[59] Direnberger, p. 39; Tirpitz, *Erinnerungen*, p. 364.
[60] *U. A.*, 15. Ausschuss, II, 147-48.
[61] *Ibid.*, 4. Reihe, XII (1), 54-56, esp. the notes.

ters of state or other high officials, parliamentarians, industrialists, agriculturists, journalists, etc., did not come to Kowno, the headquarters of *Ober-Ost*." [62]

At first relations between the two eastern commanders and Bethmann were friendly.[63] General Ludendorff, the dominating figure of the team, in a series of enlightening letters to Alexander Wyneken, editor of the *Königsberger Allgemeine Zeitung*, repeatedly expressed his agreement with Bethmann Hollweg. On December 7, 1915, two days before Bethmann's Reichstag address, Ludendorff had a long conversation with the Chancellor. " I found him in a thoroughly determined mood," the General wrote to Wyneken, " and presented to him the views known to you." Ludendorff's aims apparently were more far-reaching than those of Bethmann in his speech of December 9. But he realized that " it is easy to speak and make demands for a man who does not have full responsibility. It is necessary to put oneself in the position of the responsible leader. To expect, at this stage, binding decisions from him would, in my opinion, be premature." [64] Yet even if the Chancellor was slow in making up his mind, Ludendorff was certain that

he will do so in the end and in a strong fashion. Whatever we can do from here, shall be done. I certainly hope that the Field-Marshal [i. e., Hindenburg] will not lend his word to a rotten peace. To my greatest satisfaction complete agreement in this matter exists between the Field-Marshal and myself. I know how much the Chancellor listens to the Marshal. I am, therefore, completely reassured in this direction.

Here we have a first hint of possible later conflict between Bethmann and the Supreme Command. It is doubtful if Ludendorff would have written as he did had he known of the influence which the Social Democrats had upon Bethmann's speech of December 9. As it was, the General deplored the strong agitation against Bethmann, for " of new men, none would be better, and in many ways perhaps worse."

[62] E. von Eisenhardt-Rothe, *Im Banne der Persönlichkeit* (Berlin, 1931), p. 148; *Ober-Ost* was the region on the Eastern front under the command of Hindenburg and Ludendorff.

[63] Haussmann, p. 36; Lutz, *German Empire*, I, 326.

[64] L. G. von dem Knesebeck, *Die Wahrheit über den Propagandafeldzug und Deutschlands Zusammenbruch* (München, 1927), pp. 151 ff.

Ludendorff's next letter, in January 1916, is not quite so favorable as his earlier one, though it still supports the Chancellor.

God knows, I don't agree with everything the Chancellor does, and I wish he showed more impulsive strength. But he is not responsible for everything. . . . Criticism is easier than doing a thing oneself, as I often have experienced. We here stick to the Chancellor, for we lack a man who could replace him. The only candidate known thus far, we decidedly oppose.[65]

The last statement refers to General von Falkenhayn, whose strained relations with Hindenburg and Ludendorff we have already mentioned. In the same letter Ludendorff insisted again on " a strong peace and an increase of power."

In February, the General reproached the Conservatives for opposing Bethmann, whom he considered excellent, and for supporting Falkenhayn as his successor.[66] Again in March he " thought it well that Bethmann remained." [67] The government's vacillation in the submarine question, however, brought a first note of disapproval, not so much against the Chancellor, as against the government in general. " As an honest man," Ludendorff wrote to Wyneken in the summer of 1916, " I must confess my views, so that it cannot be said later that I have been faithless towards men whom I have supported until now." Here we have a definitely ominous note. As to the future of Belgium, he wrote a little later: " Belgium's dependence must be economic, military, and political. Only this triad will create something complete. Economic dependence alone is not enough. No one apparently any longer considers annexation. I leave the question open whether we shall have to take Liège for military reasons." [68]

The Ludendorff-Wyneken correspondence is interesting not only because it shows a more moderate and human Ludendorff than the virtual dictator we shall encounter later on, but also because it shows the beginnings of a slow change from agreement to opposition in the relationship between Bethmann and Ludendorff. As yet, in the middle of 1916, agreement was almost complete, though one cannot help noticing between the lines of Ludendorff's letters the admission that a different Chancellor might be desirable,

[65] *Ibid.*, pp. 152-53.
[66] Westarp, II, 125.
[67] Knesebeck, p. 156.
[68] *Ibid.*, pp. 157-58.

if the right one could be found. The right one, we shall see, was never found, and Ludendorff's repeated statements during this early period, when he was still open-minded on the subject, that Bethmann was the best man available, were borne out by later events. It was the lack of a suitable counterpart in the civilian field which was largely responsible for the power which Ludendorff was to assume over civil as well as military affairs during the second half of the war. The initial step, on August 29, 1916, which made Hindenburg Chief of Staff and gave Ludendorff the newly-created position of First Quartermaster General, was taken, paradoxically enough, with Bethmann's blessing and active support.[69] The added pressure of public opinion, which blamed Falkenhayn for the failures of German military policy in 1916, especially at Verdun, sufficed to bring about the change of command. It came at a time when military setbacks necessitated either extreme moderation in dealing with the Allies, or else powerful exertion in the military field. We have seen throughout Bethmann's real preference for the former, while Hindenburg and Ludendorff advocated a policy of "impulsive strength." The unifying factor of common opposition to Falkenhayn had disappeared. Conflict between the civilian and military, thus far hidden, was imminent, though it did not actually arise until the first part of 1917.

Administration of the Conquered Areas

Before we discuss the extra-governmental forces which helped to shape Germany's policy of war aims during the second year of war, we must briefly examine what happened to the areas in Western Europe under German domination during the first half of the war. Perhaps we can learn from Germany's administrative measures in occupied France and Belgium, to what extent she intended to translate her theoretical discussion of westward expansion into reality. Germany's administrative policy in these areas, of course, began very shortly after the outbreak of war. Yet it developed slowly, in a trial and error method, and did not show its characteristic traits until almost two years later. Most of our discussion here will be concerned with the administration of Belgium, where both immediate and future problems were more complex than in

[69] Bethmann Hollweg, II, 43 ff.

the occupied regions of northeastern France. In the latter, things were relatively simple. Real interest, except on the part of the most extreme annexationists, existed only for the acquisition of Briey and Longwy, and here both official and unofficial views agreed that outright annexation would be most desirable. On October 31, 1914, the region in question was put under German Civil Administration. For the mines and the numerous iron works, a special "protective administration" was set up, consisting of three mining specialists. They were aided by a permanent "advisory council" made up of industrialists who had special interests in France's iron deposits, among them Emil Kirdorf, Louis Röchling, General von Schubert (head of the Lorraine Stumm works), Kloeckner, Springorum (of Hoesch) and Krupp's representative Frielinghau.[70]

As to the economic measures taken by Germany in occupied France, they clearly revealed her leading interest in the Briey-Longwy region: the mining of iron ore. Most of the mines were soon reopened and were kept in operation throughout the war, though, as we have already pointed out, their immediate significance has been somewhat overrated. The remaining works of this highly industrialized region were forced to remain idle, unless they produced vital military supplies.[71] Soon a policy of exploitation set in, which did not assume really destructive proportions, however, until the later period of the war. How far this exploitation was dictated by immediate necessity, and how far it was due to the desire of Germany's industrialists to destroy the harmful rivalry of their French competitors is difficult to decide. It is perhaps safe to say that in the first period of the war, with certain exceptions, the former motive prevailed. It was after the change of August 1916 in the German Supreme Command, that a more thorough policy of exploitation was entered upon, about which more will be said below.

The situation in Belgium turned out to be considerably more complex. The rapid advance of the German armies in August 1914 had suddenly brought this whole nation under German domination. To meet the urgent need for some kind of administration, the

[70] *Vorwärts*, Nov. 1, 1914; Friedensburg, p. 114; E. Schrödter, *Die Eisenindustrie unter dem Kriege* (Essen, 1915), pp. 11 ff.

[71] *Ibid.*; O. Brandt, *Wirtschaftskultur und Deutsche Verwaltung der Besetzten Gebiete in Feindesland* (Essen, 1915), p. 18.

4

retired Marshal von der Goltz was appointed Governor of the
Generalgouvernement of Belgium on August 25 and was given
almost unlimited powers, responsible only to the Emperor.[72] In
his administrative work, the Marshal was at first aided by those
members of the Belgian civil service who had remained behind
when the Belgian government went into exile. But as a quick
ending of the war became increasingly unlikely, a more permanent
governmental organization was found necessary, using German
personnel, though many of the lower positions remained in Belgian
hands. On October 13, 1914, the Governor General officially assumed the powers of the Belgian King, and while he continued to
handle the military functions of his position, the civil administration was organized into a separate department under the
direction of Dr. von Sandt as *Verwaltungschef*. This Civil Administration was considered part of the German civil service, and as
such it was responsible to the Chancellor and his Secretary of the
Interior. A dual arrangement of this kind naturally contained
the seed of much future friction.[73] The administrative subdivision
of the country into nine provinces was maintained, but on
December 3, 1914, the Belgian provincial governors were replaced
by German military governors. Among them was the head of the
Army League, General Keim, who became governor of the province of Limburg, while the National Liberal leader Bassermann,
another noted annexationist, was made *aide-de-camp* to the
governor of Antwerp.[74] As time went on and need arose, certain
additional governmental agencies were created to deal with specific
problems, such as the Political Section under Baron von der
Lancken. But on the whole the administrative framework remained
as set up during the first months of the war.

The psychological effect which this creation of an independently
organized Belgian state had upon the German people was considerable. The reward which so many Germans hoped to reap
from the war had here assumed its tangible form. The more
thoroughly organized the administration of Belgium became, the

[72] F. von der Goltz, "Generalfeldmarschall von der Goltz als Generalgouverneur
in Belgien," *Deutsche Rundschau*, vol. 51 (1925), p. 105.

[73] On the administrative organization of Belgium see L. Volkmann, *Das Generalgouvernement Belgien* (Leipzig, 1917), pp. 29 ff.; L. von Köhler, *Die Staatsverwaltung der besetzten Gebiete—Belgien* (Stuttgart, 1927), *passim*.

[74] Raad van Vlaanderen, *Les Archives du Conseil de Flandre* (Brussels, 1928),
p. xvii; *Vorwärts*, Nov. 1, 1914; Keim, p. 203.

more firmly did many people, in Germany and elsewhere, believe that Germany had come into Belgium to stay. The administration of old Marshal von der Goltz did not last very long. His heart was not really in his work, but on the battlefield with the German army. In his dealings with the Belgian people, moreover, he failed to show the firmness which his military superiors expected. As result of a specific disagreement over the collection of contributions from the Belgians, he was relieved of his position as Governor General on November 7, 1914. The issue—whether to collect 200 million francs, as the Supreme Command wanted, or merely 50 million, as von der Goltz thought feasible—was symptomatic of a basic problem which was not to be decided until much later: was Belgium to be administered for her own good and only secondarily for that of Germany, or was she to be exploited for the benefit of her conquerors? It took two years to find an answer to this question, and when it finally came, it was in favor of the second alternative.[75]

The successor of von der Goltz, Baron von Bissing, was very different from his retiring and unpretentious predecessor. Holding court at *Château Trois Fontaines* near Brussels, Bissing liked to think of the Belgian problem as pretty much his private concern and of himself as subject to no authority except that of the Emperor.[76] "Wild Moritz," as he was called, was undoubtedly the most influential and, strangely enough, the most constructive of the German administrators of Belgium. His views on the future of that country played a significant role in the controversy over western war aims. On the day of his appointment, von Bissing had a talk with Walter Rathenau at the Berlin *Automobilklub*, in which he asked the industrialist's advice, how he might best fulfill his mission as Governor of Belgium. "If you plan to administer Belgium," Rathenau told him, "you must know whether you are to administer the country on behalf of Germany or of Belgium." Bissing agreed, and Rathenau added: "You must administer Bel-

[75] C. Freiherr von der Goltz, *Denkwürdigkeiten* (Berlin, 1929), p. 370; F. von der Goltz, *Deutsche Rundschau*, vol. 51, p. 119; C. von Delbrück, *Die wirtschaftliche Mobilmachung in Deutschland 1914* (München, 1924), pp. 156-57; Keim, p. 210.
[76] K. Bittmann, *Werken und Wirken*, (3 vols., Karlsruhe, 1924), III, 116-17; U. Rauscher, *Belgien heute und morgen* (Leipzig, 1915), pp. 4-5. On Bissing see R. P. Osswald, "Bissing," *Deutsches Biographisches Jahrbuch* (Berlin, 1928), II, 35-54.

gium for Belgium," to which the General replied: " Those are also approximately my views." [77]   Here, then, were the two alternatives, and Bissing's subsequent statements and his policy show that he was much aware of the dual role which he had to fulfill as governor of Belgium and representative of Germany.

I have two tasks [he said in a speech on June 19, 1915] which are equally important. As administrator of this country I have to care for its welfare and prosperity. I am of the opinion that a squeezed lemon has no value and that a dead cow will give no milk. It is, therefore, necessary and important, that a country which has such importance for Germany economically and otherwise, is kept alive, and that the wounds of war are healed as much as possible. But I am obligated, at the same time, to consider carefully the advantages and disadvantages of this policy for Germany. We want to avoid any injury to Germany's industry through a revival of Belgian industry, and we hope that it will be possible to find some compromise which will be useful to both countries right at this time. Such an understanding will also be useful to Belgium's future, no matter what we think it may be.[78]

What exactly did Bissing think the future of Belgium should be? For a while he hoped for some governmental directives, and in February 1915 he complained to the Prussian Minister of War, General von Wrisberg, that the government left him completely in the dark as to its intentions on the future of Belgium.[79]   In an interview with the *Norddeutsche Allgemeine Zeitung*, von Bissing held that it was not his business to engage in politics, but that " everything we do here [in Belgium], all conditions, under which we live, would be made much easier if the Belgians knew what finally would become of them." [80]   In the absence of any guidance from Berlin, Bissing finally had to decide on his own what he thought the future of Belgium should be. In his public statements he made it perfectly clear that in his opinion Germany should in some form keep the lands she had conquered. " What has been entrusted to us," he said on the Kaiser's birthday, January 28, 1916, " we want to hold on to." [81]   Statements like this, which he made repeatedly, created the impression, correct for the early days

---

[77] Haussmann, pp. 20-21.

[78] Bittmann, III, 5.

[79] E. von Wrisberg, *Erinnerungen an die Kriegsjahre im Kgl. Preussischen Kriegsministerium* (3 vols., Berlin, 1921-22), II, 131.

[80] *Chronik des Deutschen Krieges*, III, 325-27.

[81] Grumbach, p. 20; " Rudiger " [A. Wullus], *Flamenpolitik* (Brussels, 1921), p. 13.

of the war, that the Governor General desired the annexation of Belgium.[82] In late 1915, Bissing wrote another memorandum on the future of Belgium, mostly for his own use. He sent a copy of it to General Keim, who kept it until after the Governor's death in 1917. It was then published as Bissing's " Political Testament," with the statement, not entirely true, that " to the day of his death, von Bissing remained faithful to the opinions set forth in his memorandum." The memorandum still expressed General Keim's views on the subject of Belgium as late as 1925; but von Bissing's ideas on the form, if not the substance, of Germany's Belgian policy changed under the influence of later events.[83] The memorandum, though it never specifically says so, leaves no doubt in the reader's mind that the Governor's true aim was Germany's complete domination of Belgium. He stresses the military, naval, and economic advantages which Germany stood to gain from Belgium, and belittles the objections usually raised against incorporating a large foreign group into the German Empire. Still a policy of trying to conciliate the Belgian people, Bissing holds, will not work, pointing to the example of Germany's failure to assimilate her Polish and French minorities before the war. " For years to come we must maintain the existing state of dictatorship," he says. " Belgium must be seized and held, as it now is, and as it must be in the future."

These were the views of the Governor General of Belgium. He wanted to administer the country which had been put under his care in such a way that as little lasting harm be done to it as possible. In this he was motivated not by sympathy for the fate of a defeated nation so much as by the hope that Belgium would ultimately fall under permanent German domination as a result of the war.[84] From the German point of view, this was an eminently far-sighted and constructive policy, though based on the unjustified assumption that Germany would win the war. We must now briefly examine to what extent this policy was successful during the first years of the war.

It is impossible here to go into the details of Germany's Belgian policy.[85] All we can hope to do is discuss those measures which

[82] Tirpitz, *Erinnerungen*, p. 443; C. von Delbrück, *Mobilmachung*, pp. 168, 254.

[83] Keim, p. 224. For the text of the memorandum, see von Bissing, " Politisches Testament," *Das Grössere Deutschland*, May 19, 1917.

[84] V. Naumann, *Profile*, p. 310.

[85] See von Köhler, *Staatsverwaltung*, and H. Pirenne, *La Belgique et la guerre*

pointed towards the perpetuation of Germany's domination. In spite of von Bissing's hopes, it was in the economic field that such measures were least apparent.[86] Belgian industry had suffered remarkably little destruction from the invasion of the German armies, and efforts to resume production were made soon after the establishment of the *Generalgouvernement*.[87] Yet except for the mining of coal, these efforts turned out to be a failure.[88] The confiscation of raw materials under the direction of Walther Rathenau and his *Kriegsrohstoffabteilung* (who thus ignored the advice he himself had given to Bissing) for use in essential German war industries, and the refusal of Belgian industrialists and workers to co-operate in producing goods for the enemy, were the chief reasons for this failure. To this we must add the dependence of Belgian industry on foreign sources of raw materials and markets, both of which were closed as a result of the war. Even if the German Supreme Command (which was responsible for the confiscation of materials) and the Belgian people had been willing, a return to normalcy would have been very difficult. Another factor, though not very easy to substantiate, was the opposition of Germany's industrial interests to the revival of their Belgian competitors. General von Bissing had already briefly alluded to this in his speech on June 19, 1915.[89] Germany's economic exploitation of Belgium did not reach its full measure until after the first two years of war. Needless to say, it was carried on against the spirited opposition of General von Bissing. Yet even during the early period of the war, need for both manpower and matériel on the one hand, and the unwillingness or inability of Belgian industry to co-operate with Germany's war effort on the other, necessitated

mondiale (Paris and New Haven, n. d.), both published in the German and Belgian Series respectively of the Carnegie Foundation's *Economic and Social History of the World War*.

[86] For the following, unless indicated otherwise, see H. Pirenne, *Belgique*, ch. VIII, pp. 166 ff.; J. Pirenne and M. Vauthier, *La Législation et l'administration allemandes en Belgique* (Paris and New Haven, n. d.), ch. IV, pp. 39 ff.; Ch. de Kerchove, *L'Industrie Belge pendant l'occupation allemande 1914-1918* (Paris and New Haven, n. d.), *passim*.

[87] K. Helfferich, "Der Zustand Belgiens unter der deutschen Okkupation," *Norddeutsche Allgemeine Zeitung*, Sept. 10, 1914; von der Goltz, *Denkwürdigkeiten*, pp. 350-51.

[88] Friedensburg, p. 86; A. zu Nieden, "Karl Gerstein," *Rheinisch-Westphälische Wirtschaftsbiographien* (Münster, 1932), I, pp. 513 ff. Gerstein was the director of the German coal administration in Brussels.

[89] Great Britain, *Daily Review*, Oct. 4, 1915, p. 11; H. Pirenne, *Belgique*, p. 198.

ever more stringent measures. Large numbers of machines were moved to Germany, to help in the manufacture of munitions. The confiscation of vital raw materials reached down into the individual homes of the Belgian people. Against the passive resistance of the working population, a number of edicts were passed in August 1915 and again in May 1916, making willful evasion of employment a punishable offense. At the same time an *Industriebüro* was set up to hire Belgian workers for employment in Germany.[90] The *exploitation à outrance*, however, the limitless exploitation of Belgium which in many cases bordered on outright destruction, and which included the deportation of Belgian workers to work in German factories, did not begin until late in 1916. Here, too, the change in personnel of the Supreme Command was to show its effects.[91]

If the keynote of Germany's economic policy in Belgium was exploitation rather than construction, such a policy was dictated by military necessity and did not necessarily indicate a lack of interest in maintaining a German hold over Belgium. Whenever German interests permitted, reforms were introduced into Belgium, a fact which indicates that the administration had the future of the country very much at heart. An example is the introduction of German social legislation, included in some of the early governmental pronouncements on war aims. The chief provisions for sickness, old age and accident insurance were not introduced until 1918; though the first suggestions in this respect were made in early September 1914.[92] In a letter of September 10, the Chief of the Civil Administration, Dr. von Sandt, comments on this suggestion and points out the advantages of such a policy:

Aside from giving us hope that we may win over to our side the Belgian working population, the introduction at present of social legislation would serve as preparation for the permanent annexation of parts of Belgium by the German Reich. In case such annexation should not take place, it [i. e., social legislation] will impose burdens upon Belgian industry which, because of the workers, cannot be abolished after the conclusion of peace, and will consequently weaken Belgium's ability to compete with Germany.[93]

---

[90] *Ibid.*, pp. 171, 176-77; Germany, Nationalversammlung, *Das Werk des Untersuchungsausschusses*, 3. Reihe, "Völkerrecht im Weltkrieg," (5 vols., Berlin, 1927) (henceforth cited as *U. A.*, 3. Reihe), I, 235-36.

[91] Kerchove, part II, pp. 151 ff.

[92] Köhler, pp. 169-70.

[93] Bittmann, II, 13-14.

On January 1, 1915, the first law for the protection of woman and child labor went into effect.[94]

The most far-reaching measures concerning the future of Belgium, however, were not taken in the economic or social, but in the political field. In this connection the Flemish question, mentioned in many of the annexationist programs, became of greatest importance. To understand it fully, we have to go briefly into its background.[95]

The Flemish Question

The origins of the Flemish Movement go back to the decades following the Belgian Revolution of 1830. Its primary cause was the division of Belgium's population into two very different groups: the Walloons, French by language and cultural heritage, and the Flemings, who spoke a Germanic dialect and who, though economically and socially "inferior," were conscious and proud of their historical and cultural tradition. Common opposition to Dutch oppression had unified these Latin and Germanic sections during the revolution. But when the newly created state showed a preponderance of Walloon influence, especially in its official use of the French language, opposition from the Flemings—who were numerically superior—arose very quickly. At first this opposition was a mere cultural and literary movement under the leadership of artists and writers. This preparatory period lasted until about 1873 and was superseded by a period of conflict which went up and into the World War. Some laws were passed during this period, granting on paper the equality of French and Flemish. But still, the only effective way for the Flemings to voice their grievances was in extra-governmental propaganda organizations, since the limited franchise barred the lower classes, i. e., most of the Flemings, from parliamentary representation. The electoral reforms of 1893 changed this, introducing for the first time twenty-six Socialist members into the Belgian Chamber. From now on Flemish influence was felt in the political affairs of the nation. By the time war broke out, however, little had as yet been done to

---

[94] Köhler, p. 169.

[95] For a general survey of the Flemish question see Clough, *A History of the Flemish Movement*; also K. Bährens, " Die flämische Bewegung," *Volk und Reich,* XI (1935), 3. Beiheft.

ameliorate the cultural subjection from which the majority of the Belgian people suffered.[96]

Germany's relations with the Flemish movement, though intimate at times, had never been significant. They were quite close during the 1840's and up to 1870, though entirely of a cultural nature. During the Franco-Prussian War, Flemish sentiment was largely on the German side. Towards the end of the century, and particularly with the rise of Pan-Germanism during the 1890's, Flemish relations with Germany became noticeably cooler. The Flemings did not trust the Pan-Germans, who promised to deliver their " Low German " brethren from the yoke of their " Walloon oppressors." Even the small German minority in Belgium refused to have any dealings with the Pan-German League. As a result, the Flemish movement remained almost entirely clear from Pan-German influence.[97]

Despite the almost century-old opposition of the Flemings to their government, the whole population of Belgium rallied to the defense of the country when the Germans began their invasion.[98] Some of the fiercest fighting, as a matter of fact, was done by Flemings, and their heavy losses testified to their loyalty. The complete defeat of their country, however, and the renewed attacks upon Flemish aspirations by leaders of the Walloons, soon helped to resurrect the Flemish movement. By early 1915, three different groups of Flemings could be distinguished. They all demanded a certain amount of administrative independence for Flanders, the northern and coastal region of Belgium, in which most of the Flemings were concentrated. Where they differed was in the method which each of them suggested to achieve this independence. The largest group, called " Passivists," with headquarters in Amsterdam, hoped for an independent Flanders in a free Belgium, and proposed to reach this aim by legal means, continuing the agitation for pro-Flemish legislation after the war where it had left off in 1914. At the other extreme were the " Young Flemings," also called " Activists," concentrated at Ghent, who questioned the continued existence of Belgium and instead wanted the creation of a completely independent Flemish state. Since

[96] C. Huysmans, " Le problème linguistique en Belgique," *France Libre*, I (1940), 61.

[97] T. Heyse, *La propagande Allemande en Belgique avant la guerre* (Brussels, 1925), pp. 9 ff., 26; Clough, pp. 183-84.

[98] *Ibid.*, pp. 177-78.

they could count on violent opposition rather than assistance from the Belgian government, they hoped to realize their aims during the war and with German help. A third group, which developed a little later at Antwerp, had similar views about the desirability of Flemish independence during the war; but it also desired the maintenance of the Belgian state and in that respect was close to the " Passivists." [99] There had been few demands for such administrative division of Belgium before the war, but the failure of the Belgian government to live up to most of its promises for cultural independence made a certain amount of administrative independence seem desirable to almost all Flemings.[100]

The German government, though little aware of the Flemish movement before the war, realized that any strengthening of Flemish influence and the resulting weakening of the pro-French, Walloon section, would be to its advantage. We thus find Bethmann Hollweg writing to von Sandt as early as September 2, 1914, advising him to pay special attention to the Flemish elements in Belgium, " perhaps with regard to a future understanding with Holland." [101] Again on December 16, 1914, the Chancellor, in a letter to General von Bissing, stressed the importance of German contacts with the Flemish movement and proposed the creation of a governmental agency to deal with this question. He also suggested the founding of a Flemish university at Ghent and some sort of Flemish press, to be introduced via Holland. A week later, Captain Dirr, a member of von Bissing's administration, who had made a study of the Flemish movement, suggested that his chief establish contact with the leaders of the Flemings and carry out the existing and proposed Belgian legislation concerning the use of the Flemish language, especially the instruction in Flemish and the transformation of the University of Ghent into a Flemish university.[102]

It is interesting to note that the initial suggestions for a pro-Flemish policy were made by the Chancellor, and that his specific proposals were all realized without much delay. What probably appealed to him was the possibility of thus weakening Belgium without necessitating the annexation of the country. Other fac-

[99] *U. A.*, 4. Reihe, XII (1), 40; Clough, p. 187; H. Pirenne, *Belgique,* p. 213.

[100] Clough, p. 176.

[101] O. von der Lancken Wakenitz, *Meine Dreissig Dienstjahre (1888-1918)* (Berlin, 1931), p. 213.

[102] *Ibid.,* pp. 215-16.

tors, such as genuine sympathy for the aspirations of a " Germanic " minority and the desire to establish fri~ndly relations with at least part of the Belgian population, likewise played their part.[103]

The first step to realize Bethmann's proposal was the establishment, on January 10, 1915, of an administrative agency under Dr. Schaible, to conduct German-Flemish relations. On February 13, this Commission for Flemish Affairs was incorporated into the newly created Political Section of the *Generalgouvernement* under the direction of Baron von der Lancken.[104] In a report describing the program of his Section, von der Lancken made the following revealing statement: " There is no reason, from the German point of view, to prevent political hostilities between the Belgians themselves, as long as they do not endanger military security and internal peace." [105] Prior to this he had proposed the administrative division of Belgium into two states, Flemish and Walloon, and their economic assimilation into Germany.[106]

Close relations with the Flemish " Activists " (under the leadership of a radical clergyman, Domela Nieuwenhuys Nijegaard) was one of the chief duties of the Commission for Flemish Affairs. As far back as August 25, 1914, the Germans had shown their sympathy for the Flemish movement by publishing their decrees in Flemish as well as French, giving precedence to the former.[107] On January 1, 1915, the handling of the Belgian press was entrusted to a separate Press Section, and by the end of the month the Chancellor's plan for a Belgian paper materialized. From January 20 on, the " Belgian Courier," in which German influence was concealed behind a Dutch front, appeared six times a week.[108] In February 1915, the first " Activist " paper, the *Vlaamsche Post*, made its appearance in Ghent.[109] The same month, German military authorities supplemented these propaganda activities by a campaign among Flemish prisoners of war in Germany.[110] In the summer of 1915, the first contacts were established between Ger-

---

[103] H. Pirenne, *Belgique*, p. 212; R. P. Osswald, " Flandern und Grossniederland," *Deutsch-Akademische Schriften*, XXIII (1928), 15 ff.

[104] Raad van Vlaanderen, p. xviii; " Rudiger," p. 10.

[105] *Ibid.*, pp. 10-11.

[106] *U. A.*, 4. Reihe, XII (1), 38.

[107] H. Pirenne, *Belgique*, p. 211.

[108] F. Passelecq, *Belgian Unity and the Flemish Movement*, reprinted from *The Nineteenth Century and After*, October 1916, p. 6.

[109] *Ibid.*, p. 8.

[110] Raad van Vlaanderen, pp. xviii-xix; *Frankfurter Zeitung*, Sept. 23, 1915.

mans and " Young Flemings " at Brussels. Pastor Nieuwenhuys
Nijegaard wrote a pamphlet entitled " Flanders freed from the
Southern Yoke," which contained a manifesto of the " Young
Flemings," demanding an independent Flemish state under German
protection and in close economic and military collaboration with
Germany. The similarity between this and the programs current
in Germany is striking. Yet Nijegaard warned against German
annexation of Belgium or Flanders, stressing the latter's love of
independence and pointing out the obvious fact that the Flemings
were not Germans.[111]

Although the more far-reaching measures, such as the administrative division of Belgium into a Flemish and a Walloon section,
were not taken until later, the suggestions made by Bethmann
Hollweg and others of following the trends of pre-war developments, were carried out during the first half of the war. In addition to using the Flemish language in their administrative decrees,
the Germans now began the rigorous enforcement of earlier Belgian language laws which made sure that Flemish was used in the
correspondence between the government and the Flemish provinces
and that children received elementary instruction in their mother
tongue.[112]

More important still than these linguistic decrees were the
German measures to transform the University of Ghent into a
Flemish institution. The demand for a university of their own
had been among the outstanding pre-war grievances of the Flemings. To supply a sufficient number of teachers capable of conduct-
ing classes in Flemish and thus to utilize the various linguistic reforms, advanced instruction in Flemish was considered a primary
necessity. A Flemish university, most Flemings felt, would also
ultimately raise the cultural and thus the economic level of the
Flanders region.[113] The struggle for such a university had flared
up with particular violence during the years just prior to 1914.
The argument used against it by both Walloons and the Catholic
clergy, that Flemish was not a " cultural " language, aroused deep-
felt resentment among the Flemings. Here was opportunity for

[111] J. D. Domela Nieuwenhuys Nijegaard, *Flandern vom südlichen Zwang befreit*
(Leipzig, 1916), esp. pp. 53, 73.
[112] Pirenne-Vauthier, *Législation*, pp. 246 ff.; Clough, p. 192.
[113] *U. A.*, 4. Reihe, XII (1), 41; C. L. Becker, *German Attempts to Divide
Belgium* (Boston, 1918), p. 317.

the German government, urged on by the radical elements of the Flemish population, to ingratiate itself with a substantial part of the Belgian people. We found Bethmann Hollweg calling von Bissing's attention to this question in December 1914. But it took a whole year before the project could be approached in earnest, and almost another year before it was at least partly realized. Attempts to introduce the teaching of Flemish gradually into the University of Ghent failed, when its faculty refused to resume instruction. On December 31, 1915, therefore, the university was transformed by decree into a purely Flemish institution. For a while the transformation remained on paper only, since most professors, under the leadership of Henri Pirenne and Paul Fredericq, refused to conduct courses in Flemish. Only after the leaders of the opposition had been jailed and additional instructors had been found, could the University of Ghent be formally opened on October 21, 1916. The necessary students were secured by liberal scholarship grants, but their sentiments were pro-Flemish or pro-Dutch rather than pro-German. On the whole, the venture was only partly successful, since many Flemings refused to receive their much-wanted university from the hands of the enemy.[114]

The examples we have given of Germany's administrative measures in Belgium during the first two years of war show a general tendency to create conditions which could not be undone without considerable effort after the war, and which would be to Germany's advantage in case she maintained her hold over Belgium. Von Bissing as well as von Sandt frankly admitted these underlying tendencies in their private correspondence.[115] Any opinion to the contrary was frowned upon. A member of the administration, Karl Bittmann, for instance, had added a prefatory note to a memorandum he had written on the future of Belgium, in which he had said: "I fear, yes, I foresee that we shall not emerge victorious

[114] T. Heyse, ed., *L'Université flamande* (Ghent, 1918-19), *passim.*; Becker, pp. 318-20; H. Pirenne, *Belgique,* pp. 216 ff.; Pirenne-Vauthier, *Législation,* p. 89; K. Nyrop, *The Imprisonment of the Ghent Professors* (London, 1917). In the controversy over the university an important role was played by von Bissing's son, a professor at the university of Munich and member of the Belgian administration. The "crown prince" shared the views of his father on the future of Belgium and expressed them in numerous pamphlets, e. g., F. W. von Bissing, *Die Universität Gent, Flandern und das Deutsche Reich* (Leipzig, 1916); *Deutschlands Stelle in der Welt* (München, 1915); *Westliche Kriegsziele* (Weimar, 1917); *Wünsche und Ziele* (München, 1918).

[115] Pirenne-Vauthier, *Législation,* pp. 88-89, 92; Bittmann, III, 13-14.

from this struggle. And if we are beaten, our enemy will prepare
our fate for us, rather than our preparing his." Such pessimism
was most undesirable for a member of the German Imperial Administration, and von Sandt tore up the note when it reached
him.[116]

It is difficult to get much evidence on the views of any but the
leaders of Germany's Belgian administration. But the few comments we find of lower officials, such as the note by Bittmann, are
by no means as radical and hopeful as those made by men higher up.
Bittmann himself was opposed to von Bissing's Flemish policy, as
were his colleagues von Santen and von Lutz; and both Baron von
der Lancken and his assistant Count Harrach did not always share
the illusions of von Bissing and of ardent annexationists like General Keim or Admiral Schröder, commander of Bruges.[117] Outsiders, who visited Belgium after she had been under German
occupation for more than a year, expressed highest admiration for
the efficiency of its administration; but at the same time they
could not help feeling that much of it was artificially imposed upon
an unwilling people and that the hope of ever winning the Belgians
over to their new masters or of making a lasting impression upon
their way of life was futile.[118]

However great the hopes of some people, especially von Bissing,
may have been, they did not assume real significance as long as
they were not backed by the supreme political authority of the
Reich. It is in connection with the administrative developments in
Belgium, and particularly with the Flemish question, that the
Reichstag speech of the Chancellor on April 5, 1916, reveals its
real meaning as the most important and specific of his public
utterances on the future of Western Europe. " Here [i. e., in Bel-
gium] too," he said, " will be no *status quo ante*. Here, too, fate
will not retrace its steps. Germany cannot again abandon to
Latinization the tribe of the Flemings which has been kept down
so long." [119] What is this but an endorsement of the policy of the
Generalgouvernement, and an implied promise to maintain a development which would eventually result in the break-up of the

[116] *Ibid.*, pp. 41-48.
[117] *Ibid.*, p. 67 and *passim*.; Naumann, *Dokumente*, pp. 157-58, 168; C. von Delbrück, *Mobilmachung*, pp. 171 ff.
[118] Westarp, II, 15; Haussmann, p. 55.
[119] See above, p. 73.

Belgian state and the domination of its remnants by Germany? Among the different factors influencing the Chancellor's stand on war aims, the administrative developments in Belgium are of the utmost importance. They, more than any other force, presented an effective obstacle to any non-annexationist peace settlement. The pressure of a small annexationist minority, of public opinion, and of political parties, even his own commitments in favor of a strong peace, might be ignored by the Chancellor, if a real chance to end the war through a moderate peace offered itself. But the *faits accomplis* which von Bissing—with the Chancellor's acquiescence and, at times, active co-operation—was eagerly creating in his western domain, proved to the German people, and to the world at large, that Germany had come into Belgium to stay.

The Political Parties During the Second Year of War

If Bethmann Hollweg, during the second year of war, looked hopefully to the parties of the Reichstag for signs of moderation, he was sure to be disappointed. The tendency towards annexationism, which we found during the first months of the war, became, if anything, stronger as time went on. The most vociferous demands in favor of far-reaching annexations in east and west continued to come from the parties of the Right, notably the National Liberals. On June 2, 1915, and again two months later, they voiced the usual demands for political, military, and economic " attachment " of areas in western Europe.[120] These same views, found at the beginning of the second year of war, when Germany's successes in the east justified a certain optimism, were still held in late May 1916, in the face of heavy losses suffered during the Verdun offensive. On May 21, 1916, the National Liberals repeated their earlier conviction that only an " extension of the land and sea frontiers of the Empire in the east and the west " could give the German people the necessary guarantees for military, political, and economic security. England they still considered Germany's *Hauptfeind*, to be defeated by unlimited submarine warfare.[121].

[120] *Schulthess*, vol. 56 (1), p. 211; *Vorwärts*, June 3, 1915; *U.A.*, 4. Reihe, XII (1), 67. Some National Liberals opposed their party's annexationist stand; see Haussmann, pp. 40-41.

[121] *Schulthess*, vol. 57 (1), p. 234; Great Britain, *Daily Review*, May 31, 1916, p. 7; *Vorwärts*, June 18, 1915 and Sept. 5, 1916; Grumbach, pp. 37-39, 74.

Among National Liberal leaders, the head of the party, Ernst Bassermann, was one of the most ardent advocates of German expansion. We have already mentioned his activities as member of the German administration in Brussels and his affiliation with industrial interests through his membership on numerous boards of directors.[122]   A sympathizer of Heinrich Class and his radical aims—" I endorse every word of it," he said of Class' famous memorandum—Bassermann shared the Pan-German leader's deep aversion to Bethmann Hollweg. " How can we get rid of the scoundrel? " he asked Class in early 1915. " Everybody at the front realizes that the war will be lost if we keep him." [123]   Only as long as Bethmann seemed to be in favor of a strong peace did Bassermann refrain from open attacks.[124]

Bassermann's own annexationist statements are numerous but of the usual vagueness, so they need not concern us in detail.[125] Typical is an article he wrote for the *Magdeburgische Zeitung* on January 1, 1916, advocating a peace " which will bring us the territorial acquisitions in the east and west which are necessary for our security." [126]   Other prominent National Liberals joined their leader. Gustav Stresemann—Reichstag deputy, member of the Navy League, leader of his party in Saxony, where he was closely allied with industrial interests, and chief influence behind the *Bund der Industriellen*—delivered an address on German foreign policy before the Reichstag, which not only contained the usual references to " Germany's strengthening in the east and west," but which also stressed eloquently those forces in Germany which drove her into westward expansion, the anti-British *Drang nach Westen*:

When " Michael the Dreamer " [127] became " Michael the Seafarer," when the political unification and the development of our economic strength came, when Hamburg and Bremen became what they are, when the Rhine-

---

[122] *Salings Börsen Jahrbuch für 1914-15* (3 vols., Berlin, 1914), II, 501, 657, 967, 1488, 1501, 1667, 2082, 2144; G. Stresemann, *Reden und Schriften* (2 vols., Dresden, 1926), I, 146.

[123] Class, *Strom*, pp. 355-56.

[124] Westarp, II, 308; Knesebeck, pp. 153-54.

[125] For examples see Grumbach, pp. 71, 76-78; Great Britain, *Daily Review*, April 29, 1916, p. 7; *Reichstag*, vol. 307, p. 1526.

[126] Grumbach, p. 77.

[127] The German equivalent of " John Bull " or " Uncle Sam " is a dreamy looking farmer with a night-cap called " Michel," to emphasize the quality of good-natured unworldliness, which the Germans consider their outstanding characteristic.

land-Westphalia region developed the great foundation of its economic strength, when we created the seaports for the German world trade that insured Germany's economic position in the world, then began the economic struggle, even before the clash of arms came. England's whole history shows this struggle against us.[128]

What, in Stresemann's opinion, would be Germany's chances in this struggle after the war? Turning against those of his countrymen who saw Germany's field of expansion primarily in the east and in Central Europe, Stresemann held:

Our future does not lie in the east, and the struggle for world markets we will not give up; for if we give up, England's purpose will be achieved. With the first ship that leaves Cuxhaven and Bremerhaven, this struggle for world markets begins anew and will be carried on with all the German businessman's intensity and joy of producing. The world was our field and will be so in the future.

To maintain Germany's world-wide economic sway, " access to the sea " and " naval bases in the wide world " were necessary.[129]

Stresemann's friend and biographer, von Rheinbaben, has gone out of his way to cover up this annexationist agitation of the hero of Locarno and recipient of the Nobel Peace Prize. We may allow for a change of heart on the part of Stresemann during the postwar years; but to say, as Rheinbaben does, that " he opposed emphatically the annexationists," is incorrect.[130]

In the Prussian House of Representatives, the National Liberal deputies Fuhrmann, Friedberg, and Bacmeister represented the annexationist program of their party.[131] Even the moderate Schiffer was not opposed to " tangible securities " and an extension of Germany's frontiers if military necessity made such measures seem desirable.[132] Finally, the official publication of the party, *Nationalliberale Blätter*, and the party-dominated press carried frequent articles in favor of westward expansion.[133]

The two Conservative parties likewise continued along their earlier course. The Free Conservatives passed a resolution in December which demanded " a Germany more powerful and enlarged beyond her present frontiers by the retention, as far as possible, of

---

[128] *Reichstag*, vol. 307, pp. 866-70.
[129] For further speeches by Stresemann see Grumbach, pp. 73-74.
[130] R. von Rheinbaben, *Stresemann the Man and Statesman* (N. Y., 1929), p. 107.
[131] Grumbach, p. 70; *Tägliche Rundschau*, Aug. 25, 1915; *Vorwärts*, June 25, 1915.
[132] *Reichstag*, vol. 306, p. 173.
[133] Grumbach, pp. 75-90.

the territories now occupied, and further damages for the outlay of money." [134] Its leader, Baron von Zedlitz und Neukirch, reiterated these aims in speeches before the Prussian House of Representatives and in a number of newspaper articles.[135]

The larger and more important Conservative Party presented its stand in September 1915, proclaiming as the most important aim of the war " the defeat of England, who has brought about the war and who will never cease to threaten and injure our position in the world and our future development." It hoped for a " permanent, honorable peace, which secures the foundation of the German future," and supported " all annexations necessary for this purpose." [136] The leader of the party, von Heydebrand, was rather sparing with his remarks. At the end of the first year of war he hoped for " a stronger and greater Germany." [137] A year later, on August 14, 1916, he asked for an extension of Germany's western frontier into France. About Belgium he said: " I do not say annex, I am not speaking of that—no, but to bring into our hands, in the military and political and economic sense, what we must have in order to hold at the heart of England the pistol she has hitherto held at ours." [138] The Conservative press, especially the *Deutsche Tageszeitung* and the agrarian *Kreuzzeitung* followed the party-line.[139] There continued to be some disagreement among the Conservatives as to whether Germany's chief field of territorial expansion lay in the east or west. Professor Schiemann, for instance, who wrote a weekly column on foreign affairs for the *Kreuzzeitung*, hinted at the possibility of an understanding with England shortly after the outbreak of war, and was violently attacked by Ernst Reventlow in the *Deutsche Tageszeitung*. To maintain peace in their own ranks, the Conservatives refused to print Schiemann's answer, whereupon he resigned his position with the *Kreuzzeitung*. He was succeeded by Professor Otto Hoetzsch, who always worked in close collaboration with Count Westarp.

[134] Great Britain, *Daily Review*, Dec. 13, 1915, p. 15; H. Michaelsen, *Deutsche Kriegszielkundgebungen* (Berlin, 1916), p. 12.

[135] Grumbach, pp. 45, 53-56.

[136] Lutz, *German Empire*, I, 333-34; Michaelsen, p. 10; *Reichstag*, vol. 306, pp. 238, 744; vol. 307, pp. 875, 1263.

[137] *Kreuzzeitung*, July 31, 1915.

[138] *Schulthess*, vol. 57 (1), p. 396; Great Britain, *Daily Review*, Aug. 29, 1916, p. 6.

[139] *Deutsche Tageszeitung*, Aug. 8, Dec. 9, 1915; Jan. 29, March 1, 18, April 1, May 18, 1916; *Kreuzzeitung*, July 29, 1915 and especially Jan. 1, 1916.

The group within the Conservative Party which, quite naturally, was most concerned over too one-sided a policy of western expansion, was the Agrarian League. Its leader, Dr. Roesicke, repeatedly tried to moderate Reventlow's anti-British stand. To stress Germany's enmity for England, he held, would easily lead to neglecting her agricultural expansion and colonization of the east.[140]

The Center Party's first lengthy declaration on war aims came in October 1915. It was kept in the usual vague terms: " The terrible sacrifices which the war imposed upon our people, call for an increased protection of our country in the east and west through acquisitions of territory which (regardless of what constitutional forms they shall take) will keep the enemy from suddenly attacking us again." [141] Specific statements concerning the future of Western Europe in general and of Belgium in particular were not made at this early stage of the war. But the majority of the party agreed that the *status quo ante* should not be re-established. Interpreting the Chancellor's speech of the same day, Spahn said on April 5, 1916: " Belgium must not remain a bulwark of England. As a necessary consequence she will fall into our hands politically, militarily, and economically." [142]

It was Mathias Erzberger, who in a letter to Bethmann Hollweg on June 28, 1915, discussed the settlement of the Belgian question in more specific terms. He proposed the following " as a practical solution which also will make possible peace with England ":

Customs union with introduction of German economic legislation, and complete abolition of the Belgian army, leaving only a police force. Lease of the ports of Ostende and Zeebrugge for 99 years, with the reservation that Germany can break the lease if she reaches a final understanding with England. Community of railways, leaving local employees in charge, and the creation of a central administration in Brussels. Appointment of a German Governor General with far-reaching veto powers. Perhaps abdication of the King in favor of his son, who will be educated in Germany. Payment of indemnities and surrender of Belgian governmental coal mines and of Belgium's foreign concessions. Acquisition of Belgium's Congo Colonies. etc.[143]

---

[140] Westarp, II, 34-36; Tirpitz, *Erinnerungen,* p. 493.

[141] Wacker, p. 8; Michaelsen, pp. 13, 15-16.

[142] *Reichstag,* vol. 307, p. 856. See also Grumbach, p. 93, for similar speeches in the Prussian and Bavarian Parliaments. The south German branch of the Center Party on the whole was more annexationist than the north: e. g., *Münchner Neueste Nachrichten,* July 16, 1916.

[143] Westarp, II, 53-54.

Such was Erzberger's minimum program at the end of almost a year of war. To understand it we must remember that he had just joined Thyssen's board of directors. This fact particularly explains his war aims in France, described in the same letter: " From France the ore-basin of Briey and Longwy, a better frontier along the Vosges, the acquisition of Belfort or at least the dismantling of this fortress. The payment of a high indemnity." There is no evidence to show that Erzberger changed these views during the second year of the war.

The policy of the Center Party was thus not quite uniform but varied between moderate and more extreme annexationism.[144] This difference was also reflected in the two leading Centrist papers, the annexationist *Kölnische Volkszeitung* and the moderate Berlin *Germania*.[145] Yet even the latter was not opposed to " a tangible prize of victory," better access to the sea and the elimination of the " gates of invasion " which so badly affected the strategic position of Germany.[146] On the whole the Center Party agreed that Belgium should be kept as a kind of pawn until peace came, and that she should not again fall under the influence of France and England.[147]

The program of the Progressives was in many ways similar to that of the Center, though perhaps a little more moderate. On August 18, 1915, the Progressive Reichstag delegation passed the following resolution:

Equally removed from the systematic repudiation of all territorial aggrandizement and from limitless projections of annexations, the delegation considers that it is indispensable to assure the future of the Empire by military and economic measures as also by necessary extensions of the frontier, and to organize, for the free competition of peoples, conditions, which in the national domain as on a free sea, will guarantee the free expansion of the German people's energies.[148]

To make any more definite statement was considered premature. On December 4-5, the Central Committee of the party stated its opposition to the *status quo ante* and its hope for lasting protec-

---

[144] Wacker, pp. 6, 13-14. A small minority opposed to all annexations was of no significance at this early date.

[145] *Ibid.*, p. 10.

[146] *Germania*, Feb. 15, 1916.

[147] Wacker, p. 11.

[148] Ostfeld, p. 10; Dahlin, p. 45.

tion against attacks.[149]   During the Reichstag debate on April 6, 1916, the Progressive leader von Payer again held that the *status quo ante* would be impossible after the war, and added more specifically: "A Belgium will remain, to be sure; but this Belgium will be different, inside and out, from the Belgium of August 1914." [150]   These were moderate statements, but they were not opposed to annexations.   Some members, Müller-Meiningen for instance, went further in their demands, hoping for the outright annexation of Belgium; [151] while others were much more moderate than their party's declarations.[152]

Two figures among the Progressives merit special treatment: the "moderate" Friedrich Naumann and the radical Gottfried Traub.   Friedrich Naumann has quite wrongly been included among the most moderate of Progressives.   As early as October 10, 1914, he had suggested to Under-Secretary Wahnschaffe that Belgium be divided among France, Holland, Luxemburg, and Germany, thus wiping her completely off the map.[153]   As the war progressed, Naumann became more moderate, though he still maintained his earlier view that Belgium had to disappear in order to deliver Germany from a constant threat.   In June 1915 he again proposed its division between France and Holland.[154]   If this seems a rather harsh proposal, it should perhaps be pointed out that Naumann was not moved by chauvinism or economic greed, but by a sincere desire to prevent the recurrence of a similarly destructive war.   "The main thing," he wrote to the pacifist Quidde on August 10, 1915, "is to draw the future frontiers of Europe so that they will not be a hindrance to peaceful development." [155]   If Germany's security demanded certain corrections along the eastern and western frontiers, he wrote, such corrections were justified.[156]

It is in this constructive spirit that we should view Naumann's plan for a Central European Confederation, embodied in his well-known book *Mitteleuropa*.   First published in October 1915, it was

---

[149] *U.A.*, 4. Reihe, XII (1), 68.

[150] *Reichstag* vol. 307, p. 862; Ostfeld, pp. 10-11.

[151] Kanner, I, 13-14; *Berliner Tageblatt*, June 23, 1916; E. Müller-Meiningen, *Belgische Eindrücke und Ausblicke* (München, 1916), pp. 29, 34.

[152] Ostfeld, p. 11.

[153] Th. Heuss, *Friedrich Naumann* (Stuttgart, 1937), pp. 478-79; *U.A.*, 4. Reihe, XII (1), 37.

[154] Kanner, I (2), 90.

[155] Heuss, p. 480.

[156] F. Naumann, "Ein erster Friedensklang," *Hilfe*, Dec. 16, 1915, pp. 805-06.

soon widely discussed both in Germany and abroad. What Nau-mann suggested, briefly, was a slowly growing, voluntary Central European federation, built around the already existing Dual Alli-ance of Germany and Austria-Hungary, and including most of the small states and nationalities of Central Europe. It was to be economic rather than political in character, although Naumann hoped that ultimately it would go beyond the mere artificial and utilitarian stage. It is incorrect, therefore, to see in his *Mitteleu-ropa* plans merely another embodiment of Germany's wartime expansionism. What distinguishes them from the ordinary set of war aims is their genuinely constructive character as a "posi-tive contribution to the future well-being of the mid-European peoples." [157]

Gottfried Traub, a defrocked Protestant pastor, represents the more extreme side of Progressive annexationism. One of the lead-ing propagandists, he saw in Germany's eastern and western expan-sion the only guarantee for the maintenance of Europe's peace.[158] To spread his ideas more effectively, he published a series of leaflets, *Eiserne Blätter*.[159] Later on, Traub became a member of the Inde-pendent Committee for a German Peace and of the Fatherland Party, two ultra-annexationist organizations.[160] It should be noted that Traub was not the only annexationist among Protestant clergy-men. There is definitely more evidence of strong war aims among the Protestant than among the Catholic clergy, due, most likely, to the close relationship between the Protestant Church and the Prussian state.[161]

If, as this survey has shown, the bourgeois parties of the Center and Right maintained and even increased their annexationist senti-ment during the second year of war, the Social Democrats, with equal determination, tried to uphold their anti-annexationist stand. On June 9, 1915, for instance, several hundred of its leading mem-bers demanded that the party take a decisive stand against the

---

[157] H. C. Meyer, " Mitteleuropa," Summary.

[158] Grumbach, pp. 105-06; *Kölnische Zeitung,* May 24, 1916; E. von Dryander, *Erinnerungen aus meinem Leben* (Bielefeld, 1926), p. 275.

[159] G. Traub, *Eiserne Blätter* (Dortmund, n. d.), esp. nos. 14, 26, 28, 34, 38, 39, 61, 68, 72, 80, 87.

[160] Scheidemann, *Memoiren,* I, 283, 412.

[161] Generalsuperintendent D. Klingemann, *Wofür wir kämpfen* (Witten, n. d.), esp. pp. 9-10; Grumbach, p. 65; J. Massart, *Belgians under the German Eagle* (London, 1916), pp. 213 ff.; *Reichstag,* vol. 310, p. 3719.

growing clamour for annexations. Unless some action was taken, they threatened, the Socialist Party might break up.[162] It was partly as a result of this internal pressure that Ebert and Scheidemann addressed a letter to Bethmann Hollweg in which they protested against the Petition of the Six Economic Organizations and stressed the Socialists' desire for an early peace. " The annexation of Belgium," it read, " would isolate Germany as well as increase and enlarge the coalition against us. Peace must not bring us more enemies but more sympathies." A brief resumé of the letter, ending in the sentence " the people do not want annexation, the people want peace," was published in the *Vorwärts*, which was promptly seized by the censor.[163]

On August 14-16, 1915, the Socialist Reichstag delegation and the Party Committee held a joint meeting to consider the question of war aims. Reports were submitted by David and Bernstein, and since David's expressed the views of the majority, it was subsequently published as the Socialist Party's peace program. Three of its five points will interest us here. In its first point the memorandum was against the territorial aims of Germany's enemies, especially against France's demand for Alsace-Lorraine. To secure Germany's economic development after the war, the second point asked for the " open door," the most favored nation clause, and the " freedom of the seas." Most interesting, however, is the fourth point. As published in the *Vorwärts* on August 24, it read:

Remembering that the annexation of territories with foreign populations is against the right of self-determination and that, besides, the internal unity and strength of the German national state are only thus weakened and its political relations to the foreign countries greatly prejudiced, we oppose the shortsighted politicians' plans of conquest which have this aim.[164]

Yet the original manifesto had contained an additional last sentence: " We therefore consider the restitution of Belgium necessary for the sake of Germany's interests no less than for the sake of justice." This sentence, as we have already seen, had been

---

[162] Grumbach, pp. 443-45; Scheidemann, *Memoiren*, I, 339 ff. Haase, Kautsky, and Bernstein published a manifesto to the same effect in the *Leipziger Volkszeitung* of June 19, 1915.

[163] *Vorwärts*, June 26, 1915; Westarp, II, 175; Grumbach, pp. 429-31.

[164] Lutz, *German Empire*, I, 331-32.

omitted because of governmental interference, since it was feared that the military authorities would object to it.[165]

The minority report of Eduard Bernstein at the August 14-16 meeting was never published in Germany. It went still further than David's report, demanding not only the restitution of Belgium, but the payment of indemnities to make up for the damages that nation had suffered as a result of the war. For regions whose nationality was contested, moreover, the report suggested plebiscites, a practice easily applicable to Alsace-Lorraine.[166] Such differences of opinion within the Socialist Party had existed from the beginning of the war, and they were not limited to a few individuals. We have already mentioned the two existing opposition groups. The more radical one around Liebknecht and Rosa Luxemburg was of minor importance. Liebknecht's repeated Reichstag interpellations in favor of a non-annexationist peace were usually left unanswered.[167] He was finally drafted, and when he staged a one-man public protest on May 1, 1916, shouting " Down with the war! Down with the government! " he was imprisoned and not released until October 1918.[168] The larger opposition group under Hugo Haase and Ledebour was much more effective. Scheidemann tells of the growing friction between this group and the rest of the party. It came to the surface in a speech of Hugo Haase before the Reichstag on March 24, 1916, which led to a fight with his party and the secession of himself and seventeen of his followers. Forming at first the *Sozialdemokratische Arbeitsgemeinschaft*, it was not until April 8, 1917, that Haase organized the *Unabhängige Sozialdemokratische Partei Deutschlands*.[169] In general, this group distinguished itself from the majority of the party not so much in its war aims as in the more violent methods it used to fight annexationism. At the same time, the Haase minority was willing to make certain sacrifices, if necessary, to gain peace. It was ready, for instance, to submit the question of Alsace-Lorraine to a plebiscite, which the rest of the party definitely refused to do.[170] In April 1916, Haase demanded " the political restoration of Bel-

[165] Westarp, II, 176.

[166] Grumbach, p. 449.

[167] *Reichstag*, vol. 307, pp. 221, 448.

[168] Scheidemann, *Memoiren*, I, 356.

[169] L. Bergsträsser, *Geschichte der Politischen Parteien in Deutschland* (Berlin, 1924), pp. 114 ff.; Haussmann, pp. 57-58; Scheidemann, *Memoiren*, I, 351 ff.

[170] *U. A.*, 4. Reihe, XII (1), 59-60.

gium, and not only that, but also its political and economic independence." [171]

The Majority Socialists, as the Social Democratic Party was now called, clarified their stand on war aims once again in a petition in August, which asked that the war be ended as soon as possible. It was signed by *ca.* 900,000 persons. Simultaneously a resolution was published which held that "like the chauvinistic annexationists in the countries of the Entente, influential German circles set forth war aims and propagate plans of conquest which will incite the people of those countries to the strongest resistance." In contrast to these annexationists, the resolution requested "a peace which will make friendship of neighboring peoples possible and which will secure the territorial integrity, independence, and freedom of economic development of our country." [172]

It is impossible to treat in detail the many speeches and writings by prominent socialists stressing this opposition against annexations and expressing a real longing for peace.[173] Taken as a whole, they are an indication of the change which many Germans, especially of the lower classes, underwent during the second winter of the war. Far from giving the majority of people the political reforms they so ardently desired, war had imposed additional restrictions upon the freedom of press and assembly. It had also brought severe shortages of food and other essentials, and had inflicted heavy losses in human lives. All these factors help to explain why the enthusiasm of the early days of war now evaporated and a sincere desire for peace arose in its place. In July 1916, the *Büro für Sozialpolitik* made a survey of public opinion: "The temper of the masses is at present so bad in many places, that every mention of a war aim beyond the *status quo* which the majority [referring to the Social Democrats] might venture to disseminate, would result in numerous voters going over to the minority." [174] Many German letters intercepted by the Allies, as well as other contemporary accounts reveal a widespread hope for peace, particularly among the urban population and the soldiers at the front.[175]

---

[171] *Reichstag*, vol. 307, p. 885.

[172] Lutz, *German Empire*, I, 347.

[173] For additional material see Grumbach, pp. 429-59.

[174] *U. A.*, 4. Reihe, V, 101.

[175] *Ibid.*, VI, 89; Dahlin, pp. 83-85; *Briefe aus Deutschland* (n. pl., 1916), no. 5,

In contrast to the lower classes, the upper bourgeoisie and nobility not only continued to enjoy their political and social privileges, they also suffered less from the deprivations of war. In some cases, even, they seemed to be growing rich on lucrative war contracts. No wonder, then, that the gulf between the two extremes of German society soon became ever wider.[176] Added to the already existing differences, and soon overshadowing them in importance, was the growing suspicion that the war was continued merely to satisfy the egotism and annexationist greed of the " classes." Wahnschaffe described this feeling as early as June 28, 1915, in a letter to Valentini, head of the Kaiser's *Geheimes Zivilkabinett*:

The longing for peace among the workers is very great, and is only kept from breaking out openly through the efforts of their leaders. The violent agitation of the Right feeds the suspicion, that the government might continue the war—out of desire for conquests—longer than the protection of the Fatherland requires. Also, that the Chancellor, who is trusted not to have any fantastic plans and to be guided only by his sense of duty, might be overthrown. The agitation of the Right does not remain secret. I have often warned that this annexationist propaganda will only benefit the radical wing of Social Democracy.[177]

The controversy over annexations had become the battle-ground on which Socialists and Germany's ruling classes continued their pre-war conflicts.

Not all Socialists, however, were opposed to annexations. The rise of a right wing within the party, on the beginnings of which we have commented earlier, continued in 1915 and 1916. The Socialist deputy Suedekum, for instance, wrote in July 1915: " No objections can be raised to necessary steps taken to ensure the safety of our frontiers, and to open up far-reaching economic relations with European states." [178] On December 21, 1915, the right wing held a separate meeting at which its leader, David, is reported to have said: " We do not want to close our eyes to the necessity of conquering certain territories. It is entirely out of the question, for instance, that we again hand back the conquered

passim.; Kanner, III, 6, 9, and *passim.*; E. O. Volkmann, *Der Marxismus und das deutsche Heer im Weltkriege* (Berlin, 1925), p. 282.

[176] A. Rosenberg, *Die Entstehung der Deutschen Republik 1871-1918* (Berlin, 1928), pp. 86-88, 99.

[177] Westarp, II, 175.

[178] Great Britain, *Daily Review*, July 29, 1915, pp. 4-5.

Russian areas to Russian absolutism." The secret report of the
Berlin president of police, von Jagow, from which this excerpt of
David's speech was taken, then goes on to describe the meeting:
" Peus [another Socialist] agreed with David. He had received
hundreds of letters from party-members who all wanted to keep
the soil which had been conquered with so much blood. . . . Lensch
and Suedekum represented a similar point of view. Landsberg,
too, was mentioned as a member of this group." [179] The deputies
Geck, Quarck, and Marum, as well as some Socialist papers and
journals, likewise followed a moderately annexationist policy.[180]
Yet interesting as these right-wing pronouncements of German
socialism may be, they had little influence upon the party's general
policy.

As during the first year of the war, the split over the question
of war aims between bourgeois parties and Social Democrats led
to a number of interesting debates in the Reichstag. The longing
for peace among the lower classes did not affect the parties of the
middle—Center and Progressives—until late in 1916 and early 1917,
so it did not yet assert itself in the Reichstag session of December
9, 1915. The cause for the debate on that day was a petition,
presented by Scheidemann, that the government state its conditions of peace and reiterating the usual opposition to annexations.[181]
Bethmann Hollweg's reply, already discussed, was followed by an
interesting speech of Landsberg, who belonged to the right wing
Socialists. He regretted the fact that Bethmann did not give his
aims in detail,

especially since the Chancellor's words indicated that his conditions of peace
might well be worth hearing. . . . The Chancellor demanded securities
against frivolous attacks. Well, if there are such securities, we all want
them. The Chancellor declared his readiness to conclude an honorable
peace, and I did not gather from his speech that he imposed any unreasonable conditions on our adversary. That for me is decisive. What is understood in detail by securities, will have to be discussed once the negotiations
have begun.

Landsberg concluded, as Scheidemann had done before him, opposing the " reconquest " of Alsace-Lorraine by France.[182] This was

[179] Westarp, II, 292.
[180] Grumbach, pp. 112-17; Michaelsen, pp. 29-30.
[181] *Reichstag*, vol. 306, pp. 430-31; Scheidemann, *Memoiren*, I, 379-80.
[182] *Reichstag*, vol. 306, p. 445.

by no means unconditional opposition against annexation, instead it indicated that the Social Democrats might be willing to wink at certain post-war adjustments. The radical wing under Haase and Ledebour was aware of this fact and voiced its protest in a subsequent meeting of the Socialist Reichstag delegation.[183]

The bourgeois parties, including the smaller ones (Poles, Danes, German-Hanoverians, Bavarian Farmers' League, etc.) presented their views in a separate petition, read after Scheidemann's speech, which asked for a peace which would secure " the military, economic, financial, and political interests of Germany in their totality and by all means, including the necessary acquisitions of territory." The *Kriegszielmehrheit* had made its third united stand; and as Westarp points out, for the first time it had specifically referred to the necessity for territorial acquisitions.[184]

This majority, made up of the two Conservative parties, National Liberals, Center, and Progressives, also took a united stand on the submarine controversy, which became prominent in the winter and spring of 1915-16.[185] Certain difficulties in connection with this question, however, temporarily disturbed concerted action in regard to war aims, and the parties again made separate statements on the subject in the Reichstag debate of April 5-6, 1916. Their fundamental agreement on the war aims problem, however, was nevertheless maintained.

The general tenor of the speeches delivered during these two days, some of which we have quoted already, expressed little that was new. Westarp demanded that Germany keep Belgium closely in hand. Stresemann opposed the *status quo ante* for that country and desired Germany's " military, political, and economic supremacy "; the Centrist Spahn and the Progressive von Payer spoke in a similar vein.[186] The only opposition came from the Socialists; and even here, remarkably enough, it was neither unanimous nor unequivocal. While Haase, for the Independents, demanded the complete restoration and independence of Belgium, and Friedrich Ebert, for the majority, opposed the annexationist plans of the other parties, the speech of Philipp Scheidemann did not com-

---

[183] Ph. Scheidemann, *Der Zusammenbruch* (Berlin, 1921), p. 21; Scheidemann, *Memoiren*, I, 381.

[184] *Reichstag*, vol. 306, p. 437; Westarp, II, 55.

[185] *Ibid.*, pp. 127-28.

[186] *Reichstag*, vol. 307, pp. 856, 862, 869, 875.

pletely shut the door to annexations. " One has to be a political simpleton," he said, " to think that a whole continent has gone up in flames, that millions have been destroyed and killed, and that not a single boundary-stone, which some diplomat, long since dead, set up at one time, will be moved." [187] Scheidemann later denied that he intended this remark to be in favor of annexations. The bourgeois press, however, acclaimed it as such.

What Scheidemann said about annexations [the *Kölnische Volkszeitung* wrote on April 7, 1916] can be endorsed by any bourgeois politician. . . . Once we begin moving boundary stones and abandon the principle not to annex, it will be simply a question of power and military necessity, whether the boundary-stone will be moved to the Vistula and the Meuse, or still farther. . . . The Social Democrat Scheidemann is even closer to the " Annexationists " than the Progressive von Payer.[188]

In view of these annexationist speeches, including Scheidemann's statement, and the far-reaching speech of Bethmann during the same session, the debate of April 5-6, 1916 may be considered the high-water-mark of annexationism in the German Reichstag during the first two years of war.

The Annexationists Continue Their Agitation

Nobody could be more delighted than the annexationists with these manifestations of expansionist hopes, which they themselves had helped to create. The *Kriegszielbewegung*, and its component parts, Pan-Germanism and the industrialists, had done their most important work in the early, formative stage, the evolution of war aims. The second year saw mostly a continuation of their earlier agitation, and the perfection of their organization in the " Independent Committee for a German Peace." It is also during this period that the *Kriegszielbewegung* definitely gained additional and effective allies from the ranks of Germany's professors. The so-called " Petition of the Intellectuals " was the first fruit of this alliance.

Because of the Pan-German practice of avoiding the limelight whenever possible, there are few direct statements on war aims by the League itself and its leaders during the second year of the war. In October 1915, a series of articles by outstanding Pan-

[187] *Ibid.*, pp. 858, 885, 890.
[188] Grumbach, pp. 97-98, 114-15.

Germans appeared in the ultra-annexationist journal *Der Panther* (edited by Axel Ripke, an eastern annexationist),[189] in which Class demanded the annexation of Belgium and the coast of Northern France, supplemented by annexations in the east and overseas.[190] In the same number, General von Gebsattel, second in command of the League, advocated Germany's westward expansion into Belgium and Northern France to the mouth of the Somme. To keep these regions under firm domination he suggested the mass-migration of the natives to make room for German settlers.[191] The third member of the triumvirate of Pan-German leaders, the chief secretary of the League, Baron von Vietinghoff-Scheel, defined his aims in a memorandum entitled "The Guarantees of Germany's Future."[192] He stressed Germany's need for expansion to the east and for military security in the west. To gain the latter, he wrote, "it is sufficient to shape our frontier on one flank in such a fashion that we can dominate militarily all possible opponents from this flank." Any land acquired for this purpose, of course, must be secured free from its original inhabitants.[193]

The various publications directly or indirectly under Pan-German influence followed the same line.[194] In August 1916, a new magazine, *Deutschlands Erneuerung*, was planned, which first appeared in 1917. The list of its founders and editors indicates its highly annexationist character. Besides Class, they included Wolfgang Kapp, Houston Stewart Chamberlain, Baron von Liebig, and Professors Max von Gruber, von Below, Schäfer, and Seeberg.[195] Some of the League's auxiliary organizations likewise continued their annexationist agitation. The Army League addressed a petition to Bethmann in which it asked for the annexation of Belgium as a basis of future operations against England and France.[196] The

---

[189] A. Ripke, "Der Kampf um die Ostsee," in W. van der Bleek, ed., *Die Vernichtung der englischen Weltmacht* (Berlin, 1915), pp. 170 ff.

[190] H. Class, "Der alldeutsche Verband," *Der Panther*, no. 10, Oct. 1915, pp. 1140-45.

[191] Freiherr von Gebsattel, "Das Gebot der Stunde," *ibid.*, pp. 1178 ff.

[192] L. von Vietinghoff-Scheel, *Die Sicherheiten der deutschen Zukunft* (Leipzig, 1915).

[193] *Ibid.*, pp. 21-23, 28.

[194] *Alldeutsche Blätter*, XXVI, Jan. 15 and March 4, 1916; *Tägliche Rundschau*, April 6 and July 28, 1916.

[195] M. Lehmann, *Verleger J. F. Lehmann* (München, 1935), p. 43.

[196] Auskunftsstelle Vereinigter Verbände, *Gedanken und Wünsche zur Gestaltung des Friedens* (Berlin, 1917), pp. 50 ff.; *Die Wehr*, June 1915, p. 13; July, 1915, p. 15; Sept., 1915, p. 15.

Navy League brought its aims before the Chancellor in June 1916, desiring, as might be expected, the Flanders coast and Germany's political and military influence over the rest of Belgium.[197]

The German Colonial Society likewise presented a definite program of war aims during this period. Though its president, Duke Johann Albrecht of Mecklenburg, was a Pan-German, the Society did not always favor co-operation with the League. Even so, there can be no doubt that the two organizations were closely related in spirit.[198] In July 1915, the *Kolonialwirtschaftliches Komitee*, the economic section of the Society, hoped for the " development and enlargement of German colonial possessions " as sources of raw-materials and markets.[199] A year later, the Society itself issued its claims in a specific declaration. Colonies were necessary, it said, if Germany was to remain a great power. At the same time, however, the expansion of Germany's territorial basis in Europe was considered necessary. A strong fleet and a chain of naval stations were required to defend this future colonial empire, which should not be limited to Africa (as most colonial programs declared) but should include holdings in the Far East as well. Better than most other declarations on war aims, this one showed how one claim would lead to the next, and how westward expansion in Europe, colonial expansion across the seas, and a strong naval policy all went into the making of the *Drang nach Westen*.[200]

Direct evidence on the annexationist agitation of the great industrialists is scarcer during the second year of the war than during the first. Yet the evidence there is shows continued propagandist activity on the part of heavy industry in favor of an annexationist peace. In September 1915, for instance, the firm of Thyssen, supported by Erzberger, repeated the demand for the annexation of the Briey basin and added the annexation of Belgium as a desirable aim.[201] Very interesting is another petition of January 2, 1916, by Reinhard Mannesmann, oldest of the six Mannesmann brothers, whose pre-war attempts to secure for their firm the exploitation of Morocco's rich iron and copper supplies had been a

---

[197] Auskunftsstelle Vereinigter Verbände, *Gedanken und Wünsche,* 1917 edition, pp. 65-67.
[198] Class, *Strom,* p. 85.
[199] Michaelsen, pp. 31-32.
[200] *Kreuzzeitung,* July 6, 1916.
[201] " A," *Erzberger,* p. 19.

prominent factor in the Morocco crisis of 1911.[202] The petition, as might be expected, again dealt with Morocco, a region otherwise rarely mentioned in the discussion of war aims.

If Morocco should come under German influence at the conclusion of peace, the undersigned [i. e., Reinhard Mannesmann] can see in it such gain for the Fatherland and for private firms, that he is ready to hand over without charge half of his lands suitable for stock-farming and agriculture, to be used for the settlement of war invalids or for any other purpose designated by the government of the Reich.

In addition, Mannesmann promised " to surrender one-half of the net profit [derived from mining concessions] for war invalids or any other purpose desired by the Reich's government." [203]

To these petitions of individual firms must be added those of industrial and commercial organizations. In September 1915, the Hansa League, a commercial interest group, held a meeting to draw up its program of war aims. The League had joined five of the famous Six Economic Organizations in a petition to the Chancellor on March 10, 1915, asking for the free discussion of war aims.[204] In its declaration of September 15, it demanded the freedom of the seas, an extension of Germany's frontiers, the restoration of her colonies, and a moderate indemnity.[205] Of the industrial organizations, the *Verein Deutscher Eisen-und Stahlindustrieller* held a meeting in Berlin on December 10, 1915, and in a telegram to Bethmann asked for a peace which would give Germany " the necessary extension of her frontiers." [206] The *Zentralverband Deutscher Industrieller,* almost simultaneously, hoped that " the goverment would refuse all conditions of peace that might endanger, not only in maritime and strategic, but also in economic respects, the future security of the German Empire." [207] Interesting in this connection is a meeting of the Provincial Diet of the Rhine Province (in which western German industry was heavily represented) during the first week of February 1916. Baron von Rheinbaben, *Oberpräsident* of

---

[202] Mannesmann, pp. 8 ff.

[203] *Ibid.,* p. 59; E. Staley, " Mannesmann Mining Interests and the Franco-German Conflict over Morocco," *The Journal of Political Economy,* vol. 40 (1932), pp. 52-72.

[204] See above, p. 43.

[205] *Schulthess,* vol. 57 (1), p. 385. The president of the League, Dr. Riesser, published his own expansionist views in *England und Wir* (Leipzig, 1915).

[206] *Vorwärts,* Dec. 11, 1915.

[207] *Mitteilungen des Kriegsausschusses der Deutschen Industrie,* Dec. 11, 1915, no. 75; Great Britain, *Daily Review,* Aug. 8, 1916, p. 16.

the Province, close friend of Stresemann's and annexationist himself, presided. Annexationist speeches, particularly about Belgium, were received with applause by an audience consisting largely of influential industrialists.[208]

One of the chief sources of industrial influence, however, was the press. We have seen how under the direction of Hugenberg and the *Wirtschaftsvereinigung*, a number of news and advertising agencies had been set up, whose purpose among other things was to gain influence over the editorial policy of the provincial press through clever use of the substantial advertising contracts which heavy industry was able to hand out.[209] Some papers, especially the *Rheinisch-Westphälische Zeitung* and the *Post*, were known as industrialist mouthpieces and their statements on war aims bore this out.[210] A major addition to Hugenberg's propaganda machine during the second year of the war was the acquisition in March 1916 of the well-known firm of Scherl, which published a number of leading papers and periodicals. Hugenberg, who became the real force behind the company, had conducted the negotiations leading to its purchase as the head of a group of Ruhr industrialists—Krupp, Kirdorf, Beukenberg and Müser.[211]

The " Petition of the Intellectuals " and the " Independent Committee for a German Peace "

Most of the propaganda in favor of an expansionist peace continued to come from the co-ordinated efforts of various annexationist groups, the *Kriegszielbewegung*. Its first major achievement, as we have seen, had been the Petition of the Six Economic Organizations, presented on May 20, 1915. It was followed a month later by the so-called Petition of the Intellectuals. The reason for this petition, according to Westarp, was

to give more emphasis to the petitions of the economic organizations through support of large sections of the population, in order that the propagation of far-reaching war aims on the part of the economic organizations would not give the impression that these aims were based exclusively on selfish, materialistic and non-patriotic feelings.[212]

[208] Grumbach, pp. 146-47. On Rheinbaben see *Kölnische Zeitung*, May 8, 1916.
[209] *Vorwärts*, Nov. 22, 1915.
[210] *Rheinisch-Westphälische Zeitung*, Aug. 12, Nov. 16, 1915; April 15, 1916.
[211] Bernhard, pp. 65-73; Kriegk, pp. 52-53; " Junius Alter," *Nationalisten*, pp. 147-48.
[212] Westarp, II, 166.

5

Again Class claims to have been the originator, laying the ground-work as far back as March 1915. As in the case of the Economic Organizations he realized that the less the Pan-German League and himself appeared in the picture, the more likely his plan was to succeed. So he sent Baron von Vietinghoff-Scheel to Berlin in late March to make the necessary preparations.[213] Class first planned to turn the matter over to Dietrich Schäfer; but the latter had taken exception to the Pan-German scheme of annexing land " free from its inhabitants," so he refused to co-operate with Class to the extent of directing negotiations for the Petition of the Intellectuals, though he was ready to assist in its preparation. The position intended for Schäfer was taken over by Reinhold Seeberg, professor of theology. He was assisted by a " preparatory committee " consisting chiefly of professors from the university of Berlin. Besides Schäfer it included the historian Otto Hintze, the political scientist Hermann Schumacher, Otto von Gierke, professor of law, and " strangely enough " (according to Class) the two historians Friedrich Meinecke and Hermann Oncken, whose views on war aims, on the whole, were rather moderate.[214] The remaining members of the committee were Emil Kirdorf, former ambassador von Reichenau (who during the war and with Class' recommendation became president of the *V. D. A.*), Admiral von Grumme-Douglas, Andreas Gildemeister, and Friedrich von Schwerin.[215]

On April 26, 1915, the Seeberg Committee held its first conference. At the start the Pan-German Andreas Gildemeister submitted a draft memorandum which, except for minor alterations, was accepted. It was then put before a larger audience in June, and invitations were sent out for a general meeting on June 20.[216] This meeting, attended by several hundred outstanding industrial, military, and academic figures, was a great success. The opening

---

[213] Class, *Strom,* p. 395.

[214] Class, *Strom,* p. 362; Schäfer, *Leben,* p. 169. All these men were authors of at least one work on war aims. Dietrich Schäfer alone published *ca.* 150 books and pamphlets, many of which dealt with the future peace settlement. The participation of Meinecke and Oncken was due to a misunderstanding on their part and was subsequently withdrawn. Meinecke, *Erinnerungen,* pp. 202-04.

[215] Class, *Strom,* p. 395; Schwerin is an excellent example of the versatile character of the typical German annexationist. By profession he was *Regierungspräsident* of the district of Frankfurt a. O. In addition he was a close friend of Hugenberg's, member of the Pan-German League, opponent of Bethmann, member of the " Independent Committee " and editor of the annexationist *Deutschlands Erneuerung.*

[216] *Ibid.,* pp. 395-96.

address by Professor Seeberg referred to war aims in rather general terms, but Professor Schäfer's address, "Our people among the powers" was more specific.[217] The main speeches were given by Schwerin and Professor Schumacher on eastern and western aims respectively.[218] Schumacher's speech was very detailed and emphatic in its far-reaching demands for the annexation of Belgium and parts of eastern France.[219] The draft of Seeberg's committee was then submitted and unanimously approved. Copies were mailed to a long list of influential persons with the request to attach their signatures. Altogether 1,347 names were collected within a very short time. Of these, the largest contingent of 352 came from professors, 252 from artists, writers, and journalists, and 158 from clergymen and teachers. More than half thus came from so-called "intellectual" circles, which accounts for the name usually applied to Gildemeister's memorandum. Other professions, however, were not absent: 182 representatives of commerce and industry, 148 justices and lawyers, 145 high state officials, 52 agrarians, 40 members of various parliaments, and 18 retired generals and admirals completed the list. There were no signatures from the working class.[220]

As to the Petition itself, it registered, according to Class, "complete agreement" with the war aims of the Pan-German League. The following excerpts give the gist of the document.[221] Its first point dealt with the future of France and was unusually specific:

We want to do away once and for all with the French danger. . . . For that purpose, a thorough improvement of our whole western frontier, from Belfort to the Channel coast is needed. We must, if possible, conquer part of the northern French Channel coast, to be strategically more secure against England and to gain a better access to the open sea. . . . The key enterprises and possessions are to be transferred to German hands. France will have to take in the previous owners and reimburse them. The part of the population taken over by Germany will be given no influence in the affairs of the Reich. It is furthermore necessary . . . to impose without mercy a high indemnity upon France. . . . We should also remember that this country has disproportionately large colonial possessions.

---

[217] *Akademische Blätter*, Aug. 1 and Sept. 16, 1915.
[218] Class, *Strom*, p. 396.
[219] Text in Grumbach, pp. 171-73.
[220] Auskunftsstelle Vereinigter Verbände, *Gedanken und Wünsche*, 1915 edition, pp. 21, 31.
[221] For text see *ibid.*, pp. 21 ff.

About Belgium, the petition asked that Germany keep the country "politically, militarily, and economically closely in hand," else Belgium "would become nothing but a highly threatening base for English attacks." Economically, Belgium would give Germany "a tremendous increase of power." And the addition of the Flemings would prove a valuable asset to German folkdom. As in the case of France, the inhabitants "were to be given not the slightest political influence in German affairs." Only the third out of five points dealt with German war aims in the east, where the petition demanded land for the settlement of German farmers. The fourth point treated at length the colonial future of Germany and her war aims against England. Even though the war with Russia had been particularly active and glorious, it held, "we must never forget for a moment that this war, in its last analysis, is a war of England against Germany's world economy and against her naval and overseas prestige." Germany, therefore, should knit the European continent into an economic whole, revive her overseas trade, and restore and enlarge her colonial holdings in Africa and elsewhere. The interdependence of a strong continental base, a powerful fleet, and an extensive colonial empire, stressed in the declaration of the Colonial Society, we find repeated here. A chain of naval stations and the loosening of England's hold over Egypt would reestablish the freedom of the seas.[222] The fifth and last point, dealing with indemnities, included demands not only for the costs of war, but also for reparations, pensions, and funds for the restoration and increase of the German army. "If we could get into the position of imposing an indemnity upon England, . . . no sum could be too large. . . . But it will probably be primarily, if not exclusively France who will be in line for a financial indemnity. We must not hesitate, out of false mercy, to burden her most heavily."

In a sweeping conclusion, the Petition of the Intellectuals warned the government that a weak peace might arouse dissatisfaction among the German people and thus bring about the fall of the monarchy.

---

[222] There was considerable interest among German annexationists in the future of Egypt: G. Roloff, *Eine ägyptische Expedition als Kampfmittel gegen England* (Berlin, 1915); R. Hennig, *Der Kampf um den Suezkanal* (Stuttgart, 1915); P. Rohrbach, *Bismarck und Wir* (München, 1915), pp. 39-45; D. Trietsch, *Die Welt nach dem Kriege* (Berlin, 1915), p. 29.

A statesman who returns without Belgium—soaked with German blood—, without strong extensions of the frontier in east and west, without a substantial indemnity, and, before all, without the most ruthless humiliation of England, such a statesman will have to expect not only the worst discontent from the lower and middle classes about the increased burden of taxation; he will also find much bitterness among leading circles, which will endanger internal peace and may even affect the foundations of the monarchy. The disappointed nation would believe that it sacrificed in vain the flower of its youth and manhood.

The petition was not sent to the Chancellor and other dignitaries until July; and since it violated censorship restrictions, it was promptly banned and confiscated. Even so, it continued to circulate and its contents soon became known abroad, where they did anything but help the German cause.

On July 29, 1915, Professor Seeberg invited a small group which had shown particular interest in the Petition to a meeting at the Hotel " Kaiserhof " in Berlin. Of the ten persons present, Seeberg and Schäfer were the only remaining representatives of the original academic section of the " preparatory committee." The other members of the committee, Kirdorf, von Reichenau, von Grumme-Douglas, Gildemeister and von Schwerin were present; also the National Liberal Paul Fuhrmann, the historian Eduard Meyer, and the secretary of the meeting, Massmann. After a brief report on the success of the petition, Seeberg resigned his position and the preparatory committee officially terminated its activities. At the same meeting, however, its former members re-constituted themselves as a new group, this time under the leadership of Dietrich Schäfer, the so-called *Unabhängiger Ausschuss für einen Deutschen Frieden*.[223] Heinrich Class claims to have been the originator of this annexationist creation also.[224] The membership of the Independent Committee was larger than that of the preparatory committee, with about forty members by the middle of 1916 and more than three hundred more or less loosely attached followers. Some of these we have already met: the leaders of the Agrarian League, Roesicke and von Wangenheim, Wolfgang Kapp, Dr. Hirsch, and professor von Gruber. Other prominent additions were Carl Duisberg (Director of the Bayer Chemical Trust), Karl Röchling (of the Saar industrial family) Paul Wilhelm Vogel

[223] Schäfer, *Leben*, pp. 171-72.
[224] Class, *Strom*, p. 398.

(President of the Saxon Diet and second in command of the National Liberal Party) and *Reichsrat* Buhl (a leading figure both in the National Liberal Party and in Bavarian politics). Professor Stahlberg of Berlin became secretary of the new committee and Professor Kulenkampff was made its treasurer.[225]

As time went on, particularly after the Committee revealed its identity in the summer of 1916, branches developed in most German cities, and by 1917 we find several hundred members, including most of the annexationists we have thus far encountered in this study.[226] The Independent Committee had become the most important annexationist organization of war-time Germany. Its strength was less the quantity than the quality of its members. There were first, and perhaps most numerous, the representatives and leaders of German heavy industry: Beukenberg, the two brothers Kirdorf (Emil and his less well-known brother Adolf), Duisberg, Poensgen, Ziese, Häuser (of the Höchst Dye Works), Beumer, Friedrichs, Hirsch, Wilhelm Meyer, and Roetger. There were editors of annexationists papers and periodicals (Bacmeister, Rippler, and Bäcker), prominent Protestant figures (Klingemann and Fischer), Professors (von Gierke, von Below, von Gruber, Schiemann), Admirals (von Knorr, Kalau vom Hofe), and many well-known annexationist propagandists like Fabarius, Reventlow, Prince Otto zu Salm-Horstmar, and Gustav Stresemann. These names present barely one-tenth the talent, wealth and power assembled behind the Independent Committee, the one and only purpose of which was the propagation of far-reaching annexationist war aims.

Compared to its immediate forerunner, the preparatory committee for the Petition of the Intellectuals, the Independent Committee had a considerably smaller contingent of university professors. Three of the original members, Hintze, Meinecke, and Oncken had even withdrawn their signatures from the Petition. But as a group the academic profession still took first place among the writers of annexationist propaganda. It would take too much space to discuss the writings and speeches of men like Zitelmann and Schumacher of Bonn, Brandenburg and Hans Meyer of Leipzig, Fester and von Bissing of Munich, Spahn of Strassburg, von Liebig of

---

[225] Schäfer, *Leben*, p. 172.

[226] For a partial list of members see Unabhängiger Ausschuss, *An das Deutsche Volk* (Königsberg, 1917), pp. 3 ff.

Giessen, Hettner and Hampe of Heidelberg, and von Schulze-Gaevernitz of Freiburg.[227] The most numerous academic pronouncements came from the University of Berlin, where Schäfer, Eduard Meyer, von Gierke and Seeberg held forth. Their colleagues Conrad Bornhak, Wilhelm Kahl, Werner Sombart, and even the moderate Hans Delbrück likewise contributed their share of propagandist writings.[228] In July 1916, a group of Berlin professors—von Gierke, Kahl, Meyer, Schäfer, Wagner, and von Wilamowitz-Möllendorf—issued a joint appeal in favor of strong war aims.[229] It would be wrong to attribute to these men the same egotistical motives and class ambitions we can detect behind the aims of most other annexationists. At the same time, it would be equally wrong to belittle or underestimate the influence of these academic contributions to the subject of war aims. To wave them aside as unrealistic utterance of uninfluential intellectuals would be to ignore the high prestige which the academic profession enjoyed in the German Empire. To find their war aims supported by men of world reputation and eminent specialists in their respective fields was a windfall to Germany's annexationists. The array of historical, economic, geographic and ethnographic arguments which these intellectuals lined up in defense of large-scale annexations supplied valuable ammunition to the propaganda of the annexationists. The German professors became the " brain trust " behind the *Kriegszielbewegung.*

One of the chief duties of the Independent Committee was the framing of a new declaration on war aims to take the place of the confiscated Petition of the Intellectuals. A memorandum by Professor Schäfer, entitled *Zur Lage* answered the requirements, though its tone was much milder than that of the Petition. It was

---

[227] For a list of annexationist writers and members of the Committee see Schäfer, *Leben,* p. 210. For examples of their writings see: E. Zitelmann, *Das Schicksal Belgiens beim Friedensschluss* (München, 1915); E. Brandenburg, *Deutschlands Kriegsziele* (Leipzig, 1917); H. Meyer in *Frankfurter Zeitung,* April 9, 1916 (2d ed.); R. Fester, *Die Wandlungen der belgischen Frage* (Halle, 1918); F. W. von Bissing, *Westliche Kriegsziele* (Weimar, 1917); M. Spahn, *Im Kampf um unsere Zukunft* (M. Gladbach, 1915); von Liebig in *Berliner Neueste Nachrichten,* June 26, 1915; A. Hettner, *Die Ziele unserer Weltpolitik* (Berlin, 1915); K. Hampe, *Belgiens Vergangenheit und Gegenwart* (Leipzig, 1915); G. von Schulze-Gaevernitz, *La Mer libre* (Stuttgart, 1915).

[228] Grumbach, pp. 159, 201, 348-49; W. Sombart, *Händler und Helden* (München, 1915), esp. pp. 143-44; H. Delbrück, *Bismarck's Erbe* (Berlin, 1915), pp. 202 ff.

[229] *Schulthess,* vol. 57 (1), pp. 369-70.

published on New Year's Day 1916 and over 300,000 copies were distributed.[230] From France it demanded the Briey-Longwy region and a better frontier along the Vosges mountains. Belgium should become politically, militarily and economically dependent upon Germany, and the suppressed Flemings were to be " saved." The first large-scale meeting of the Committee was in June 1916 in Berlin. Schäfer gave the opening address and then introduced a resolution which asked for the usual set of western war aims.[231] In August of 1916, another meeting of the Independent Committee decided to present its war aims to a wider audience in a proclamation entitled " To the German People." [232] It was signed by most of the members of the Committee plus about two hundred additional outstanding personalities. The proclamation itself was drafted in rather general terms to evade the restrictions of censorship.[233]

Another one of the functions of the Independent Committee was to serve as national headquarters for the numerous local organizations of annexationists springing up all over Germany and to supply them with materials for speeches, pamphlets, handbills, etc.[234] The interesting feature of these local organizations was the way in which various annexationist groups co-operated in their propagandist activities. In Düsseldorf, for instance, the Pan-German League, the Army League, various athletic clubs, and the *Verein Deutscher Eisenhüttenleute* worked together for the dissemination of strong aims. In Karlsruhe another such group existed under the leadership of the local Independent Committee. In Hamburg the Conservative Parties, the Center Party, and the Agrarian League held joint meetings with the Pan-German League and the Army League. In Chemnitz, Frankfurt a. M., Königsberg, and other major cities, similar collaboration existed.[235] Special

---

[230] D. Schäfer, *Zur Lage* (Berlin, 1916); Schäfer, *Leben,* pp. 173-74; *Berliner Tageblatt,* Aug. 12, 1916.

[231] K. Jagow, ed., *Dietrich Schäfer und sein Werk* (Berlin, 1925), p. 120; Schäfer, *Leben,* p. 188.

[232] Schäfer, *Krieg,* II, 10; Unabhaengiger Ausschuss, *An das Deutsche Volk!* (Königsberg, 1917).

[233] The Independent Committee also put its whole weight behind the growing agitation for the unlimited use of submarines: *Schulthess,* vol. 57 (1), p. 126; *Reichstag,* vol. 417, pp. 381 ff.

[234] Wortmann, p. 16.

[235] *Vorbilder zur Organisation* (n. pl., n. d.), Monkemöller Collection, Hoover Library, Stanford, Calif.; *Schulthess,* vol. 57 (1), p. 396; Grumbach, p. 148;

efforts were made to organize the nationalists of Bavaria and to arouse the people of Southern Germany in general. In March of 1916, a group of some one hundred leading Munich citizens published the *Richtlinien für Wege zum dauernden Frieden* which asked for the usual German domination over Belgium, the annexation of the ore-regions and some frontier rectifications from France, a large German colonial Empire in Central Africa, and naval stations to ensure the freedom of the seas.[236] The next step in the growth of an annexationist group in Munich was "a confidential discussion in July of 1916 between leading men of South Germany on the political situation."[237] Out of this meeting developed the "Committee of Principles for the Roads to a lasting Peace," which was nothing but the Munich branch of the Independent Committee.[238] Professor Emil Kraepelin, member of the Independent Committee, Gottfried Traub, Count Reventlow, and the Centrist Schlittenbauer were among its founders. It was from these same circles that a delegation approached King Ludwig demanding a strong peace, unrestricted submarine warfare, and expressing strong opposition to Bethmann Hollweg. Of the eleven delegates, seven at least were members of the Independent Committee. The King, whose sympathies were definitely with the annexationists, as we have already seen, still urged the petitioners to have confidence in the responsible leaders of the Empire.[239]

The relationship between the Independent Committee and the annexationist parties of the Right was a close one. Count Westarp refrained from joining the Committee so as not to tie the hands of his party; but his attitude towards Dietrich Schäfer and Professor Stahlberg "was based on trust and sympathy."[240] The National Liberals were less hesitant in their co-operation and several of their leaders—Fuhrmann, Stresemann, Vogel, and Buhl—were among the members of the Committee. But annexationist agitation after 1915 was not limited to the Independent Committee. Other combinations of nationalist groups continued to

---

Hamburger Nachrichten, Sept. 15, 1916; A. Lanick, *Klarheit über die Kriegsziele* (Heidelberg, 1917), p. 127.

[236] Auskunftsstelle Vereinigter Verbände, *Gedanken und Wünsche*, 1917 edition, pp. 32-36.

[237] *Weser Zeitung*, July 29, 1916.

[238] Dahlin, pp. 68-69.

[239] *Schulthess*, vol. 57 (1), p. 387.

[240] Westarp, II, 167.

collaborate whenever the necessity for a united stand arose. The two chief causes for such collaboration were the demands for a strong peace and for unlimited submarine warfare as a means of winning such a peace; and the main obstacle to their realization was seen in Bethmann Hollweg's basic moderation. The questions of war aims, submarine warfare, and opposition to the Chancellor thus became closely interrelated.

The Campaign Against Bethmann Hollweg

There had been a number of attacks against Bethmann Hollweg, ever since his moderate stand on the subject of war aims was first suspected; but during the summer of 1915 these attacks increased both in volume and violence.[241] At the same time lack of agreement on a suitable successor—ex-chancellor von Bülow, von Tirpitz, Falkenhayn and Baron von Rheinbaben were all named as possibilities—proved a severe handicap to the campaign for the Chancellor's dismissal.[242] A further obstacle was the support which Bethmann enjoyed from the Emperor. The fact that William II seemed to agree with the " weak " policy of his Chancellor caused much consternation among annexationists. They tried to explain the Kaiser's attitude as the result of the alleged seclusion in which he was purposely kept by the supporters of moderation. To penetrate this seclusion, a letter was addressed to the Kaiser in January 1916, by a group of notables, including Schäfer, Prince Otto zu Salm-Horstmar, Admiral von Knorr, Baron von Gebsattel, Count von Roon, and other members of the Independent Committee. The letter pointed out that in the opinion of the signatories, the direction of Germany's policy was in the hands of men who lacked the confidence of the ablest and most faithful supporters of the monarchy. It would do great harm to the existing system, it continued, " if peace . . . would not bring a prize of victory to our people, justifying the terrible sacrifices of blood that have been made." Finally, to voice their grievances more effectively and specifically, the authors of the letter asked the favor of a personal audience. But William's answer was negative and highly indignant at this attempt to influence the decisions of the Crown.[243]

[241] Hutten-Czapski, II, 212-14.
[242] Westarp, II, 303.
[243] Schäfer, *Leben*, pp. 173-74; H. von Treuberg, *Zwischen Politik und Diplomatie* (Strassburg, 1921), p. 84.

Aside from these co-operative moves against Bethmann Hollweg and his submarine and war aims policy, we find several individual attacks between the end of 1915 and the middle of 1916, three of which merit separate discussion because of the considerable stir they caused at the time. The first was a book by Professor Hans von Liebig, *Die Politik von Bethmann Hollwegs*, published in December 1915.[244] Written in three parts, it levelled a violent attack upon Bethmann's policy, mostly during the pre-war years. The book was the brain-child of the Munich publisher J. F. Lehmann, prominent in annexationist circles, whose plan was further developed in conversations with Heinrich Class, General von Gebsattel, and Carl Caesar Eiffe, another prominent Pan-German propagandist. Liebig was then commissioned to write the book and Lehmann published it at his own expense.[245] To outwit the censor, two editions were printed in great secrecy. One, a volume of ordinary size, was mailed in small quantities. It could easily be detected and was promptly confiscated. When the authorities thought they had the matter well in hand, 3,000 copies, printed on very thin paper, were sent out as first class mail and most of them reached their destination.[246] Most of von Liebig's book dealt with the pre-war period and the outbreak of war. When he came down to the present, he demanded the usual annexations especially in Western Europe.

The second attack against Bethmann appeared in May 1916 and was distributed in about 300 typewritten copies.[247] Its author was Wolfgang Kapp, *Generallandschaftsdirektor* of East Prussia and one of the most important supporters of the annexationist cause. He was a member of the Pan-German League as well as the Independent Committee and co-editor of *Deutschlands Erneuerung*, though he did not really become well-known until he wrote his attack upon Bethmann Hollweg.[248] Despite its brevity, his pamphlet summed up admirably the attitude of the *fronde* against

[244] H. von Liebig, *Die Politik von Bethmann Hollwegs* (München, 1919), 3 parts in 2 vols.

[245] Lehmann, pp. 252-54.

[246] *Ibid.*, pp. 40-41; *Berliner Tageblatt*, Aug. 16, 1916.

[247] W. Kapp, " Die nationalen Kreise und der Reichskanzler " (Königsberg, 1916). Typescript at the Hoover Library, Stanford, Calif.

[248] For a discussion of Kapp see " Junius Alter," *Nationalisten*, pp. 28 ff.; L. Schemann, *Wolfgang Kapp und das Märzunternehmen vom Jahre 1920* (München, 1937).

the Chancellor. Point by point he attacked and demolished Bethmann's domestic and foreign policy, suggesting the Chancellor's
dismissal as the only remedy. His first point of attack was Germany's moderate submarine policy, which Kapp blamed on Bethmann's submissive attitude towards the United States and his
belief that victory over England was impossible. He then went
on to deal with Bethmann's war aims, singling out his Belgian
policy for special attack:

> The Chancellor has stated clearly that Belgium, which once he indicated
> as a pledge in hand, will be surrendered—though only in return for real
> guarantees, so that she will not again become an outpost of our enemies—
> but surrendered, and that is the decisive thing. . . . The guarantees
> demanded by the Chancellor, even if " real," cannot help us at all. For
> he was thinking only of negative guarantees against the plans of our
> opponents. What we need, however, are positive guarantees for our future
> as a world power. We can only obtain such guarantees if we do not give
> up Belgium but under some form, especially by retaining the coast, take
> her under political, economic, and military control. That is exactly what
> the Chancellor does not want.[249]

Actually there was nothing in Bethmann's statements to justify
Kapp's accusation. As a matter of fact, Bethmann's speech of
April 5, 1916, as we have seen, was the most far-reaching of his
public statements about German war aims and had been welcomed
as such by most annexationists. The opposition we find in Kapp's
memorandum, therefore, can only be understood if we realize how
closely in his mind, as in that of almost all annexationists, the
question of war aims was related to the problem of internal reforms. The same argument already used by General von Gebsattel,
by the Petition of the Intellectuals, and by Count Westarp to
describe this relationship, we find again repeated by Kapp:

> Our brave nation, which in this struggle for its national existence has borne
> incomparable sacrifices with never-wanting self-denying inspiration, expects
> the most from this peace. It dare not be deprived of the reward for these
> sacrifices. It has a valid claim to the magnificence whose development is
> opened by the victories of our arms. Should it be disappointed in its lofty
> expectations, the destructive results on our internal political life and their
> reaction upon the Reich's foreign policy would be enormous. An irremedi-
> able weakening of the government would take place which would immensely
> strengthen parliament and would endanger the future of the German
> Empire.

---

[249] Kapp, p. 25.

On the other hand, after a glorious peace, " a strong popular Empire of highest splendor will arise which will empower Germany to the greatest political, economic, and cultural productivity. . . . Only then shall we escape from the democratic swamp into which we should be drawn undoubtedly after a lukewarm peace." [250]

No one before had more strongly voiced the fear, that a weak peace would hasten the rise of that despised Western product called democracy. Nor had any annexationist ever stated more frankly his opposition to the two most burning questions of German internal politics—the reform of Prussia's suffrage and the introduction of a parliamentary regime. About the first, Kapp wrote: " In discussing the domestic development of the German people . . . the importance has been wrongly placed upon the suffrage demands and their realization. The basis of true political freedom is economic independence and the economic self-determination of the individual "—a doctrine which was attractive to the middle class, but held little consolation for the lower class. As to granting a larger share of influence in the affairs of the Reich to political parties, the memorandum held that the government,

to preserve its reputation . . . must not let the reins be taken from its hands by political parties; otherwise it is to be feared that unity of action will be destroyed, that the government will be driven to the defensive by the unreasonable demands of the parties, and that because of the resulting political complications general dissatisfaction and disillusionment will take place instead of improvement, as had been hoped.[251]

Statements like these must be kept in mind to understand the hatred of the annexationists towards Bethmann, about whose sympathies with domestic reforms they never had any doubt.

The third example of anti-Bethmann propaganda appeared under the pseudonym " Junius Alter " in June 1916.[252] The author, probably, was Franz Sontag, editor of the *Alldeutsche Blätter*, though it may have been a co-operative venture.[253] Like Liebig's book, the " Junius Alter " pamphlet dealt largely with Bethmann's pre-war and domestic policy and contained little on war aims.

[250] Lutz, *German Empire*, I, 101-02.

[251] *Ibid.*, p. 106.

[252] " Junius Alter," *Das Deutsche Reich auf dem Wege zur geschichtlichen Episode* (München, 1919), first published in June 1916.

[253] M. Wenck, *Alldeutsche Taktik* (Jena, 1917), pp. 18, 21; Class, *Strom*, p. 339; Westarp, II, 169.

Two thousand copies were distributed and when the censor intervened, the book reappeared under a new title and the pseudonym " *Drei Deutsche*." [254]

The immediate results of these attacks upon his person and policy were two Reichstag speeches by Bethmann on June 5-6, 1916. " I know that no party in this House [he said on June 5] approves of agitation which uses falsehoods or invective. But unfortunately the pirates of public opinion frequently abuse the flag of the nationalist parties. . . . It is bitter to have to fight the lies of our enemies. Slander and defamation at home are just shameful." [255] The press, almost unanimously, joined the Chancellor against his attackers, though the indignation displayed by a paper like the *Deutsche Tageszeitung* did not sound especially sincere.[256] " There can be no doubt [Georg Bernhard of the *Vossische Zeitung* observed with insight] that a large number of the attacks upon the Chancellor's alleged attitude towards the question of peace are made from motives of internal policy. . . . Doubtless those, who view a change of the existing forces in domestic policy with alarm, often use foreign policy as a pretext to vent their anger on him." [257] Other observers shared this interpretation. " They speak of peace terms and they really mean the Prussian franchise," the banker Paul von Schwabach wrote to a friend in July 1916.[258] Eventually the war aims controversy always revealed its roots in German domestic affairs.

This alarm of the ruling classes, that war might bring reforms which in turn would curtail their privileges was, of course, by no means unfounded. Bethmann Hollweg had hinted at such reforms as early as December 1914. More specific hints and the first tangible evidence of impending changes occurred during the first half of 1916 in the Emperor's speech from the throne on January 13, and the introduction on May 1 of legislation removing some of the most irksome restrictions upon labor unions.[259] It was felt,

---

[254] " Drei Deutsche," *Deutsche Reichspolitik seit 14. Juli 1909*, cited in *Schulthess*, vol. 57 (1), p. 386.

[255] *Reichstag*, vol. 307, pp. 1510 ff.

[256] See Thimme, *Bethmann Hollweg*, pp. 128-29 for a survey of press reactions to Bethmann's speech.

[257] *Ibid.*, p. 129.

[258] Schwabach, pp. 300, 310; M. Weber, *Max Weber, ein Lebensbild* (Tübingen, 1926), p. 577.

[259] Westarp, II, 222 ff., 257 ff.

therefore, that only a change of government, i. e., the dismissal of Bethmann Hollweg, and the conclusion of a strong peace might stem the tide of reforms. The agitation for strong war aims hoped to achieve both. The basic aim of the *Kriegszielbewegung* during the second as during the first year of the war was the maintenance and strengthening of the existing political, social, and economic order. In that it was supported by most of the *Kriegszielmehrheit*.[260] It was in the face of this opposition that the Chancellor had to develop and formulate his war aims.

There were, of course, just as during the first year of war, large numbers of annexationist articles, pamphlets and books, not directly connected with annexationist organizations. With a few exceptions—notably the writings of professors already mentioned—these are significant merely as an indication of the prevalence of annexationist views in Germany despite rigid censorship regulations.[261] Among their authors were such well-known names as Count Reventlow, Dr. Carl Peters, Paul Rohrbach, and Count Hoensbroech. Of special interest are the views on war aims which Prince Bülow, Bethmann's predecessor, put forth in his *Deutsche Politik* in May 1916. " The result of this war," he wrote, " must be positive, not negative. . . . The simple restoration of the *status quo ante bellum* would not be a gain but rather a loss to Germany." [262] In a letter to Theodor Wolff in July 1916, Bülow repeated these views, which received high praise from the annexationist press, though they did not fundamentally differ from Bethmann's declarations.[263] Bülow's middle-of-the-road policy may well have been determined by the fact that he hoped to replace Bethmann and again become Chancellor. He could not afford to antagonize either annexationist or moderate circles.

Annexationist papers likewise continued their agitation.[246] At a meeting of the *Verein Deutscher Zeitungsverleger* in July 1915, its president, Robert Faber—publisher and editor of the National Liberal and annexationist *Magdeburgische Zeitung*—proposed the founding of an association of newspapermen for the discussion of

---

[260] *Ibid.*, p. 124; *Reichstag*, vol. 308, pp. 1708-09.

[261] For examples see Grumbach, pp. 270 ff., 290 ff., 327 ff.; Great Britain, Foreign Office, *German Opinion on National Policy since July 1914*, part III (London, 1920), *passim.*

[262] B. von Bülow, *Deutsche Politik* (Berlin, 1916), pp. xii, 88-89.

[263] Wolff, *Marsch*, p. 120; *Rheinisch-Westphälische Zeitung*, July 3, 1916.

[264] Grumbach, pp. 56 ff., 78 ff., 94 ff., 106 ff., 115 ff.

war aims. His plan was accepted and the first meeting of the "Club 1914-15" took place in September 1915. Of the newpaper publishers present, "there was hardly one who was not in favor of territorial acquisitions for the security of Germany." The second and last meeting of the group took place in November 1915.[265]

The "Moderates" Launch a Counter-Offensive

The only real and consistent opposition to the ultra-annexationists, as we have already seen, came from among the ranks of the Social Democrats. Other individuals and groups, though they had the reputation of being anti-annexationist, merely differed from the radical annexationists in the extent of their war aims. The fact, however, that these moderates came from the same social background as the annexationists made the rivalry between the two groups extremely bitter at times. During this second year of the war, we may trace a very distinct tendency towards more effective organization among these moderates, running parallel to the rise of the annexationist Independent Committee.

Although the negotiations leading to the Petition of the Intellectuals were carried on secretly, the men who held less radical views on the future peace settlement knew that such a proclamation was on its way.[266] On July 7, 1915, therefore, about fifty of them, under the leadership of the former ambassador to England, Count Hatzfeld, met in Berlin to discuss the Belgian problem. The majority of those present, e. g., Professors Kahl, Seering, and the former Colonial Secretary Dernburg, were opposed to any kind of annexation. After an impressive speech by Hans Delbrück, a smaller committee (Delbrück, Kahl, Dernburg, August Stein of the *Frankfurter Zeitung* and Theodor Wolff of the *Berliner Tageblatt*) was formed to frame a declaration expressing the views of the meeting. Two days later the newly-formed committee met at Delbrück's house and approved a memorandum drafted by Theodor Wolff. Like the Petition of the Intellectuals, it was sent to a number of leading personalities, and 141 signatures were finally attached to it. Compared to the almost tenfold number which Seeberg collected for his petition, this was very meager.[267] Wolff's

---

[265] Knesebeck, pp. 59-60.

[266] Haussmann, p. 37.

[267] Wolff, *Marsch*, pp. 269-70; Schäfer, *Leben*, pp. 170-71; Hutten-Czapski, II, 213; V. Valentin, *Deutschlands Aussenpolitik von Bismarck's Abgang bis zum Ende des Weltkrieges* (Berlin, 1921), pp. 252, 270.

petition, addressed to the Chancellor, opposed " the annexation or attachment (*Angliederung*) of politically independent . . . peoples." At the same time it insisted that the areas which Germany had conquered " should not become a bulwark " for Germany's enemies. " The German people," the petition concluded, " can only make a peace which offers a secure basis for the strategic needs and the political and economic interests of the country, as well as for the unhindered use of its strength and spirit of enterprise at home and on the free seas." [268] Among the signatories of the petition were many famous names. Aside from the participants in the meeting of July 7, we find the former ambassadors Count Monts (Italy), Wolff-Metternich (England) and von Stumm (Spain); the former Secretary of State Prince Henckel von Donnersmarck, the banker Franz von Mendelssohn, the industrialist Karl Friedrich von Siemens, and the Protestant *Superintendent* of Berlin, Friedrich Lahusen. As was the case with the Petition of the Intellectuals, the largest group among the signatories consisted of university professors, most of them well-known—e. g., Albert Einstein, Ernst Troeltsch, Adolph Harnack, Gustav von Schmoller, Gerhard Anschütz, and Max Weber. Compared to the Petition of the Intellectuals, historians were noticeably absent, as were representatives of heavy industry. Aside from these differences, however, the social background of the signatories of both petitions was very much the same.[269] Most of the leaders of moderate or anti-annexationist groups who had made separate declarations during the first year of war now joined forces behind Wolff's Petition (Baron von Tepper-Laski of the *Bund Neues Vaterland*, Professor Kahl of the *Freie Vaterländische Vereinigung*, and Professors Quidde and Schücking of the *Deutsche Friedensgesellschaft*), just as the various annexationist individuals and groups had rallied behind the Independent Committee. One of the so-called moderates, Albert Ballin, refused to sign the petition. As the main reason he gave the omission of colonial aims and the necessity for a German lease over the port of Zeebrugge.[270] Ballin's statements during the later part of 1915, however, showed increasing moderation and a real desire for peace.[271]

[268] Grumbach, pp. 409-11.
[269] For a list of signatories see *Preussische Jahrbücher*, vol. 162 (1915), pp. 169 ff.
[270] Wolff, *Marsch*, pp. 269-70.
[271] Huldermann, pp. 244, 246-47; Stubmann, pp. 261-62.

The next major step in the movement for moderate aims was again a parallel development to the *Kriegszielbewegung*. As a counter-weight to the Independent Committee, the *Deutscher Nationalausschuss für einen Deutschen Frieden* was founded on June 6, 1916, under the presidency of Prince Wedel, former German *Statthalter* of Alsace-Lorraine.[272] The idea to found an organization for the propagation of moderate war aims had apparently originated with Matthias Erzberger, who wrote a memorandum on the subject in April 1916.[273] Among its founders, besides Erzberger, were Wahnschaffe, Hammann (chief of the Foreign Office press section), and Riezler, an indication of the government's interest in the National Committee. Its large propaganda bureau, under the direction of Ulrich Rauscher and Peter Breuer of the *Frankfurter Zeitung* seems to have received governmental financial support.[274] The motto of the National Committee was " to stay equally clear of the giddiness of the peacemakers and of the greediness displayed in the proclamations of the Pan-Germans." [275] Prince Wedel stressed the necessity for close collaboration between his Committee and the government and held that Germany should only make such annexations as her military, economic, and political security required. Such terms, of course, were similar to Bethmann Hollweg's and did not mean the renunciation of any and all annexations.[276] The National Committee hoped to win peace with England by restoring the independence of Belgium (with certain " guarantees ") and to seek territorial compensations in the east and across the sea.[277] " With the annexation of the Belgian coast and even Calais, we can never reach peace with England," Prince Wedel wrote in July 1916.[278] Nor would such German expansion along the Atlantic coast prove an effective threat to Great Britain. England will always remain strong due to her insular position,

[272] Sometimes this committee is called *Deutscher Nationalausschuss für Vorbereitung eines ehrenvollen Friedens*.

[273] Westarp, II, 185-86; Rupprecht, I, 455.

[274] Westarp, II, 185-86; Schäfer, *Leben*, p. 188. In 1917 another moderate organization was founded in Frankfurt, called *Volksbund für einen Verständigungsfrieden*: see Werner, pp. 238-39.

[275] Westarp, II, 186.

[276] F. Lienhard, ed., "Statthalterbriefe aus Elsass-Lothringen," *Der Türmer*, XXVI (1924), 536 ff.

[277] *U. A.*, 4. Reihe, XII (1), 51.

[278] Lienhard, *Der Türmer*, XXVI, 538-39.

Dernburg held. "To destroy British power we would have to erase England from the map." [279]

The main intellectual force behind the moderates was Professor Hans Delbrück. In a controversy with the annexationist *Deutsche Tageszeitung* in April 1916 he defined his position (and that of his fellow moderates) as follows: "The difference between the *Deutsche Tageszeitung* and myself lies in the fact that it considers England the most dangerous enemy of Germany's future, while I think Russia is." [280] Both Hans Delbrück and Paul Rohrbach hoped to extend Germany's sphere of influence by liberating the suppressed nationalities of Eastern Europe. Looking back upon his controversies with the ultra-annexationists, Delbrück said in 1926:

I often used to say openly: my annexationist aims are in no way smaller than those of others! They are only different. They are such that the others can accept them. . . . Both Rohrbach and I have always emphasized, the great idealistic aim of Germany must be the freedom and independence of small peoples. . . . This was at the same time in the interest of Germany's power.[281]

The National Committee, like the Independent Committee, included many great names. The professors Harnack, von Liszt, and Oncken; the Progressive deputies Haussmann, Naumann, and von Payer; ex-ambassador von Stumm, Director Heineken of the North German Lloyd, Paul von Schwabach, and the Social Democrat Suedekum. The best indication, however, of how little the National Committee differed from its rival organization is the fact that several leading industrialists were, at least temporarily, among its members: August Thyssen, the brothers Röchling, Peter Kloeckner, and Baron von Bodenhausen-Degener (a director of Krupp's and member of the Mannesmann Board of Directors).[282]

After publishing a proclamation against the Pan-German League in July, the National Committee planned a major propaganda campaign with meetings in thirty-nine cities for the second anniversary of the outbreak of war.[283] The central office of the Independent Committee, on July 22, consequently addressed a circular to its

---

[279] Kanner, III, 98-99.
[280] *Deutsche Tageszeitung*, April 5, 1916.
[281] *U.A.*, 4. Reihe, XII (1), 51-52, notes 1 and 2.
[282] *Schulthess*, vol. 57 (1), p. 346; Great Britain, *Daily Review*, Aug. 3, 1916, p. 3.
[283] *Schulthess*, vol. 57 (1), p. 345.

local representatives asking them to send large numbers of annexationists to these meetings to present the views of the Independent Committee. There would be quite a few speakers for the National Committee, the circular said, who were really members of the Independent Committee, and from whose speeches little need be feared. But if something were said against the aims of the Independent Committee which could not be immediately contradicted, the representatives of the latter were to hold meetings of their own to counteract the bad effects of the moderates' attack.[284] The most important of the meetings was the one in Berlin at which Professor Harnack attacked war profiteering and advocated a mild kind of state socialism. This promptly resulted in the resignation of the above-mentioned industrialists from the National Committee.[285]

The many similarities between the membership and to some extent even the aims of the Independent and National Committees naturally suggested co-operation between the two. A meeting of representatives from both groups was called in the fall of 1916 but failed to reach an agreement.[286] The meeting was held at the Pringsheim Palais in Berlin, headquarters of the *Deutsche Gesellschaft 1914*. This remarkable club had been founded in 1915 by General von Moltke, with Colonial Secretary Solf as president. Its purpose was to perpetuate the unity which the outbreak of war had brought to the German people, and " to offer German men from all professions and classes, regardless of party affiliations, the possibility of unprejudiced and informal social intercourse." [287] Membership was only by invitation and dues were high. The following is a brief selection from its list of famous members: [288] There was a handful of right-wing Social Democrats—Lensch, Suedekum, and Fendrich; there were the Secretaries of State Solf, Helfferich, Wahnschaffe, and Zimmermann; the generals von Moltke, von Kessel, von Kluck, and von Perthes; the admirals von Capelle, von Holtzendorff, Truppel and Büchsel; the industrialists Thyssen, Siemens, Rathenau, and Kirdorf; the bankers von Schwabach, von Men-

---

[284] *Ibid.*, p. 380.

[285] *Kölnische Zeitung*, Aug. 12, 1916; Great Britain, *Daily Review*, Aug. 26, 1918, p. 8.

[286] Schäfer, *Leben*, p. 189.

[287] Moltke, pp. 443-44; Deutsche Gesellschaft 1914, *Satzung* (n. pl., n. d.), copy at the Hoover Library, Stanford, Calif.

[288] For a list of members see *Berliner Tageblatt*, Nov. 29, 1915.

delssohn, Salomonsohn and von Friedländer-Fuld; the Reichstag deputies Erzberger, Bassermann, and von Payer; the artists Gerhart Hauptmann, Max Liebermann, Max Reinhardt and Ludwig Thoma; the professors Hans Delbrück, Kahl, Lepsius and von Gierke; the publishers and editors Mosse, Ullstein, Rippler, and Theodor Wolff. The *Gesellschaft 1914* was not an annexationist organization. It was a political club in which extreme annexationists mingled with moderate annexationists, the former being in the majority, offering an excellent place for informal discussion and exchange of views.[289]

A similar, though much smaller group, was the *Mittwochsgesellschaft*, founded by Bassermann and including von Moltke, von Kluck, Stresemann, Stinnes, Hugenberg, Rathenau, Professor Hoetzsch, Westarp, von Heydebrand, Roesicke, and the Socialists David, Heine, and Suedekum.

Both these clubs played a not unimportant part behind the scenes. They established connections in what was for Germany a completely new form, between the government on the one hand, and members of parliament, journalists, leaders of industry, bankers and people from every department of public life on the other; and by means of these easy and unceremonious relationships they often exerted more influence on German policy and the direction of the war, especially in critical moments, than did the censored press or " public opinion," or even the Houses of Parliament, which after all sat within hearing of the Entente.[290]

The discussion of Germany's western aims during the second year of the war is thus complete. As was pointed out at the beginning, the tendencies of the first year continued throughout the second. The policy of Bethmann Hollweg, moderate by inclination, became increasingly, though vaguely, annexationist, under the pressure both of events (the development of a German administration in the occupied areas) and propaganda (from annexationists both inside parliament and out). The longer the war continued without a definite statement from the government against the annexation of western areas and in favor of the platform of August 4, 1914, the more difficult such a statement became. Yet even during the second year, the publication of Belgian documents, which helped to justify the demands of the annexationists

[289] Weber, p. 568.

[290] Kessler, pp. 230-31; Westarp, II, 11. During the last year of war an exclusively Pan-German club was founded, the *Donnerstagsgesellschaft*.

in the eyes of the German people, continued.[291]   One cannot but feel that it was fear of the annexationists which prompted the Chancellor to make statements more radical than he himself believed in.[292]   Faced with continuous demands for large war aims, he admitted to Valentini in the spring of 1915: "I can do nothing against it.   The psychology of our people has been so poisoned by boasting during the last 25 years, that it would probably become timid if we were to prohibit it." [293]

[291] *Norddeutsche Allgemeine Zeitung,* July 29, 31, Aug. 4, 1915.

[292] See the interesting comments of Delbrück and Schwertfeger in *U. A.,* 4. Reihe, XII (1), 42, note 1.

[293] Valentini, p. 226; see also Max Weber's comment in Weber, p. 577.

Chapter III

A HOUSE DIVIDED

CHANCELLOR VS. SUPREME COMMAND
(SEPTEMBER 1916–JULY 1917)

NOT ONLY the first, but to some extent the second year of the war must be considered a formative period in the history of German war aims. But when military reverses during the summer of 1916 made an early, negotiated peace desirable, if not necessary, the situation changed. The third year of the war, then, was a year of declarations and feelers for peace. The tension which had developed over the question of war aims was thus brought out into the open and made the remainder of the war a succession of internal crises. These crises were intensified by an increasing divergence of views between the civilian and military heads of the German government, beginning with the change of military command on August 29, 1916.[1]

The first open indication of Germany's willingness for peace was the Peace Note of December 12, 1916. The vague ideas concerning a post-war settlement, found in the statements of the German government during the first two years of war, now by necessity had to crystallize into specific peace terms. In spite of its negative results, therefore, the peace offer of December 12, 1916, stands as one of the key events in the history of German war aims.

The Peace Note of December 12, 1916

We have already briefly sketched the military situation chiefly responsible for Bethmann Hollweg's growing skepticism during the summer of 1916.[2] The attempts at mediation of President Wilson, therefore, thus far treated in a desultory fashion, suddenly seemed to offer a welcome chance for terminating the war. On August 31, 1916, a meeting of German military and civilian authorities took place at headquarters in Pless. Here is Helfferich's account:

[1] Bethmann Hollweg, II, 31.
[2] See above, p. 74.

The Chancellor . . . gave us a picture of the situation which he considered extremely serious, in spite of the confidence of Hindenburg and Ludendorff. We had to do everything possible to gain peace. The only way out, in his opinion, led through Wilson, and this way had to be taken, even if the prospects were uncertain. . . . We should tell Wilson that we were ready to give up Belgium, with the one reservation that we would settle our relations with that country after its restitution through direct negotiations.[3]

The immediate result of Bethmann's desire for peace was a telegram on September 2 to Germany's ambassador in Washington, Count Bernstorff: " Would peace mediation by Wilson be possible and successful if we were to guarantee Belgium's unconditional restoration? Otherwise the unrestricted U-boat war will have to be carried out in dead earnest." [4] The alternative of peace or unlimited submarine warfare, as we shall see, was no exaggeration.

Before we continue our discussion of the negotiations between Berlin and Washington, a word about the simultaneous attempts at a separate peace with Russia. There had been various minor moves in this direction during 1916, as for instance the conversations of Hugo Stinnes with the Japanese minister to Sweden in March 1916 and of Max Warburg with the Vice-President of the Russian Duma, Protopopov, in June the same year.[5] We have already discussed the chief reasons for their failure. Sentiment in favor of such a settlement, however, continued among certain people in Germany, especially the parties of the Right.[6] During the fall of 1916, Hugo Stinnes was once again sent to Sweden, this time to confer with Protopopov. The use of the prominent industrialist for these missions is further proof of the influence he wielded in German affairs. But negotiations came to nothing and all chances for a separate peace with Russia were wrecked when the Central Powers resurrected the Kingdom of Poland in November 1916.[7]

Germany's efforts to secure President Wilson's services as mediator were rather slow in bringing results. It was not until after he had been re-elected on November 9, that Wilson finally began

[3] Helfferich, pp. 335-36.
[4] Forster, p. 47.
[5] Ibid., p. 43; Brunauer, " Peace Proposals," pp. 41 ff.
[6] Helfferich, p. 336; Kronprinz Wilhelm, pp. 157, 167; Rupprecht, II, 50-51.
[7] U. A., 4. Reihe, XII (1), 43 ff.

drafting his own peace note.[8] The wave of anti-German feeling (due largely to the deportation of Belgian workers) which swept Allied and neutral countries at this time, necessitated further postponement of mediation. But some time earlier, the plan had already arisen in Germany of issuing a direct declaration in favor of peace, which might strengthen those minorities in Allied countries willing to enter into peace negotiations. Bethmann had first thought of it in the summer of 1916. Subsequently he received similar suggestions from other quarters, notably Helfferich and Haussmann.[9] In late October the Chancellor broached his plan to Hindenburg and the Kaiser. Both agreed to it, the former with some hesitation, the latter with enthusiasm, seeing himself already in the role of a world savior.[10]

Germany's ally, Austria-Hungary, was likewise in favor of any measures that might lead to a speedy termination of the war. Already during his visit to Germany on October 17, 1916, her foreign minister Count Burian had discussed the possibility of such a peace offer with the German Chancellor. Here we have the beginnings of a series of three-cornered negotiations over desirable peace terms between Burian, Bethmann, and Hindenburg, which lasted from October until the middle of November and which throw important light on the war aims of the Central Powers. The fact that Hindenburg was consulted at each step of the negotiations indicates the influence which Germany's military leaders had already gained over decisions which belonged primarily in the political sphere. Burian's terms of October 17, as far as they had any bearing on Western Europe and colonies, were as follows: [11] (1) The restoration of Belgium as a sovereign state with sufficient guarantees to ensure Germany's legitimate interests. (2) Full territorial integrity of France. (3) Return of German colonies and German annexation of the Congo State. (4) No indemnities for Germany, except perhaps the granting of commercial advantages. (5) Treaties to guarantee the freedom of the seas. (6) Renunciation of all agreements between the Allies which might prevent the resumption of normal economic relations after the war.[12]

---

[8] Helfferich, pp. 336-37; Valentin, *Aussenpolitik*, p. 308; Bernstorff, pp. 305-06.

[9] Bethmann Hollweg, II, 151; Helfferich, p. 339; Haussmann, pp. 72-73; Max von Baden, p. 49.

[10] Helfferich, pp. 339-40.   [11] *U. A.*, 15. Ausschuss, II, 80.

[12] The last point was directed against the Allied Economic Conference of Paris

Bethmann's own peace proposals were ready by late October.[13] His suggestions differed in several respects from those of Burian. In regard to Belgium, guarantees for Germany's security were to be gained through negotiations with King Albert. If such guarantees could not be won, Germany should annex a strip of territory including Liège, to protect her western industrial areas. As to France, all except the area of Briey-Longwy should be evacuated. In return for this evacuation, France would have to pay an indemnity. Both these provisions presented an increase over Burian's demands. The only concession Bethmann made was that Germany would give up some of her colonial holdings in the Pacific. Here we have—except for his private statements during the first months of the war—the Chancellor's first specific program of war aims. Compared to the aims of the ultra-annexationists, it was not very extreme; yet it was not exactly against annexations either. Aside from strategic motives, industrial considerations appear in the choice of areas suggested for outright annexation. These included the French ore regions as well as the country around Liège, the Campine, one of the richest European coal deposits, as yet hardly tapped. These, then, were some of the "real guarantees and securities" which the Chancellor had hinted at in most of his public utterances during the first years of the war.

On November 5 Hindenburg gave his own comments on Bethmann's peace proposals. His views, as was to be expected, went still further.[14] In addition to the annexation of Liège and vicinity, he demanded Belgium's economic attachment to Germany, German ownership of railways, and her right to military occupation. He also suggested specifically the exploitation of the mineral resources of the Campine, which Hugo Stinnes had told him about in numerous conversations.[15] Hindenburg agreed that Germany should keep the Briey-Longwy region and suggested further improvements of the Franco-German frontier. Germany should also receive an

in June 1916, which accepted a series of resolutions in favor of close economic co-operation between the Allies as well as post-war boycott of the Central Powers: C. Rothe, *Weltkrieg gegen Deutsche Wirtschaft* (Hamburg, 1932), pp. 21 ff.; W. Prion, *Die Pariser Wirtschaftskonferenz* (Berlin, 1917), pp. 82-85; *Schulthess*, vol. 57 (2), pp. 217 ff.

[13] *U. A.*, 15. Ausschuss, II, 84-85.

[14] *Ibid.*, p. 86.

[15] Raphäel, *Stinnes*, p. 97. On the significance of the Campine see P. Krusch, *Die nutzbaren Lagerstätten Belgiens, ihre geologische Position und wirtschaftliche Bedeutung* (Essen, 1916).

indemnity in return for her evacuation of France. England might pay a similar indemnity for the evacuation of Belgium. Additional suggestions dealt with the incorporation of Luxemburg into the German Confederation and the acquisition of the Congo State.

Bethmann's reply to Hindenburg's program agreed on the whole with the latter's recommended changes of his original plan.[16] The one objection Bethmann raised was against Hindenburg's demand for an indemnity to make up for Germany's evacuation of Belgium. England, he held, would certainly oppose such a demand, which would result in an immediate failure of negotiations; furthermore, the withdrawal of Germany was intended as a *quid pro quo* for the return of her colonies and perhaps the acquisition of the Congo State; and finally, such an indemnity seemed unjustified to Bethmann in view of the fact that Belgium had been paying 40 million francs per month since her invasion in 1914. Hindenburg, on November 7, replied that the war indemnity for the evacuation of Belgium might well consist in economic concessions, and that at any rate the monthly payment of tribute should be raised considerably above 40 million francs. The same day Bethmann reported a kind of combined program (made up of his own and Hindenburg's terms) to the Emperor and the Supreme Command as basis for a reply to Count Burian. Both the Kaiser and Hindenburg agreed to this program, so the following terms were communicated to Burian a week later: Belgium will be reconstituted as a sovereign state with specific guarantees for Germany. If these guarantees can not be agreed upon, Liège with adjacent territory will be annexed; return of French occupied areas (in exchange for an indemnity), except for strategic and economic frontier improvements; Luxemburg's adherence to the German Empire as a federal state; return of Germany's former colonies and a general re-distribution of colonial holdings in which Germany is to receive the Congo State; reimbursement to German individuals and firms for losses suffered abroad during the war; renunciation of all agreements limiting the re-opening of normal trade and traffic between all countries, and establishment of the freedom of the seas. Burian's terms, presented to Bethmann on the same occasion, agreed on the whole with the German government's program.

The aims, on the basis of which Germany was willing to enter into peace negotiations, had thus been decided upon and all the

---

[16] For this and the following see *U. A.*, 15. Ausschuss, II, 87.

government needed was an opportunity for presenting its Peace Note. The program, of course, was still full of ambiguities. The "guarantees" which Germany hoped to gain from Belgium, as we have seen in our discussion of war aims thus far, might easily develop into "veiled annexation." Hindenburg, in a conversation with Count Westarp in November 1916 again mentioned Germany's right of military occupation, German ownership of railways plus the port of Antwerp, and the dissolution of the Belgian army.[17] The Emperor himself told Prince Bülow in the autumn of 1916: "Albert shall keep his Belgium, since he too is King by Divine Right. . . . Though, of course, he'll have to toe the line there. I imagine our future relationship as rather that of the Egyptian Khedive to the King of England."[18] Bethmann's comment about the negotiations of November 1916 was: "In settling these war aims, a maximum of political aims was combined with a minimum of military aims. It was of course a matter of compromise."[19]

Such compromise was still possible at this time. Relations between the Chancellor and the Emperor were, as always, very good. And even between Bethmann and Hindenburg things at first went without much friction;[20] though already Hindenburg complained to Westarp about the indecision and weakness of Germany's policy. He objected particularly to von Jagow, who was "an intelligent man, but not one who can bang his fist on the table" (which, in the eyes of German nationalists, was a necessary prerequisite for any diplomat). Jagow finally resigned on November 22 and was replaced by his associate Zimmermann. Even a successor to Bethmann Hollweg was seriously considered late in 1916 by Hindenburg.[21]

Meanwhile the public in general, as well as the political parties and annexationists, were unaware of the negotiations for a governmental peace program. There were two interesting Reichstag debates prior to December 12. The first, on October 11, again showed the split over the question of annexations between bourgeois parties and Social Democrats. The former took decided exception to Scheidemann's statement: "Whatever is French shall remain

[17] Westarp, II, 62-63.
[18] B. Prince von Bülow, *Memoirs* (3 vols., London, 1932), III, 281-82.
[19] *U. A.*, 15. Ausschuss, I, 231.
[20] Haussmann, p. 76.
[21] Westarp, II, 335; Haussmann, p. 77.

French; whatever is Belgian shall remain Belgian; and whatever is German shall remain German." [22] The main issue of the debate, however, was in connection with Bethmann Hollweg's hints, on September 28, at post-war domestic reforms. Here we find Bassermann supporting the Chancellor's views, while Count Westarp vehemently opposed any plans for reform, a clear indication of the conflict between the National Liberals' domestic and foreign policy.[23] The second debate took place after Bethmann Hollweg's speech before the Reichstag's Main Committee on November 9, 1916, in which he claimed never to have designated the annexation of Belgium as Germany's war aim.[24] Only the Social Democrats opposed dishonorable conditions of peace for Belgium. The parties of the *Kriegszielmehrheit* once again took an almost unanimous stand. Gröber for the Center Party, Bassermann for the National Liberals, and von Gamp and Westarp for the two Conservative parties made the usual statements to the effect that Belgium should remain politically, militarily, and economically in German hands. The Progressive von Payer demanded guarantees that German influence would be maintained.[25]

The *Kriegszielbewegung* likewise continued its agitation, with Schäfer's Independent Committee leading the way. On September 14 Bethmann Hollweg received a delegation consisting of Schäfer and a number of other annexationists. The discussion dealt chiefly with the submarine problem, but it also touched on war aims. Ten days later Schäfer addressed an annexationist petition to the Reichstag entitled " The Demand of the Hour." [26] On October 15 a large meeting of the Committee took place in Berlin at which Count Reventlow gave the main speech.[27] A new addition to the *Kriegszielbewegung* was founded at this time in Munich under the absurd name of *Volksausschuss für rasche Niederkämpfung Englands*. The chief speaker at its first meeting was Pastor Traub. " We have a right before God and man," he said, " to extend our frontiers in such a manner that our enemies will find it difficult in the future to attack us again." [28]

---

[22] *Reichstag*, vol. 308, pp. 1693-94, 1707 ff.
[23] *Ibid.*, pp. 1712-15, 1723-25.
[24] Thimme, *Bethmann Hollweg*, p. 163.
[25] *Ibid.*, pp. 166-67; Westarp, II, 62.
[26] Schäfer, *Leben*, pp. 191-92.
[27] *Schulthess*, vol. 57 (1), p. 474; Haussmann, p. 69.
[28] *Schulthess*, vol. 57 (1), p. 428; *Münchner Neueste Nachrichten*, Sept. 19, 1916.

The agitation of the industrialists for annexations and unlimited submarine warfare was going on hand in hand with their exploitation of the conquered lands in Western Europe.

In October [1916] I was invited by the Foreign Office to go with a group of correspondents to Essen, Cologne, and the Rhine valley industrial centers [writes an American correspondent]. In Essen I met Baron von Bodenhausen and other directors of Krupp's. In Düsseldorf at the *Industrieklub* I dined with the steel magnates of Germany and at Homburg-on-the-Rhine I saw August Thyssen, one of the richest men in Germany and the man who owns one-tenth of Germany's coal and iron fields. The most impressive thing about this journey was what these men said about the necessity for unrestricted submarine warfare. Every man I met was opposed to the Chancellor.[29]

On October 24, the *Bund der Industriellen* held its yearly meeting at which its vice-president Stresemann gave the main address, pointing out the need of German industry for raw-materials and the importance of the conquered areas in the west as possible sources for such materials.[30]   The following day, representatives of the *Bund der Industriellen* and the *Zentralverband deutscher Industrie*, both among the famous Six Economic Organizations, united to form the *Deutscher Industrierat*. This German Industrial Council in a telegram to the Emperor expressed confidence " that the German Reich will emerge from this war strengthened, enlarged, and secured against new attacks in east and west." [31]

The German press continued to make use of whatever loopholes the censor left to discuss the post-war settlement. The Chancellor's Reichstag addresses usually supplied the necessary excuse to advance annexationist views by way of comment or criticism.[32] Constant pressure against the government's policy of restricting the freedom of the press finally brought results. On November 27, 1916, " the objective discussion of war aims " was permitted, barring unfair attacks on those holding opposing views.[33]   At the same time, the German press was officially advised: " The welfare of

[29] C. W. Ackerman, *Germany the next Republic?* (N. Y., 1917), p. 145.

[30] Bund der Industriellen, *Bericht über die 18. Generalversammlung* (n. pl., n. d.); G. Stresemann, " Industrie und Krieg," *Veröffentlichungen des Bundes der Industriellen*, no. 9a (n. pl., n. d.).

[31] Bund der Industriellen, *Bericht*, p. 42.

[32] Thimme, *Bethmann Hollweg*, p. 167; Great Britain, General Staff, *Daily Review of the Foreign Press, Enemy Press Supplement*, I, Nov. 23, 1916, 7-9.

[33] *Schulthess*, vol. 57(1), p. 559; Germany, Kriegspresseamt, *Zensurbuch für die deutsche Presse* (Berlin, 1917), see under " Kriegsziele."

the Reich requires that we demand on principle that not a foot of blood-soaked soil is relinquished before the enemy has promised us corresponding equivalents." [34] Most newspapers made use of this long hoped-for opportunity to voice their war aims; yet little was said that had not been said before and in almost identical words. Papers already known for their far-reaching aims, like the *Deutsche Tageszeitung*, merely became a little more outspoken in their demands; while others, like the *Berliner Tageblatt* continued their moderate course. [35] In general one is struck by the prevalence of western and colonial over eastern aims, especially in conservative and industrialist papers. [36] Some writers preached moderation, stressing the idea that the territories held in the west were primarily pledges to be exchanged against Germany's former colonies, now in the hands of the Allies. [37] Even Professor Schäfer, though hoping to make large gains in the west, realized that such gains would depend on a favorable military outcome of the war, and that some of his exalted hopes might easily be disappointed. [38]

Finally, the moderate National Committee of Prince Wedel also came out with a public statement on war aims which included a strong, defensible colonial empire, the freedom of the seas, and a war indemnity " corresponding to our sacrifices." But " above all, strategically necessary rectifications of the frontier. . . . The catchword ' policy of conquest ' must not discourage us." [39]

It was into this annexationist agitation that the Peace Note of December 12 came like an explosion. Not the slightest effort had been made to prepare public opinion. The fact that such a radical move could be made at this time shows that the German government, if it chose to act strongly, was not hampered by constitutional limitations or public opinion. Even so, the phrasing of the Peace Note was not entirely free from outside pressure. As we shall see presently, no specific aims were published in connection with it, largely out of fear that the public might not approve of the Bethmann-Burian program. [40] It was thus another half-measure,

---

[34] K. Mühsam, *Wie wir belogen wurden* (München, 1918), pp. 89 ff.

[35] *Deutsche Tageszeitung*, Nov. 30, 1916; *Berliner Tageblatt*, Dec. 4, 1916.

[36] *Post*, Nov. 28, 1916; *Kölnische Zeitung*, Dec. 1-2, 1916; *Vossische Zeitung*, Dec. 6, 1916.

[37] *Münchner Neueste Nachrichten*, Nov. 28, 1916; *Leipziger Tageblatt*, Nov. 28, 1916.

[38] *National Korrespondenz*, Dec. 2, 1916.

[39] *Schulthess*, vol. 57 (1), p. 537; *Kölnische Volkszeitung*, Jan. 17, 1917.

[40] Brunauer, " Peace Proposals," p. 62.

doing nothing to clear the air by laying down a definite governmental set of aims.

The Supreme Command, always somewhat skeptical about the feasibility of the Peace Note, had agreed to it on two conditions: that the military situation, especially in Rumania, be favorable at the time of its publication, so it could not be interpreted abroad as a sign of weakness; and that the *Hilfsdienstgesetz*, introducing compulsory labor service for Germans outside the armed forces, be passed by the Reichstag. The fall of Bucharest on December 6 and the acceptance of the *Hilfsdienstgesetz* four days previous fulfilled these conditions, and both military and civilian authorities agreed that the time had come to publish the German peace offer. Last minute attempts of the Supreme Command to pledge the government to conclude only " the peace which Germany needs," were thwarted by Bethmann Hollweg " because of the vagueness and the varied intrepretation " which might be given the term " useful peace." [41] On December 12, 1916, the German note was handed to Joseph C. Grew, American *chargé d'affaires*, to be transmitted to the Allied governments. After an introductory passage, which stressed the fact that the Central powers did " not seek to crush or annihilate their adversaries," the note continued:

Conscious of their military and economic strength and ready to carry on to the end, if they must, the struggle that is forced upon them, but animated at the same time by the desire to stem the flood of blood and to bring the horrors of war to an end, the four allied powers propose to enter even now into peace negotiations. They feel sure that the propositions which they would bring forward, and which would aim to assure the existence, honor, and free development of their peoples, would be such as to serve as a basis for the restoration of a lasting peace. If, notwithstanding this offer of peace and conciliation, the struggle should continue, the four allied powers are resolved to carry it to a victorious end, while solemnly disclaiming any responsibility before mankind and history.[42]

The two most outstanding characteristics of the note are its vagueness and its defiant tone. Such overbearing language did anything but convey a willingness to make concessions in return for an early peace.

The German people were introduced to the Peace Note in Bethmann's Reichstag speech of December 12.[43] Until the previous

---

[41] E. Ludendorff, *Urkunden der Obersten Heeresleitung* (Berlin, 1920), pp. 310-11.

[42] Lutz, *German Empire*, I, 398-99.

[43] *Reichstag*, vol. 308, pp. 2331-32.

evening, when the Chancellor invited representatives of the bourgeois parties to acquaint them with the events planned for the next day, nothing had been officially known about the impending offer by either parties or press.[44] Bethmann told party representatives that a program of concrete peace terms (which he refused to reveal) had been agreed upon among the Central Powers, and that, for bargaining purposes, it was only to be released at the future peace conference. He also expressed doubt that the peace proposal would be accepted by the Allies, but hoped that it would put their aggressive leaders in an embarrassing position with their own people.[45] The reaction of most parties to the government's surprise move was one of opposition (as in the case of National Liberals and Conservatives) or annoyance at not having been consulted beforehand (as with the Center Party). Only the Progressives, who became increasingly moderate in their war aims during the second half of 1916, were " overjoyed." [46] Against the votes of Conservatives, National Liberals, and Minority Socialists, the Reichstag decided to refrain from a debate after the Chancellor's speech, so as to give to the world at least the semblance of unity behind the government's policy.[47]

Since there was no chance for discussion in the Reichstag, most of the criticism was voiced in the press. The parties of the Right opposed the Peace Note because it might be interpreted as a sign of weakness, and both the extreme Right and Left wanted more specific statements on Germany's war aims. The Conservative Party demanded a peace which must " in fact guarantee the German future." [48] The *Deutsche Tageszeitung* complained because such concrete terms had not been discussed beforehand with representatives of the various parties. The industrialist *Berliner Neueste Nachrichten* stated in complete frankness that the best thing that could happen would be the rejection of the Peace Note by the Allies. The *Post, Kölnische Zeitung, Leipziger Tageblatt*, and *Berliner Lokal Anzeiger* all favored the " pitiless continuation of the war with all means at our disposal," in case of such rejection.

---

[44] Westarp, II, 74; J. Seeberg, *Wilson's Botschaft der 14 Punkte vom 8. Januar 1918 im Urteil der grossen deutschen Tagespresse vom Januar bis zum Oktober 1918* (Berlin, 1936), Diss. Berlin, p. 12.

[45] Westarp, II, 74.

[46] Haussmann, pp. 79-80; Wacker, pp. 17-18.

[47] Thimme, *Bethmann Hollweg*, p. 181.

[48] *Kreuzzeitung*, Dec. 13, 1916.

6

The moderate *Frankfurter Zeitung* and *Berliner Tageblatt*, as well as the Socialist *Vorwärts* were hopeful that the offer might have favorable results, though they too regretted its vagueness.[49] The veteran industrialist and annexationist Emil Kirdorf, who had just been elected to the Main Committee of the Pan-German League, expressed his disappointment with the events of December 12 in a letter to Heinrich Class.[50] The publication of the Peace Note had its immediate, and to industrialists most alarming, repercussions on the German stock market. " In Berlin the joyfully received Peace Offer of the Central Powers showed its first effects in directing all interest almost exclusively towards so-called peace stocks, while armament stocks were little noticed and in part heavily offered." The same applied to dynamite and mining stock.[51]

Abroad, the reception of Germany's note was anything but friendly. The French Premier Briand, on December 13, called it " an attempt to split the Allies and to demoralize their peoples." Russia's Foreign Minister Pokrovsky accused Germany of " seeking a breathing space by making deceitful offers of a permanent peace." Sonnino for Italy and Lloyd George for Great Britain made similar statements.[52] The official reply of the Allies on December 30 accused the Central Powers of making " a calculated attempt to influence the future course of the war, and to end it by imposing a German peace," and refused " to consider a proposal which is empty and insincere." [53]

In the midst of these events, on December 21, President Wilson published his own long-awaited mediation proposals, asking for the mutual exchange of views on the future peace. The German government expressed its approval five days later and suggested a meeting of delegates from the belligerent nations at a neutral place.[54] The jingo press opposed Wilson's note, charging partiality to the Allies. Moderates and Socialists, on the other hand, were definitely pleased to see another chance for the termination of war.[55] The Allies in their reply on January 10, 1917, asked for

---

[49] For a survey of press reaction see Great Britain, *Enemy Supplement*, I, Dec. 21, 1916, p. 5 and Dec. 28, 1916, pp. 5-6.

[50] Bacmeister, p. 139.

[51] *Berliner Tageblatt*, Dec. 13, 1916, 2d ed.

[52] *U. A.*, 4. Reihe, XII (1), 78; Forster, pp. 50-52.

[53] G. L. Dickinson, *Documents and Statements Relating to Peace Proposals and War Aims* (N. Y., 1919), p. 9.

[54] *U. A.*, 4. Reihe, XII (1), 78; Brunauer, " Peace Proposals," p. 75.

[55] Great Britain, *Enemy Supplement*, I, Jan. 4, 1917, 2.

the evacuation and restoration of the countries occupied by the Central Powers, and hinted at the return of Alsace-Lorraine to France and the break-up of the Austro-Hungarian and Ottoman Empires. They furthermore refused to deal with the Central Powers on a basis of equality.[56]

The discrepancy between the aims of the Allies and the terms, as yet unpublished, of the German government, makes it perfectly clear that a negotiated peace at this stage of the war was difficult, if not impossible. Neither side was in a desperate enough position to make the concessions necessary to satisfy the other side. The fact that both German and American peace attempts had failed, moreover, had the most significant results for the further conduct of the war by Germany. Since the Peace Note had been primarily the Chancellor's idea, its failure brought him a serious loss of prestige, much to the delight of his many opponents.[57] From now on the influence of the Supreme Command became an ever more decisive factor in Germany's political as well as military affairs. At the same time, the Allied refusal of the German offer kindled among many Germans, who had begun to waver under the growing hardships of a seemingly endless war, a new spirit of determination to fight to the end. The outcome of Germany's peace offensive was thus a resurgence of war spirit, and with it of annexationist feeling, in some of its strongest manifestations. This expansionist patriotism seemed to derive added justification from the far-reaching official pronouncements of the Allies. The growing conviction that the only alternative from now on was victory or complete and utter defeat became one of the most powerful arguments of annexationist propagandists. The most immediate result of the failure of the Peace Note and of Wilson's efforts was the declaration of unlimited submarine warfare by the German government on January 9, 1917.

Exploitation à Outrance

Before we discuss Germany's war aims policy any further, we must examine developments in the occupied regions of Western Europe at a time when Germany proclaimed her willingness for

---

[56] *U. A.*, 4. Reihe, XII (1), 79.

[57] C. Duisberg, *Abhandlungen, Vorträge und Reden aus den Jahren 1882-1921* (Berlin, 1923), pp. 815-17.

peace. The most illuminating events again occurred in Belgium, but a few words must first be said about France.

Germany's main interest, as we have pointed out, was in the Briey region. But this was only a small fraction of the French territory under German occupation. The rest, one of the most important industrial sections of France, was by no means neglected by the German authorities. Early in 1916, two hundred army specialists had completed a survey of over four thousand industrial firms in northeastern France and had published their findings in a voluminous report.[58] It was this report which prompted the accusations of the French government after the war, that the ultimate aim of Germany's occupation policy was the permanent crippling of French competition through destruction of her industrial equipment.[59] There is nothing in the German report to serve as direct proof of this accusation. Its purpose, according to the preface, was simply " to give a preliminary view of the repercussions which the damaging of individual branches of [French] industry will probably have upon Germany." To do this, the report examined in great detail each individual industry and showed how much competition there was between that industry and its German counterpart before the war, and how much of the machinery destroyed by war had originally been bought in Germany. The answers to these questions were of greatest importance to German industrialists (who had been supplied with copies of this highly confidential report). Coal mining in northern France, for instance, had suffered so seriously through German destruction of mines and machinery that it would take years to return to pre-war conditions. The best solution, the report hints, would be the outright annexation of France's mineral regions. If that should be impossible, Germany still would profit from the destruction of France's coal mines, since it would necessitate French importation of German coal. Finally, there was a further advantage, since not only the mines themselves but much of the machinery had been destroyed or confiscated. Here Germany would also profit after the war, since no

---

[58] Germany, Generalquartiermeister, *Die Industrie im besetzten Frankreich* (München, 1916). A less complete survey was published by a member of Germany's administration of occupied France: A. Günther, *Das besetzte Französische Gebiet* (München, 1918).

[59] Friedensburg, pp. 101 ff.; L. de Launay, *France-Allemagne* (Paris, 1917), pp. 26 ff.

other country specialized, as she did, in mining equipment.[60] It should be pointed out that the conclusions here presented were not drawn in the document, nor is there any proof that they existed in the minds of its authors. But they are inevitable and obvious on the basis of the material presented.

In regard to iron mining, the report treated in detail Germany's pre-war penetration into the Briey-Longwy basin.[61] Compared to coal-mining, destruction in this field had been negligible. France's iron industry, on the other hand, presented a different picture. Here " war damages, looked at individually, are not very great," the report said, " yet on the whole they are very considerable. They stem mostly from confiscation of raw-materials and machinery." In another place the report held that the production of each of the great iron works had been thrown back by several years. Since new factories had been built elsewhere in France heavy industry would not gain so great an advantage from this fact as might be expected. The large-scale damage done to France's iron industry, moreover, would deeply arouse French sentiment and thus affect adversely Germany's exports of machinery and raw-materials after the war.

In a similar fashion the report dealt with all branches of French industry in the occupied region. The machine and textile industries had been hit particularly hard by German dismantling of factories, so there would very likely be a post-war boom for Germany's manufacturers of textile machines, since German machines were unsurpassed in this field. Both France's dye works and her paper industry had suffered such damage that they would take years to recuperate. In one paper factory alone almost 90 tons of copper had been carted off by the invaders.[62]

These were some of the topics treated in much greater detail than is possible here. The general conclusions of the report, either openly expressed or left to be drawn by the reader, were as follows: (1) The occupied section was one of the most important of France, containing one-fifth of her factories and commercial establishments, and producing 84 per cent of her iron and 76 per cent of her steel. (2) Economically speaking, this region was almost self-sufficient, little dependent upon its French hinterland, and on the

[60] Germany, Generalquartiermeister, *Die Industrie*, pp. 19 ff.
[61] *Ibid.*, pp. 52 ff.
[62] *Ibid.*, pp. 65, 147, 158 ff., 164 ff., 167.

whole an area of surplus rather than deficiency. (3) So powerful a region presented dangerous competition to Germany. The report, as we have pointed out, made no specific suggestions how to remedy this situation other than to hint at certain "special measures" that might be taken to turn matters to Germany's advantage. The most effective "special measure" which suggests itself is of course the perpetuation of some form of German control over the whole occupied district. (4) The destructive effects of the war gave Germany at least a temporary advantage over her French competitors. French exports would cease until her industries had been rebuilt, which in some cases might take several years. So it was up to Germany to make the best possible use of this lapse by invading former French markets. (5) At the same time the rebuilding of French industry could itself be turned to Germany's advantage. Of 247,740 machines found in occupied France, 34,462, i. e., almost 14 per cent, were of German origin. Many of these machines had been destroyed or dismantled during the war, and despite the unavoidable post-war opposition to Germany, orders for their replacement would probably be given to German firms.

The army's report on France's economy did not suggest the annexation of all of occupied France, or the destruction of French industry to kill its competitive force. It was merely a presentation of data, lending itself to highly suggestive interpretations. In addition, it testified to the large-scale destruction of French industry, at first due to combat, but since the middle of 1916 increasingly due to German confiscation of machines and materials. To what extent these destructions were dictated by the necessities of a war economy severely pinched by Great Britain's blockade, and to what extent they were simply motivated by a desire to kill French industrial competition is impossible to say.

In Belgium, the two parallel developments, economic exploitation and administrative growth, went through some of their most important phases during the latter part of 1916 and early 1917. In the economic field, two events stand out most prominently: the infiltration of Germany's western industrialists into Belgium's key industries, and the deportation of Belgian workers to be employed in German factories.

On August 30, 1916, a first meeting of German industrialists took place in Brussels, General von Bissing presiding. Its purpose was the creation of a company for the exploitation of Belgium's industrial resources. Krupp's director Hugenberg gave his views on the matter as follows:

Once such a company has been founded in Belgium, with German capital and official support, the weight of events will act in such a way that the Reich can no longer escape the consequences which morally and politically result from it. I don't see the whole matter at all as a business venture, but as a political sacrifice which we have to make in this as in other instances, because the interest of the whole, of which we are a part, demands it.[63]

The outcome of deliberations was the founding, on October 12, 1916, of three companies—the *Industriegesellschaft 1916 m. b. H.*, the *Bodengesellschaft 1916 m. b. H.*, and the *Verkehrsgesellschaft 1916 m. b. H.*[64] Among the founders and directors were Hugenberg, Stinnes, Kirdorf, Beukenberg, and Reusch.[65] The purpose of these companies was the acquisition of Belgian industrial and other holdings, to increase and perpetuate Germany's influence. Their first action was the liquidation and acquisition of Belgium's gas, water, and electrical companies, owned by France and England, for a price far below their actual value, which was not to be paid until six months after the conclusion of peace.[66] If this was a "political sacrifice," to use Hugenberg's words, it was one which brought Germany's industrialists handsome profits.[67]

The events just described are merely an example of the general trend which dominated Germany's Belgian policy after the middle of 1916. The growing conviction that victory had to be won soon or never, necessitated the concentrated use of every ounce of material and strength at the disposal of the Central Powers. With the rise of Hindenburg and Ludendorff to the leadership of the army, considerations of immediate necessity rather than long-range planning began to determine Germany's administration of her own resources as well as those of the occupied territories. General von Bissing's constructive policy of not killing the milk-producing cow now gave way to a policy of merciless exploitation for the imme-

[63] Germany, Nationalversammlung, *Die Deutsche Nationalversammlung im Jahre 1919 in ihrer Arbeit für den Aufbau des neuen deutschen Volksstaates* (9 vols., Berlin, n. d.), VII, 169; Anonymous, *Wer hat den Krieg verlängert?* (n. pl., 1919), p. 4.

[64] Brinckmeyer, pp. 32-33.

[65] Germany, *Die Deutsche Nationalversammlung*, VII, 166-67.

[66] Raphaël, *Stinnes*, p. 96.

[67] Köhler, pp. 139 ff.

diate benefit of Germany's war machine.[68] That such measures would result in the elimination of most of their Belgian competitors only helped to endear this policy to Germany's industrialists.[69]

Aside from this material exploitation of Belgium, we find, again under military pressure, the compulsory use of her manpower in Germany's industry. It presents another example of the powerful and disastrous influence of Germany's industrialists.[70] On September 16, 1916, at a meeting of representatives of the army (Prussia's Minister of War von Wrisberg and the delegate of the Supreme Command, Lt. Col. Bauer) and a number of German industrialists (Röchling, Kloeckner, Duisberg, von Siemens, Rathenau, Springorum, Vögler, et al.) the serious shortage of manpower for the increased production of the so-called "Hindenburg Program" was discussed.[71] The policy of hiring Belgian workers through a special agency, the *Industriebüro*, had not been very successful. Yet the closing of factories and the refusal of Belgian workers to collaborate with the enemy, resulted in large numbers of unemployed behind the German lines, which presented a grave problem to the occupying forces. It was at the meeting in September that Carl Duisberg and Walther Rathenau suggested compulsory labor service in German factories for these Belgians, partly to solve the problem of unemployment, but mostly to increase the dwindling ranks of German labor. The driving force among industrialists behind this policy of deportations was Hugo Stinnes.[72] The chief opposition to it came from Germany's Belgian administration, notably General von Bissing.[73] Already in March 1916, he had refused a request of the War Ministry to force 400,000 Belgians to work in Germany, one of his chief objections being that such a move would create a very harmful impression abroad.[74]

[68] Kerchove, p. 8; Davignon, *Belgien*, p. 121.

[69] W. Martin, "Notes de Guerre" (typescript at the Hoover Library, Stanford, Calif.), p. 365; *U. A.*, 4. Reihe, VII(1), 276; E. Fitger, "Politische Kriegsziele für Handel und Industrie," *Handel und Industrie*, XXV (1916), 776-77; Kerchove, pp. 153-55.

[70] For detailed treatment see F. Passelecq, *Déportation et travail forcé des ouvriers et de la population civile de la Belgique occupée (1916-1918)* (Paris, 1928); A. Henry, *Etudes sur l'occupation Allemande en Belgique* (Brussels, 1920), pp. 81 ff.

[71] *U. A.*, 3. Reihe, I, 382, 387.

[72] Mendelssohn Bartholdy, p. 232; Lancken, p. 233; Raphaël, *Stinnes*, p. 98.

[73] *U. A.*, 3. Reihe, I, 323 ff.

[74] Köhler, p. 148.

On September 15, a day before the meeting of the industrialists, von Bissing repeated his refusal.[75] " I must express my serious objections to such a measure," he said. " It is difficult to realize, economically harmful, and politically dangerous." Turning against the growing interference in the affairs of Belgium, he added: " His Majesty the King and Emperor has handed to me the administration of the country by an order which makes me responsible to him alone. As long as the Emperor holds to it, I must refuse any interference in my affairs." [76] The decisive meeting came on September 29, 1916. The representative of the Supreme Command stressed the need of additional workers for Germany's munitions industry, adding " that the outcome of the whole war depends on this." Against such an appeal and a renewed request by leading western industrialists, von Bissing could not hold out, and he finally gave in on October 6, 1916.[77] The first transports of workers were sent on October 26-27, 1916, the last ones on February 10, 1917. By that time some 66,150 Belgians had been deported to Germany. Unnecessary cruelty and faulty organization resulted in considerable sickness and about 1,250 deaths among the deported. When the transports were finally stopped, it was due chiefly to the pressure of neutral opinion.[78] The fact that the German government's Peace Note appeared at a time when these deportations were in full swing, did much to weaken its effectiveness. Yet there was little the government could do, according to Bethmann Hollweg. " It is exceedingly difficult, yes impossible, for the Reich's Chancellor to put aside a measure about which the military authorities say ' if this measure is not carried out, we cannot hope to win the war.' " [79]

If von Bissing's policy of careful planning for the future gave way to a policy of immediate exploitation, this did not mean that Germany's plans about Belgium's ultimate fate had changed. " If we do not get Belgium into our sphere of power," Bissing wrote to Gustav Stresemann on June 14, 1917, " and if we do not govern it in German fashion . . . the war is lost. . . . The coast must be our frontier. . . . This will release us from the ' wet triangle.' "

[75] *Ibid.*, pp. 151-52.
[76] Bittmann, III, 144 ff.
[77] *Ibid.*, p. 149; Köhler, pp. 151-52.
[78] *U. A.*, 3. Reihe, I, 197, 210; *U. A.*, 15. Ausschuss, II, 124.
[79] *Ibid.*, I, 224.

And a month later, the Governor wrote: " We must make it clear from the outset, that Belgium belongs to us by right of conquest and defer to a later occasion the decision what form its self-government shall take." [80] Not only did von Bissing uphold his aim of bringing Belgium under German domination, but he also tried to maintain, in the face of army pressure, as much of his constructive policy as possible. On February 22 he wrote to Ludendorff:

Your Excellency must be aware that the policy of the Reich urgently demands that I create values in the administration of the country entrusted to my care, which will outlast the war. If I endeavour to administer this country in such a way as to help Germany's world-reputation, and if I strive to create conditions which will permit us to use Belgium after the war as a means of extending Germany's world-position, I have only one aim: to render the results of war productive to our Fatherland.[81]

The German army's policy of exploiting Belgium's resources and manpower was paralleled by administrative measures which deeply affected the future of the country. In October 1916, for instance, the Flemish University of Ghent was finally opened with appropriate ceremony, and subsequently two separate departments of public education were created for the Flemish and Walloon sections.[82] The most important event however, was the complete administrative separation of the two ethnic groups in early 1917. Suggestions for such a policy had been made during the first half of the war, but lack of agreement among the various Flemish factions had delayed action.[83] The first step, therefore, had to be the unification of the " activists " behind a common program. Germany's December Peace Note, suggesting the possibility of an early peace, hastened this process, and after a preliminary discussion, a Flemish National Congress, attended by some 250 " activist " representatives, and assisted by the German government, met in Brussels, on February 4, 1917. Out of this group an executive " Council of Flanders " was chosen, which now became the guiding element of the Flemish movement.[84] In a manifesto, the Council

[80] General von Bissing, *General von Bissing's Testament* (London, 1917), pp. 31-32, 36.

[81] Ludendorff, *Urkunden*, pp. 131-32.

[82] *Die flämische Hochschule in Gent*, Reden zur feierlichen Übergabe und Wiedereröffnung, gehalten am 20., 21., und 24. Oktober 1916 (Berlin, 1917); Becker, p. 323.

[83] " Rudiger," p. 48; Osswald, " Bissing," pp. 51-52.

[84] *U. A.*, 4. Reihe, XII (1), 104-05; T. Heyse, *La Genèse du Conseil de Flandre* (Brussels, 1924), pp. 5-6; " Rudiger," p. 17; Becker, p. 324.

proclaimed as its aim the administrative separation and cultural autonomy of the Flemish and Walloon parts of the Belgian state.[85] Its claim to some 125,000 followers was exaggerated, most likely the number was closer to 20,000.[86] From the first the Council worked in close agreement with the Germans, although not all of its members favored such collaboration.[87] A representative of Germany's civil administration in Belgium was attached to it and attended its weekly meetings.[88] In March, a delegation of several Council members went to Berlin and was received by the Chancellor.[89] After presenting their program for the administrative separation of Belgium, Bethmann promised the delegates Germany's support in their aspirations.

The linguistic frontier must, as soon as possible, become the frontier between two separate administrative districts, unified only under the command of the Governor General. The joint efforts of German officials and representatives of the Flemish people will succeed in reaching this aim. . . . We shall be happy to discuss with the Council of Flanders the means which will lead to the aspired aim. . . . The German Reich will do everything possible at the peace conference and beyond to further and secure the free development of the Flemish people.[90]

The annexationist press took this statement to be a promise that their hopes for Germany's future control over Belgium would be fulfilled, and pro-Flemish agitation, especially among the Independent Committee, received fresh encouragement.[91] Such agitation was considered necessary, since most Germans seemed little concerned over their Flemish brethren.[92] Two propaganda societies were now founded—the *Gesellschaft zur Pflege der deutsch-flämischen Beziehungen* and the *Deutsch-Flämische Gesellschaft*. In September 1917, they were joined, under the latter name, with the ex-ambassador and Pan-German von Reichenau as president. To understand its real character, we need only look at the list of sponsors, which included von Bissing, his successor von Falken-

[85] *Deutscher Geschichtskalender*, 1917, I, 396 ff.
[86] Raad van Vlaanderen, p. ix; " Wie tief geht die flämische Bewegung? " *Deutsche Stimmen*, XXIX (1917), 645.
[87] Raad van Vlaanderen, pp. xxix, xxxv.
[88] Clough, pp. 199-200; Köhler, pp. 42, 192 note 46.
[89] *Schulthess*, vol. 58 (1), pp. 239-40.
[90] Thimme, *Bethmann Hollweg*, p. 213.
[91] Great Britain, *Enemy Supplement*, I, March 22, 1917, 246; Schäfer, *Leben*, p. 215.
[92] Clough, p. 182; Pirenne, *La Belgique*, 209-10.

hausen, von Tirpitz, Kapp, Reventlow, Traub, von Wangenheim, Schäfer, and Westarp.[93]   In the Reichstag, finally, the Flemish question was the subject of many speeches and debates.[94]

Bethmann Hollweg himself, in a letter to Hindenburg on March 7, 1917, showed that he was perfectly aware of the advantages which a Belgium, divided into a Flemish and a Walloon section, offered to Germany:

> The German interests which we are furthering by this policy are clear. The fate of Belgium depends upon the final success of our armies. But whatever happens, a Belgium whose international organization is separate and in which a Flemish majority is free from the domination of the pro-French Walloon minority, will be more easily made useful to German interests than the Belgian state under its present form.[95]

The contemplated administrative separation, as this statement proves, found Germany's official support not simply because of her sympathy for the suppressed Flemings, but because it provided a means of maintaining Germany's influence over Belgium. If the wishes of the Flemish people had been the real concern of the government, the protest of the "passivists" on March 10, 1917, against the activities of the " Council of Flanders " should have made more of an impression than it actually did.[96]   Hindenburg's reply to the Chancellor's letter is likewise very interesting, since it throws more definite light on Germany's economic exploitation of Belgium.

> Since we have made these promises to the Flemings, I can no longer maintain the point of view that we should push the unlimited exploitation to such a point that the need for peace arises with great force among the Belgian people. But Belgium must nevertheless be weakened economically to a greater extent than the German people. Only thus can we render her economically dependent upon ourselves.[97]

Here we have a frank confession that Germany's economic policy in Belgium had as its motive not merely need for matériel and manpower, but the weakening of the country, so as to facilitate Germany's post-war domination.   In a way, therefore, both eco-

[93] Schäfer, *Leben*, p. 215; " Rudiger," pp. 363-64; *Schulthess*, vol. 58(1), p. 303; Westarp, II, 82.
[94] *Reichstag*, vol. 309, pp. 2416 ff., 2472 ff.
[95] Raad van Vlaanderen, p. xxiv; Clough, p. 185.
[96] *Ibid.*, p. 201; Becker, pp. 327 ff.
[97] Raad van Vlaanderen, p. xxiv.

nomic exploitation and administrative division were measures closely related to Germany's Belgian war aims.

On March 21, 1917, less than three weeks after Bethmann's promise to the Council of Flanders, General von Bissing signed the decree for the administrative separation of Belgium. Both he and von Sandt had opposed unsuccessfully this too rapid development. The decree called for the creation of two administrative districts, Flanders and Wallonia, separated according to language and governed from Brussels and Namur, respectively, with ultimately a system of self-government for both sections.[98] The division of Belgium was the last major act of General von Bissing. On April 18, 1917, he died, after a brief illness. He had been one of the leading figures in the history of German war aims, and the most effective resistance to the haphazard policy which had become characteristic of German-Belgian relations since the end of 1916. Bissing's long-range policy had brought him the reproach, mostly inspired by the Supreme Command, that he treated the Belgians too kindly. Whenever possible, he tried to deny these accusations. " I am sure of Your Majesty's approval," he wrote to William II two weeks before his death, " if I consider Germany's interests the sole guide of my policy in Flanders as well as Wallonia; even if I can only realize that German interest by over-riding the protestations of the two sections of the population." [99] We may sum up von Bissing's Belgian policy in his own words of April 6, 1917. Belgium, he held, because of the measures taken by Germany during the war, imposed

upon the German Empire the debt of honor to extend, after the war, a protective hand over the two parts of the country. Only on that condition can Germany's power and influence be exercised in the political, economic, and military sphere of Flanders and Wallonia; only thus can the Fatherland draw any profit from the activity which we have spent here, and the two sections of Belgium enjoy in peace and security the fruits of the benefits which they owe Your Majesty.[100]

Annexationist Reaction to the Peace Note of December 12, 1916

The most important period in the World War, not only in relation to war aims but to Germany's affairs in general, was the

---

[98] Köhler, p. 42; Clough, p. 203; Osswald, " Bissing," p. 52.
[99] " Rudiger," pp. 56 ff.
[100] " Rudiger," p. 59.

period immediately following the Peace Note of December 12, 1916. In the field of war aims, this period witnessed a series of official and unofficial declarations, issued with the more or less sincere indignation resulting from the Allied refusal of the German peace offer. At the same time, events of much greater importance occurred with the beginning of unlimited submarine warfare on February 1, and the subsequent declaration of war by the United States. Finally, parallel to these manifestations of an iron-fisted foreign policy, we find in Bethmann's speeches during this period the clearest and most far-reaching promises of domestic reform given thus far. This last development, culminating in the Kaiser's Easter Message on April 7, 1917, although belonging in the field of domestic developments, ultimately had considerable bearing upon the war aims problem.

Despite the incompatibility of German and Allied secret war aims, the German peace offer might have succeeded had Germany been a little more specific, particularly in regard to Belgium. The Allies, while officially rejecting Germany's Peace Note, still sent out feelers via neutral sources indicating their interest in "the restoration and complete independence of Belgium." [101] At the same time, the German government continued negotiations with Washington over President Wilson's mediation proposal, though these negotiations were carried on half-heartedly and without the essential declaration about the future of Belgium.[102] Bethmann Hollweg gives as reason why he did not make such a declaration "the blunt attitude of the Entente" towards the December note.[103] It was the reply of the Allies which seemed to justify the clamor of military and naval authorities as well as annexationists for stronger war aims and an all-out submarine campaign. The decision in favor of the latter, reached on January 9, 1917, ended for the time being all chances for a negotiated peace.[104] The fact, moreover, that this major step was taken so hurriedly and so shortly after the German peace offer, helped to confirm Allied belief in the insincerity of that offer. It also showed on how slim a support the Chancellor's Peace Note really had rested.

The first official opposition inside Germany to the government's

[101] Brunauer, "Peace Proposals," pp. 72-73.
[102] Forster, pp. 57-58; Bernstorff, pp. 321 ff.; U. A., 15. Ausschuss, II, 129.
[103] Ibid., I, 235.
[104] Ibid., II, 131; Brunauer, "Peace Proposals," pp. 44-45, 72.

Peace Note came a week after its publication. On December 19, the navy, for the first time, came out with a series of war aims, asking for Germany's domination over the Belgian coast.[105] Four days later, Hindenburg followed suit and asked for a strong peace and the immediate beginning of unlimited submarine warfare.[106] The next in line was Secretary Solf, who on December 26 presented his colonial program, the main feature of which was a large and compact African Empire.[107] Even the Emperor, usually quite moderate, held that "from now on there could no longer be any question of obliging France and Belgium, that King Albert, after having refused our efforts for the third time could no longer be permitted to return to Belgium, and that the Flanders coast had to become German."[108] Three days later, on January 5, William, in a proclamation, summed-up Germany's hurt pride and renewed determination to continue the war. "In righteous indignation over the enemy's insolence," he told his soldiers, "and in the desire to defend our most sacred possessions and to secure for the Fatherland a happy future, you must harden into steel. Our enemies did not want the conciliation which I offered them. With God's help our weapons shall force them to it."[109]

Added to these official statements was the widespread propaganda for a ruthless war and a strong peace, which we shall discuss below. The immediate outcome of this universal pressure was the Chancellor's consent to unrestricted submarine warfare on January 9.[110] It is impossible here to discuss in detail the submarine controversy which was in so many ways related to the war aims problem.[111] It was in connection with this controversy that the first real conflict developed between Bethmann and the Supreme Command. "We can no longer work with him," Ludendorff said in January 1917; and Hindenburg admitted that only the absence of a suitable successor kept him from asking for Bethmann's dismissal.[112] The Chancellor was only too well aware of this situation

---

[105] *U. A.*, 4. Reihe, XII(1), 92; Solf, *Die Lehren*, p. 24 and *passim*.

[106] Ludendorff, *Urkunden*, pp. 315-16; *U. A.*, 4. Reihe, XII(1), 92.

[107] *Ibid.*, p. 92; Great Britain, *Enemy Supplement*, I, Nov. 9, 1916, p. 4.

[108] *U. A.*, 15. Ausschuss, II, 113.

[109] Lutz, *German Empire*, I, 400. King Ludwig of Bavaria expressed the same sentiment: *Schulthess*, vol. 58(1), p. 17.

[110] Ludendorff, *Urkunden*, pp. 322-24.

[111] *Ibid.*, pp. 315 ff.; Helfferich, pp. 351 ff.; Westarp, II, 90.

[112] Eisenhardt-Rothe, p. 55; F. von Bernhardi, *Denkwürdigkeiten aus meinem Leben* (Berlin, 1927), pp. 461-63; Direnberger, p. 18.

and realized that his continued opposition to the unrestricted use of the submarine weapon would only postpone but not settle the issue and might very well lead to his dismissal, which he considered harmful at this time. He therefore yielded, against his better judgment, and unrestricted submarine warfare actually began on February 1, 1917.[113]

Before this irrevocable step was taken, however, another official statement on German war aims was made to President Wilson. Aware of the fact that Germany might begin her submarine campaign, Wilson had notified the Chancellor that he still saw a chance for mediation and asked for a confidential program of German war aims.[114] These aims, which the German government thus far had refused to reveal, were agreed on in negotiations between civil and military authorities on January 29. They were immediately communicated to ambassador Bernstorff in Washington, who handed them to Colonel House on January 31.[115] The German terms, including those dealing with the east, and differing little from the program agreed on between Germany and Austria on November 15 as the basis for the December Peace Note, read as follows:

Restitution of the part of Upper Alsace occupied by the French.
A frontier which would protect Germany and Poland economically and
    strategically against Russia.
Restitution of colonies in form of an agreement which would give Germany
    colonies adequate for her population and economic interest.
Restitution of those parts of France occupied by Germany under reservation
    of strategic and economic changes of the frontier and financial
    compensations.
Restoration of Belgium under special guarantee for the safety of Germany
    which would have to be decided on by negotiations with Belgium.
Economic and financial mutual compensation on the basis of the exchange
    of territories occupied and to be restituted at the conclusion of peace.
Compensation for the German business concerns and private persons who
    suffered by the war. Abandonment of all economic agreements and
    measures which would form an obstacle to normal commerce and
    intercourse after the conclusion of peace, and instead of such agree-
    ments reasonable treaties of commerce.
The freedom of the seas.[116]

---

[113] Westarp, II, 152; Bethmann Hollweg, II, 169.
[114] Forster, p. 59.
[115] *U. A.*, 4. Reihe, XII (1), 82.
[116] Seymour, II, 431-32; Ludendorff, *Urkunden*, p. 343. For an appraisal of these terms see E. C. Brunauer, *Has America Forgotten?* (Washington, 1941), pp. 13-14.

These general terms must be read, of course, in the light of the Hindenburg-Bethmann correspondence of early November 1916, which had mentioned indemnities, the annexation of the Briey-Longwy region, of the country around Liège, and of the Belgian Congo. It is most doubtful whether the Allies would ever have agreed to enter into negotiations on the basis of a program which refused to consider so essential a question as Alsace-Lorraine and did not promise the unconditional restoration of Belgium. As it was, the submarine declaration made any further negotiations impossible.

But if these German aims went too far for the Allies, they did not go far enough for many people in Germany. On January 31, 1917, the members of the Reichstag's Main Committee were informed of the government's program. According to Helfferich, all bourgeois parties opposed the moderation of Germany's official aims and expressed the wish " that the Chancellor, if it comes to peace negotiations, should not feel himself bound to this program." [117] To understand this attitude of the political parties and to realize the outside pressure to which the Chancellor was subjected, we must again briefly examine the body of extra-governmental opinion on war aims and the submarine question, immediately following the failure of the Peace Note.

The Reichstag did not resume its sessions until February 22, 1917. We are therefore deprived of this important sounding board during the crucial weeks after December 12, 1916, and depend almost entirely on occasional statements, speeches, and proclamations. We have already mentioned the opposition of Conservatives and National Liberals to the Note and its specific terms as revealed on January 31, 1917. On December 23, Bethmann tried vainly to reach an agreement with Count Westarp. The latter wanted the Flanders coast and considerably more far-reaching guarantees from Belgium than the Chancellor was willing to ask.[118] When the government failed to notify the parties of the decision in favor of submarine warfare, the Conservatives spent most of January in violent anti-Bethmann agitation.[119] As General Hoffmann remarked with insight: " The Conservatives are not shouting so loud because they are worried that something might happen

[117] Helfferich, p. 374; Westarp, II, 82.
[118] *Ibid.*, pp. 318-19.
[119] *Ibid.*, pp. 151-53.

to the Fatherland, but because they are afraid that they might lose some of their political power." [120] Germany's ruling class saw in the unrestricted use of the submarine the only means to gain a victorious peace, which in turn, they felt, was necessary to maintain the existing political and social order. The National Liberal views on the submarine question as usual were much like those of the Conservatives.[121] As to war aims, Bassermann and Stresemann asked that Germany keep Belgium and Briey-Longwy. The Flemings should be supported in their attempts at liberation from the Walloons, and the region of Flanders should remain in German hands completely.[122] The Center Party was likewise in favor of unrestricted submarine warfare, even before Germany's attempts at a negotiated peace had failed. It was the resolution voted by the Centrist Reichstag delegation on October 16, 1916, endorsing submarine warfare, which had created a parliamentary majority in favor of an unrestricted submarine campaign and thus had helped to isolate Bethmann Hollweg.[123] " We are done with notes! " the Centrist deputy Bell exclaimed at a meeting of his party in January. " Let us take the sword into our hands. Not the word but the sword must now decide! " [124] Only a small minority, including, surprisingly enough, Erzberger, opposed the government's policy. Erzberger, influenced by Germany's unfavorable military situation, grew increasingly moderate in his war aims, until he finally became the driving force behind the Reichstag's Peace Resolution on July 19, 1917.[125]

As we move towards the left, both the majority of the Progressives and the Socialists were opposed to unrestricted submarine warfare. The former, however, supported the government's policy, once it had been definitely decided upon.[126] When the Budget Committee of the Reichstag was notified on January 31, 1917, of the impending start of the submarine campaign, the Socialists David and Hoch took a decided stand against it, while the repre-

---

[120] Hoffmann, *Aufzeichnungen*, I, 152.

[121] Westarp, II, 155.

[122] Lanick, pp. 114-17; Bassermann in *Deutsche Stimmen*, Dec. 25, 1916; G. Stresemann, " Eine Atempause im Weltkriege," *ibid.*, Jan. 10, 1917; *Schulthess*, vol. 58(1), p. 99.

[123] Helfferich, p. 357; *U. A.*, 4. Reihe, VIII, 68.

[124] Wacker, p. 18.

[125] *Ibid.*, pp. 22-23.

[126] Ostfeld, pp. 14-16; Scheidemann, *Memoiren*, I, 391.

sentatives of the Center and the Progressives acquiesced. Only the National Liberals and the two Conservative Parties were definitely in favor of the government's decision.[127]

If the stand of Socialists and Progressives on the submarine issue was one of complete or partial opposition, both parties agreed that the rejection of the Peace Note and the annexationist ambitions of the Allies required a renewed stiffening of German resistance. The Social Democrats defined their stand as follows:

Through the refusal of peace negotiations offered by Germany and her allies, the governments of the enemy powers have taken upon themselves the heavy responsibility of continuing the war. They intend to carry out their openly expressed policy of annexations that will mean the ruin and lasting subjugation of the Central Powers. In view of this situation, the German Social Democratic Party once more declares its firm determination to fight on until a peace ensuring the vital interests of the German people has been reached.[128]

Germany's six leading trade and labor unions told Bethmann on January 16: "The Entente's answer removes every doubt that Germany is waging a war of defense. In the full understanding that the existence of our country and of its people is at stake, we shall mobilize the full effort of the working classes to the utmost." [129]

The press, even more clearly than the sparse declarations of the political parties, showed an almost general determination to continue the "war of defense." [130] There was a difference of tone, however, between the annexationist and moderate press. While the former seemed relieved that the spectre of a moderate peace had passed, the latter was sincerely disappointed that such a peace had not been achieved. But after the far-reaching terms of the Allies became known, even some of the moderate papers began asking for a more substantial settlement. On January 23, 1917, the clerical *Germania* opposed the return to the *status quo ante* in Belgium and demanded indemnities and colonies. The liberal *Frankfurter Zeitung*, on January 17, and again on February 7 wanted a German protectorate over Belgium and the annexation of Briey, Longwy, Verdun, and Belfort. Admiral von Truppel in

---

[127] Westarp, II, 155-56.
[128] Forster, p. 57; *Sozialdemokratie und Kriegsziele* (n. pl., n. d.), *passim*.
[129] Lutz, *German Empire*, I, 401-02.
[130] Great Britain, *Enemy Supplement*, I, Jan. 4, 1917, pp. 4-5.

the *Tag* (February 6) proclaimed the navy's favorite aim, the Flanders coast.

The most violent reaction to the refusal of Germany's peace offer came from those annexationist groups which we have collectively called the *Kriegszielbewegung*. "We can thank God upon bended knee, that our enemies didn't accept the peace offer of December 12," Heinrich Class exclaimed at a meeting in Hamburg.[131] On New Year's Day, Dietrich Schäfer put out a new edition of his annexationist pamphlet and his Independent Committee subsequently held a meeting in the Prussian House of Deputies which was so well attended that thousands had to be turned away.[132] The other annexationist organizations followed suit. The Pan-German League came out of its self-imposed retirement and demanded Belgium, parts of France, and the launching of unrestricted submarine warfare.[133] It was at this time that a Pan-German group bought the *Deutsche Zeitung* (appointing Dietrich Schäfer and Houston Stewart Chamberlain as editors) and an industrial group, notably Krupp and Stinnes, bought the *Berliner Lokalanzeiger*, both to be used for annexationist propaganda.[134] The Six Economic Organizations likewise indicated that the aims which had originally brought them together in May of 1915 were still adhered to in January 1917.[135] One of the most important of the associations, the Agrarian League, held a meeting in February, also attended by industrial representatives, at which its president, von Wangenheim, demanded that the future peace be signed with the German sword, and not with the "old romantic goose-quills of the bureaucrats and diplomatists, or the pliable gold-nibbed fountain-pen of the bankers." [136] Dr. Roetger, representing the Central Union of German Industrialists at the meeting, advised that Germany conclude a peace settlement in which she could keep the regions she had conquered, especially Belgium. In this he was supported by the Conservative Wildgrube, who had just been elected to the Reichstag on an annexationist platform.[137]

---

[131] *U. A.*, 4. Reihe, VII(1), 175.

[132] D. Schäfer, *Nochmals: Zur Lage* (n. pl., 1917); Schäfer, *Leben*, p. 209; *Kreuzzeitung*, Jan. 20, 1917; Unabhängiger Ausschuss für einen deutschen Frieden, *Durch Deutschen Sieg zum Deutschen Frieden* (Berlin, 1917), p. 52 and *passim*.

[133] *Schulthess*, vol. 58(1), pp. 66-67.

[134] *Berliner Volkszeitung*, Feb. 21, 1917; Dahlin, p. 102.

[135] *Schulthess*, vol. 58(1), pp. 72-73.

[136] *Deutsche Tageszeitung*, Feb. 22, 1917; *Schulthess*, vol. 58(1), pp. 154 ff.

[137] Great Britain, *Enemy Supplement*, I, Nov. 18, 1916, p. 14; Dec. 14, 1916, p. 10.

Another one of the leading annexationist groups, the *Auskunfts-stelle Vereinigter Verbände*, founded in 1915 under the direction of the industrialist Poensgen, also held a meeting in January, at which Gottfried Traub and various representatives of the associations affiliated with the *Auskunftsstelle* expressed their determination to hold out until a victorious peace had been won.[138] The *Aus-kunftsstelle* served as a kind of central clearing house for the different annexationist organizations. Its directors, besides Poensgen, included von Reichenau of the *V. D. A.* and Gustav Stresemann, and among its members were many familiar annexationists— Bacmeister, von Vietinghoff-Scheel, Traub, Stahlberg, Fabarius, Gildemeister, Hirsch, Schäfer, Roesicke, Kirdorf, Kapp, and Ripke. The organizations represented in the *Auskunftsstelle* included the Six Economic Organizations, the Pan-German League, the Army League, the Association of Germans Abroad, and many minor groups.[139] The membership of the *Auskunftsstelle* reveals once again how most of the propaganda for extensive war aims was carried on, for patriotic or selfish reasons, by a small minority. Certain names we find repeated whenever and wherever a strong peace was demanded. To give their private ambitions the appearance of enjoying widespread support, new propagandist organizations were constantly being founded by these annexationists. The *Auskunftsstelle,* the " Independent Committee," the " Committee for the Rapid Overthrow of England," and the " Committee for the Guiding Principles on the Road to a Lasting Peace," these groups were nothing more than the same small but influential group of annexationists each time in a different guise. To Germany's enemies, this constant stream of annexationist propaganda was a valuable means of maintaining the fighting spirit of their peoples. " The wild proclamations of the Pan-Germans," a confidential report of the official French propaganda bureau said in February 1917, " are as good as cash to us and to all other nations united to fight Germany's arrogance." [140]

---

[138] O. Poensgen, *Was haben die Engländer gegen uns?* (Berlin, 1917), p. 17.

[139] Auskunftsstelle Vereinigter Verbände, *Gedanken und Wünsche zur Gestaltung des Friedens,* 1917 edition, *passim.*

[140] France, Maison de la Presse, *Geheimbericht,* no. 7, Feb. 1917, edited by Conrad Haussmann (n. pl., n. d.), pp. 5, 8-9; *U. A.,* 4. Reihe, VII (2), 337.

Annexationism and Domestic Reform

During the month of January, as the preceding section shows, the controversy between the government and the annexationists over war aims had been temporarily overshadowed by the immediate effects of the German peace offer and the general demand for strong measures against the Allies. This demand had culminated in the unrestricted use of the submarine, which was put into effect on February 1. During the next two months, the war aims controversy not only reappeared with renewed vigor, but additional force was injected into it by the problem of domestic reform which assumed ever-growing importance.

Between the beginning of total submarine warfare and the resumption of Reichstag sessions on February 22, the Bavarian and Prussian diets served on several occasions as platforms for the discussion of war aims, both being in favor of German westward expansion. In the Bavarian Lower House, the Centrist Held demanded that " Germany must hold Belgium militarily and economically," and even several of the Liberal deputies were against a return to the *status quo ante.* Of special interest is the speech of the Pacifist Professor Quidde in which he agreed that after the rejection of Germany's peace offer her war aims had to change and become more radical.[141]

The debates in the Prussian House of Representatives on February 20-22 were not quite so unanimously in favor of strong aims. The determination of pursuing the war to a victorious end, so prominent during the weeks immediately following the Peace Note, had begun to wear thin by the middle of February. The Socialist deputy Hué struck a discordant note when he denied the claim, so universally accepted by protagonists of the *Drang nach Westen,* that the annexation of the Briey-Longwy region was of vital necessity to Germany. Instead he suggested that the close collaboration between the German coal and French iron industries, so prominent before 1914, be resumed at the end of the war. The Centrist Bell and the National Liberals, notably Beumer and Fuhrmann, took exception to Hué's speech. Fuhrmann remarked quite correctly that the concessions of German industrialists in

---

[141] *Schulthess,* vol. 58(1), pp. 94-95; Great Britain, *Enemy Supplement,* I, Feb. 15, 1917, 133.

France would most likely be lost, if Germany should return this region to French domination after the war.[142]

The Reichstag resumed its sessions on February 22, and soon the debate turned to the refusal of Germany's peace offer and the question of war aims. As far as the first was concerned, all parties, except the Socialists, agreed that Germany should no longer adhere to the terms that served as the basis for her peace note.[143] As to war aims, Bethmann Hollweg's first Reichstag speech on February 27 reopened the question with a very vague reference. " I have repeatedly said all that I could say about the direction and intention of our terms. To end the war through a lasting peace which will grant us compensation for all the injuries suffered and which will secure the existence and future of a strong Germany—that is our aim." [144] In the debate following this speech, most of the bourgeois parties took a strong stand on war aims; but Count Westarp went further than any speaker had ever gone in the German Reichstag. The program of December 12, he held, was completely out of the question now and should be replaced by the demands for the annexation of the Briey basin, the Flanders coast, the port of Antwerp, Belgium's mineral and coal deposits, a large colonial empire, and substantial indemnities.[145] Spahn for the Center Party, agreed with the necessity for indemnities and asked for Germany's economic domination over Belgium.[146] The National Liberals Schiffer and Stresemann expressed similar views.[147] The Progressive Haussmann agreed with Bethmann that the discussion of war aims at this stage was " unfruitful." Only Scheidemann opposed outright the expansionist demands of the other parties.[148] There can be little doubt that the sum of these annexationist statements was in part responsible for the decisive steps which we saw the government take during March in regard to the administrative division of Belgium.

The topic of war aims, however, was giving way increasingly to the debate over domestic reforms at this point. Little had been done in this respect since the Kaiser's speech of January 13, 1916. The question did not really become acute until 1917, when many elements—the food shortage, the controversy over the law con-

---

[142] *Schulthess*, vol. 58 (1), pp. 144, 149.
[143] *Reichstag*, vol. 309, pp. 2368, 2393.
[144] *Ibid.*, p. 2375.
[145] *Ibid.*, pp. 2403, 2407-08.

[146] *Ibid.*, pp. 2382, 2512.
[147] *Ibid.*, pp. 2416, 2472.
[148] *Ibid.*, p. 2483.

cerning entails, and the impending split within the Social Democratic Party—increased the feeling of domestic insecurity and
unrest.[149] In his speech on February 27, therefore, Bethmann felt
it wise to hold out some promise of domestic reform. After stressing the indebtedness of the nation to the loyalty and self-sacrifice
of its poorest sons, he continued: " Whenever we shall come to re-
arrange political rights, it will not be a question of rewarding our
people for what it has done—this conception has always seemed
degrading to me—but of finding the right political and governmental expression for this people." [150] Received with enthusiasm by
the Socialists and with approval by the Progressives, Centrists and
National Liberals, Bethmann's statements were heavily attacked
by the Conservatives.[151] In two more speeches, one on March 14
before the Prussian Lower House, the other on March 29 before
the Reichstag, Bethmann dealt with the necessity for internal reforms.[152] Again all parties except the Conservatives gave undivided
approval to the Chancellor's statements.[153] " A historic event,"
Conrad Haussmann wrote after the speech of March 14. " Bethmann has openly joined the Left and the struggle for power begins
in the midst of war and under the leadership of the Chancellor." [154]
After the speech on March 29, the parties presented their views on
the subject. Progressives, Centrists, and Socialists gave their approval to Bethmann's policy. " If once the danger is passed and
nothing has been done," the Socialist Noske threatened, " we shall
know how to obtain for the people what they claim; if it cannot
be obtained in a peaceful way, then we shall claim it in a sharp
and determined fight! " [155] Gustav Stresemann for the National
Liberals delivered the longest and most ardent plea in favor of
immediate reform. " It is the opinion of my political friends and
my party delegation," he said, " that the time has come to begin
the reorganization of affairs in Germany and in the Federal
States." [156] Count Westarp alone stood firmly opposed to the
reforms of the Prussian franchise, which he termed " an internal

[149] Westarp, II, 228; Bethmann Hollweg, II, 171-72.
[150] *Reichstag*, vol. 309, p. 2375.
[151] *Ibid.*, pp. 2386, 2399, 2832, 2477, 2404; *U. A.*, 4. Reihe, VIII, 161-62.
[152] *Reichstag*, vol. 309, pp. 2866-67; Thimme, *Bethmann Hollweg*, pp. 218-19.
[153] *Ibid.*, pp. 221, 236.
[154] Haussmann, p. 91.
[155] *Reichstag*, vol. 309, pp. 2832, 2842, 2846.
[156] *Ibid.*, p. 2855.

affair of Prussia," and to the extension of parliamentary rights, the two most vital reform demands.[157] The outcome of the debates on March 29 and 30 was the creation of a Constitutional Committee " for the study of constitutional questions, in particular the composition of the representative body and its relations to the government." [158] The problem of granting a larger measure of influence to the Reichstag, if not solved, had at least been taken in hand. Developments abroad, the outbreak of the Russian Revolution in March, and the declaration of war by the United States in April, only helped to increase Germany's domestic tension. To keep the initiative in the face of growing pressure for the reform of Prussia's franchise, Bethmann Hollweg entered into immediate negotiations with his colleagues in the Prussian Ministry and with the Emperor. The result of their hurried deliberations was the famous " Easter Message " of April 7, 1917, which promised the abolition of the Prussian three-class electoral system and the reform of the Upper House, both of which were to come right after the war.[159]

The effect of these internal developments was not really felt until the summer of 1917. Knowing the determined opposition of the Conservatives to internal reform, we now must be prepared for a war to the knife against the Chancellor, whose policy threatened the very existence, so the Conservatives felt, of their whole way of life. " The icy silence of the Conservatives," the *Vorwärts* wrote after Bethmann's speech on March 14, " clearly signified the death sentence for the Chancellor." [160] The battle against Bethmann was on, and one of the major battle-fields, as always, was the question of war aims. The conflict over internal reforms threatened to disrupt even the close alliance between National Liberals and Conservatives which the war aims controversy had established. Yet the Conservatives gained powerful allies in their anti-Bethmann campaign among the Supreme Command, especially General Ludendorff, to whom the Easter Message was little more than a concession to the *Zeitgeist* and the Russian Revolution.[161]

It was at this time, in late February, that an incident occurred,

[157] *Ibid.*, pp. 2857-64.
[158] Lutz, *German Empire*, I, 258-61.
[159] *U. A.*, 4. Reihe, VIII, 164-65.
[160] Thimme, *Bethmann Hollweg*, p. 221.
[161] Bethmann Hollweg, II, 191.

the so-called " Adlon Meeting," which indicated to what lengths
the enemies of Bethmann would go to bring about his fall.   The
first hint that something was under way came when a number of
prominent people received invitations to a meeting on February
25, 1917, at the Hotel " Adlon " in Berlin, allegedly to listen to an
address on the condition of German's chemical industry.   The real
purpose of the conference was to discuss the ways and means of
bringing about the fall of Bethmann Hollweg and the invitation
was accompanied by detailed plans for the creation of a large
anti-Bethmann movement.   A committee was to be formed whose
task should be " the planning of meetings in all large cities," the
" winning of newspaper support," the " provision of financial resources," and the " drafting of a resolution to the Reichstag and
other quarters," especially the Emperor and General Ludendorff.
Drafts of such resolutions were submitted with the invitations.
They all contained the request that Hindenburg be made Bethmann's successor and that a stronger policy be followed in regard
to Belgium and the submarine question.   The following draft of a
letter to General Ludendorff gives an idea of the tone and contents
of these documents:

The Field-Marshal, because of his absolute indispensability is positively
irremovable. Imperial favor or disfavor cannot touch him. He alone,
together with you, is guardian of Germany's life and honor and thus
guardian of the Hohenzollern dynasty as wearer of the Imperial Crown
and the Royal Crown of Prussia, for both crowns will roll into the dust
if we do not win the war and win soon. What the Field-Marshal really
desires will be done, and if it should come to a conflict—either Hindenburg
or Bethmann Hollweg—the removal of Bethmann Hollweg will be certain.
The future of our people and its dynasty require that such a conflict be
brought about. The *furor teutonicus*, demanded with so much justification
by the Field-Marshal, cannot be kindled by Bethmann Hollweg and his
associates, who have not a glimmer of this *furor*. I beg you to put this
letter before the Field-Marshal.[162]

Again the relationship between a victorious outcome of the war
and the continuation of the existing political and social order is
clearly emphasized.   To achieve such a victory and to maintain
the Hohenzollern dynasty, the appointment of a regent, e. g., Hindenburg, who might take the direction of affairs out of the hands
of the Emperor, was felt necessary by some people.[163]

[162] *Reichstag*, vol. 309, pp. 2489-90; *Berliner Tageblatt*, Feb. 25, 1917.
[163] In this connection see the plans for the establishment of a government by

The invitation to the "Adlon" meeting was issued by Count Paul Hoensbroech and signed by Emil Kirdorf and Admiral von Knorr. It also mentioned a number of illustrious names as patrons—the industrialist Körting, Prince von Salm-Horstmar, Count Luxburg, and the lawyer Petzold, founder of the Committee for the Rapid Overthrow of England and member of the Managing Committee of the Pan-German League. The invitation also stated that Count Westarp was expected, that the meeting might last all day, and that it was not intended to compete with the Independent Committee, but was meant as an additional effort in the same direction. "Two horses do more than one in pulling a wagon," was how the invitation put it.[164]

It was sheer accident that a copy of the document fell into the hands of Conrad Haussmann, who immediately published a report of the whole matter in the *Stuttgarter Beobachter* (Feb. 25) and caused considerable embarrassment to the "Adlon" conspirators.[165] Fuhrmann, Schäfer, and Westarp immediately denied that they had intended to take part in the conference, the latter's comment being that "at present" such meetings should be avoided.[166] As a result of the unwanted publicity, the meeting was only attended by some 29 people, with the industrialist Duisberg as the moving spirit. Despite some violent speeches—one of them suggesting that far from introducing the more liberal Reichstag franchise into Prussia, the Prussian franchise should be used in Reichstag elections—most of the resolutions proposed in the invitation failed to be adopted.[167] Beginning as a serious plot against the Chancellor and his moderate associates, the Adlon meeting ended as a rather insignificant "conspirators' matinée." But even so, it showed the deep hatred with which a small minority regarded the first minister of their country. "Traitor" and "scoundrel" were the mildest of the epithets thrown at Bethmann by Conservative members of the Prussian Upper House, hysterical with fear lest they lose their traditional power.[168] It was only a matter of months before their

Imperial Council, discussed in the Prussian Upper House, as a means of limiting the Kaiser's power: Bernhardi, p. 429.

[164] *Berliner Tageblatt*, Feb. 25, 1917; Westarp, II, 171.

[165] Haussmann, p. 87.

[166] Great Britain, *Enemy Supplement*, I, March 8, 1917, p. 200; *Kreuzzeitung*, Feb. 26, 1917; *Reichstag*, vol. 309, p. 2491.

[167] Westarp, II, 171; Haussmann, p. 90.

[168] Bernhardi, p. 461.

dream, the dismissal of the "grave-digger of the German people" would come true.

Bethmann Hollweg vs. the Supreme Command

During the late winter and early spring of 1917, the discussion of war aims had been overshadowed by the important question of internal reforms. Or we might say that the place of foreign war aims had been temporarily taken over by domestic aims. But the fact that the war, despite many German victories, had brought nothing but misery to the majority of Germans, made itself felt not only in the domestic, but also in the foreign affairs of the Reich, even if only slightly. While still deeply involved in the fight over internal issues, Bethmann Hollweg found time to accept the invitation of Austria's new foreign minister, Count Czernin, to discuss problems vital to both members of the Dual Alliance, in particular the question of an early peace.[169] The results of these conversations were embodied in a memorandum, which stated as the minimum program agreed upon by the two statesmen the withdrawal of their troops from the occupied regions and the restoration of the *status quo ante*. In case the war should end favorably, Germany planned to expand primarily towards the east and Austria-Hungary towards the southeast.[170] On the whole this memorandum of March 27 was not a very clear or confident document, yet the growing weakness of Germany's chief ally made any more optimistic program impossible. Already the Austrian government had embarked on its secret negotiations with France, Emperor Karl's brother-in-law, Prince Sixtus, serving as go-between.[171] On April 12, Count Czernin issued his famous secret memorandum which stated that Austria-Hungary had reached the limit of her endurance and that her support could not be counted upon beyond the end of the summer:

I do not think that the internal situation in Germany is widely different from what it is here. I am only afraid that the military circles in Berlin are deceiving themselves in certain matters. I am firmly convinced that

---

[169] R. Fester, *Die politischen Kämpfe um den Frieden* (*1916-1918*) *und das Deutschtum* (Berlin, 1938), p. 48; *U. A.*, 4. Reihe, XII (1), 92.

[170] *Ibid.*, p. 200

[171] Graf A. von Demblin, *Czernin und die Sixtus Affaire* (München, 1920); R. Fester, *Die Politik Kaiser Karls und der Wendepunkt des Weltkrieges* (München, 1925); Forster, pp. 91 ff.

Germany too, like ourselves, has reached the limit of her strength, and the responsible political leaders in Berlin do not seek to deny it. . . . If the monarchs of the Central Powers are not able to conclude peace within the next few months, it will be done for them by their peoples, and then will the tide of revolution sweep away all that for which our sons and brothers fought and died.[172]

Simultaneous with Austria's attempts for a separate peace, the German government made some half-hearted efforts of its own.[173] At the same time, however, the Germans drew up their most far-reaching program of war aims to date. The Kaiser, never too happy about the Easter Message, which circumstances and the Chancellor had forced upon him, now abandoned his usual moderation and tried to regain his self-confidence by demanding a strong peace. On April 17, he asked Bethmann to put up more determined opposition to the widespread demand for a non-annexationist peace. In reply the Chancellor drafted a set of eastern aims, which were much too general for the Kaiser's taste. It was no longer possible, William II held, to treat the problem of war aims in a dilatory fashion. If disagreement should arise over these aims between Chancellor and Supreme Command, he, the Emperor, would serve as arbiter. The agreement between Bethmann and the Kaiser, one of the few permanent elements in an otherwise very unstable situation, had temporarily been shaken. And the same day, April 20, Hindenburg asked Bethmann to draw up minimum terms for negotiations both with Germany's allies and ultimately with her enemies.[174]

The outcome of these various requests for a program of war aims was the conversations at General Headquarters in Kreuznach on April 23, 1917. The protocol of the meeting gives in detail the results of the negotiations.[175] In regard to Belgium, Germany was to maintain her military control until the country was politically, economically, and militarily "ripe" for an offensive and defensive alliance with Germany. During this probationary period, Germany had the right of occupation and supervision over Belgium's communications, expecially her railways, which were to be merged with the German railway system. How long this intermediary

---

[172] Lutz, *German Empire*, I, 408-12.

[173] Lancken, pp. 257-58; R. Recouly, *Les négociations secrètes Briand-Lancken* (Paris, 1933).

[174] *U. A.*, 4 Reihe, XII (1), 93.

[175] *Ibid.*, pp. 200-02.

stage was to last, was to be determined solely by German interests. However the fortress of Liège with its surrounding territories and the Flanders coast should remain permanently in German hands, or else be leased for 99 years. The southeastern tip of Belgium, around Arlon, adjoining the French basin of Longwy, was to be ceded outright or else might be ceded to Luxemburg and the latter then included in the German Empire as a federal state. From France, the usual cession of the Briey-Longwy district and frontier rectifications were demanded. Undoubtedly with some simultaneous Franco-German negotiations in mind, a few minor concessions to France were considered, but they were to be at the expense of Belgium rather than Germany.[176] The question of colonies and naval stations was left to future discussion.

This program, we should note, went considerably further than the terms agreed upon five months earlier as the basis for the December Peace Note. Especially in regard to Belgium, there was wide divergence between " the restoration of Belgium under special guarantees . . . to be decided on by negotiations with Belgium," as communicated to Colonel House on January 31, 1917, and this program of veiled annexation.[177] In the light of his negotiations a few weeks earlier with Count Czernin, it is surprising to find Bethmann Hollweg agreeing to such far-reaching demands. Yet agree he did, at least outwardly, both during the meeting and afterwards.[178] On May 15, he told the cheering Reichstag that he was " in full agreement " with the Supreme Command on the question of war aims.[179] Such agreement, however, was only apparent. On the first of May 1917, Bethmann attached a note to the minutes of the Kreuznach meeting, in which he blamed Ludendorff for urging the Emperor to insist on a specific program of war aims.

The General probably hoped to bring about my fall because of disagreements over war aims, which at present might easily be possible; or else he thought he could tie me down, so that I could not start negotiations on a cheaper basis (Peace Offer of Dec. 12). I have signed the minutes because my resignation over such fantastic matters would be ridiculous. But I shall not let myself be tied in any way by these minutes. If somewhere and somehow possibilities arise for peace, I shall pursue them.[180]

---

[176] Lancken, p. 258; Scheidemann, *Memoiren*, II, 5.
[177] Seymour, II, 431-32.
[178] Valentini, p. 152.
[179] *Reichstag*, vol. 310, p. 3397.
[180] Westarp, II, 85.

In a letter to Count Hertling several months later, Bethmann repeated that he gave in to the Kreuznach program because the Emperor, under the influence of the Supreme Command, desired it. At the beginning of the negotiations, he adds, the demands of the army, both in the east and west, went even further than the terms finally agreed upon.[181]

The question of colonial and maritime aims, postponed at Kreuznach, was settled subsequently on May 18, 1917.[182] If Germany should succeed, after the war, in building up a Central African Empire, the Admiralty suggested, she must acquire the necessary naval stations to maintain communications with her overseas possessions during a future war. The stations suggested as most useful for this purpose were: (1) In the Atlantic, all or part of the Azores plus Dakar with the surrounding territory of Senegambia, which could serve as valuable military base against the recruiting of French native troops from France's Central African possessions. (2) In the Mediterranean, the Albanian port of Valona, to be connected with Germany by railway via Austria-Hungary. (3) The question of naval stations in the Indian Ocean depended on whether or not Germany would keep her East African colony. If so, East African ports as well as the Portuguese section of the Malay island of Timor would be desirable. (4) In the Pacific, Germany should hold on to her possessions in New Guinea and the Bismarck Archipelago, and in addition acquire the island of New Caledonia for its nickel and cobalt deposits. Wireless stations were to be established on the islands of Yap and Tahiti. In China, the memorandum held, economic rather than military stations should be founded. Not included in these suggestions, but equally desired, were the Faroe Islands belonging to Denmark.[183] The German Colonial Office, according to the Admiralty, was in agreement with these demands. On June 7, Colonial Secretary Solf gave a speech in Leipzig, in which he asked for the return and extension of Germany's colonies, especially in Central Africa.[184] He differed from his colleagues in the Admiralty, however, in that he did not insist on the Belgian coast as base for a powerful fleet to maintain his colonial empire. It was this omission which caused

[181] *U. A.*, 4. Reihe, XII (1), 142-43.
[182] *Ibid.*, pp. 209-10.
[183] Brunauer, *Has America Forgotten?*, p. 14.
[184] *Schulthess*, vol. 58 (1), pp. 626 ff.

the annexationists to suspect that his whole colonial program had no other purpose than to divert the attention of the German people from territorial expansion on the European continent, especially in Belgium.[185]

It is difficult to determine who originated the term *Mittelafrika* which by 1917 had become almost as current a term as *Mitteleuropa*, and was part of nearly all programs for a future peace. The chief advantages of a large and compact empire in the heart of the dark continent were its strength and self-sufficiency in time of war, preventing another such rapid collapse of most of her colonial possessions as Germany had witnessed at the outset of the World War.[186] Few problems arose in connection with the question of *Mittelafrika*, except the fundamental one whether Germany should expand on the European continent as well as overseas, or whether her European conquests should simply serve as pledges, to be exchanged at a future conference against an enlarged Central African Empire. The more precarious Germany's military position became, the more the latter view gained ground. Emil Zimmermann, " the most industrious preacher of the *Mittelafrika* gospel," definitely preferred a Central African Empire to the coast of Flanders.[187] On the other hand, a proponent of the opposite school admonished his countrymen in 1917: " Forget about your colonies, if it means that in return you would have to make substantial sacrifices on the continent! Here are the roots of your strength, and if you grow powerful here, you will also again get the necessary colonies." [188]

There was one other field of possible German expansion, which was of particular concern to the United States, namely South America. Despite some pre-war agitation for a greater degree of German influence over that continent in general and the region of Southern Brazil in particular the topic of South America was rarely

[185] Wolff, *Vollendete Tatsachen*, p. 182; *Deutsche Tageszeitung*, June, 9, 1917; *Tägliche Rundschau*, June 10, 1917.

[186] The best-known contemporary work is Emil Zimmermann, *Das deutsche Kaiserreich Mittelafrika als Grundlage einer neuen deutschen Weltpolitik* (Berlin, 1917).

[187] E. Zimmermann, *The German Empire of Central Africa* (London, 1918), pp. 13-14.

[188] A. Rudolph, *Lieber deutscher Michel* (Leipzig, 1917), p. 50. For additional writings on colonial aims see O. Karstedt, *Koloniale Friedensziele* (Weimar, 1917); Germany, Kriegspresseamt, *Unsere Kolonien* (Berlin, 1918); P. Leutwein, *Mitteleuropa-Mittelafrika* (Dresden, 1917).

mentioned in the discussion of German war aims.[189] There were a few pamphlets and articles on the subject, but they only proposed the establishment of closer economic and cultural rather than political ties between Germany and South America.[190] On September 1, 1915, an " Economic Association for South America " had been founded in Berlin, under the presidency of Bernhard Dernburg, former Colonial Secretary.[191] The Allies made the most of whatever expressed sentiment there was in Germany for expansion in South America, so that the semi-official *Norddeutsche Allgemeine Zeitung* found it necessary on March 15, 1916, to deny that Germany had any intention of annexing or even slowly penetrating South America. The final denial came from Bethmann Hollweg himself on April 5, 1916.[192]

Not only the army and navy, but the Kaiser himself, in a letter to Bethmann, now came forth with a set of war aims of his own. In addition to demands on the continent, which closely followed the Kreuznach discussions of the previous month, he also mentioned a large *Mittelafrika* and a series of naval stations. His letter closed " with some sharp remarks and reprimands to the Chancellor, who, after three years of war, had as yet produced nothing positive about war aims, so that he [the Emperor] was obliged to draw up a program of war aims according to his own wishes and those of his armed forces." [193] The truth of the matter was that Bethmann was still pursuing the vacillating policy which, in his endeavor to preserve German unity, he had followed since the beginning of the war. Such a policy was possible as long as there was no power strong enough to challenge it. It worked in face of annexationist opposition, for though violent in its manifestations, that opposition had lacked sufficient political power to make itself felt. But with the Supreme Command rapidly becoming the dominant power in Germany, this vacillation was no longer possible.[194] Still in view of the generally unfavorable situa-

---

[189] On Germany's pre-war ambitions in South America see Great Britain, *German Opinion*, II, 75 ff.; " Germanus Liber," *Deutschland und England* (Wien, 1918), p. 18; D. Perkins, *Hands Off!* (Boston, 1940), p. 211.

[190] E. de Magalhães, " Germany and South America," *Nineteenth Century and After*, vol. 81 (1917), pp. 67-80.

[191] *Schulthess*, vol. 56 (I), p. 452.

[192] Thimme, *Bethmann Hollweg*, p. 101.

[193] *U. A.*, 4 Reihe, XII (1), 109-10.

[194] Rupprecht, II, 168.

7

tion and the growing moderation of most of Germany's political parties, Bethmann saw no reason why his statements on war aims should become either more radical or more specific. It was in a very pessimistic mood that he gave the last Reichstag address of his career on May 15, 1917. Both Social Democrats and Conservatives had presented interpellations demanding specific statements on war aims, and it was in this connection that the Chancellor defined his position:

To make such a statement at the present moment would not serve the interests of the country. I must, therefore, decline to make one. . . . It comes to this: Shall I immediately give our enemies the assurance that they can prolong the war indefinitely without danger of losses to themselves? Shall I inform these enemies that, come what may, we shall under all circumstances be the people which renounces . . . ? Shall I nail down the German Empire in all directions by a one-sided statement which comprises only one part of the total peace conditions, renounces the successes gained by the blood of our sons and brothers, and leaves everything else in a state of suspension? No! I reject such a policy. . . . We did not go to war, and we are not fighting now against almost the whole world to make conquests, but only to secure our existence and firmly establish the future of the nation. A program of conquest is as little helpful in achieving victory and ending the war as a program of renunciation. . . . In full confidence we can trust that we are approaching a satisfactory conclusion. Then the time will come when we can negotiate with our enemies about our war aims, regarding which I am in full harmony with the Supreme Command.[195]

Here we have the Chancellor's own explanation for the vagueness and vacillation of his war aims policy. And his stand found support elsewhere.

With such declarations [Helfferich points out] the Chancellor could satisfy neither the Right nor the Left. And yet I am still of the opinion that his attitude was the only correct, the only possible one. Either our enemies were ready to give up their aims of conquest and annihilation, in which case the Chancellor's repeated declarations that we were ready to be satisfied with our defensive aims, offered a sufficient basis for the opening of peace negotiations, or else our enemies—as was really the case—were not ready to resign their aims . . . in which case the proclamation of all the details of our peace program could not lead to negotiations. . . .[196]

Yet Helfferich's analysis completely overlooks the fact that Germany's aims, as defined before December 12, 1916, and again on

[195] Lutz, *German Empire*, I, 354-58.
[196] Helfferich, p. 306.

April 23, 1917, were anything but defensive. Furthermore, although the Allied governments, confident in their final victory, were unwilling to conclude a negotiated peace, Germany's sincere willingness to conclude such a peace, if supported by specific declarations, especially on the crucial subject of Belgium, would have made a deep impression on public opinion in Allied countries, and in turn forced the Allies to look more favorably upon peace negotiations. It was not the futility of stating moderate aims, but the fear of the opposition such aims would arouse among the annexationists and the Supreme Command that was responsible for the continued uncertainty of the Chancellor's statements. Only in private conversations did Bethmann give specific proof of his moderation. One such occasion came in his talk with the Papal nuncio on June 26, 1917.

There had been earlier attempts of the Holy See to serve as mediator between the Allies and the Central Powers.[197] The major move was not made till the summer of 1917, and it culminated in the Papal Peace Note of August 1, 1917. The negotiations leading up to this note go back to the end of June, when Monsignore Pacelli in a conversation intimated to Bethmann Hollweg that it might be of considerable help to the Pope's peace efforts if Germany could give some confidential information about her real aims. Bethmann agreed and stressed Germany's readiness for peace.

In reply to the question about war aims in Belgium [Bethmann tells us] I replied that we should restore her complete independence. It would be irreconcilable with this independence, however, if Belgium would fall politically, militarily, and financially under the domination of England and France, who would then use this domination to Germany's disadvantage. To the question, finally, about Germany's plans with regard to Alsace-Lorraine, and whether the German government was ready to make territorial concessions to France, I replied that, in case France was willing to reach an understanding, peace would not fail because of this problem. By way of certain mutual frontier rectifications, a way might be found.[198]

These terms, though very general, were considerably milder than the ones agreed on at Kreuznach two months earlier, and there is no reason to doubt their sincerity. According to his statements

---

[197] Brunauer, " Peace Proposals," p. 174.

[198] Bethmann Hollweg, II, 212-13; see also: T. von Bethmann Hollweg, " Friedensmoeglichkeiten im Fruehsommer 1917," *Deutsche Allgemeine Zeitung*, Feb. 29, 1920; H. J. T. Johnson, *Vatican Diplomacy in the World War* (Oxford University Press, 1933), pp. 24 ff.

after the war, Bethmann Hollweg was prepared not only to restore
Belgium, but to pay several billions by way of reparation to that
country.[199] The Papal nuncio was highly satisfied with the results of the conversation.[200] It was held, however, without the
knowledge of the Supreme Command, and it is doubtful whether
Bethmann could have maintained his moderate stand against the
certain opposition from this quarter as well as from the annexationists. His resignation, little more than two weeks later, was to
prove fatal to the further developments of the papal move.

The Fall of Bethmann Hollweg

Before we discuss the events of July which led to the fall of
Bethmann and to the subsequent failure of the Papal Peace Note,
we must briefly look at the changing attitude of Germany's political parties towards the war aims question. The renewed determination, after the Allied refusal of the December peace move, to
hold out until the very end, slowly began to give way to a growing
desire for peace. The slogan for such a peace—" no annexations
and no indemnities "—was supplied by the Russian Revolution.
It held particular fascination for the poorly clad and underfed
masses behind the Social Democrats. The growing radicalization
of German political life had just resulted in the final split between
the Majority and the Independent Socialists, which we have mentioned earlier. To hold their ground, the Majority Socialists were
forced to become ever more radical themselves so that, except on
war credits, there was actually little disagreement between the two
Socialist parties. The most notable expression of this growing
popular unrest was the first major strikes during April of 1917.
In Berlin alone, more than 200,000 metal and munitions workers
quit work to protest against the lack of food and fuel.[201] Halle
and Braunschweig followed the Berlin example. In Leipzig
strikers went beyond the usual economic grievances to demand
universal suffrage and an immediate peace without annexations.[202]
Simultaneous reports of the *Büro fuer Sozialpolitik* and a poll by
the *Münchener Post* gave further proof of the desire among workers
and soldiers for a speedy non-annexationist peace.[203]

---

[199] *U. A.*, 15. Ausschuss, I, 235.   [201] Scheidemann *Zusammenbruch*, pp. 60 ff.
[200] Helfferich, p. 476.   [202] *Ibid.*, p. 65; Rosenberg, p. 194.
[203] R. H. Lutz, *The Causes of the German Collapse in 1918* (Stanford, 1934),
p. 96; Naumann, *Dokumente*, p. 456.

The Majority Socialists themselves came out with a manifesto which stressed the relationship between internal reform and war aims: " We demand the immediate abolition of all inequalities of civil rights in *Reich*, state, and community as well as the abolition of any kind of bureaucratic regime and its replacement by the decisive influence of parliament." The Manifesto welcomed the Russian Revolution and its determination " to prepare a general peace without annexations and indemnities on the basis of the free international development of all peoples. . . . It is our duty to fight the dreams of power of an ambitious chauvinism, to urge the government to renounce clearly all policy of conquest, and, as soon as possible, to bring about peace negotiations on this basis." [204] The Kaiser, prompted by Hindenburg, expressed alarm at the publication of the Manifesto and asked Bethmann " to suggest some kind of countermeasures "; but since most of the harm had already been done, no such measures were taken. Count Westarp asserts that the Socialist resolution played a major role in bringing about the Kreuznach meeting of April 23 and its extensive set of war aims.[205]

If the Socialist manifesto alarmed the Kaiser, it came as a definite shock to the parties of the Right. " The resolution of the Social Democratic Party," a Conservative counter-manifesto said, " would, if realized lead our country to the abyss. . . . It contains the great danger that, through continuous weakening of our monarchical institutions and complete democratization of our political organism, the domestic future of the German Reich may be severely harmed." The National Liberals defined their attitude in a resolution which referred to their original declaration of May 16, 1915, in favor of strong war aims. At the same time they expressed hope for a " new orientation of Germany's internal political life through greater parliamentary influence." [206] This put the National Liberals between the two extremes, the Socialists, who demanded a peace without annexations and far-reaching internal reforms, and the Conservatives, who were for a strong peace abroad and the maintenance of the existing order at home.

The views on war aims of all parties were brought out in the

[204] *U. A.*, 4. Reihe, XII (1), 128-29. A still more specific Socialist program for a post-war settlement was drawn up for the International Socialist Conference at Stockholm in June, 1917: Scheidemann, *Memoiren*, II, 5-21.

[205] Westarp, II, 85.

[206] *U. A.*, 4. Reihe, XII (1), 130.

Reichstag debates of May 15, which dealt with Conservative and Socialist interpellations introduced on May 3.[207]   The Conservative interpellation was presented by Dr. Roesicke, who wanted " an increase of Germany's power and territory and the collection of an indemnity, not only for the injury and hardships which the war brought upon us, but also for the expenditures which the war directly imposes upon us." [208]   Scheidemann, in turn, reiterated his party's demand for a peace without annexations and indemnities. He spoke sharply against the Pan-Germans and other annexationists and threatened with revolution if the German government should try to continue the war merely for the sake of conquests. Minor territorial changes along the frontier, Scheidemann said, would be all right, if settled by mutual agreement.[209]   The Chancellor's reply to these speeches, which we have already discussed, failed to grant the requests of either Conservatives or Social Democrats. His noncommittal attitude found the approval, however, of the majority of bourgeois parties, the Center, Progressives, and National Liberals. In their name Peter Spahn declared: " We are satisfied if the government pursues neither boundless plans of conquest nor bind itself to a peace without annexations or indemnities." [210]   The *Kriegszielmehrheit* which had taken a uniform stand on war aims through almost three years of war had here been replaced by a different group, held together primarily by a common stand on internal reform. Its seemingly united stand on war aims, however, was to be of short duration only. The Peace Resolution of July 19, as we shall see, made the National Liberals abandon this newly-formed majority, which instead acquired the Social Democrats as permanent allies. But prior to July, the bourgeois parties in their majority still favored a moderately strong peace rather than Scheidemann's peace of understanding.[211]   Their declaration of May 15 had merely turned against the extremes of Socialists and Conservatives, but had not renounced annexations on principle.

Though the parliamentary *Kriegszielmehrheit* was dead, the *Kriegszielbewegung* was still very much alive. The Social Democratic Manifesto of April 19 had hardly been out before the annexa-

---

[207] Westarp, II, 86-87; *Reichstag*, vol. 321, Anlagen nos. 774-75.
[208] *Ibid.*, vol. 310, p. 3389.
[209] *Ibid.*, pp. 3390-95.
[210] *Ibid.*, p. 3398.
[211] Wacker, pp. 24-28; Ostfeld, pp. 20-21.

tionists swung into action. The Independent Committe was ready with a counter-resolution of its own.[212] On May 1, the Pan-German League urged its local branches to hold meetings of protest against the Socialist resolution.[213] The Agrarian League published a " Manifesto for a German Peace." [214] The Colonial Society came out once more for Solf's program, especially in *Mittelafrika*.[215] On May 3, over sixty leagues and associations, under Pan-German leadership, published a joint statement against a Scheidemann peace. " Only a peace with indemnity," it said, " with an increase of power and the acquisition of land can make permanently secure for our nation its national existence, its position in the world, and its economic freedom of development." [216] Public meetings and constant pressure upon governmental leaders by letter and telegram completed the anti-socialist campaign.[217]

As in the case of the political parties, the question of internal reform was of great concern to the annexationists. Dietrich Schäfer, in an article published in the annexationist *Panther*, held it was wrong to fight over domestic issues while the existence of the country was at stake.[218] Heinrich Class expressed his opposition to the growth of German democracy.[219] Diederich Hahn of the Agrarian League, summed up the annexationists' opposition to domestic reform: " When they continually speak of *Neuorientierung*, we must say straight out: Have we had a rotten system hitherto? Have we just emerged from a decline? Has our monarchical Germany failed? No. It stands gloriously before all the world as victor—if only it will. There must be no *Neuorientierung* for the German system." [220] In early July ten professors, led by Delbrück, Meinecke and von Harnack, came out in favor of immediate reform of the Prussian franchise.[221] Four days later, ten

---

[212] Schäfer, *Leben*, p. 218; *Schulthess*, vol. 58 (1), pp. 438-39.

[213] *Ibid.*, pp. 465-66.

[214] K. Heller, *Der Bund der Landwirte bezw. Landbund und seine Politik* (Kulmbach, 1936), Diss. Würzburg, p. 45; *Bund der Landwirte*, no. 19, May 12, 1917.

[215] *Schulthess*, vol. 58 (1), p. 663.

[216] *Ibid.*, pp. 480-81; Schäfer, *Leben*, p. 210.

[217] Unabhängiger Ausschuss, *Deutschlands Zukunft und der deutsche Friede* (Berlin, 1917); *Norddeutsche Allgemeine Zeitung*, May 29, 1917.

[218] Schäfer, *Leben*, p. 218.

[219] *Deutsche Zeitung*, June 16, 1917.

[220] *Deutsche Tageszeitung*, April 25, 1917.

[221] Schäfer, *Leben*, p. 217; Max von Baden, p. 108.

others, including von Gierke, Eduard Meyer, Theodor Schiemann and Reinhold Seeberg considered such an immediate change a great misfortune and hoped that victory would be gained first.[222] What the annexationists hoped was, that victory would bring large gains and thus help people forget their demands for internal reforms; and this hope was fully shared by at least one governmental agency—the Supreme Command.

Ever since the accession of Hindenburg and Ludendorff, the annexationists had tried to establish some kind of open contact with the Supreme Command. A favorite method was to get the army to support some annexationist program. " One makes resolutions in the well-known sense of the annexationists," the *Münchner Neueste Nachrichten* describes the usual procedure, " and then a harmless telegram is sent to Hindenburg in which there is naturally not a syllable about the details. Then, if the Field-Marshal amiably replies to the amiable greeting, Hindenburg's ' endorsement ' has been given to the principles of the resolutions about which he knows nothing." [223] Such telegrams were sent in great numbers from most large cities, usually after meetings of the Independent Committee. When Ludendorff's attention was called to this fact, he refused to do anything about it and instead insisted that Hindenburg continue to send answers to the wires he re-received.[224] The truth of the matter was that the Supreme Command was entirely in sympathy with the annexationists. The only way of bolstering army morale, in its opinion, was to hold out the promise of a worthwhile peace, a " Hindenburg peace." In June 1917, a memorandum was drawn up under the direction of Major Nicolai, chief of the army's propaganda and intelligence section, which dealt with the question of peace as it should be presented to the German soldier.

A German victory is necessary and possible and presents the only way to gain a peace which corresponds to the sacrifices made. . . . Our propaganda has the purpose of proving that a peace of renunciation or of understanding will not fulfill the needs of the German people but that only a victory and its consequences at the peace conference will bring about happy conditions for the German people and for each individual class.[225]

---

[222] *Schulthess*, vol. 58 (1), p. 679.
[223] *Münchner Neueste Nachrichten*, May 25, 1917.
[224] *U. A.*, 4. Reihe, VII (1), 384.
[225] H. Thimme, *Weltkrieg ohne Waffen* (Stuttgart, 1932), pp. 250-51; Lehmann, pp. 139-41; *Vorwärts*, June 5, 1917.

We now come to the fateful two weeks in July 1917, so crammed full with important events, most outstanding among them the "resignation" of Bethmann Hollweg. There had been considerable discontent during the first half of 1917, when the government failed to carry out the Kaiser's Easter promise of domestic reforms. As the year went on, the ineffectiveness of Germany's U-boat campaign caused additional uneasiness. People had put complete confidence behind this last trump card, and had expected that England would collapse within a few months. But despite large numbers of monthly sinkings, England's resistance continued undiminished and the end of the war seemed as far away in July as it did in January. It was Mathias Erzberger who, on July 4, first gave word to this growing discontent. After the U-boat war had failed to live up to expectations, he held, other ways had now to be found to end the war. Yet the aims of Social Democracy— "no annexations, no indemnities"—were entirely too negative. Instead Erzberger suggested returning to the initial program of a defensive war.[226] In a second speech, two days later, Erzberger made a still more decisive thrust. Citing specific figures on the U-boat campaign, he pointed out that England could never be seriously enough affected by German sinkings to be knocked out of the war. It was time, therefore, according to Erzberger, that a majority of the Reichstag declare itself in favor of a peace of understanding, based on the "war of defense" formula of August 1914. The 25,000 Pan-Germans, he held, should simply be ignored. It was cheaper to build asylums for them than to continue the war for another year. The German people should never have to reproach its representatives, Erzberger concluded, with the terrible words "too late!"[227]

The effect of Erzberger's speech, both in the Reichstag's Main Committee, where it was delivered, and outside, was "crushing." It seemed to bear out all the worst fears current in Germany. Immediately the "reformist" parties—National Liberals, Center, Progressives and Social Democrats—got together to discuss such joint measures as might appear feasible after Erzberger's speech. All four parties agreed on the necessity of internal reforms, but on the question of the Reichstag peace resolution which Erzberger had proposed, the National Liberals differed from the rest and

---

[226] *U. A.*, 4. Reihe, VIII, 72.
[227] *Ibid.*, pp. 108-11; Scheidemann, *Memoiren*, II, 29-30.

refused to co-operate.[228] The Conservatives, of course, were equally opposed to any such resolution, and to the introduction of internal reforms. " We would rather win ourselves to death (*totsiegen*) than to succumb cowardly," Count Westarp summed up his party's attitude.[229] At the same meeting of the Reichstag's Main Committee Bethmann Hollweg, for the last time, defined his views. He said nothing really new, but pointed out that he had always insisted that Germany was waging a defensive war. To make another declaration in favor of peace now, after the failure of the December Note, would be harmful; far from increasing the desire for peace among Germany's adversaries, it would most likely have the opposite effect. He was opposed, therefore, to such a move.[230]

Events now happened in rapid succession. The Center Party decided the same day that the continuation of Bethmann in office was undesirable because he had led the Reich at the outbreak of war and thus would find it difficult to negotiate an early peace. It was suggested that he resign whenever he felt it his duty to do so.[231] Two days later, Stresemann added his party's attacks to those of Erzberger and demanded the Chancellor's withdrawal. Stresemann confessed that he was still an annexationist, but that he also desired the introduction of much-needed governmental reforms. His speech was not very clear, except in its unequivocal request for Bethmann's resignation.[232] Here, then, we find two of Germany's major parties demanding a change of personnel in the Reich's chief executive office. This in itself was something entirely new and one of the first indications that a greater degree of parliamentary influence was close at hand. The motives of the two parties for demanding such a change differed. In the case of the Center Party it was allegedly the desire for an early peace which prompted its anti-Bethmann stand; while in the case of the National Liberals it was the Chancellor's weak and vacillating domestic and foreign policy which was responsible. In both cases the fact that Erzberger as well as Stresemann favored the candidacy of Prince Bülow—who had made certain promises of greater par-

---

[228] Haussmann, p. 99; Scheidemann, *Memoiren*, II, 34; Scheidemann, *Zusammenbruch*, p. 86.

[229] Westarp, II, 340.

[230] *U. A.*, 4. Reihe, VIII, 120-25.

[231] *Ibid.*, p. 78.

[232] *Ibid.*, pp. 125-31; Scheidemann, *Memoiren*, II, 36.

liamentary influence—played a considerable role.[233]   The Center, more than any other party, stood to gain from any increase of parliamentary power.   Its position as the largest intermediary party would give it the decisive voice in most future political issues and thus put it in an excellent bargaining position.   Only thus can we understand Erzberger's attitude during the July crisis. His initial concern over the submarine question, increased by his knowledge of the Czernin memorandum of April 12, had been perfectly sincere.[234]   Yet if the conclusion of peace was his only aim, why try to overthrow a Chancellor known for his moderation? And why overthrow him in collaboration with the National Liberals and, as we shall see presently, the Supreme Command, both known for their annexationist aims?[235]   It is difficult to fathom Erzberger's motives, especially if we consider that both before and after the July Peace Resolution he still favored the annexation of the Briey-Longwy iron region, a fact which made any negotiated peace impossible from the outset.[236]

As a result of these repeated attacks, Bethmann, on July 10, offered his resignation, but William II refused to accept it.[237]   At the same time one of the requests of the new Reichstag majority was now granted.   The decision to apply, as soon as possible, the liberal Reichstag franchise to the elections of the Prussian Lower House was reached in negotiations between Bethmann, the Prussian Ministers of State, the Kaiser and the Crown Prince.   An Imperial decree to that effect was published on July 12.[238]   This measure went far towards pacifying the Socialists and it strengthened the Progressives in their always loyal support of the Chancellor.[239]   It seemed as though the crisis had once more been negotiated.

At this point another force entered the conflict.   The Supreme Command, worried over the demand for a Peace Resolution, had finally decided that Bethmann's government was unable to cope with the situation.   Already on July 7, Hindenburg and Ludendorff had made a hurried trip to Berlin to counteract the results of

---

[233] *Ibid.*, p. 77; Wacker, p. 43.
[234] *Ibid.*, pp. 29-30; Erzberger, pp. 251 ff.
[235] Helfferich, p. 444.
[236] Germany, *Deutsche Nationalversammlung*, VII, 319, 324.
[237] Westarp, II, 353.
[238] *Ibid.*, pp. 350 ff., 517.
[239] Helfferich, p. 449; Haussmann, pp. 117, 121-22; Ostfeld, p. 35.

Erzberger's speech the previous day. Bethmann, however, had prevailed on that occasion and the two military leaders were told by the Kaiser to return to Headquarters.[240] A second attempt to intervene, this time successful, was made on July 12. It consisted of two parallel moves, both with the identical goal of forcing the Emperor to drop his Chancellor. The first was a meeting between the Crown Prince and party delegates to discuss the Reichstag's attitude towards Bethmann. This entirely unprecedented meeting was arranged by the prince's former political adviser, the Conservative Baron von Maltzahn, and by a representative of the Supreme Command, Colonel Bauer.[241] All parties present, except the Progressives and Social Democrats, were in favor of a change in the Chancellorship; and even the Socialists' support of Bethmann was somewhat lukewarm.[242] The minutes of the meeting, unknown to the participants, were kept in detail, to prove to the Emperor that Bethmann no longer enjoyed the support of the parties. Subsequently, the National Liberals and Center addressed letters to William II demanding the Chancellor's dismissal.[243] The second and more decisive move came directly from Supreme Headquarters. The Kaiser had called in Bethmann to discuss the situation, when a telephone call from Kreuznach announced that Hindenburg and Ludendorff had just handed in their resignation, since they refused to work any longer with Bethmann Hollweg. The Emperor ordered the two commanders to report to Berlin immediately; but he also complained to Bethmann about the impossible situation in which Hindenburg's and Ludendorff's action had placed him. The Chancellor declared that the loss of these two important figures was, of course, out of the question, and the next day, July 13, he sent in his own resignation. As the main reason for his decision he gave the opposition of the Reichstag, to conceal the fact that he had given way to military pressure. His request was granted the same day.[244]

---

[240] Scheidemann, *Memoiren*, II, 38.

[241] Haussmann, p. 150; M. Bauer, *Der grosse Krieg in Feld und Heimat* (Tübingen, 1921), pp. 141-42, 204.

[242] *U. A.*, 4. Reihe, VIII, 79-80; Westarp, II, 357 ff.; Helfferich, pp. 449-51.

[243] Haussmann, pp. 121-24.

[244] Bethmann Hollweg, II, 229, 235; E. Ludendorff, *Meine Kriegserinnerungen 1914-1918* (Berlin, 1920), pp. 361-62. Excerpts from Bethmann's diary, not included in his memoirs, which came to the author's attention after this study was already in print, stress the significance of the problem of Prussian electoral reform in the events leading to the Chancellor's dismissal. Braun, pp. 31-35.

We have presented a mere outline of the " Chancellor Crisis " of July 1917. Considered separately, the attitudes of individuals and parties were often contradictory. The three major issues— internal reform, Peace Resolution, and Bethmann's continuation in office—were closely interwoven at all times. Some people, notably the Conservatives and the army, were opposed to all three. Others, the National Liberals for instance, only opposed the Chancellor and the Peace Resolution; while the Center was merely opposed to Bethmann. The decisive point was that everyone—except the Progressives and, to a lesser extent, the Socialists—was against Bethmann and in favor of a change. In the light of this opposition Bethmann's fall need not cause any surprise. The question of war aims which was behind so much of this opposition, again played the dominant role in the July crisis.[245] The fact, however, that Bethmann's fall came at a time when a parliamentary majority in favor of reforms and a moderate peace dominated the scene, was most deplorable. Because if there was any man willing to realize the aims of this majority, it was Bethmann. " The tragic fact is," the Centrist Fehrenbach said after Bethmann's resignation, " that this man, who tried to gain peace with every means at his disposal, had to fall when the German Reichstag decided in favor of a Peace Resolution." [246] And yet it had been the attitude of the Center Party which had initiated Bethmann's dismissal. If it had drawn the logical conclusion from its desire for a Peace Resolution, it should have turned against the most determined opponents of such a resolution, the Supreme Command, and supported Bethmann Hollweg. In that case the forces that were for the Chancellor would have matched those opposed to him. This unrealistic attitude of the Center Party was almost entirely the work of Erzberger, who used all his political skill to win the reluctant majority of his party over to his side.[247]

July 13, 1917, was an important date, a turning point in the history of the World War, at least for Germany. With Bethmann Hollweg went the one political figure who, if no match for the strong personalities of Hindenburg and Ludendorff, at least was powerful enough to delay the complete ascendancy of the military authorities over the political affairs of the nation. The two mili-

[245] *U. A.*, 4. Reihe, XII (1), 134-36.
[246] *Reichstag*, vol. 310, p. 3575.
[247] Wacker, pp. 41-43; *U. A.*, 4. Reihe, VIII, 83.

tary leaders, who now became the virtual rulers of Germany, possessed many of the qualities which Bethmann lacked. Compared to the retiring, schoolmasterly " philosopher of Hohenfinow " they were popular heroes. And while their successful career and military value gave them an almost unassailable position, their lack of constitutional responsibility and political experience enabled them to favor a more definite and determined course in Germany's non-military affairs than the ever cautious Bethmann had been willing to pursue. It was not so much that the actual war aims of the government became more chauvinistic; it was the attitude behind the program of war aims which changed with the retirement of Bethmann Hollweg. No matter what promises the latter had held out for a future peace, most Germans assumed, correctly, that his own sympathies were always on the moderate side, for a peace of understanding rather than a peace of victory. The Supreme Command, on the other hand, though it never openly stated any more far-reaching aims than Bethmann, was known to be in favor of a strong peace. For the first time the annexationists thus found full sympathy and support from the German government. In the realm of war aims, this change was the most significant result of Bethmann's fall.

Chapter IV

THE STRANGE CASE OF GEORG MICHAELIS
(JULY 1917–OCTOBER 1917)

WHILE Bethmann's fall was a serious blow to the moderate cause, the subsequent months nevertheless were easily the most hopeful in the history of German war aims. For a while it appeared as though moderation might triumph over annexationism, in the Reichstag's Peace Resolution, and as though a Papal offer to mediate between the belligerents might bring about a negotiated peace. The fact that neither of these hopes materialized was due to the fact that annexationism had entered the German government in the person of Bethmann Hollweg's successor.

Michaelis and the Peace Resolution of July 19, 1917

The first task before the victors in the July crisis was the selection of a suitable Chancellor. The fact that such a selection had not been made before is a sad comment upon the shortsightedness of Bethmann's adversaries, who soon discovered that it was far easier to engage in destructive criticism than to suggest positive remedies. On the evening of July 17, after Bethmann's resignation had become a certainty, the Conservatives gave a party to celebrate the long awaited event. "The next morning," Count Westarp tells us, "we had more than just a physical hangover. The fulfillment of a long-desired event often brings new disappointments and worries. This the politician discovers, particularly when he has hoped or worked for the dismissal of a leading statesman without making sure of his successor." [1] There were, of course, several more or less serious candidates, among them the Minister President of Bavaria, Count Hertling, ex-ambassador Bernstorff, Admiral von Tirpitz, and Prince Bülow. [2] Even General von Bernhardi, whose pre-war writings had supplied the Allies with

---

[1] Westarp, II, 467.
[2] Hutten-Czapski, II, 384; Fester, *Kämpfe*, p. 95.

some of their most effective anti-German propaganda, was mentioned.[3] The most influential backing was enjoyed by Bülow, who was the favorite not only of the Supreme Command, but also of Stresemann, Erzberger and the Empress, "who had much more influence upon the Kaiser during the war than is usually assumed."[4] Her influence was not sufficient, however, to overcome her husband's opposition.[5] The Reichstag, so influential in overthrowing Bethmann, was completely disregarded in the choice of his successor, whose selection was made with utter disregard for the importance of the Chancellor's position, especially in time of war.

The man who was chosen in a very off-hand manner was Dr. Michaelis, definitely a "dark horse." As Food Commissary for Prussia he had recently delivered a strong speech before the Lower House, sufficient qualification, at least in the eyes of the Supreme Command, to entrust him with the leadership of German affairs. Nobody was more surprised than Michaelis at the honor so suddenly thrust upon him—though it took him little time to make up his mind. What doubts he had about his qualifications for so important an office were dispelled when he came upon the daily message of his Moravian Brotherhood. "Do not fear and be dismayed," it said, "for the Lord, your God, will be with you in everything you do." Without enquiring any further into the duties and immediate problems of his new job, he accepted the call of God and his country little more than fifteen minutes after the proposition was first made to him.[6] Yet the issues facing the new Chancellor were so numerous and complex as to baffle the most experienced politician, let alone a complete novice like Michaelis, who admittedly knew little more about the affairs of Germany than he had learned from the daily press.[7] While the Supreme Command, the parties of the Right, and the annexationists expected him to gain a strong peace, and to counteract, as far as possible, the Reichstag Peace Resolution, the parties of the Center and Left, and with them the majority of Germans, hoped that he would conclude an early and moderate peace on the basis

[3] Bernhardi, pp. 476-77.
[4] Hutten-Czapski, II, 384; Westarp, II, 354.
[5] *U. A.*, 4. Reihe, VIII, 84; Valentini, pp. 159 ff., 168-69.
[6] G. Michaelis, *Für Staat und Volk* (Berlin, 1922), p. 321; F. Ritter von Lama, *Die Friedensvermittlung Papst Benedikts XV. und ihre Vereitelung durch den deutschen Reichskanzler Michaelis* (München, 1932), p. 47, note 10.
[7] Haussmann, p. 131.

of the same Resolution.[8] In the struggle between the Reichstag majority and the Supreme Command, the attitude of the chief executive was of tremendous importance. The negotiations surrounding the July Peace Resolution were to show to which of the two camps the new Chancellor belonged.

The afternoon of Bethmann's resignation, July 13, Hindenburg and Ludendorff invited a delegation from the moderate Reichstag majority to discuss the proposed Peace Resolution. The day before Hindenburg had told William II that such a resolution would "weaken the army's strength and power of resistance," and he had asked that the government prevent such a declaration.[9] But in their talk with the majority leaders, the army heads took a more moderate stand. They objected not so much, they said, to the general idea of a Peace Resolution, but rather to the weak tone of the Reichstag draft. Hindenburg wanted "a little more pepper" put into it, and Ludendorff suggested that it demand a "peace of adjustment" (*Ausgleich*) rather than a "peace of understanding." As an example of such an adjustment he mentioned Germany's strategic position against Belgium, where some changes were much in order.[10] From this it appears as though the Supreme Command was not basically opposed to the Resolution. But from a subsequent conversation which Hindenburg and Ludendorff had with the Conservatives Heydebrand and Westarp, we get a somewhat different impression. Because now they demanded that the Resolution be dropped entirely, because of its possible effect abroad.[11] It was this outright opposition of the Supreme Command to the Peace Resolution which became ever more outspoken in subsequent discussions.

On July 14, the day after his appointment, Michaelis himself received the majority parties, in the presence of Hindenburg and Ludendorff. In the meantime the text of the Resolution, as it had been decided upon up to this point, had been published prematurely in a number of radical papers, a fact which deeply disturbed the Chancellor and Supreme Command.[12] It was impossible, there-

---

[8] *U.A.*, 4. Reihe, VIII, p. 85.

[9] Bethmann Hollweg, II, 229; Helfferich, pp. 451-52.

[10] Scheidemann, *Memoiren*, II, 39-40; F. von Payer, *Von Bethmann Hollweg bis Ebert* (Frankfurt, 1923), p. 36; Erzberger, p. 264; Haussmann, p. 127.

[11] Westarp, II, 468-69.

[12] Scheidemann, *Zusammenbruch*, pp. 95-97; Payer, *Bethmann Hollweg*, pp. 37-38.

fore, to kill the Resolution altogether; instead Michaelis and Hindenburg now tried at least to prevent an official vote on the Resolution. When the majority parties refused to agree to this, Michaelis in turn reserved his final judgment in the matter until he had been able to study the Resolution more carefully. The general impression Michaelis gave at this meeting was that he tended towards the Supreme Command rather than the Reichstag majority in his stand on the Peace Resolution.

This impression was confirmed the next day, when Chancellor and Supreme Command played host to the parties of the Right. Both Michaelis and Hindenburg deplored that the Peace Resolution, because of its publication two days earlier, could not be prevented altogether. But when Count Westarp expressed concern over the future, Hindenburg and the Chancellor assured him that Germany " would have a free hand at the peace conference, since the military situation, as it had developed by that time, would be fully exploited, despite the Resolution." [13] The attitude of both military and civilian authorities towards the Peace Resolution, as these various discussions show, was at best one of acquiescence, certainly not of agreement. They refrained from a more pronounced opposition simply because it might complicate matters for the new Chancellor and endanger the granting of war credits by the Socialists.[14]

Michaelis' first appearance before the Reichstag was to be on July 19, in the same session in which the Peace Resolution was to be voted upon. During the preceding days, the Chancellor and the Parties discussed the former's inaugural address, and Michaelis promised to express his agreement with the Resolution.[15] Count Westarp, when he heard of these discussions, immediately called on Michaelis and repeated his party's opposition to the Resolution. The Chancellor again stressed the fact that " he was determined to reach, at the peace conference, an understanding and adjustment which would make full use of our military advantages." [16] There certainly could no longer be any doubt as to where his sympathies were.

---

[13] Westarp, II, 469-70.
[14] Scheidemann, *Zusammenbruch*, p. 101; Lama *Friedensvermittlung*, pp. 56-57; Knesebeck, p. 160.
[15] Scheidemann, *Zusammenbruch*, pp. 103-05; Erzberger, p. 266.
[16] Westarp, II, 471.

The Peace Resolution of the German Reichstag was officially presented on July 19, 1917.[17] After reiterating Germany's defensive stand of August 4, 1914, it said:

The Reichstag strives for a peace of understanding and the permanent reconciliation of peoples. Forced territorial acquisitions and political, economic, or financial oppressions are irreconcilable with such a peace. The Reichstag also rejects all plans which aim at economic isolation and hostility among nations after the war. Freedom of the seas must be guaranteed. Only an economic peace will prepare the ground for friendly intercourse between the nations. The Reichstag will strongly promote the creation of international judicial organizations. However, as long as the enemy governments will not enter upon such a peace, as long as they threaten Germany and her allies with conquests and coercion, the German nation will stand together as one man and steadfastly hold out and fight until its own and its allies' right to life and development is secured. The German nation is invincible in its unity. The Reichstag knows that in this respect it is in harmony with the men who in heroic struggle are defending the Fatherland. The undying gratitude of the whole people is assured them.[18]

This official text of the Peace Resolution differs in one important, though little noticed detail from the version published prematurely in the *Vorwärts* on July 14. Instead of referring simply to the preceding statement on German unity, the agreement of " the men who in heroic struggle are defending the Fatherland " (i. e. the army and especially its leaders) originally referred to the whole Resolution. The change was suggested by Scheidemann, at the request of Ludendorff, who objected to a sentence which might imply the Supreme Command's agreement with the Reichstag's peace move.[19]

The Resolution was passed by 212 votes, against the 126 votes of the Right and the Independent Socialists (who wanted a more far-reaching statement).[20] Its influence upon government policy, as we shall see, was insignificant. Nor did it affect the attitude of the Allies one way or the other.[21] The terms " forced territorial acquisitions and political, economic, or financial oppressions," did not exclude the various schemes for Germany's post-war domination of Belgium. " With the Peace Resolution," a German critic observes correctly, " the German government might have con-

[17] *Reichstag*, vol. 310, pp. 3573-76.
[18] Lutz, *German Empire*, II, 282-83.
[19] Scheidemann, *Zusammenbruch*, p. 102.
[20] *Reichstag*, vol. 310, pp. 3598-3600.
[21] *U. A.*, 4. Reihe, III, 369-70.

quered half the world." [22]   Even so, as far as the German masses were concerned, the Peace Resolution expressed for the first time a widespread longing for an early peace. Popular restlessness and discontent already had found sporadic expressions in numerous popular demonstrations demanding bread and peace.[23]   Soldiers' letters, collected by the government and used in the post-war deliberations of the Reichstag Investigating Committee, testify to the prevalence of identical views at the fighting fronts.[24]   On July 31, 400 sailors of the H. M. S. "King Albert" joined the Independent Socialist Party and asked for a speedy peace on the basis of "no annexations and no indemnities." [25]   Even among officers, though predominantly annexationist, we find indications of growing moderation.[26]

The policy of the government, however, was little affected by this popular longing for peace. To be sure, Michaelis' speech on July 19 outwardly adhered to the Resolution. After stressing the inviolability of Germany's territorial integrity, he continued:

By way of agreement and adjustment we must guarantee the vital conditions of the German Empire on the continent and overseas. The peace must provide the basis for a lasting reconciliation among nations. It must, as is expressed in your Resolution, prevent the further incubation of hostility among nations by erecting economic barriers. It must provide a guarantee that the armed alliance of our enemies does not evolve into an economic offensive alliance against us. These ends are attainable within the limits of your Resolution as I understand it.[27]

On first sight this looks like a full endorsement of the Reichstag's policy, and it was taken as such by the majority parties.[28]   Yet already at the July 19 meeting, the Independent Socialist Haase pointed to the qualifying phrase "as I understand it," which had not appeared in the speech as submitted earlier to the majority parties, and which seemed to permit different interpretations of

[22] Rosenberg, *Republik*, p. 163.
[23] Dahlin, pp. 123-24.
[24] *U. A.*, 4. Reihe, V, 182 ff., 262 ff., VI, 65-66, 151; XI (1), 424.
[25] Rosenberg, *Republik*, p. 172.
[26] H. von Stein, *Erlebnisse und Betrachtungen aus der Zeit des Weltkrieges* (Leipzig, 1919), p. 112; Michaelis, p. 332; Thimme, *Weltkrieg ohne Waffen*, p. 203; O. Lehmann-Russbüldt, *Warum erfolgte der Zusammenbruch an der Westfront?* (Berlin, 1919), p. 12; *Frankfurter Zeitung*, Sept. 12, 1917.
[27] *Reichstag*, vol. 310, p. 3572.
[28] *U. A.*, 4. Reihe, VIII, 88-89; *Reichstag*, vol. 310, pp. 3577-80.

the Resolution.[29]   The press, particularly of the Right, was not slow to interpret this clause as an attempt on the part of Michaelis to evade the restrictions of the Resolution. In his Memoirs, Michaelis tries to explain the insertion of the famous phrase as an unintentional slip.[30]   But in the light of his statements before and after July 19, there can be no doubt that he viewed the Peace Resolution with disapproval and intended not to have it tie his hands at a future peace conference.   "I am most confident," he wrote in reply to a Pan-German protest against the Peace Resolution, " that our excellent military position will help us to gain a peace which will permanently secure the vital interests of the German Reich on the continent and overseas ";[31] and in a letter to the Crown Prince, Michaelis made no secret of his real views on the Reichstag move.   "The notorious Resolution," he wrote, " has been passed by 212 votes to 126, with 17 not voting. Through my interpretation of it I have exorcised its chief danger. With the Resolution we can ultimately conclude any peace we like." [32]

It took the majority parties a little while longer to catch on to the Chancellor's two-faced policy. The first shock came from a different quarter. The day following the July 19 meeting, the Emperor, for the first time in almost two decades, received delegates from all parties (except the Independent Socialists) at the Ministry of the Interior for an informal exchange of views. As was to be expected, the " exchange " consisted largely of little monologues delivered by William II; and in these monologues he advanced rather startling views, completely at variance with the peace policy of the Reichstag. The idea of a " peace of adjustment " (a term carefully avoided by the Reichstag) was excellent, he said. The word " adjustment," according to William, meant that Germany would simply take away money, raw materials, etc., from her adversaries. The Kaiser then outlined his plans for what he called the " Second Punic War " against England, in which the whole continent, under Germany's leadership, would destroy Britain's world domination. The delegates of the moderate parties became increasingly uncomfortable, especially when, referring to Germany's recent victories on the Galician front, the Emperor

---

[29] *Ibid.,* p. 3585.
[30] Michaelis, pp. 328-29; *U. A.,* 4. Reihe, VII (1), 75.
[31] Werner, pp. 266-67, note 421.
[32] *U. A.,* 4. Reihe, VII (2), 390-91; Scheidemann, *Memoiren,* II, 53.

remarked: "Where my guards appear, there is no room for democracy." Far from establishing closer understanding between monarch and parliament, the meeting left a most unfortunate impression with all but the most enthusiastic and blind admirers of the Hohenzollern regime.[33] On August 1, 1917, third anniversary of the outbreak of war, the Kaiser tried to remedy this impression by paying at least lip-service to a non-annexationist peace. In a proclamation to the German people, he said: "Our people may rest assured that German blood and industry are not staked for the shadow of a hollow ambition, nor for plans of conquest and bondage, but for a strong, free Empire in which our children will be able to live in security." [34] But this conciliatory gesture failed to correct the impression created by his earlier statements.

If the German government's attitude towards the Peace Resolution was, as these statements show, doubtful, its support by the majority parties was not unanimous either.[35] The most sincere supporters of a peace of mutual understanding were the two Socialist parties.[36] But this did not mean that Germany's whole working class was in favor of a non-annexationist peace. On August 2, the *Freier Ausschuss für einen deutschen Arbeiterfrieden* was formed at Bremen. Its aims were the safeguarding of Germany's frontiers, the acquisition of land for settlement, freedom of the seas, and a war indemnity.[37] Three days later, representatives of the *Verband der wirtschaftsfriedlichen nationalen Arbeitervereine im Rheinisch-Westphälischen Industriegebiet*, an association of national workers' organizations representing some 30,000 workers of the Ruhr met at Dortmund, to oppose "the Peace Resolution of the so-called Reichstag majority." Instead they demanded "a peace which will guarantee an indemnity for the sacrifices imposed by the enemy and protect the borders of Germany against all dangers of a future attack, and which will offer the working population the opportunity of a secure livelihood and unhindered development." [38] A group of Protestant workers' associations like-

---

[33] Erzberger, pp. 52-54; Scheidemann, *Memoiren*, II, 54-57; Westarp, II, 473-74; Helfferich, p. 473.

[34] Lutz, *German Empire*, II, 299.

[35] Payer, *Bethmann Hollweg*, p. 38; *U. A.*, 4. Reihe, XII(1), 137.

[36] *Vorwärts*, Sept. 25, 1917; *U. A.*, 4. Reihe, XII(1), 139.

[37] *Schulthess*, vol. 58(1), p. 741.

[38] *Handel und Industrie*, XXVI, Aug. 25, 1917, p. 528.

wise came out in favor of a strong peace.[39] The reason for these manifestations of annexationism among the workers was their belief that the advantages of an enlarged Germany would ultimately be shared by the lower classes and not merely remain restricted to a small percentage of the population.

There also was some opposition in Progressive ranks against the Peace Resolution, among men like Körte, Traub, or Müller-Meiningen. The latter did not want to restrict the government's freedom of action if certain territorial gains should seem necessary for strategic reasons.[40] Pastor Traub's annexationism finally drove his party to protest and to force his withdrawal in October.[41] As time went on, however, this annexationist faction gained more adherents, though in October the Progressive Party still declared its support of the Resolution, pointing out that the Resolution proposed a peace of understanding and not a peace of renunciation.[42]

The Center Party's position as usual, was not quite so clear as that of the other parties. It was from Erzberger's speeches before the Main Committee of the Reichstag in early July, that the Peace Resolution had originated.[43] But while he was able to win over the Reichstag delegation of his party, considerable opposition against the Peace Resolution remained within the rank and file of the Center Party.[44] Even before the Resolution had been passed, the *Kölnische Volkszeitung* started to collect signatures for a Hindenburg peace.[45] Particularly in Bavaria, the stronghold of Centrist annexationism, a regular anti-Erzberger front arose, under the leadership of Schlittenbauer and Heim.[46] To rally the party behind the policy of its Reichstag delegation, a meeting was called for July 23, at which Erzberger successfully defended his policy, reading the Czernin memorandum of April 12 to explain his pessimistic outlook. A statement was then issued which said that the Central Committee of the Center Party was in favor of a " peace

---

[39] *U. A.*, 4. Reihe, XII (1), 137-38; F. Behrens, *Was der deutsche Arbeiter vom Frieden erwartet* (Hagen, 1917).

[40] *U. A.*, 4. Reihe, XII (1), 137.

[41] *Vossische Zeitung*, Oct. 15, 1917.

[42] *U. A.*, 4. Reihe, XII (1), 137-39; Wortmann, p. 103.

[43] Wacker, pp. 35-36.

[44] *Ibid.*, p. 138; K. Bachem, *Vorgeschichte, Geschichte und Politik der Deutschen Zentrumspartei* (9 vols., Köln, 1930-32), IX, 437.

[45] *U. A.*, 4. Reihe, XII (1), 137.

[46] *Schulthess*, vol. 58 (1), 797.

of understanding and adjustment which will guarantee Germany's political security and economic development." [47] As the military situation improved during the second half of 1917, the anti-Erzberger faction became more prominent, but the Reichstag delegation officially maintained its favorable stand on the July Resolution.[48]

One result of Erzberger's activities during July of 1917 was his resignation from the Thyssen concern, apparently at the request of August Thyssen himself.[49] This did not mean, however, that he had given up hoping for Germany's domination over the French iron district of Briey-Longwy, which had been the cause of his close relations with the firm of Thyssen.[50] In a conversation with Prince Max of Baden, shortly after July 19, Erzberger stated that the Peace Resolution would help him to gain this French region by way of negotiation! [51]

While the majority parties were thus not entirely united behind the Peace Resolution, the opposition parties contained some moderate elements who opposed a further continuation of the war and favored a peace of understanding.[52] Some Conservatives and a moderate section of the National Liberals had almost voted for the Peace Resolution.[53] The National Liberals as a whole were opposed to the Peace Resolution not so much because they still desired large annexations but because they felt that the German government should declare its willingness for a peace of understanding not through a public announcement but through other channels.[54] Still the National Liberals refused to agree beforehand to relinquish all territorial gains in a future peace, regardless of the outcome of the war. " If our flag should be waving over Calais," Stresemann wrote in July, " and if we should thus establish a German Gibraltar on the Atlantic, who could make us relinquish it, if we were able to maintain ourselves militarily? . . . We wish to gain every possible security in the east and west, and whatever we

[47] Wacker, p. 39.
[48] *Ibid.*, pp. 56, 89.
[49] *Vossische Zeitung*, Sept. 12, 1917.
[50] Westarp, II, 551.
[51] Max von Baden, p. 114.
[52] H. Delbrück, *Krieg und Politik*, part II, 1916-17 (Berlin, 1919), pp. 296-97.
[53] *Reichstag*, vol. 310, p. 3600; Westarp, II, 472.
[54] *Reichstag*, vol. 310, p. 3585; *U. A.*, 4. Reihe, VII (1), 6.

can get in the way of colonies and sea-power." [55]   The Peace Resolution, according to Stubmann, another National Liberal deputy,
was " unbusinesslike to the highest degree, since it almost entirely
eliminated the risk run by our enemies for originating and continuing the war." [56] Arguments like these were typical for a party
which primarily drew its support from industrial and business
interests. As time went on, and the Peace Resolution proved
ineffective, the National Liberal Party reverted to its earlier
annexationist stand.[57]

As for the Conservatives, they repeatedly tried to reach an
agreement with the National Liberals for a united stand against
the Peace Resolution. A Conservative declaration of July 19
opposed the Resolution and demanded a strong peace. " We shall
continue," it said, " to hold irrevocably to the views we have
always held about the gains which peace shall bring to the German
Fatherland." The military situation alone should determine what
these gains might be, and it would be the duty of the German
government, in close collaboration with the Supreme Command,
to make the most of that situation.[58] The chief objections raised
against the Peace Resolution by Conservative annexationists were
the familiar ones that, while it would strengthen the power of
resistance among Germany's enemies, it would weaken the very
same power within Germany.[59] Subsequently both Conservative
parties published almost identical declarations asking for annexations and indemnities. Significantly enough, both declarations
came out against the introduction of parliamentary government
into Germany and of the equal franchise into Prussia.[60] The tide
of peace and democracy was rising in Germany, threatening to
engulf and destroy traditional powers and privileges. A last determined stand, a rally of all available forces in favor of a Greater
Germany abroad and the *status quo* at home was the demand of
the hour. It found its answer in the founding of the *Vaterlandspartei.*

[55] G. Stresemann, " Gedanken zur Krisis," *Deutsche Stimmen*, XXIX (1917),
430.
[56] P. Stubmann, " Dreissig nationalliberale Thesen zur heutigen politischen Lage,"
ibid., p. 579.
[57] *U. A.*, 4. Reihe, XII (1), 138.
[58] *Reichstag*, vol. 310, p. 3584.
[59] Westarp, II, 336; *U. A.*, 4. Reihe, XII (1), 138.
[60] *Schulthess*, vol. 58 (1), pp. 907, 927; *U. A.*, 4. Reihe, VII (1), 6.

The Vaterlandspartei

The Peace Resolution, though it failed in its immediate objectives, served as an effective banner around which the new coalition of the middle and lower classes gathered in their struggle against the existing order. It was in this coalition which lasted into and through the Weimar Republic that the supporters and beneficiaries of the Hohenzollern regime saw their most dangerous enemy. They realized correctly that the aims of the majority parties were not limited to the Peace Resolution, but included the much more important reform of the German government and the Prussian franchise. The fact that the reforming parties could count on the sympathy and active co-operation of many National Liberals did not help to decrease the concern of Conservatives and annexationists. It is not surprising, therefore, to find immediate and ardent agitation against the Peace Resolution from the ranks of the chief expansionist organizations.

As soon as Dietrich Schäfer heard that a movement demanding a peace of understanding was under way, he first sent a note of protest to twenty leading papers and then called together his Independent Committee.[61] " The Reichstag," the Committee stated " which was elected under entirely different circumstances, does not have the right of thus gambling away the future of the German people." Yet neither these declarations, nor a request to Michaelis that he prevent the Reichstag from voting on the Resolution, had any success. The only thing left seemed to be to write articles in favor of a strong peace.[62]

The Pan-German League likewise found the Peace Resolution sufficient cause for a new outburst of annexationist agitation. According to the *Vorwärts*, the *Weserzeitung* was bought at this time by a Pan-German group and turned into another effective propaganda weapon.[63] On July 28, the League came out with a formal protest against the Peace Resolution.[64] The same day, President von Strantz of the Army League added his voice to the growing chorus of opposition.[65] Finally, on August 9, a joint mani-

---

[61] Schäfer, *Leben*, p. 209; *Schulthess*, vol. 58 (1), p. 698.

[62] Schäfer, *Krieg*, II, 11; Schäfer, *Leben*, p. 209; *Tägliche Rundschau*, July 26, 1917.

[63] *Vorwärts*, July 26, 1917.

[64] *Alldeutsche Blätter*, XXVII, July 28, 1917.

[65] K. von Strantz, " Unsere territorialen Faustpfänder," *Handel und Industrie*, XXVI (1917), 461-62.

festo against the Resolution was published by a long list of annexationist organizations, most notably the Independent Committee, the Pan-German League, the Navy League, and the *Ostmarkenverein*.[66] In September, most of these groups joined forces behind the *Hauptvermittlungsstelle Vaterländischer Verbände*, another of the many combines of annexationist organizations, this time under the direction of Dietrich Schäfer and the Pan-German Admiral Count Baudissin.[67]

The trouble with most of these organizations was that they were not popular movements but small, though highly influential pressure groups. Their membership, as we have seen throughout, overlapped considerably; as the Socialist Landsberg told the Reichstag in October 1917: " Pan-German League, Army League, Navy League, Colonial Society, League of the Eastern Marches, Independent Committee for a German Peace—they are always the same men, only the name of the firm changes." [68] As the moderate opposition to strong war aims became more powerful and vociferous, it seemed desirable to counteract this opposition by a large-scale movement in favor of a strong peace. Less than two months after the Peace Resolution had passed the Reichstag, the *Vaterlandspartei* was born.

Its plan originated with Wolfgang Kapp. During July and August of 1917, he discussed with a number of prominent East Prussians the project for a movement to combat the Peace Resolution, and it was decided to select that region, already famous for the Wars of Liberation, as the birthplace of the new organization.[69] On August 31 these plans were submitted to a meeting in Berlin, attended by most leaders of the *Kriegszielbewegung*, who pledged the support of their organizations.[70] On September 2, anniversary of the Battle of Sedan, the new party introduced itself to the German people with a lengthy manifesto, which set forth the following platform:

The German *Vaterlandspartei* aims at welding together the whole energy of the Fatherland without distinction of party politics. . . . The German

---

[66] *Schulthess*, vol. 58 (1), p. 748.

[67] *Deutschlands Erneuerung*, I (1917), 765.

[68] *Reichstag*, vol. 310, p. 3714.

[69] Wortmann, pp. 27-28.

[70] Schäfer, *Leben*, p. 220. Those present included Kapp, Tirpitz, Schäfer, Duke Johann Albrecht of Mecklenburg, Baron von Wangenheim, von Reichenau, and C. C. Eiffe.

Vaterlandspartei will not enter into rivalry with patriotically minded political parties. . . . It is a party of union. It does not, therefore, contemplate setting up its own parliamentary candidates. When peace is proclaimed, it will dissolve. It wants no internal strife. . . . However any individual may view the vexing questions of internal politics, decisions on these are to be postponed till after the war. Then our heroes will have returned from the battlefield and will be able to co-operate in the internal construction of the Empire. Now victory is all that matters! . . . The stature of German freedom towers sky-high above the freedoms of fake democracies and their vaunted blessings, of which English hypocrisy and Wilson prate in order thereby to undermine Germany, who stands impregnable against their weapons. . . . We will have no peace of starvation. . . . If we willingly bear with distress and deprivation, the German people will gain a Hindenburg peace, which will repay us the price of the immense sacrifices and exertions. Any other peace means a devastating blow to our future development. The stunting of our position in the world and intolerable accompanying burdens would destroy our commercial position and all the prospects of our working classes.[71]

The manifesto was signed by twenty prominent citizens of East Prussia, all members of the upper middle class, an inauspicious start for an organization that expected to develop into a popular movement.[72] As far as the contents of the manifesto were concerned, it had little to say on war aims and dealt almost exclusively with the question of domestic reforms. What the *Vaterlandspartei* apparently hoped to do was to sidetrack the issue of reform until after the war. Such a stand, of course, was in flat contradiction to the policy of the majority parties as well as to the Kaiser's Easter Message and his promise of July 11, 1917 to accomplish the reform of the Prussian franchise during the war.[73] The opposition immediately seized upon this point, so that the *Vaterlandspartei* found it advisable to drop from its program the statement which relegated the discussion of reforms to the post-war period. Yet even so, the party was never able to outlive its reactionary reputation.

As regards war aims, the Sedan Manifesto simply mentioned a Hindenburg Peace. At the first meeting of the party, on September 24, Admiral von Tirpitz elaborated briefly on this point. " We must demand," he said, " that not England, but Germany become the protector of Belgium. . . . It is likewise our moral duty to protect the Flemings against renewed suppression. . . .

---

[71] *Norddeutsche Allgemeine Zeitung*, Sept. 2, 1917; Lutz, *German Empire*, I, 368-70.

[72] Wortmann, p. 29.

[73] *U. A.*, 4. Reihe, XII (1), 145.

The tremendous war which Germany is fighting is not for Germany's sake alone but in reality for the freedom of the European continent and its peoples from the all-devouring tyranny of Anglo-Americanism." [74] Germany's " protection " of Belgium, the official publication of the *Vaterlandspartei* said, should be maintained by means of close economic and military ties between the two countries, very much like the *Angliederung* of Belgium proposed in annexationist circles.[75] Frontier rectifications (Briey-Longwy), eastern annexations, colonial acquisitions, and an indemnity completed a program which, though considerably milder than many statements during the first half of the war, was still highly annexationist.[76] It should be noted that the chief argument to defend such strong war aims was not that they would add to the greater wealth and glory of the Fatherland—such glowing tales no longer aroused much enthusiasm among a war-weary people. Now we find a different approach, dwelling on the negative results, the " intolerable burdens " and the " devastating blows " which a moderate peace would bring to all Germans, including the workers. " Germany's salvation, honor and future are at stake! " the September Manifesto concluded.[77] With appeals to the basic emotions of greed and fear, the annexationists hoped to transform their small pressure group into a large popular movement.

A look at the organization and membership of the *Vaterlandspartei* however, shows that this attempt was only partly successful.[78] At the head of the party was Admiral von Tirpitz, with the Duke of Mecklenburg as honorary president and Kapp as vice-president. In the various governing committees we find a further array of familiar annexationists: Traub, Schäfer, von Reichenau, von Buhl, Class, von Below, and von Wangenheim. Most of these men were leaders of annexationist organizations, whose activities remained unaffected by the rise of the *Vaterlandspartei*. The doubtful reputation of the Pan-German League made it desirable for the new movement to disclaim any close relation with it.[79] Yet the collaboration between members of the

[74] *Schulthess*, vol. 58 (1), p. 814; Wortmann, p. 41.

[75] *Katechismus der Deutschen Vaterlandspartei* (Berlin, 1917), pp. 7-9.

[76] Landesverein der Deutschen Vaterlandspartei im Königreich Sachsen, *Warum muss ich der Vaterlandspartei beitreten?* (n. pl., n. d.), pp. 11-14.

[77] Lutz, *German Empire*, I, 370.

[78] Wortmann, pp. 66 ff.

[79] *Ibid.*, p. 46; G. von Below, *Das gute Recht der deutschen Vaterlandspartei* (Berlin, 1917), p. 3.

League and the new party was close, and in many local branches the new organization was run by members of the League.[80] Between the Independent Committee and the party, such collaboration was openly acknowledged and welcomed. Taking over the Committee's complete set of over 2,000 experienced local representatives, the *Vaterlandspartei* concentrated on large-scale propaganda campaigns, leaving to Schäfer's group the further definition and elaboration of war aims.[81] The result was the rise of more than 2,500 local groups by the middle of 1918, with 1.25 million members. Geographically the main strength of the *Vaterlandspartei* was in the Conservative regions of northern and eastern Germany. It was much weaker in the democratic and Catholic west and south.[82] As to the social and economic background of its members, it is difficult, without a complete membership list, to arrive at final conclusions. Opponents of the party charged that it was primarily a party of the upper classes, heavily supported by the great industrialists. Attempts to disprove these accusations, such as the study by Wortmann, do not actually present sufficient evidence to the contrary. If there should be any doubt in our minds as to the background of the party's supporters, we need only look at its anti-democratic and expansionist program. Hugo Stinnes, Wortmann claims, was not a member, though "a number of gentlemen from heavy industry, who played a political role in other respects . . . were interested in the *Vaterlandspartei*." [83] On the whole, the party followed pretty closely the social pattern already established for most of the other annexationist organizations.[84] In their attempt to prove the democratic character of the party, its defenders point to several groups of workers who expressed their support. Yet the number of workers involved is too small to substantiate the claim that the *Vaterlandspartei* enjoyed wide working-class support.[85]

The activities of the *Vaterlandspartei* differed little from those of most other organizations of its kind. Its press section supplied the annexationist press with suitable news and articles. In its

[80] Werner, p. 241.
[81] Wortmann, pp. 47, 69; Jagow, p. 123.
[82] Wortmann, pp. 72-73; *U. A.*, 4. Reihe, XII(1), 148.
[83] *Ibid.*, pp. 76, 94; "Die Not der Zeit und die Vaterlandspartei," *Handel und Industrie*, XXVI (1917), 637-38.
[84] Wortmann, pp. 71, 76.
[85] *Ibid.*, p. 77; *Deutschlands Erneuerung*, II (1918), 78.

own publishing house the party produced large quantities of annexationist propaganda as well as its official publication—*Mitteilungen der Deutschen Vaterlandspartei*. Special departments within its central office were set up to supply speakers and recruit organizers of new local branches and to carry on propaganda among the recalcitrant working population.[86] All members were urged to cooperate by enlisting new supporters and by propagating the party's aims in speeches, articles, and pamphlets, in which the question of domestic reforms was to be avoided.[87]

As regards the attitude of the political parties towards the *Vaterlandspartei*, the Right, always in favor of far-reaching annexations, put no obstacles in the way of its members if they wished to join.[88] Nevertheless the National Liberals were not so closely allied with the *Vaterlandspartei* as the Conservatives. Particularly in Bavaria, the former took a rather negative stand towards the new party.[89] The Conservatives, on the other hand, gave it constant support and urged their members to join.[90] The same was done by the predominantly Conservative Agrarian League, whose President, von Wangenheim, was one of the leading figures of the *Vaterlandspartei*.[91]

With the majority parties, the case was somewhat different. As adherents of the Peace Resolution, they were naturally against an organization whose chief purpose was to fight that Resolution. But as we have already pointed out, the rank and file of these parties was not always in complete agreement with the policy of their Reichstag delegations, a fact which is borne out if we examine the attitude of each party towards the new *Vaterlandspartei*. The Center, more than any other of the majority parties, had been split in its stand on the July Resolution. In October, its leaders asked all members to stay out of all new parties or party-like organizations; but even so a number of prominent Centrists, mostly of the aristocratic right wing, became members of Kapp's organization.[92]

The Progressive Party likewise urged its members " to stay clear

[86] Wortmann, pp. 68-69.

[87] *Ibid.*, p. 70.

[88] Vaterlandspartei, *Das deutsche Volk und der Friede* (Berlin, 1918), pp. 11 ff., 15-16.

[89] *U. A.*, 4. Reihe, XII (1), 149.

[90] Westarp, II, pp. 526, 622.

[91] Heller, pp. 45-46.

[92] Wortmann, pp. 74-75, 99-103.

from any support of the Fatherland Party, since its existence endangers internal unity and since it aims particularly at the prevention of domestic reforms during the course of the war." [93] A number of its members, however, became dissatisfied with the policy of its Reichstag delegation, and a group of them voiced their opposition in a memorandum against the Peace Resolution and its "peace of renunciation." So we need not be surprised to find several Progressives among the founders of the *Vaterlandspartei*. The majority, however, observed party discipline and did not join.[94]

From the ranks of the Majority Socialists, of course, hardly a single member joined the new party. On the contrary, it is from this quarter more than from any other that the most effective propaganda against the Kapp movement was carried on. To the socialists and their press, the *Vaterlandspartei* consisted "largely of people who profit from the war," and who "were the chief enemies of equal franchise." [95] It was chiefly this last point which caused most Germans to oppose the *Vaterlandspartei*. Far from winning for itself the reputation of unselfish patriotism, the party combined and personified the most hated aspects of a declining regime.

Opposition to the new movement outside the Reichstag developed just as naturally as against other annexationist organizations. In October, thirty-two members of the faculty of Heidelberg objected to the founding and propaganda of the party.[96] Among its most outspoken enemies were Hans Delbrück and Friedrich Meinecke. In the October number of his *Preussische Jahrbücher,* Delbrück reproached the *Vaterlandspartei* for postponing internal reforms and demanding Germany's domination over Belgium. The *conditio sine qua non* for a peace with Great Britain, he observed correctly, was the restitution of Belgium. As an equivalent for giving up continental expansion, he proposed the creation of a large German colonial empire.[97] It was the Belgian problem which formed the central topic of his pamphlet "Against the Lack of Confidence," published in the fall of 1917. Delbrück

---

[93] *U. A.,* 4. Reihe, XII (1), 148.
[94] Wortmann, pp. 104-06.
[95] *Ibid.,* pp. 106-11.
[96] *Ibid.,* p. 77.
[97] H. Delbrück, "Die deutsche Vaterlandspartei," *Preussische Jahrbücher,* vol. 170 (1917), pp. 154-57.

denied the annexationist claim that German control of Belgium and the Flanders coast was an essential condition for the protection of Germany's western industrial region.[98] His most consistent attacks were directed against the leader of the *Vaterlandspartei*, Admiral von Tirpitz, driving force behind Germany's demands for the Flanders coast.[99] The defense of the Fatherland Party against Delbrück's attacks was taken up by Professor von Below, and the result was a controversy which was neither dispassionate nor dignified.[100] Meinecke's writings were chiefly directed against the reactionary internal policy of the new party.[101] Stressing the close relationship between domestic and foreign affairs, he felt that Germany, in the long run, could withstand the pressure of her enemies only if she introduced a government which corresponded to the wishes of her people. Only under these conditions would the German soldier be willing to sacrifice everything for the protection of his country. Germany's territorial integrity must be maintained; but to go beyond and engage in territorial expansion might easily divert attention from the vital necessity of domestic reforms and thus lead to the suppression not merely of foreign populations but of the German people as well.

Just as the Petition of the Intellectuals in 1915 had resulted in a petition of the moderates, and the founding of the Independent Committee had found its counterpart in the German National Committee, so the Fatherland Party gave birth to its own antithesis, the *Volksbund für Freiheit und Vaterland*.[102] Its spiritual fathers were the Berlin professors Meinecke, Troeltsch, and Herkner. Its purpose was to organize the opposition against the *Vaterlandspartei*, and its program, briefly, was " the continuation of the foreign and domestic policy of Bethmann Hollweg." Stressing the equivalence of both policies, internal and external, the *Volksbund* worked " for the rallying of popular forces during the war, the immediate introduction of internal freedom, and a popu-

---

[98] H. Delbrück, *Wider den Kleinglauben*, Eine Auseinandersetzung mit der Deutschen Vaterlandspartei (Jena, 1917), pp. 7 ff.

[99] *Preussische Jahrbücher*, vol. 173 (1917), p. 277.

[100] Below, *Vaterlandspartei, passim.*

[101] F. Meinecke, " Vaterlandspartei und deutsche Politik," *Hilfe*, Nov. 22, 1917; *Frankfurter Zeitung*, Nov. 25, 1917. See also Meinecke, *Erinnerungen*, pp. 164, 224-27, 243 ff.

[102] For the following see Wortmann, pp. 94-98; *U. A.*, 4. Reihe, XII (1), 149; Meinecke, *Erinnerungen*, p. 235.

8

lar, lasting peace." Compared to its rival, the *Volksbund* remained small and ineffective, lacking both the means and the talent for an effective propagandist movement. Despite their continuous open controversies, *Volksbund* and *Vaterlandspartei* (like the Independent and National Committees before them) tried repeatedly to come to some agreement. The negotiations showed that there were few basic and insurmountable differences of opinion in regard to war aims, a fact which we have discovered throughout in our comparisons of "moderates" and "annexationists." The main disagreement was over the question of internal reforms, where both groups maintained opposing positions. Though outwardly, the *Vaterlandspartei* tried to erase the impression that it was merely a tool of reaction—"we are neither conservative nor liberal [an official declaration of the party said] neither agrarian nor industrial, neither Army League nor Pan-German." [103] But it soon appeared that the Fatherland Party, far from bringing unity, only aggravated existing conflicts and disunity. Instead of creating a true popular movement, it simply added another annexationist and reactionary organization to the large number already existing. Instead of giving new strength to the government, it often proved embarrassing to the authorities. Measured against the ambitious plans of its founders, the *Vaterlandspartei* was a decided failure; which does not mean, however, that it was not one of the most effective and powerful organizations of the *Kriegszielbewegung*.[104]

The Government and the Vaterlandspartei

There remains one other important point to be discussed in connection with the *Vaterlandspartei*, namely, its relations with Germany's civil and military authorities. Upon the attitude of the latter, success or failure of the new movement depended to a considerable extent. A clear governmental stand against it, added to the already existing opposition of the Reichstag majority, would have been a decisive blow to the annexationist cause. As it turned out, the government's policy was far from uniform. The reply of Michaelis to the telegram announcing the founding of the new party was noncommittal.[105] He admits in his Memoirs that he

---

[103] Wortmann, p. 45.
[104] *U. A.*, 4. Reihe, XII (1), 151-52; VIII, 96, 376.
[105] *Ibid.*, XII (1), 149.

had more in common with the supporters of the new party than with its opponents; yet his " adherence " to the Peace Resolution, he says, made any close collaboration impossible.[106]

This lack of central direction left it up to each government department to determine its own course of action, thus creating considerable confusion. Prussia's Minister of the Interior, Drews, published a decree in October, granting governmental officials the right to join the new party, provided they did not participate in its propaganda.[107] While it caused a stir and repeated discussions in the Prussian Lower House, the decree did not prevent the open agitation among state officials for the Fatherland Party.[108] At the same time, the Prussian Minister of Culture gave his subordinates complete freedom in their relations with the party, and vigorous annexationist propaganda was introduced into German schools.[109] To the German people, these developments seemed to bear out the not unfounded suspicion that the government's sympathy was with the annexationists rather than the moderate majority of the Reichstag.[110]

This popular suspicion received added support from the policy of Germany's military authorities. Due to pressure from the *Vaterlandspartei*, the Prussian Ministry of War had issued an order permitting officers to join the new party. A decree of November 30, 1917, withdrew this order, but failed to prevent numerous cases of individual collaboration between army officers and the Fatherland Party.[111] Admiral Bachmann, former Chief of the Admiralty, declared that the new decree did not affect the German navy but was limited to the army only.[112] Admiral von Krosigk, chief of the Atlantic naval station at Wilhelmshaven, advised his officers to get around the restrictions imposed on November 30 by having their wives join the party and paying a double membership fee. As a result, large-scale annexationist propaganda was carried on within Germany's navy.[113]

[106] *Ibid.*, p. 150.

[107] Wortmann, pp. 44, 88.

[108] *Reichstag*, vol. 310, p. 3718; Wolff, *Vollendete Tatsachen*, p. 244; *Vorwärts*, Sept. 18, 1917; *Frankfurter Zeitung*, Sept. 19, 1917.

[109] Wortmann, p. 93; Great Britain, *Enemy Supplement*, IV, Sept. 12, 1918, 527; E. Hauptmann, *Kriegsziele* (Langensalza, 1917), *passim.*

[110] Helfferich, p. 494.

[111] Wortmann, p. 93; Heinrich Prinz von Schönburg-Waldenburg, *Erinnerungen aus kaiserlicher Zeit* (Leipzig, 1929), pp. 289-91.

[112] *U. A.*, 4. Reihe, IX (1), 30.

[113] *Ibid.*, pp. 29, 170, 234.

The chief reason for the spread of such agitation through army ranks was the support it received from the Supreme Command. We have seen how half-heartedly Hindenburg and Ludendorff had acquiesced in the Reichstag's Peace Resolution. " Unfortunately," Ludendorff wrote to Alexander Wyneken on August 13, 1917, " my offensive in Galicia was not quite ready yet. I believe it has shown that all talk is nonsense as long as the sword is at work. I, therefore, did not take the Peace Resolution too tragically." In the same letter he outlined a program for a patriotic revival very much like the policy inaugurated by the *Vaterlandspartei* a month later.[114] It is quite in line with Ludendorff's whole attitude toward the Peace Resolution that he should welcome the rise of that party. " I maintained no relations with it [i. e. the Fatherland Party]," he says in his Memoirs. " Yet in the interest of the conduct of war, I highly welcomed its activities. If it went too far in its aims, that did no harm. The tempest of war would keep it in its proper bounds." [115] Here was a movement to fan the enthusiasm of the German people, enabling them to withstand the sacrifices of another winter of misery. So wherever possible, the Supreme Command gave its support to the " morale-building " policy of the annexationists. Late in September, Hindenburg released a statement intended to boost the confidence of the German people:

I have been informed by the War Minister that it has been frequently asserted in an unauthorized quarter that, according to statements made by myself and General Ludendorff, threatening economic collapse and exhaustion of military resources are forcing us to peace at any price. I do not desire that our names should be connected with such utterly false assertions. I declare, in full agreement with the Imperial Government, that we are equipped in both the military and economic sense for further fighting and victory.[116]

The army had various means of its own by which to spread propaganda for stronger war aims. There was first the *Kriegspresseamt*, which published and distributed writings of patriotic and annexationist character, although after the Peace Resolution it tried to avoid the controversial subject of war aims.[117] Of greater

---

[114] Knesebeck, pp. 160-61.

[115] Ludendorff, *Kriegserinnerungen*, p. 369.

[116] Lutz, *German Empire*, I, 370.

[117] W. Nicolai, *Nachrichtendienst, Presse und Volksstimmung im Weltkrieg* (Berlin, 1920), p. 115; Germany, Kriegspresseamt, *Bericht über die Tagung vom*

significance was the so-called *Vaterländischer Unterricht*, the army's most direct way of counteracting, within its own ranks, the effects of the Peace Resolution. Its guiding principles were first laid down in a document dated July 29, 1917, signed by General Ludendorff. " Idle talk of peace," it said, " just like pessimism, will prolong the war." Instead it was necessary " to fight on, until we have broken our enemies' will of destruction and created stable conditions for our economic development." In case Germany's enemies should attempt " through peace negotiations, to deprive us of the fruits of our victory and especially to strangle our chances of economic development, it must be made clear to all soldiers that we should be ready to re-open our struggle in order to gain our war aim, i. e., the safeguarding of our future." [118] These statements did not make clear whether the question of war aims was to be made part of the *Vaterländischer Unterricht*. A ruling of September 1917 held that " discussions of war aims are not really the subject of patriotic instruction." There would be no objection, however, to an officer's telling his own views on this subject to his men, if he were asked to do so.[119]

The *Vaterländischer Unterricht*, carried on by officers whose whole background made them adherents of the annexationist cause, often developed into outright propaganda for the aims of the *Vaterlandspartei*. The activities of the two are so closely interwoven, and in most cases so similar, that it is difficult to tell where the one left off and the other began. Here are the instructions given by their superior officer to a group of officers in charge of patriotic instruction:

It is not in place, neither now nor when enlightening the men, to discuss whether Belgium or parts of eastern France ought to be annexed or not. But one thing must be made clear to the soldier: If, when they have recovered after a German victory, our enemies should develop a longing to undertake a renewed attempt to throttle us, then Germany's arm and Germany's sword must not be paralyzed again, as was done in 1914, owing to Belgium's geographical position and hostility.[120]

War aims were not the only subject treated in the army's instruction program. It also dealt with domestic problems. A pamphlet

7. *bis 10. August 1917 in Berlin* (Berlin, 1917), pp. 73, 80; and *Unsere Kolonien* (Berlin, 1918), *passim*.
[118] Nicolai, pp. 119, 122.
[119] *Ibid.*, p. 124.
[120] *U. A.*, 4. Reihe, VII (1), 133 ff.

" for official use only " and entitled " World Democracy " had this to say:

> We are waging a double war: on fronts in the east and the west. . . . Prusso-German heroes are fighting world democracy; and at home, behind the front, we are waging exactly the same war with those who remained at home: the struggle of our national kingdom of the sword against world democracy. . . . In the spring of 1917, when the Tsar had been dethroned and the democratic constitution introduced in Russia . . . it was said in Germany: we Germans are " backward " as compared with the Russians. . . . The democratic parties of the German Reichstag began to attack our powerful monarchy, the Kaiser's power of command, and the Prussian suffrage system. They wanted to compel the conclusion of a peace of renunciation by means of strikes and street demonstrations. . . . Those who do not stop the democratic and international efforts at the threshold are working for the enemy, they are not working for true freedom and equality but for the interests of an international band of swindlers.[121]

Here we have the creed of Germany's ruling classes on the evils of domestic reform and a moderate peace. The pamphlet fore-shadows the *Dolchstosslegende* which later on explained Germany's defeat as a collapse not of the German army but the home front, undermined by the ideas of internationalism and democracy.

The question of annexationist propaganda within the German army was made the subject of a Socialist Reichstag interpellation on October 6, 1917, which presented a wealth of concrete evidence on the various methods used in this agitation.[122] Membership lists for the *Vaterlandspartei* were circulated among soldiers; famous annexationists, like Bacmeister, Traub, and Schäfer were asked to give speeches at the front and in army hospitals; annexationist pamphlets were distributed by the thousands, including one by General Keim which demanded the Flanders coast for Germany; soldiers were forced to attend meetings which advocated a strong peace and which went so far as to suggest that the originators and chief supporters of the Peace Resolution, especially Scheide-mann and Erzberger, be given a good beating, thrown into prison, or better still—be shot! The replies of the Prussian Minister of War, von Stein, to these Socialist charges, did not satisfactorily disprove the fact of widespread annexationist propaganda within the armed forces. The evidence on the subject is not sufficient to reach any definite conclusion on the extent of such propaganda,

---

[121] Lutz, *German Collapse*, pp. 235-36; *Frankfurter Zeitung*, April 29, 1918.
[122] *Reichstag*, vol. 310, pp. 3714 ff., 3767 ff 3778 ff.; Schäfer, *Leben*, p. 223.

but nobody reading the debates of October 6-9 can help being impressed by the material cited. The German government and army might outwardly dissociate themselves from the *Vaterlandspartei*; yet there can be little question that their sympathies continued to be with the annexationists rather than the more moderate Reichstag majority. If there is still any doubt on this score, it will disappear as we deal with the second important peace attempt of 1917, the Papal Peace Note of August 1.

The Papal Peace Note of August 1, 1917

The origin of the Vatican's peace move goes back to the last weeks of Bethmann Hollweg's administration, notably the conversation between Bethmann and Pacelli on June 26, 1917. The favorable reaction of the German government and the Reichstag's Peace Resolution, together with indications of Austria's desire for peace, prompted Pope Benedict, on August 1, to address a Peace Note to the belligerent powers.[123] Besides general statements about disarmament, international arbitration, and freedom of the seas, the Note referred to the basic questions of indemnities and territorial settlements. In regard to both, it suggested mutual renunciation; this would mean the evacuation of France and Belgium by Germany, in return for receiving back her colonies from the Allies. As for remaining territorial problems, such as France's demand for Alsace-Lorraine, they were to be settled by peace negotiation. What the Papal Note proposed, briefly, was the return to the *status quo ante bellum.*[124]

It is impossible to go into the details of the complicated negotiations connected with the Papal Note, between, as well as within, the belligerent powers. Germany's policy, to a varying degree, was determined by her civil and military authorities, with the Reichstag asserting its influence and claiming a voice in the deliberations. Parallel developments, notably the peace feelers sent directly to Great Britain by Germany's new foreign secretary, Richard von Kühlmann, complicated the situation still further. As perhaps the most important attempt at a negotiated peace during the whole course of the war, the events of August and September 1917 have been the subject of considerable research; yet thus far no satisfactory answer has been given to some of their

[123] Lama, pp. 72-75.   [124] Forster, pp. 128-29.

more puzzling aspects and to the question of how close they came to being successful.[125]

The Papal Note was handed to the German government on August 15.[126] Before that date, however, important developments had occurred, clarifying the government's stand on war aims, which had been somewhat ambiguous since the Peace Resolution. On July 24, five days after that Resolution had passed the Reichstag, Pacelli once again visited Berlin, this time presenting a more specific peace program of seven points which closely resembled the later Note of August 1.[127] Michaelis' reaction to these terms was favorable, yet he held that a definite answer could not be given before Vienna had been consulted. This was done at a meeting between Michaelis and Czernin on August 1. Germany's comments on the Pacelli note of July 24, presented on that occasion, demanded that, together with her former colonies, she receive additional overseas holdings at the peace conference. The settlement of Franco-German territorial issues and the conditions of Belgium's restitution should be left to separate negotiations.[128] These terms differed little from those drawn up in November 1916 as basis for Germany's Peace Note of December 12, 1916. Eight months of growing peace sentiment, culminating in the July Resolution, apparently had little effect upon the German government's official war aims. This fact was borne out further at a discussion in Kreuznach on August 9 between Chancellor and Supreme Command. In regard to Belgium it was recognized that the future of Anglo-German relations depended upon the fate of that country. Still the army, for military reasons, repeated its demands of April 23, 1917. " Belgium must remain in our hands as a special state, so as to enable us to draw up troops along the Franco-Belgian frontier, protected against England by the Flemish coast. . . . In case we cannot thus chain Belgium to ourselves, we must at least have Liège and the adjacent terrain to the north, for the protection of the industrial region of Aix-la-Chapelle." [129] Luxemburg should

---

[125] Lama's books, despite their bias, present a wealth of material. See also Forster, pp. 126-41; Brunauer, *Peace Proposals*, pp. 176 ff.; Johnson, pp. 30-39; M. Spahn, *Die päpstliche Friedensvermittlung* (Berlin, 1919); Meinecke, *Erinnerungen*, p. 230; and especially R. von Kühlmann, *Erinnerungen* (Heidelberg, 1948), pp. 475 ff.

[126] Lama, p. 82.

[127] *Ibid.*, p. 66.

[128] R. Fester, *Die Politik Kaiser Karls*, p. 191.

[129] *U. A.*, 4. Reihe, XII (1), 98, 205.

eventually be united with Germany. As to France, " the coal and iron region of Briey-Longwy (together with its northward projection into Belgium) is economically indispensable to us. About the form of this political union, French feeling may be taken into consideration. A westward extension of Metz's sphere of influence, however, is desirable." [130]

These were the terms given to Czernin when he again visited the German capital on August 14-15. But while on August 1 Michaelis had been anxious to conclude peace before winter set in, the Kreuznach conversations had changed his views. Peace was still desirable, he held, yet the first move had to come from the Allies. Czernin's suggestion that Germany give up Alsace-Lorraine in exchange for Poland was emphatically refused and the demands of the Supreme Command of August 9 were repeated instead. Especially in Belgium, " far-reaching military and economic influence " was to be secured.[131] Czernin in turn pointed out that neither the Allies nor Belgium would ever give in to such terms, which presented " a severe obstacle to peace " and were in direct opposition to the aims of the Reichstag majority.[132] Yet the matter actually was no longer in the hands of the Chancellor. Negotiations during the first half of August clearly indicated that the spirit of the Peace Resolution was dead and that Michaelis was completely under the influence of Hindenburg and Ludendorff.

The Papal Note, as soon as it became generally known, aroused the opposition of the annexationists. " If Germany entered into negotiations on the Papal basis," the industrialist *Düsseldorfer Generalanzeiger* wrote, " she would emerge not only vanquished, but ruined for all time." [133] The Independent Committee likewise protested to Michaelis against the restitution of Belgium, which was emerging as the central point of the Pope's appeal for peace.[134] The *Vaterlandspartei* held its first large meeting of protest in late September with many annexationist speeches, notably one by Admiral Tirpitz.[135] " Why does the Pope step forward at this precise moment? " Gottfried Traub asked on August 30, " I know

[130] *Ibid.*, pp. 205-06; Rupprecht, II, 238, 244, 247.

[131] *U. A.*, 4. Reihe, XII (1), 99, 206-08.

[132] Czernin, p. 219.

[133] *Düsseldorfer Generalanzeiger*, Aug. 19, 1917; *Kreuzzeitung*, Aug. 18, 1917; *Reichsbote*, Aug. 17, 1917.

[134] Schäfer, *Leben*, p. 215.

[135] Deutsche Vaterlandspartei, *Deutsche Ziele* (Berlin, 1917), *passim*.

no other answer but because England is in a bad way. . . . Why in the very year of the jubilee of the Reformation should we accept a peace negotiated by the Pope? " [136]　The purely political issue of the Papal Note was thus transformed into a religious one.

This was the general situation when, on August 20, Michaelis called a preliminary meeting with the party leaders to discuss the Papal Note. General agreement was registered on the refusal to give up Alsace-Lorraine, while on the future of Belgium considerable difference of opinion prevailed. The Chancellor took this occasion to try and explain away the clause " as I understand it " of his July 19 speech and to assure the parties once more of his loyalty towards the Reichstag Resolution. Yet the Social Democrats expressed their suspicion of his stand on war aims. It was becoming increasingly evident that Michaelis' attitude was merely one of paying lip-service to the Resolution. At the same time, however, a speech by von Kühlmann, favoring right rather than might as guiding principle of a successful foreign policy was well received.[137]　Baron von Kühlmann had succeeded Zimmermann on August 6 when the latter's involvement in a series of diplomatic blunders made his continuation in office impossible. At 44, the new Foreign Secretary could already look back upon a successful diplomatic career, including the important position as First Secretary at the German Embassy in London at the outbreak of war. In this latter capacity he had conducted the negotiations for an Anglo-German colonial agreement, intended to decrease the tension between the two countries. During the war he had represented Germany at the Hague and in Constantinople. An able diplomat he combined an acute business sense with an artistic temperament. Unlike von Jagow and Zimmermann before him, whose activities had been overshadowed by the influence and personality of Bethmann, Kühlmann, during the few months he was in office, was to play an influential role. Despite his background—he owned an estate in Bavaria and his father had been director of the Anatolian Railway—which should have predestined him for the conservative-annexationist camp, he had the reputation of being moderate, liberal, and an Anglophile.[138]　Shortly after he became Foreign

---

[136] *Magdeburger Zeitung*, Aug. 31, 1917.

[137] Helfferich, pp. 477-79; Michaelis, pp. 358 ff.

[138] Wolff, *Vollendete Tatsachen*, pp. 215-16; H. Nicolson, " Marginal Comment," *The Spectator*, March 2, 1945, p. 194; Meinecke, *Erinnerungen*, pp. 204-10, 217-18.

Secretary Kühlmann defined his views on foreign policy in a memorandum addressed to Michaelis. Its basic idea was that Germany's
military and domestic situation required the earliest possible conclusion of peace. While the question of Alsace-Lorraine made any
compromise between Germany and France impossible, Kühlmann
held, the situation with regard to England was different. " Once
the leading English statesmen know for sure that the specifically
British aims (freedom of the Belgian coast and liberation of Belgium in general) can be had without a winter campaign, we can
be certain that they will press France to give up her aspirations in
Alsace-Lorraine." [139] It should be Germany's aim, therefore, to
approach England with concessions on the question of Belgium and
thus drive a wedge between the Allies. These views, of course,
were much closer to the Papal Note than the aims expressed at
the Kreuznach discussion of August 9. It seemed as though the
moderates had found their champion in Richard von Kühlmann.

On August 21 a Committee of Seven had been appointed by
the Reichstag to represent its views in drafting the answer to
Benedict XV. The Committee consisted of five members from
the majority parties — Erzberger, Fehrenbach, the Progressive
Wiemer and the Socialists Ebert and Scheidemann—and two from
the parties of the Right—Westarp and Stresemann.[140] Its first
meeting took place on August 28. Michaelis, Kühlmann, and several members of the *Bundesrat* were likewise present. The question of Belgium again occupied the center of discussion, the representatives of the majority parties asking that Germany, in her
answer to the Pope, make a clear statement on the future of Belgium. The only open opposition to such a statement came from
Westarp, who wanted to wait and let the Allies take the first step.
Michaelis apparently agreed with this, as did Kühlmann, the latter
in a private conversation with Westarp. An open statement on
Belgium, he felt, would impose unilateral restrictions on the German
government.[141]

Up to the end of August, the situation was relatively simple;
but now suddenly complications arose, chiefly because of the at-

---

The most revealing source on Kühlmann is his *Erinnerungen*. T. Rhodes, *The Real
von Kühlmann* (London, 1925) is of little value.
[139] Korostowetz, pp. 296-98. For an excellent brief analysis of Kühlmann's aims
by a close friend, see Meinecke, *Erinnerungen*, pp. 205-08.
[140] Lama, pp. 108 ff.
[141] Scheidemann, *Zusammenbruch*, pp. 106 ff.; Westarp, II, 535.

tempts of Kühlmann and Michaelis to enter into direct negotiations with Great Britain, using Madrid rather than Rome as intermediary. There were several indications of England's willingness to discuss peace, avoiding the obstacle of Alsace-Lorraine and arriving at the kind of settlement which Kühlmann suggested in his September 3 memorandum. At the same time, on August 30, another letter of Pacelli's arrived, which quoted a statement of the British government to the effect that a German declaration on the future of Belgium was a prerequisite of any future negotiations. The Pope, therefore, urged the German government to state clearly its intention of granting Belgium's independence, with reparation for all damages caused by the war, and to specify what guarantees Germany would require for ensuring Belgium's political, military, and economic neutrality. Here, then, were two separate peace moves. For reasons never quite clear, Michaelis and Kühlmann decided to rely on the latter's British contacts rather than on the mediation of the Holy See.[142] The results of such a decision were twofold: First of all, the answer to the Papal Note had to be treated in a dilatory fashion; or, if that should prove impossible, it had to be framed as vaguely as possible, so as not to weaken Germany's bargaining position through an early declaration on Belgium. In addition, the Kaiser and the Supreme Command had to be won over to Kühlmann's plan for secret negotiations with Great Britain, in which the restitution of Belgium was to be used as bait, inducing England to talk peace and to force France to do the same.

The answer to the Papal Note of August 1 was to be the subject of a second meeting of the Committee of Seven on September 10. The task before Michaelis and Kühlmann was to dissuade the representatives of the majority parties from demanding a statement on Belgium. The plans for direct Anglo-German negotiations were considered too delicate to be divulged to the Committee, though hints were dropped to the main advocate of a declaration on Belgium, Scheidemann, on September 9.[143] The Pacelli letter of August 30, with its demand for such a declaration, was likewise kept from the Committee. Michaelis and Kühlmann

---

[142] Brunauer, "Peace Proposals," pp. 181 ff.; Lama, pp. 149 ff. In his Memoirs, published after the completion of this study, Kühlmann gives as the main reason for his decision his knowledge that the French government intended to give a negative reply to the Papal Note. Kühlmann, pp. 477, 486-87.

[143] Scheidemann, *Zusammenbruch*, pp. 110-11.

succeeded at the meeting of September 10 in keeping a specific reference to Belgium out of the answer to the Pope, though as a compromise a reference to the July Peace Resolution was included.[144] Despite the fact that Pacelli, who on September 13 was shown a draft of this vague reply, told Michaelis that it was unsatisfactory and would most likely mean the end of the Pope's peace efforts, the document was officially communicated to Rome on September 19.[145]

The door to a peace of understanding through papal mediation was thus being closed, though not completely shut. There was still Pacelli's letter of August 30, emphasizing the significance of Belgium and asking for a specific statement about its future. Yet this chance was likewise spoiled on September 24 in a letter from Michaelis to Pacelli, which said that at present a statement on Belgium was impossible, but that "before too long" the Imperial government hoped to be more specific.[146] By the end of September, therefore, the Papal peace move had definitely failed. Still, there remained the possibility of direct negotiations with England, and it was this second peace attempt which now begins to occupy the center of the stage.

The Bellevue Conference

The plans for a separate peace with England were the subject of a special "Crown Council" meeting on September 11 at the Bellevue Palace in Berlin. The Kaiser had been first informed of this peace plan on September 9, and he had agreed that it might present a good chance for terminating the war. The night prior to the Bellevue conference, however, Michaelis was roused by an Imperial messenger, bearing a letter from William II in which he objected to the plan submitted to him the previous day. The navy, the message said, had been promised the Flanders coast, and it was necessary, therefore, to keep some hold over the Belgian port of Zeebrugge and to acquire additional naval stations in the Mediterranean. Kühlmann, when he learned of the Kaiser's change of heart, was ready to hand in his resignation; yet in a talk between William II and Michaelis on the morning of September 11,

---

[144] *Ibid.*, p. 113; Erzberger, p. 279; Westarp, II, 536; Lama, pp. 201 ff., 270 ff.; Kühlmann, pp. 478-79, 484-85.

[145] *U. A.*, 4. Reihe, VII (2), 28-29.

[146] *Ibid.*, VII (1), 76. On the still less favorable Allied attitude see Forster, pp. 130-31.

the Emperor again gave his Chancellor a free hand in respect to Belgium.[147]

The Bellevue Conference was opened by Michaelis, who hinted at existing peace possibilities which required Germany's unconditional renunciation of Belgium. Both Hindenburg and Ludendorff agreed to give up the Flanders coast; yet the latter insisted on maintaining Germany's hold over Liège and its neighborhood to protect the Rhineland industrial region. The Chief of the Admiralty, Admiral von Holtzendorff, moreover, insisted on the necessity of holding the coastal region as well. Michaelis and Kühlmann once more pleaded their case for a clear statement on Belgium and finally appealed to the Emperor for a decision. William agreed with their view of the situation and gave Michaelis a free hand for his negotiations, provided they would be successful before the end of the year. At the same time he asked the Supreme Command and the navy to concur in his decision.[148] To all appearances, the results of the conference were highly favorable to the plans of Kühlmann and Michaelis. Yet a closer analysis of the attitude of the major participants during and shortly after the meeting reveals quite a different picture.

The Chancellor's opposition to the Supreme Command during the Bellevue Conference certainly was a departure from his earlier subservience to the wishes of Hindenburg and Ludendorff. For once he had freed himself from the Supreme Command's influence—or so it seemed. The following day, September 12, he sent separate letters to the Kaiser and the Army and Navy Commands, summing up the conversations of the previous day. His letter to the Kaiser mentioned the exclusion of English influence and the solution of the Flemish question, but was emphatic on the restitution of Belgium. Not so the letters to Hindenburg and Holtzendorff. " I incorporate into our plans for negotiation," he wrote to the Field-Marshal, " as demands of the Supreme Command, which in your opinion must be maintained, that both of you [Hindenburg

---

[147] Michaelis, pp. 344-45. For a slightly different version, see Kühlmann, pp. 480-81.

[148] Helfferich, pp. 479-80; Michaelis, pp. 347-50; Ludendorff, *Kriegserinnerungen*, pp. 415 ff.; Ludendorff, *Urkunden*, pp. 428 ff. According to Kühlmann, Hindenburg and Ludendorff also opposed giving up the Flanders coast. To make everyone feel better the Kaiser then promised that after victory his navy would visit the ports of South America and enforce the payment of high reparations. Kühlmann had these remarks omitted from the minutes. Kühlmann, p. 482.

and Ludendorff] demand, for the protection of our western industry, first of all Liège and the surrounding area." In addition
Michaelis mentioned the close economic *Anschluss* between Belgium and Germany.[149] The courage with which Michaelis defended
his stand on the Belgian question at the Bellevue Conference had
deserted him almost immediately. It took a stronger man than
this unimaginative Prussian official to stand up to the overpower-
ing influence of Hindenburg and Ludendorff. The choice before
Michaelis was to adopt the moderate and conciliatory policy of the
Reichstag majority, or the strong and aggressive policy of the
opposition, the annexationists, and the Supreme Command. His
social and political background predetermined his choice in favor
of the second alternative; and both the army and the navy were
ready to take advantage of the Chancellor's change of heart.[150]

On September 14, Ludendorff, in the form of a lengthy memorandum, laid down the main points of his statement at the Bellevue
meeting.[151] Stressing the fact that the position of the Allies, both
at home and at the front was not so favorable as that of the Central Powers, he advocated an early peace only on condition that it
would secure Germany's economic and military future. In the
west, therefore, protection of Germany's industrial regions was a
prime necessity. The iron basin of Lorraine, he held, needed a protective barrier. The fact that this barrier at the same time included
additional iron mines was of added advantage to Germany's limited
supply of ore. The Ruhr, likewise, required for its protection the
fortress of Liège and adjacent territories. Annexation of the Meuse
region as far south as St. Vith was the only means of securing the
strategic security of northwestern Germany. In addition, the General wrote, " We must push back the Anglo-French army still
further. This can only be done by joining Belgium so closely to
ourselves economically, that she will also seek political *Anschluss*.
The economic *Anschluss* cannot be realized without strong military
pressure through extended occupation and without seizing Liège.
The neutrality of Belgium is a phantom which cannot really be
counted upon." As for Flanders, Ludendorff held, it would only
become a vital necessity to Germany if England should gain a foothold on the continent, at Calais for instance. Otherwise Belgium's

---

[149] Michaelis, pp. 352-53; Westarp, II, 493.
[150] Michaelis, pp. 325 ff.
[151] Ludendorff, *Urkunden*, pp. 428 ff.; Westarp, II, 552 ff.

economic union with Germany and the separation of the Flemings and Walloons would suffice. Such co-operation between Germany and Belgium, furthermore, would draw Holland into Germany's orbit and give the latter a still stronger position against England. A large colonial empire in Africa, commercial concessions in South America, a series of naval stations, and close commercial ties with Denmark completed Ludendorff's set of war aims.[152] Their primary motive, of course, was military, and their justification was approved by simultaneous statements of German strategic experts.[153] In view of the belief, held in military circles, that France and England contemplated improving their military collaboration by means of one or two underwater tunnels, and in view of the proximity of Germany's western industrial regions to the frontier, such strategic considerations have a certain degree of plausibility. Yet by the middle of 1917 it was no longer a question of how to achieve the most ideal post-war strategic position for Germany, but rather how to make the most of a situation which, despite outstanding military successes in the past, was none too favorable.[154]

The motives of the Supreme Command, however, were not exclusively military, even though Ludendorff tries to give that impression.[155] In view of the close relationship between industrialists and the leaders of the army, it was more than a mere coincidence that the projected westward extension of Germany's Lorraine border covered almost exactly the valuable Briey-Longwy region.[156] As for Belgium, there was the same co-existence of military and economic motives. The annexation of the Liège district was to be accompanied by German economic penetration of the whole country. On September 16, in a talk with Count Westarp, Ludendorff defined more closely the term "economic penetration," asking for a customs-union with Germany, community of railways and ports, uniform laws of banking and exchange, common social legislation, and penetration of Belgium's industry, specifically the Campine region, by German capital, with forced liquidation of French holdings.[157]

[152] Ludendorff, *Urkunden*, pp. 432-33.

[153] *U. A.*, 4. Reihe, II, 108; Ludendorff, *Urkunden*, p. 432 note.

[154] *U. A.*, 4. Reihe, II, 117-18; H. von Kuhl, *Der Weltkrieg 1914-1918* (Berlin, 1929), p. 272.

[155] Ludendorff, *Kriegserinnerungen*, p. 415.

[156] Ludendorff, *Urkunden*, p. 432 note.

[157] Westarp, II, 552.

Here we have a set of war aims which go further than anything the German government had ever proclaimed during the first three years of the war. On September 15, 1917, four days after the Bellevue meeting, and encouraged by Michaelis' letter several days earlier, Hindenburg sent the Chancellor Ludendorff's memorandum of September 14, stating that it was " entirely in accordance " with his own views. In the same letter he stressed the necessity for an extensive military occupation of Belgium by German forces and objected to the idea " that there should be any question of compensation " for war damages on the part of Germany.[158] On September 27 Hindenburg requested Michaelis to deny the rumour that the Crown Council had given up Belgium, a request which the Chancellor fulfilled promptly, as we shall see. Only the Flanders coast, Hindenburg held, had been relinquished at Bellevue, and only on condition that peace would be won before the end of the year.[159] As far as the Supreme Command was concerned, the agreement reached on September 11 was dead, or at least its original interpretation had been basically changed.

A further attack on the Bellevue program was launched by the navy. On September 14, Holtzendorff wrote the following letter to Michaelis:

I beg to be allowed to make clear once more . . . that the annexation of Belgium as such has never been advocated by me. On the other hand, since my appointment to my present post, I have met with His Majesty's complete assent as well as that of the Supreme Command to the demand for the maintenance of our maritime position on the Flemish coast. . . . Opinion must be unanimous with regard to the great importance inherent in the retention of the maritime triangle Zeebrugge-Bruges-Ostend, in German hands—that is the kernel of the demands I have advocated. What the surrender of this stretch of coast would mean for the future prosperous and peaceful development of the German Empire is apparently underestimated in many quarters. His Majesty's remark that we should not be spared the Second Punic War obliged me to point out that I am firmly convinced that this war will be directly provoked if Germany remains unprotected on the Flemish coast. These are the reasons why I must advise holding on to our position there.[160]

Hindenburg's letter of September 15 supported the Admiral's claims. " I cannot conceal from myself," it said, " that in the navy

---

[158] *U. A.*, 4. Reihe, II, 140; III, 314.
[159] *Ibid.*, p. 318.
[160] *Ibid.*, II, 141.

and in extensive patriotic circles a renunciation of the Flemish coast will be felt as a heavy blow which will be tempered only if the compensations adjudged by Your Excellency to the navy become actual facts. General Ludendorff and I think of these compensations as taking the form of naval bases in and outside of our colonies." [161] Finally, in a personal letter to the Chancellor on September 15, Germany's former Secretary of the Navy, Admiral von Tirpitz, expressed similar views. Opinion on the strategic importance of the Flanders coast, however, was by no means unanimous. Unofficial naval experts (such as Vice-Admiral Galster and Captain Persius) pointed out that while the possession of that region would fail to open the English Channel to Germany, it would prove a permanent thorn in England's side and thus a constant danger to world peace. Germany would become committed to a naval policy far beyond her means and out of character with a primarily continental power.[162]

As for the Kaiser's attitude towards the Michaelis-Kühlmann proposal of September 11, it had not been entirely positive either but had hinted at certain compensations or necessary conditions to be fulfilled in return for Germany's restitution of Belgium. These included the exclusion of England's influence over Belgium, economic safeguards, and the solution of the Flemish question.[163] We have already mentioned William's hesitation and change of heart prior to the Bellevue Conference. In a long letter to Michaelis, written in October 1926, William II once more explained his attitude: "I naturally had to attach certain conditions to the final and complete renunciation of Belgium, which I felt absolutely necessary in the interest of securing a future peace." [164] The Crown-Prince, who had likewise taken part in the Bellevue meeting, was more moderate than his father. He afterwards confided to Helfferich that any opportunity for a decent peace had to be seized and that such a peace should not fail because of a single German demand, no matter how important.[165] Count Czernin tells of a visit he paid the Prince on the western front in the fall of 1917, finding him extremely moderate and conciliatory. When the Aus-

[161] Lutz, *German Collapse*, p. 46.

[162] K. Galster, " Flandern," *Preussische Jahrbücher*, vol. 170 (1917), pp. 117-21; *Frankfurter Zeitung*, Nov. 21, 1917; Persius, pp. 66 ff.

[163] *U. A.*, 4. Reihe, VII (1), 75-76; Michaelis, pp. 349-50.

[164] *U. A.*, 4. Reihe, VII (2), 14-15.

[165] Helfferich, p. 480.

trian Foreign Minister met Ludendorff shortly afterwards, the latter reproached him: " What have you done to our Crown Prince? He has suddenly been ' deflated.' But we have re-inflated him." [166]

If in the light of these various qualifying statements made by the participants in the Bellevue Conference we once more appraise its results, we come to the conclusion that it did anything but pronounce in favor of the unconditional and complete restoration of Belgium. Yet the rumour that it had done just that leaked out during the week following September 11 and produced the usual reaction in annexationist circles. " A cry of holy wrath would go through the nation," the *Tägliche Rundschau* wrote, " if it proved true, this story that no semi-official writer today dares to deny." The *National-Liberale Korrespondenz*, official organ of the National Liberal Party wrote: " It is quite unthinkable that the German government should declare that it has no interest in the fate of Belgium. It is quite out of the question that Germany should ever again withdraw her protecting hand from the Flemings, who have come by the destined course of this war into a saving contact with their former Motherland." The Conservative *Kreuzzeitung* reprimanded the government for its unbusinesslike attitude in the matter of Belgium. " The man who, when he puts up his horse for sale, offers it with the statement that he is already resolved on no account to keep it, that he has no moral right to do so, and that he can only do so to his own detriment, will not get much of a price for it." The rest of the annexationist press wrote along similar lines.[167] This annexationist outcry, produced in some cases at the instigation of Ludendorff, put additional pressure upon the already wavering government.[168] On September 28, the Chancellor found it necessary, at Hindenburg's request, to declare before the Main Committee of the Reichstag, that the German government still had an entirely free hand for possible peace negotiations, also as far as Belgium was concerned.[169]

Despite these developments, Kühlmann, who had not been

[166] Czernin, p. 97; Bethmann Hollweg, II, 209; Naumann, *Profile*, pp. 125-26; Rupprecht, II, 336. The Bavarian Crown Prince was equally moderate, while his father clung to his annexationist views as late as January 1918: *Naumann, Dokumente*, pp. 256, 263, 328-29.

[167] Great Britain, *Enemy Supplement*, II, Oct. 4, 1917, pp. 689 ff.; Oct. 11, 1917, pp. 729 ff.

[168] Knesebeck, p. 162; Ludendorff, *Urkunden*, pp. 445-46.

[169] Helfferich, p. 491.

informed of Michaelis' correspondence with the Emperor and the Supreme Command, proceeded with his secret negotiations, on the assumption that the decisions reached at Bellevue were still valid.[170] Using his friend, the Marquis de Villalobar, Spanish ambassador to Brussels, as an intermediary, Kühlmann sent a message to England, declaring Germany's willingness to enter into peace negotia tions on the basis of complete restoration of Belgium and the corre sponding Allied guarantee of Germany's territorial integrity. There are still several doubtful points in the history of the Villalobar mediation, such as the uncertainty whether the full statement on Belgium was ever communicated to the British.[171] In addition, Anglo-French confidence, strengthened by the knowledge of Czernin's April 12 memorandum which revealed the weakness of Austria, was less receptive for offers of a negotiated peace. The German move was deprived of its secrecy when Balfour put it before a meeting of Allied diplomatic representatives on October 6, 1917. By the middle of October, Germany's secret negotiations with England, themselves largely responsible for the failure of the simultaneous Papal Peace Note, had in turn failed to achieve their objective.[172]

The Fall of Michaelis

The Papal Note, as one of the most serious attempts to reach a negotiated peace, has been the object of considerable speculation. In trying to determine the causes of its failure, we may say generally that neither the Allies nor Germany were ready and in a desperate enough military position to be wholeheartedly in favor of returning to the absolute *status quo ante bellum*. In the case of Germany, the failure of the Kerensky government to carry out its summer offensive foretold the imminent breakdown of Russia, which in turn would enable Germany to concentrate her forces in a knockout blow against the west. The German Supreme Command saw every reason to be optimistic.

It has been said with much justification that a clear statement by the German government on the future of Belgium, such as was desired by the majority of the Reichstag and by many influential

---

[170] *U. A.*, 4. Reihe, VII (1), 10; Kühlmann, pp. 483-87.

[171] Lama, pp. 217 ff.; Meinecke, *Erinnerungen*, p. 218. Kühlmann, while stressing some of the difficulties of Villalobar's mission, does not fully explain its failure. Kühlmann, pp. 485-86.

[172] Forster, pp. 137-38.

people throughout Germany, might have strengthened the moderate groups within the Allied countries and facilitated the opening of peace negotiations.[173] The responsibility for this failure to include a specific reference to Belgium in the various communications to the Holy See must be sought somewhere among the people responsible for drafting these communications, and here the Chancellor takes first place. The dominating influence of the Supreme Command over his decisions largely explains the two-faced and vacillating policy of Michaelis and it is unnecessary to attribute his sabotage of the Papal peace efforts to his ardent Protestantism, which objected to a peace settlement via the good offices of Rome.[174] Michaelis' letters of September 12 to Hindenburg and Holtzendorff show that his refusal to fulfill Pacelli's repeated requests for a declaration on Belgium had its roots in the Chancellor's real preference for the stronger war aims of the Supreme Command. This preference ultimately led him beyond the merely negative action of omitting a reference to Belgium from Germany's note to the Papacy of September 19. Michaelis' letter to Pacelli on September 24, which remained unknown to both Reichstag and Supreme Command, definitely mentioned that " the views and necessary demands of the Imperial government, especially with respect to Belgium," would be presented " in the not too distant future." This statement implied anything but the unconditional restitution of Belgium and presented an inexcusable digression from the policy laid down in the Chancellor's negotiations with the Committee of Seven. It was this letter which dealt the Papal Peace Note its final blow.[175]

More sincere was the attitude of the Foreign Secretary. If he was against an open statement on Belgium, it was because he adhered to the theory that such a valuable pledge should not be openly renounced without gaining some equally important concession in return.[176] A statement of his predecessor, Zimmermann, on October 4, supports this position. " Our negotiators," he wrote, " are not put in a very enviable position if everything is being sur-

---

[173] Max von Baden, p. 123; Haussmann, p. 144; Scheidemann, *Memoiren*, II, 89-92; H. Stegemann, pp. 389-90; Naumann, *Dokumente*, pp. 275-76, 278; M. Hoffmann, *Der Krieg der versäumten Gelegenheiten* (München, 1923), p. 232; *U. A.*, 4. Reihe, VII (1), 11.

[174] This is the main thesis of von Lama.

[175] *U. A.*, 4. Reihe, VIII, 147-48.

[176] *Ibid.*, pp. 136-37.

rendered before we sit down at the conference table." [177]   On September 20, the moderate Colonel von Haeften asked Kühlmann to make a public statement on Belgium, hinting that the Supreme Command would approve such action.   The Secretary, however, refused " to sell this particular horse " at this time, saving it for a better bargain.   This incident has earned Kühlmann much reproach.   Yet it should be pointed out that the public statement, desired by the Supreme Command, was to include a reference to " the economic *Anschluss* of Belgium to the German Reich," which would immediately and finally have spoiled whatever chances for an Anglo-German rapprochement existed at the time.[178]   The chief reproach against Kühlmann should be that he overestimated the willingness of the British government to come to an agreement with Germany and consequently neglected the opportunity presented by the Papal Note of appealing to the more real peace sentiment among the Allied peoples.   For a professional diplomat, however, the Secretary's choice was logical, and compared to Michaelis, there is nothing to suggest that his action was due to annexationist sympathies or influences; it was entirely dictated by considerations of expediency.

The Reichstag's role in the developments of August and September 1917 is perhaps least to blame for the failure of the Papal peace effort.   It is true that the Committee of Seven should have insisted more firmly upon a clear statement on Belgium, to be included in the official German reply to the Pope, rather than be satisfied with a general reference to the July Resolution.[179]   Had its members been aware of Pacelli's letter of August 30, stressing the importance of such a statement, we can be certain that they would have insisted on its inclusion in the note of September 19. As it turned out, not only did Michaelis keep Pacelli's letter from the Committee, but, as we have just seen, he also answered it in a way which made it clear that Germany had no intention of giving up Belgium unconditionally.   It is most doubtful that a mere declaration on Belgium, which did not touch on such vital questions as Alsace-Lorraine and the South Tyrol, would have been

[177] Knesebeck, p. 107.

[178] Max von Baden, p. 145; Ludendorff, *Kriegserinnerungen*, p. 412; F. Meinecke, " Kühlmann und die Päpstliche Friedensaktion von 1917," *Sitzungsberichte der Preussischen Akademie der Wissenschaften* (Berlin, 1928), Phil.-Hist., pp. 174 ff., 187-90.

[179] *U. A.*, 4. Reihe, VIII, p. 381.

sufficient inducement for the Allies to enter into peace negotiations. One thing is certain, however, that without such a declaration Germany could never expect to get Great Britain to the conference table. If there was a real opportunity for a negotiated peace in the fall of 1917, through Germany's open renunciation of Belgium, the chief responsibility for its failure lies with Georg Michaelis.

It was not very long after the final steps in the Papal peace move had been taken, that the "Hundred Days" of Michaelis came to a sudden close. The initial misgivings about his lack of experience and ability had turned out to be only too true. Appointed without the consultation of the Reichstag, he had been unable to hide for very long the fact that on the crucial question of the Peace Resolution his views differed fundamentally from those of the majority parties. Nor was his stand on the issue of domestic reforms any more favorable. As early as December 1914, he had said: "What democrat can raise the demand for parliamentary government in Germany, after watching the pitiful fiasco of such government in England and of Republicanism in France?"[180] The resentment which his famous phrase "as I understand it" had caused among the majority parties, was equalled if not surpassed by the effect of his reference to internal affairs in the same speech. "I am not willing," he said, "to have the conduct of affairs taken from my hands."[181] In his Memoirs, Michaelis explains his failure to follow up Bethmann Hollweg's promise for the reform of the Prussian franchise:

I had to inherit from Bethmann the royal message concerning the introduction of equal franchise into Prussia. . . . The equal franchise was to increase the number of Social Democrats in the Prussian Lower House to far beyond one hundred. This rearrangement would have been achieved essentially at the expense of the parties of the Right, which would have meant a radical departure from hitherto prevailing Prussian policy. We therefore realized that all possible safeguards, capable of weakening these radical results, had to be worked into the franchise law as well as the bill concerning the Upper House.[182]

These divergences of opinion between Chancellor and Reichstag resulted in a succession of internal crises, of which the discussions in the Reichstag's Main Committee on August 22, and the Reichstag debates of October 6 were outstanding examples. The fact,

[180] Wolff, *Vollendete Tatsachen*, pp. 221-22.
[181] *Reichstag*, vol. 310, p. 3573.
[182] Michaelis, p. 365.

moreover, that the annexationist and Conservative press and the newly-founded *Vaterlandspartei* treated Michaelis as their man, did not improve his standing in the eyes of his numerous political opponents.[183] Ever since early September, therefore, forces were at work for his dismissal.

The whole matter came to a head in the Reichstag meeting of October 9. The Chancellor's opponents were already much worked up over the debate on annexationist propaganda within the armed forces, which had been going on since October 6. On October 9, the Independent Socialist Dittmann continued to attack this " Pan-German propaganda," and dealt with the recent disturbance in the German navy, as a result of which some sailors had been given sentences of death or life imprisonment " for expressing their political opinions." [184] Michaelis, after some very pointed remarks against the Independent Socialists, referred the matter to his Secretary of the Navy. The latter, Admiral von Capelle, asserted that three members of the Independent Socialist Reichstag delegation had been guilty of advising and assisting the crews of German warships in their plan to cripple the German fleet by a widespread campaign of disobedience.[185] His revelation came as a bombshell. Independent Socialists, Majority Socialists, Progressives and to a lesser extent the Center Party violently protested against this unsubstantiated attack upon their colleagues.

It is inconceivable [the Majority Socialist Ebert said] at a time when our country is in a most difficult position, when the unification of all our people's forces should be the government's highest duty, that the government should try to put part of our people—no matter how large or small— outside the law. . . . Such an act, such a declaration, could only be made by a government which . . . is unconscious of its great responsibility and unequal to its high and important task. . . . I say openly: we shall welcome each day that will bring us closer to the liberation of the German people from this government.[186]

Here we have the death-sentence of the Michaelis regime. Events now moved rapidly.[187] The majority parties, with the collaboration

---

[183] Valentini, p. 173.

[184] *Reichstag*, vol. 310, pp. 3766 ff.; *U. A.*, 4. Reihe, IX (1 & 2), *passim*; H. Neu, *Die Revolutionäre Bewegung auf der Deutschen Flotte 1917-1918* (Stuttgart, 1930).

[185] *Reichstag*, vol. 310, pp. 3773-74.

[186] *Ibid.*, p. 3794.

[187] On the events of Oct. 9 and after see Helfferich, *Weltkrieg*, pp. 505 ff.; Westarp, II, 483 ff.; Valentini, pp. 174 ff.; *U. A.*, 4. Reihe, VIII, 100 ff.

of the National Liberals, held a series of joint meetings and drew up a letter to the Emperor, suggesting the appointment of a new Chancellor.   Against such pressure, there was little William II could do, especially since the question of war credits was about to become acute once again.   Among possible candidates suggested from various sides to succeed Michaelis, were Prince Bülow, Max von Baden, von Kühlmann, Count Hatzfeld, Solf, and Count Hertling.   Michaelis was most reluctant to give up the position in which he had cut such an unfortunate figure.   For a while it appeared as though the Chancellorship and the Prussian Prime-Ministership, traditionally united in one person, might be held separately, the Bavarian Count Hertling taking over the former and Michaelis remaining in the latter.   In view of the fact, however, that as Prime Minister of Prussia Michaelis could have obstructed the necessary franchise reforms, such a suggestion met the opposition of the majority parties.   On October 31, therefore, Michaelis resigned, and the following day Count Hertling was appointed Chancellor of the Reich.

Chapter V

THE VICTORY OF THE ANNEXATIONISTS —
THE DEFEAT OF GERMANY
(NOVEMBER 1917–SEPTEMBER 1918)

THE HISTORY of German war aims during the last year of the war, particularly as concerns Western Europe, is a melancholy tale. The struggle between the Reichstag majority and the expansionists ended with a victory of the latter, and whatever expectations had been aroused by the Peace Resolution and the Papal Peace Note were now shattered. While the majority of Germans still clung to the futile hope of an early negotiated peace, a small minority of annexationists, with the active co-operation of the Supreme Command and the acquiescence of a weak civil government, continued to pursue its ambitious policy to the bitter end.

Count Hertling and the Supreme Command

The circumstances of Count Hertling's appointment differed most significantly from the selection of his predecessor. While in Michaelis' case the Reichstag had not been informed, let alone consulted, the days prior to November 1 were spent in careful negotiations with the leaders of the majority parties. There were a number of objections to Hertling's candidacy, and it was due chiefly to Kühlmann's successful handling of the situation that the parties finally gave their support to the Bavarian Prime Minister.[1] Parliamentary government had won a triumph. For the first time in the history of the German Empire, the Reichstag had been able to overthrow a Chancellor entirely by itself and to take part in the selection of his successor. Not only that—in discussions with Hertling, prior to his appointment, the inter-party committee, made up of the majority parties and National Liberals, had secured his adherence to a five-point program which included a demand for the earliest possible presentation of a Prussian franchise bill, less stringent handling of censorship and assembly restrictions, and

---

[1] Max von Baden, pp. 150-51; Helfferich, *Weltkrieg*, p. 512.

in the field of foreign policy the program laid down in the answer to the Pope of September 13, 1917, i. e., the note sent to Rome on September 19. It is this last point which is of chief interest here. Instead of tying the new Chancellor to a definite program of war aims in general and the crucial problem of Belgium in particular, this demand was at best a veiled adherence to the vague Peace Resolution of July 19, 1917, which could be interpreted almost any way. The Reichstag had missed its opportunity of imposing a moderate peace program upon the new government. Maybe the fact that besides Hertling's appointment, the Progressive von Payer and the National Liberal Friedberg were made Vice-Chancellor and Vice-President of the Prussian Ministerial Council respectively, was considered sufficient guarantee for a moderate governmental course.[2]

The selection of Hertling, on the whole, seemed a fortunate one. As President of the *Bundesrat's* Committee on Foreign Affairs he had gained experience in the field of foreign policy. He also looked back on a distinguished parliamentary career as member of the Reichstag from 1875 to 1912, a valuable asset in future dealings with that body. In addition, as one of the outstanding members of the Center Party's conservative wing, he could expect to command the allegiance of this important party. And finally, in view of growing friction between Bavaria and Prussia, the appointment of a South-German seemed a singularly astute move. The most apparent drawback to the new Chancellor was his age—he was over 75. It remained to be seen to what extent the old gentleman was capable of holding his own against Germany's real rulers, the Supreme Command.

The first weeks of Hertling's chancellorship were a most promising period of domestic peace, embellished by spectacular successes of Austro-German forces on the Isonzo front. The public discussion of war aims and peace negotiations was temporarily in abeyance. In private conversation the Chancellor expressed moderate views, favoring a peace of understanding, opposing annexations, and approving plans for the exploitation of the Briey-Longwy region by way of commercial agreements rather than through annexation.[3] On November 29, Hertling delivered his inaugural address before the Reichstag. On war aims his statements were noncommittal:

[2] *U. A.*, 4. Reihe, VIII, 106-07.   [3] Naumann, *Dokumente*, pp. 297-98.

From the first day our war aim has been the defense of the Fatherland, the inviolability of its territory, and the freedom and independence of its economic life. We are therefore able to greet the Pope's appeal for peace with joy. The spirit from which our reply to the Papal Note proceeded still lives today, but our enemies should understand once and for all—this answer signifies no *carte blanche* for a criminal prolongation of the war. For the continuation of this terrible massacre, for the destruction of irreplaceable cultural values, for the insane mutilation of Europe, our enemies alone bear the responsibility. They will have to bear the consequences.[4]

Hertling's statements on other vital issues, notably internal reforms, were no more specific. The fact, however, that on December 5 the Prussian Reform Bill was officially presented to the Prussian Lower House quieted any fears on that count.

The high respect of his former Reichstag colleagues and the sufficiently ambiguous character of his statements made for a friendly reception of Hertling by almost all parties.[5] "We consider the new government an improvement," Scheidemann said, "provided that it sticks to its program." Count Westarp expressed the "deep respect" of himself and his political friends for the new Chancellor. He objected, however, to the inclusion of the Peace Resolution into Germany's answer to the Pope, which Hertling had indicated in his speech. Stresemann raised a similar objection but then went on to say that the Peace Resolution had been superseded by events anyway and did therefore no longer tie the hands of the government. Only the Independent Socialist Haase injected a critical note into his speech, citing a statement which Hertling was reported to have made earlier before the Bavarian Lower House. "No binding promises concerning the Belgian question have been made to Rome," Hertling had said, "and it would not be advisable to make any definite proposals about Belgium at this time. . . . The *status quo ante*, especially in regard to Belgium, is no longer possible, the Belgium *quo ante* does no longer exist." Haase also read a telegram which Hindenburg had sent in reply to a congratulatory message of the Pan-German League. "Every one must admit," it concluded, "that our Rhenish-Westphalian industry would be greatly endangered through a Belgian state leaning towards England and France." Here were indications that the attitude of the government would not be greatly changed with the

---

[4] *Reichstag*, vol. 311, pp. 3945-46.
[5] For the following see *ibid.*, pp. 3949, 3953, 3961.

appointment of a new chief executive. Additional proof of this fact was to appear shortly.

On November 29, the prominent British Conservative and ex-Foreign Secretary, Lord Lansdowne, wrote a letter to the *Daily Telegraph,* urging the conclusion of an early peace and pointing to Belgium as the most significant issue of the war.[6] Like the peace-feelers in late September, Lansdowne's letter failed to have any specific results, though it testified again to the central significance of the Belgian question. What was the new Chancellor's attitude on that question? The Supreme Command was determined to find out. On December 11, 1917, Hindenburg suggested to Hertling a re-definition of Germany's Belgian aims:

The basis of our intentions in Belgium is the memorandum of the Kreuznach discussion on April 23, 1917, approved by his Majesty the Kaiser: " Belgium will continue to exist and will be taken under German military control until it is ripe politically and economically for a defensive and offensive alliance with Germany. . . . Nevertheless, for reasons of military strategy, Liège and the Flanders coast, including Bruges, will remain permanently in Germany's possession (or on a 99-year lease). The cession of this territory is an imperative condition for peace with England. The foreland of Liège must include Tongeren and the railway line Liège-Stavelt-Malmédy. . . . The occupation must secure the advance of the German army against France on the Franco-Belgian frontier." The Supreme Command repeated these demands at the conference in Kreuznach with Your Excellency's predecessor on the 9th August, 1917. . . . In the discussion presided over by His Majesty in Berlin on the 11th September, 1917, it was decided after great hesitation to renounce the permanent occupation of the Flemish coast, if at this price peace could be obtained this year and if in addition the British would leave France. . . . The presupposition which led to the Crown Council taking this decision, no longer holds good. Since, in addition, our military situation has developed especially favorably, I can no longer recognize the necessity for a partial renunciation of the military demands but must prefer them once more to their full extent, as laid down unanimously in the Kreuznach conferences of 23rd April and 9th August 1917. I therefore consider that a fresh decision with regard to the Belgian question is necessary.[7]

This request of Hindenburg's to reconsider the question of Belgium was taken up at a meeting in Kreuznach on December 18. Belgium, it was decided at this time, should be brought under German influence through economic measures, military occupation, and continuation of the Flemish policy, as agreed at the Bellevue

[6] Max von Baden, pp. 155 ff.; Helfferich, *Weltkrieg,* pp. 591-92; Haussmann, p. 157.
[7] *U. A.,* 4. Reihe, III, 265-66. Translation in Lutz, *German Collapse,* pp. 88-89.

Conference on September 11. Beyond that, however, "an agreement with Belgium should be obtained to the effect that the Belgian coast, which we have fortified, must not come under English influence, but that the Belgians must pledge themselves to protect this coast under all circumstances in the interest of Germany and Belgium." [8] While not going so far as the program of April 23, these demands of December 18 certainly came close to the aim of Germany's naval authorities for a hold over the Flemish coast. In regard to Luxemburg it was decided to incorporate the Grand Duchy into Germany as a federal state. To overcome the objections of its inhabitants, study at German universities was to be encouraged and facilitated. No reference seems to have been made to France at the December 18 meeting. Earlier in the month, however, the liaison officer between the Foreign Office and the Supreme Command, von Grünau, had been asked by Hertling to sound out the army on the question of giving up some of Germany's aims in the Briey region. On December 14 he reported:

I do not want to pass on the suggestion about Briey at present as conditions are unfavorable for a good reception of it and the impression would be created that Your Excellency wishes to be very lenient towards France. They are feeling very big here at present and are entertaining ideas of smashing the enemy. I would advise rather raising the question when its practical decision is necessary.[9]

From December 1917 on, Germany's attention was almost exclusively absorbed by the negotiations with Russia at Brest-Litovsk. On December 15, an armistice had been signed between Germany and Russia, and a week later the first peace congress of the World War was under way. Prior to the departure of the German delegation the various party leaders were given an opportunity of expressing their views on the Russo-German settlement. While both Scheidemann and Erzberger insisted on a firm adherence to the July Peace Resolution, the Centrist Fehrenbach, supported by Westarp, declared that the Resolution had lost its validity.[10] On December 24, Germany and Russia agreed on the principle of "no annexations and indemnities" as basis for a post-war settlement, provided the Allies were willing to join in a general settlement on the same terms. Despite this last evasive clause, which invalidated

[8] *U. A.*, 4. Reihe, XII (1), 216-17.
[9] Lutz, *German Collapse*, pp. 48-49.
[10] Westarp, II, 566.

the agreement from the start, since neither England nor France would ever subscribe to it, the Supreme Command and the annexationist press were furious at this policy of complete renunciation.[11] Over this issue there grew up a serious controversy between Germany's political and military leaders, which ultimately boiled down to the fundamental issue, the question of responsibility for the conduct of the Reich's political affairs. Without going into detail we may say that Hertling and Kühlmann gained at least a nominal victory when, on January 24, the Kaiser took their side against Hindenburg and Ludendorff.[12]

Although this January crisis had primarily grown out of the eastern question, the west had also played its part. On January 2, General Ludendorff, in a statement before the *Bundesrat's* Committee on Foreign Affairs once again defined the Supreme Command's war aims in the west, in terms with which we are sufficiently familiar.[13] Hertling's attitude towards these aims did not quite satisfy the Supreme Command. At the height of the January crisis, Hindenburg wrote to the Emperor, complaining about the negotiations at Brest-Litovsk and including the following brief reference to Belgium:

In all the conferences with the Imperial Chancellor over which Your Majesty presided, we pointed out the importance of secure frontiers as a vital question for Germany. It is doubtful whether such frontiers will be obtained, and this causes me the greatest anxiety. . . . In the discussions with regard to Belgium I have encountered nothing but the greatest reserve on the part of the Imperial government with regard to military demands.[14]

Hindenburg's suspicion of the government's attitude on Belgium, however, was unjustified. The very same day that Hindenburg wrote to the Emperor, January 7, Hertling wrote a letter to Hindenburg in which he referred to the contemplated offensive on the western front:

If, therefore, the proposed new offensive under your Excellency's experienced leadership, supported by the heroic courage and will to victory of our soldiers, leads, by the grace of God, to the complete success hoped for, we shall be in a position to lay down the terms for a peace to be concluded with the western powers which will be necessary after the war to secure

---

[11] Helfferich, p. 541.
[12] *U. A.*, 4. Reihe, II, 58 ff.; Direnberger, pp. 86-87.
[13] *U. A.*, 4. Reihe, VIII, 272.
[14] Lutz, *German Collapse*, p. 25.

our frontiers, our economic interests, and our international position. I hope that we shall succeed in convincing the Reichstag, with the exception of the Social Democrats, of this. Efforts in this direction will not be wanting.[15]

Kühlmann, in a memorandum on January 10, defined the government's position still more clearly. "The Belgian question," he wrote, "was very thoroughly dealt with in a Crown Council at Kreuznach in the presence of His Majesty. There is no cause at present for a modification of the attitude adopted by the Imperial Chancellor."[16] In a letter to the Emperor on January 23, Hertling enlarged upon these views. To go beyond the general principles laid down at earlier discussions with the Supreme Command was premature, he held, and would tie Germany's hands at the future peace conference.

It need not be especially stressed that questions of military security will not be overlooked. In what way they will be achieved, depends upon the political and military situation at the time peace is concluded. We shall have to take into consideration how far our future economic and political relations to this neighbor [i. e. Belgium] and especially the development of our Flemish policy will diminish the probability of a future war with her and thus decrease the necessity for military safeguards.[17]

These various pronouncements of Count Hertling make it perfectly clear that by January of 1918 the Chancellor, as far as war aims were concerned, was definitely on the side of the Supreme Command. As further proof we may cite his conversation with the Conservative leader von Heydebrand on January 17, in which he said that Germany now had an entirely free hand in the west, that there would be no more peace offers, and that the Peace Resolution of July 19 was completely and definitely dead.[18] The same day an interesting document was sent to the Chancellor's liaison officer with the Supreme Command, Count Limburg-Stirum. Drafted by Under-Secretary of State von Radowitz, it was endorsed by Hertling. The following passage is of special interest:

The Supreme Command, the Kaiser, and the Crown Prince insist that the Chancellor at this time, through an appropriate declaration before the Reichstag, withdraw publicly and positively from the Resolution of July 19. The Chancellor, like the authorities just mentioned, holds the opinion that the assumptions under which the government agreed to the Resolution

---

[15] *Ibid.*, p. 33.

[16] *Ibid.*, p. 35.

[17] *U. A.*, 4. Reihe, II, 62.

[18] Westarp, II, 549.

no longer hold good, and that consequently the government has a free hand against the Western Powers.[19]

The Supreme Command had succeeded completely in making its views on western war aims prevail. It had been assisted in its "conversion" of Hertling by the various groups of annexationists, who at this time launched another major propaganda offensive.

Supreme Command and Kriegszielbewegung

There is some evidence that the army actually approached the leaders of heavy industry, asking them to increase their annexationist propaganda. The result of the request is said to have been the creation of an industrial propaganda fund.[20] If the responsibility for the renewed wave of industrial propaganda at the end of 1917 cannot definitely be placed, its actual existence cannot be overlooked. The most important example is the petition presented by the *Verein deutscher Eisen-und Stahlindustrieller* and the *Verein deutscher Eisenhüttenleute,* under the presidency of Albert Vögler, director of the Stinnes concern.[21] Based on the research of two of the most eminent German authorities in the field of mining geology, Professors Beyschlag and Krusch of the Prussian Royal Geological Academy, the memorandum went into a most careful examination of Germany's post-war supply of iron ore. Its conclusions were as follows: Germany's domestic supplies of ore would last only about forty to fifty years. It was thus highly desirable to find additional sources of supply, and the most suitable region was French Lorraine. To secure a steady supply from the Briey basin, however, its military occupation and domination by Germany was absolutely necessary. Mere treaty arrangements to guarantee Germany's share in the mineral riches of France were not sufficient. Already before the World War, German owners of French mines had faced a great many obstacles and in most cases had to conceal their ownership behind French directors. These difficulties would be multiplied after the war, if Germany's influence in the Briey district rested entirely on paper guarantees. Not only for economic, but for strategic reasons as well, the petition continued,

---

[19] *U. A.,* 4. Reihe, II, 337.

[20] *Ibid.,* I, 238.

[21] Verein Deutscher Eisen- und Stahl-Industrieller und Verein Deutscher Eisenhüttenleute, *Zur Einverleibung der französisch-lothringischen Eisenerzbecken in das deutsche Reichsgebiet* (Berlin, 1917).

9

Germany's western border must be extended, so that even the most powerful guns cannot reach industrial establishments in German Lorraine. Not only did the Briey-Longwy area constitute ancient German soil, but France would still keep some of the world's richest iron deposits in Normandy; though even here France must grant Germany the rights she had before the war. The annexations which the memorandum suggested would not merely favor the industrialists, but the working classes as well. While lack of iron-ore would cause unemployment and result in the mass-migration of workers (who thus were lost to the armed forces) the annexation of French Lorraine would provide work for at least 30,000 additional miners. And finally, the production of fertilizer as a by-product from the phosphorous minette ore was of vital significance to German agriculture. The whole German people, therefore, stood to profit from the annexation of Briey-Longwy. On the other hand, " if this opportunity is missed," the petition concluded, " the German people, in a future war, will be doomed to destruction." As in the case of Germany's military authorities, the final argument of the industrialists was preparation for future war, the " Second Punic War," about the certainty of which there never seemed the slightest doubt.

There were other similar products of industrial propaganda at this time. The firm of Thyssen published a pamphlet entitled " The significance of the Briey Basin for Germany's Economic and Military Future," demanding the iron deposits of French Lorraine.[22] One of Krupp's directors, Ernst Haux, in several speeches before the employees of the Krupp works, stressed the proximity of Germany's industrial regions to the frontier. The French, Haux pointed out, could have destroyed important sections of German Lorraine through long-range guns at the outbreak of war, if they had chosen to do so. To prevent such danger once and for all, Germany should acquire a protective *glacis* which would keep her enemies at a safe distance.[23]

In view of the vital significance which the French iron regions had for German heavy industry, these writings are understandable. The fact that so many of them appeared at this time can be explained by the threatening increase of plans proposing to

[22] Gewerkschaft " Deutscher Kaiser," *Die Bedeutung des Briey-Beckens für Deutschlands volkswirtschaftliche und militärische Zukunft* (n. pl., 1917)

[23] E. Haux, *Was lehrt uns der Krieg?* (n. pl., n. d.), pp. 32-36.

solve the iron-ore problem by commercial agreements rather than conquest. The additional encouragement from Hindenburg and Ludendorff sufficed to keep alive the fondest hopes of German industrialists.[24]

Together with the Supreme Command and heavy industry, the annexationists launched a frontal attack upon the exponents of moderate war aims. The Pan-German League at its yearly meeting in October passed a resolution containing the standard set of annexationist aims, with special emphasis on Belgium.[25] Heinrich Class' famous memorandum on war aims came out in a revised edition, including suggestions for the racial and cultural improvement of the German " master race." [26] The Independent Committee had stepped out of the limelight and made room for the *Vaterlandspartei*; though Dietrich Schäfer continued to be active. " A peace without an extension of Germany's sphere of power and without indemnities," he wrote on December 31, " would be equal to our destruction." [27] Colonial demands continued to be the most generally accepted war aim. Both the Colonial Society and Colonial Secretary Solf constantly repeated their arguments for a large *Mittelafrika* and for a series of naval stations.[28]

The *Vaterlandspartei* took the lead in annexationist propaganda. Its president, Admiral von Tirpitz, was constantly on the move, addressing large meetings in all parts of Germany. On November 10 he told a Munich audience that it was Germany's mission to serve as protector of Belgium.[29] Later in the month, in two overflow meetings at Dresden he again dealt with his favorite subject— Belgium. Several Saxon Ministers of State were present at these meetings and supported Tirpitz, a fact which led to a heated debate in the Saxon Lower House.[30] On November 30 the Admiral ad-

---

[24] G. Raphaël, *Krupp et Thyssen* (Paris, 1925), pp. 180-81; *Vossische Zeitung*, Feb. 5-7, 1918; *Düsseldorfer Tageblatt*, Feb. 24, 1918; *Der Metallarbeiter*, March 2, 1918.

[25] *Schulthess*, vol. 58(1), pp. 859-60.

[26] H. Class, *Zum deutschen Kriegsziel* (München, 1917), pp. 31, 50; Werner, pp. 233-35.

[27] Schäfer, *Leben*, p. 222.

[28] Auskunftsstelle Vereinigter Verbände, *Gedanken und Wünsche*, 1917 edition, pp. 69-70; *Kölnische Zeitung*, Nov. 24, 1917; *Norddeutsche Allgemeine Zeitung*, Dec. 22, 1917, March 13, 1918; *Deutscher Kurier*, Feb. 11, 1918; *Schulthess*, vol. 59(1), p. 103.

[29] Wortmann, p. 47.

[30] *Deutsche Tageszeitung*, Nov. 21, 1917; *Schulthess*, vol. 59(1), p. 17.

dressed six thousand persons at Essen, heart of the Ruhr district. The rich coal region of the Belgian Campine, he said, " must not be allowed to fall into English hands, to be developed into a powerful rival to our Rhenish-Westphalian territories. On the contrary, it must be made part of our economic strength, in opposition to Anglo-Americanism." [31]   The Fatherland Party's opposition to the Reichstag's Peace Resolution came out at almost every meeting.[32] On November 28 it asked the Reichstag to give up the Resolution " as once and for all superseded by recent events," and instead " to manifest a firm will for the achievement of a peace which will assure all the essentials of Germany's existence." [33]

To complete the picture of annexationist agitation during the last months of 1917, we should also mention the large number of pamphlets and books dealing with war aims that continued to flood the German market. They can be divided into two groups, according to the significance of their authors. A large number of them were unknown and it is surprising that their uninteresting writings ever found publishers and readers.[34] Yet others were written by some of Germany's outstanding intellectual figures who thus gave added prestige to the clamor of the annexationists. The Leipzig historian Erich Brandenburg gave an intelligent discussion of German territorial needs which, in the west, agreed in most respects with the aims of the government and Supreme Command.[35] Alfred Hettner, the Heidelberg geologist, advocated the annexation of Briey-Longwy, but was dubious about keeping a German foothold in Belgium. There was some justification, in his opinion, for the annexation of small sections, especially Liège. But on the whole, Hettner believed, a truly neutral Belgium was possible and he suggested that the country be given up in exchange for Germany's

[31] *Deutsche Tageszeitung*, Dec. 1, 1917; *Rede des Grossadmirals von Tirpitz am Freitag, den 30. November in Essen* (n. pl., n. d.).

[32] Wortmann, p. 49.

[33] *Deutsche Tageszeitung*, Nov. 30, 1917 (ev. ed.).

[34] The following are examples from a much longer list: A. Konietzko, *Unsere Wirtschaftliche Zukunft bei einem Verzichtfrieden* (Weimar, 1917); F. Lauterbach, *Wenn wir heimkehren* (Leipzig, 1917); L. Schwering, *Belgien, der Angelpunkt des Weltkrieges* (Regensburg, 1917); H. O. Schmidt, *Deutschlands Friede und Freiheit* (Dresden, 1917); A. Meister, *Unser belgisches Kriegsziel* (Münster, i. W., 1917); A. Stoll, *Deutsche Kriegsziele im Westen* (Cassel, 1917); R. C. Hentsch, *Friedensziele—Kriegsziele* (Annaberg, 1917).

[35] E. Brandenburg, *Deutschlands Kriegsziele* (Leipzig, 1917), esp. pp. 43 ff., 77 ff., 86 ff.

pre-war colonies.[36] The historian Ziekursch favored the usual
" veiled annexation " for Belgium which would give Germany
maximum advantages without the disadvantages of a large foreign minority.[37] Other distinguished contributors to the discussion and propagation of war aims included Georg von Below, who
suggested the division of Belgium between France and Germany,
and the geographer Felix Hänsch.[38] The significance of these
writings, however, must not be overrated. They presented few
new arguments and probably were always read by the same annexationist clique. There was a time at the beginning of the war when
the writings of such authorities did much to mold public opinion.
But after more than three years of unfulfilled hopes, most Germans had made up their minds in favor of a moderate peace, and
few were affected by the constant repetition of hollow promises
on the part of a small minority. The most interesting characteristic again noticeable in some of these annexationist pamphlets
was a change of emphasis from the advantages to the necessities
of annexations, from the economic motive of gain to the strategic
motive of protection. But even that generalization holds true for
a limited number of writings only. The majority wrote in 1917
as they had written in 1914, utterly oblivious of any changes in
Germany's military and political situation.

The annexationists were alarmed not merely over the prospect
of having to abandon their dreams of westward expansion. There
was the equally if not more important threat of domestic reform,
which became acute with the rise of parliamentary government and
the introduction of the Prussian Franchise Bill on December 5
(the bill was promptly relegated to a Committee, from which it
did not emerge until April 30, 1918).[39] " The controversy over
war aims," Prussia's Minister of the Interior wrote on February
13, 1918, " which at present dominates the domestic scene in Germany, has been able to gain its depth and intensity only because
each side recognizes in the representative of opposing peace demands also its opponent in domestic issues." [40] On December 8,

---

[36] A. Hettner, *Der Friede und die deutsche Zukunft* (Stuttgart, 1917), pp. 176 ff.,
182 ff., 194 ff.

[37] J. Ziekursch, *Was soll aus Belgien werden?* (n. pl., 1917), esp. pp. 21 ff.

[38] Below, *Kriegs-und Friedensfragen*, pp. 47 ff.; F. Hänsch, *An der Schwelle des
grösseren Reiches* (München, 1917), pp. 21 ff., 51 ff.

[39] *U. A.*, 4. Reihe, VIII, 184-87.

[40] Volkmann, *Der Marxismus*, p. 298.

Germany's "classes," alarmed at these internal developments, founded a subsidiary organization to the *Vaterlandspartei*, the *Bund der Kaisertreuen*. "The *Deutsche Vaterlandspartei* fights against the same enemies we fight against, to gain a peace for Germany that will secure its further development. But it has publicly and definitely declared that it will take no part in the domestic controversies of Germany. In this direction the *Bund der Kaisertreuen* will supplement it."[41] The influence of the organization, which included a number of high-ranking political, military, and industrial figures, was considerable; it claimed, for instance, to have had a hand in the later dismissals of the Kaiser's chief political adviser, von Valentini, and of Foreign Secretary von Kühlmann. The *Bund* opposed "the plaintive lamentations for peace," and instead demanded a strong settlement. Though "what good would the most glorious victories, the most favorable peace settlement do us, if the proud structure of the German Reich should be shaken in its foundations by democratization?" one of its propagandists asked.[42] Conservative and annexationist organizations like the Pan-German and the Agrarian Leagues joined in this anti-reform campaign.[43] At a meeting of the latter, in February 1918, the Conservative Wildgrube revealed most clearly the true cause for the concern of his class and party over the question of reform. "We wish for the maintenance of the German and Prussian monarchy," he said, "not for the sake of the dynasty, but for our own sake. Germany will be monarchical, or she will not be at all."[44] Here we have, stripped of all its patriotic verbiage, the naked fear of Germany's ruling classes, to whom democracy meant the loss of their traditional powers and privileges.

In their domestic concerns, as in the field of war aims, the annexationists enjoyed the support of the Supreme Command. "I have never been for the Prussian franchise," Ludendorff wrote on December 16, "I think it is a great mistake. . . . The reconstruction of Germany is really more important than questions of franchise."[45] And again on January 1, 1918, he wrote:

I always hope that the Prussian franchise falls through. If I didn't have that hope, I would advise the conclusion of any peace. With this franchise

---

[41] *U. A.*, 4. Reihe, XII (1), 146.

[42] "Senex," *Deutscher Kaiser hoere Dein Volk* (Berlin, 1918), pp. 2, 7, 12, 14-15.

[43] *Schulthess*, vol. 58 (1), pp. 859-60; Heller, p. 47.

[44] *Berliner Tageblatt*, Feb. 19, 1918.   [45] Knesebeck, p. 163.

we cannot live. . . . Let the disturbances come. I would rather endure a terrible end than endless terror. Are there no more fighters left? Can the best among us be frightened by the bogie of " internal unrest? " To look the danger straight in the eye and then at it! Only thus can we win; and if we should lose it would be better than acting against one's conviction.[46]

Of all Ludendorff's statements, this is the most revealing. It shows that to him as to any Conservative and annexationist, the war was lost if concessions along democratic lines had to be made to the German people. The constant stress on the strategic necessity as the only argument for western annexations is belied by his statement that once the Prussian franchise had been conceded, any peace would suit him. To prefer a terrible end to endless terror may serve as a suitable maxim for the ruthless policy the Supreme Command pursued during the last six months of the war. To avoid endless terror, Ludendorff put everything on one card, an all-out offensive against the west. The loss of this offensive left as the only alternative the terrible end, the collapse of the German Empire.

Political or Military Offensive?

There were a number of Germans in early 1918 who realized that a military offensive against the west was not the only way to achieve peace. Instead they suggested that Germany precede this military offensive with a political offensive to arrive at a negotiated settlement. It was in this connection that the problem of Belgium once more emerged as the basic issue between Germany and the west. This fact was made clear both in a speech by Lloyd George on January 5, which placed particular emphasis on the future of Belgium,[47] and in President Wilson's message to Congress of January 8, citing the famous Fourteen Points as basis for a post-war settlement. Hertling dealt with Wilson's program in an address before the Reichstag Main Committee on January 24, 1918:

As far as the question of Belgium is concerned, my predecessors have repeatedly declared that at no time during the war the annexation of Belgium by force has been part of Germany's program. The Belgian question belongs to the whole group of questions whose details will have to be settled at the peace negotiations. As long as our adversaries do not openly accept the idea that the territorial integrity of the allied nations [i. e. the Central Powers] forms the only possible basis for peace negoti-

---

[46] *Ibid.*, p. 164.   [47] Max von Baden, pp. 195 ff.

ations, I must insist on the position taken thus far and refuse to take the matter of Belgium out of the discussion of the whole peace problem.[48]

These are vague and careful words which do not exclude the possibility of Belgian restoration. But we must remember that they were primarily directed at President Wilson and were therefore intended to be moderate. Hertling's real views on the subject, as shown in his letter to the Emperor the day before, were by no means as conciliatory. Nor did he fool his listeners. The majority parties, despite some earlier indications of disagreement, once more united in their criticisms of the Chancellor's speech, pointing directly at its chief weakness. "A definite statement of the German government on Belgium," Erzberger said, "would be most effective. The Chancellor, to be sure, treated the question negatively; but it should be treated positively." [49] Then came Scheidemann: "The complete and honest restoration of Belgium, including her political independence, is our duty of honor. . . . I should have greatly hoped that the Chancellor, in regard to Belgium, had said clearly and openly: we are ready to relinquish her, on the condition, of course, that our opponents for their part give up their plans for the infringement of Germany's integrity." Scheidemann concluded with the ominous words: "We Social Democrats shall do all we can for our country and people. But we shall never think of risking our lives for a government that does not fulfill its duties towards the people." Finally Friedrich Naumann expressed his own and his party's agreement with what his colleagues had said before him. "A positive word," he said, "should be spoken about Belgium. We must not put everything on the card of victory." [50]

The problem of political *vs.* military offensive was summed up and put before General Ludendorff in an extensive memorandum, dated February 11, and signed, among others, by Friedrich Naumann, Alfred Weber, and Robert Bosch.[51] Its authors pointed out that the increasing unrest at home and the economic weakness of the Central Powers made the conclusion of an early peace an imperative necessity. If the impending offensive was the only method to gain such a peace, the German people would willingly endure its hardships. The task, therefore, was to make the people see that the offensive, if it did come, was unavoidable. To do this, the military offensive should be preceded by a political offensive

---

[48] *U. A.*, 4. Reihe, VIII, 301-02.
[49] *Ibid.*, XII (1), 140-41.
[50] *Ibid.*, pp. 141-42.
[51] *Ibid.*, II, 136-39.

which will compel Lloyd George to declare openly that he wishes to continue the war for the sake of Alsace-Lorraine. This aim can be achieved by an unequivocal declaration regarding the future restoration of the sovereignty and integrity of Belgium. That is the postulate of the British and American peace parties. . . . This declaration with regard to Belgium would break down the unbroken determination behind the lines in the enemy countries and build it up anew in Germany. The declaration should be made as soon and as clearly as possible and also quite publicly. . . . The fruitful soil for war propaganda in enemy countries and for the anti-war agitation in Germany has been entirely created by the obscurity of the statements made by the German government.

The memorandum summed up the possible results of the political action it proposed, which would either be the fall of the British war cabinet and its substitution by a moderate ministry, or the formation of a new chauvinistic government under Lloyd George and against the will of the British people. With the former, Germany could easily conclude a satisfactory peace, while the latter would present a decisive obstacle to Great Britain's conduct of the war and thus facilitate German victory. The document closed with the prophetic statement:

A terrible responsibility rests at present on the leaders of the government; it is still possible to retain the good will of the masses. All healthy forces among the German workmen tend to reject the forces making for disorganization. But the government must assist them. It has in its power to allow the disintegrating forces to become a great destructive power in Germany or to condemn them to lasting impotency.[52]

General Ludendorff was sufficiently impressed with the memorandum to reply at length on February 22. But he restricted himself entirely to the military aspects of the contemplated offensive, pointing out that for the first time since the early days of the war, the withdrawal of Russia gave Germany a choice on the western front between offensive and defensive, and that he had to make use of this chance to attack before American assistance to the Allies would turn the scales against Germany. The central idea of the memorandum, to precede the military by a political offensive, using a declaration on Belgium as an entering wedge to weaken the enemies' power of resistance, was completely ignored by the General.[53]

The idea of a propaganda offensive against England had been suggested by other people ever since the major spring campaign

---

[52] Lutz, *German Collapse*, pp. 41-45.   [53] *U. A.*, 4. Reihe, II, 92-93.

had been decided upon.[54] In January, Colonel von Haeften presented Ludendorff with an elaborate proposal for such a move. Its purpose should be to make clear to the British people that the only obstacle to peace was Lloyd George's imperialistic policy.

The right words are victorious battles, and the wrong words are lost battles. If we desire to gain a victory behind the English front to prepare our victory on the battle-field, we must choose such words as will enable the patriotic peace party in England to step before their people and say: If you follow us, the road to negotiations will be clear, and the honor and security of England will be assured.[55]

Ludendorff " urgently recommended " Haeften's memorandum to the Chancellor, a fact which has been taken as proof of the Supreme Command's consent to a political offensive.[56] This would be true if the most essential part of Haeften's memorandum, the demand for a clear statement on Belgium, had not been omitted before the document was handed to the government.[57] In view of the Supreme Command's aims in regard to Belgium, a promise of its restitution was, of course, out of the question. On February 5, at a meeting between German and Austrian political and military leaders, Ludendorff once more made clear his attitude on this point:

A peace which only guarantees the territorial *status quo* would mean that we lost the war. . . . Matters are still uncertain as far as the west is concerned. But if we keep our old frontiers there, we shall be in a less favorable position after the war than before. . : . We must improve the protection of our western coal regions through rectifications of the frontier. To a peace which offers less, we of the Supreme Command cannot agree. It can only be ordered from above.[58]

To make matters complete, the Chief of the High Seas Fleet, Admiral Scheer, supported by Admiral von Holtzendorff, once more brought the navy's claims for the coast of Flanders to the attention of the Supreme Command.[59] Yet a statement on Belgium was the *conditio sine qua non* of a peace settlement with

---

[54] Rupprecht, II, 330, 332, 336.

[55] Ludendorff, *Urkunden*, pp. 473-78.

[56] Max von Baden, p. 201; Eisenhardt-Rothe, pp. 126 ff., *U. A.*, 4. Reihe, III, 263, 267-69.

[57] Max von Baden, p. 201, note 2.

[58] *U. A.*, 4. Reihe, XII (1), 220; Max von Baden, pp. 236-37.

[59] " Rudiger," p. 82.

England. Without the reference to Belgium, Haeften's proposal was as meaningless as all of Germany's earlier official statements on war aims. The Colonel himself had said in the section that was later omitted: " We have always offered the English peace party weapons which were of no use to it, while they were of considerable use to the English war party." [60]

The question of a political offensive was further broached by the famous armchair strategist and historian, Hermann Stegemann. Viewing the situation from neutral Switzerland, he addressed his important observations to Conrad Haussmann. Stegemann agreed that Germany's military situation was more favorable than ever before. Yet he doubted that an offensive in the west, even though successful, would knock one of the Allies out of the war. Quite the contrary, he held, it might only serve to unite Germany's adversaries still more closely. On the other hand, the very fact of Germany's military superiority, which was universally recognized, might be used as effectively as an actual offensive to terminate the war.

Only if an understanding—made easier through a clarification of the Belgian question (my *ceterum censeo*)—cannot be achieved in the course of a few weeks, only then the two-edged weapon of an offensive must be used. Its qualification as a surgical instrument remains doubtful, but its use could then be considered necessary. Today that is not yet the case.[61]

Conrad Haussmann related Stegemann's views to Ludendorff, but failed to receive a clear reply.[62]

One of the chief advocates of a peace offensive against England, the later Chancellor, Prince Max of Baden, finally put the matter directly before Hertling.[63] The Chancellor was most skeptical of England's willingness to discuss peace and was afraid that a German declaration on Belgium would only cause Allied jeers. Most important, however, was Hertling's unwillingness to oppose the Supreme Command. He had the firm belief that the two military leaders would gain peace, and a better peace, by military means. The Vice-Chancellor, von Payer, was more amenable to Prince Max's suggestion, but he also had all his hopes set on the impend-

[60] Max von Baden, p. 201, note 2.

[61] *U. A.*, 4. Reihe, II, 96-98.

[62] C. Haussmann, *Aus Conrad Haussmanns politischer Arbeit* (Frankfurt a. M., 1923), p. 105.

[63] Max von Baden, pp. 231 ff.

ing offensive. The Foreign Secretary, on the other hand, was extremely pessimistic, believing neither in the success of a military or peace offensive, nor that the Supreme Command could be made to agree to the latter. Only Dr. Solf saw eye-to-eye with the Prince, but his influence was insufficient to bring about a statement on Belgium. Ex-Chancellor von Bethmann Hollweg, likewise convinced of the necessity to clarify publicly Germany's stand on Belgium before going into the spring offensive, went to see Hertling, but had no more luck than Prince Max. Nor was a visit which the latter paid to Ludendorff any more successful. The unequivocal declaration on the future of Belgium, not in itself perhaps a sufficient inducement for the British government to enter into peace negotiations, but surely a necessary prerequisite of such negotiations, had once again failed to materialize.

In addition to these various suggestions for a peace offensive, there were again several peace moves and feelers between the Central and Allied Powers during the spring of 1918. Aside from the fact that in almost every case the question of Belgium soon emerged as the central issue, these secret negotiations had little effect upon the main course of events. Most outstanding were the conversations at the Hague, in early March, between Colonel von Haeften and the German-American Jacob Noeggerath, and the series of meetings in Switzerland between President Wilson's friend, Professor Herron, and notable German liberals, such as Conrad Haussmann, Professor Quidde, and Professor Jaffé, which lasted from December 1917 into November 1918.[64] Other peace attempts never actually reached the stage of negotiation.[65]

On February 25, Count Hertling appeared before the Reichstag, which had resumed its sessions on February 19, to deliver his second address before a plenary session. Again he referred to Belgium in the customary terms:

It has been repeatedly said from this place that we do not think of retaining Belgium or of making the Belgian state a component part of the German Empire, but that we must, as was also set forth in the Papal Note of August 1, be safeguarded from the danger that a country with which after the war we desire to live again in peace and friendship should become an object or jumping-off ground of enemy machinations. The means

---

[64] *Ibid.*, pp. 242 ff.; *U. A.*, 4. Reihe, I, 21; "Herron Papers," (12 vols. of typescript at the Hoover Library, Stanford, Calif.), vols. II and IV; Lutz, *German Empire*, I, 469 ff.

[65] Eisenhardt-Rothe, pp. 98 ff.; Hertling, pp. 57-58.

of reaching this end and thus serving the general world peace would be the subject of discussion at such a meeting. If, therefore, a proposal in this direction came from the opposite side, let us say from the government at Le Havre [i. e. the Belgian government in exile], we should not adopt an antagonistic attitude, even though the discussion, as a matter of course, could at first not be binding.[66]

As usual there was enough vagueness in the Chancellor's words to permit almost any interpretation. "We should like to live in peace and friendship with Belgium," Scheidemann said on February 26, "as the Chancellor remarked yesterday. That can only be done, of course, with a people whose independence is really safeguarded." Von Heydebrand, on the other hand, interpreted Hertling's speech as a demand for Germany's political, military, and economic domination over Belgium. Stresemann likewise was confident that the Chancellor's statement on Belgium permitted the guarantee of Germany's interests. The Progressive Wiemer understood the speech as a promise not to keep Belgium, as did Erzberger, the latter adding the warning not to underestimate the effect on neutral nations if Germany should insist on pursuing power-politics in Belgium, the " darling of the world." [67]

The last chance for a clear official statement on Belgium came on March 18, 1918, when Count Hertling presented the Treaty of Brest-Litovsk, signed on March 3, to the Reichstag. There were some indications that England might be willing to talk peace if such a statement were made.[68] Yet despite several requests, the Chancellor made no reference to Belgium. "We are ready," he concluded his brief speech, " to make further heavy sacrifices. . . . The responsibility for all this bloodshed will fall upon the heads of those who in frivolous obduracy refuse to listen to the voice of peace." [69] Three days later, on the afternoon of March 12, Germany's artillery along the whole sector between Arras and La Fère opened fire, sounding the beginning of the great spring offensive and the end for a peace by negotiation.

In the light of subsequent events, it seems strange that the German government did not avail itself of the opportunity presented by the proposed peace offensive. There was so little to be lost by a declaration on Belgium, and perhaps everything to be

---

[66] *Reichstag*, vol. 311, p. 4140.
[67] *Ibid.*, pp. 4163, 4176, 4182, 4191, 4220-21.
[68] Max von Baden, pp. 246-47.
[69] *Reichstag*, vol. 311, p. 4426.

gained. Disregarding the unanswerable question whether such an offensive, if attempted, would have succeeded, how can we explain the almost suicidal manner in which Germany's statesmen led their country to its destruction?

If we look at the situation as it presented itself to these men in the spring of 1918, we must realize that on the whole events could not have happened very differently from the way they actually did. One basic idea should be clear after reviewing the events of the preceding months: Germany's governing forces refused to proclaim the unconditional renunciation of Belgium not so much because they doubted Great Britain's willingness to talk peace, but because they did not really want to see the complete independence of Belgium re-established. We have traced the relentless insistence of the Supreme Command on far-reaching strategic improvements of Germany's western frontier, which included the annexation of parts of France and the " veiled annexation " of most of Belgium.[70] To Hindenburg and Ludendorff, a war which failed to secure these aims, was a lost war. This attitude may be wrong or narrow-minded, but it was none the less real, backed by a stubborn determination which found its only parallel in the simultaneous demands of France's military authorities for the strategic frontier of the Rhine. To the German army, therefore, there really existed no alternative. It was Belgium or nothing.

The civil branch of the government, though not so insistent on strong western aims as the army, nevertheless favored such westward expansion and was willing to hold out for whatever gains might be made in that region. But even if there had been sentiment in favor of a *status quo ante* settlement in the west, as in fact there was on the part of Baron von Kühlmann, it could not have asserted itself against the dominating influence of the Supreme Command. The old Chancellor willingly submitted to the army's decisions, which converted the question of Belgium, primarily a territorial and political problem, into a strategic and military one. The Foreign Secretary had discovered at Brest-Litovsk that it was difficult to oppose the will of Ludendorff. And the Kaiser, though usually on the side of moderation, could always be swayed to an opposite point of view.

The fact of intrinsic unwillingness or at best great reluctance to give up Germany's western conquests received additional support

[70] Valentini, p. 190.

from events in the east. The feeling of achievement and the optimism that went with the successful conclusion of a treaty which fulfilled a large share of Germany's expansionist dreams, helped to keep alive the desire for the western counterpart of the *Drang nach Osten*. Why should a premature declaration jeopardize the chance of establishing once and for all Germany's security on the European continent, especially when the impending offensive on the western front had all likelihood of success? This last fact we must always keep in mind. It was only after the failure of this military venture that the lost opportunity of making a declaration on Belgium assumed such great importance. As things stood in March of 1918, with a powerful army ready to finish the war within a few months, a statement on Belgium, in the opinion of the Supreme Command, might have weakened the German people's power of resistance at a time when it was needed more than ever before.

The German People and Brest-Litovsk

In our analysis of Germany's policy prior to the 1918 spring offensive we have thus far dealt only with the attitude of the German government and have omitted dealing with the German people. While the former was most reluctant to give up any of its strategic war aims, the chief concern of the latter was to gain peace at the earliest possible opportunity. This longing of the German masses for peace had little chance of expressing itself, except in direct revolutionary action, mass protests and strikes.[71] On January 28, 1918, the largest event of this kind prior to the November Revolution occurred, when 400,000 workers in Berlin alone quit work. The close interrelationship between this act and the question of war aims is made clear in the demands of these strikers, the first point of which reads: " Speedy conclusion of peace without annexations and indemnities, on the basis of the self-determination of peoples." [72] Nor was this longing for peace restricted to the lower classes. Around the middle of February 1918, the *Frankfurter Zeitung* addressed a memorandum to the Supreme Command, which emphasized the whole country's hope for peace. " The course of events," it said, " might be such that considerable sections of the people will prefer any peace, peace at any price, to the continuation of the war." [73]

[71] Rosenberg, pp. 196-97, 201.
[72] *U. A.*, 4. Reihe, XII (1), 152; VI, 184.   [73] *Ibid.*, II, 114-15.

Although the German people's desire for peace was beyond question, and they were willing to conclude such a peace without making any territorial gains, this does not mean that they objected to a peace settlement which managed to realize some of Germany's war aims. Only the lower classes behind the Socialist Parties truly believed in " no annexations and indemnities " as a matter of principle. The attitude of most middle class moderates, averse to strong war aims, was the result not so much of deep-felt opposition to German expansionism, but of a common-sense realization that such expansionism was dangerous, if not impossible, since it would arouse the permanent opposition of Germany's adversaries. We have seen that it took three years to form a moderate majority within the German Reichstag. As long as there was no really vital and controversial issue, this majority had held together pretty well. But when it was confronted with the *fait accompli* of the Treaty of Brest-Litovsk, which violated all possible principles of moderation, the parties did not rise to fight but acquiesced.

The peace settlement with Russia was an illustration of the way in which the Supreme Command could make the wildest annexationist dreams come true. It deprived Russia of the most valuable parts of her European possessions—Poland, the Baltic States, and the Ukraine—placing the areas, if not under the direct sovereignty, at least under the influence of the Central Powers. There were certain mitigating circumstances that help to explain Germany's eastern policy; but there can be no doubt that this treaty was one of the most blatant manifestations of German expansionism and as such was a tremendous boon to Allied propaganda. It now was evident what Germany meant when she spoke of " real guarantees and securities " and refused to be more specific. Looked at in the light of Brest-Litovsk, the future of Western Europe, in case of a German victory, was a dismal one indeed.

If only the representatives of the German people had shown that they were not in accord with their government's annexationist policy! But quite the opposite happened. Only the Social Democrats launched a slight protest against the treaty and refused to vote on it. Erzberger, on the other hand, went so far as to state that " the peace which we have concluded in the East stays entirely within the bounds of the July 19th Resolution. Wherever it deviates from those principles it represents only temporary police

measures." [74] The German Reichstag had proved to the world that
it might talk peace when the going was tough—as was the case in
the summer of 1917—but that it was unwilling to stand up for its
convictions when the situation improved. Some doubts remained
with the delegates, to be sure. On March 21, the majority parties,
with the collaboration of the National Liberals, published a resolution expressing their hope that the government would help the
peoples liberated from the Russians to set up their own governments, according to the principle of self-determination. [75] Germany's actual policy in the east, which assumed all the aspects of
veiled annexation, soon aroused further opposition and criticism
from German moderates. [76] But the harm had been done and these
belated protests, while weakening the German home-front, did
nothing to remedy the situation east of the Vistula.

To explain the attitude of the majority parties we must remember that there had always been considerable anti-Russian feeling
among German moderates and socialists. To those among them
who could convince themselves that the Treaty of Brest-Litovsk
primarily intended the liberation of Russia's western provinces, its
acceptance was made easy. Others, especially the Social Democrats, argued that the treaty at least put an end to the war in
the east and was thus an important milestone on the road to a
general peace settlement. To oppose it would only prolong the
war and perhaps lead to an equally hard peace imposed upon
Germany by the Allies. As far as the bourgeois parties were concerned, we must not underestimate the prestige which the Supreme
Command enjoyed in the eyes of most Germans. While their own
attempts at a policy of moderation and negotiation had found
little response in the Allied camp, Ludendorff's policy of the sword
seemed once again to have lived up to its reputation of infallibility.
Since the chief aim of most Germans was to end the war, why,
they felt, should they object if this could be done with some territorial or economic gains into the bargain? Why—and here we
see the connection with the west—should the Supreme Command
not be given an opportunity to try against the Allies what had
been accomplished with such evident success in the east? We
have noticed that, up to the beginning of the spring offensive,
the majority parties insisted on the restoration of Belgium. Yet
to go one step further and insist on a public declaration of such a

[74] *Ibid.*, XII(1), 142-43.   [75] *Ibid.*, p. 143.   [76] Dahlin, pp. 324-26.

policy required more determination, unity of purpose, and courage than the Reichstag majority possessed. As in other periods of history, the sin of the majority of Germans was one of omission rather than commission, the willingness to acquiesce in the decisions made by men who had the courage of translating their convictions and ambitions into reality.

Annexationism during the Spring Offensive

Germany's offensive in the west started with a series of brilliant successes which seemed to fulfill the Supreme Command's most hopeful expectations. Somewhat prematurely, as it turned out, the Emperor awarded the Iron Cross with gold rays (a decoration given only once before to Blücher after the battle of Belle-Alliance) to Hindenburg, four days after fighting began. Germany's forces achieved several outstanding victories and were able to maintain their initiative against the Allies into the summer; yet they failed to deliver the one decisive blow which might force the other side to sue for peace. The danger of " winning herself to death " became increasingly more real for Germany as the campaign dragged on.

The German people, of course, were unaware of all this. As usual victories on the military front strengthened the position of the annexationists at home, and as a result we find the last major outburst of expansionist propaganda during the spring of 1918. In the light of later events, these manifestations are difficult to understand. Yet at the time they seemed entirely justified. The period of comparative moderation, ushered in by the July Peace Resolution, had come to an end. The day once more belonged to the annexationists, and they made the most of it.

At a meeting on April 14, the Pan-German League re-defined its position on war aims. Only a month before, the League had suffered a major set-back when six of its more prominent members, all of them National Liberal Reichstag deputies, under the leadership of Stresemann, had resigned their membership " in view of the inner political attitude and the unprecedented method of fighting against the National Liberal Party indulged in by the *Deutsche Zeitung*, founded by the Pan-German League." The fight for strong war aims, however, was not much affected by the secession, since the former members specifically declared that their step would not involve any change in their " work for a strong guarantee of

the German future." [77]   At the April meeting, after the main speech
by Count Reventlow, that never-tiring apostle of German westward expansion, a resolution was adopted professing once again
the League's " adherence to its war aims drawn up at the beginning
of the war." " Before all things Belgium must remain firmly in
German hands, from a military, political, and economic point of
view. . . . The German people must demand from the sense of
duty of the Reichstag that it give up the decision of July 19, 1917,
and following the historical events, stand for the war aim which
arises out of the military situation." [78]   Other organizations of the
Kriegszielbewegung likewise came out for strong war aims.   On
April 9, General Keim, addressing the Army League, demanded
the annexation of Belgium as proposed in the late. General von
Bissing's famous testament. [79]   Ten days later, the Vaterlandspartei
held its second general meeting which brought forth a manifesto
similar to the Pan-German one of April 14. [80]   The activities of
the Independent Committee became still more closely affiliated
with the Fatherland Party when Dietrich Schäfer became the
latter's Vice-President in March of 1918. [81]

A word should be said, perhaps, about the widespread demand
for an indemnity, found in most annexationist writings of this
period.   It was not a new war aim, but had always formed a kind
of appendix to most war-aims programs.   As the war continued,
and financial burdens increased, this financial aim had assumed
growing significance.   Especially in connection with Germany's war
loans, the hope for substantial indemnities supplied an important
incentive for investment. [82]   On various occasions during late 1917
and early 1918, the matter had been the subject of debates in
the Prussian, Bavarian and Saxon Diets and substantial indemnities had been demanded in both places. [83]   Various industrial and
commercial organizations constantly reiterated these financial de-

[77] Werner, p. 249; Norddeutsche Allgemeine Zeitung, March 13, 1918.

[78] Vossische Zeitung, April 15, 1918 (ev. ed.).

[79] Kreuzzeitung, April 10, 1918.

[80] Great Britain, Enemy Supplement, III, May 2, 1918, 1081; Wortmann, p. 52.

[81] Schäfer, Leben, p. 221. For additional annexationist statements see K. Jünger,
ed., Vom kommenden Weltfrieden (Siegen, 1918), passim.

[82] Germany, Reichsbank, Leitfaden und Nachschlagewerk zur Werbearbeit zur
VII. Kriegsanleihe (n. pl., 1917), p. 14.

[83] Vorwärts, Nov. 29, 1917; P. Dehn. Nicht ohne Kriegsentschädigung (Halle,
1918), pp. 37 ff.; Münchner Neueste Nachrichten, Feb. 9, 1918.

mands.[84] Some writers on the subject went one step further and
tried to figure out the amount Germany required to pay her war
debts and losses. They arrived at figures anywhere between 120
and 190 billion marks, which they hoped to collect from the Allies
after the war.[85]

The great industrialists likewise welcomed Germany's initial military successes.[86] In April, the *Vossische Zeitung* circulated a ques-
tionnaire among the leaders of German industry, asking for their
aims in regard to France. Ernst von Borsig, partner in one of Germany's leading machine manufacturing concerns, wanted Briey-
Longwy, since the Allied threat of economic reprisals after the
war would limit Germany's foreign sources of iron-ore. August
Thyssen stressed the strategic necessity of the same region for the
protection of Germany's steel production. Stinnes' director Albert
Vögler went so far as to call "the acquisition of the iron district
of Briey and Longwy . . . a question of life and death for the
German iron industry."[87] Also at this time, Jacob Reichert, secretary of the *Verein Deutscher Eisen—und Stahlindustrieller*, wrote
two pamphlets pointing out the advantages to be gained from the
annexation of France's iron regions.[88] The Christian labor unions
shared these views. "If we are able to conclude a powerful peace,"
their leader Stegerwald said in April 1918, "we want such a peace
under all circumstances"; and the *Deutsche Metallarbeiter*, organ
of the Christian metal and foundry workers' union, in an article
on April 6, 1918, specifically demanded the Briey-Longwy basin.[89]

As was to be expected, the Supreme Command shared the
optimism of its annexationist friends, though its better insight into
the country's real military situation should have advised greater
caution in the discussion of war aims. "The events of the past
months," Hindenburg wrote to Hugenberg on March 31, 1918,
"prove that the kind of victory we need for Germany's political

[84] Dehn, pp. 32-33; *Weserzeitung*, May 2, 1918.

[85] Dehn, pp. 40-41; P. Franz, *Der Bankerott-Friede* (München, 1918), pp. 2 ff.;
M. Kögl, "Finanzlage und Kriegsentschädigungsfrage," *Handel und Industrie*,
XXVII (1918), 99-100.

[86] Hugenberg, pp. 190-91.

[87] *Vossische Zeitung*, April 7, 1918.

[88] J. Reichert, *Aus Deutschlands Waffenschmiede* (Berlin, 1918), pp. 107-09; J.
Reichert, *Was sind uns die Erzbecken von Briey und Longwy?* (Berlin, 1918),
passim.

[89] *U. A.*, 4. Reihe, VII(1), 34; G. W. Schiele, *Wie der rechte Deutsche Arbeiterfrieden aussehen muss* (Nürnberg, 1918), *passim*.

and economic future can no longer be wrested from us." [90] On
April 16, the Field Marshal joined the annexationists in urging
the Reichstag to declare itself " for a strong German peace, which
alone can preserve us from a future war." [91] General Ludendorff
likewise maintained his plans for some kind of German hold over
Belgium.[92] On May 25, a discussion took place at Brussels between the Supreme Command and members of the Belgian administration, on the post-war settlement. All present, particularly Governor General von Falkenhausen, Hindenburg, and Ludendorff,
agreed that Germany's occupation of Belgium ought to last at
least ten years, and longer, if necessary. Certain sections, Hindenburg pointed out, should be annexed permanently. This applied
particularly to Liège, to protect the industrial region of Aix-la
Chapelle and to keep an eye on Brussels. " To those in Berlin,"
he said, " we must use as a threat that we have to annex Liège
no matter what, if we cannot chain Belgium solidly to Germany."
During the period of occupation, the Belgians would, of course,
only be permitted to have a police force. Later on, perhaps, if
Germany's community of interest with Flanders was definitely
assured, a Flemish army might be organized. The central government would have to be kept as weak as possible, von Falkenhausen
held. And finally, about the Flanders coast, Ludendorff pointed
out that it would " decide the next war. Time will show if it is
possible to replace the German marines by Flemish ones. The
coast must be protected against a land encirclement from the direction of the French frontier." [93] Here we have one of the frankest
expositions of the Supreme Command's plans for Belgium. Reduced to essentials it foresaw one of two alternatives: either Belgium became completely subservient to German influence, or else
Germany would continue her occupation of the country indefinitely.
The former would mean " veiled annexation "; the latter open
annexation, though it might not be called that. Of special interest
is Ludendorff's statement on the Flemish coast, about which the
army had thus far been hesitant to commit itself. In early April,
under the influence of the German successes on the western front,
Admiral von Holtzendorff had produced another memorandum on
this question, so close to the heart of German naval authorities and
annexationists. The main points of the Admiral's memorandum

[90] Kriegk, p. 40.
[91] *Reichstag*, vol. 311, p. 4574.
[92] Rupprecht, II, 399-400.
[93] " Rudiger," pp. 83-85.

dealt with the creation of a Duchy of Flanders under German protection and the cession of Wallonia to a "royalist" France.[94] Nothing shows better the narrow and unrealistic outlook under which some annexationists drew up their war aims, guided exclusively by the particular requirements of their own department. Politically, geographically, and most of all economically, the permanent separation of the Flemish and Walloon sections was an unwise if not impossible scheme. Whoever held the coast would by necessity also dominate its hinterland, a fact which many annexationists realized only too well, though for tactical reasons they preferred to keep quiet about it.

The Future of Belgium

Before examining the attitude of the government and parties during this Indian Summer of annexationism, we must consider briefly developments in occupied Belgium, to discover what bearing they might have upon the situation in Germany. We need not discuss in any great detail the economic exploitation of the occupied areas, which was largely dictated by the demands of a German economy restricted by Great Britain's blockade. There was also an element of interference by German industrialists who saw in destruction the most effective way of throttling their inconvenient Belgian competitors.[95] The real and most willful damage was not done until the retreat of the German troops after the failure of the 1918 offensive. Yet already on October 16, 1917, Director Middendorf of the Section for Commerce and Industry of the German administration of Belgium pointed out that, if the war would last another year and a half, Belgium's resources, except for coal and phosphates, would be completely exhausted, a warning which he repeated in June of 1918.[96] Besides the destruction of industries through confiscation of vital materials, the liquidation of industrial enterprises and their transfer into German hands went on apace. The purpose behind these measures, as Ludendorff pointed out once more in a letter to the Secretary of the Interior, Helfferich, on October 20, 1917, was to create *faits accomplis* for the post-war period.[97] The rule that only predominantly French and British

[94] Hertling, pp. 92-93.
[95] A. Erkelenz, "Die geschichtliche Schuld der deutschen Schwerindustrie," *Hilfe*, Jan. 1, 1924, pp. 3-6.
[96] Kerchove, p. 152.
[97] *Wer hat den Krieg verlängert?*, pp. 4-5.

enterprises in Belgium could thus be liquidated was soon evaded by special provisions.[98] Alongside these more destructive aspects of Germany's industrial activity should be mentioned her attempts to open up the rich coal deposits of the Campine region.[99] If German war-time economy required the thorough exploitation of all possible sources of raw materials, we should not conclude from the resulting destruction that Germany had no intention of keeping Belgium after the war. In a meeting of the Section of Commerce and Industry, the eventual affiliation of Belgian and German industries was discussed in detail. It was agreed to make the revival of each Belgian industry dependent on its utility to Germany, and to distinguish between Belgian industries which were harmful to their German competitors and those which were not.[100]

Still more interesting than these economic questions was the simultaneous growth of administrative separation between Flemings and Walloons. We have already traced developments up to the death of General von Bissing and the formation of a culturally independent Flemish region under the leadership of a Council of Flanders. The new Governor General, Baron von Falkenhausen, like his two predecessors a retired General and well-preserved septuagenarian, lacked von Bissing's political foresight and talent for organization. So it is not surprising that he became a willing tool in the hands of the Supreme Command, whose views on the future of Belgium predominated from then on. On September 11-12, 1917, for instance, the Governor General, in an exchange of views with Helfferich, advocated economic collaboration between Germany and Belgium (railroads, tariff union, monetary union, Campine), close relations between Germans and Flemings, and substantial military guarantees, in short the kind of program Hindenburg and Ludendorff were suggesting at this same time.[101]

On May 19, 1917, Falkenhausen received the delegates of the Council of Flanders, who expressed their loyalty to Germany and their hope that the existing administrative separation between Flanders and Wallonia would eventually develop into a political separation, with a special government for Flanders. Falkenhausen's answer carefully avoided the word " independence " when referring to the future of the Flemings and did not conceal the fact that he

---

[98] Germany, *Nationalversammlung*, VII, 16.
[99] Keim, pp. 217-18; Hertling, p. 20.
[100] Kerchove, pp. 158-59.
[101] Dahlin, pp. 95-96.

envisaged future developments under the protection of Germany.[102]
On August 29, 1917, the new Chancellor, Michaelis, received a
similar delegation of the Council and promised to adhere to Bethmann Hollweg's promises of March 3, 1917, to the effect that
Germany would secure the free development of the Flemings at
the peace conference.   Other minor concessions were made by the
German government, such as the introduction of Flemish as official
language of Flanders and the formation of a Flemish guard, the
Rijkswacht.[103]   At the same time the German government studied
the administrative division of the Austro-Hungarian Empire, as a
possible guide for the handling of the Belgian problem.[104] Despite
this activity, Ludendorff, on November 28, 1917, complained about
the absence of a clear and determined line in the dealings between
the Political Section of the Government General and the Flemings.
The Chief of the Political Section, Baron von der Lancken, pointed
out in his answer, that the Flemings, as a people, had too strong a
sense of independence ever to become entirely the object of German
policy and that Germany would be successful only if a certain
amount of freedom were left to the Flemings in shaping their own
destiny.[105] Similar warnings against the opposition of many Flemings to any close collaboration with Germany had been frequent
since the early days of the war.[106]   Nor did the Flemish policy of
the German government meet with the undivided approval of all
members of the Government General. The head of the civil administration, von Sandt, and many of his associates, did not share
the usual predilection for the Flemings, and many officers of the
occupation force looked down upon the pro-German " activists " as
traitors. The economic importance of the Walloons, finally, made
many people hesitate to alienate that important section of the
Belgian population.[107]

The main desire of the Flemings, as they had pointed out to
Falkenhausen on May 19, 1917, was to transform the already existing administrative separation into political independence. On December 22, 1917, therefore, the Council of Flanders, in a surprise

[102] Raad van Vlaanderen, p. xxix.

[103] Clough, pp. 211-12.

[104] Lutz, *German Empire*, I, 361.

[105] *U. A.*, 4. Reihe, XII (1), 105-06.

[106] *Frankfurter Zeitung*, Aug. 9, 1917; *Berliner Tageblatt*, June 26, 1918; Rauscher,
p. 42.

[107] " Rudiger," pp. 60-61.

move, proclaimed the independence of the province of Flanders. This came as a decided shock to the German government, and the Council did not get permission to publish its proclamation until the word " autonomy " had been substituted for " independence." [108] Even so, Germany's civil and military authorities differed on the desirability of announcing the proclamation. Both Falkenhausen and Ludendorff desired that it be made public, and it was chiefly due to their pressure that Count Hertling finally acquiesced. Ludendorff's chief argument was that the declaration of Flemish autonomy would strengthen the Flemish movement inside the Belgian army and thus weaken that army's power of resistance.[109] In a letter to one of his army friends, on February 15, 1918, the General gave additional and more plausible reasons: " I consider the division of Belgium into Flanders and Wallonia," he wrote, " one of the surest means of realizing our chief war aim in Belgium, the destruction of Anglo-French influence by economic conquest and eventually by political conquest of the country." [110] This statement was made at the same time that some people in Germany suggested the opening of a political offensive through a declaration on the unconditional restoration of Belgium.

As a result of Ludendorff's intervention, the Flemings, on January 20, 1918, proclaimed their autonomy. The same day a new Council of Flanders was " elected " by acclamation. It adopted a six-point program, which included the complete political independence of Flanders and her freedom to deal directly with foreign powers. The publication of this program was promptly forbidden by the Germans, who preferred to leave to the future any final decision on Flanders.[111] On March 7, 1918, the Governor General received a delegation of the new Council and declared once again that he intended to keep Bethmann Hollweg's promises of March 3, 1917. The Proclamation of December 22, 1917, he interpreted as an indication of Flemish desire to be liberated from the Walloons. The conditions of their autonomy, however, would have to be determined at the future peace conference.[112] At the request of General Ludendorff, Hertling likewise received some members of the Coun-

---

[108] Becker, pp. 332-33; Clough, p. 204.
[109] " Rudiger," pp. 68-69, 286.
[110] *Ibid.*, p. 82.
[111] *Schulthess*, vol. 59 (2), pp. 343-45.
[112] *Leipziger Tageblatt*, March 8, 1918, (ev. ed.); *Schulthess*, vol. 59 (2), p. 345.

cil on July 26, 1918, and told them that he shared Bethmann Hollweg's views on the Flemish question.[113]

These rather nebulous promises, postponing the settlement of the problem until a future date, did not satisfy the Council of Flanders. On June 20, therefore, it published another manifesto demanding the political, cultural, and economic independence of Flanders.[114] While the industrial *Kölnische Zeitung* applauded this declaration for a " Flanders free and Flemish, in close economic relations to its natural hinterland, Germany," the German government remained noncommittal.[115] The reason for this attitude is interesting. It seems that the administrative separation which Germany herself had introduced, had turned out to be a doubtful blessing and had resulted in considerable difficulties and confusion. Events had proved that the complete political separation of Flanders and Wallonia was undesirable from an economic point of view.[116] This was taken into account when the Government General drew up its own program for the future of Belgium in early April of 1918. Economically, far-reaching collaboration with Germany was suggested, with such details as the establishment of a customs and monetary union and German influence over rail and waterways. Of particular interest, however, are the proposals for Belgium's future political organization. The separation between Flemings and Walloons was to be carried through as planned, yet for economic reasons a certain amount of unity was to be maintained by means of a common ruler and common ministries for both sections of the country.[117]

The question is—why did the Germans bother to maintain the division of Belgium, if it caused them such difficulties and was economically harmful? The answer, given on several occasions by Ludendorff, was that the principle of " divide and rule " presented many advantages to Germany.[118] " It matters very little to the Central Powers whether or not Belgium is divided into the two states of Flanders and Wallonia," a confidential memorandum of the Government General read. " What does matter is that we shall profit from this linguistic dualism which so divides and breaks

[113] " Rudiger," pp. 286-87; Raad van Vlanderen, pp. 434-35.
[114] *Schulthess*, vol. 59 (2), pp. 347-48.
[115] *Norddeutsche Allgemeine Zeitung*, June 26, 1918.
[116] C. von Delbrück, *Mobilmachung*, p. 254; Winnig, pp. 413-14.
[117] *U. A.*, 4. Reihe, XII (1), 106; VII (1), 32.
[118] " Rudiger," pp. 82, 286-87.

up the Belgian people that German public opinion will see the necessity of our occupying Belgium." [119] The duration of such an occupation, it was decided on May 25 by the Supreme Command and the Government General, was to be at least ten years.[120] It was to be discontinued only on condition that Germany's influence over the country in general and Flanders in particular had been securely established. The general agreement registered again on this occasion, as well as the general developments in Belgium during 1917 and early 1918, shows that the annexationism current in Germany had the full support of the Belgian administration. There was considerable difference of opinion about the details of Belgium's future among the leading members of the Government General. But there is no indication that the latter ever advocated the unconditional restitution of Belgium, necessary prerequisite for a negotiated peace.

The Fall of Kühlmann

The German government, during the spring of 1918, left the field of war aims pretty much to the Supreme Command and its annexationist friends. The negotiations at Brest-Litovsk having been concluded, the peace settlement with Rumania was now being discussed at Bucharest. It was in connection with the German Foreign Secretary's presence at the Rumanian capital, that the annexationists tried to play one of their less savory tricks, trying to bring about Kühlmann's fall. The Secretary's moderation had long been a matter of concern to the proponents of far-reaching war aims. Already in March of 1918 Kühlmann had been warned against the constant agitation for his dismissal, carried on by the great industrialists, notably Stinnes.[121] In April, the Secretary was again involved in some of his efforts to open direct and secret negotiations with the British government.[122] On April 23, the *Deutsche Zeitung* published an article accusing von Kühlmann of damaging the reputation of the German Empire by his nightly excursions into the Bucharest *demi-monde* during his negotiations with Rumania.[123] As was to be expected, the article caused a considerable stir, though in a way quite different from what its authors had

[119] Raad van Vlaanderen, p. 499.
[120] *Ibid.*
[121] *U. A.*, 4. Reihe, VIII, 261.
[122] Haussmann, pp. 187, 190-91; Max von Baden, p. 266.
[123] Haussmann, p. 189; Werner, p. 270.

expected. The German press was unanimous in its denunciation of the methods used in attacking one of the Reich's chief political figures. Vice-Chancellor von Payer, for the government, sued the editor of the *Alldeutsche Blätter*, chief source of the mud-slinging against Kühlmann.[124] The affair, in itself of little consequence, shows to what depths of bad taste the annexationists were willing to stoop to realize their aims. If they were concerned over the dignity of their country, this was one way how not to maintain it, because the impression this incident left abroad was anything but favorable.[125]

In view of the wave of annexationism that swept over Germany in the spring of 1918, the moderate Reichstag majority found it difficult to withstand the many requests for repudiating publicly its Peace Resolution of July 19, 1917. Only the Socialists maintained unwaveringly, or almost unwaveringly, their anti-annexationist stand.[126] Speakers of both the Center and Progressive Parties, on the other hand, pointed out that because the enemy had refused to accept their peace offer Germany's hands were now free to make whatever settlement she desired.[127] At a meeting of the Center Party's Rhineland branch, the Reichstag deputy Trimborn asserted that his party would approve any peace settlement in the west as it had done in the east.[128] Erzberger, on the other hand, published a declaration in May upholding the validity of the Reichstag Resolution; but in view of the elastic interpretation that Resolution had received, particularly by Erzberger himself, such a statement had only limited value.[129] The Progressives, likewise, had their share of members who desired that the party dissociate itself from the Peace Resolution. The Progressive deputy Fischbeck had published an article to that effect in April and was supported by several of his colleagues, notably Müller-Meiningen and Schulze-Gaevernitz. The majority of the party, however, under the leadership of Friedrich Naumann, declared its continued adherence to the July Resolution.[130]

[124] Great Britain, *Enemy Supplement*, III, May 9, 1918, 1124.

[125] A French punster referred to the German Foreign Secretary as *Ridi culmann, embrasseur d'Allemagne*. Kühlmann claims that the attack against him was inspired by persons " close to the Supreme Command." Kühlmann, pp. 564-65.

[126] Winnig, p. 416.

[127] *Norddeutsche Allgemeine Zeitung*, April 6, 1918.

[128] *Ibid.*, April 7, 1918; *Reichstag*, vol. 311, p. 4155.

[129] *Germania*, May 23, 1918.

[130] Haussmann, p. 187; Ostfeld, p. 54.

These various manifestations show that we must not overestimate the continued vitality of the Resolution as the chief binding force on the Reichstag majority. It was with some justification that Gustav Stresemann, at a meeting of his National Liberals, could say: " Practically we have brought it to this, that a conclusion of peace, in opposition to the policy of July 19, has been agreed to by all the bourgeois parties." [131] What kept the majority together was not so much its common moderation in the field of foreign policy as its united demand for the reform of Prussia's franchise. On April 30, the franchise bill came up for its second reading in the Prussian House of Deputies. Its key provisions, in favor of equal franchise, had been replaced by a complicated system of plural suffrage, which robbed the bill of its most essential features. Count Hertling gave a serious warning to the deputies among whom the anti-reform parties of the Right predominated. " Equal franchise," he said, " will come, if not today, then within a measurable length of time. It must come either without disturbances or after serious internal conflicts." [132] Yet extensive discussions of the bill failed to bring any substantial change, and on July 4, after its fourth reading, the bill was passed in its adulterated form and equal franchise had been defeated.[133] Not only in external policy, therefore, but in the much more important domestic field, the forces of annexationism and reaction had their last great success. Coming so shortly before the final catastrophe, such narrow-minded insistence on obsolete privileges seems difficult to comprehend. But we must remember that to most of the beneficiaries of the Hohenzollern regime, the loss of these privileges was at least as vital a threat as the military defeat of their country.

The optimism of the annexationists, however, was hardly justified by events on the western front. By the end of March, one week after the start of the offensive, Germany's first thrust against the Anglo-French lines between the Scarpe and Oise rivers had spent its force. Its objective, the break through the Allied front, the separation of the French and British armies, and the defeat of the latter, had failed. A second offensive, this time on the Armentières sector, beginning on April 9, and culminating on April 25 in the successful attack upon the key position of Kemmel, likewise

---

[131] *Berliner Tageblatt*, March 11, 1918.

[132] Lutz, *German Empire*, II, 435.

[133] *U. A.*, 4. Reihe, VIII, 187-90.

brought the Germans outstanding successes, but failed to effect the decisive break which alone could re-convert the struggle in the west into a war of movement. It took another month before the German armies had sufficiently recovered so that another major attack could be undertaken. It was during this period of waiting that some doubts began to appear among the German people about the success of the great military venture. "The public doesn't read the army communiqués any more," Conrad Haussmann wrote to Haeften in May. "It is uncertain about the offensive, whether it is still going on or whether it is to start all over again. Public opinion in villages and cities is very quiet." [134]

From this atmosphere of doubt grew another series of plans for a peace offensive, such as we witnessed during the first months of 1918. Hermann Stegemann, in early May, summed up Germany's position as "excellent—but hopeless," hopeless because she had missed her chance of making a special declaration on Belgium before the military offensive began. Such a declaration, he held, "would either have made the offensive superfluous or else would have increased its effectiveness one hundred-fold." [135] Yet other people believed that a political offensive was still possible at this point. On June 1, Crown Prince Rupprecht wrote to Hertling, whom he knew intimately from the latter's days as Bavaria's first minister: "At one time I myself supported the idea of joining Belgium with the German Reich in some form. But I have now changed my mind, aside from other reasons, because I am convinced that the only way which can lead us to peace is a declaration to the effect that we intend to maintain Belgium's independence untouched." Count Hertling's answer on June 5 expressed agreement. "As far as Belgium is concerned," he wrote, "I agree with Your Royal Highness that the *Angliederung* of the country to the German Reich is not to be desired; some difficulty will be created by the administrative separation, introduced during the occupation." [136] This view was certainly more moderate than Hertling's public utterances. But even so, it did not touch upon Prince Rupprecht's main suggestion for an open declaration of Germany's disinterestedness in Belgium.

Of further interest in this connection is a lengthy memorandum which the German Crown Prince handed to his father in July. Since the military situation was such as to make a victorious conclusion of the war most unlikely, at least in the near future, the

---

[134] Haussmann, p. 197.   [135] Max von Baden, p. 275.   [136] Hertling, pp. 140-42.

Crown Prince suggested that Germany try once again to reach a negotiated peace through neutral channels. For that purpose a clear definition and statement of her war aims was a prime necessity. " Of course we want to keep Alsace-Lorraine," the Crown Prince wrote, " and we also want back our colonies. Perhaps we may also demand the Briey basin. But on the other hand we should agree to renounce a war indemnity and to restore Belgium...." Germany already had enough unreliable foreign minorities within her boundaries, he held, without increasing their number by extending her hold over Belgium. To keep the Flanders coast would be unacceptable to England and of little use to Germany, since its ports were not very well suited as naval bases.

In addition [the Prince concluded] the coast would force us to maintain a fleet at least equal to that of England, which we would hardly be able to do. We therefore better agree that Belgium will remain independent, neither pay nor receive an indemnity, may not keep an army, and recognize Germany's economic equality with the states of the Entente.[137]

How widespread the idea for a political offensive had become is shown by the fact that some German newspapers now began writing about it. On May 22, in a widely discussed article, the *Neue Preussische Zeitung* suggested that Germany open such an offensive by declaring her specific official war aims, especially towards England. The *Vorwärts* (on June 1) and the *Kölnische Zeitung* (on June 3) supported this proposal, while annexationist papers like the *Deutsche Zeitung*, the *Deutsche Tageszeitung*, and the *Kölnische Volkszeitung* came out in sharp opposition.[138] Most remarkable, however, was a series of articles in favor of a negotiated peace published in the *Kreuzzeitung* during the first days of June 1918.[139] Even though its editors insisted that they did not agree with their contents and that the idea behind them differed widely from that of the July Peace Resolution, the fact that they were published in a paper notorious for its annexationism created a considerable stir.[140] The same paper, on June 6, advocated the annexation of the Briey-Longwy region, but admitted, as had been pointed out before, that Germany might secure her necessary supplies of iron ore by means of a treaty with France on the model of her petroleum convention with Rumania.[141]

[137] Bauer, p. 219.
[138] Seeberg, pp. 55-57.
[139] Helfferich, p. 625.
[140] *Kreuzzeitung*, June 5, 1918.
[141] For a similar suggestion see *Europäische Staats-und Wirtschaftszeitung*, May 11, 1918.

More important still was a second memorandum of Colonel von Haeften, dated June 3, 1918, and repeating the ideas first expressed by him on January 14. Already on May 19, Prince Max von Baden, during a visit to the front, had asked Ludendorff to attempt another peace settlement before Germany spent her last bit of offensive strength. The General had agreed, but a new German offensive against the French between Noyon and Rheims required his immediate and undivided attention. Starting on May 27, along the slopes of the *Chemin des Dames*, this renewed attack again did not go beyond its initial successes and had to be broken off on June 13. It was at the height of Germany's successful advance that von Haeften handed his memorandum to Ludendorff.[142] The document made specific suggestions for a political offensive, to be carried out by a number of prominent unofficial persons, just before Germany launched the final thrust of her military offensive. It differed in one essential respect from the original draft of Haeften's proposal of January 14, as well as from most of the other suggestions of its kind: it was quite noncommittal on the key problem of Belgium. " Though it would be wrong, at this time, to make official declarations on the question of Belgium," it said, " it would . . . be most effective if some more or less private personalities would open the question . . . in the manner of the public declarations made thus far by the present and former Chancellors." [143]

Despite his current military successes, Ludendorff read Haeften's memorandum with great care and asked that it be sent immediately to Hertling. In a covering note Ludendorff warmly supported the Colonel's proposed peace offensive.[144] On his return to Berlin, therefore, von Haeften was called in to discuss his document with Hertling and Kühlmann. Both of them immediately put their finger upon its chief weakness when they questioned the success of a peace offensive as long as the government and Supreme Command disagreed on the fundamental question of Belgium. After Haeften assured them that an agreement on this crucial point could be achieved, since Ludendorff had expressed quite moderate views on the subject, Hertling and Kühlmann gave their approval and asked the Colonel to take over the direction of the project.[145]

[142] Haussmann, p. 200.   [144] *Ibid.*, pp. 195-96.
[143] *U. A.*, 4. Reihe, II, 342. [145] *Ibid.*, p. 197.

After the suggestions for a political offensive from Prince Rupprecht as well as the Supreme Command, the matter was brought to Count Hertling's attention for a third time by Secretary of State Helfferich.[146] But despite these repeated warnings, the Chancellor failed to pursue Haeften's suggestion, a fact which has brought him much unjustified criticism. The main reason for Hertling's hesitation was a memorandum from his Press Chief, Deutelmoser, which pointed to the most startling aspect of the Haeften memorandum, namely, that Germany's military leaders seemed to doubt the chance of ending the war by mere military means. Before Haeften's suggestion could be carried out, Deutelmoser said, agreement had to be established between the government and the Supreme Command, not only on questions of foreign but of domestic policy as well. In addition, the Reichstag would have to be taken into confidence and its co-operation secured.

The most essential point on which agreement had to be reached between civil and military authorities was the question of Belgium; and here, as should be clear from developments thus far, agreement was impossible. Haeften's confidence in Ludendorff's moderation was mostly wishful thinking and the result, probably, of his own moderation. It was contradicted not only by Haeften's statement in late 1918, citing as Ludendorff's aim the maintenance of Germany's military, political, and economic influence over Belgium, but also by the General's own views expressed at the Brussels meeting on May 25 and on other occasions.[147] In the light of all earlier and subsequent developments, it seems most unlikely that the Supreme Command should have agreed to the unconditional restitution of Belgium in June of 1918. The only criticism one can justifiably direct against Germany's political leaders is that they did not call von Haeften's bluff and ask the army for its views on Belgium. Yet since the answer was sure to be unsatisfactory, their failure to ask for it should not cause any great surprise.

If collaboration on a peace offensive between civil and military authorities was thus difficult, the Haeften memorandum had made a sufficiently strong impression to bring about an independent move by Germany's Foreign Secretary. On June 24, Kühlmann was suddenly asked to substitute for Count Hertling and to address the Reichstag. Coming at the end of a strenuous day, the Secretary's improvised speech, delivered in a tone of weary resignation,

---

[146] Helfferich, pp. 625-26.   [147] *U. A.*, 4. Reihe, II, 369.

10

was definitely one of his less successful performances.[148] He made
some general and meaningless statements on Germany's war aims
and explained once again that the question of Belgium would have
to be treated together with all other problems at the future peace
conference, and that Germany could not restrict her freedom of
action by a unilateral declaration. This, in reality, was the most
significant part of Kühlmann's address, since it closed the door
on any opportunity for peace negotiations by means of a clear
statement on Belgium.[149] But the real sensation of the day was
caused when the Secretary of State hinted at the information he
had gained from Haeften's memorandum. "Without some exchange of views," he said, "considering the tremendous extent of
this war of coalitions and the number of powers . . . involved in it,
an absolute end can hardly be expected from military decisions
alone, without recourse, to diplomatic negotiations." [150] This pessimistic confession, that the war could no longer be won by mere
military measures, might have been overlooked, had it not been for
the vigilance of Count Westarp, who immediately rose to attack
Kühlmann's speech as a threat to Germany's morale at home and
at the front.[151] Nor did the Supreme Command hide its indignation at the Secretary's speech. Though it was primarily due to
the memorandum of one of its own officers, among the chief points
of that same memorandum had been the suggestion to keep the
government itself from engaging in any peace move and to leave
the matter up to unofficial figures of public life. Kühlmann's
speech, therefore, though justified, was most unwise. Its immediate result was that Ludendorff told Haeften to give up his efforts
for a political offensive.[152] Both Hertling and Kühlmann tried to
remedy the situation by explanations before the Reichstag on
June 25.[153] The annexationists, especially the *Vaterlandspartei*,

---

[148] *Reichstag*, vol. 312, pp. 5607 ff.

[149] Stegemann, *Erinnerungen*, pp. 460-61.

[150] *Reichstag*, vol. 312, pp. 5611-12. Kühlmann himself explains his speech as
only partly motivated by the Haeften memorandum. Its main purpose was to
support another one of his peace feelers towards England by stating openly the
need for a " peace of understanding." Kühlmann, pp. 569 ff., esp. pp. 573-74, 576.

[151] *Reichstag*, pp. 5634-35. Westarp reportedly phoned the Supreme Command immediately after Kühlmann's speech to point out that some of its statements could
be used as basis for an attack against the Foreign Secretary. Kühlmann, p. 575.

[152] *U. A.*, 4. Reihe, II, 200-03; Helfferich, pp. 627 ff.; Hertling, pp. 55, 75-76, 116 ff.,
131 ff.; Payer, *Bethmann Hollweg*, ch. IV.

[153] *Reichstag*, vol. 312, pp. 5640 ff.

joined the Conservatives and National Liberals in condemning a statement which merely told the unpleasant truth.[154] Kühlmann was able to remain in office for another two weeks, and in view of the impression his dismissal would make both abroad and at home, it was by no means an easy decision to let him go.[155] If the Kaiser finally had to tell the Secretary that they had to sever their relations, it was due almost entirely to pressure from Hindenburg and Ludendorff, who refused to have any more dealings with him. To the annexationists, the dismissal of this relatively liberal and moderate official was a major victory. The Supreme Command, against the wishes of Emperor and Chancellor, achieved on July 8 what the *Deutsche Zeitung* had tried without success on April 23, using, as in the case of Bethmann Hollweg's dismissal, their unassailable position in the military sphere to enforce their will in the political field.[156]

Events surrounding the Kühlmann crisis had shown a dangerous lack of collaboration between Germany's political and military authorities. In late June, therefore, Count Hertling decided to move to Supreme Headquarters at Spa, so as to be able to maintain closer personal contact with Hindenburg and Ludendorff. Discussions of vital issues began immediately, and on July 2-3, during von Kühlmann's absence, they turned to a re-definition of Germany's Belgian war aims. The results were embodied in the following statement:

Belgium must remain under German influence, so that she cannot again fall under Anglo-French domination, and thus offer our enemies bases for their armies. For that purpose we must demand the separation of Flanders and Wallonia into two separate states, united only by personal union and economic arrangements. Belgium must, through customs union, community of railways, etc., be brought into closest relation with Germany. For the time being there must be no Belgian army. Germany must secure for herself a long period of occupation with gradual withdrawal in such a way that the Flanders coast and Liège will be evacuated last. The complete evacuation depends on Belgium's attaching herself to us as closely as possible. In particular we must have complete and absolute certainty about Belgian measures for the protection of the Flanders coast.[157]

---

[154] Wortmann, p. 53; Westarp, II, 609.

[155] Payer, *Bethmann Hollweg*, pp. 69-70.

[156] *U. A.*, 4. Reihe, II, 203 ff. *The Bund der Kaisertreuen* likewise claimed a share in Kühlmann's dismissal: Great Britain, *Enemy Supplement*, IV, Aug. 15, 1918, 381. Kühlmann gives a full account of his parting discussion with the Emperor for whom he felt considerable admiration and affection. Kühlmann, p. 579.

[157] *U. A.*, 4. Reihe, II, 346-47.

Here we have additional proof of the Supreme Command's continued optimism and its unwillingness to give up any of its western aims. The old Chancellor, already subservient to the wishes of the military before the spring offensive, now gave in completely to the two men who better than anyone else knew the true state of Germany's military strength. On July 11 he travelled to Berlin to report the Foreign Secretary's dismissal to the Reichstag, and to assure the deputies that the change in personnel—the former Admiral von Hintze had been selected as Kühlmann's successor—did not mean any change in policy.[158] On the same occasion, Hertling referred to the question of Belgium, repeating in sufficiently ambiguous terms the results of the July 2-3 meeting. Germany did not intend keeping Belgium permanently, he held.

Belgium is a pledge (*Faustpfand*) in our hand, to be used at future negotiations. . . . We must protect ourselves in the conditions of peace against the danger of Belgium's turning into a base for the advance of our enemies; we must protect ourselves not only in the military, but also in the economic sense. . . . If we succeed, in addition, in agreeing with Belgium on the political questions which touch Germany's vital interests, we have the definite prospect of finding the best safeguard against future dangers which may threaten us from Belgium or from England and France via Belgium.[159]

In many ways these words remind one of Bethmann Hollweg's vague utterances on the same subject during the first three years of war, and they permitted the same variety of interpretation. While the *Berliner Tageblatt* stressed the moderation of Hertling's speech, the *Kölnische Volkszeitung* welcomed the demand for Germany's economic, political, and military control over Belgium.[160] The annexationist *Deutsche Tageszeitung* was against the declaration, however ambiguous, of Germany's Belgian aims; [161] and the *Vaterlandspartei* published a protest on July 14, refusing

to participate in the attempts to read this or that meaning into the statements [of the Chancellor]. For us Belgium is not merely a pledge. For the security of a lasting peace, real German power in Belgium must defend the economy of the country from Anglo-American exploitation, the Flemings from Gallicisation, German land and German industry from the devastations of a future war, and not least, the seas from English tyranny.[162]

---

[158] *Ibid.*, p. 207.
[159] *Ibid.*, XII (1), 156-57.
[160] *Ibid.*, VII (1), 34; *Berliner Tageblatt*, July 12, 1918 (ev. ed.).
[161] *Deutsche Tageszeitung*, July 13, 1918.
[162] Wortmann, p. 54.

If they had only known how closely their aims really agreed with those of the government, the annexationists could have saved much of their verbal thunder.

The Final Months

On July 15, the Supreme Command launched its last major offensive on the Rheims-Soissons front. In a conversation with the new Foreign Secretary, Ludendorff was confident that this time the enemy's defeat would be decisive.[163] For once, however, even the usual initial successes failed to materialize, since the French were not taken by surprise and were able to withdraw into prepared positions beyond the range of German artillery. On July 16, therefore, the Supreme Command had to break off operations and on the following day withdrew to the northern bank of the Marne. On July 18, a French countermove, making effective use of tanks, laid a deep breach into the German positions southwest of Soissons. At last the tide had turned; the initiative had shifted from the Germans to the Allies. The attempt to reach a military decision before the arrival of American reinforcements had failed. General Ludendorff realized that the situation was most serious, but still hoped to withstand Allied attacks, which now had to be expected with increasing force and frequency.[164] The orderly withdrawal of German troops into new positions seemed to uphold this view, and a letter of Under-Secretary of State von Radowitz on August 1 testifies to the continued confidence of the Supreme Command.[165] "Five times thus far during the war," Ludendorff remarked to Count Hertling, "I had to withdraw my troops, and still was able, in the end, to beat the enemy. Why shouldn't I succeed a sixth time?"[166]

This last vestige of hope was destroyed, or better, should have been destroyed, when on August 8, 1918, large masses of Allied tanks broke the German lines on the Albert-Moreuil sector. This "darkest day" in the history of the German army, as Ludendorff called it, at first convinced the Supreme Command that the game was up.[167] "We have reached the limit of our endurance," the Emperor summed up the situation. "The war must be ended.

[163] *U. A.*, 4. Reihe, II, 387.
[164] Ludendorff, *Kriegserinnerungen*, pp. 543, 545-46.
[165] *U. A.*, 4. Reihe, II, 381-82.
[166] Hertling, p. 146.
[167] Ludendorff, *Kriegserinnerungen*, pp. 547 ff.; Scheidemann, *Memoiren*, II, 175.

. . ." [168] A meeting was called at Spa on August 13-14, to discuss the situation which had been so profoundly changed a few days earlier. The conviction of the Supreme Command that Germany, by an effective defensive, was still able to exhaust the enemies' military strength and force them to sue for peace, made Ludendorff continue to insist on the far-reaching Belgian war aims drawn up on July 3. Again the political leaders bowed to the judgment of those most qualified to render it. Attempts at a negotiated peace were to be considered at a future date, when the right moment offered itself, "after the next success on the western front." The idea that such a time might never come, that it was already too late for such attempts, since Germany's position in the west had been so severely shaken, seems not to have occurred to anyone at the Spa conference.[169]

Despite the army's continued optimism, the civilian authorities thought it advisable to make some further attempts at a negotiated peace settlement. On August 14, von Hintze told the Bavarian Count Törring, who had been carrying on secret negotiations with the Belgian government since March, that Germany would agree to discuss the complete political and economic independence of Belgium. While going far beyond any concessions the Supreme Command was willing to make, the proposal, as submitted by Count Törring to the Belgian ambassador at Bern, still insisted on the solution of the Flemish question, failed to mention a German indemnity to Belgium, and made its restitution dependent on the return of Germany's colonies. Under the circumstances, the Belgian government, in an official communiqué of September 19, refused to consider such a conditional offer.[170] On August 15, von Hintze, with equally small success, had also informed the government of the United States of his Belgian war aims: "No annexation, no vassal or similar relationship of dependence, good economic relations, guarantees of political and economic independence, also from our adversaries." [171] At an earlier date, such peace offers might have been successful. After August 8, Germany's opponents could afford to wait until Germany was willing to make peace on their own terms.

[168] A. Niemann, *Kaiser und Revolution* (Berlin, 1928), p. 43.
[169] *U. A.*, 4. Reihe, II, pp. 223 ff.
[170] *Schulthess*, vol. 59 (2), pp. 349 ff., *U. A.*, 4. Reihe, III, 351-52.
[171] *U. A.*, 4. Reihe, II, 235, 393-94.

These last minute attempts at a negotiated peace, moreover, were still over-shadowed by expressions of expansionist war aims. In its refusal to give in, to recognize its own failure, German annexationism revealed once again all those qualities which had made it such a powerful force during four years of war—its patriotism, its greed, and its fear of having to give up some of its cherished privileges. As war aims capable of realization, the pronouncements after the middle of August can no longer be taken seriously; as indications of the deep hold which annexationism had over its victims, these belated expressions are of considerable significance.

On August 19, von Hintze tried once more to have Ludendorff make a concession on Belgium. Two days later, the General replied that he could not approve of the *status quo ante*, and von Hintze the same day told a meeting of party leaders about the Supreme Command's confidence in Germany's ability to hold out until she could reach a satisfactory peace settlement.[172] On August 20, Solf, speaking before the *Deutsche Gesellschaft 1914* on German and British war aims, intended to make a clear statement on Belgium. He was prevented by the Foreign Office, which feared opposition from the Supreme Command.[173] Four days later, Vice-Chancellor von Payer and Count Hertling drafted another statement on Belgium, for which they asked the approval of Hindenburg and Ludendorff. This was given only after several qualifying clauses had been inserted, reserving the Flemish question for future discussions with Belgium and making the restoration in general dependent on the return of Germany's colonies. Finally the declaration was not to be used as such, but was to be carefully concealed in a speech which Payer delivered on September 10, and which even then caused Ludendorff's disapproval.[174] Nothing shows better the stubborn blindness of Germany's military authorities towards the real danger than this wrangling over the details of a statement which, even in its original form, had by no means advocated the unconditional restoration of Belgium. The Payer-Ludendorff negotiations, it has been said, remind one of two men playing a leisurely game of chess aboard a rapidly sinking ship.[175]

[172] *Ibid.*, pp. 236-37; Westarp, II, 563.

[173] Max von Baden, pp. 292-93; *Schulthess*, vol. 59 (1), pp. 254 ff.; Schwabach, pp. 257-58.

[174] Payer, *Bethmann Hollweg*, p. 274; F. von Payer, *Mein Lebenslauf* (Stuttgart, 1932), p. 59.

[175] Rosenberg, p. 225.

The course of events leading up to the final crisis now became ever more complicated. Austria's desire to get out of the war as soon as possible necessitated von Hintze's visit to Vienna in early September, where he discussed the question of war aims with Austria's new Foreign Secretary, Count Burian. Germany's aims, as presented on September 5, were held in most general terms. In regard to Belgium they simply advocated "no appropriation (*Besitznahme*) of Belgium, but no privileges for other powers either."[176]

In the meantime, events on the western front had gone from bad to worse and on September 3 Count Hertling asked Hindenburg's views on the military situation. When no answer had been received by September 9, von Hintze went to Headquarters, where he found continued confidence. The Foreign Secretary on this occasion also reported Austria's contemplated peace proclamation to the Supreme Command. Hindenburg opposed such a move, but at least he agreed to submit to the immediate mediation of a neutral power, which led to an unsuccessful last minute attempt at a negotiated peace through the Queen of the Netherlands.[177]

Despite Germany's efforts to prevent such a step, Austria's peace note was published on September 15, with very serious effects on German public opinion. The leaders of the various parties immediately asked to see the Chancellor, who once again assured them that all was well and that there was no cause for alarm.[178] In general it can be said that, while the Supreme Command, not always very successfully, was keeping the government in the dark as to the real gravity of the military situation, the latter handed the same note of optimism on to the people's representatives. The explanation for such a policy was partly lack of courage to face reality, partly the fear that full knowledge of the seriousness of Germany's position would undermine public morale. As things turned out, a terrible shock was inflicted on the German people when suddenly, a few weeks later, they were confronted by defeat.

It is only through ignorance of the true military situation that we can explain the final outbursts of German annexationism during September of 1918. This ignorance, however, was not so complete as some of the annexationists themselves try to make us believe. On August 12, for instance, the Kaiser's new political

[176] *U. A.*, 4. Reihe, XII (1), 224. [177] *Ibid.*, II, 240 ff. [178] *Ibid.*, pp. 245-46.

adviser, von Berg, asked Westarp to use his influence in moderating the discussion of war aims in the annexationist press. This the Count refused to do. Instead the Conservatives clung to their large war aims to the very last minute. On September 26, Westarp declared before the Reichstag Main Committee that his party continued to adhere to its Belgian demands and to a large indemnity. " The renunciation of Belgium and of indemnities," he wrote in the *Kreuzzeitung* on September 29, " will not bring us one step closer to peace." On September 30, the Count repeated the same ideas in his last address on war aims, and he would have continued to do so had not political events—the resignation of Count Hertling and Germany's request for an armistice—advised greater moderation.[179]

Much of the responsibility for the stubborn adherence of the Conservative leader to strong war aims was due directly to the influence of the Supreme Command. Rumor had it in September that the National Liberals were about to come out in favor of a moderate program, such as laid down in Payer's speech of September 10, on the understanding that the Supreme Command agreed to it. Westarp asked Ludendorff if the Supreme Command had made a statement to that effect and whether the General would object if the Conservatives continued to adhere to their western aims. Ludendorff replied: " The Conservative Party shall stick to its war aims. . . . I should deplore the declaration of the National Liberal Party." [180]

The *Kriegszielbewegung* likewise kept up its agitation to the very last minute. " We have no use for a peace of understanding," General von Liebert said in early September, " because it would mean our ruin "; and he went on to make the usual demands for annexations in Western Europe and overseas.[181] On September 2, the *Vaterlandspartei* celebrated its first anniversary with a meeting advocating a strong peace.[182] Three weeks later, on September 24, it came out with another one of its rousing manifestoes.[183] Despite the government's continued assurance to the contrary, however, some of the annexationists began to suspect that perhaps their dreams might not come true after all. The *Frankfurter Zeitung* recognized " in the present tone of the Pan-Germans a

[179] Westarp, II, 560-64; *U. A.*, 4. Reihe, III, 325.
[180] Westarp, II, 563-64.
[181] *Berliner Tageblatt*, Sept. 2, 1918.
[182] *Frankfurter Zeitung*, Sept. 3, 1918.
[183] Wortmann, pp. 57-58.

new and unwonted quietude, even sadness. Their time, they feel, has gone by." [184]

It is unnecessary to go into the events directly leading up to Germany's request for an armistice on October 3, 1918. The decision to take this momentous step was reached by the Supreme Command on the afternoon of September 28, largely under the influence of Bulgaria's collapse. It came as a complete surprise and shock to the government and the people, especially in view of the army's constant assurance that Germany could hold out until a successful peace was won. It had been due chiefly to the army's confident attitude that the government hesitated to renounce publicly its hopes for some measure of German influence over Western Europe. On September 24, Count Hertling delivered his last important address before the Reichstag Main Committee. When he came to the subject of Belgium, the Chancellor repeated almost exactly the explanations which Bethmann Hollweg had given in 1914 for Germany's violation of Belgian neutrality. His speech expressed moderation, to be sure, but not in specific enough terms to indicate that the government was aware of the fact that the *Drang nach Westen* had lost all chance of realization.[185]

Even after the Supreme Command requested the government to enter into negotiations for an armistice, expansionist hopes were still expressed by German political and military figures. On September 27, Hindenburg wanted the annexation of Briey and Longwy as one of the armistice conditions, but Ludendorff had sense enough to realize that the time for such demands had gone by.[186] The next day, Solf spoke at the University of Munich, in the presence of King Ludwig of Bavaria, and expected not only the return of Germany's colonies, but also a redistribution of African holdings, in which Belgium, France, and Portugal had to give up some of their disproportionate colonial wealth.[187] After the government, on October 4-5, had officially asked President Wilson for an armistice on the basis of his Fourteen Points, all justification for such continued hopes of gain disappeared once and for all. But even so there are instances of the army's *Vaterländischer Unterricht* insisting, as late as the middle of October, that Germany had won

---

[184] *Frankfurter Zeitung,* Aug. 29, 1918 (ev. ed.).
[185] *U. A.,* 4. Reihe, VIII, 310-11.
[186] *Ibid.,* II, 405.
[187] *Kölnische Zeitung,* Oct. 1, 1918.

the war and all she had to do now was to secure the fruits of victory.[188] The Independent Committee and its president, on October 10 and 16, came out against a peace based on Wilson's program.[189] On October 17, Dietrich Schäfer wrote that the Committee " believes to serve the Fatherland by continuing to represent the views which form the basis of its endeavors; for the future belongs to them." [190] On October 23, in a speech before the Reichstag, the former Secretary of the Interior, Count von Posadowsky-Wehner, once more brought up the question of Belgium and implied that Germany should try to maintain a certain amount of influence in that region.[191] And finally, on October 30, following a similar proposal of Hindenburg's six days earlier, the *Vaterlandspartei* suggested that Germany refuse the Allied demands and continue the war as the only means of winning a tolerable peace.[192]

We need not extend the discussion of these death-struggles of annexationism any further. If they seem prolonged and painful, we must remember how much there was at stake for the men whose plans for German expansion had exerted such profound influence on the policy of their country. There were already many indications that the defeat of annexationism was not to be limited to the territorial sphere. On October 4, when Germany's military collapse had become unavoidable, the Supreme Command had finally used its influence to settle the question of Prussian reforms. The result of its intercession was the acceptance, on October 24, of equal franchise for Prussia. The annexationists had suffered a second, at least equally serious defeat in the domestic sphere. The close relationship between a strong peace and the continued enjoyment of the privileged position of Germany's ruling classes, here found its final confirmation. It was to be a matter of weeks before the decisive defeat at the front was followed by the complete and utter collapse of the German political order.

---

[188] Thimme, *Weltkrieg*, p. 204.
[189] Schäfer, *Leben*, pp. 226-28.
[190] Jagow, p. 124.
[191] *Reichstag*, vol. 314, p. 6203.
[192] Wortmann, p. 62.

CONCLUSION

WE HAVE come to the end of the Great War and Germany's attempts to extend her political and economic influence over much of the European continent and overseas. The anti-climax to more than four years of great expectations did not come until several months later, when the war aims of the Allies won their triumphal victory at the Peace Conference of Paris. Instead of acquiring the ore basin of Briey and Longwy, Germany had to cede Alsace and Lorraine to France. Instead of gaining all or part of Belgium, she was forced to give up the districts of Eupen and Malmédy. The dream of a large *Mittelafrika* not only failed to materialize, but Germany lost even the colonies she held before 1914. And finally, far from being able to regain the expenses of the war from their enemies, the Germans had to shoulder the whole burden of misery and destruction which the war had caused to all the world. Annexationism, as the final outcome of the war showed, was a universal problem, not confined to one particular nation. What differences existed between the two groups of powers were of objective rather than of principle. Viewed in the light of four years of annexationist propaganda and the treaties of Brest-Litovsk and Bucharest, the kind of peace settlement which a victorious Germany would have imposed upon her western opponents would most likely have equalled, if not surpassed, the one she was forced to sign at Versailles. Nevertheless, the German people have been almost unanimous in their condemnation of the Versailles Treaty; and ironically enough, the most vociferous denunciations of its terms have come from the very circles that were most outspoken in favor of annexations during the First World War.

It is difficult to sum up a topic as complex as the present one, not the least because it is a study of unfulfilled ambitions. As with any development which fails to reach its logical conclusion, a discussion of the effects of German expansionist plans on the history of the Empire will move as much in the realm of speculation as in the realm of fact. Still, there are two final questions that should be answered on the basis of the material presented in this study. One concerns the general influence of the problem of war aims on German affairs during the war; the second the role which various factors and factions within Germany played in the propagation of war aims—in other words: who was responsible for the *Drang nach Westen?*

In the field of foreign affairs, the question uppermost in the minds of historians has been whether the continued declaration of German war aims was responsible for the failure to reach a peace of understanding during the course of the war. To answer this question one has to consider not merely Germany's war aims, but those of her opponents as well. To use a concrete example: while the problem of Belgium, because of Great Britain's insistence on Belgian independence, developed into one of the crucial obstacles to a negotiated peace, the problem of Alsace-Lorraine was just as important to Germany as Belgium was to Great Britain. If Germany failed to renounce Belgium, France made it perfectly clear that she never intended to give up her demand for the return of Alsace-Lorraine. Nevertheless, there were several situations—and here we enter the realm of speculation—in which a clear statement on Belgium might have resulted in peace negotiations. England might have been willing to break her commitments under the secret treaties of London and make a separate peace with Germany; or else she could bring sufficient pressure to bear on France, so that the latter would give up her aims in Alsace-Lorraine; or maybe a clear German statement would have strengthened the peace-loving groups within the Allied nations, who in turn might have forced their governments to negotiate peace with Germany. Considering these various possibilities, a clear German statement on Belgium would have been decidedly worth trying. Not to have made it remains a grave blunder of German foreign policy during the World War.

In trying to evaluate the influence of war aims upon domestic affairs in Germany, we are on somewhat safer ground. Entering the war with a number of internal problems, the solution of which had long been overdue, the German people soon found this solution postponed not only for the duration of the war, but most likely for an indefinite period. Annexationism in its most outspoken form became the main province of the upper classes, in their vain hope of maintaining their own political and social supremacy. To the lower classes it appeared, with much justification, that the war was being carried on for the sake of foreign gains, which in turn would only serve to perpetuate domestic injustices. To have thus maintained and intensified the political, social, and economic cleavages among the German people at one of the most critical periods of its existence is one of the serious responsibilities of annexationism.

How large a part these foreign and domestic influences of annexationism played in shaping the history of the German Empire during the World War is difficult to say. To realize their magnitude, we do well to remember the effect of war aims on the dismissal of such important political figures as Bethmann Hollweg and Kühlmann, both of them victims of the annexationists. We should also remember the many attempts to arrive at a negotiated peace settlement, all of them condemned to failure because of the war aims, declared or implied, of the two groups of belligerents. And finally, we should bear in mind the internal strife and disunity created by four years of wrangling over war aims which contributed decisively to the weakening and final collapse of Imperial Germany.

As to the problem of responsibility, it is a more difficult and controversial one. The great number of factors involved in the propagation of German war aims makes it difficult to assign to each a due share of liability for the blunders committed in the handling of the war aims problem. Although the German government entered the war without specific aims, it would have been unrealistic, after the successes of Germany's armed forces, to expect this state of affairs to last. Germany in 1914 was no longer the saturated power she had been under Bismarck. An extension of territory, the gain of new fields of commercial activity, and the acquisition of additional sources of raw material were looked upon as absolute necessities to a growing and highly industrialized country. The German government, therefore, should have drawn up a realistic program of war aims, moderate in scope but specific in character. This program should have been so designed as to concentrate on one of the major fields of possible expansion—east, west, or overseas—and thus, by driving a wedge between the Allied Powers, make possible the kind of negotiated peace which had become an unavoidable necessity since the failure of the Schlieffen plan in 1914. In addition to such specific aims, a series of general principles might have completed a program which, much in the way of President Wilson's Fourteen Points, would have won the support of the majority of Germans, thus making possible a more effective conduct of the war.

Instead, the Imperial government preferred to leave the question of war aims vague and undecided, clinging to the concept of a war of defense, which few people in Germany and still fewer outside really believed. Left without direction from above but encouraged by the ambiguity of official pronouncements, the German people embarked upon a heated controversy over war aims, which destroyed the last vestige of internal unity created by the outbreak of war. Instead of counteracting this confusion of minds by publishing a definite set of aims, the government preferred to suppress this public discussion, thus only increasing its intensity. Abroad, the failure to come out clearly for or against annexations, viewed in connection with these unofficial utterances in favor of far-reaching war aims, created an atmosphere of suspicion, which made any peace short of complete German or Allied victory impossible.

The responsibility for initiating this policy of vagueness and confusion belongs to Bethmann Hollweg. It was he who set the style for the kind of war aims statement open to almost any interpretation which was then followed by his two successors. While moderate in his aims the uncertainty of Bethmann's statements was a direct boon to his annexationist opponents, to whose attacks he finally succumbed. Bethmann's chief motive was a sincere desire to maintain Germany's internal unity by avoiding the disagreement inherent in the vital question of war aims. But even though his own aims were moderate it would be incorrect to consider the Chancellor averse to any expansion whatsoever. Like most of his countrymen, Bethmann was willing to await the outcome of war before deciding on a definite set of aims. Any premature declaration, he felt, would only limit this German choice. Where Bethmann differed from his successors was in his willingness to give up whatever hopes of gain he had, if in return a negotiated peace could be won. The question what might have happened if his dismissal had not come in the midst of the Papal peace move, is one of the most interesting points of speculation of the whole World War.

After the middle of 1917, the direction of affairs shifted from the hands of the political to those of Germany's military authorities. While outwardly the ambiguous policy on war aims continued, there was no longer much doubt as to the annexationist ambitions of those in command. The fact that this change occurred when popular sentiment in Germany and elsewhere grew increasingly desirous of peace, was most deplorable. The primary motive behind the war aims of the Supreme Command was the attempt to secure, once and for all, Germany's position in Western Europe. Ludendorff's views on the fundamental strategic significance of Belgium should have made him realize, however, that Germany's desire of keeping Belgium was matched by an equally strong Allied determination to prevent Germany from gaining too powerful a position there. As the war progressed, it became increasingly clear that there were only two possible alternatives: a German victory, enabling her to do with Belgium as she pleased, or a negotiated peace, requiring first and foremost that Germany give up Belgium. There appear to have been a few brief instances during the spring of 1918, especially in his conversations with von Haeften, when Ludendorff was more moderate on the subject of Belgium; though to declare this moderation openly, he felt, might seriously affect the morale of the German army. The view held by Bethmann Hollweg, that it was a sufficiently great achievement for Germany to have withstood successfully the large coalition of her enemies, was foreign to the military mind. Both Hindenburg and Ludendorff shared the mistaken belief that the average soldier would only continue fighting if he was shown sufficiently large war aims. If anything, the opposite was true. As the hardships of war increased most soldiers were indignant at the suggestion of continuously risking their lives for the sake of ultimate material gains.

Although politically unsound, the strategic motives behind the army's stubborn annexationism are understandable from the point of view of its own limited, military sphere. The unfortunate part was that the Supreme Command gained such a predominating influence over the direction of German affairs. The absence of any suitable counterweight in the political field tended to centralize complete political as well as military responsibility in the hands of General Ludendorff. His strong and domineering personality played a not insignificant part in this process. As a result the necessary and mutually corrective division of control between military and political authorities disappeared. In addition we must remember the close relationship between Ludendorff and the small but powerful annexationist minority, based on a community of war aims and a deep affinity of social background and political belief. The constant contact between the Supreme Command and Germany's barons of industry suggests that the motives which prompted the annexationism of the German army were not always and exclusively military. Ludendorff's uncompromising adherence to strong war aims was the most important single influence in Germany's misguided efforts to extend her sphere of influence to the west. Although his attitude was determined by the needs of his country, these needs were seen entirely through the eyes of his profession and class. On the one hand they included the necessary strategic improvements enabling the General Staff to be prepared for the next war; and on the other such material and territorial gains as would ensure the maintenance of the existing political and social order. There was really little difference between Ludendorff and most of the radical annexationists, except that the General was in a position where he could enforce his annexationist views.

In discussing the attitude of the German people towards war aims, we have distinguished between the large and inarticulate masses and their parliamentary representatives. The views of the first group are difficult to ascertain. It seems fairly certain, however, that the majority of Germans, under the influence of early military successes, were in favor of more or less strong aims. As the war progressed, this stand became more moderate. The change, which became pronounced some time in 1916, ended in a widespread longing for peace among the lower classes. This fact was not due to any greater degree of political insight on the part of this group over its social and economic betters, but rather to the fact that the common people in Germany suffered more deeply from the hardships of war. It was partly for that reason that the change of attitude from annexationism to moderation was not reflected in the German Reichstag until the middle of 1917. Despite the absence of constitutional provisions to that effect, the influence of the Reichstag became ever greater as the war continued. Its role in the dismissal of both Bethmann Hollweg and Michaelis signified the change from bureaucratic to parliamentary regime. But unfortunately little use was made of this newly-won power to demand a voice in the government's foreign policy. The 1917 Peace Resolution was as far as the majority of the Reichstag was willing to go. As soon as the military situation improved, it reverted to its earlier acquiescence in the decisions of Germany's political and military leaders, as shown in the stand taken on the Treaty of Brest-Litovsk. In the majority of its middle class, the

German people resembled those " tree-frog annexationists " whose war aims changed with the news from the front. Only the Socialists, with some exceptions, maintained a consistently and courageously anti-annexationist platform from the first day of the war to the last.

There remains the small group of annexationists to which we have devoted so much of our discussion. Granted the German civil government was too vague and not always moderate in its aims, granted many Germans changed their views according to the success or failure of the armed forces, still there were several critical situations in which the feeling of moderation might have gained the upper hand had it not been for the vigilance of the annexationist groups and individuals organized behind the *Kriegs-zielbewegung*. It was this numerically unimportant but politically, financially, and intellectually powerful minority which took the lead in the evolution of a German program of war aims. Among these radical annexationists, the great industrialists played a particularly important role. There may be some doubt as to the motives of some of the members of the *Kriegszielbewegung* whose patriotism was more important than their greed; there is no doubt as we deal with men like Thyssen, Stinnes, Kirdorf, Hugenberg, Kloeckner, Beukenberg, and their lesser known associates. To these men Germany's westward expansion meant specific material gains, and Germany's failure to expand meant specific material losses.

It was a combination of elements, then, industrialists, Pan-Germans, the parties of the Right, and the Supreme Command, that was responsible for the stubborn propagation of large war aims, which condemned the German people to remain at war until the bitter end. Each of these forces had its own particular reasons for wanting to hold out for far-reaching territorial gains; yet one aim most of them had in common—to ensure through a successful peace settlement the continuation of the existing order, to their own advantage, and to the political and economic detriment of the majority of the German people.

BIBLIOGRAPHICAL NOTE

A full reference for each work used in this study is given on the page of its first citation. The number of this page can be found in the index, under the name of the respective author. Space does not permit giving a complete and critical bibliography of the works consulted. Such a list is given in the earlier version of this study: "Drang nach Westen" (typescript at the Widener Library, Harvard University, Cambridge, Mass.), pp. 529-73. Most of the research is based on published material, much of which, because of German censorship regulations, was privately printed and is scarce. The bulk of it is available at the Hoover Library, Stanford, California.

State Department restrictions have made it impossible for the author to examine unpublished documentary materials from the German archives captured at the end of the recent war. Scholars who are acquainted with the materials, however, have been very helpful in checking certain conclusions reached in this study.

The main documentary source for the study of German war aims, as for the study of any aspect of German history during the First World War, was published in connection with the Reichstag's postwar investigation into the causes of Germany's collapse in 1918: Germany, Nationalversammlung, *Das Werk des Untersuchungsausschusses*, 4. Reihe, "Die Ursachen des Deutschen Zusammenbruchs im Jahre 1918," 12 vols. (Berlin, 1925-1929). Of special importance is vol. XII (1), E. O. Volkmann, "Die Annexionsfragen des Weltkrieges." Vol. XII (2) by M. Hobohm has never been published. R. H. Lutz has edited a one volume selection in English from the above series, entitled *The Causes of the German Collapse in 1918* (Stanford, 1934). Other important material may be found in Germany, Nationalversammlung, Untersuchungsausschuss über die Weltkriegsverantwortlichkeit, *Stenographische Berichte über die öffentlichen Verhandlungen des 15. Untersuchungsausschusses*, 2 vols. (Berlin, 1920). The debates of the Reichstag for the war period have been published as *Verhandlungen des Reichstages*, XIII. Legislaturperiode, II. Sitzung, vols. 306-308. They contain valuable evidence on the attitude of both the government and the political parties towards the problem of war aims.

No period in German history has been so thoroughly covered by personal memoirs and recollections as the First World War. There is hardly a major or even minor figure who has not left his impressions for posterity. While almost all of these volumes yield some information on war aims, some are more useful than others. The second volume of T. von Bethmann Hollweg's *Betrachtungen zum Weltkriege*, 2 vols. (Berlin, 1921) gives a dispassionate analysis of the author's political activity during the war. The apologia of his successor, G. Michaelis' *Für Staat und Volk* (Berlin, 1922), does not succeed in its purpose but contains useful information. The career of Count Hertling has been described by his son, Karl Graf von Hertling, *Ein Jahr in der Reichskanzlei* (Freiburg, 1919). The last of the Imperial Chancellors, Prinz Max von Baden, in his *Erinnerungen und Dokumente* (Stuttgart, 1927), throws important light on the events prior to Germany's collapse in 1918. The memoirs both of William II and of Hindenburg are disappointing, not only in respect to war aims. General E. Ludendorff, on the other hand, has presented his case with vigor, if not always impartiality, in his *Meine Kriegserinnerungen 1914-1918* (Berlin, 1920) and his *Urkunden der Obersten Heeresleitung über ihre Tätigkeit 1916-1918* (Berlin, 1920). The same can be said for Admiral A. von Tirpitz, both in his *Erinnerungen* (Leipzig, 1919) and in the second volume of his *Politische Dokumente*, 2 vols. (Hamburg, 1924-1926), which contains important documentary material on war aims. Karl Helfferich, *Der Weltkrieg* (Berlin, 1919) gives a historical account of the war, interspersed with the author's personal recollections. Richard von Kühlmann's substantial *Erinnerungen* (Heidelberg, 1948) rounds out the picture on the governmental side.

Several of Germany's party leaders likewise have left us their memoirs. Outstanding is the Conservative Count Westarp's *Konservative Politik im letzten Jahrzehnt des Kaiserreiches*, 2 vols. (Berlin, 1935), the second volume of which deals with the war period. Philipp Scheidemann in his *Memoiren eines Sozialdemokraten*, 2 vols. (Dresden, 1928) and *Der Zusammenbruch* (Berlin, 1921) presents the story from the Socialist side. Matthias Erzberger's *Erlebnisse im Weltkriege* (Stuttgart, 1920) attempts to explain—not always too successfully and reliably—his own activities and those of the Center Party. There are two reliable and useful accounts by Progressives: Conrad Haussmann, *Schlaglichter* (Frankfurt a. M., 1924), and Friedrich von Payer, *Von Bethmann Hollweg bis Ebert* (Frankfurt, 1923). Among the writings of non-political figures, the memoirs of Heinrich Class, President of the Pan-German League, *Wider den Strom* (Leipzig, 1932), are easily the most significant, though unfortunately they cover only the first part of the war. Alfred Hugenberg's *Streiflichter aus Vergangenheit und Gegenwart* (Berlin, 1927) contains some valuable material, while Dietrich Schäfer's *Aus meinem Leben* (Berlin, 1926) is less important. The Austrian journalist Victor Naumann had frequent contact with leading German figures, about which he tells in his *Dokumente und Argumente* (Berlin, 1928) and *Profile* (München, 1925). The same applies to his colleague and compatriot, Heinrich Kanner, who has left " The Papers of Dr. Heinrich Kanner of Vienna " (3 vols. of typescript at the Hoover Library, Stanford, California). Of the large number of remaining memoirs, diaries, and other first-hand accounts, the following deserve special mention: Kronprinz Rupprecht von Bayern, *Mein Kriegstagebuch—In Treue Fest*, 3 vols. (München, 1929); R. von Valentini, *Kaiser und Kabinettschef* (Oldenburg, 1931); M. Hoffmann, *Die Aufzeichnungen des Generalmajors Max Hoffmann*, 2 vols. (Berlin, 1930); E. von Eisenhardt-Rothe, *Im Banne der Persönlichkeit* (Berlin, 1931); Graf J. H. Bernstorff, *Deutschland und Amerika* (Berlin, 1920); Oskar Freiherr von der Lancken Wakenitz, *Meine Dreissig Dienstjahre* (*1888-1918*) (Berlin, 1931); P. von Schwabach, *Aus meinen Akten* (Berlin, 1926).

It is impossible to discuss or even cite the numerous writings advocating German westward expansion that appeared during the First World War. The bibliography in the earlier version of this book, mentioned above, contains more than two hundred items in this category. For additional references see Great Britain, Foreign Office, *German Opinion on National Policy since July 1914* (London, 1920); also Germany, Kriegsamtsstelle Leipzig, *Verzeichnis der Aufklärungsmittel* (Leipzig, 1918). A good selection of annexationist statements is S. Grumbach, *Das annexionistische Deutschland* (Lausanne, 1917), though it covers only the first two years of the War. Much material on war aims, not otherwise obtainable, can be found in *Schulthess' Europäischer Geschichtskalender 1914-1918* (München, 1919-1921), an excellent chronicle of events, edited by

Ernst Jaeckh and Karl Hönn. A study of the German press and periodicals, especially after the lifting of censorship restrictions on November 27, 1916, yields important evidence on the attitude of the public towards expansionism. The official press digest of the British army: Great Britain, General Staff, *Daily Review of the Foreign Press*, with its Confidential and its Enemy Press Supplements, gives excellent surveys and analyses of German opinion.

Among secondary works, the only major contribution in the field of war aims is E. O. Volkmann's volume in the Fourth Series of the *Untersuchungsausschuss* (cited above), which presents invaluable material, but fails to treat the subject exhaustively and impartially. There are several studies on various aspects of the war aims problem, none of them outstanding: E. Dahlin, *French and German Public Opinion on Declared War Aims 1914-1918* (Stanford, 1933); H. Ostfeld, *Die Haltung der Reichstagsfraktion der Fortschrittlichen Volkspartei zu den Annexions—und Friedensfragen in den Jahren 1914-1918* (Kallmünz, 1934), Diss. Würzburg; F. Wacker, *Die Haltung der Deutschen Zentrumspartei zur Frage der Kriegsziele im Weltkrieg 1914-1918* (Lohr, 1937), Diss. Würzburg. The numerous attempts at a negotiated peace settlement, so closely related to the war aims question, have been treated more successfully. E. C. Brunauer's " The Peace Proposals of Germany and Austria-Hungary " (Stanford, 1927, typescript at the Stanford University Library) is still useful. The same author's *Has America Forgotten?* (Washington, 1940) is a more recent brief reminder of Germany's World War expansionism. K. Forster, *The Failures of Peace* (Washington, 1941) gives a clear survey over the many peace moves. Some of these moves have been the subject of separate studies. F. von Lama, *Die Friedensvermittlung Papst Benedikts XV. und ihre Vereitelung durch den deutschen Reichskanzler Michaelis* (München, 1932) gives a full, though biased, account of the Papal peace move in 1917. A more impartial account is H. J. T. Johnson, *Vatican Diplomacy in the World War* (N. Y., 1933). Various attempts to reach a separate peace between France and Germany are treated in R. Recouly, *Les Négociations secrètes Briand-Lancken* (Paris, 1936).

There are no competent studies on the World War activities of the more important annexationist organizations. M. S. Wertheimer, *The Pan-German League 1890-1914* (N. Y., 1924) stops short of the war and needs some revision. L. Werner, *Der Alldeutsche*

Verband 1890-1918 (Berlin, 1935), while glorifying the League's aims, belittles its influence. K. Wortmann's account of the Fatherlands Party, *Geschichte der Deutschen Vaterlandspartei 1917-1918* (Halle, 1926) is sound in its facts but biased in its interpretation. There is no treatment of the Independent Committee for a German Peace, though there is some material on it in K. Jagow, ed., *Dietrich Schäfer und sein Werk* (Berlin, 1925) and in D. Schäfer, *Der Krieg 1917/18* (Leipzig, 1920). The story of the so-called " moderate " organizations, which were opposed to far-reaching war aims, is told in W. Kahl, *Die Freie Vaterländische Vereinigung* (Berlin, 1915); F. W. Förster, *Mein Kampf gegen das militaristische und nationalistische Deutschland* (Stuttgart, 1920); O. Lehmann-Russbüldt, *Der Kampf der Deutschen Liga für Menschenrechte, vormals Bund Neues Vaterland, für den Weltfrieden 1914-1927* (Berlin, 1927); and Friedrich Meinecke, *Strassburg, Freiburg, Berlin 1901-1919, Erinnerungen* (Stuttgart, 1949).

Germany's aims and activities in France and Belgium, before and during the war, are the subject of an excellent memorandum by A. H. Brooks and M. F. Lacroix, " The Iron and Associated Industries of Lorraine, the Sarre District, Luxemburg, and Belgium," *United States Geological Survey*, Bulletin 703 (Washington, 1920). For a more recent and less thorough treatment see F. Friedensburg, *Kohle und Eisen im Weltkrieg und in den Friedensschlüssen* (Berlin, 1934). Germany's war-time administration of France is described in G. Gromaire, *L'Occupation Allemande en France 1914-1918* (Paris, 1925). For Belgium see J. Pirenne and M. Vauthier, *La législation et l'administration allemande en Belgique* (Paris, 1926); L. von Köhler, *Die Staatsverwaltung der besetzten Gebiete : Belgien* (Stuttgart, 1927); and Ch. de Kerchove, *L'Industrie Belge pendant l'occupation allemande 1914-1918* (Paris, 1927). The Flemish movement, which assumed such importance during the war, is traced from its beginnings in S. B. Clough, *A History of the Flemish Movement in Belgium* (N. Y., 1930). Raad van Vlaanderen, *Les Archives du Conseil de Flandre* (Brussels, 1928), and " Rudiger " [A. Wullus], *Flamenpolitik* (Brussels, 1921) include much material on Germany's relations with the Flemish movement.

There is no thorough and unbiased treatment of the political influence of Germany's big industrialists. Existing works are either entirely favorable or unfavorable and usually suffer from insufficient evidence. Among the favorable are P. Arnst, *August*

Thyssen und sein Werk (Leipzig, 1925); W. Bacmeister, *Emil Kirdorf, Der Mann, Sein Werk* (Essen, 1936); H. Brinckmeyer, *Hugo Stinnes* (München, 1921); and O. Kriegk, *Hugenberg* (Leipzig, 1932). As antidotes to these eulogies the following may be found useful, though, as their titles suggest, they tend to be sensational in character and the factual basis for their conclusions is usually slim: L. Lania, *Gruben, Gräber, Dividenden* (Berlin, 1925); "Morus" [L. Lewinsohn] *Das Geld in der Politik* (Berlin, 1930); G. Seldes, *Iron, Blood, and Profits* (N. Y., 1934); K. Heinig, *Hugo Stinnes und seine 600 000 Arbeiter* (n. pl., n. d.). G. Raphaël's *Hugo Stinnes, Der Mensch, Sein Wirken* (Berlin, 1925) and his *Krupp et Thyssen* (Paris, 1925) take a more neutral position. The same applies to P. Ufermann and C. Hüglin, *Stinnes und seine Konzerne* (Berlin, 1924).

Finally, as a general survey of German history during the First World War, Arthur Rosenberg, *Die Entstehung der Deutschen Republik 1871-1918* (Berlin, 1928) remains unsurpassed. To its penetrating analysis of the major issues underlying German affairs, including that of war aims, the present study owes a great deal.

INDEX

301

11